Lecture Notes in Computer Science 9698

Commenced Publication in 1973
Founding and Former Series Editors:
Gerhard Goos, Juris Hartmanis, and Jan van Leeuwen

More information about this series at http://www.springer.com/series/7407

Fabrice Kordon · Daniel Moldt (Eds.)

Application and Theory of Petri Nets and Concurrency

37th International Conference, PETRI NETS 2016
Toruń, Poland, June 19–24, 2016
Proceedings

 Springer

Editors
Fabrice Kordon
Université Pierre and Marie Curie
Paris
France

Daniel Moldt
Department Informatik
Universität Hamburg
Hamburg
Germany

ISSN 0302-9743 ISSN 1611-3349 (electronic)
Lecture Notes in Computer Science
ISBN 978-3-319-39085-7 ISBN 978-3-319-39086-4 (eBook)
DOI 10.1007/978-3-319-39086-4

Library of Congress Control Number: 2016939067

LNCS Sublibrary: SL1 – Theoretical Computer Science and General Issues

Printed on acid-free paper

This Springer imprint is published by Springer Nature
The registered company is Springer International Publishing AG Switzerland

Preface

This volume constitutes the proceedings of the 37th International Conference on Application and Theory of Petri Nets and Concurrency (Petri Nets 2016). This series of conferences serves as an annual meeting place to discuss progress in the field of Petri nets and related models of concurrency. These conferences provide a forum for researchers to present and discuss both applications and theoretical developments in this area. Novel tools and substantial enhancements to existing tools can also be presented. This year, the satellite program of the conference comprised three workshops, two Petri net courses, two advanced tutorials, and a model checking contest.

Petri Nets 2016 was co-located with the Application of Concurrency to System Design Conference (ACSD 2016). Both were organized by the Faculty of Mathematics and Computer Science of the Nicolaus Copernicus University. It took place in Toruń, Poland, during June 19–24, 2016. We would like to express our deepest thanks to the Organizing Committee chaired by Łukasz Mikulski for the time and effort invested in the local organization of this event.

This year, 42 regular papers were submitted to Petri Nets 2016. The authors of the submitted papers represented 29 different countries. We thank all the authors. Each paper was reviewed by at least three reviewers, three and a half on average. The Program Committee (PC) meeting took place electronically, using the EasyChair conference system for the paper selection process. The PC selected 16 papers for presentation, among them three are tool papers. The program also included four invited talks. After the conference, some authors were invited to submit an extended version of their contribution for consideration in a special issue of a journal.

We thank the PC members and other reviewers for their careful and timely evaluation of the submissions before the meeting and the fruitful discussions during the electronic meeting. The Springer LNCS team and the EasyChair system provided excellent support in the preparation of this volume. We are also grateful to the invited speakers for their contribution:

- Ian Foster, University of Chicago, who delivered the Distinguished Carl Adam Petri Lecture
  "Reasoning About Discovery Clouds"
- Manfred Broy, Technical University of Munich
  "From Actions, Transactions, and Processes to Services"
- Slawomir Lasota, University of Warsaw
  "Decidability Border for Petri Nets with Data: WQO Dichotomy Conjecture"
- Jetty Kleijn, Leiden University
  "On Processes and Paradigms"

June 2016

Fabrice Kordon
Daniel Moldt

Organization

Steering Committee

W. van der Aalst, The Netherlands
G. Ciardo, USA
J. Desel, Germany
S. Donatelli, Italy
S. Haddad, France
K. Hiraishi, Japan
J. Kleijn, The Netherlands
F. Kordon, France
M. Koutny, UK (Chair)

L.M. Kristensen, Norway
C. Lin, China
W. Penczek, Poland
L. Pomello, Italy
W. Reisig, Germany
G. Rozenberg, The Netherlands
M. Silva, Spain
A. Valmari, Finland
A. Yakovlev, UK

Program Committee

Gianfranco Balbo	University of Turin, Italy
Kamel Barkaoui	Cedric-Cnam, France
Robin Bergenthum	FernUniversität in Hagen, Germany
Luca Bernardinello	Università degli studi di Milano-Bicocca, Italy
Hanifa Boucheneb	Ecole Polytechnique de Montréal, Québec, Canada
Didier Buchs	CUI, University of Geneva, Switzerland
Lawrence Cabac	University of Hamburg, Germany
Piotr Chrzastowski-Wachtel	Institute of Informatics, Warsaw University, Poland
José Manuel Colom	University of Zaragoza, Spain
David de Frutos Escrig	Universidad Complutense, Spain
Raymond Devillers	ULB, Bruxelles, Belgium
Henri Hansen	Tampere University of Technology, Finland
Monika Heiner	Brandenburg University at Cottbus, Germany
Vladimir Janousek	Brno University of Technology, Czech Republic
Joost-Pieter Katoen	RWTH Aachen University, Germany
Ekkart Kindler	Technical University of Denmark, DTU Compute, Denmark
Fabrice Kordon (Chair)	LIP6/UPMC, France
Lars Kristensen	Bergen University College, Norway
João M. Fernandes	Universidade do Minho, Portugal
Hiroshi Matsuno	Yamaguchi University, Japan
Łukasz Mikulski	University of Toruń, Poland

Andrew Miner	Iowa State University, USA
Daniel Moldt (Chair)	University of Hamburg, Germany
Madhavan Mukund	Chennai Mathematical Institute, India
Pascal Poizat	Paris Ouest University and LIP6, France
Artem Polyvyanyy	Queensland University of Technology, Australia
Riadh Robbana	LIP2 - INSAT - University of Carthage, Tunisia
Stefan Schwoon	ENS de Cachan/Inria, France
Natalia Sidorova	Technische Universiteit Eindhoven, The Netherlands
Pawel Sobocinski	University of Southampton, UK
Yann Thierry-Mieg	Laboratoire d'Informatique Paris 6, France
Antti Valmari	Tampere University of Technology, Finland
Wil van der Aalst	Eindhoven University of Technology, The Netherlands

Workshops and Tutorials Chairs

Jetty Kleijn	University of Leiden, The Netherlands
Wojciech Penczek	Polish Academy of Sciences, Poland

Organizing Committee Chair

Łukasz Mikulski	Nicolaus Copernicus University, Poland

Tools Exhibition Chair

Marcin Piatkowski	Nicolaus Copernicus University, Poland

Publicity Chair

Kamila Barylska	Nicolaus Copernicus University, Poland

Additional Reviewers

Amparore, Alvio	Herajy, Mostafa
Barros, Joao Paulo	Hiraishi, Kunihiko
Barylska, Kamila	Kaminski, Benjamin Lucien
Beccuti, Marco	Kilinç, Görkem
Chakraborty, Souymodip	Langar, Mahjoub
Cordero, Francesca	Lawrence, David
Costa, Aniko	Linard, Alban
De Pierro, Massimiliano	Liu, Fei
Dehnert, Christian	Lodaya, Kamal
Franceschinis, Giuliana	Machado, Daniel
Gomes, Luis	Magnin, Morgan
Haustermann, Michael	Martos-Salgado, María

Miyamoto, Toshiyuki
Mosteller, David
Moutinho, Filipe
Piatkowski, Marcin
Pomello, Lucia
Puerto Aubel, Adrian
Racordon, Dimitri
Ribeiro, Óscar R.

Rohr, Christian
Rosa-Velardo, Fernando
Sfaxi, Lilia
Valero, Valentin
Wagner, Thomas
Wu, Hao
Yamaguchi, Shingo

Invited Talk

On Processes and Paradigms

Jetty Kleijn

LIACS, Leiden University, P.O. Box 9512, 2300 RA, The Netherlands
h.c.m.kleijn@liacs.leidenuniv.nl

Summary

Understanding the causal relations between occurrences of actions during a run of a distributed system is crucial for reasoning about the behaviour of such systems. Knowledge of dependencies between events (occurrences of actions) may facilitate the identification of different (sequential) observations belonging to the same run. The resulting equivalence classes (*traces*) comprise observations that have the same underlying events and agree on their dependencies. The elements of a trace thus share a common dependency structure the closure of which defines an invariant labelled relational structure that characterises the trace. For systems modelled by Petri nets, dependencies between events during a run of a net are determined by local interactions of transitions as made visible in the corresponding *process*, *i.e.* an unfolding of the net according to the given execution. Abstraction from places in combination with a closure operation then leads to a causality semantics in terms of relational structures labelled with transition names. Consequently, a trace semantics and a process semantics of a Petri net model 'fit together' if the labelled relational structures they associate with concurrent runs are always in agreement. A classical example of such fitting is provided by Elementary Net (EN) Systems, see, *e.g.*, [5]. For this fundamental class of Petri nets, the process semantics fits through partial orders with the classical Mazurkiewicz' traces [4] consisting of firing sequences and defined using a structural independence relation on transitions.

In this lecture, we will present a generalisation of this semantical theory to the case that observations are represented by sequences of steps (sets of one or more simultaneous events) rather than sequences of single occurrences and apply it to extended EN systems. In case of EN systems and their step sequences, two transitions that can be observed consecutively in any order can also be observed (in an equivalent observation) as occurring in a single step, and vice versa. This property reflects the 'true concurrency paradigm'. Consequently, for this net model, the structure of runs can still be described in terms of partial orders.

In general however, the relational structures obtained from sets of step sequences are no longer partial orders but rather rely on dependence relations that can describe events as being 'unordered but never simultaneous' and 'always ordered or simultaneous'. Such global relationships between events in sets of related observations of a system identify the concurrency paradigm to which it adheres, with the least restrictive, most general paradigm making no assumptions at all. The order structures that correspond to this most general paradigm have been characterised in [2]. They can capture any history, *i.e.* any set of labelled structures underlying the step sequences that form the observations of a run. Moreover, these general order structures match exactly with *step traces* [1], a generalisation of Mazurkiewicz' traces to equivalence classes of step sequences, based on simultaneity and sequentialisation relations between actions to swap and split steps.

EN systems with inhibitor arcs and mutex arcs are a system model for the most general concurrency paradigm [3]. We will demonstrate that their process semantics and step trace semantics fit together through the general order structures identified above.

Acknowledgement The work presented is based on and extends earlier work with Ryszard Janicki, Maciej Koutny, and Łukasz Mikulski.

References

1. Janicki, R., Kleijn, J., Koutny, M., Mikulski, Ł.: Step traces. Acta Inf. **53** (1), 35–65 (2016). http://doi.org/10.1007/s00236-015-0244-z
2. Janicki, R., Kleijn, J., Koutny, M., Mikulski, Ł.: Characterising concurrent histories. Fundam. Inform. **139**(1), 21–42 (2015). http://doi.org/10.3233/FI-2015-1224
3. Kleijn, J., Koutny, M.: Mutex Causality in Processes and Traces of General Elementary Nets. Fundam. Inform. **122** (1–2), 119–146 (2013). http://doi.org/10.3233/FI-2013-785
4. Mazurkiewicz, A.: Trace Theory. In: Brauer, W., Reisig, W., Rozenberg, G. (eds.) Petri Nets: Applications and Relationships to Other Models of Concurrency, LNCS, vol. **255**, pp. 279–324. Springer, Heidelberg (1987). http://doi.org/10.1007/3-540-17906-2_30
5. Rozenberg, G., Engelfriet, J.: Elementary Net Systems. In: Reisig, W., Rozenberg, G. (eds.) Lectures on Petri Nets I: Basic Models, LNCS, vol. **1491**, pp. 12–121 Springer, Heidelberg (1998). http://doi.org/10.1007/3-540-65306-6_14

Contents

Applications

Conformance Checking

Time and Stochastic Models

Structural Methods

Distinguished Carl Adam Petri Lecture

Reasoning About Discovery Clouds

Ian Foster[1,2]([✉])

[1] Argonne National Laboratory, Argonne, IL 60439, USA
[2] The University of Chicago, Chicago, IL 60637, USA
foster@uchicago.edu

Abstract. A discovery cloud is a set of automated, cloud-hosted services to which individuals may outsource their routine and not-so-routine research tasks: finding relevant data, inferring links between data, running computational experiments, inferring new knowledge claims, evaluating the credibility of knowledge claims produced by others, designing experiments, and so on. If developed successfully, a discovery cloud can accelerate and democratize access to data and knowledge tools and the collaborative construction of new knowledge. Such systems are also fascinating to consider from a reasoning perspective because they integrate great complexity at multiple levels: the underlying cloud-based hardware and software, for which issues of reliability and responsiveness may be paramount; the knowledge bases and inference engines that sit on that cloud substrate, for which issues of correctness may be less well defined; and the human communities that form around the discovery clouds, and that arguably form as much as part of the cloud as the hardware, software, and data. I raise questions here about what it might mean to reason about such systems. I do not provide any answers.

1 Introduction

I am a researcher who seeks to advance knowledge by building systems. I build systems for two reasons: because I believe strongly in the power of automation (Whitehead: Civilization advances by extending the number of important operations which we can perform without thinking about them [1]) and because experience teaches that it is only when we build systems that we learn how people use them in practice. Perhaps because of this predilection for engineering, I have little experience with the theory that was at the core of Carl Petri's work [2]. Instead, therefore, I will write here about the nature of the systems that I want to build in the coming decade, and the modeling challenges that they may introduce. I will be delighted if this presentation spurs discussions of how theory and modeling can be applied to such systems.

2 The Changing Nature of Science

The world of science is changing rapidly due to rapid evolution in sensor technologies, digitization of existing (e.g., textual) data sources, and increasingly

F. Kordon and D. Moldt (Eds.): PETRI NETS 2016, LNCS 9698, pp. 3–10, 2016.
DOI: 10.1007/978-3-319-39086-4_1

powerful computers. These developments have many implications for the nature of both discovery and knowledge. The opportunities inherent in so-called big data are widely discussed: for example, the ability to learn, via examination of large numbers of examples, how to label objects in images [3], translate text from one human language to another [4], or even synthesize explanatory theories for natural phenomena [5]. So too are the challenges: the massive quantities of data that must be stored and processed, the uncertain nature of knowledge based on data mining or deep learning, and the difficulty of maintaining privacy when many information is integrated from many sources. Supercomputers, too, present exciting new opportunities, allowing the implications of theoretical models to be explored in unprecedented detail and sensitivity to unknown parameters. Increasingly, also, data and simulation are being combined, with data used to calibrate or validate theoretical models and computational simulations used to explain data or propose new experiments.

These developments have two interesting consequences. First, the scale and complexity of the data, software, and computing hardware required to understand natural phenomena (in the case of science) or design new systems (in the case of engineering) grows every larger. Increasingly, therefore, the individual investigator must outsource important elements of the discovery process to remote computing systems, whether a curated database, a supercomputer simulation, or a machine learning process. I use the term *discovery cloud* to denote the resulting environment, and discuss some of its attributes below.

Second, our understanding of new discoveries or new engineered systems is increasingly often based on our understanding of, or faith in, the various elements of this discovery cloud. In part, the issue is that our understanding is increasingly encoded in algorithms rather than equations [6], to the extent that, arguably, "applied computer science is now playing the role which mathematics did from the seventeenth through the twentieth centuries: providing an orderly, formal framework and exploratory apparatus for other sciences" [7]. Equally importantly, the machinery that is used to execute, and in many cases construct, these algorithms becomes part of our explanatory apparatus.

3 Discovery Engines

Not so long ago, a researcher or engineer conducted their work on the basis of their own observations of the natural world, the knowledge of others as obtained from personal correspondence or the library, and a suite of mathematical tools. Results were communicated in the form of scientific articles or products, which others could review and test.

The rapidly growing data volumes and use of computational methods referred to above, as well as other related factors such as increasingly collaborative research and greater methodological complexity, are transforming the nature of investigation in many fields. Increasingly, research depends on the ability to search and compute over large quantities of data, at scales that are not easily supported in a typical investigator's lab. Thus, we see the emergence of a new form of instrument: the storage, computing, data, and code required to allow community analysis of a large dataset—what I term a *discovery engine* [8]. Many individuals and groups may work on a single discovery engine over a period of months or years, asking different questions, and producing 10s or even 1000s of publications. The community needs to have access to the datasets and the analysis and visualization tools, along with all of the provenance needed to interpret, reproduce, and extend results.

Successful discovery engines have been developed within a few disciplines and projects: see, for example, the Sloan Digital Sky Survey's SkyServer [9], the SEED system for microbial genomes [10,11], the MG-RAST metagenomics server [12], and what Szalay calls Open Numerical Laboratories [13]. The Sloan survey, for example, has collected imaging data for more than 35 % of the sky with photometric observations of ∼500 million objects and spectra for more than 3 million objects. Importantly, SDSS does not simply provide the community with access to raw data: the SkyServer provides a range of interfaces for querying and accessing the data, including the CasJobs interface [14] for running computationally intensive SQL queries. As of March 2016, use of SDSS data has resulted in >5,800 refereed papers with >245,000 citations.

The SEED was first established in 2004, at a time when large numbers of sequenced bacterial genomes were being produced, with the goal of producing superior annotations (e.g., labeling genes with their functional role) for the first 1,000 sequenced genomes. To this end, the SEED team pioneered a new approach to genome annotation based on the annotation of subsystems by expert annotators across many genomes. Users upload genomes the system for automated analysis and annotation; genes are called by comparison to the knowledge maintained within the SEED system. As of 2013, >12,000 users worldwide had annotated >60,000 distinct genomes. The related MG-RAST server, launched in 2007, has as of March 2016 processed 239,314 metagenomes totalling >100 trillion base pairs for >12,000 users.

These usage data illustrate the outsize impact that discovery engines can have on their communities. Importantly, the systems cited are all easily accessible by researchers with limited information technology experience and resources. They thus serve to both empower researchers who could not otherwise easily analyze data from new instruments, and as loci for collaboration around that data.

4   The Discovery Cloud

While the discovery engine is relatively new to science, similar entities have existed for some time, and indeed on much larger scales, within industry. The Google search engine is a massive collection of data, organized and processed so as to permit rapid query by any web user and presumably yet more powerful computations by Google employees. So too are the Amazon catalog and Face-Book social network. And these services are just three (albeit large) instances of a vast array of *cloud services* on which businesses, consumers, and indeed society as a whole increasingly rely. The full spectrum of cloud services encompass a tremendous variety of computational and data-oriented services to which businesses and consumers can outsource tasks that until recently were performed either manually or on personal computers: for example, booking travel, managing travel information, writing documents, organizing photographs, or tracking customer relationships. The convenient and cost structures of these services are such that small businesses, in particular, often choose to outsource essentially all of their IT to such software-as-a-service (SaaS) providers [15–17]. And SaaS providers themselves frequently outsource responsibility for providing the computing and storage that they need to operate to infrastructure-as-a-service (IaaS) providers, such as Amazon Web Services, Microsoft Azure, and Google cloud, and leverage capabilities provided by platform as a service (PaaS) systems [18].

Scientists make frequent use of consumer cloud services in their work, using for example Google Docs or GitHub for collaborative authoring, Skype for communication, and DropBox for data sharing. But such usage is still incidental to the main business of science: the painstaking steps by which experiments are designed However, a growing number of services are emerging that provide on-demand access to functions more directly relevant to scientific practice. In addition to the discovery engines listed above, we can point to Google Scholar for searching papers and retrieving citation information, Globus services for data transfer and sharing [19], the nanoHUB system for nanotechnology simulation software [20], and iPlant (now CyVerse) services [21].

If enough such science services [22] can be assembled, we can establish the *Discovery Cloud* [23], a set of services that (a) address directly the data lifecycle and computational challenges faced by researchers; (b) allow rapid adoption within advanced discovery tools, without requiring substantial technical expertise or local infrastructure; and (c) adapt easily to varied disciplinary needs and rapidly evolving science requirements. Such services will enable state-of-the-art discovery and education within those labs that today struggle with IT challenges, while also accelerating work within even the best-resourced labs by slashing time spent on mundane and routine activities. It will thus allow researchers to compete and indeed prosper in a world of increasingly large, noisy, and complex datasets and ever more sophisticated computation. The availability of powerful commercial cloud platforms allow the Discovery Cloud to focus on developing, adapting, and integrating higher-level services, including those that were originally developed for enterprise or big science collaborations, and delivering the resulting tools through a framework designed specifically to meet the needs of researchers.

While our vision for the Discovery Cloud is expansive, it is firmly rooted in practical experience. Over the past five years we have developed and operated Globus [19]—a collection of cloud-hosted services designed specifically to address SML data management challenges [24] and platform requirements [25]. The results of this experiment have been positive: Globus services have been incorporated into many thousands of research workflows worldwide. The rapid growth of usage combined with overwhelmingly positive feedback, has highlighted the value of service-based delivery of scientific capabilities.

We anticipate the Discovery Cloud building on this experience, leveraging proven services (e.g., Globus authentication, identity management, data transfer, data sharing), while supporting the development and integration of new capabilities, providing a platform to simplify the creation of new services while reducing development and operations costs, and creating new mechanisms that directly address the inherent sustainability challenges of research software.

The Discovery Cloud can also create opportunities for new research projects focused on the nature of research. The fact that a greater number of research tasks are digitally mediated makes it possible, in principle, to treat research processes as objects of study in their own right. The resulting metaknowledge [26] can provide insights into the nature of effective research strategies [27].

5   Reasoning About Discovery Clouds

In a Discovery Cloud environment, substantial parts of an end-to-end research workflow will routinely be outsourced to cloud services. Workflow results will often depend on data and computation maintained by sophisticated discovery engines that are frequently updated with new data, inferences, and inference methods.

In this context, issues relating to the documentation, integrity, and reproducibility of research results can become far more challenging than in a pre-cloud environment. For example, consider the following questions: Which specific data products were used to obtain a result? What code was executed to create a dataset? What do I need to do to reproduce a result? Is my computation deterministic? How do I account for a result obtained from machine learning service that uses neuromorphic hardware [28]? What steps should I follow to reproduce a result? Who is authorized to alter data? What work do I need to redo upon correcting an error in an input dataset?

Each of these questions will often be straightforward to answer when working only on a personal computer. Answering them in a Discovery Cloud environment may be much harder, given that a singe computation may engage many services, each with different internal processes and policies.

Another set of research challenges relate to the often complex computational workflows associated with data-intensive scientific applications. These workflows may span many services and sites and involve thousand or millions of distinct computational steps. Increasingly, higher-level workflow management systems (e.g., Galaxy [29], Pegasus [30], Swift [31], Taverna [32]) are used to express and manage such processes. Petri nets have been used to express and reason about workflows [33] but are not yet mainstream, perhaps because they are viewed as being less expressive than other approaches.

The solution to these challenges may be to develop new approaches to reasoning about distributed systems, that focus on the data and code maintained by different services rather than on service interactions. (It may be interesting to focus on specifying events in a data elements lifecycle and the actions that should be taken when certain events occur [34,35].) I would certainly like a discovery engine service to maintain versioning information for its code and data.

But that information is less useful if (as will often be the case) code and data are changing frequently. Some code changes will be relevant to my science and others will not. Some data changes will effect the results that I obtain, while others do not. (The magnitude of the change may also be important.) Are there invariants that I would like a discovery engine to maintain for me, with methods for notifying me when invariants no longer hold? I will also want the Discovery Cloud as a whole to maintain the integrity of my data, which implies a need to reason about properties such as confidentiality, authorization, and data replication.

6   Summary

In science as in business, large-scale automation and outsourcing can slash costs and democratize access to powerful big data and computational services. The Discovery Cloud thus has the potential to accelerate discovery across a range of disciplines and problems.

The Discovery Cloud environment also poses challenges in terms of scientific method: as research processes are distributed over cloud services, it can become harder to document provenance, validate results, and ensure reproducibility. These challenges may motivate new approaches to reasoning about distributed systems, for example to focus on the data that a set of distributed services maintain, and the computations that they perform, rather than on service interactions.

Acknowledgements. I am grateful to the organizers of Petri Nets 2016 for the opportunity to contribute this article to the proceedings. This work is supported in part by the US Department of Energy contract DE-AC02-06CH11357.

References

1. Whitehead, A.N.: Introduction to Mathematics. Williams and Norgate, London (1911)
2. Murata, T.: Petri nets: properties, analysis and applications. Proc. IEEE **77**(4), 541–580 (1989)
3. Quoc, V.L.: Building high-level features using large scale unsupervised learning. In: IEEE International Conference on Acoustics, Speech and Signal Processing, pp. 8595–8598. IEEE (2013)
4. Koehn, P.: Statistical Machine Translation. Cambridge University Press, Cambridge (2009)
5. Daniel, D.L., Lipson, H.: Learning symbolic representations of hybrid dynamical systems. J. Mach. Learn. Res. **13**(1), 3585–3618 (2012)
6. Honavar, V.G., Hill, M.D., Yelick, K.: Accelerating science: a computing research agenda. A white paper prepared for the Computing Community Consortium committee of the Computing Research Association (2016). http://cra.org/ccc/resources/ccc-led-whitepapers/
7. Djorgovski, S.G.: Virtual astronomy, information technology, and the new scientific methodology. In: 7th International Workshop on Computer Architecture for Machine Perception, pp. 125–132. IEEE (2005)

8. Foster, I., Ananthakrishnan, R., Blaiszik, B., Chard, K., Osborn, R., Tuecke, S., Wilde, M., Wozniak, J.: Networking materials data: accelerating discovery at an experimental facility. In: Joubert, G., Grandinetti, L. (eds.) Big Data and High Performance Computing (in press, 2015)
9. Gray, J., Szalay, A.S., Thakar, A.R., Kunszt, P.Z., Malik, T., Raddick, J., Stoughton, C., vandenBerg, J.: The SDSS SkyServer - public access to the sloan digital sky server data. In: ACM SIGMOD, pp. 1–11 (2002)
10. Overbeek, R.A., Disz, T., Stevens, R.L.: The SEED: a peer-to-peer environment for genome annotation. Commun. ACM **47**(11), 46–51 (2004)
11. Overbeek, R., Olson, R., Pusch, G.D., Olsen, G.J., Davis, J.J., Disz, T., Edwards, R.A., Gerdes, S., Parrello, B., Shukla, M., Vonstein, V., Wattam, A.R., Xia, F., Stevens, R.: The SEED and the rapid annotation of microbial genomes using subsystems technology (RAST). Nucleic Acids Res. **42**(D1), D206–D214 (2014)
12. Meyer, F., Paarmann, D., D'Souza, M., Olson, R., Glass, E.M., Kubal, M., Paczian, T., Rodriguez, A., Stevens, R., Wilke, A., Wilkening, J., Edwards, R.A.: The metagenomics RAST server - a public resource for the automatic phylogenetic and functional analysis of metagenomes. BMC Bioinform. **9**(1), 386 (2008)
13. Szalay, A.S.: From simulations to interactive numerical laboratories. In: 2014 Winter Simulation Conference, pp. 875–886. IEEE Press (2014)
14. O'Mullane, W., Li, N., Nieto-Santisteban, M., Szalay, A., Thakar, A., Gray, J.: Batch is back: CasJobs, serving multi-TB data on the Web. In: IEEE International Conference on Web Services, pp. 33–40. IEEE (2005)
15. Chong, F., Carraro, G.: Architecture strategies for catching the long tail. MSDN Library, Microsoft Corporation, pp. 9–10 (2006)
16. Dubey, A., Wagle, D.: Delivering software as a service. The McKinsey Quarterly, May 2007
17. Foster, I., Vasiliadis, V., Tuecke, S.: Software as a service as a path to software sustainability. Technical report (2013). doi:10.6084/m9.figshare.791604
18. Lawton, G.: Developing software online with platform-as-a-service technology. Computer **41**(6), 13–15 (2008)
19. Foster, I.: Globus online: accelerating and democratizing science through cloud-based services. IEEE Internet Comput. **15**(3), 70–73 (2011)
20. Madhavan, K.P.C., Beaun, D., Shivarajapura, S., Adams, G.B., Klimeck, G.: nanoHUB.org serving over 120,000 users worldwide: its first cyber-environment assessment. In: 10th IEEE Conference on Nanotechnology (IEEE-NANO), pp. 90–95. IEEE (2010)
21. Goff, S.A., Vaughn, M., McKay, S., Lyons, E., Stapleton, A.E., Gessler, D., Matasci, N., Wang, L., Hanlon, M., Lenards, A., et al.: The iPlant collaborative: cyberinfrastructure for plant biology. Front. Plant Sci. **2** (2011)
22. Foster, I.: Service-oriented science. Science **308**(5723), 814–817 (2005)
23. Foster, I., Chard, K., Tuecke, S.: The discovery cloud: accelerating and democratizing research on a global scale. In: International Conference on Cloud Engineering (2016)
24. Chard, K., Tuecke, S., Foster, I.: Efficient and secure transfer, synchronization, and sharing of big data. IEEE Cloud Comput. **1**(3), 46–55 (2014)
25. Ananthakrishnan, R., Chard, K., Foster, I., Tuecke, S.: Globus platform-as-a-service for collaborative science applications. Concurrency Comput.: Pract. Exp. **27**(2), 290–305 (2015)
26. Evans, J.A., Foster, J.G.: Metaknowledge. Science **331**(6018), 721–725 (2011)
27. Rzhetsky, A., Foster, J.G., Foster, I.T., Evans, J.A.: Choosing experiments to accelerate collective discovery. Proc. Natl. Acad. Sci. **112**(47), 14569–14574 (2015)

28. Mead, C.: Neuromorphic electronic systems. Proc. IEEE **78**(10), 1629–1636 (1990)
29. Goecks, J., Nekrutenko, A., Taylor, J., et al.: Galaxy: a comprehensive approach for supporting accessible, reproducible, and transparent computational research in the life sciences. Genome Biol. **11**(8), R86 (2010)
30. Deelman, E., Singh, G., Mei-Hui, S., Blythe, J., Gil, Y., Kesselman, C., Mehta, G., Karan, V., Berriman, G.B., Good, J., et al.: Pegasus: a framework for mapping complex scientific workflows onto distributed systems. Sci. Program. **13**(3), 219–237 (2005)
31. Wilde, M., Foster, I., Iskra, K., Beckman, P., Zhang, Z., Espinosa, A., Hategan, M., Clifford, B., Raicu, I.: Parallel scripting for applications at the petascale and beyond. Computer **11**, 50–60 (2009)
32. Hull, D., Wolstencroft, K., Stevens, R., Goble, C., Pocock, M.R., Li, P., Oinn, T.: Taverna: a tool for building and running workflows of services. Nucleic Acids Res. **34**(suppl 2), W729–W732 (2006)
33. Van der Aalst, W.M.P.: The application of Petri nets to workflow management. J. Circuits, Syst. Comput. **8**(01), 21–66 (1998)
34. Simonet, A., Fedak, G., Ripeanu, M.: Active data: a programming model to manage data life cycle across heterogeneous systems and infrastructures. Future Gener. Comput. Syst. **53**, 25–42 (2015)
35. Simonet, A., Chard, K., Fedak, G., Foster, I.: Using active data to provide smart data surveillance to e-science users. In: 23rd Euromicro International Conference on Parallel, Distributed and Network-Based Processing, pp. 269–273. IEEE (2015)

Invited Talks

From Actions, Transactions, and Processes to Services

Manfred Broy[✉]

Institut für Informatik, Technische Universität München, 80290 Munich, Germany
broy@in.tum.de
http://wwwbroy.informatik.tu-muenchen.de

1 Introduction

For the problem domain of business process engineering we introduce, model, and formalize notions of business processes such as action, actor, event, business process, and business transaction. In addition, for the solution domain of service-oriented architectures (SOA) we introduce, model, and formalize notions of service, service composition, service-oriented architecture, and layered SOA in a systematic way. We do that by a rigorous mathematical system model. For that purpose, we first develop a basic mathematical system model for formalizing fundamental concepts of processes and services. The goal is to provide a minimal set of formal modeling concepts, nevertheless expressive enough to formalize key notions and concepts in business process engineering and service-oriented architectures capturing also their mutual relationships. This way, the relationship between central notions in business process models is captured formally, which provides a basis for a methodology for deriving the systematic specification and design of service-oriented architectures from business process modeling. The purpose of the approach is manifold; one goal is a clear definition of terminology, concepts, terms, and models in business process modeling and SOA; another goal is a rigorous formal basis for the specification, design, and development of business processes and, in particular, SOAs. We end up with a strictly formal concept for the development steps from business process models to services as part of a SOA-oriented development process.

This is an extended abstract of [Broy 15].

2 Business Process Design

When designing business processes and, in turn, developing business transaction and workflow support software, concepts of domain modeling in terms of business processes and software based business applications are needed. In consequence, various notions and modeling concepts of two disciplines, namely software engineering and business process engineering, have to be related, harmonized, integrated, and conceptually unified. The challenge is to provide a comprehensive modeling framework expressive enough to support the development steps in the construction of service-oriented architectures (SOA) on the basis of business process models.

In the development of a SOA for business applications, it is first to capture and work out the goals and requirements in the application domain. Then based on these

© Springer International Publishing Switzerland 2016
F. Kordon and D. Moldt (Eds.): PETRI NETS 2016, LNCS 9698, pp. 13–19, 2016.
DOI: 10.1007/978-3-319-39086-4_2

requirements we work out the business processes. Finally, we determine which parts of the software processes are to be supported by computer-based services to derive from them the software requirements and specifications, further on the software service architecture, and finally service implementations. For carrying out such development tasks, models, and modeling concepts are applied both from the field of business process modeling and model based software and system development – more specifically from the field of service-oriented architecture.

Our main concern is to provide formal models for processes and formal models for service-oriented systems in terms of their interfaces to model key notions in business process engineering. We use process models to model notions like *business process* and *business process transaction*. We use the notion of systems and system interface behavior to model business services. One of our goals is to relate these notions to the concept of services as studied in service-oriented architectures.

We aim at a synergy between the problem domains of business process engineering and that of formal system modeling. For both areas, we work out formal concepts as a basis for engineering service-oriented architectures (SOA).

Remark: Avoiding clashes in engineering terminology.
One delicate difficulty for our approach is a terminological clash between two disciplines, that of "business process engineering" and that of "formal process modeling". This difficulty is immediately recognized when studying the general term "process" in the field of event processing. Moreover, in the field of business processes, the term "business process" is used differently addressing a number of different notions like the business process of an organization, the instance of the business process during a day of operation, or the business process of a business transaction as an instance of a specific business case; in formal system modeling, formal models of discrete processes are introduced as generic concepts for modeling discrete activities.

End_of_Remark

For service-oriented architecture we formalize the notion of the service layer leading to the concept of service-layered architecture.

3   Fundamentals in Discrete Process Modeling

Modeling discrete processes is one of the challenges in the development of automation systems – be it in business automation or in production automation.

The term process is used for many quite different notions and concepts. It is used for behavior described by a system or by a system model, execution mechanism (a Petri-net, for instance), or for a particular instance of behavior of a system or system execution mechanism model (an occurrence net for a Petri-net). In addition, given such an instance of behavior, we may consider certain sub-behaviors representing (smaller) instances of behavior.

This shows that we deal with three forms of notions of processes and their description:

• process descriptions (by modeling concepts) with which we associate

- sets of instances (scenarios) of behavior, the members of which are
- instances (scenarios) of behaviors.

In the following, we use the word "process" strictly for an instance of behavior. So we get the following terminology:

- a system description (of a business system), called a *process specification,* describes a
- *set of (business) processes* where
- *(business) processes* are instances of system behavior (representations of system executions).

In this terminology, a process is used to denote the run ("history") of a system like an occurrence net represents an instance of behavior of a Petri-net. A Petri-net is an example of a process specification. Since we can identify in a given process several sub-processes, a process can also be understood as describing sets of (sub-)processes. This general approach of understanding the term process is used in the following in a more concrete and detailed form by introducing a modeling theory for processes.

4 Process Descriptions and Instances Business Process Engineering - Notions and Concepts

In business process engineering, the concept of a process is essential. The term "business process" is used in business process engineering in a very generic way. It addresses the process (in the sense of instance) of a particular business transaction as well as the process of a particular sub-organization as well as the comprehensive set of activities of an entire company or even a network of companies. In this section, we introduce a taxonomy of slightly different form for capturing business processes and their specification.

A business process consists of a set of business actions[1] (often called "steps") executed by business actors. Their actions are in some logical, causal, and temporal relationship.

For a business process and its specification, we introduce several views and structures. We take the following fundamental viewpoint onto business processes. In a business process, actors execute a set of actions. This way we obtain two essential notions:

- business actions (singe steps of activity in a process)
- business actors (humans or machines that carry out actions).

In addition, we might consider business objects and business data as they are used to capture the states related to business transactions. Business actions usually have certain effects on business objects. They may change states of business objects and they may consume or produce events that relate to actions in terms of the exchange of messages (or even exchange of material or energy). We do not consider business objects

---

[1] Note that the choice of a set of actions determines also the granularity of the model of a business process. This granularity can be changed by replacing an action by a set of sub-actions or vice versa.

and business data, in particular, in the following; they can be added, however, in a straightforward manner to the approach.

Actors are humans or computer systems that carry out actions. By carrying out actions, actors provide specific services. While carrying out services actors may observe certain actions executed by other actors. These observations may trigger actors to executions of further actions.

This leads to another key notion in business process engineering, the notion of a service, more precisely to the notion of a

- business service.

A business service is carried out (provided) by some business actor or a set of actors (the service provider); it consists of a business process generated by the actor in reaction to the process and the actions the actor observes. The set of actions the actor observes (which form a sub-process of the overall process) are called its *service input*, the set of actions generated by the actor (which also form a process) are called its *service output*.

To illustrate our notions, we sketch the example of a web shop with the help of our previously introduced terminology. Words referring to key concepts are put in italic. The web shop operates by carrying out a number of *actions*. The ordering of a product in the web shop by a customer is done by a set of actions by the customer and the web shop forming a *business transaction (instance)*. The structure of all possible business transactions can be described by a *business transaction specification*. Within a given time interval (one hour, one day, one month, one year) a set of business transactions is carried out; they form what we call a *business transaction flow* (for instance, the process of the web shop consisting of all actions and transactions carried out in one year). Note that there may be and usually are dependencies between the individual business actions and business transactions that occur within a business transaction flow. There are various ways to describe such dependencies (for instance, business objects) and derive sub-transactions (sub-processes) from a business transaction flow.

There are several ways to define the notion of a *business process*. It addresses the set of transactions that serve a certain business purpose ("business purpose viewpoint"):

(a) We may call the set of all possible business transactions business process.
(b) We may call the set of all possible business transaction flows business process.
(c) We may call an instance of a business transaction business process.

We tend to follow position (c) where we include (b) since the business transaction flows include the business transactions as sub-transactions ("sub-processes"). We call what is addressed by (a) and (b) the business process specification. For our running example, the business process specification describes all the business transaction flows and also the set of all possible business transactions of the web shop.

5   From Business Processes to Service-Oriented Architectures

Services and service-oriented architectures (SOA) have received much attention in recent years for good reasons (see [Broy 05], [Broy et al. 07]). When dealing with large systems, it is generally recognized that we need appropriate abstractions. These abstractions have to be useful for the implementation of systems, but they are even more urgently needed for the design and specification of domain specific aspects of information processing systems. Service-oriented architectures aim, in particular, at structuring software systems not so much governed by technical concepts of implementation but rather driven by concepts of the application domain with its domain-specific terms and conditions.

We understand service-oriented architecture as an approach that follows classical general goals and principles of software system construction such as modularity, application domain orientation, and strict concentration onto the user-centric functionality of systems. These principles are in response to the growing demand of putting emphasis on system evolution and maintenance with flexible response to changing requirements. In addition, SOA is expected to lead to a higher quality of software systems in terms of changeability, adaptability, interoperability, and reusability. In the following, we introduce a basic formal model for services as they are used in service-oriented architectures.

A further important issue is a methodological one defining what are systematic steps of the development of service architectures starting from high-level requirements and use cases. In this section, we give a very short and brief preliminary description of how such a top-down development methodology could look like.

We characterize the proceeding by the following steps:

1. We give *use cases*. In each use case, we describe scenarios of service use that correspondent very directly to scenarios that can be formally seen as service instances.
2. From the scenarios, we derive *service processes* they can be described by process diagrams or by interaction diagrams. To do these diagrams we also have to formalize the service messages. The service messages can be directly identified from the service use cases.
3. In the processes, we have steps, which are done manually and steps, which are done by the software systems. Therefore, it is an important decision which of the steps in the systems are done manually and which of the steps are done by the software.
4. By identifying steps that are to be done by software, we can derive from the service processes, the *service hierarchy* as well as *services instances* for each of the services in the hierarchy.
5. For each of the services, we define its *service interface behavior*. Perhaps, we decide to introduce additional auxiliary services that provide small service provision networks for the services to implement.
6. From this, we get on one hand *service architectures* and a black box descriptions of each of the services involved.
7. The black box view of the provided services, have to be correctly represented by the service composition, including a *layered architecture* in terms of a *stack of internal services*.

This shows, how service architectures can be worked out in a top-down fashion. In fact, we could also use the same approach in a bottom up development. What we finally get is an artifact model for service-oriented architecture where all of the ingredients of a service architecture are given that are more less as described by the notion and concept model by the introduced mathematical techniques.

6   Conclusion

In this paper, we base the formalization of SOA concepts on the theory of processes and process oriented service functions. We can use all concepts such as

- service separation
- service refinement
- service specification and implementation.

for the engineering of SOA systems.

An interesting question addresses the difference between object- and service-orientation (OO vs. SO). For a number of practical SOA approaches the answer is not obvious, in particular, when OO concepts are used to represent services. However, there is a significant difference between OO and SOA that has to be understood to see the advantages of SOA over OO:

- Typically, OO-concepts are sequential and method-invocation oriented,
- SOA approaches are, by nature, taking into account time, parallel and concurrent computation and explicitly support of distribution, interaction, and time.

Of course, we may use OO-concepts to implement SOA, but these concepts are too weak to represent SOA ideas explicitly. The strength of SOA can be fully exploited only by a dedicated modeling framework addressing interaction and concurrency explicitly.

By the constructions introduced, we provide the following foundations:

- We describe general models for several important notions and terms in business process modeling.
- We introduce a very compact general formal model and theory for processes and services.
- Due to the form of models, we can define formally the relationship between these notions and how they interact with each other.
- The main idea is to use this as a foundational framework for a methodology and development processes for business systems.

The ultimate goal is to provide a foundation for a formalized approach to service-oriented architectures. Service-oriented architectures claim to be the better approach to develop main business process applications. A key issue here is the step from a descriptive approach to processes where processes are described as structures of activities to an input/output oriented view, which we call services. By our notion, we capture formally the heart of the idea of business process modeling and the formal step from business process modeling into SOA.

References

[Aalst, Stahl 01] van der Aalst, W., Stahl, C.: Modeling Business Processes: A Petri Net-Oriented Approach. MIT Press, Cambridge (2011)

[Broy, Stølen 01] Broy, M., Stølen, K.: Specification and Development of Interactive Systems: Focus on Streams, Interfaces, and Refinement. Springer, New York (2001)

[Broy 03] Broy, M.: Modeling services and layered architectures. In: König, H., Heiner, M., Wolisz, A. (eds.) Formal Techniques for Networked and Distributed Systems. LNCS, vol. 2767, pp. 48–61. Springer, Berlin (2003)

[Broy 04] Broy, M.: The semantic and methodological essence of message sequence charts. Sci. Comput. Program. SCP **54**(2–3), 213–256 (2004)

[Broy 05] Broy, M.: Service-Oriented systems engineering: specification and design of services and layered architectures – the Janus approach. In: Broy, M., Grünbauer, J., Harel, D., Hoare, T. (eds.) Engineering Theories of Software Intensive Systems, pp. 47–81. Springer, Dordrecht (2005)

[Broy et al. 07] Broy, M., Krüger, I., Meisinger, M.: A formal model of services. TOSEM - ACM Trans. Softw. Eng. Methodol. **16**, 1 (2007)

[Broy 11] Broy, M.: Towards a theory of architectural contracts: schemes and patterns of assumption/promise based system specification. In: Broy, M., Leuxner, C., Hoare, T. (eds.) Software and Systems Safety - Specification and Verification. NATO Science for Peace and Security Series D: Information and Communication Security, vol. 30, pp. 33–87. IOS Press, Amsterdam (2011)

[Broy 10] Broy, M.: Multifunctional software systems: structured modeling and specification of functional requirements. Sci. Comput. Program. **75**, 1193–1214 (2010)

[Broy 15] Broy, M.: From actions, transactions, and processes to services. In: Irlbeck, M., Peled, D., Pretschner, A. (eds.) Dependable Software Systems Engineering. NATO Science for Peace and Security Series D: Information and Communication Security, vol. 40, pp. 42–78. IOS Press, Amsterdam (2015)

[Großkopf et al. 09] Großkopf, A., Decker, G., Weske, M.: The Process: Business Process Modeling Using BPMN. Meghan-Kiffer Press, Tampa (2009)

[Haar 00] Haar, Stefan: Occurrence net logics. Fundam. Inf. **43**(1–4), 105–127 (2000)

[Küster-Filipe 06] Küster-Filipe, J.: Modeling concurrent interactions. Theoret. Comput. Sci. **351**, 203–220 (2006)

[Petri 62] Petri, C.A.: Kommunikation mit Automaten. Institut für instrumentelle Mathematik der Universität Bonn (1962)

[Thurner 04] Thurner, V.: Formal fundierte Modellierung von Geschäftsprozessen. Dissertation, TU München, Munich (2004)

[Torka 13] Torka, P.: Dienstorientierte Architekturen: Eine konzeptuelle Herleitung auf Basis eines formalen Prozessmodells

[Winskel, Nielsen 95] Winskel, G., Nielsen, M.: Models for concurrency. In: Abramsky, S., Gabbay, D., Maibaum, T. (eds.) Handbook of Logic in Computer Science. Semantic Modeling, vol. 4, pp. 1–148. Oxford Science Publications, Oxford (1995)

Decidability Border for Petri Nets with Data: WQO Dichotomy Conjecture

Sławomir Lasota$^{(\boxtimes)}$

Institute of Informatics, University of Warsaw, Warsaw, Poland
sl@mimuw.edu.pl

Abstract. In Petri nets with data, every token carries a data value, and executability of a transition is conditioned by a relation between data values involved. Decidability status of various decision problems for Petri nets with data may depend on the structure of data domain. For instance, if data values are only tested for equality, decidability status of the reachability problem is unknown (but decidability is conjectured). On the other hand, the reachability problem is undecidable if data values are additionally equipped with a total ordering.

We investigate the frontiers of decidability for Petri nets with various data, and formulate the *WQO Dichotomy Conjecture*: under a mild assumption, either a data domain exhibits a well quasi-order (in which case one can apply the general setting of well-structured transition systems to solve problems like coverability or boundedness), or essentially all the decision problems are undecidable for Petri nets over that data domain.

1 Introduction

We investigate the model of Petri nets with data, where tokens carry values from some data domain, and executability of transitions is conditioned by a relation between data values involved. One can consider *unordered data*, like in [26], i.e. an infinite data domain with the equality as the only relation; or *ordered data*, like in [24], i.e. an infinite densely totally ordered data domain. One can also consider a more general setting of Petri nets over an arbitrary fixed data domain $\mathbb{A}$. In Sect. 2 we provide such a general definition of *Petri nets with atoms* $\mathbb{A}$, parametric in a relational structure $\mathbb{A}$. For instance, unordered and ordered data are modeled by $\mathbb{A} = (\mathbb{N}, =)$ and $\mathbb{A} = (\mathbb{Q}, \leq)$, respectively. We want to emphasize here that the idea seems not at all new, as similar net models have been proposed already in the early 80ies: high-level Petri nets [13] and colored Petri nets [19]. Since then, similar formalisms seem to have been rediscovered, for instance constraint multiset rewriting [5,8,9].

Equivalently, Petri nets with atoms are just reinterpretation of the classical definition of Petri nets with a relaxed notion of finiteness, namely orbit-finiteness, where one allows for orbit-finite sets of places and transitions instead of just finite ones; this is along the lines of [3,4].

The work is partially supported by the Polish National Center of Science 2012/07/B/ST6/01497.

F. Kordon and D. Moldt (Eds.): PETRI NETS 2016, LNCS 9698, pp. 20–36, 2016.
DOI: 10.1007/978-3-319-39086-4_3

It is well known that the reachability problem is undecidable for Petri nets with ordered data, while the decidability status of this problem for unordered data is a intriguing open problem. In this note we do not embark on investigation of the reachability problem. Instead, we concentrate on the termination problem, the boundedness problem, the coverability problem, and alike, jointly called here *standard problems*. Again, it is well known that standard problems are decidable for Petri nets with ordered data [24] (and in consequence also for Petri nets with unordered data), as the model fits into the framework of well-structured transition systems of [11]. Most importantly, the structure of ordered data admits, in a certain technical sense explained in Sect. 5, a well quasi-order (wqo).

The decidability status of standard problems depends on the choice of atoms $\mathbb{A}$, and the purpose of this note is to investigate the decidability border. In order to make it possible to finitely present Petri nets and its configurations, and in particular to consider Petri nets as input to algorithms, we restrict to relational structures $\mathbb{A}$ that are *homogeneous* [25] and *effective* (the formal definitions are given in Sect. 4). On one side, in Sect. 5 we provide a simple but general decidability result that works under the sole additional assumption that $\mathbb{A}$ admits a wqo (which generalizes the decidability result for ordered data [24]). On the other side, in Sect. 3 we provide an example of an effective homogeneous structure $\mathbb{A}$ that makes all standard problems for Petri nets undecidable; further such examples are mentioned in Sect. 6. An observation that none of this examples admits a wqo naturally leads to the *WQO Dichotomy Conjecture* formulated in Sect. 6: for a homogeneous effective structure $\mathbb{A}$, either $\mathbb{A}$ admits a wqo (and then the standard problems are easily decidable), or all the standard problems are undecidable for Petri nets with atoms $\mathbb{A}$. It seems that either confirming or falsifying this conjecture would be very interesting: in the former case one can expect a deeper insight into the power of wqo-based methods, while in the latter case one would have to come up with a completely new approach to deciding properties of Petri nets with data.

In this note we do not use the recent approach to forward analysis of well-structured transition systems based on *idea completion* [10]. In [17] this approach have been recently applied to compute Karp-Miller trees for Petri nets with unordered data. The procedure does not generalize however to other structures $\mathbb{A}$ that admit a wqo, for instance to ordered data.

2 Petri Nets with Atoms

Atoms. A model of data Petri nets, to be defined below, is parametric in the underlying logical structure; the structure can be seen as data domain. Thus in the sequel we always assume a fixed a countable relational[1] structure $\mathbb{A}$, which we call *atoms*. Here are some example structures of atoms:

---

[1] Restriction to only relational structures is for the sake of simplicity.

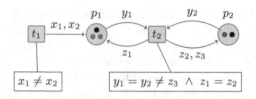

Fig. 1. A Petri net with equality atoms with places $P = \{p_1, p_2\}$ and transitions $T = \{t_1, t_2\}$. Different atoms are depicted through differently colored tokens.

- *Equality atoms*: natural numbers with equality $\mathbb{A} = (\mathbb{N}, =)$; equally well any other countable infinite set could be used instead of natural numbers $\mathbb{N}$, as the only available relation is equality.
- *Total order atoms*: rational numbers with the natural order $\mathbb{A} = (\mathbb{Q}, \leq)$; again, any other countable infinite dense total order without extremal elements could be used instead.
- *Timed atoms*: $\mathbb{A} = (\mathbb{Q}, \leq, +1)$ extending total order atoms with the binary relation $x + 1 = y$.

Note that every structure in the above list extends the preceding one by some additional relations. In the sequel we always assume that the vocabulary (signature) Σ of $\mathbb{A}$ is finite and contains the equality $=$.

Petri Nets with Atoms. We define a model that extends classical place/transition Petri nets. A *Petri net with atoms* $\mathbb{A}$ consists of two disjoint finite sets of places P and of transitions T, the arcs $A \subseteq P \times T \cup T \times P$, and two labelings:

- arcs are labelled by pairwise disjoint finite nonempty sets of variables;
- transitions are labelled by first-order formulas over the vocabulary Σ of $\mathbb{A}$, such that free variables of the formula labeling a transition t belong to the union of labels of the arcs incident to t.

Example 1. As an illustrating example, consider a Petri net with equality atoms with two places p_1, p_2 and two transitions t_1, t_2 depicted on Fig. 1. Transition t_1 outputs two tokens with arbitrary but distinct data values onto place p_1. Transition t_2 inputs two tokens with the same data value, say a, one from p_1 and one from p_2, and outputs three tokens: two tokens with arbitrary but equal data values, say b, one onto p_1 and the other onto p_2; and one token with a data value $c \neq a$ onto p_2. Note that transition t_2 does not specify whether $b = a$, or $b = c$, or $b \neq a, c$, and therefore all three options are allowed. Variables y_1, y_2 can be considered as input variables of t_2, while variables z_1, z_2, z_3 can be considered as output ones; analogously, t_1 has no input variables, and two output ones x_1, x_2.

From syntactic point of view, the net in Fig. 1 can be considered to be over *any* atoms $\mathbb{A}$, as we always assume equality relation to be available in $\mathbb{A}$.

The formal semantics of Petri nets with atoms is given by translation to multiset rewriting. Given a set X, finite or infinite, a finite multiset over X is a finite (possible empty) partial function from X to positive integers. In the sequel let $\mathcal{M}(X)$ stand for the set of all finite multisets over X. A *multiset rewriting system* $(\mathcal{P}, \mathcal{T})$ consists of a set $\mathcal{P}$, and a set of rewriting rules:

$$\mathcal{T} \subseteq \mathcal{M}(\mathcal{P}) \times \mathcal{M}(\mathcal{P}).$$

Configurations $C \in \mathcal{M}(\mathcal{P})$ are finite multisets over $\mathcal{P}$, and the step relation $\longrightarrow$ between configurations is defined as follows: for every $(I, O) \in \mathcal{T}$ and every $M \in \mathcal{M}(\mathcal{P})$, there is the step ($+$ stands for multiset union)

$$M + I \longrightarrow M + O.$$

For instance, a classical Petri net induces a multiset rewriting system where $\mathcal{P}$ is the set of places, and $\mathcal{T}$ is essentially the set of transitions, both $\mathcal{P}$ and $\mathcal{T}$ being finite. Configurations correspond to markings.

A Petri net with atoms $\mathbb{A}$ induces a multiset rewriting system $(\mathcal{P}, \mathcal{T})$, where $\mathcal{P} = P \times \mathbb{A}$ and is thus infinite. Configurations are finite multisets over $P \times \mathbb{A}$ (cf. a configuration depicted in Fig. 1). The rewriting rules $\mathcal{T}$ are defined as

$$\mathcal{T} = \bigcup_{t \in T} \mathcal{T}_t,$$

where the relation $\mathcal{T}_t \subseteq \mathcal{M}(\mathcal{P}) \times \mathcal{M}(\mathcal{P})$ is defined as follows. Let ϕ denote the formula labeling the transition t, and let X_i, X_o be the sets of input and output variables of t. Every valuation $v_i : X_i \to \mathbb{A}$ gives naturally raise to a multiset M_{v_i} over $\mathcal{P}$, where $M_{v_i}(p, a)$ is the (positive) number of variables x labeling the arc (p, t) with $v_i(x) = a$. Likewise for valuations $v_o : X_o \to \mathbb{A}$. Then let

$$\mathcal{T}_t = \{\, (M_{v_i}, M_{v_o}) \mid v_i : X_i \to \mathbb{A}, \ v_o : X_o \to \mathbb{A}, \ v_i, v_o \vDash \phi \,\}.$$

Like $\mathcal{P}$, the set of rewriting rules $\mathcal{T}$ is infinite in general.

As usual, for a net N and its configuration C, a run of (N, C) is a maximal finite, or infinite sequence of step starting in C. A configuration of N is *reachable* from C if it appears in some run of (N, C).

Remark 1. Petri nets with equality atoms are equivalent to (even if defined differently than) unordered data Petri nets of [24]. An even different but equivalent definition, in the style of vector addition systems, have been used in [17]. Another equivalent model is ν-PNs of [26] but *without* name creation: indeed, name creation considered in [26] is generation of a *globally* fresh atom, while in Petri nets with equality atoms it is only possible to generate a *locally* fresh one. Petri nets with total ordered atoms are equivalent to ordered data Petri nets of [24]. Finally, Petri nets with timed atoms subsume many timed extensions of Petri nets, including timed Petri nets [1] and timed-arc Petri nets [18].

Fig. 2. A pair of configurations related by $\preceq$, in the case of equality atoms. One witnessing automorphism maps black to blue, blue to brown, and preserves red; the other one maps black to red, red to blue, and blue to brown. (Color figure online)

Orbit-Finiteness. An *atom automorphism* is an automorphism of $\mathbb{A}$ with itself, that is a bijection $\mathbb{A} \to \mathbb{A}$ such that for every n-tuple $(a_1, \ldots, a_n)$ and every n-ary relation r in $\mathbb{A}$, $r(a_1, \ldots, a_n)$ holds if, and only if $r(f(a_1), \ldots, f(a_n))$ holds. For instance, in the case of equality atoms these are all bijections of $\mathbb{N}$, in the case of total order atoms these are all monotonic bijections of $\mathbb{Q}$, and in the case of timed atoms these are monotonic bijections of $\mathbb{Q}$ that preserve integer differences.

We define an action of atom automorphisms on configurations: for a configuration C and an atom automorphism π, let $C \cdot \pi$ denote a configuration obtained from C by applying π to every atom carried by every token in C. Using the action, we define a quasi-order (i.e., a reflexive and transitive relation) on configurations: $C \preceq C'$ if $C \cdot \pi \sqsubseteq C'$ for some atom automorphism π, where $\sqsubseteq$ stands for multiset inclusion (cf. Fig. 2). If $C \preceq C' \preceq C$ then $C \cdot \pi = C'$ for some atom automorphism π, in which case we call C and C' equivalent. Note that the step relation is invariant under the equivalence: for equivalent C, C', if $C \longrightarrow D$ then $C' \longrightarrow D'$ for some D' equivalent to D. This is due to the fact the transitions are specified in the first-order logic which is clearly invariant under atom automorphisms.

A set of configurations $\mathcal{C}$ is *orbit-finite* if it is finite up to the equivalence. In other words, $\mathcal{C}$ is contained in a finite union of orbits, where an orbit of a configuration C is defined as $\{ C \cdot \pi \,|\, \pi \text{ an atom automorphism} \}$. Similarly one can define orbits, and orbit-finiteness, for any other set on which an action of atom automorphisms is defined.

Remark 2. Our presentation is in the style of [14,26], in order to keep it simple. Interestingly, an equivalent but more abstract definition can be provided, by following the approach of [3]. In this approach, a model of computation is reinterpreted with finiteness relaxed to orbit-finiteness. In case of Petri nets this boils down to allowing orbit-finite sets of places and transitions instead of finite ones only. Following the approach, one would consider the set $\mathcal{P}$ directly as places, and the set $\mathcal{T}$ as transitions of a net. For ω-categorical structures $\mathbb{A}$, including all homogeneous relational structures [25], both $\mathcal{P}$ and $\mathcal{T}$ are orbit-finite sets.

Standard Decision Problems. We focus on classical decision problems, like the *termination problem*: does a given (N, C) admit only finite runs? The structure of atoms is considered as a parameter, and hence itself does not constitute part of input. Concerning representation of input, the net N is represented by finite sets P, T, A and appropriate labelings with variables and formulas. Representation of a configuration C will be discussed in Sect. 4. Another classical problem is the *place non-emptiness problem* (markability): given (N, C) and a place p of N, does (N, C) admit a run that puts at least one token on place p?

In order to define some other standard problems we need to take the action of atom automorphisms on configurations into account. For instance, a Petri net with atoms has typically infinitely many reachable configurations, and hence the classical boundedness question is not interesting. Thus we say that (N, C) is *bounded* if the set of reachable configurations is orbit-finite. This defines the appropriate variant of the *boundedness problem*. The *coverability problem* we define as follows: given N, C and C', is there a configuration C'' of N reachable from C with $C' \preceq C''$? In the same vein one translates other decision problems to nets with atoms, for instance the *evitability problem*: given (N, C) and a finite set $\mathcal{C}$ of configurations of N, is there a run of (N, C) whose all configurations are in $\uparrow \mathcal{C} = \{ C' \mid \exists C \in \mathcal{C}. \ C \preceq C' \}$?

All the decision problems mentioned above we jointly call *standard problems*. These should be considered as examples rather that an exhaustive list – the results reported in the sequel keep holding for many other problems not mentioned above (we refrain however from an attempt of characterization of all such problems). An example of the problem for which the results *do not* hold is the place-boundedness problem, which is decidable for equality atoms (as shown in [17], using the forward analysis via computation of a Karp-Miller tree), but undecidable for total order atoms [24]. Also, we do not consider here the 'hard' decision problems, like reachability or liveness.

3   Undecidability

As already mentioned, decidability status of standard problems depends on the choice of data domain $\mathbb{A}$. Before stating a general decidability result for a wide class of structures $\mathbb{A}$ (cf. Sect. 5), in this section we exhibit an undecidable case – we sketch a proof of undecidability of the standard problems when tokens are allowed, roughly speaking, to carry pairs of equality atoms. Formally speaking, we consider Petri nets with atoms

$$\mathbb{A}_2 \ = \ (\mathbb{N}^2, =_1, =_2, =_{12}),$$

where $=_1$, $=_2$, and $=_{12}$ are binary relations describing, respectively, equality on the first coordinate, equality on the second coordinate, and equality of the first coordinate of the first argument with the second coordinate of the second argument. We show that Petri nets with atoms $\mathbb{A}_2$ can faithfully simulate computations of Minsky counter machines.

In the sequel consider a fixed deterministic Minsky machine $\mathcal{M}$ with two counters c_1, c_2, and states Q. We will sketch a construction of a Petri net N over $\mathbb{A}_2$ that simulates the computation of $\mathcal{M}$ from the initial state with the initial counter values $c_1 = c_2 = 0$. The net will have the following transitions:

$$T \ = \ \{z_1, z_2, d_1, d_2, i_1, i_2, i'_1, i'_2, t_1, t_2\}$$

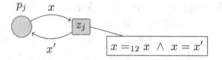

Fig. 3. Transition z_j simulating zero test of counter c_j. The equality $x = x'$ is a shorthand for $x =_1 x' \land x =_2 x'$. For simplicity, the places corresponding to control states of $\mathcal{M}$ are omitted.

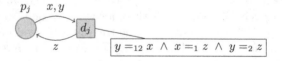

Fig. 4. Transition z_j simulating decrement operation on counter c_j.

and its places will include, except for a number of auxiliary ones, the following places:

$$\{p_1, p_2, q, r\} \cup Q \subseteq P.$$

In particular, every state of $\mathcal{M}$ will have a corresponding place in N. The idea is to represent a value $c_j = n$ by storing $n + 1$ tokens on place p_j, carrying atoms

$$(a_1, a_2), (a_2, a_3), \ldots, (a_n, a_{n+1}), (a_{n+1}, a_1),$$

for some arbitrary but distinct $a_1, \ldots, a_{n+1} \in \mathbb{N}$. Intuitively, if atoms were considered as directed edges, a value n of a counter is represented by a directed cycle of length $n + 1$. The initial configuration C of N encodes counter values $c_1 = c_2 = 0$, by placing on p_1 and p_2 an atom (a, a), for some arbitrary $a \in \mathbb{N}$, corresponding to a self-loop. In addition, C contains a token on the place corresponding to the initial state of $\mathcal{M}$.

Zero Test: A zero test on a counter c_j is performed by a transition z_j that inputs one token from p_j (cf. Fig. 3). The transition detects a self-loop using the constraint $x =_{12} x$, where x is the input variable. The input token is output back onto place p_j in order to preserve the representation of the counter value.

Decrement: The decrement operation on a counter c_j is simulated, roughly speaking, by replacing two consecutive edges on a cycle by one edge; using the condition $y =_{12} x$ we can enforce that the edge y follows the edge x on the cycle. This is achieved by a transition d_j (cf. Fig. 4) that inputs from p_j two tokens carrying atoms (a, a') and (a', a''), for arbitrarily chosen pairwise different $a, a', a'' \in \mathbb{N}$, and outputs to p_j one token carrying (a, a'').

Increment: Slightly more complicated is the simulation of the increment operation on a counter, as it involves creating a fresh natural number that must be different from all currently used ones. In the first step of the simulation, the net

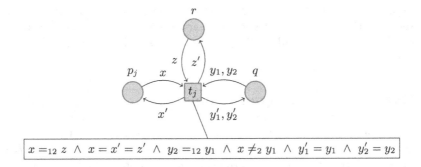

Fig. 5. Transition t_j constituting the crucial part of simulation of increment operation on counter c_j.

executes a transition i_j that inputs a token (a, a') from p_j and outputs, for an arbitrarily chosen $a'' \in \mathbb{N}$ different than a and a', two tokens carrying (a, a'') and (a'', a') onto an auxiliary place q. In addition, let the transition output a token carrying (a'', a') onto place r. In the very last step of the simulation, two tokens will be moved from place q to p_j by a transition i'_j, and a single token will be removed from r. The aim of the remaining steps is to check that a'' does not currently appear on place p_j. To this aim the net traverses the cycle stored on p_j, starting from the edge (a'', a'). The traversal is done by iterative execution of the transition t_j, depicted on Fig. 5, that uses the place r to store the current edge in the course of traversal. The condition $x =_{12} z$ ensures that the edge x, picked up from place p_j, follows the edge z on the cycle. The equalities $x = x' = z'$ enforce that the edge x is put both back to q_j, and also copied to r. Finally, the condition $x \neq_2 y_1$ checks that the edges x and y_1 have different endpoints.

Note that replacing $x \neq_2 y_1$ by $x =_2 y_1$ would allow to detect that a'' does appear on the cycle, which means that a'' has been chosen incorrectly in the first step of the simulation. Note also that replacing $x \neq_2 y_1$ by $y_1 =_{12} x$ allows to detect that the endpoint of x equals a, and thus the traversal can be finished. Finally, observe that the case when the incremented counter has value $c_j = 0$ needs a separate treatment.

We have thus sketched a construction of a net N and configuration C such that the place corresponding to the halting state of $\mathcal{M}$ is nonempty in some reachable configuration of (N, C) if, and only if, the machine $\mathcal{M}$ halts. This entails undecidability of the place non-emptiness, coverability and evitability problems. Furthermore, (N, C) terminates if and only if the machine $\mathcal{M}$ halts. This entails undecidability of the termination and boundedness problems.

Proposition 1. *The standard problems are undecidable for Petri nets with atoms $\mathbb{A}_2$.*

A similar undecidability argument can be given for Petri nets with slightly simpler atoms $\mathbb{A}'_2 = (\mathbb{N}^2, =_1, =_2)$. In contrast to this, all the standard problems are decidable for Petri nets with atoms $\mathbb{A}_1 = (\mathbb{N}^2, =_1, =)$, which will become apparent shortly. Below we investigate in more detail the decidability border between those atoms that admit decidability of classical decision problems and those atoms that do not.

4   Effective Homogeneous Atoms

In this section and in the next one we are going to stay on the decidable side. In this section we prepare the ground: we define the class of structures $\mathbb{A}$ we are going to restrict to, namely *effective homogeneous* ones [25]. This restriction will guarantee, in particular, that configurations of a Petri net can be finitely presented and thus input by an algorithm. We will also provide an operation of *wreath* product that preserves effective homogeneity. In the next section we will state a general decidability result for Petri nets over effective homogeneous atoms $\mathbb{A}$, using the setting of well-structured transition systems [11].

For two relational Σ-structures $\mathcal{A}$ and $\mathcal{B}$ we say that $\mathcal{A}$ *embeds* in $\mathcal{B}$, written $\mathcal{A} \trianglelefteq \mathcal{B}$, if $\mathcal{A}$ is isomorphic to an induced substructure of $\mathcal{B}$, i.e. to a structure obtained by restricting $\mathcal{B}$ to a subset of its domain. This is witnessed by an injective function[2] $h : \mathcal{A} \to \mathcal{B}$, which we call *embedding*. The class of finite structures that embed into $\mathbb{A}$ we denote by AGE($\mathbb{A}$).

Homogeneous Structures. A Σ-structure $\mathbb{A}$ is *homogeneous* if every isomorphism between two finite induced substructures of $\mathbb{A}$ extends to an automorphism of $\mathbb{A}$. (Intuitively, the 'position' of a finite induced substructure inside $\mathbb{A}$ depends only on its isomorphism type.) For instance, equality atoms and total order atoms are homogeneous structures. In the latter case finite induced substructures are just finite total orders, and every isomorphism between any two such total orders does extend to a monotonic bijection from $\mathbb{Q}$ to $\mathbb{Q}$. Timed atoms are not homogeneous: no isomorphism between two induced 2-element substructures $\{-1, 3\}$ and $\{0.5, 2.5\}$ extends to an automorphism of timed atoms, as the distances between -1 and 3, and between 0.5 and 2.5, are different integers.

There is a one-to-one correspondence between infinite countable homogeneous structures, and classes of finite structures over the same vocabulary that are closed under isomorphisms and induced substructures, and satisfy the *amalgamation property*[3] (such classes of structures are called *Fraïssé classes*). In one direction, the class AGE($\mathbb{A}$), for a homogeneous Σ-structure $\mathbb{A}$, is a Fraïssé class. In the other direction, a Fraïssé class of finite Σ-structures induces a unique up to isomorphism homogeneous Σ-structure via the construction of *Fraïssé limit* [12]. In particular, $(\mathbb{N}, =)$ is the Fraïssé limit of finite pure sets (structures with $=$ as the only relation) and $(\mathbb{Q}, \leq)$ is the Fraïssé limit of finite total orders.

---

[2] We deliberately do not distinguish a structure $\mathcal{A}$ from its domain set.

[3] A class has amalgamation property if for every two embeddings $h_1 : \mathcal{A} \to \mathcal{B}_1$ and $h_2 : \mathcal{A} \to \mathcal{B}_2$ there is a structure $\mathcal{C}$ and two embeddings $g_1 : \mathcal{B}_1 \to \mathcal{C}$ and $g_2 : \mathcal{B}_2 \to \mathcal{C}$ such that $g_1 \circ h_1 = g_2 \circ h_2$ (see [12,25] for details).

Many other natural classes of structures have the amalgamation property: finite graphs, finite directed graphs, finite partial orders, finite equivalence relations, finite tournaments, etc. Each of these classes induces, as the Fraïssé limit, a homogeneous relational structure. For instance finite graphs induce the *universal graph* (called also random graph) [12], which is the infinite countable graph that results with probability 1, if every pair of vertices is related by an edge with probability p, irrespectively of the choice of the probability as long as $0 < p < 1$. Therefore, every finite graph G embeds into the universal graph, and if G embeds into another finite graph H then every embedding of G into the universal graph extends to an embedding of H. Along the same lines, finite partial orders induce the universal partial order, finite tournaments induce the universal tournament, etc. The Fraïssé limit of the finite equivalence relations is $(\mathbb{D}, R, =)$, where $\mathbb{D}$ is a countably-infinite set and R is an infinite-index equivalence relation over $\mathbb{D}$ s.t. each one of the infinitely-many equivalence classes is itself an infinite subset of $\mathbb{D}$. This structure is isomorphic to $(\mathbb{N}^2, =_1, =)$ and can be used to model data with *nested* equality, where one can check whether two elements belong to the same equivalence class and, if so, whether they are actually equal. Examples of homogeneous structures abound, see for instance [25].

From this point on we assume atoms to be a Σ-structure $\mathbb{A}$ satisfying the following two conditions:

(A1) $\mathbb{A}$ is a homogeneous countable infinite relational structure.
(A2) the following *age problem* for $\mathbb{A}$ is decidable: given a finite Σ-structure $\mathcal{A}$, decide whether $\mathcal{A} \trianglelefteq \mathbb{A}$.

Such structures $\mathbb{A}$ we call *effective homogeneous*. All the structures $\mathbb{A}$ mentioned so far, except for timed atoms, are effective homogeneous.

Among various good properties, homogeneous structures admit quantifier elimination: every first-order formula is equivalent to (i.e., defines the same set as) a quantifier-free one. Therefore, from now on we may assume wlog. that formulas labeling transitions are quantifier-free.

Wreath Product. Given two relational structures $\mathbb{A} = (A, R_1, \ldots, R_m)$ and $\mathbb{B} = (B, S_1, \ldots, S_n)$, their *wreath product* is the relational structure $\mathbb{A} \otimes \mathbb{B} = (A \times B, R'_1, \ldots, R'_m, S'_1, \ldots, S'_n)$, where

- $((a_1, b_1), \ldots, (a_k, b_k)) \in R'_i$ if $(a_1, \ldots, a_k) \in R_i$, and
- $((a_1, b_1), \ldots, (a_k, b_k)) \in S'_j$ if $a_1 = \cdots = a_k$ and $(b_1, \ldots, b_k) \in S_j$.

Intuitively, $\mathbb{A} \otimes \mathbb{B}$ is obtained by replacing each element in $\mathbb{A}$ with a disjoint copy of $\mathbb{B}$. For instance, $(\mathbb{N}, =) \otimes (\mathbb{N}, =)$ is exactly $\mathbb{A}_1 = (\mathbb{N}^2, =_1, =)$. More generally, one can model data with k-*nested* equality: take $\mathbb{B}_1 = (\mathbb{N}, =)$ and, for each $k \geq 1$, let $\mathbb{B}_{k+1} = \mathbb{B}_1 \otimes \mathbb{B}_k$. Up to isomorphism, $\mathbb{B}_k$ is the structure $(\mathbb{D}, R_1, \ldots, R_k)$ with k nested equivalence relations $R_1, \ldots, R_k$ over an infinite set $\mathbb{D}$, where R_1 has infinitely many infinite equivalence classes, R_{i+1} refines every equivalence class of R_i into infinitely many classes, for $i = 1, \ldots, k-1$; and the finest relation R_k is the equality.

The wreath product preserves effective homogeneity: first, if $\mathbb{A}$ and $\mathbb{B}$ are homogeneous then the same holds for $\mathbb{A} \otimes \mathbb{B}$, and second, the age problem for $\mathbb{A} \otimes \mathbb{B}$ reduces to the same problem for $\mathbb{A}$ and $\mathbb{B}$ [7]. As an example, the wreath product $(\mathbb{Q}, \leq) \otimes (\mathbb{N}, =)$ is, up to isomorphism, the universal total quasi-order, i.e. the Fraïssé limit of all finite total quasi-orders.

5 Well-Structured Petri Nets

Fix an effective homogeneous Σ-structure $\mathbb{A}$. For a set X, let $\mathrm{AGE}(\mathbb{A}, X)$ denote the set of all functions $\mathcal{A} \to X$, where $\mathcal{A} \in \mathrm{AGE}(\mathbb{A})$. In other words, $\mathrm{AGE}(\mathbb{A}, X)$ contains finite induced substructures of $\mathbb{A}$ labeled by elements of X.

Finite Representations. Recall that a configuration is a finite partial function from $\mathbb{A} \times P$ to positive integers, which can be reformatted into a total function $\mathcal{A} \to \mathcal{M}(P)$ from a finite (possibly empty) induced substructure $\mathcal{A}$ of $\mathbb{A}$ to finite multisets[4] over P. Thus from now on we consider configurations as elements of

$$\mathrm{conf}(\mathbb{A}, P) \quad = \quad \mathrm{AGE}(\mathbb{A}, \mathcal{M}(P)).$$

By homogeneity of atoms, two configurations $C : \mathcal{A} \to \mathcal{M}(P)$ and $D : \mathcal{B} \to \mathcal{M}(P)$ are equivalent if, and only if, the two domain structures $\mathcal{A}$, $\mathcal{B}$ are related by an isomorphism $h : \mathcal{A} \to \mathcal{B}$ that preserves labels: $C(a) = D(h(a))$ for every $a \in \mathcal{A}$. Similarly, $C \preceq C'$ if, and only if, there is an embedding $h : \mathcal{A} \to \mathcal{B}$ that *increases* labels: $C(a) \sqsubseteq D(h(a))$ for every $a \in \mathcal{A}$ (recall that $\sqsubseteq$ stands for multiset inclusion).

Recall that the step relation is invariant under equivalence: equivalent configurations have equivalent successor configurations. Thus to represent a configuration it is enough to know the equivalence class of a configuration; furthermore, by homogeneity it is enough to know the isomorphism type of the domain structure $\mathcal{A}$. Therefore configurations of a Petri net with homogeneous atoms can be finitely represented (up to isomorphism of the domain structure), which makes the model amenable to algorithmic analysis.

Well Quasi-orders. By *skeleton* of a quasi-order $(X, \leq)$ we mean the partial order obtained as the quotient of X by the equivalence relation that relates every two elements $x, y \in X$ satisfying $x \leq y \leq x$. We call two quasi-orders $(X, \leq)$ and $(X', \leq')$ *skeleton-isomorphic*, and write $(X, \leq) \cong (X', \leq')$, if their skeletons are isomorphic.

A quasi-order $(X, \leq)$ lifts naturally to $\mathrm{AGE}(\mathbb{A}, X)$: for $f : \mathcal{A} \to X$ and $g : \mathcal{B} \to X$, let $f \trianglelefteq_{(X, \leq)} g$ if there is an embedding $h : \mathcal{A} \to \mathcal{B}$ such that $f(a) \leq g(h(a))$ for every $a \in \mathcal{A}$. For instance, for equality atoms we obtain the natural lifting of $(X, \leq)$ to finite multisets over X, and for total order atoms we obtain Higman ordering of finite sequences X^* over X with respect to the base

---

[4] We could further restrict the codomain to *nonempty* finite multisets over P.

order $(X, \leq)$ (see e.g. [10] for formal definitions). When $(X, \leq) = (\mathcal{M}(P), \sqsubseteq)$, one obtains the quasi-order of configurations:

$$(\text{AGE}(\mathbb{A}, \mathcal{M}(P)), \trianglelefteq_{(\mathcal{M}(P), \sqsubseteq)}) \quad \cong \quad (\text{conf}(\mathbb{A}, P), \preceq).$$

A *well quasi-order* (WQO) is a quasi-order $(X, \leq)$ such that for every infinite sequence $x_1, x_2, \ldots$ of elements of X, there are positions $i < j$ with $x_i \leq x_j$. Equivalently, a WQO is a well founded quasi-order without infinite antichains. For two skeleton-isomorphic quasi-orders, if one is a WQO than the other is a WQO too. For the rest of this section assume that

(A3) for every WQO $(X, \leq)$, the lifted quasi-order $(\text{AGE}(\mathbb{A}, X), \trianglelefteq_{(X, \leq)})$ is a WQO (we say in this case that $\mathbb{A}$ *preserves* WQO).

For example, both equality atoms and total order atoms preserve WQO. Indeed, if $(X, \leq)$ is a WQO then $(\text{AGE}((\mathbb{N}, =), X), \trianglelefteq_{(X, \leq)})$ is a WQO, which is a generalization of Dickson's Lemma; and $(\text{AGE}((\mathbb{Q}, \leq), X), \trianglelefteq_{(X, \leq)})$ is a WQO as well, which is exactly Higman's Lemma [16]. Interestingly, for a suitably defined structure of atoms (a forest order, see [2] for details) one can also provide a similar model-theoretic reformulation of Kruskal's lemma [22].

When $\mathbb{A}$ preserves WQO then $(\text{AGE}(\mathbb{A}), \trianglelefteq)$ is necessarily a WQO. We do not know whether the converse holds, and thus the following question is open:

Question 1. For every homogeneous $\mathbb{A}$ such that $(\text{AGE}(\mathbb{A}), \trianglelefteq)$ is a WQO, and for every WQO $(X, \leq)$, is the lifted quasi-order $(\text{AGE}(\mathbb{A}, X), \trianglelefteq_{(X, \leq)})$ a WQO?

Let's concentrate on an important special case, when $(X, \leq) = (\text{AGE}(\mathbb{B}), \trianglelefteq)$ for some homogeneous structure $\mathbb{B}$. We observe that $\text{AGE}(\mathbb{A}, \text{AGE}(\mathbb{B}))$, containing induced substructures of $\mathbb{A}$ labeled by induced substructures of $\mathbb{B}$, is essentially the same set as $\text{AGE}(\mathbb{A} \otimes \mathbb{B})$, containing induced substructures of the wreath product. Furthermore, the lifted quasi-order coincides with the embedding quasi-order on $\text{AGE}(\mathbb{A} \otimes \mathbb{B})$. Formally, the following two quasi-orders are isomorphic:

$$(\text{AGE}(\mathbb{A}, \text{AGE}(B)), \trianglelefteq_{\trianglelefteq}) \quad \cong \quad (\text{AGE}(\mathbb{A} \otimes \mathbb{B}), \trianglelefteq). \tag{1}$$

This leads to a 'weaker' version of Question 1 (in the sense that the positive answer to Question 1 implies the same answer to the following one):

Question 2. For every homogeneous structures $\mathbb{A}, \mathbb{B}$ such that both $(\text{AGE}(\mathbb{A}), \trianglelefteq)$ and $(\text{AGE}(\mathbb{B}), \trianglelefteq)$ are WQOs, is $(\mathbb{A} \otimes \mathbb{B}, \trianglelefteq)$ a WQO?

Note that the answer to Question 2 is positive in the special case when $\mathbb{A}$ *preserves* WQO.

We stress upon importance of the homogeneity assumption, as one can easily come up with a non-homogeneous counterexample to both questions, for instance taking $\mathbb{A} = (\mathbb{N}, +1)$.

Well-Structured Petri Nets with Atoms. We are now going to use the setting of well-structured transition systems of [11] to derive a general decidability result. Consider in the sequel a fixed effective homogeneous Σ-structure $\mathbb{A}$ that preserves WQO, and a fixed Petri net with atoms $\mathbb{A}$. We need to check a number of assumptions required for the decidability results of [11].

By decidability of the embedding problem one easily deduces that the step relation is computable. Indeed, a satisfying valuation of variables of a formula corresponds to an embedding of finite structure $\mathcal{A}$ in $\mathbb{A}$, and thus one can compute all (up to isomorphism) valuations satisfying a quantifier-free formula that labels a transition, by enumerating all finite Σ-structures $\mathcal{A}$ of bounded size. In particular one can compute successors $\{\,C' \mid C \longrightarrow C'\,\}$ of a given configuration C (note that the successor set is finite, up to isomorphism of the domain structure). The ordering $\preceq$ is also easily decidable.

Like for classical Petri nets, step relation of a Petri net with atoms $\mathbb{A}$ satisfies a compatibility condition with respect to $\preceq$: if $C \prec D$ and $C \longrightarrow C'$ then there exists a configuration D' with $C' \prec D'$ and $D \longrightarrow D'$. This property, combined with the invariance of step relation under equivalence, implies *strong strict compatibility* of [11].

Let $\uparrow C = \{\,C' \mid C \preceq C'\,\}$ denote the upward closure of C. By compatibility, the predecessor set $\mathrm{pred}(\uparrow C) = \{\,C' \mid C' \longrightarrow C'' \in \uparrow C\,\}$ is upward closed. As $\mathbb{A}$ preserves WQO, $(\mathrm{conf}(\mathbb{A}, P), \preceq)$ is a WQO and hence the set $\mathrm{pred}(\uparrow C)$ has only finitely many minimal elements. Using decidability of the embedding problem one shows the property called *effective pred bases* in [11]: given a configuration C, the finite set $\min(\mathrm{pred}(\uparrow C))$ is computable.

We have thus completed the check-list: $(\mathrm{conf}(\mathbb{A}, P), \longrightarrow, \preceq)$ is a well-structured transition system that satisfies all assumptions of Theorems 3.6, 4.6, 4.8 and (if skeleton of $(\mathrm{conf}(\mathbb{A}, P), \preceq)$ is considered) Theorem 4.11 in [11]. Therefore we may state the following general decidability result:

Theorem 1. *If $\mathbb{A}$ is an effective homogeneous structure that preserves WQO then the standard problems are decidable for Petri nets with atoms $\mathbb{A}$.*

This generalizes the decidability result of [24], and applies to a range of different structures of atoms including, among the others, equality atoms, total order atoms, and all structures obtained from them by the wreath product. Indeed, using the following generalization of the isomorphism (1):

$$(\mathrm{AGE}(\mathbb{A}, \mathrm{AGE}(\mathbb{B}, X)), \trianglelefteq_{\trianglelefteq_{(X, \leq)}}) \quad \cong \quad (\mathrm{AGE}(\mathbb{A} \otimes \mathbb{B}, X), \trianglelefteq_{(X, \leq)}),$$

one easily shows that wreath product, in addition to preservation of effective homogeneity, also preserves WQO-preservation: if homogeneous structures $\mathbb{A}$ and $\mathbb{B}$ preserve WQO then $\mathbb{A} \otimes \mathbb{B}$ also does. For instance, in the case of nested equality atoms $\mathbb{A}_1 = (\mathbb{N}, =) \otimes (\mathbb{N}, =)$, the lifted quasi-order is skeleton isomorphic to the natural ordering of $\mathcal{M}(\mathcal{M}(X))$ finite multisets over finite multisets over X; and when atoms is the wreath product $(\mathbb{Q}, \leq) \otimes (\mathbb{N}, =)$ of total order atoms and equality atoms, the lifted quasi-order is skeleton-isomorphic to the Higman ordering of $\mathcal{M}(X)^*$ finite sequences of finite multisets over X.

The decision procedures solving the standard problems, as derived from [11], can be actually directly encoded in the one of recently developed programming languages designed for manipulating infinite definable structures: LOIS [21] or Nλ [20].

6   The WQO Dichotomy Conjecture

What is the crucial difference between atoms $\mathbb{A}_1 = (\mathbb{N}^{(2)}, =_1, =)$ and $\mathbb{A}'_2 = (\mathbb{N}^{(2)}, =_1, =_2)$ that makes Petri nets with the former atoms decidable, while Petri nets with the latter atoms undecidable? We claim that the crucial difference is that the quasi-order $(\mathrm{conf}(\mathbb{A}_1, P), \preceq)$ is a WQO, while the quasi-oder $(\mathrm{conf}(\mathbb{A}'_2, P), \preceq)$ is not. All quasi-orders considered by us are well founded (as P is finite), hence the difference lies in existence of an infinite antichain in $(\mathrm{conf}(\mathbb{A}'_2, P), \preceq)$.

The induced substructure of $\mathbb{A}$ with domain $A \subseteq \mathbb{A}$ we call below the *substructure induced by A*. For the encoding of counter values in the undecidability proof in Sect. 3 we have actually used an infinite antichain $\{\mathcal{A}_1, \mathcal{A}_2, \ldots\}$ in $(\mathrm{AGE}(\mathbb{A}_2), \trianglelefteq)$, namely one that contains, for every $n \geq 1$, the substructure $\mathcal{A}_n$ of $\mathbb{A}_2$ induced by:

$$A_n = \{(a_1, a_2), (a_2, a_3), \ldots, (a_{n-1}, a_n), (a_n, a_1)\},$$

for some arbitrary but pairwise different $a_1, \ldots, a_n \in \mathbb{N}$. Note that when one moves to $\mathbb{A}'_2$, the substructures $\mathcal{A}'_n$ induced by the same subsets A_n do not form an antichain any more; indeed, for $n < m$, an arbitrary injection $A_n \to A_m$ is an embedding of $\mathcal{A}'_n$ into $\mathcal{A}'_m$. In order to adapt the undecidability proof to Petri nets with atoms $\mathbb{A}'_2$, we can use another infinite antichain, namely one that contains, for every $n \geq 1$, the substructure of $\mathbb{A}'_2$ induced by:

$$A'_n = \{(a_1, b_1), (a_2, b_1), (a_2, b_2), (a_3, b_2), \ldots, (a_n, b_{n-1}), (a_n, b_n), (a_1, b_n)\},$$

for some arbitrary but pairwise different $a_1, \ldots, a_n \in \mathbb{N}$, and arbitrary but pairwise different $b_1, \ldots, b_n \in \mathbb{N}$. We leave it as an exercise to check that this is an antichain in $(\mathrm{AGE}(\mathbb{A}'_2), \trianglelefteq)$, and to adapt the undecidability proof.

Interestingly, for all structures $\mathbb{A}$ not preserving WQO that have been mentioned so far, one easily comes up with an infinite antichain $\{\mathcal{A}_1, \mathcal{A}_2, \ldots\}$ admitting an undecidability argument similar to the one in Sect. 3. For instance, in the case of the random graph atoms, take as $\mathcal{A}_n$ a cycle of length n, and in the case of the directed random graph, take as $\mathcal{A}_n$ a directed cycle of length n.

For the universal partial order $(\mathbb{D}, \leq)$, take as $\mathcal{A}_n$, for $n \geq 1$, a crone partial order (cf. Fig. 6) consisting of $2n$ elements $a_1, \ldots, a_n, b_1, \ldots, b_n \in \mathbb{D}$ such that $a_i \leq b_j$ if and only if $i = j$, or $i = j + 1$, or $i = 1$ and $j = n$, and moreover $\{a_1, \ldots, a_n\}$ and $\{b_1, \ldots, b_n\}$ are pairwise incomparable w.r.t. $\leq$. One readily verifies that this is an antichain. Essentially, the antichain provides an encoding of finite cycles into partial orders.

For the universal tournament, take as $\mathcal{A}_n$, for $n \geq 7$, an n-element tournament obtained from an n-element total order $a_1 < a_2 < \ldots < a_n$ by

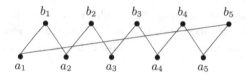

Fig. 6. A crone partial order $\mathcal{A}_5$.

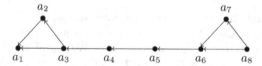

Fig. 7. A tournament $\mathcal{A}_8$ [15,23]. All missing edges are oriented from left to right.

reversing edges (a_1, a_3), (a_{n-2}, a_n), and all edges (a_i, a_{i+1}) (cf. Fig. 7). Again, this is essentially an encoding of finite cycles into tournaments. A formal proof that $\{\mathcal{A}_n \mid n \geq 7\}$ is an antichain can be found in [15,23]. We encourage the reader to try reusing some of the antichains listed above in the undecidability proof.

We do not know whether every homogeneous structure not preserving WQO admits a similar encoding of finite cycles. Formally, we do not know the answer to the following question:

Question 3. When $\mathbb{A}$ is an effective homogeneous structure not preserving WQO, are all the standard problems undecidable for Petri nets with atoms $\mathbb{A}$?

We conjecture positive answers to Questions 1–3. Put explicitly, we formulate the following:

Conjecture 1 (WQO Dichotomy). For every effective homogeneous infinite countable relational structure $\mathbb{A}$ over a finite vocabulary, exactly one of the two conditions hold:

– $(\textsc{Age}(\mathbb{A}), \trianglelefteq)$ is a WQO;
– the standard problems are undecidable for Petri nets with atoms $\mathbb{A}$.

Any answers to Questions 1–3 will be interesting. If the conjecture is proved, this would shed a new light on the decidability border, and on the power of WQO-based methods. On the other hand, in order to falsify the conjecture one has to come up with a completely new method for solving (some of) the standard problems for Petri nets with data.

The conjecture is easily confirmed for atoms $\mathbb{A}$ ranging over a restricted subclass of homogeneous graph, or homogeneous directed graphs, using the classification result by Cherlin [6].

Remark 3 An analogous conjecture can be stated for other models of computation. For instance, instead of the standard problems for Petri nets with atoms, one can consider the universality problem for nondeterministic finite automata with one register, or the emptiness problems for alternating automata with one register (cf. [2]).

Acknowledgments. In first place, I am very grateful Wojtek Czerwiński and Paweł Parys, with whom I currently work on the WQO Dichotomy Conjecture, for many fruitful discussions and for reading a draft of this paper. Furthermore, I thank Sylvain Schmitz for our discussion and for his interesting ideas towards resolving the conjecture. Finally, I would like to thank my colleagues: Mikołaj Bojańczyk, Lorenzo Clemente, Bartek Klin, Asia Ochremiak and Szymek Toruńczyk for the joint research effort on sets with atoms, a long-term research project, of which the present note constitutes a small part.

References

1. Abdulla, P.A., Nylén, A.: Timed petri nets and BQOs. In: Colom, J.-M., Koutny, M. (eds.) ICATPN 2001. LNCS, vol. 2075, pp. 53–70. Springer, Heidelberg (2001)
2. Bojańczyk, M., Braud, L., Klin, B., Lasota, S.: Towards nominal computation. In: Proceedings of the POPL, pp. 401–412 (2012)
3. Bojańczyk, M., Klin, B., Lasota, S.: Automata theory in nominal sets. Logical Methods Comput. Sci. **10**(3), 1–44 (2014). Paper 4
4. Bojańczyk, M., Klin, B., Lasota, S., Toruńczyk, S.: Turing machines with atoms. In: LICS, pp. 183–192 (2013)
5. Cervesato, I., Durgin, N.A., Lincoln, P., Mitchell, J.C., Scedrov, A.: A meta-notation for protocol analysis. In: Proceedings of the CSFW 1999, pp. 55–69 (1999)
6. Cherlin, G.: The classification of countable homogeneous directed graphs and countable homogeneous n-tournaments. Memoirs of the American Mathematical Society, vol. 621. American Mathematical Society (1998)
7. Clemente, L., Lasota, S.: Reachability analysis of first-order definable pushdown systems. In: Proceedings of the CSL 2015, pp. 244–259 (2015)
8. Delzanno, G.: An overview of MSR(C): a clp-based framework for the symbolic verification of parameterized concurrent systems. Electr. Notes Theor. Comput. Sci. **76**, 65–82 (2002)
9. Delzanno, G.: Constraint multiset rewriting. Technical report DISI-TR-05-08, DISI, Universitá di Genova (2005)
10. Finkel, A., Goubault-Larrecq, J.: Forward analysis for wsts, part I: completions. In: Proceedings of the STACS 2009, pp. 433–444 (2009)
11. Finkel, A., Schnoebelen, P.: Well-structured transition systems everywhere! Theor. Comput. Sci. **256**(1–2), 63–92 (2001)
12. Fraïssé, R.: Theory of Relations. North-Holland (1953)
13. Genrich, H.J., Lautenbach, K.: System modelling with high-level petri nets. Theor. Comput. Sci. **13**, 109–136 (1981)
14. Haddad, S., Schmitz, S., Schnoebelen, P.: The ordinal-recursive complexity of timed-arc Petri nets, data nets, and other enriched nets. In: Proceedings of the LICS 2012, pp. 355–364 (2012)
15. Henson, W.: Countable homogeneous relational structures and $\aleph_0$-categorical theories. J. Symb. Logic **37**, 494–500 (1972)
16. Higman, G.: Ordering by divisibility in abstract algebras. Proc. London Math. Soc. (3) **2**(7), 326–336 (1952)
17. Hofman, P., Lasota, S., Lazic, R., Leroux, J., Schmitz, S., Totzke, P.: Coverability trees for petri nets with unordered data. In: Jacobs, B., Löding, C. (eds.) FOSSACS 2016. LNCS, vol. 9634, pp. 445–461. Springer, Heidelberg (2016). doi:10.1007/978-3-662-49630-5_26

18. Jacobsen, L., Jacobsen, M., Møller, M.H., Srba, J.: Verification of timed-arc petri nets. In: Černá, I., Gyimóthy, T., Hromkovič, J., Jefferey, K., Královič, R., Vukolić, M., Wolf, S. (eds.) SOFSEM 2011. LNCS, vol. 6543, pp. 46–72. Springer, Heidelberg (2011)
19. Jensen, K.: Coloured petri nets and the invariant-method. Theor. Comput. Sci. **14**, 317–336 (1981)
20. Klin, B., Szynwelski, M.: SMT solving for functional programming over infinite structures. In: Mathematically Structured Functional Programming (accepted for publication, 2016)
21. Kopczyński, E., Toruńczyk, S.: LOIS: an application of SMT solvers (submitted, 2016). http://www.mimuw.edu.pl/~erykk/lois/lois-sat.pdf
22. Kruskal, J.B.: Well-quasi-ordering, the tree theorem, and Vazsonyi's conjecture. Trans. Am. Math. Soc. **95**(2), 210–225 (1960)
23. Latka, B.J.: Finitely constrained classes of homogeneous directed graphs. J. Symbolic Logic **59**(1), 124–139 (1994)
24. Lazić, R.S., Newcomb, T., Ouaknine, J., Roscoe, A.W., Worrell, J.B.: Nets with tokens which carry data. In: Kleijn, J., Yakovlev, A. (eds.) ICATPN 2007. LNCS, vol. 4546, pp. 301–320. Springer, Heidelberg (2007)
25. Macpherson, D.: A survey of homogeneous structures. Discrete Math. **311**(15), 1599–1634 (2011)
26. Rosa-Velardo, F., de Frutos-Escrig, D.: Decidability and complexity of petri nets with unordered data. Theor. Comput. Sci. **412**(34), 4439–4451 (2011)

Petri Net Synthesis

Characterising Petri Net Solvable Binary Words

Eike Best, Evgeny Erofeev, Uli Schlachter, and Harro Wimmel$^{(\boxtimes)}$

Parallel Systems, Department of Computing Science,
Carl von Ossietzky Universität, D-26111 Oldenburg, Germany
{eike.best,evgeny.erofeev,uli.schlachter,
harro.wimmel}@informatik.uni-oldenburg.de

Abstract. A word is called Petri net solvable if it is isomorphic to the reachability graph of an unlabelled Petri net. In this paper, the class of finite, two-letter, Petri net solvable words is studied. A linear time, necessary condition allows for an educated guess at which words are solvable and which are not. A full decision procedure with a time complexity of $O(n^2)$ can be built based on letter counting. The procedure is fully constructive and can either yield a Petri net solving a given word or determine why this fails. Algorithms solving the same problem based on systems of integer inequalities reflecting the potential Petri net structure are only known to be in $O(n^3)$. Finally, the decision procedure can be adapted from finite to cyclic words.

Keywords: Binary words · Labelled transition systems · Petri nets · Synthesis

1 Introduction

The relationship between a Petri net and its reachability graph can be viewed from a system analysis or from a system synthesis viewpoint. In system analysis, a system could, for instance, be modelled by a marked Petri net whose (unique) reachability graph serves to facilitate its behavioural analysis [9]. We may get various kinds of interesting structural results for special classes of Petri nets. For example, if the given system is described by a marked graph, then its reachability graph enjoys a long list of useful properties [7]. In system synthesis, a behavioural specification is typically given, and a system implementing it is sought. For example, one may try to find a Petri net whose reachability graph is isomorphic to a given labelled transition system [1]. We may get structural results of a different nature in this case. For example, [4] describes a structural characterisation of the class of marked graph reachability graphs in terms of a carefully chosen list of graph-theoretical properties.

This research has been supported by DFG (German Research Foundation) through grants Be 1267/15-1 ARS (Algorithms for Reengineering and Synthesis), Be 1267/14-1 CAVER (Comparative Analysis and Verification for Correctness-Critical Systems), and Graduiertenkolleg GRK-1765 SCARE (System Correctness under Adverse Conditions).

© Springer International Publishing Switzerland 2016
F. Kordon and D. Moldt (Eds.): PETRI NETS 2016, LNCS 9698, pp. 39–58, 2016.
DOI: 10.1007/978-3-319-39086-4_4

Region theory [1] establishes an indirect characterisation of the class of Petri net reachability graphs. This characterisation essentially consists of an algorithm solving many systems of linear inequalities derived from a given transition system [5,10]. By its linear-algebraic nature, it provides little insight into the structural properties of Petri net reachability graphs. The aim of the present paper is to complement this indirect characterisation by a direct one, and to show that such a direct characterisation can lead to different, time-efficient, algorithms for checking synthesisability. However, we shall limit ourselves to a special class of transition systems, namely to finite, non-branching ones having at most two edge labels. That is, we study the class of binary, finite or cyclic words (possibly with some finite initial part). We shall obtain a characterisation of the Petri net synthesisable ones amongst them, along with corresponding algorithms.

In a first step, we shall develop a necessary criterion that must hold for finite, binary, synthesisable words. This will frequently allow us to spot non-synthesisable words in linear time. In a second step, we shall provide charac-terisations of binary, synthesisable words in the finite as well as in the cyclic case with a quadratic time complexity, allowing for a faster decision procedure than via the region based approach. More specifically, the structure of the paper is as follows. Section 2 contains some basic definitions about labelled transition systems, Petri nets, and regions. Section 3 describes properties of synthesisable words leading to a necessary criterion for synthesisability. Sections 4 and 5 char-acterise synthesisable word in the finite case and in the cyclic case, respectively. Section 6 compares an implementation of our results with the region based algo-rithms of Synet [5] and APT [10]. Section 7 concludes the paper.

2   Basic Concepts, and Region-Based Synthesis

2.1   Transition Systems, Words, and Petri Nets

A *finite labelled transition system with initial state* is a tuple $TS = (S, \rightarrow, T, s_0)$ with nodes S (a finite set of states), edge labels T (a finite set of letters), edges $\rightarrow \subseteq (S \times T \times S)$, and an initial state $s_0 \in S$. A label t is enabled at $s \in S$, denoted by $s[t\rangle$, if $\exists s' \in S: (s, t, s') \in \rightarrow$. A state s' is reachable from s through the execution of $\sigma \in T^*$, denoted by $s[\sigma\rangle s'$, if there is a directed path from s to s' whose edges are labelled consecutively by σ. The set of states reachable from s is denoted by $[s\rangle$. A sequence $\sigma \in T^*$ is allowed, or firable, from a state s, denoted by $s[\sigma\rangle$, if there is some state s' such that $s[\sigma\rangle s'$. We use $\sigma|_s \sigma'$ as an abbreviation for $s_0[\sigma\rangle s[\sigma'\rangle$. Two labelled transition systems $TS_1 = (S_1, \rightarrow_1, T, s_{01})$ and $TS_2 = (S_2, \rightarrow_2, T, s_{02})$ are isomorphic if there is a bijection $\zeta: S_1 \rightarrow S_2$ with $\zeta(s_{01}) = s_{02}$ and $(s, t, s') \in \rightarrow_1 \Leftrightarrow (\zeta(s), t, \zeta(s')) \in \rightarrow_2$, for all $s, s' \in S_1$.

A *word over* T is a sequence $w \in T^*$, and it is *binary* if $|T| = 2$. For a word w and a letter t, $\#_t(w)$ denotes the number of times t occurs in w. A word $w' \in T^*$ is called a *subword* (or *factor*) of $w \in T^*$ if $\exists u_1, u_2 \in T^*: w = u_1 w' u_2$. A word $w = t_1 t_2 \ldots t_n$ of length $n \in \mathbb{N}$ uniquely corresponds to a finite transition system $TS(w) = (\{0, \ldots, n\}, \{(i - 1, t_i, i) \mid 0 < i \leq n \wedge t_i \in T\}, T, 0)$.

An *initially marked Petri net* is denoted as $N = (P, T, F, M_0)$ where P is a finite set of places, T is a finite set of transitions with $P \cap T = \emptyset$, F is the flow function $F : ((P \times T) \cup (T \times P)) \rightarrow \mathbb{N}$ specifying the arc weights, and M_0 is the initial marking (where a marking is a mapping $M : P \rightarrow \mathbb{N}$, indicating the number of tokens in each place). A side-place is a place p with $p^\bullet \cap {}^\bullet p \neq \emptyset$, where $p^\bullet = \{t \in T \mid F(p, t) > 0\}$ and ${}^\bullet p = \{t \in T \mid F(t, p) > 0\}$. A transition $t \in T$ is enabled at a marking M, denoted by $M[t\rangle$, if $\forall p \in P : M(p) \geq F(p, t)$. The firing of t leads from M to M', denoted by $M[t\rangle M'$, if $M[t\rangle$ and $M'(p) = M(p) - F(p, t) + F(t, p)$. This can be extended, as usual, to $M[\sigma\rangle M'$ for sequences $\sigma \in T^*$, and $[M\rangle$ denotes the set of markings reachable from M. The reachability graph $RG(N)$ of a bounded (such that the number of tokens in each place does not exceed a certain finite number) Petri net N is the labelled transition system with the set of vertices $[M_0\rangle$, initial state M_0, label set T, and set of edges $\{(M, t, M') \mid M, M' \in [M_0\rangle \wedge M[t\rangle M'\}$. If a labelled transition system TS is isomorphic to the reachability graph of a Petri net N, we say that N *PN-solves* (or simply *solves*) TS, and that TS is *synthesisable* to N. We say that N solves a word w if it solves $TS(w)$. We frequently identify the states of TS with the markings of N then, writing e.g. $s(p) \geq F(p, t)$.

2.2   Basic Region Theory, and an Example

Let a finite labelled transition system $TS = (S, \rightarrow, T, s_0)$ be given. In order to synthesise – if possible – a Petri net with isomorphic reachability graph, T must, of course (since we do not consider any transition labels), be used directly as the set of transitions. For the places, $\frac{1}{2} \cdot (|S| \cdot (|S| - 1))$ state separation problems and up to $|S| \cdot |T|$ event/state separation problems have to be solved, as follows:

- A *state separation problem* consists of a set of states $\{s, s'\}$ with $s \neq s'$ where s and s' must be mapped to different markings in the synthesised net. Such problems are always solvable if $TS = TS(w)$ originates from a word w, for instance by introducing a counting place which has j tokens in state j.
- An *event/state separation problem* consists of a pair $(s, t) \in S \times T$ with $\neg(s[t\rangle)$. For every such problem, one needs a place p such that $M(p) < F(p, t)$ for the marking M corresponding to state s, where F refers to the arcs of the hoped-for net.

For example, in Fig. 1, TS_1 is PN-solvable, since the reachability graph of N_1 is isomorphic to TS_1. Note that N_1 has exactly two transitions a and b, which is true for any net solving a binary word over $\{a, b\}$. By contrast, TS_2 is not PN-solvable. The word *abbaa*, from which TS_2 is derived, is actually one of the two shortest non-solvable binary words (the other one being *baabb*, its dual under swapping a and b).

To see that *abbaa* (viz., TS_2) is not PN-solvable, we may use the following argument. State $s = 2$ generates an event/state separation problem $\neg(s[a\rangle)$, for which we need a place q whose number of tokens in the marking corresponding to state 2 is less than necessary for transition a to be enabled. Such a place q

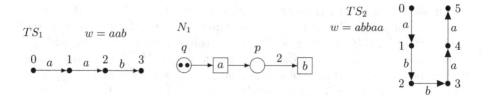

Fig. 1. TS_1 and TS_2 correspond to aab and $abbaa$, respectively. N_1 solves TS_1. No Petri net solution of TS_2 exists.

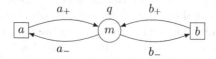

Fig. 2. A place with four arc weights a_-, a_+, b_-, b_+ and initial marking m

has the general form shown in Fig. 2. We now show that such a place does not exist.

In order to present this proof succinctly, it is useful to define the *effect* $\mathbb{E}(\tau)$ of a sequence $\tau \in T^*$ on place q. The effect of the empty sequence is $\mathbb{E}(\varepsilon) = 0$. The effect of a sequence $a\tau$ is defined as $\mathbb{E}(a\tau) = (a_+ - a_-) + \mathbb{E}(\tau)$, and similarly, $\mathbb{E}(b\tau) = (b_+ - b_-) + \mathbb{E}(\tau)$. For instance, $\mathbb{E}(abbaa) = 3 \cdot (a_+ - a_-) + 2 \cdot (b_+ - b_-)$. In general, $\mathbb{E}(\tau) = \#_a(\tau) \cdot \mathbb{E}(a) + \#_b(\tau) \cdot \mathbb{E}(b)$.

If q (as in Fig. 2) prevents a at the marking corresponding to state 2 in $abbaa$ (cf. TS_2 in Fig. 1), then it must satisfy the following inequalities: $a_- \leq m$, since state 0 enables a; $a_- \leq m + \mathbb{E}(abba)$, since state 4 enables a; $m + \mathbb{E}(ab) < a_-$, since q prevents a at state 3. Using $\mathbb{E}(abba) = \mathbb{E}(ab) + \mathbb{E}(ab)$, it is immediate to see that this set of inequalities cannot be solved in the natural numbers.

2.3   Worst Case Complexity of the General Algorithm

In a word of length n, the equation system for a single event/state separation problem comprises $n + 1$ inequalities, n for the states $0, \ldots, n - 1$ and one for the event/state separation. In binary words, we have $n + 2$ such problems, one for every state $0, \ldots, n - 1$ and two for the last state. A word w of length n is PN-solvable if and only if all $n + 2$ systems, each having $n + 1$ inequalities and five unknowns a_-, a_+, b_-, b_+, m, are solvable in $\mathbb{N}$.

Suppose that we solve this special case (with five unknowns) by Khachiyan's algorithm [6]. Solving $O(n)$ systems of inequalities, we may roughly expect a running time of $O(n^3)$.

3   Necessary Conditions for Solvability

As a first step of characterising solvable words over $\{a, b\}^*$, and quoting various related partial results from [2], we develop a necessary criterion with a linear time complexity. From this we will get a good idea of how solvable words are structured and can easily sort out the majority of unsolvable words just by looking at them.

Proposition 1. [2] SOLVABILITY OF SUBWORDS.
If $w = xvy$ with $x, y \in \{a, b\}$ is solvable, then xv and vy are also solvable.

The reverse does not hold, of course, otherwise there would be no unsolvable words at all. With $x \neq y$ though, solvability can be propagated:

Proposition 2. [2] SOLVABILITY OF awb FROM aw AND wb.
If both aw and wb are solvable, then awb is also solvable.

This also holds for bw and wa, of course. It is also possible to prefix a solvable word by its first letter.

Proposition 3. [2] PREFIXING SOLVABLE WORDS BY THEIR FIRST LETTER.
Let v be a solvable word starting with a letter $x \in \{a, b\}$. Then, xv is solvable.

An unsolvable word w is *minimal* if all subwords of w are solvable. For this, it is sufficient that for $w = xvy$ with $x, y \in \{a, b\}$ both xv and vy are solvable. So, due to Proposition 2, minimal unsolvable words must start and end with the same letter. They are also restricted to which subwords aa or bb can be contained:

Proposition 4. [2] NEVER aa AND bb INSIDE A MINIMAL UNSOLVABLE WORD.
If a minimal non-solvable word is of the form $u = a\alpha a$, then either α does not contain the factor (subword) aa or α does not contain the factor bb.

Propositions 3 and 4 together now also suggest a restriction for solvable words. Solvable words may contain both aa and bb as subwords, but only if one of these subwords appears at the beginning of the word, created by the prefixing mechanism of Proposition 3. This is indeed the case:

Proposition 5. NEVER aa AND bb IN SOLVABLE WORDS AFTER INITIAL a^+.
Let $w \in \{a, b\}^*$ be a solvable word, decomposable into $w = a^n b\alpha$ with $n \geq 1$ and $\alpha \in \{a, b\}^*$. Then, $b\alpha$ does not contain the factor aa or it does not contain the factor bb.

Proof: Assume w contains both factors aa and bb in $b\alpha$. Select "neighboring" factors aa and bb, such there is no other factor aa or bb in between. Since neither chosen factor is at the start of the word, w can be decomposed into $w = \beta ab^i \underline{bb}(ab)^j \underline{aa}\gamma$ or $w = \beta ba^i \underline{aa}(ba)^j \underline{bb}\gamma$ with $\beta, \gamma \in \{a, b\}^*$ and $i, j \geq 0$. The neighbors aa and bb have been underlined. W.l.o.g. let us assume the latter form.

Let $N = (P, T, F, M_0)$ be a Petri net solving w and select states s, s', and s'' such that $w = \beta|_{s'} ba^i a|_s a(ba)^j b|_{s''} b\gamma$. Since b cannot fire at s, there must be a place $p \in P$ with $s(p) < b_-$ (compare Fig. 2). At s' and s'' the transition b can fire, so $s'(p) \geq b_- \leq s''(p)$ holds. As firing a enables b again after s, a must produce tokens on p and $\mathbb{E}(a) > 0$. Since b does not remain enabled from s' to s, it has to consume tokens from p, so $\mathbb{E}(b) < 0$. Computing the token differences on p between our chosen states we then obtain

$$0 > s(p) - s'(p) = (i+1) \cdot \mathbb{E}(a) + \mathbb{E}(b) \ \text{ and}$$
$$0 < s''(p) - s(p) = (j+1) \cdot \mathbb{E}(a) + (j+1) \cdot \mathbb{E}(b).$$

Comparing the lines gives $\mathbb{E}(a) > -\mathbb{E}(b) > (i+1) \cdot \mathbb{E}(a)$, which is a contradiction, i.e. w is not solvable.   □ 5

This reduces the potentially solvable words to the regular expression

$$a^* b^+ (ab^+)^* (a|\varepsilon) \ \mid \ b^* a^+ (ba^+)^* (b|\varepsilon) \ \mid \ \varepsilon,$$

where in the first subexpression aa may only occur at the beginning of the word and in the second one the roles of a and b are switched. The following results are shown for the first expression only, but hold for both, of course.

If we compare two different blocks of the form ab^+ in the regular expression we find that their lengths must be nearly equal.

Lemma 1. BLOCK LENGTHS DIFFER BY AT MOST 1.
  Let $w \in a^* b^+ (ab^+)^* (a|\varepsilon)$ be a word that contains both $bab^i a$ and $abb^i b$ with $i \geq 1$ as subwords. Then, w is not solvable.

Proof: Consider first the case $w = \alpha|_s bab^i|_{s'} (abb^i)^k abb^i|_{s''} b\beta$ with $\alpha, \beta \in \{a, b\}^*$. If there are more or less than $i + 1$ b's in any of the intermediate $k \geq 0$ blocks we can choose factors $bab^i a$ and $abb^i b$ that are closer together (possibly even having an a in common). Assume p to be a place of a Petri net solving w with $s'(p) < b_- \leq s(p)$, i.e. $\mathbb{E}(bab^i) = s'(p) - s(p) < 0$. Due to Parikh equivalence, $\mathbb{E}(bab^i) = \mathbb{E}(abb^i)$, we know $s''(p) = s'(p) + (k+1) \cdot \mathbb{E}(abb^i) < s'(p) < b_-$, which is a contradiction to b being enabled at s''.

The second case, $w = \alpha|_s abb^i b^j (bab^i)^k|_{s'} bab^i|_{s''} a\beta$ with $\alpha, \beta \in \{a, b\}^*$ and $j, k \geq 0$, we also obtain by choosing the factors – first $abb^i b$, then $bab^i a$ this time – as close together as possible. Assume p to be a place with $s'(p) < a_- \leq s''(p)$, then with $s''(p) - s'(p) = \mathbb{E}(bab^i) = \mathbb{E}(abb^i) > 0$ and $\mathbb{E}(b) > 0$ (since firing b at s' enables a), we obtain $s(p) = s'(p) - k \cdot \mathbb{E}(bab^i) - j \cdot \mathbb{E}(b) - \mathbb{E}(abb^i) < s'(p) < a_-$. This contradicts a being enabled at s.   □ 1

Solvable words must then fulfill a kind of balancing property where the blocks of b's must almost all have almost the same length.

Proposition 6. BALANCING PROPERTY.

Let $w = a^k b^{x_1} a b^{x_2} \ldots a b^{x_n}$ with $k \geq 0$, $n \geq 2$, $x_1, \ldots, x_n \geq 1$. Then, the following hold:

1. w solvable $\Rightarrow x_j - 1 \leq x_i$ for $2 \leq i \leq n-1$, $2 \leq j \leq n$.
2. wa solvable $\Rightarrow x_j - 1 \leq x_i$ for $2 \leq i, j \leq n$.
3. If $k > 0$ the above implications also hold for $j = 1$.

Proof: Assume there are i and j such that one of the above implications does not hold. Then, w (or wa) contains the subwords $bab^{x_i}a$ (since $i \geq 2$) as well as $abb^{x_i}b$ as a (possibly trivial) prefix of ab^{x_j}. Lemma 1 shows that the word is not solvable, yielding a contradiction.   □ 6

The first block of b's can have arbitrary length (e.g., both $abab^9 ab^9 ab^9 a$ and $b^9 abbabbabba$ are solvable). The last block of b's cannot be longer, but it can be much shorter than the average b-block if no final a follows; e.g. $ab^9 ab^9 ab^9 ab$ is solvable while $abababab^9$ is not. In the former case, we may even append some more b's.

Lemma 2. PROLONGING THE LAST b-BLOCK.

Let $w = a^k b^{x_1} a b^{x_2} a \ldots a b^{x_n}$ be a solvable word with $k \geq 0$ and $x_i - 1 > x_n$ for all $1 \leq i < n$. Then, $w' = a^k b^{x_1} a b^{x_2} a \ldots a b^{x_n + 1}$ is solvable.

Proof: Consider the case $k \leq 1$ first. Assume $N = (P, T, F, M_0)$ to be a Petri net solving $w = a^k b^{x_1} a b^{x_2} \ldots a b^{x_i-1}|_{s'} a b^{x_i-1}|_{s''} ba \ldots b|_s a b^{x_n}|_f$ with a place p that prevents b at some s' before s. Then, $s'(p) < b_-$ and $s''(p) = s'(p) + \mathbb{E}(a b^{x_i-1}) \geq b_-$, i.e. $\mathbb{E}(ab^{x_i-1}) > 0$. With $s(p) \geq b_+$ (b fires directly before s) and $\mathbb{E}(b) < 0$ (b fires directly before s'), we conclude $f(p) = s(p) + \mathbb{E}(ab^{x_n}) \geq b_+ + \mathbb{E}(ab^{x_n}) = b_+ + \mathbb{E}(ab^{x_i-1}) - \mathbb{E}(b^{x_i-1-x_n}) > b_+ - (x_i - 1 - x_n) \cdot \mathbb{E}(b) \geq b_+ - \mathbb{E}(b) = b_-$. Therefore, a place p preventing b at such s' cannot prevent b at the end of w. At s, b can be prevented by a new place q with $b_- = 1$, $b_+ = 0$, $a_- = 0$, $a_+ = \min\{x_1, \ldots, x_{n-1}\}$, and an initial token count of $(\sum_{i=1}^{n-1} x_i) - (n - 2 + k) \cdot \min\{x_1, \ldots, x_{n-1}\}$ (which is non-negative). Then, $s(q) = 0$ and $f(q) = s(q) + a_+ - x_n > 0$. A place preventing a (except after the last a) must have $\mathbb{E}(b) > 0$, so it cannot prevent b at the end either. After the last a, a new place with $\#_a(w)$ initial tokens, $a_- = 1$, and $a_+ = 0$ can disable any further a. With these modifications, a place preventing b at the end of the word w is not needed to prevent any other occurrence of a or b any more. We can now delete all places preventing b at the end of w from N and create a new place with $1 + \sum_{i=1}^n x_i$ tokens, $b_- = 1$, and $b_+ = 0$, to prevent b after w' is complete. The modified Petri net solves w'.

In case $k > 1$, we cut off all leading a's but one, apply the above proof, and then reprepend the missing a's using Proposition 3.   □ 2

Deleting one b from each block of b's will also not turn a word unsolvable.

Lemma 3. LENGTH REDUCTION OF b-BLOCKS.

Let $w = a^k b^{x_1} a b^{x_2} a \dots a b^{x_n} a^j$ with $j \in \{0,1\}$, $k \geq 0$, and $x_1, \dots, x_n \geq 2$ be a solvable word. Then, also $w' = a^k b^{x_1-1} a b^{x_2-1} a \dots a b^{x_n-1} a^j$ is solvable.

Proof: For $k > 1$, cut off all leading a's but one, apply the following proof for $k = 1$, and reprepend the missing a's using Proposition 3. So, let now $k \leq 1$. In case $j = 1$, we apply the proof to the word wb [and w'], which by Lemma 2 and Proposition 1 is solvable if and only if w is. If $k = 0$ we use the words w and bw', where $k = 0$ and $j = 1$ are, of course, combinable, and w' is solvable if bw' is. After applying the above modifications, note that with the homomorphism $h(a) = ab$ and $h(b) = b$, we get $h(w') = w$.

Let N be a Petri net solving w. For each place p with arc weights a_+, a_-, b_+, and b_- let $i_p := \max\{0, -a_+ - \mathbb{E}(b)\}$ and define a place p' for a new Petri net N' with $M'_0(p') := M_0(p) + i_p$, $b'_- := b_- + i_p$, $b'_+ := b_+ + i_p$, $a'_- := a_- + i_p$, and $a'_+ := a_+ + \mathbb{E}(b) + i_p$. In all cases, $a'_+ - a'_- = \mathbb{E}(ab)$ and $b'_+ - b'_- = \mathbb{E}(b)$ and all new arc weights (especially a'_+) are non-negative. By induction over the length of prefixes of w', the state reached in N' after some prefix v of w' is the state reached in N after the corresponding prefix $h(v)$ of w plus the additional $(i_p)_p$. We conclude that w' and only w' can fire in N', i.e. N' solves w'.   □ 3

This lemma suggests that comparing the lengths of b-blocks are more important for solvability than computing their absolute lengths. Our necessary criterion, being a summary of the results of this section, establishes this intuition more formally as follows:

Theorem 1. LINEAR TIME NECESSARY CRITERION.

If a word $w \in \{a,b\}^*$ is solvable, it is the empty word $w = \varepsilon$ or it has the form $w = a^k b^{x_1} a b^{x_2} a \dots a b^{x_n} a^j$ or $w = b^k a^{x_1} b a^{x_2} b \dots b a^{x_n} b^j$, where $j, k, n, x_1, \dots, x_n \in \mathbb{N}$ with $j \leq 1$, $n \geq 0$ and there is some $x \in \mathbb{N}$ such that $x_2, \dots, x_{n-1} \in \{x, x+1\}$ and $x_n \leq x + 1$. Furthermore, if $j > 0$ also $x_n \in \{x, x+1\}$, and if $k > 0$ also $x_1 \leq x + 1$.

The criterion is in linear time as we can detect the structure of a word w by going over it once from left to right. Remembering the block lengths that occurred so far allows us to check if the next block also has a valid length.

What we do not know so far is when a block may have length $x + 1$ in the criterion, and when only length x is allowed. E.g., *ababababbabba*, *ababbababba*, *ababbabbaba*, *abbababbaba*, and *abbabababba* are all solvable while *abbabbababa* is not. One could suspect that the high number of early b's makes the latter word unsolvable. This will be made precise in the following section.

4   Characterisation of Solvable Binary Words

For a decomposition $w = u|_s xv$ with $x \in \{a, b\}$, let us call $y \in \{a, b\}$ with $y \neq x$ *separable at s* iff we can construct a Petri net with transitions a and b and one place p such that w can be fired completely and at s, y is not enabled.

Theorem 2. CHARACTERISATION OF SOLVABLE WORDS.

A word $w \in \{a, b\}^*$ is solvable if and only if the following formula holds for $x = a \wedge y = b$ as well as for $x = b \wedge y = a$:

$$\forall \alpha, \beta, \gamma, \delta : (w = \alpha y \beta x \gamma y \delta \Rightarrow \#_y(y\beta) \cdot \#_x(x\gamma) > \#_x(y\beta) \cdot \#_y(x\gamma)).$$

Proof: We need to show that for any decomposition $w = u|_s x v$ with $x \in \{a, b\}$, the other letter $y \neq x$, $y \in \{a, b\}$ is separable at s if and only if the above formula holds for all decompositions of $u = \alpha y \beta$ and $v = \gamma y \delta$. We outsource this proof to Lemma 4. Disabling a and b at the end of the word is trivially done by putting $|w|$ tokens on a new place, from which each transition takes one token upon firing. □ 2

Lemma 4. CHARACTERISATION OF SEPARABLE STATES.

For a word $w \in \{a, b\}^*$ let $w = u|_s x v$ be an arbitrary decomposition with $x \in \{a, b\}$. Let $y \in \{a, b\}$ with $y \neq x$ be the other letter in our alphabet. Then, y is separable at s if and only if

$$\forall \alpha, \beta, \gamma, \delta : (w = \alpha y \beta|_s x \gamma y \delta \Rightarrow \#_y(y\beta) \cdot \#_x(x\gamma) > \#_x(y\beta) \cdot \#_y(x\gamma)).$$

Proof: "⇒": Let p be a place (of some Petri net) enabling y at s' and s'' but not at s in a decomposition $w = \alpha|_{s'} y\beta|_s x\gamma|_{s''} y\delta$. Since p disables y at s but not at s'', the number of tokens on p must increase from s to s'', and also from s to the first y after s, where only letters x are present. Thus, x effectively increases the token count on p, i.e. $\mathbb{E}(x) > 0$.

Assume firing y would not lower the token count on p. Since y is enabled at s', it will also be enabled at every state afterwards, even at s. So, p would not disable y at s. We conclude that y effectively removes tokens from p, i.e. $\mathbb{E}(y) < 0$.

Since y can fire at s' but not at s, tokens are consumed by $y\beta$, i.e. $\#_y(y\beta) \cdot (-\mathbb{E}(y)) > \#_x(y\beta) \cdot \mathbb{E}(x)$. From s to s'', for analogous reasons, tokens are produced on p, so $\#_x(x\gamma) \cdot \mathbb{E}(x) > \#_y(x\gamma) \cdot (-\mathbb{E}(y))$. Multiply the first inequality by $\#_x(x\gamma)$ and the second one by $\#_x(y\beta)$, then divide both by $-\mathbb{E}(y)$ to make them comparable:

$$\#_y(y\beta) \cdot \#_x(x\gamma) > \#_x(y\beta) \cdot \frac{\mathbb{E}(x)}{-\mathbb{E}(y)} \cdot \#_x(x\gamma) > \#_x(y\beta) \cdot \#_y(x\gamma).$$

"⇐": Let $S' := \{s' \mid \exists \alpha, \beta : w = \alpha|_{s'} y\beta|_s xv\}$ and $S'' := \{s'' \mid \exists \gamma, \delta : w = u|_s x\gamma|_{s''} y\delta\}$. Denoting by $\#_x(s', s)$ the number of occurrences of x between states s' and s (and analogously for y and for pairs of states (s, s'')), let us define ratios of y and x in $\mathbb{Q} \cup \{-\infty, \infty\}$ via

$$r_{max}(s) := \min_{s' \in S'} \left\{ \frac{\#_y(s', s)}{\#_x(s', s)} \right\} \quad \text{and} \quad r_{min}(s) := \max_{s'' \in S''} \left\{ \frac{\#_y(s, s'')}{\#_x(s, s'')} \right\}.$$

In case $S' = \emptyset$ we assume the minimum $r_{max}(s)$ to be ∞ as a default value, if $S'' = \emptyset$ the maximum $r_{min}(s)$ will be $-\infty$. $\#_x(s, s'')$ and $\#_y(s', s)$ cannot be zero (as there is an x directly after s and a y after s' and s''), so no ambiguos fraction $\frac{0}{0}$ can occur. If $\#_x(s', s)$ is zero, we assume the (obvious) default value of ∞ for this fraction. See Fig. 3 for a visualisation.

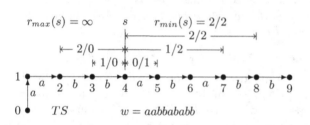

select $\frac{3}{2} \in]2/2, \infty[$

$(\mathbf{2} - 1$ tokens on p at $s)$

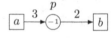

avoid neg. init.marking:

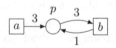

Fig. 3. TS corresponding to $aabbababb$ with a state s at which b must not occur. We compute maximal/minimal b/a-ratios $r_{min}(s)/r_{max}(s)$ for words starting with b ending at s and starting at s ending in front of a b, respectively. The production/consumption ratio for a place p in a Petri net prohibiting b at s must fall into the open interval $]r_{min}(s), r_{max}(s)[$. A loop around b can be added to prevent a negative initial marking.

We now show that $r_{max}(s) > r_{min}(s)$. This is trivial in case one of the two assumes its default value ∞ or $-\infty$. Otherwise, for all decompositions $w = \alpha|_{s'}y\beta|_s x\gamma|_{s''}y\delta$ with $s' \in S'$ and $s'' \in S''$, we get $\#_y(y\beta) \cdot \#_x(x\gamma) > \#_x(y\beta) \cdot \#_y(x\gamma)$. We now select those $s' \in S'$ and $s'' \in S''$ that yield the ratio values $r_{max}(s)$ and $r_{min}(s)$ in the above definitions, respectively. For these two states we obtain:

$$r_{max}(s) = \frac{\#_y(s', s)}{\#_x(s', s)} = \frac{\#_y(y\beta)}{\#_x(y\beta)} > \frac{\#_y(x\gamma)}{\#_x(x\gamma)} = \frac{\#_y(s, s'')}{\#_x(s, s'')} = r_{min}(s).$$

We now create a Petri net with two transitions x and y and a single place p that will disable y at s but not at any other state in $S' \cup S''$. In a first step, let us choose arc weights $y_- \in \mathbb{N}^+$ (from p to y) and $x_+ \in \mathbb{N}^+$ (from x to p) such that

$$r_{max}(s) > \frac{x_+}{y_-} > r_{min}(s),$$

which is obviously possible; compare Fig. 3. Furthermore, let us assume there are $y_- - 1$ tokens on p at state s, so p disables y at s. Choose any state $s' \in S'$, then

$$\frac{\#_y(s', s)}{\#_x(s', s)} \geq r_{max}(s) > \frac{x_+}{y_-}.$$

In case $\#_x(s', s) > 0$, we can multiply with this value and with y_- to obtain

$$\#_y(s', s) \cdot y_- > \#_x(s', s) \cdot x_+.$$

In case $\#_x(s', s) = 0$ the above inequality is trivially true, since s' is immediately followed by a y. The inequality shows that there are more tokens on p in s' than in s. Due to our choice of $y_- - 1$ tokens for s, y is not disabled at s' by p.

Analogously, for a state $s'' \in S''$, we have

$$\frac{x_+}{y_-} > r_{min}(s) \geq \frac{\#_y(s, s'')}{\#_x(s, s'')}$$

and by multiplying with the non-zero denominators we get

$$\#_x(s, s'') \cdot x_+ > \#_y(s, s'') \cdot y_-.$$

So, at s'' there are more tokens on p than at s, and p cannot disable y at s''.

It remains to be shown that there are always at least zero tokens on p at any possible state. This is already known for all states from $S' \cup S''$ (having at least y_- tokens) and for all states $\hat{s}$ immediately following a state from $S' \cup S''$ (only y_- tokens are consumed). Since from such an $\hat{s}$ until the next state in $S' \cup S''$ only x occurs in the word w, the number of tokens will only be increased. So, all states beginning with the first state from $S' \cup S''$ in the word w are covered. Before this first state, only letters x occur in w, so it suffices to check if the initial state of the Petri net has at least zero tokens on p.

If the initial state s_0 is in $S' \cup S''$, we are done. Otherwise, we compute the initial number of tokens via $s(p) = y_- - 1$ in w: $n := y_- - 1 + \#_y(s_0, s) \cdot y_- - \#_x(s_0, s) \cdot x_+$. Only in case of an initial marking $n < 0$ we have a problem. This can be easily solved, though, by creating an arc from y to p with weight $F(y, p) := -n$ and replacing the values for the reverse arc weight and the initial marking by $F(p, y) := y_- - n$ and $M_0(p) := n - n = 0$. The additional $-n$ tokens are never used up but are always needed for y, so they will neither allow any additional firing of y nor prevent any required one.   □ 4

Proposition 7. SHARED SEPARATING PLACES.

Let $w = u|_s xv|_{\hat{s}} xz$ be a solvable word with $x \in \{a, b\}$ and with two states s, $\hat{s}$ after which the same letter x occurs. Then, for s and $\hat{s}$, we can use the same place for the separation if and only if the open intervals $]r_{min}(s), r_{max}(s)[$ and $]r_{min}(\hat{s}), r_{max}(\hat{s})[$ (from the proof of Lemma 4) have a non-empty intersection.

Proof: The first direction of the proof of Lemma 4 shows that the arc weight ratio $\frac{x_+}{y_-}$ of the occurring letter x compared to the separation letter y must lie inside the open interval. If one separation place is enough for both states, the arc weight ratio must fall into both open intervals. Similarly, if the intervals have a non-empty intersection, the arc weight ratios in the second part of the proof of Lemma 4 can be chosen identical, so the same place is generated for both states. The different separation states may require a different number of loops at y to prevent a negative initial marking. In this case, the higher number of loops will always suffice.   □ 7

Let us take a look at the word $w = aabbababb$ from Fig. 3 again. For states followed by an a we get $r_{min}(0) = \max\{\frac{0}{2}, \frac{1}{2}, \frac{2}{3}, \frac{3}{4}, \frac{4}{4}\} = 1$, $r_{max}(0) = \infty$ with the interval $]1, \infty[$, $r_{min}(1) = \max\{\frac{0}{1}, \frac{1}{1}, \frac{2}{2}, \frac{3}{3}, \frac{4}{3}\} = \frac{4}{3}$, $r_{max}(1) = \infty$ with the interval $]\frac{4}{3}, \infty[$, $r_{min}(4) = \max\{\frac{0}{1}, \frac{1}{2}, \frac{2}{2}\} = 1$, $r_{max}(4) = \min\{\frac{2}{0}, \frac{1}{0}\} = \infty$ with $]1, \infty[$, and $r_{min}(6) = \max\{\frac{0}{1}, \frac{1}{1}\} = 1$, $r_{max}(6) = \min\{\frac{3}{1}, \frac{2}{1}, \frac{1}{0}\} = 3$ with $]1, 3[$. The value $\frac{3}{2}$ lies in all open intervals, so we get one place p with $\mathbb{E}(a) = 3$ and $\mathbb{E}(b) = -2$ and at most $2 - 1 = 1$ tokens on it at each of the four states. Backward calculation of the initial state gives 1, -2, -1, and -2 tokens for the states 0, 1, 4, and 6, respectively. We set $b_- = 2 + 2$, $b_+ = 2$ to obtain zero tokens in the initial marking. For states followed by b we have $r_{min}(2) = \max\{\frac{0}{2}, \frac{1}{3}\} = \frac{1}{3}$, $r_{max}(2) = \min\{\frac{2}{0}, \frac{1}{0}\} = \infty$, $r_{min}(3) = \max\{\frac{0}{1}, \frac{1}{2}\} = \frac{1}{2}$, $r_{max}(3) = \min\{\frac{2}{1}, \frac{1}{1}\} = 1$, $r_{min}(5) = \max\{\frac{0}{1}\} = 0$, $r_{max}(5) = \min\{\frac{3}{2}, \frac{2}{1}, \frac{1}{0}\} = 1$, $r_{min}(7) = -\infty$, $r_{max}(7) = \min\{\frac{4}{3}, \frac{3}{3}, \frac{2}{1}, \frac{1}{0}\} = 1$, $r_{min}(8) = -\infty$, $r_{max}(8) = \min\{\frac{4}{4}, \frac{3}{4}, \frac{2}{2}, \frac{1}{1}\} = \frac{3}{4}$. We are inside all intervals if we choose $\frac{2}{3} \in]\frac{1}{2}, \frac{3}{4}[$ for a new place q with $\mathbb{E}(b) = 2$, $\mathbb{E}(a) = -3$, and at most $3 - 1 = 2$ tokens at any of these states. We compute for the initial marking 8, 6, 7, 7, 6 tokens (for the five states), so by the proof of Lemma 4 six initial tokens are enough to enable a where it occurs in w, but not anywhere else. Adding a place f with 9 tokens to prevent a and b at the end, we obtain the net in Fig. 4.

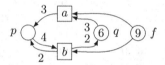

Fig. 4. A Petri net solving the word $aabbababb$

In all examples we examined so far, all the open intervals $]r_{min}(s), r_{max}(s)[$, for the same separation letter, had a common intersection. With one additional place needed to prevent a and b at the end of a word, we therefore believe:

Conjecture 1. SOLUTIONS FOR BINARY SOLVABLE WORDS NEED ≤ 3 PLACES.

For any solvable word $w \in \{a, b\}^*$ there is a Petri net with at most three places solving it.   □ Conjecture 1

The following algorithm for the Petri net synthesis for a finite word w is in $O(|w|^2)$:

Algorithm 1. ABSolve

Input: $w \in \{a, b\}^*$
Output: A Petri net $N = (P, \{a, b\}, F, M_0)$ solving w if it exists
  $P \leftarrow \emptyset$, $F \leftarrow \emptyset$, $M_0 \leftarrow \emptyset$
  for $i = 0$ **to** $|w| - 1$ **do** {separation point s}
    $r_{min}[i] \leftarrow -\infty$, $r_{max}[i] \leftarrow \infty$ {defaults}
    $N[0] \leftarrow 0$, $N[1] \leftarrow 0$ {for counting a's and b's}
    if $w[i] = 'a'$ **then** $R \leftarrow 1$ **else** $R \leftarrow 0$ {fraction selector}
    for $j = i - 1$ **down to** 0 **do** {compute r_{max}}
      if $w[j] = 'a'$ **then** $N[0] \leftarrow N[0] + 1$ **else** $N[1] \leftarrow N[1] + 1$
      if $w[j] \neq w[i]$ **and** $r_{max}[i] > \frac{N[R]}{N[1-R]}$ **then** $r_{max}[i] \leftarrow \frac{N[R]}{N[1-R]}$
    endfor
    $N[0] \leftarrow 0$, $N[1] \leftarrow 0$
    for $j = i + 1$ **to** $|w| - 1$ **do** {compute r_{min}}
      if $w[j - 1] = 'a'$ **then** $N[0] \leftarrow N[0] + 1$ **else** $N[1] \leftarrow N[1] + 1$
      if $w[j] \neq w[i]$ **and** $r_{min}[i] < \frac{N[R]}{N[1-R]}$ **then** $r_{min}[i] \leftarrow \frac{N[R]}{N[1-R]}$
    endfor
    if $r_{min}[i] \geq r_{max}[i]$ **then return** {unsolvable}
  endfor
  $S \leftarrow \{0, \ldots, |w| - 1\}$ {unprocessed intervals}
  while $S \neq \emptyset$ **do**
    choose $I \subseteq S$ with $|\{w[i] | i \in I\}| = 1$ and $\bigcap_{i \in I}]r_{min}[i], r_{max}[i][\neq \emptyset$
    $S \leftarrow S \backslash I$
    choose $\frac{m}{n} \in \bigcap_{i \in I}]r_{min}[i], r_{max}[i][$
    $P \leftarrow P \cup \{p_I\}$
    $\ell \leftarrow w[\min I]$ {doesn't matter which $i \in I$}
    if $\ell = 'a'$ **then** $F(a, p_I) \leftarrow m$, $F(p_I, b) \leftarrow n$ **else** $F(b, p_I) \leftarrow m$, $F(p_I, a) \leftarrow n$
    compute the minimal $M_0(p_I) \in \mathbb{Z}$ for $i \in I$ from $M(p_I) = n - 1$
      {via backward firing $M_0[w[0] \ldots w[i-1]\rangle M$}
    if $M_0(p_I) < 0$ **and** $\ell = 'a'$ **then**
      $F(b, p_I) \leftarrow F(b, p_I) - M_0(p_I)$, $F(p_I, b) \leftarrow F(p_I, b) - M_0(p_I)$, $M_0(p_I) \leftarrow 0$
    if $M_0(p_I) < 0$ **and** $\ell = 'b'$ **then**
      $F(a, p_I) \leftarrow F(a, p_I) - M_0(p_I)$, $F(p_I, a) \leftarrow F(p_I, a) - M_0(p_I)$, $M_0(p_I) \leftarrow 0$
  endwhile
  return $(P, \{a, b\}, F, M_0)$

Note that the first part (with the **for**-loops) is obviously quadratic, and the **while**-loop is run two times if Conj. 1 holds and at most $|w|$ times otherwise. For the choice of I, select one interval and intersect consecutively with any other interval unless the intersection would become empty, resulting in $O(|w|)$ time. The choice of $\frac{m}{n}$ can be done in constant time unless some "optimal" value is sought. The computation of $M_0(p_I)$ by backward firing is in $O(|w|)$. So, overall, the **while**-loop is in $O(|w|^2)$ in the worst case.

For an enumeration of all solvable words (ordered by length) without synthesising Petri nets, we would need to remember all solvable words of the same length and their $r_{max}[i]$-values (in a breadth-first manner). If we append a letter x to some word w, all comparisons of r_{min} and r_{max} for wx have already been done when we inspected w, except (possibly) for the comparison of $r_{max}[i]$ with the ratio of the subword from position i to $|wx| - 1$, for each i. Starting with $i = |wx| - 1$ and counting down, these comparisons can be done in linear time. So our enumeration takes at most $O(|w|)$ time per solvable word w.

The algorithm ABSolve can be adapted for k-bounded Petri nets (where in every reachable marking every place has at most k tokens). Note that when choosing $\frac{m}{n}$, both $m \leq k$ and $n \leq k$ must hold, so the number of options does not depend on $|w|$. We need to check, though, if the created place could have more than k tokens on it (in linear time for fixed m, n by "firing" the word and computing the maximal token difference). Unluckily, it is possible that the intersection of intervals of the form $]r_{min}(s), r_{max}(s)[$ does not allow for a valid choice of m and n while there are valid choices for each interval separately. So, if we create one place for each interval we could do the second half of ABSolve in $O(k^2 \cdot |w|^2)$ (the first half remaining unchanged), but an optimal solution with as few places as possible is much harder to gain.

5 Cyclic Solvable Words

A word $w = t_1 \ldots t_n$ (with $t_i \in T$) is *cyclic solvable* if the transition system $TS_{cyc}(w) = (\{0, \ldots, n\}, \{(i-1, t_i, i) \mid 0 < i < n \land t_i \in T\} \cup \{(n, t_n, 0)\}, T, 0)$ is solvable. $TS_{cyc}(w)$ represents the infinite word w^ω. A Petri net solving $TS_{cyc}(w)$ reproduces its initial marking by firing w and allows for the (infinite) firing of w^ω.

Theorem 3. CHARACTERISATION OF CYCLIC SOLVABLE BINARY WORDS.
A word $w \in \{a, b\}^+$ is cyclic solvable if and only if $\forall x, y \in \{a, b\} \forall \alpha, \beta, \gamma, u, v$:

$$(x \neq y \land w = uv \land vu = x\alpha y\beta) \Rightarrow \#_x(x\alpha) \cdot \#_y(w) > \#_y(x\alpha) \cdot \#_x(w).$$

Proof: "$\Rightarrow$": Let N be the Petri net solution for w. Due to the reproduction of the initial marking we can fire w arbitrarily often, i.e. for $ww = uvuv$ we can investigate the decomposition of $vuvu = x\alpha|_{s'}y\beta|_s x\alpha|_{s''}y\beta$. Looking at the subword from s' to s'', by Lemma 4 we know $\#_y(y\beta) \cdot \#_x(x\alpha) > \#_x(y\beta) \cdot \#_y(x\alpha)$. Since $\#_y(w) = \#_y(x\alpha) + \#_y(y\beta)$ and $\#_x(w) = \#_x(x\alpha) + \#_x(y\beta)$, the ratio of y to x ($\in \mathbb{Q} \cup \{\infty\}$) in w must lie between those of $x\alpha$ and $y\beta$:

$$\frac{\#_y(y\beta)}{\#_x(y\beta)} > \frac{\#_y(w)}{\#_x(w)} > \frac{\#_y(x\alpha)}{\#_x(x\alpha)}.$$

The latter inequality completes this direction of the proof.

"$\Leftarrow$": Consider a decomposition of the 'rolled out' version w^ω of w

$$\ldots |_{s'} \hat{w}^i|_{\hat{s}'} y\beta|_s x\alpha|_{\hat{s}''} \tilde{w}^j|_{s''} y \ldots$$

where $\hat{w} = y\beta\gamma$ and $\tilde{w} = \delta x\alpha$ (with some $\gamma, \delta \in \{a, b\}^*$) have the same Parikh vector as w and $i, j \geq 0$. Note that $x\alpha$ and $y\beta$ may each have a length up to $|w| - 1$, so they might not add up to w. If we show that all possible finite subwords from some s' to s'' around our separation point s fulfill the condition of Lemma 4, the lemma is applicable with the result of y being separable at s. Since s is chosen arbitrarily, the infinite word w^ω is solvable and thus w is cyclic solvable.

If $x\alpha$ is a factor in w, we know $\#_x(x\alpha) \cdot \#_y(w) > \#_y(x\alpha) \cdot \#_x(w)$. If $x\alpha = uv$ is distributed such that $w = vy\gamma u$, we come to the same conclusion by using the rolled version $uvy\gamma$ in the precondition. For $y\beta$, consider the rolled version $x\gamma y\beta$ of w (with γ chosen accordingly). We then know $\#_x(x\gamma) \cdot \#_y(w) > \#_y(x\gamma) \cdot \#_x(w)$ and conclude that the ratio of x and y in w must be between those of $x\gamma$ and $y\beta$, i.e.

$$\frac{\#_y(y\beta)}{\#_x(y\beta)} > \frac{\#_y(w)}{\#_x(w)} > \frac{\#_y(x\gamma)}{\#_x(x\gamma)}.$$

Overall, we get

$$\frac{\#_y(y\beta)}{\#_x(y\beta)} > \frac{\#_y(w)}{\#_x(w)} > \frac{\#_y(x\alpha)}{\#_x(x\alpha)},$$

which is the precondition for Lemma 4 at $\hat{s}'$ and $\hat{s}''$. We can now argue that

$$\frac{\#_y(y\beta)}{\#_x(y\beta)} > \frac{\#_y(\hat{w}y\beta)}{\#_x(\hat{w}y\beta)} > \frac{\#_y(w)}{\#_x(w)}$$

(and analogously for $x\alpha$ and $x\alpha\tilde{w}$). Just note that $\hat{w}$ and w have the same Parikh vector, so the same number of x and y in it. The argument can be applied repeatedly until $\hat{w}^i$ and $\tilde{w}^j$ are reached and we get

$$\frac{\#_y(\hat{w}^i y\beta)}{\#_x(\hat{w}^i y\beta)} > \frac{\#_y(w)}{\#_x(w)} > \frac{\#_y(x\alpha\tilde{w}^j)}{\#_x(x\alpha\tilde{w}^j)}.$$

So, the precondition for Lemma 4 is fulfilled for arbitrary s' and s'' that are followed by y, and by arbitrary s followed by x. Lemma 4 is applicable and y is separable at s. This concludes the proof.   □ 3

Note that with increasing i and j the ratios of y and x in the words $\hat{w}^i y\beta$ and $x\alpha\tilde{w}^j$ converge against $\frac{\#_y(w)}{\#_x(w)}$ (without ever reaching it). Thus, the open interval in Lemma 4 from which we can choose the arc weight ratio for the place p to be created turns into a single point $\frac{\#_y(w)}{\#_x(w)}$ – independently of the separation point, as long as we prevent the same transition y. We conclude:

Proposition 8. NETS FOR CYCLIC SOLVABLE WORDS.

If $w \in \{a, b\}^+$ is cyclic solvable, there is a Petri net solving it that has at most two places. The arc weights of these places are determined by the ratios $\frac{\#_a(w)}{\#_b(w)}$ and $\frac{\#_b(w)}{\#_a(w)}$, respectively.

Take the word $w = ababbab$ as an example. We check prefixes ending before some b first. The $\frac{a}{b}$-ratio must be better than in w, i.e. $> \frac{3}{4}$. This is true for a (∞), aba (2), $abab$ (1), and $ababba$ (1). Then, rotate the front a to the end ($babbaba$) and check again (now for the $\frac{b}{a}$-ratio $> \frac{4}{3}$, and prefixes ending before an a): b (∞), $babb$ (3), and $babbab$ (2). We continue until we end up rotating back to w. Here, everything is ok and w is cyclic solvable. The Petri net solving it is depicted in Fig. 5. Note, however, that at this point of the development, we do not know about its initial marking; it is only the next proposition which allows us to compute it.

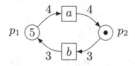

Fig. 5. A Petri net solving the word $(ababbab)^\omega$

Let us call a word $w \in \{a,b\}^+$ *minimal cyclic solvable* if it is cyclic solvable and there is no shorter word v, $|v| < |w|$, with $v^\omega = w^\omega$.

Proposition 9. TOKEN COUNT FOR CYCLIC SOLVABLE WORDS.
Let $w \in \{a,b\}^+$ *be minimal cyclic solvable. There is a Petri net* $N = (\{p_1, p_2\}, \{a,b\}, F, M_0)$ *solving* w^ω *such that for all* $M \in [M_0\rangle$, $M(p_1) + M(p_2) = |w| - 1$.

Proof: From Proposition 8 we have a Petri net solution with two places and two transitions and know that we may choose arc weights $F(p_1, a) = F(a, p_2) = \#_b(w)$ and $F(p_2, b) = F(b, p_1) = \#_a(w)$. Thus, $\forall M \in [M_0\rangle$: $M(p_1) + M(p_2) = M_0(p_1) + M_0(p_2)$. Let $w[i]$ be the ith letter of w and let M_i markings with $M_{i-1}[w[i]\rangle M_i$ for $1 \le i \le |w|$. Then, $M_0 = M_{|w|}$ and due to minimal cyclic solvability of w, $M_i \ne M_j$ for $0 \le i < j < |w|$ (otherwise, $v^\omega = w^\omega$ for some rotation v of $w[i+1] \ldots w[j]$). We conclude $|[M_0\rangle| = |w|$. Since $|P| = 2$, there are at most $M_0(p_1) + M_0(p_2) + 1$ reachable states in N, i.e. $M_0(p_1) + M_0(p_2) \ge |w| - 1$. Assume, $n := M_0(p_1) + M_0(p_2) \ge |w|$. Then, markings $(\#_b(w) + k, \#_a(w) + \ell)$ with $k, \ell \ge 0$ must be unreachable as they allow firing of both transitions. The remaining possible markings $(0, n)$, $\ldots$, $(\#_b(w) - 1, n - \#_b(w) + 1)$ and $(n, 0)$, $\ldots$, $(n - \#_a(w) + 1, \#_a(w) - 1)$ are exactly the $|w| = \#_a(w) + \#_b(w)$ markings reachable in N. Now, $(0, n)[b\rangle(\#_b(w), n - \#_b(w))$ would reach an unreachable marking, a contradiction. Thus, $M_0(p_1) + M_0(p_2) = |w| - 1$. □ 9

Algorithm 2 for cyclic solving of a word w is obviously in $O(|w|^2)$.

Lemma 5. SOLVABLE BINARY WORDS OF THE FORM vw^ω.
Let $v \in \{a,b\}^+$ *and* $w \in \{a,b\}^+ \backslash (a^+ \cup b^+)$. *The infinite word* vw^ω *is solvable if and only if* w *is cyclic solvable and* v *is a postfix of* w^i *for some* $i \ge 1$.

Proof: "⇒": For arbitrary late parts of vw^ω, Lemma 4 results in the same conditions as for w^ω, i.e. if vw^ω is solvable by $N = (\{p_1, p_2\}, \{a,b\}, F, M_0)$, so is w^ω (possibly with a different initial marking). W.l.o.g. let w be minimal cyclic solvable (otherwise rewrite vw^ω accordingly). If v is not a postfix of w^i (with i such that $|v| \le |w^i|$), we find u, x, y with (w.l.o.g.) $v = xau$ and $w^i = ybu$,

---

Algorithm 2. ABCycSolve

Input: $w \in \{a, b\}^+$
Output: Petri net solving w^ω if it exists
  compute $W[0] \leftarrow \#_a(w)$, $W[1] \leftarrow \#_b(w)$
  $m_0 \leftarrow 0$, $m \leftarrow 0$ {tokens available for a}
  for $i = 0$ **to** $|w| - 1$ **do** {rotations of w}
    $v \leftarrow w[i] \ldots w[|w| - 1]w[0] \ldots w[i - 1]$
    if $v[0] = 'a'$ **then** $R \leftarrow 0$ **else** $R \leftarrow 1$ {fraction selector}
    $N[0] \leftarrow 0$, $N[1] \leftarrow 0$ {for counting a's and b's}
    for $j = 0$ **to** $|v| - 1$ **do** {prefixes of v}
      if $v[0] \neq v[j]$ **and** $N[R] * W[1 - R] \leq W[R] * N[1 - R]$
      then return {unsolvable}
      if $v[j] = 'a'$ **then** $N[0] \leftarrow N[0] + 1$ **else** $N[1] \leftarrow N[1] + 1$
    endfor
    if $v[0] = 'a'$ **then** $m \leftarrow m - W[1]$ **else** $m \leftarrow m + W[0]$ {fire}
    if $m < 0$ **then** $m_0 \leftarrow m_0 - m$, $m \leftarrow 0$
  endfor
  $F(p_1, a) \leftarrow \#_b(w)$, $F(a, p_2) \leftarrow \#_b(w)$, $F(p_2, b) \leftarrow \#_a(w)$, $F(b, p_1) \leftarrow \#_a(w)$
  return $(\{p_1, p_2\}, \{a, b\}, F, \{p_1 \to m_0, p_2 \to |w| - 1 - m_0\})$

---

and $M_0[xa\rangle M[uyb\rangle M$ for some marking M. Since w contains an a and a b, w.l.o.g. p_1 receives tokens from b and delivers to a, and p_2 covers the other direction. Thus, $M(p_1) + M(p_2) \geq F(b, p_1) + F(a, p_2) = \#_a(w) + \#_b(w) = |w|$, contradicting Proposition 9.

"$\Leftarrow$": If v is a postfix of w^i we can rewrite vw^ω as u^ω with u and w being rotations of each other, and thus having the same Petri net solving them by Theorem 3, differing only at the initial marking.   □ 5

So, words vw^ω with $\#_a(w) > 0 < \#_b(w)$ are solvable only if they can be rewritten as u^ω. Checking words in which w contains only one letter, we get:

Lemma 6. SOLVABLE BINARY WORDS OF THE FORM va^ω.
  Let $v \in \{a, b\}^+$. The infinite word va^ω is solvable if and only if $v \in b^*a^*$.

Proof: "$\Leftarrow$": If $\#_b(v) > 0$, the Petri net $N = (\{p_1, p_2\}, \{a, b\}, F, M_0)$ with $F(p_1, a) = F(a, p_1) = \#_b(v)$, $F(p_2, b) = 1 = F(b, p_1)$, $M_0(p_2) = \#_b(v)$, and $M_0(p_1) = 0$ solves va^ω. With $\#_b(v) = 0$, the trivial Petri net $(\emptyset, \{a\}, \emptyset, \emptyset)$ is a solution.

"$\Rightarrow$": Assume $v \notin b^*a^*$, then a decomposition $va^\omega = u|_s a|_{s'} b|_{s''} a^\omega$ exists. A place p preventing a at s' exists with $s'(p) - s(p) = \mathbb{E}(a) < 0$. Thus, a cannot fire infinitely often at s''.   □ 6

Summing up these lemmas, we obtain the following theorem for words that consist of a finite prefix and a cyclic remainder.

Theorem 4. SOLVABLE CYCLIC BINARY WORDS WITH A PREFIX.
  A word vw^ω with $v, w \in \{a, b\}^*$ is solvable if and only if $w = \varepsilon$ or vw^ω can be rewritten as a cyclic solvable word u^ω or it has the form a^+b^ω or b^+a^ω.

6   Experimental Results

In an implementation of the general synthesis algorithm using the region-based approach, it is very likely that one of the freely available ILP solvers is employed. Since such solvers usually implement the simplex algorithm, our theoretical considerations of Sect. 2.3 are of limited practical value and need to be complemented by benchmarks. In particular, while the simplex algorithm can have exponential run times, it frequently allows a system of linear equations to be solved in linear time, which is much better than Khachiyan's worst case complexity.

To see how our algorithm fares compared to the region-based approach, we used the tools Synet and APT, both of which can synthesise Petri nets, and let all three run on the same computer. APT and our algorithm ABSolve have been implemented in Java while Synet was written in OCaml, which is known to produce efficient code. For each single test that was done we randomly generated 4000 words meeting certain criteria and fed them to all tools (including a pseudo-tool "no-op" doing virtually nothing), trying to synthesize the whole set of words. From the composite result we computed the average run time per word.

We made tests for words in $(a|b)^x$ with a fixed word length $x \in \{1, \ldots, 700\}$, i.e. 700 tests times 4000 words per tool, and again for words from $(ab|abb)^x$, where we expected a higher probability for solvable words. (Note that for $x = 1$ randomisation means we tested the words a and b each about 2000 times, but e.g. at $x = 50$ it is extremely unlikely that we tested the same word twice.) Fig. 6 (upper left) shows the results for $(a|b)^x$ on a logarithmic time scale. ABSolve is about a factor 10^3 faster than APT and Synet, and by the same factor slower than "no-op". In the upper right we normalised all curves by dividing all values of each curve by its value at $x = 350$. Due to the linear time scales we can see that ABSolve and APT both seem to have run time $O(n)$ while Synet shows a clearly parabolic curve, i.e. $O(n^k)$ with $k > 1$. The lower left part of the figure shows the results for $(ab|abb)^x$. The times are higher than for $(a|b)^x$, but this seems to be mostly due to the increased word length. We then tried to compare random sets of *solvable* words with sets from all words. From about $x = 40$ upwards it takes a lot of time to randomly generate solvable words (by randomly creating words and then picking the solvable ones) as solvable words become scarce. The lower right part of the figure shows that solvable words take distinctly more time with APT or ABSolve than arbitrary ones. This is the result of quick fail strategies in both algorithms (we stop checking at the first unsolvable system of equations or the first empty open interval, respectively). It also explains the linear run time for ABSolve and APT (we expect at least quadratic for solvable words) and the visible hook at the beginning of the curve for ABSolve in the other three pictures. Synet has identical times for solvable and for arbitrary words and was thus left out of the picture. A likely reason for this is the missing quick fail mechanism, at least in our version of Synet.

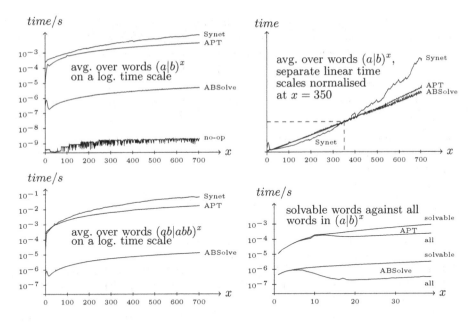

Fig. 6. Tests were done for random sets of 4000 words for each x with $1 \leq x \leq 700$ where words stem from $(ab|abb)^x$ (lower left) or $(a|b)^x$ (the other three pictures). Time scales are linear (but different for each curve) in the upper right picture and logarithmic in the others.

7   Concluding Remarks

In this paper, the class of Petri net synthesisable binary words has been studied in depth. We have presented a linear-time necessary condition for solvability representing an educated guess (Theorem 1), as well as quadratic time characterisations for finite binary words and for cyclic binary words (Theorems 2 and 3). The proof of Theorem 2 can easily be turned into a proof of a conjecture stated in [2], the main difference being that the latter is formulated for minimal unsolvable (rather than general) words. The algorithms derived from our quadratic-time characterisations allow to check solvability considerably more quickly than a general synthesis algorithm could. This has been confirmed both by the theoretical estimates contained in this paper and by experimental validation.

It would be interesting to consider extensions and ramifications. For example, we know of no results characterising PN-solvable acyclic labelled transition systems with few branching points, or with some other regular structure. The work described in [4] is an exception, a reason being that the cyclic structure of marked graph reachability graphs is particularly harmonious. Extending the results from binary words to words over a larger alphabet should also be worthwhile, and does not seem to be easy.

The present work could also be of interest in a wider context, as it might entail nontrivial necessary conditions for the solvability of an arbitrary labelled transition system. If the latter is solvable, then finding a PN-unsolvable structure in it may have a strong impact on its structure or shape. Also, words are persistent in the sense of [8] and tractable by the method described in [3]. However, they form (in some sense) a worst case and still lead to many region inequalities. It could therefore be interesting to check more closely whether the work described here can be of any benefit in enhancing the method described in [3].

Acknowledgments. We would like to thank Raymond Devillers for his very helpful suggestions to improve this paper and Valentin Spreckels for his valuable support in computing the experimental data.

References

1. Badouel, É., Bernardinello, L., Darondeau, P.: Petri Net Synthesis, 339 p. Springer, Heidelberg (2015). ISBN 978-3-662-47966-7
2. Barylska, K., Best, E., Erofeev, E., Mikulski, L., Piątkowski, M.: On binary words being Petri net solvable. In: Carmona, J., Bergenthum, R., van der Aalst, W. (eds) Proceedings of the ATAED 2015, pp. 1–15 (2015). http://ceur-ws.org/Vol1371
3. Best, E., Devillers, R.: Synthesis of bounded choice-free Petri nets. In: Aceto, L., Frutos Escrig, D. (eds) Proceedings of the 26th International Conference on Concurrency Theory (CONCUR 2015), LIPICS, Schloss Dagstuhl - Leibniz-Zentrum für Informatik, Dagstuhl, pp. 128-141 (2015). doi:10.4230/LIPIcs.CONCUR.2015. 128
4. Best, E., Devillers, R.: Characterisation of the state spaces of live and bounded marked graph Petri nets. In: Dediu, A.-H., Martín-Vide, C., Sierra-Rodríguez, J.-L., Truthe, B. (eds.) LATA 2014. LNCS, vol. 8370, pp. 161–172. Springer, Heidelberg (2014)
5. Caillaud, B.: http://www.irisa.fr/s4/tools/synet/
6. Khachiyan, L.: Selected Works, Moscow Center for Mathematical Continuous Education, ISBN 978-5-94057-509-2, 519 pages (2009). (in Russian)
7. Murata, T.: Petri nets: properties, analysis and applications. Proc. IEEE **77**(4), 541–580 (1989)
8. Landweber, L.H., Robertson, E.L.: Properties of conflict-free and persistent Petri nets. J. ACM **25**(3), 352–364 (1978)
9. Reisig, W.: Understanding Petri Nets: Modeling Techniques, Analysis Methods, Case Studies, 211 p. Springer, Heidelberg (2013). ISBN 978-3-642-33278-4
10. Schlachter, U. et al.: (2013). https://github.com/CvO-Theory/apt

The Power of Prime Cycles

Eike Best[1(✉)] and Raymond Devillers[2]

[1] Department of Computing Science,
Carl von Ossietzky Universität Oldenburg, 26111 Oldenburg, Germany
`eike.best@informatik.uni-oldenburg.de`
[2] Département d'Informatique, Université Libre de Bruxelles,
Boulevard du Triomphe - C.P. 212, B-1050 Bruxelles, Belgium
`rdevil@ulb.ac.be`

Abstract. In this paper, we shall examine properties of labelled transition systems which are motivated by system synthesis. Most of them are necessary conditions for synthesis by Petri nets to be successful. They can be checked in a pre-synthesis phase, allowing the immediate rejection of transition systems not satisfying them as non-synthesisable. The order of checking such conditions plays an important role in pre-synthesis optimisation. It is particularly desirable to know which conditions are implied by others, especially if the latter can be machine-verified more simply than the former. The purpose of this paper is to describe some mathematical results exhibiting a number of such implications.

Two properties called strong cycle-consistency and full backward determinism, respectively, are particularly hard to check. They are generalised counterparts of the marking equation of Petri net theory. We show that under some circumstances, they may be deduced from other properties which are easier to check. Amongst these other properties, the prime cycle property plays a particularly important role, not just because it is strong enough to imply others, but also because it is interesting to be checked on its own, if synthesis is targetted towards choice-free Petri nets.

Keywords: Choice-free Petri nets · Cyclic behaviour · Labelled transition systems · System synthesis

1 Introduction

Some Background. In Petri net synthesis [1], a labelled transition system is viewed as a specification for which a Petri net implementation with the same behaviour is sought. Petri net synthesis is useful, for instance, in case a sequential specification is given by a labelled transition system, and a smaller, concurrent implementation is aimed at.

E. Best—Supported by DFG (German Research Foundation) through grants Be 1267/15-1 ARS (Algorithms for Reengineering and Synthesis) and Be 1267/14-1 CAVER (Comparative Analysis and Verification for Correctness-Critical Systems).

© Springer International Publishing Switzerland 2016
F. Kordon and D. Moldt (Eds.): PETRI NETS 2016, LNCS 9698, pp. 59–78, 2016.
DOI: 10.1007/978-3-319-39086-4_5

Synthesis may be directed at specific classes of implementations, for instance at choice-free Petri nets. Such nets are defined by the absence of concurrency-unrelated choices; they have applications in hardware design [14] as well as in manufacturing [20,25], and allow a distributed implementation [7]. In tight synthesis (such as considered here, and largely in [1]), "the same behaviour" means that the reachability graph of a target Petri net should be isomorphic to a given source transition system, and that the Petri net's transitions should correspond uniquely to the labels of the transition system (thus there are no silent transition, no two transitions with the same label, and no transition with a sequence of labels). Such synthesis supports the physical distribution of Petri nets [4,17,18].

Both theoretically and algorithmically, the synthesis problem has been solved for finite transition systems [1,16] and, partially, for infinite ones [15]. The algorithms described in [1] are polynomial for place/transition Petri nets [23] and exponential for 1-bounded Petri nets, for which the problem is NP-complete [2]. All general algorithms, even when polynomial, are very costly. If the given transition system specification has n states, $O(n^2)$ transitions, and m labels, then $(n \cdot (n+1)/2) + O(n \cdot m)$ systems of inequalities, each having $O(n)$ inequations and $O(m)$ variables, have to be solved for a Petri net to be created. Even allowing for the fact that m may be considerably smaller than the set of states, n is usually a very large number. The entire algorithm tends to be of the order of n^6 or slightly less. This is problematic for all but relatively small n.

Motivation. The present paper is part of an on-going effort to alleviate the computational burden implicated by the general Petri net synthesis algorithm, and to improve failure information. For example, it was shown in [8,10] that if a given labelled transition system satisfies a list of properties, then it can be synthesised into a marked graph [13], even without solving a single linear inequality system. In effect, this provides a structural characterisation of such transition systems.

In more general cases, however, such a characterisation seems out of reach, and our approach is to minimise, by mathematical analysis, the number and size of linear inequality systems that need to be solved. In [9], it was shown that if the given transition system satisfies a number of structural preconditions (much weaker than the ones for marked graphs), then synthesis can be sped up by restricting the necessary linear inequation systems to small subsets of states. In effect, this approach suggests splitting synthesis into two phases: a first one –pre-synthesis–, in which the preconditions are scrutinised (and a transition system is rejected if it does not satisfy them), and a second one –proper synthesis–, in which the remaining (minimised but unavoidable) part of the general synthesis algorithm is carried out.

Remarkably, while some of these preconditions may be hard to check individually during pre-synthesis, some are not too difficult to verify once other ones have already been checked, and others may be verified simultaneously. In the present paper, we shall examine a list of properties which are inspired by (more precisely: are necessary for) a labelled transition system to be Petri net synthesisable. The main purpose of this investigation is to find dependencies between these properties. This allows pre-synthesis algorithms to be optimised by fine-tuning the order in which they are checked.

In addition, synthesis can be optimised, in the sense that some unsuitable input is rejected as early as possible, revealing structural reasons for such a rejection and for the implied (and inevitable) failure of synthesis, without actually carrying it out. The designer is then free to use the structural information in order to inspect his transition system as to which parts (if any) might be in need of re-design. This kind of information tends to be more useful than the error messages issued by a general synthesis algorithm, which typically just state that some of the many inequation systems are unsolvable. For an idea, the reader is referred to Appendix A below.

Structure. In Sect. 2, a list of relevant properties of labelled transition systems is defined and explained on some examples. Some of these properties are "local" (i.e., pertaining only to single states and their immediate surroundings), others are "global" (i.e., pertaining to the relationship between pairs or triples of states which might be very far from each other in the transition system, with long paths between them). Section 3 explains why these properties are important in the context of choice-free Petri net synthesis, and recalls a number of results from previous papers which will heavily be used here. In Sects. 4 and 5, we concentrate on deriving two rather unwieldy global properties, called strong cycle-consistency and full backward determinism, respectively, from other ones that are easier to check, in particular the property that the label counts of each small cycle are relatively prime. A summary can be found in Sect. 6, together with some observations about the difficulty to check the needed properties. Some concluding remarks are contained in Sect. 7.

2 Labelled Transition Systems

Definition 1. LTS, REACHABILITY, PARIKH VECTORS, CYCLES. A labelled transition system with initial state, abbreviated lts, is a quadruple $TS = (S, \rightarrow, T, \imath_0)$ where S is a set of *states*, T is a set of *labels*, $\rightarrow \subseteq (S \times T \times S)$ is the *transition relation*, and $\imath_0 \in S$ is an *initial state*. A label t is *enabled* in a state s, denoted by $s[t\rangle$, if there is some state s' such that $(s, t, s') \in \rightarrow$. For $t \in T$, $s[t\rangle s'$ iff $(s, t, s') \in \rightarrow$, meaning that s' is *reachable* from s through the execution of t. For sequences $\sigma \in T^*$, $s[\varepsilon\rangle$ and $s[\varepsilon\rangle s$ are always true; and $s[\sigma t\rangle$ $(s[\sigma t\rangle s')$ iff there is some s'' with $s[\sigma\rangle s''$ and $s''[t\rangle$ $(s''[t\rangle s'$, respectively). A state s' is *reachable* from state s if $\exists \sigma \in T^* : s[\sigma\rangle s'$. The set of states reachable from s is denoted by $[s\rangle$.

A *T-vector* is a function $\Phi : T \rightarrow \mathbb{N}$, and its *support* is $supp(\Phi) = \{t \in T \mid \Phi(t) > 0\}$. When $supp(\Phi) \neq \emptyset$, the *greatest common divisor* $\gcd(\Phi)$ is defined as $\gcd\{\Phi(t) \mid t \in supp(\Phi)\}$. Two *T-vectors* $\Phi_1, \Phi_2 : T \rightarrow \mathbb{N}$ are *label-disjoint* if their supports are disjoint. For a finite sequence $\sigma \in T^*$, the *Parikh vector of* σ is a *T-vector* $\Psi(\sigma)$, where $\Psi(\sigma)(t)$ denotes the number of occurrences of t in σ. For brevity, let the support of a sequence σ be defined as $supp(\sigma) = supp(\Psi(\sigma))$. Two finite sequences are *Parikh-equivalent* if they have the same Parikh vector.

A path $s[\sigma\rangle s'$ is called a *cycle*, or more precisely a *cycle at (or around) state* s, if $s = s'$. The cycle is *nontrivial* if $\sigma \neq \varepsilon$. A nontrivial cycle $s[\sigma\rangle s$ is called *small* if there is no nontrivial cycle $s'[\sigma'\rangle s'$ (with $s, s' \in S$) such that $\Psi(\sigma') \lneqq \Psi(\sigma)$, where, by definition, $\lneqq$ equals ($\leq \cap \neq$). A path $s[\sigma\rangle s'$ is called *short* (or *short from s to s'*, to be precise), if there is no path $s[\sigma'\rangle s'$ with $|\sigma'| < |\sigma|$.   □

Note that a cycle $s[\sigma\rangle s$ is short if and only if it is trivial, i.e., $\sigma = \varepsilon$.

Definition 2. DETERMINISM, PERSISTENCE, AND OTHER LTS PROPERTIES.
A labelled transition system $(S, \rightarrow, T, \iota_0)$ is called

- *finite* if S and T (hence also $\rightarrow$) are finite;
- *totally reachable* if $[\iota_0\rangle = S$ (i.e., every state is reachable from ι_0);
- *(weakly forward) deterministic* if, for all states $s, s', s'' \in S$, and for any label $t \in T$, $s[t\rangle s'$ and $s[t\rangle s''$ imply $s' = s''$ (i.e., an executable label uniquely determines the successor state);
- *(weakly) backward deterministic* if, for all states $s, s', s'' \in S$, and for any label $t \in T$, $s'[t\rangle s$ and $s''[t\rangle s$ imply $s' = s''$;
- *fully forward deterministic* if, for all states $s, s', s'' \in S$ and for all sequences $\alpha, \alpha' \in T^*$, $(s[\alpha\rangle s' \wedge s[\alpha'\rangle s'' \wedge \Psi(\alpha) = \Psi(\alpha'))$ entails $s' = s''$ (i.e., the Parikh vector of an executable sequence uniquely determines the target state);
- *fully backward deterministic* if, for all states $s, s', s'' \in S$ and for all sequences $\alpha, \alpha' \in T^*$, $(s'[\alpha\rangle s \wedge s''[\alpha'\rangle s \wedge \Psi(\alpha) = \Psi(\alpha'))$ entails $s' = s''$;
- *persistent* if for all states $s, s', s'' \in S$, and labels $t \neq u$, if $s[t\rangle s'$ and $s[u\rangle s''$, then there is some state $r \in S$ such that both $s'[u\rangle r$ and $s''[t\rangle r$ (i.e., once two different labels are both enabled, neither can disable the other, and this leads to the same state, forming a characteristic diamond shape);
- *backward persistent* if for all states $s, s', s'' \in S$, and labels $t \neq u$, if $s'[t\rangle s$ and $s''[u\rangle s$, then there is some state $r \in S$ such that both $r[u\rangle s'$ and $r[t\rangle s''$.   □

See Figs. 1, 2 and 3 for some examples. We shall use them as running examples and refer to the transition systems shown there by their names (TS_1, TS_2, ...).

Definition 3. HOME STATES, AND OTHER CYCLICITY PROPERTIES OF AN LTS.
A state $s \in S$ of $TS = (S, \rightarrow, T, \iota_0)$ is called a *home state* if $\forall s' \in S: s \in [s'\rangle$ (i.e., s is always reachable from any state). Moreover, TS is called

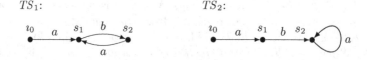

Fig. 1. TS_1 satisfies all properties of Definitions 2 to 4 (including the existence of home states) except weak and strong backward determinism (due to $\iota_0[a\rangle s_1$ and $s_2[a\rangle s_1$) and all forms of cycle-consistency (due to $\iota_0[ab\rangle s_2$ and $s_2[ab\rangle s_2$). TS_2 satisfies all properties except all forms of cycle-consistency (due to $\iota_0[a\rangle s_1$ and $s_2[a\rangle s_2$).

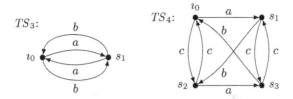

Fig. 2. TS_3 satisfies simple cycle-consistency but not mild cycle-consistency (since $\iota_0[aa\rangle\iota_0$, $\iota_0[a\rangle s_1$, $\Psi(aa) = 2 \cdot \Psi(a)$, but $\iota_0 \neq s_1$, and similarly for b). TS_3 satisfies all other properties except weak periodicity, the prime cycle property, and the disjoint small cycle property (since TS_3 has four partly overlapping small cycles $\iota_0[\beta\rangle\iota_0$, one – $\iota_0[aa\rangle\iota_0$ – with Parikh vector $(2\,0)$, another one – $\iota_0[bb\rangle\iota_0$ – with Parikh vector $(0\,2)$, and two Parikh-equivalent ones – $\iota_0[ab\rangle\iota_0$ and $\iota_0[ba\rangle\iota_0$ – with Parikh vector $(1\,1)$). TS_4 is path-disjoint (there are disjoint non-cyclic paths, for instance $\iota_0[c\rangle s_2$ and $\iota_0[a\rangle s_1[b\rangle s_2$).

- *weakly periodic* if for every $s_1 \in S$, label sequence $\sigma \in T^*$, and infinite sequence $s_1[\sigma\rangle s_2[\sigma\rangle s_3[\sigma\rangle s_4[\sigma\rangle \ldots$, either $s_i = s_j$ for all $i, j \geq 1$, or $s_i \neq s_j$ for all $i, j \geq 1$ with $i \neq j$;
- *weakly cycle-consistent* if for all $\sigma \in T^*$, $(\exists s \in S: s[\sigma\rangle s)$ implies $(\forall s', s'' \in S: s'[\sigma\rangle s'' \Rightarrow s' = s'')$;
- *simply cycle-consistent* if for all $\sigma \in T^*$, $(\exists s \in S: s[\sigma\rangle s)$ implies $(\forall s', s'' \in S, \sigma' \in T^*: (s'[\sigma'\rangle s'' \wedge \Psi(\sigma) = \Psi(\sigma')) \Rightarrow s' = s'')$;
- *mildly cycle-consistent* if for all $\sigma \in T^*$, $(\exists s \in S: s[\sigma\rangle s)$ implies $(\forall s', s'' \in S, \sigma' \in T^*: (s'[\sigma'\rangle s'' \wedge \exists q \in \mathbb{N} \setminus \{0\}: \Psi(\sigma) = q \cdot \Psi(\sigma')) \Rightarrow s' = s'')$;
- *strongly cycle-consistent* if for all $\sigma \in T^*$, $(\exists s \in S: s[\sigma\rangle s)$ implies $(\forall s', s'' \in S, \sigma' \in T^*: (s'[\sigma'\rangle s'' \wedge \exists p, q \in \mathbb{N}\setminus\{0\}: p \cdot \Psi(\sigma) = q \cdot \Psi(\sigma')) \Rightarrow s' = s'')$.

Moreover, TS will be said to have the *disjoint small cycle property* if there exist a number $n \leq |T|$ and a finite set of mutually label-disjoint T-vectors $\Upsilon_1, \ldots, \Upsilon_n: T \to \mathbb{N}$ such that

$$\{\Upsilon_1, \ldots, \Upsilon_n\} = \{\Psi(\beta)| \text{ there is a state } s \text{ and a small cycle } s[\beta\rangle s\}$$

If this property is satisfied, we shall abbreviate it to $\mathbf{P}\{\Upsilon_1, \ldots, \Upsilon_n\}$ (for **P**arikh vectors of small cycles).

Finally, TS will be said to have the *prime cycle property* if every small cycle $s[\beta\rangle s$ is *prime*, i.e., by definition, satisfies $\gcd(\Psi(\beta)) = 1$. □

Cycle-consistency specifies how the presence of a cycle determines that other, Parikh-related, paths are also cyclic. Weak cycle-consistency disallows a cycle and a non-cycle which are the same (as label sequences). Simple cycle-consistency disallows a cycle and a non-cycle to be Parikh-equivalent. Mild cycle-consistency forbids the Parikh vector of a cycle to be the multiple (by $q \geq 1$) of the Parikh vector of a non-cyclic path. Strong cycle-consistency prevents any cycle and non-cycle at all to be Parikh-related. Obviously, the cycle-consistency notions form a hierarchy: strong $\Rightarrow$ mild $\Rightarrow$ simple $\Rightarrow$ weak. It is also not hard to see that

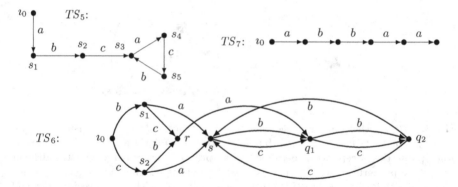

Fig. 3. TS_5 is not fully backward deterministic (since $\iota_0[abc\rangle s_3$, $s_3[acb\rangle s_3$, $\Psi(abc) = \Psi(acb)$, and $\iota_0 \neq s_3$). TS_5 is also not simply cycle-consistent (for the same reason), but it is weakly cycle-consistent (since there is no non-cyclic path acb, cba or bac). Also, TS_5 satisfies the prime cycle property. TS_6 is not weakly (hence fully) backward deterministic (since $s_1[a\rangle s$ and $s_2[a\rangle s$ but $s_1 \neq s_2$), not mildly cycle-consistent (because, e.g., $s[bbb\rangle s$ is cyclic but $s[b\rangle q_1$ is not), but simply and weakly cycle-consistent. Moreover, TS_6 does not satisfy the prime cycle property (because, e.g., $s[bbb\rangle s$ is a small, non-prime cycle), and it is path-disjoint (because, e.g., $s[b\rangle q_1$ and $s[c\rangle q_1$ with $b \neq c$). Both TS_5 and TS_6 are forward deterministic and persistent, and they have home states. TS_7 satisfies all properties of Definitions 2, 3, and 4, including the existence of a home state.

mild cycle-consistency implies weak periodicity. See Figs. 1, 2 and 3 for some examples.

Definition 4. PATH PROPERTIES OF AN LTS. A labelled transition system $TS = (S, \rightarrow, T, \iota_0)$ will be said

- to have the *short path property* if for all states $s, s' \in S$ and sequences $\sigma, \tau \in T^*$, if $s[\sigma\rangle s'$ and $s[\tau\rangle s'$ are short paths, then $\Psi(\sigma) = \Psi(\tau)$;
- and to be *path-nondisjoint* if for all states $s, s' \in S$ and sequences $\sigma, \tau \in T^*$ with $s[\sigma\rangle s'$ and $s[\tau\rangle s'$, $s \neq s'$ implies $supp(\sigma) \cap supp(\tau) \neq \emptyset$; *path-disjoint* if it is not path-nondisjoint. □

The short path property essentially means that all the short paths between two states are Parikh-equivalent, and the path-nondisjointness property is typically satisfied when we have the short path property and all the paths between two states Parikh-dominate the short paths.

3   Properties of a Synthesisable Lts

Let us first recall some basic definitions about Petri nets.

Definition 5. PETRI NETS, MARKINGS, REACHABILITY GRAPHS. A (finite, initially marked, place-transition, arc-weighted) Petri net is a tuple $N =$

(P, T, F, M_0) such that P is a finite set of *places*, T is a finite set of *transitions*, with $P \cap T = \emptyset$, F is a *flow* function $F \colon ((P \times T) \cup (T \times P)) \to \mathbb{N}$, M_0 is the *initial marking*, where a *marking* is a mapping $M \colon P \to \mathbb{N}$. A transition $t \in T$ is *enabled by* a marking M, denoted by $M[t\rangle$, if for all places $p \in P$, $M(p) \geq F(p, t)$. If t is enabled at M, then t can *occur* (or *fire*) in M, leading to the marking M' defined by $M'(p) = M(p) - F(p, t) + F(t, p)$ (denoted by $M[t\rangle M'$). A marking M' is *reachable* from M if there is a sequence of firings leading from M to M'. The set of markings reachable from M is denoted by $[M\rangle$. The *reachability graph of N* is the labelled transition system $RG(N)$ with the set of vertices $[M_0\rangle$, initial state M_0 and transitions $\{(M, t, M') \mid M, M' \in [M_0\rangle \wedge M[t\rangle M'\}$. A Petri net N is called *plain* if $cod(F) \subseteq \{0, 1\}$; a *marked graph* [13] if N is plain and $|p^{\bullet}| = 1$ and $|{}^{\bullet}p| = 1$ for all places $p \in P$; and *choice-free* if $|p^{\bullet}| \leq 1$ for all places $p \in P$. A marked Petri net $N = (P, T, F, M_0)$ is *bounded* if $RG(N)$ is finite, and *persistent* if $RG(N)$ is persistent.   □

The next proposition renders the mathematical background of our approach in precise terminology. It specifies which ones of the properties defined in the previous section are necessary for (choice-free) Petri net synthesisability.

Proposition 1. PROPERTIES OF PETRI NET REACHABILITY GRAPHS. *The reachability graph RG of a Petri net N is finite iff N is bounded. Moreover:*

- *RG is totally reachable, fully deterministic in both directions, and strongly cycle-consistent, i.e., satisfies all properties listed in Definition 2 except persistence; and all properties of Definition 3 except the existence of home states, the disjoint small cycle property, and the prime cycle property.*
- *If N is bounded and choice-free, then RG satisfies, in addition, all remaining properties of Definition 3; and all properties of Definition 4. In particular, RG is persistent, has home states and satisfies the disjoint small cycle property, the prime cycle property, the short path property and the path-nondisjointness.*

□

The proof of the first part of Proposition 1 is easy, as well as basic, in Petri net theory [23]. Total reachability arises by the definition of RG. Full determinism derives from the marking equation [23]. Strong cycle-consistency derives from the fact that every cycle determines a Petri net T-invariant, in combination with the marking equation. For the proof of the second part of Proposition 1, see [9] (more precisely: choice-free nets are clearly structurally persistent; disjoint small cycles arise from Theorem 3.1 of [9]; prime cycles arise from Lemma 3.6; and path-nondisjointness and the short path property are corollaries of Lemma 3.8 in [9]), and also [25] where it was first shown that realisable T-invariants in choice-free Petri nets enjoy stronger properties than in general nets.

If any of the properties listed in part 1 of Proposition 1 does not hold in a given TS, then Petri net synthesis necessarily fails. If any of the properties listed in the two parts of Proposition 1 does not hold, then choice-free Petri net synthesis necessarily fails. TS_7 (shown in Fig. 3) demonstrates that Proposition 1 has no converse: it satisfies all properties mentioned there, but is not realisable by any Petri net (that is, there is no Petri net whose reachability graph is isomorphic to TS_7 [5]). Figures 4 and 5 show, on the other hand, that Proposition 1 is sharp with respect to the properties of prime cycles and short paths: Both TS_8 and TS_9 have Petri net implementations (as shown in the figures), but they do not have choice-free Petri net solutions.

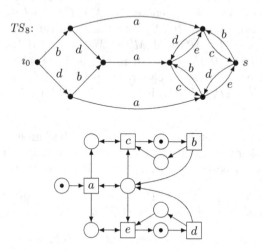

Fig. 4. Upper part: an lts which is PN-solvable but has no choice-free Petri net realisation. TS_8 satisfies all properties of Proposition 1 except the short path property (since $\imath_0[bac\rangle s$ and $\imath_0[dae\rangle s$ are not Parikh-equivalent). Lower part: non-choice-free solution of TS_8.

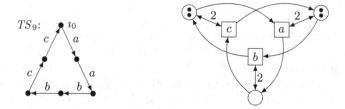

Fig. 5. Left-hand side: another PN-solvable lts without choice-free Petri net realisation. TS_9 satisfies all properties of Proposition 1 except the prime cycle property (since $\imath_0[aabbcc\rangle \imath_0$ with $gcd(aabbcc) = 2$). Right-hand side: non-choice-free solution of TS_9.

In the remaining part of this section we recall Keller's theorem, which is valuable as a tool for simplifying proofs about persistent lts, and some results about home states and small cycle decomposability.

Definition 6. RESIDUES. *Suppose that* $\tau, \sigma \in T^*$. *By* $\tau \stackrel{\bullet}{-} \sigma$, *we denote the (right) residue of* τ *left after cancelling successively in* τ *the leftmost occurrences of all symbols from* σ, *read from left to right. Formally:* $\tau \stackrel{\bullet}{-} \varepsilon = \tau$; *and* $\tau \stackrel{\bullet}{-} t = \tau$, *if* $t \notin \operatorname{supp}(\tau)$; *and* $\tau \stackrel{\bullet}{-} t = $ *the sequence obtained by erasing the leftmost* t *in* τ, *if* $t \in \operatorname{supp}(\tau)$; *and* $\tau \stackrel{\bullet}{-} (t\sigma) = (\tau \stackrel{\bullet}{-} t) \stackrel{\bullet}{-} \sigma$. □

Theorem 1. KELLER [21]. *Let* $(S, \rightarrow, T, \iota_0)$ *be a weakly forward deterministic, persistent lts. Let* τ *and* σ *be two label sequences activated at some state* s. *Then* $\tau(\sigma \stackrel{\bullet}{-} \tau)$ *and* $\sigma(\tau \stackrel{\bullet}{-} \sigma)$ *are also activated from* s. *Furthermore, the state reached after* $\tau(\sigma \stackrel{\bullet}{-} \tau)$ *equals the state reached after* $\sigma(\tau \stackrel{\bullet}{-} \sigma)$. □

An easy corollary of this result is that any weak forward deterministic and persistent lts satisfies full forward determinism, since $\sigma \stackrel{\bullet}{-} \tau = \varepsilon$ when $\Psi(\sigma) = \Psi(\tau)$ (i.e., in this case a global property is implied by local ones).

Proposition 2. FINITE PERSISTENT LTS HAVE HOME STATES [6]. *Let* $(S, \rightarrow, T, \iota_0)$ *be a finite, totally reachable, weakly forward deterministic, and persistent lts. Then there exists a home state* $\widetilde{s}$. □

Proposition 3. CYCLES MAY BE PUSHED TO HOME STATES [6]. *Let* $(S, \rightarrow, T, \iota_0)$ *be a weakly forward deterministic, persistent lts, and let* $\widetilde{s}$ *be a home state. For any cycle* $s[\rho\rangle s$ *from some state* $s \in S$, *there exists a cycle* $\widetilde{s}[\widetilde{\rho}\rangle \widetilde{s}$ *such that* $\Psi(\rho) = \Psi(\widetilde{\rho})$. □

Both propositions are easy consequences of Keller's theorem.

Proposition 4. SMALL CYCLE DECOMPOSITION. *Let* $(S, \rightarrow, T, \iota_0)$ *be a weakly forward deterministic, persistent lts with a home state. For any cycle* $s[\rho\rangle s$ *we have* $\Psi(\rho) = \sum_{i=1}^{n} k_i \cdot \Upsilon_i$ *where, for each* i, $k_i \in \mathbb{N}$ *and* Υ_i *is the Parikh vector of some small cycle.*

Proof: The proposition is obvious if ρ is small or empty.

Let us thus assume that there is a small cycle $s_i[\alpha_i\rangle s_i$ whose Parikh vector is smaller than the Parikh vector of ρ, i.e. $\Upsilon_i = \Psi(\alpha_i) \lneqq \Psi(\rho)$. From Proposition 3, both ρ and α_i may be pushed Parikh-equivalently around any home state $\widetilde{s}$, yielding $\widetilde{s}[\widetilde{\rho}\rangle \widetilde{s}$ and $\widetilde{s}[\widetilde{\alpha}_i\rangle \widetilde{s}$ with $\Psi(\rho) = \Psi(\widetilde{\rho})$ and $\Psi(\alpha_i) = \Psi(\widetilde{\alpha}_i)$. Keller's theorem can be applied, starting from $\widetilde{s}$, in the following way:

$$\widetilde{s}[\widetilde{\rho}\rangle \widetilde{s}[\widetilde{\alpha}_i \stackrel{\bullet}{-} \widetilde{\rho}\rangle \widetilde{s}$$
$$\text{and} \quad \widetilde{s}[\widetilde{\alpha}_i\rangle \widetilde{s}[\widetilde{\rho} \stackrel{\bullet}{-} \widetilde{\alpha}_i\rangle \widetilde{s}$$

The first line entails $\widetilde{s} = \widehat{s}$, since $\widetilde{\alpha}_i \stackrel{\bullet}{-} \widetilde{\rho} = \varepsilon$ on account of $\Psi(\alpha_i) \lneqq \Psi(\rho)$.

The second line then yields $\widetilde{s}[\widetilde{\rho} \stackrel{\bullet}{-} \widetilde{\alpha}_i\rangle \widetilde{s}$, that is, $\widetilde{\rho} \stackrel{\bullet}{-} \widetilde{\alpha}_i$ is cyclic around $\widetilde{s}$.

Moreover, $\Psi(\rho) = \Psi(\widetilde{\rho}) = \Psi(\alpha_i) + \Psi(\widetilde{\rho} \stackrel{\bullet}{-} \widetilde{\alpha}_i)$, again using $\Psi(\alpha_i) \lneqq \Psi(\rho)$. Resuming the decomposition for $\widetilde{\rho} \stackrel{\bullet}{-} \widetilde{\alpha}_i$, we shall eventually get the claimed result. □

Remark: The decomposition is not necessarily unique, as shown by system TS_3, depicted in Fig. 2: $\iota_0[abab\rangle\iota_0$ and $\Psi(abab) = 2 \cdot \Psi(ab) = \Psi(aa) + \Psi(bb)$. However, it is easy to see that this does not happen if small cycles are label-disjoint whenever they are not Parikh-equivalent (without overlapping supports, two different linear combinations may not be the same). This shows the importance of the next result.   □

Theorem 2. DISJOINT SMALL CYCLES ([6], WITH AN AMENDMENT). *Let $TS = (S, \rightarrow, T, \iota_0)$ be a finite and totally reachable lts which is weakly forward deterministic, persistent, and weakly periodic. Then there are n disjoint T-vectors $\Upsilon_1, \ldots, \Upsilon_n$, with $n \leq |T|$, such that $\mathbf{P}\{\Upsilon_1, \ldots, \Upsilon_n\}$ is satisfied.*

Proof (Sketch). The proof in [6] works by exploiting Proposition 3 to the effect that all small cycles can be realised Parikh-equivalently around any home state, and that at such a state, they are label-disjoint or their Parikh vectors are equal.

Actually, Theorem 2 of [6] lists weak cycle-consistency (just called "cycle-consistency" in [6]) as a further premise. However, a closer examination reveals that weak cycle-consistency is used only once in the proof. At that point, it can be replaced by a different argument not needing weak cycle-consistency.

More precisely: In Lemma 6 of [6], just after equation (3), the desired conclusion $s'[\tau\overset{\bullet}{-}\sigma\rangle s'$ is yielded by $s[\tau\overset{\bullet}{-}\sigma\rangle s$, $s[a\rangle s'$ and $a \notin \Psi(\tau\overset{\bullet}{-}\sigma)$, using Lemma 1 of [6], without the need to invoke weak cycle-consistency.   □

Remark: TS_3, depicted in Fig. 2, shows that Theorem 2 is sharp with respect to the weak periodicity property; namely, TS_3 satisfies all premises of the result, except weak periodicity, and it fails to satisfy $\mathbf{P}\{\Upsilon_1, \Upsilon_2, \Upsilon_n\}$: the four small cycles around any of the two states ι_0, s_1 have three different Parikh vectors that are, however, not label-disjoint.

4   Strong Cycle-Consistency

Our aim in this section is to derive strong cycle-consistency, which can be hard to check because it may be necessary to consider rather long paths, from other global properties which may be easier to check, together with a set of mainly local properties, namely finiteness, forward determinism, and persistence. This will be done in two steps.

In the first step (Theorem 3), the goal is to show that the disjoint small cycle property is implied by a different set of premises than those of Theorem 2, not using weak periodicity, but using, instead, the prime cycle property.

Theorem 3. DISJOINT PRIME CYCLES. *Let $TS = (S, \rightarrow, T, \iota_0)$ be a finite, totally reachable, weakly forward deterministic, persistent lts. Also, assume that TS satisfies the prime cycle property. Then TS satisfies $\mathbf{P}\{\Upsilon_1, \ldots, \Upsilon_n\}$ for some label-disjoint T-vectors $\Upsilon_1, \ldots, \Upsilon_n$ and a number $n \leq |T|$.*

Proof: Let $s \in [\iota_0\rangle$ be a home state. Such a state exists by Proposition 2. From Proposition 3, all cycles, and in particuler the small ones, may be pushed Parikh-equivalently around s. We shall thus examine the set of small cycles around s and show that they are either Parikh-equivalent or label-disjoint.

We proceed by contradiction. Let $s[\alpha_1\rangle s$ and $s[\alpha_2\rangle s$ be two non-Parikh equivalent small cycles with $supp(\alpha_1) \cap supp(\alpha_2) \neq \emptyset$, and let us choose them in such a way that α_1 has a minimal support set among the small cycles sharing labels with non-Parikh-equivalent ones.

Given α_1 and α_2, we consider the relatively prime natural numbers x, y such that

$$\frac{x}{y} = \max\left\{ \frac{\Psi(\alpha_2)(t)}{\Psi(\alpha_1)(t)} \mid t \in supp(\alpha_1) \right\} \tag{1}$$

Since $supp(\alpha_1) \neq \emptyset$, the definition is sound, and since $supp(\alpha_1) \cap supp(\alpha_2) \neq \emptyset$, $x, y \geq 1$. Now we use the cyclicity of α_1 and α_2 (repeating x times α_1 and y times α_2) and Keller's theorem in the following way, starting with state $s_1 = s$:

$$s_1 \left[\alpha_2^y \right\rangle s_1 \left[\underbrace{\alpha_1^x \overset{\bullet}{-} \alpha_2^y}_{\beta} \right\rangle s_2 \quad \text{and} \quad s_1 \left[\alpha_1^x \right\rangle s_1 \left[\underbrace{\alpha_2^y \overset{\bullet}{-} \alpha_1^x}_{\gamma} \right\rangle s_2$$

By the definition of $\overset{\bullet}{-}$, β and γ are label-disjoint, so that we may still apply Keller's theorem repeatedly:

$$s_1 \left[\beta \right\rangle s_2 \left[\beta \right\rangle s_3 \left[\beta \right\rangle s_4 \cdots$$
$$\text{and} \quad s_1 \left[\gamma \right\rangle s_2 \left[\gamma \right\rangle s_3 \left[\gamma \right\rangle s_4 \cdots$$

Since S is finite, there are two indices $i < j$ such that $s_i = s_j$. If the system is weakly backward deterministic, by following backward β and γ we immediately get that $s_i = s_1$; otherwise, since s is a home state we may push, Parikh-equivalently, the cycles $s_i[\beta^{(j-i)}\rangle s_i$ and $s_i[\gamma^{(j-i)}\rangle s_i$ around s: $s[\widetilde{\beta}\rangle s$ and $s[\widetilde{\gamma}\rangle s$ with $\Psi(\widetilde{\beta}) = (j - i) \cdot \Psi(\beta)$ and $\Psi(\widetilde{\gamma}) = (j - i) \cdot \Psi(\gamma)$.

Let us consider the Parikh vectors $\Psi(\beta)$ and $\Psi(\widetilde{\beta})$.

If a transition t is not in $supp(\alpha_1)$, then $\Psi(\beta)(t) = 0$, because $\Psi(\alpha_1)(t)$ is zero, and $\overset{\bullet}{-}$-subtracting something from it does not change the zero; hence also $\Psi(\widetilde{\beta})(t) = 0$.

For any transition $t \in supp(\alpha_1)$ realising the maximum in (1) (hence for at least one transition), we have $\Psi(\beta)(t) = 0$, because $x \cdot \Psi(\alpha_1)(t) = y \cdot \Psi(\alpha_2)(t)$.

Hence, $supp(\widetilde{\beta}) = supp(\beta) \subsetneq supp(\alpha_1)$. Then, either $s[\widetilde{\beta}\rangle s$ is a small cycle, or by Proposition 4 it is a linear combination of small cycles, all having labels in common with α_1 and a smaller support than α_1, contradicting the choice of the latter.

As a consequence, $\beta = \varepsilon$. This also implies that for every $t \in supp(\alpha_1)$, the fraction $\frac{\Psi(\alpha_2)(t)}{\Psi(\alpha_1)(t)}$ actually equals x/y, because otherwise $\Psi(\beta) = x \cdot \Psi(\alpha_1)(t) - y \cdot \Psi(\alpha_2)(t) > 0$. In particular, that also means that $supp(\alpha_1) \subseteq supp(\alpha_2)$.

If $x > y$, or if $x = y$ but $supp(\alpha_1) \subsetneq supp(\alpha_2)$, that means that $\Psi(\alpha_1) \lneq \Psi(\alpha_2)$, i.e., α_2 is not small.

If $x = y$ and $supp(\alpha_1) = supp(\alpha_2)$, that means that α_1 and α_2 are Parikh-equivalent.

If $x < y$, we have $2 \leq y$ and, since $x \cdot \Psi(\alpha_1)(t) = y \cdot \Psi(\alpha_2)(t)$ for each $t \in supp(\alpha_1)$, any prime factor of y must divide $\Psi(\alpha_1)(t)$ (it does not divide x since by definition x and y are relatively prime). Hence α_1 is not prime.

In all cases, we get a contradiction with the way we chose α_1 and α_2, so that, for any two small cycles, either they are label-disjoint or Parikh-equivalent, as claimed.   □

Example: In TS_3, consider the two overlapping small cyclic Parikh vectors

$$\alpha_1 \colon a, b \mapsto 2, 0 \quad \text{and} \quad \alpha_2 \colon a, b \mapsto 1, 1$$

We have $supp(\alpha_1) \cap supp(\alpha_2) = \{a\}$ and $b \in supp(\alpha_2) \setminus supp(\alpha_1)$. The construction yields $x = 1$ and $y = 2$, showing that α_1 is not prime.

Remark: Figure 2 shows that the prime cycle property is necessary for the conclusion of Theorem 3 to be valid. TS_3 contains two non-prime small cycles, and the non-Parikh-equivalent small cycles are not mutually label-disjoint.

In the second part of this section, our goal is to derive strong cycle-consistency from full backward determinism and the prime cycle property.

Theorem 4. DERIVING STRONG CYCLE-CONSISTENCY. *Let $TS = (S, \rightarrow, T, \imath_0)$ be finite, totally reachable, forward deterministic, persistent. Also assume that TS is fully backward deterministic and satisfies the prime cycle property. Then TS is strongly cycle-consistent.*

Proof: Assume $\imath_0[\beta\rangle s[\alpha\rangle s$, with α being a cycle around s, and $\imath_0[\gamma\rangle s_1[\alpha'\rangle s_2$. Also assume that $p \cdot \Psi(\alpha) = q \cdot \Psi(\alpha')$, for $1 \leq p, q \in \mathbb{N}$. We want to prove that $s_1 = s_2$.

The property is obvious if α is empty.

Since cycles can be pushed Parikh-equivalently to home states and home states exist, we can assume, without loss of generality, that s is a home state. By Theorem 3, we can decompose $s[\alpha\rangle s$ as

$$\begin{aligned} s\, [\, \alpha_1^{p_1} \, \ldots \, \alpha_m^{p_m} \,\rangle\, s \\ \text{with} \quad \Psi(\alpha) = p_1 \cdot \Psi(\alpha_1) + \ldots + p_m \cdot \Psi(\alpha_m) \end{aligned} \tag{2}$$

where for $1 \leq j \leq m$, $1 \leq p_j \in \mathbb{N}$ and $s[\alpha_j\rangle s$ are mutually label-disjoint small cycles. Since $p \cdot \Psi(\alpha) = q \cdot \Psi(\alpha')$, we also have a decomposition

$$q \cdot \Psi(\alpha') = p \cdot p_1 \cdot \Psi(\alpha_1) + \ldots + p \cdot p_m \cdot \Psi(\alpha_m)$$

By the prime cycle property and the label-disjointness, no prime divisor of q divides $\Psi(\alpha_j)$, and therefore, q divides $p \cdot p_j$, say $1 \leq r_j = (p \cdot p_j)/q \in \mathbb{N}$, for $1 \leq j \leq m$. Thus, we have:

$$\Psi(\alpha') = r_1 \cdot \Psi(\alpha_1) + \ldots + r_m \cdot \Psi(\alpha_m)$$
$$\text{with} \quad r_j \geq 1 \quad \text{for all} \quad 1 \leq j \leq m$$

By Keller's theorem, applied to $\iota_0[\beta\rangle s$ and $\iota_0[\gamma\rangle s_1$, we get

$$\iota_0\,[\,\beta\,\rangle\,s\,[\,\gamma\stackrel{\bullet}{-}\beta\,\rangle\,\widetilde{s}\quad\text{and}\quad\iota_0\,[\,\gamma\,\rangle\,s_1\,[\,\delta\,\rangle\,\widetilde{s}$$
$$\text{with}\quad\delta=\beta\stackrel{\bullet}{-}\gamma \tag{3}$$

Since $\widetilde{s}$ is also a home state and $s[\alpha\rangle s$, we get $\widetilde{s}\,[\,\widetilde{\alpha}\,\rangle\,\widetilde{s}$ with some $\widetilde{\alpha}$ satisfying $\Psi(\widetilde{\alpha})=\Psi(\alpha)$. More precisely, as in (2), $\Psi(\widetilde{\alpha})=p_1\cdot\Psi(\widetilde{\alpha}_1)+\ldots+p_m\cdot\Psi(\widetilde{\alpha}_m)$ for some small cycles $\widetilde{s}\,[\,\widetilde{\alpha}_j\,\rangle\,\widetilde{s}$, such that $\Psi(\widetilde{\alpha}_j)=\Psi(\alpha_j)$ for all $1\leq j\leq m$. Combining this and (3) with the assumption $s_1[\alpha'\rangle s_2$, we get

$$s_1\,[\,\alpha'\,\rangle\,s_2\quad\text{and}\quad s_1\,[\,\delta\,\rangle\,\widetilde{s}\,[\,\eta\,\rangle\,\widetilde{s},\quad\text{with}\quad\eta=\widetilde{\alpha}_1^{r_1}\ldots\widetilde{\alpha}_m^{r_m}$$

and we can apply Keller's theorem once more, getting:

$$s_1\,[\,\alpha'\,\rangle\,s_2\,[\,(\delta\,\eta)\stackrel{\bullet}{-}\alpha'\,\rangle\,\widehat{s}$$
$$\text{and}\quad s_1\,[\,\delta\,\rangle\,\widetilde{s}\,[\,\alpha'\stackrel{\bullet}{-}(\delta\,\eta)\,\rangle\,\widehat{s}$$

Note that $\Psi(\eta)=\Psi(\alpha')$. Thus, the second line gives $\widehat{s}=\widetilde{s}$, since $\alpha'\stackrel{\bullet}{-}(\delta\,\eta)=\varepsilon$ because of $\Psi(\alpha')\leq\Psi(\delta\,\eta)$. The first line then gives $s_2\,[\,\widetilde{\delta}\,\rangle\,\widetilde{s}$ for some sequence $\widetilde{\delta}$ with $\Psi(\widetilde{\delta})=\Psi(\delta)$, because of $\Psi(\alpha')=\Psi(\eta)$. In all, we have $s_1\,[\,\delta\,\rangle\,\widetilde{s}$ and $s_2\,[\,\widetilde{\delta}\,\rangle\,\widetilde{s}$, with $\Psi(\widetilde{\delta})=\Psi(\delta)$.

Full backward determinism then yields $s_1=s_2$. $\qquad\square$

Remark: TS_2 and TS_4 (shown in Figs. 1 and 2, respectively) prove that the prime cycle property is essential for the result to be valid. TS_5 (cf. Fig. 3) demonstrates that full backward determinism is needed, as well.

5 Full Backward Determinism

In this section, we show that full backward determinism (a global property, used as a premise in Theorem 4, which may be a bit hard to check in all generality) can be derived from other – more easily checkable – properties. There will be two variants of this result. In the first variant (Theorem 5), we use, additionally, mild cycle-consistency, another global property. In the second variant (Theorem 7), we use, in addition, the prime cycle property and simple cycle-consistency. It turns out that the nondisjoint path property also follows from these latter assumptions (Theorem 6).

Theorem 5. DERIVING FULL BACKWARD DETERMINISM, VARIANT 1. *Let $TS = (S,\rightarrow,T,\iota_0)$ be finite, totally reachable, forward deterministic, persistent. Also assume that TS is mildly cycle-consistent. Then TS is fully backward deterministic.*

Proof: Assume that $s_1[\gamma_1\rangle s$ and $s_2[\gamma_2\rangle s$, with $s,s_1,s_2\in S$ and $\Psi(\gamma_1)=\Psi(\gamma_2)$. We need to show that $s_1=s_2$.

The property is obvious if $\gamma_1=\varepsilon$ or $\gamma_2=\varepsilon$.

By total reachability, there are sequences α, β such that $\imath_0[\alpha\rangle s_1$ and $\imath_0[\beta\rangle s_2$. Thus $\imath_0[\alpha\gamma_1\rangle s$ and $\imath_0[\beta\gamma_2\rangle s$. An application of Keller's theorem yields

$$\imath_0\,[\,\alpha\,\rangle\,s_1\,[\,\beta\overset{\bullet}{-}\alpha\,\rangle\,s'$$
$$\text{and}\quad \imath_0\,[\,\beta\,\rangle\,s_2\,[\,\alpha\overset{\bullet}{-}\beta\,\rangle\,s'$$

One further application of Keller's theorem yields

$$\imath_0\,[\,\alpha\gamma_1\,\rangle\,s\,[\,(\beta\gamma_2)\overset{\bullet}{-}(\alpha\gamma_1)\,\rangle\,\widehat{s}$$
$$\text{and}\quad \imath_0\,[\,\beta\gamma_2\,\rangle\,s\,[\,(\alpha\gamma_1)\overset{\bullet}{-}(\beta\,\gamma_2)\,\rangle\,\widehat{s}$$

and since $\Psi(\gamma_1) = \Psi(\gamma_2)$, we get

$$s\,[\,\widetilde{\beta}\,\rangle\,\widehat{s}\ \text{and}\ s\,[\,\widetilde{\alpha}\,\rangle\,\widehat{s}$$
$$\text{with}\quad \Psi(\widetilde{\beta}) = \Psi(\beta\overset{\bullet}{-}\alpha)\text{and}\Psi(\widetilde{\alpha}) = \Psi(\alpha\overset{\bullet}{-}\beta)$$

If $s = \widehat{s}$, then both $\widetilde{\beta}$ and $\widetilde{\alpha}$ are cyclic around s with the same Parikh vectors as $\beta\overset{\bullet}{-}\alpha$ and $\alpha\overset{\bullet}{-}\beta$, respectively. Simple cycle-consistency implies $s_1 = s' = s_2$ as desired. (Note that only simple, not mild, cycle-consistency has been necessary, up to this point.)

Lastly, suppose that $s \neq \widehat{s}$. Then both $s[\widetilde{\beta}\rangle\widehat{s}$ and $s[\widetilde{\alpha}\rangle\widehat{s}$ with $\widetilde{\beta} \neq \varepsilon$ and $\widetilde{\alpha} \neq \varepsilon$.

Now we use the fact that $\beta\overset{\bullet}{-}\alpha$ and $\alpha\overset{\bullet}{-}\beta$ and thus also $\widetilde{\beta}$ and $\widetilde{\alpha}$, are label-disjoint, by the definition of $\overset{\bullet}{-}$. By applying Keller's theorem repeatedly, we find two infinite paths as follows:

$$s\,[\,\widetilde{\beta}\,\rangle\,\widehat{s}\,[\,\widetilde{\beta}\,\rangle\,\widehat{\widehat{s}}\,\ldots\quad \text{and}\quad s\,[\,\widetilde{\alpha}\,\rangle\,\widehat{s}\,[\,\widetilde{\alpha}\,\rangle\,\widehat{\widehat{s}}\,\ldots$$

By the finiteness of TS, these sequences contain two states which are the same, say $\widetilde{s}$, and thus, a nonempty cycle $\widetilde{s}\,[(\widetilde{\beta})^q\rangle\,\widetilde{s}$ and another nonempty cycle $\widetilde{s}\,[(\widetilde{\alpha})^q\rangle\,\widetilde{s}$, with some natural number $q \geq 1$. By mild cycle-consistency, $\beta\overset{\bullet}{-}\alpha$ is cyclic around s_1, implying $s_1 = s'$, and $\alpha\overset{\bullet}{-}\beta$ is cyclic around s_2, implying $s_2 = s'$.

Altogether, this entails $s_1 = s_2$ as claimed. $\qquad\qquad\square$

Remark: TS_5, as shown in Fig. 3, demonstrates that mild cycle-consistency is necessary for the theorem's conclusion to hold. TS_5 satisfies all premises of Theorem 5, except mild cycle-consistency, and is not fully backward deterministic. TS_6 shows that replacing mild cycle-consistency by simple cycle-consistency destroys the validity of the theorem, but note that in this case the small cycle is not prime.

In the second part of this section, we show that requiring the prime cycle property allows us to weaken the other premises of the previous theorem. First, it is shown that path-nondisjointness is implied.

Theorem 6. DERIVING PATH-NONDISJOINTNESS. *Let TS be finite, totally reachable, weakly forward deterministic, and persistent. Also assume that TS satisfies the prime cycle property and is weakly cycle-consistent. Then TS is path-nondisjoint.*

Proof: Suppose that $\imath_0[\delta\rangle s_1[\alpha\rangle s_2$ and $\imath_0[\delta\rangle s_1[\beta\rangle s_2$ with two label-disjoint paths α, β, i.e., $supp(\alpha) \cap supp(\beta) = \emptyset$. Suppose that $s_1 \neq s_2$ (hence $\alpha \neq \varepsilon$ and $\beta \neq \varepsilon$). We shall derive a contradiction.

By persistence and label disjointness, we find two infinite sequences as follows:

$$s_1[\alpha\rangle s_2[\alpha\rangle s_3 \ldots \quad \text{and} \quad s_1[\beta\rangle s_2[\beta\rangle s_3 \ldots$$

By the finiteness of TS, the sequence $s_1, s_2, \ldots$ contains two states which are the same. Thus, in this sequence, there is a state s_i and a number $q \in \mathbb{N} \setminus \{0\}$ such that $s_i[\alpha^q\rangle s_i$ (and also $s_i[\beta^q\rangle s_i$, but we can forget about β from now on). If $s_{i+1} = s_i$, then α is cyclic around s_i and non-cyclic around s_1, contradicting weak cycle-consistency.

Hence $s_i[\alpha\rangle s_{i+1}$ and $s_i \neq s_{i+1}$.

Next, let s be any home state and consider a sequence $s_i[\gamma\rangle s$. Let k be the maximum number of times a letter from α occurs in γ. We apply Keller's theorem in the following way, using the cyclicity of α^q (hence also of $\alpha^{k \cdot q}$) around s_i:

$$s_i [\alpha^{k \cdot q} \rangle s_i [\delta\rangle s' \text{ with } \delta = \gamma \overset{\bullet}{-} \alpha^{k \cdot q}$$
$$\text{and} \quad s_i [\gamma\rangle s [\alpha^{k \cdot q} \overset{\bullet}{-} \gamma\rangle s'$$

By $q \geq 1$ and the definition of k, $s_i[\delta\rangle s'$ is a sequence which is label-disjoint with α. Moreover, s' is also a home state since it is reachable from s.

By Proposition 4 and Theorem 3, we know that the Parikh vectors of all cycles have a disjoint decomposition into sums of Parikh vectors of small cycles around home states. So, there are mutually label-disjoint small cycles $s'[\alpha_1\rangle s', \ldots, s'[\alpha_m\rangle s'$ such that $\Psi(\alpha^q) = \sum_{1 \leq j \leq m} p_j \cdot \Psi(\alpha_j)$, with some numbers p_j; in other words,

$$q \cdot \Psi(\alpha) = p_1 \cdot \Psi(\alpha_1) + \ldots + p_m \cdot \Psi(\alpha_m)$$

Since all the α_j are not just small but also prime, and by their label-disjointness, no prime divisor of q divides $\Psi(\alpha_j)$, and therefore, q divides each of the p_j. It is thus possible to execute each α_j at s' only p_j/q times, instead of p_j times, and we get a cycle $s'[\tilde{\alpha}\rangle s'$ around s' which has the same Parikh vector as α.

Now persistency, applied to $s_i[\alpha\rangle$ and $s_i[\delta\rangle s'$, and considering also that α and δ are label-disjoint, allows to infer $s'[\alpha\rangle$ (in exactly the same order as in $s_i[\alpha\rangle$). But since $s'[\tilde{\alpha}\rangle s'$ is cyclic and $\Psi(\tilde{\alpha}) = \Psi(\alpha)$, we may use full forward determinism (implied by the premises) to conclude $s'[\alpha\rangle s'$. This contradicts $s_i \neq s_{i+1}$, by weak cycle-consistency, and ends the proof.   □

Remark: TS_4 (as depicted in Fig. 2) shows that the prime cycle property is essential for Theorem 6 to be true. The example TS_{10} (as shown in Fig. 6) demonstrates that weak cycle-consistency cannot be omitted.

Theorem 7. DERIVING FULL BACKWARD DETERMINISM, VARIANT 2. *Let $TS = (S, \rightarrow, T, \imath_0)$ be finite, totally reachable, weakly forward deterministic, and persistent. Also assume that TS satisfies the prime cycle property and is simply cycle-consistent. Then TS is fully backward deterministic.*

TS_{10}: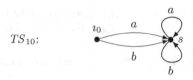

Fig. 6. TS_{10} is finite, totally reachable, weakly forward deterministic, and persistent. It also satisfies the prime cycle property but is not weakly cycle-consistent. Moreover, TS_{10} is not path-nondisjoint.

Proof: Theorem 6 implies that in the proof of Theorem 5, $s = \hat{s}$, provided the prime cycle property is added to the premises. Thus, in that case, the last step of the proof of Theorem 5 does not materialise. Hence, simple cycle-consistency, instead of mild cycle-consistency, suffices to get the desired result.   □

Remark: TS_6 (as shown in Fig. 3) satisfies all premises of Theorem 7 except the prime cycle property. This shows that omitting the prime cycle property from the set of preconditions does not allow the conclusion of the theorem to be drawn. The example TS_5 (as shown in Fig. 3) proves that simple cycle-consistency cannot be omitted, or weakened to weak cycle-consistency, either.

6   Summary and Discussion

The results of this paper can be summarised as follows: For labelled transition systems which are finite, totally reachable, weakly forward deterministic and persistent,

- weak periodicity ⇒ disjoint small cycles (Theorem 2)
- mild cycle-consistency ⇒ disjoint small cycles (Theorem 2 and the fact that mild cycle-consistency implies weak periodicity)
- prime cycles ⇒ disjoint small cycles (Theorem 3)
- prime cycles + full backward determinism ⇒ strong cycle-consistency (Theorem 4)
- mild cycle-consistency ⇒ full backward determinism (Theorem 5)
- prime cycles + weak cycle-consistency ⇒ path-nondisjointness (Theorem 6)
- prime cycles + simple cycle-consistency ⇒ full backward determinism (Theorem 7).

It turns out that the prime cycle property implies strong structural restrictions. In any pre-synthesis algorithm for choice-free Petri nets, the order of checking these properties is thus likely to have an impact on performance.

For instance, in choice-free synthesis, we might first perform some checks for total reachability (which is not entirely local but not too difficult to check), weak forward determinism and persistence, and then two global checks for prime cycles and weak cycle-consistency (possibly by incorporating them in known, fast, cycle-detection algorithms such as Johnson's [19]).[1] Then all other interesting properties – except the short path property – follow, using the theorems quoted above in a suitable order. In particular, strong cycle consistency and full backward determinism, which are hard to check individually,[2] are logically implied.

Note also that, once total reachability, weak forward determinism and persistence are known to hold for a given lts, the computation of small cycles can be limited to an arbitrarily chosen home state. Moreover, there can be no more than at most $|T|$ mutually disjoint (Parikh vectors of) cycles, where T, the set of labels, is normally much smaller than the set of states. An added benefit of such an approach is that the computed disjoint small cycle decomposition can serve as an input to dedicated synthesis algorithms, for example the one developed in [9].

If synthesis targets marked graphs (as it is the case in some applications [14,20]), then backward persistence can be added to the list of properties [8,10]. This, of course, allows full backward determinism to be derived from its weak counterpart. Prime cycles still have to be checked (otherwise, TS_3 in Fig. 2 would be a counterexample), but can be limited to Parikh vectors having entries ≤ 1 only. In fact, an initial test for live marked graphs is incorporated in the general synthesis algorithm of APT [11,24], leading to an enormous speedup when marked graphs can be synthesised. Noticeable slowdown in negative cases was avoided by performing quick-fail tests that have a high expectation of a negative outcome first. (More precisely, for example, it is tested initially whether the initial state has an incoming arrow, and if not, the entire test is skipped, because no live marked graph is then synthesisable.) This experiment shows that pre-synthesis can be implemented feasibly.

7   Concluding Remarks

The results described in this paper reveal some relationships between a variety of cycle and path properties of labelled transition systems. Such properties have been motivated by Petri net synthesis. Some of them (such as the determinism and cycle-consistency properties) must hold whenever Petri net synthesis is meant to succeed; others (such as the prime cycle property) must hold whenever choice-free Petri nets are to be synthesised. We expect that our results are helpful for the design of a pre-synthesis phase during which unsuitable transition systems are sorted out, providing some meaningful error information.

The results we obtained in this paper can be interpreted as going a small way towards a partial structural characterisation of Petri net synthesisable transition systems. However, we would like to emphasise that such an endeavour is

---

[1] This algorithm has a complexity of $O(n \cdot e \cdot \gamma)$ where n is the number of nodes of a graph, e the number of edges, and γ the number of small cycles. Thus, in our context, a bad upper bound is $O(n^3 \cdot m)$ where $n = |S|$ and $m = |T|$, which, however, still compares favourably with $O(n^6)$ for the full synthesis algorithm.

[2] Since, in brute force form, they involve, for all states $s \in S$, Parikh-comparisons of pairs of – possibly long – paths emanating from s.

extremely difficult. For instance, it has been a major task just to characterise the set of binary words corresponding to Petri net reachability graphs [5], and there are still a lot of labelled transition systems which satisfy all properties listed in Proposition 1 but do not allow to be synthesised.

In future work, we would like to discover further relationships of this kind, and more generally, to explore algorithmic improvements for synthesis. For example, the reader may have noticed that the short path property (which is a good candidate for being checked in choice-free synthesis) does not appear in one of our theorems. Indeed, though having an intuitive hunch, we do not know for sure, at the present stage, whether this property is connected to the other ones described in this paper.

Acknowledgments. The authors would like to thank Harro Wimmel and Valentin Spreckels for carefully commenting on a draft version of this paper and for checking and confirming that the assumption of weak cycle-consistency can indeed be circumvented in the proof of Theorem 2. The authors are also indebted to the anonymous reviewers for useful detailed comments.

A   Error messages of synet and APT (and pre-synthesis)

When asked to synthesise TS_2 (Fig. 1), synet [12] outputs

```
State separation failures:
  States 0 1  are not separated pairwise.
Event-state separation failures:
  Event a and states 1 are not separated.
  Event b and states 0 are not separated.
Synthesized net:
  -b:=1
```

while APT's [24] output is:

```
success: No
failedStateSeparationProblems: [[s0, s1]]
failedEventStateSeparationProblems: {a=[s1], b=[s0]}
```

Instead, our suggested pre-synthesis algorithm would issue an error message such as:

```
Synthesis not possible:
Path"a" may not be a cycle [s2 a s2]
  and a non-cycle [s0 a s1]
```

References

1. Badouel, É., Bernardinello, L., Darondeau, P.: Petri Net Synthesis. Texts in Theoretical Computer Science. An EATCS Series. Springer, Heidelberg (2015). ISBN 978-3-662-47967-4, 339 pp

2. Badouel, É., Bernardinello, L., Darondeau, P.: The synthesis problem for elementary net systems is NP-complete. Theor. Comput. Sci. **186**(1–2), 107–134 (1997)
3. Badouel, É., Darondeau, P.: Theory of regions. In: Reisig, W., Rozenberg, G. (eds.) Lectures on Petri Nets I: Basic Models. LNCS, vol. 1491, pp. 529–586. Springer, Heidelberg (1999)
4. Badouel, É., Caillaud, B., Darondeau, P.: Distributing finite automata through Petri net synthesis. J. Formal Aspects Comput. **13**, 447–470 (2002)
5. Barylska, K., Best, E., Erofeev, E., Mikulski, Ł., Piątkowski, M.: On binary words being Petri net solvable. In: Carmona, J., Bergenthum, R., van der Aalst, W. (eds.) ATAED 2015, pp. 1–15. http://ceur-ws.org/Vol-1371
6. Best, E., Darondeau, P.: A decomposition theorem for finite persistent transition systems. Acta Informatica **46**, 237–254 (2009)
7. Best, E., Darondeau, P.: Petri net distributability. In: Virbitskaite, I., Voronkov, A. (eds.) PSI 2011. LNCS, vol. 7162, pp. 1–18. Springer, Heidelberg (2011)
8. Best, E., Devillers, R.: Characterisation of the state spaces of live and bounded marked graph Petri nets. In: Dediu, A.H., Martín-Vide, C., Sierra-Rodríguez, J.L., Truthe, B. (eds.) LATA 2014. LNCS, vol. 8370, pp. 161–172. Springer, Heidelberg (2014)
9. Best, E., Devillers, R.: Synthesis of bounded choice-free Petri nets. In: Aceto, L., Frutos Escrig, D. (eds.) Proceedings of the 26th International Conference on Concurrency Theory (CONCUR 2015), LIPICS, Schloss Dagstuhl - Leibniz-Zentrum für Informatik, Dagstuhl, pp. 128–141 (2015). doi:10.4230/LIPIcs.CONCUR.2015. 128
10. Best, E., Devillers, R.: Characterisation of the State Spaces of Marked Graph Petri Nets. Accepted for publication in Information and Computation (2015). 20 pp., Extended version of [8]
11. Best, E., Schlachter, U.: Analysis of Petri nets and transition systems. In: Knight, S., Lanese, I., Lafuente, A.L., Vieira, H.T. (eds.) Proceedings of the 8th Interaction and Concurrency Experience. Electronic Proceedings in Theoretical Computer Science, vol. 189, pp. 53–67, June 2015. http://eptcs.web.cse.unsw.edu.au/paper.cgi? ICE2015.6
12. Caillaud, B.: http://www.irisa.fr/s4/tools/synet/
13. Commoner, F., Holt, A.W., Even, S., Pnueli, A.: Marked directed graphs. J. Comput. Syst. Sci. **5**(5), 511–523 (1971)
14. Cortadella, J., Kishinevsky, M., Kondratyev, A., Lavagno, L., Yakovlev, A.: Petrify: a tool for manipulating concurrent specifications and synthesis of asynchronous controllers. IEICE Trans. Inf. Syst. **80**(3), 315–325 (1997)
15. Darondeau, P.: Unbounded Petri net synthesis. In: Desel, J., Reisig, W., Rozenberg, G. (eds.) Lectures on Concurrency and Petri Nets. LNCS, pp. 413–438. Springer, Heidelberg (2004)
16. Ehrenfeucht, A., Rozenberg, G.: Partial 2-structures, Part I: basic notions and the representation problem, and Part II: state spaces of concurrent systems. Acta Informatica **27**(4), 315–368 (1990)
17. van Glabbeek, R.J., Goltz, U., Schicke-Uffmann, J.-W.: On distributability of Petri nets - (Extended Abstract). In: Birkedal, L. (ed.) Foundations of Software Science and Computational Structures. LNCS, vol. 7213, pp. 331–345. Springer, Heidelberg (2012)
18. Hopkins, R.P.: Distributable nets. In: Rozenberg, G. (ed.) Advances of Petri Nets 1991. LNCS, vol. 524, pp. 161–187. Springer, Heidelberg (1991). Applications and Theory of Petri Nets 1990

19. Johnson, D.B.: Finding all the elementary circuits of a directed graph. SIAM J. Comput. **4**(1), 77–84 (1975)
20. Júlvez, J., Recalde, L., Silva, M.: Deadlock-freeness analysis of continuous mono-T-semiflow Petri nets. IEEE Trans. Autom. Control **51**–9, 1472–1481 (2006)
21. Keller, R.M.: A fundamental theorem of asynchronous parallel computation. In: Feng, T.Y. (ed.) Parallel Processing, pp. 102–112. Springer, Heidelberg (1975)
22. Kondratyev, A., Cortadella, J., Kishinevsky, M., Pastor, E., Roig, O., Yakovlev, A.: Checking signal transition graph implementability by symbolic BDD traversal. In: Proceedings of the European Design and Test Conference, Paris, France, pp. 325–332 (1995)
23. Reisig, W.: Petri Nets. Monographs in Theoretical Computer Science. An EATCS Series, vol. 4. Springer, Heidelberg (1985)
24. Schlachter, U., et al. (2013–2016). https://github.com/CvO-Theory/apt
25. Teruel, E., Colom, J.M., Silva, M.: Choice-free Petri nets: a model for deterministic concurrent systems with bulk services and arrivals. IEEE Trans. Syst. Man Cybern. Part A **27**–1, 73–83 (1997)

Petri Net Synthesis for Restricted Classes of Nets

Uli Schlachter[✉]

Department of Computing Science, Carl von Ossietzky Universität,
26111 Oldenburg, Germany
uli.schlachter@informatik.uni-oldenburg.de

Abstract. This paper first recapitulates an algorithm for Petri net synthesis. Then, this algorithm is extended to special classes of Petri nets. For this purpose, any combination of the properties plain, pure, conflict-free, homogeneous, k-bounded, generalized T-net, generalized marked graph, place-output-nonbranching and distributed can be specified. Finally, a fast heuristic and an algorithm for minimizing the number of places in the synthesized Petri net is presented and evaluated experimentally.

Keywords: Petri net synthesis · Petri net properties · Region theory · Petri net minimization

1 Introduction

Algorithms for Petri net synthesis produce a Petri net that generates a given state space. More precisely, their task is to construct a Petri net whose reachability graph is isomorphic to a given labelled transition system (lts), although other notions of equivalence, for example language-equivalence, are possible as well.

The theory behind Petri net synthesis is based on *regions* of the lts and was developed by Ehrenfeucht and Rozenberg for partial 2-structures [25,26], which are related to elementary nets [4]. These results were later extended to pure Petri nets [1]. Another branch of research is synthesis up to language-equivalence [23,28] which has applications to process discovery, e.g. [15,29]. An overview of these results can be found in [4]. A newer and more detailed explanation is available in [2]. Besides these general results, there are also special algorithms for the synthesis of marked graphs [7], T-systems [8], and output-nonbranching Petri nets [9] (called choice-free in [9]).

Several tools for Petri net synthesis have been implemented, e.g. Synet, Petrify and GENET. The Synet tool [1,3,13] can produce general and pure P/T nets.

U. Schlachter—The author is supported by the German Research Foundation (DFG) project ARS (Algorithms for Reengineering and Synthesis), reference number Be 1267/15-1.

F. Kordon and D. Moldt (Eds.): PETRI NETS 2016, LNCS 9698, pp. 79–97, 2016.
DOI: 10.1007/978-3-319-39086-4_6

In contrast to this, Petrify [19–22] always produces 1-bounded Petri nets and allows properties like pure and free-choice to be specified for the resulting Petri net. Another tool is GENET [14, 16, 17] which can produce k-bounded Petri nets and which can over-approximate its input, if no exact solution is possible. It supports a restriction to marked graphs.

Depending on the context, different restrictions via additional properties can be useful. For example, Petrify has applications in circuit design, where the desired behaviour of a circuit is used as specification. The Petri net synthesized by Petrify provides a possible encoding of the internal states of the circuit. Synet is used with a communication protocol and the resulting Petri net models two communicating automata [13]. In more general terms, Petri net synthesis can be used to highlight possible concurrency in an lts, see e.g. [3].

All of these tools allow some specifically targeted synthesis, but they are mutually incomparable and apparently no focus was put on different classes of nets, perhaps with the exception of Petrify, which however can only synthesize 1-bounded Petri nets. What is missing is a systematic approach, starting from a synthesis algorithm that allows the entire class of P/T-nets and deriving an algorithm that can be used for a large class of targets and which may be useful in a variety of circumstances.

The purpose of the present paper is to introduce a Petri net synthesis algorithm which can also deal with various properties that the calculated Petri net should satisfy. Based on this, another algorithm is described which calculates a Petri net with a minimal number of places. An implementation of these algorithms is already available in our tool APT [11]. An overview of APT's capabilities, which go beyond Petri net synthesis, can be found in [10]. As an example application of this tool in research, our group is trying to structurally characterize the reachability graphs of some classes of Petri nets in the sense of [7–9]. For this purpose it is necessary to decide if some structure can be generated by some class of nets and helpful to get hints about where the problems are.

There is of course previous work that handles some restrictions on the synthesized Petri net, as indicated by the capabilities of the tools mentioned above. The approach of [20, 21] always produces elementary nets[1] and relies on label-splitting to produce e.g. free-choice solutions. Label-splitting produces non-injectively-labelled Petri nets. The present paper does not consider label-splitting, because this weakens isomorphic solutions to just bisimilar ones. Isomorphic reachability graphs correspond more strongly to the input of the synthesis algorithm and allow to investigate the expressivity of Petri nets. The algorithm for the synthesis of general Petri nets that is presented in [28] is extended with restrictions for elementary nets in the same paper. This is done with constraints equivalent to the ones used in the present paper. However, here these constraints are lifted to the general case of k-boundedness and pureness is also handled. Synthesis of distributed Petri nets was already examined in [3]. The present paper incorporates these results into its framework. An algorithm for the synthesis of plain Petri nets based on integer linear programming is extended with some structural

---

[1] Elementary nets correspond to pure, plain and 1-bounded Petri nets.

constraints in [29], for example pure, free-choice, marked graph and elementary net. All the properties that are not specific to a workflow context, but applicable to general Petri net synthesis, can also be handled in the framework that is presented in this paper. The encoding of these constraints is done in a similar way in this paper.

In summary, this paper presents an approach for Petri net synthesis that can deal with all previously examined classes of Petri nets and that is not limited to the synthesis of plain nets. Additionally, properties like e.g. homogeneity can be handled, which were not dealt with before.

The general approach of the algorithm is to encode the behaviour of the system into a formula that is then solved via an off-the-shelf library. Specifically, APT encodes the problem in first-order logic with linear arithmetic over integers without quantifiers (the QF_LIA logic defined in the SMT-LIB standard [5]) and uses the SMTInterpol library [18] to solve the constructed formula.

The next section introduces the general settings of lts and Petri nets, and Sect. 3 introduces region theory and presents an algorithm for Petri net synthesis without further restrictions. This algorithm is extended in Sect. 4 to support additional properties that a synthesized Petri net must have. In Sect. 5 some optimizations are presented, specifically a heuristic for removing superfluous places from the synthesized net, an approach for speeding up some detail of the algorithm, and an algorithm that calculates a Petri net with the minimal possible number of places. This section also contains an experimental evaluation of the presented optimizations.

2   Labelled Transition Systems and Petri Nets

An lts (labelled transition system with initial state) is a tuple $(S, \rightarrow, T, s_0)$, where S is a set of *states*, T is a set of *labels* with $S \cap T = \emptyset$, $\rightarrow \subseteq (S \times T \times S)$ is the *transition relation*, and $s_0 \in S$ is an *initial state*. A label t is *enabled* in a state s, denoted by $s \xrightarrow{t}$, if there is some state s' such that $(s, t, s') \in \rightarrow$. This situation is written as $s \xrightarrow{t} s'$ and means that s' is *reachable* from s through the execution of t. The definitions of enabledness and of the reachability relation are extended as usual to label sequences (or directed paths) $\sigma \in T^*$: $s \xrightarrow{\varepsilon}$ and $s \xrightarrow{\varepsilon} s$ are always true; $s \xrightarrow{\sigma t}$ $(s \xrightarrow{\sigma t} s')$ iff there is some s'' with $s \xrightarrow{\sigma} s''$ and $s'' \xrightarrow{t}$ $(s'' \xrightarrow{t} s'$, respectively). A state s' is reachable from a state s if there is a label sequence σ such that $s \xrightarrow{\sigma} s'$. A state s' is *reachable* if it is reachable from s_0. By $s^{\rightarrow}$, we denote the set of states reachable from s. The *Parikh vector* $\Psi(\sigma)$ of a sequence $\sigma \in T^*$ is a T-vector where $\Psi(\sigma)(t)$ denotes the number of occurrences of t in σ.

Two lts $(S_1, \rightarrow_1, T, s_{01})$ and $(S_2, \rightarrow_2, T, s_{02})$ over the same set of labels T are *isomorphic* if there is a bijection $\zeta : S_1 \rightarrow S_2$ with $\zeta(s_{01}) = s_{02}$ and $(s, t, s') \in \rightarrow_1$ $\iff (\zeta(s), t, \zeta(s')) \in \rightarrow_2$, for all $s, s' \in S_1$.

A labelled transition system $(S, \rightarrow, T, s_0)$ is called *finite* if S and T (hence also $\rightarrow$) are finite sets. It is *deterministic* if for any reachable state s and label t,

$s \xrightarrow{t} s'$ and $s \xrightarrow{t} s''$ implies $s' = s''$ and it is *totally reachable* if $S = s_0^{\rightarrow}$ and $\forall t \in T : \exists s \in s_0^{\rightarrow} : s \xrightarrow{t}$.

A *spanning tree* of a totally reachable lts $(S, \rightarrow, T, s_0)$ is an lts $(S, \rightarrow', T, s_0)$ with $\rightarrow' \subseteq \rightarrow$ so that for every $s \in S$ there is a unique $\sigma \in T^*$ with $s_0 \xrightarrow{\sigma} s$. The Parikh vector of σ for a given $s \in S$ is called Ψ_s.

A (finite, initially marked, place-transition, arc-weighted, unlabelled) Petri net is a tuple (P, T, F, M_0) such that P is a finite set of *places*, T is a finite set of *transitions*, with $P \cap T = \emptyset$, F is a *flow* function $F : ((P \times T) \cup (T \times P)) \to \mathbb{N}$, and M_0 is the *initial marking*, where a *marking* is a mapping $M : P \to \mathbb{N}$, indicating the number of *tokens* in each place. $F(p, t) = w > 0$ (resp. $F(t, p) = w > 0$) means that there is an *arc* from p to t (resp. from t to p) with *arc weight* w. A transition $t \in T$ is *enabled by* a marking M, denoted by $M[t\rangle$, if for all places $p \in P$, $M(p) \geq F(p, t)$. If t is enabled at M, then t can *occur* (or *fire*) in M, leading to the marking M' defined by $\forall p \in P : M'(p) = M(p) - F(p, t) + F(t, p)$ (notation: $M[t\rangle M')$. The *reachability graph of* N, with initial marking M_0, is the labelled transition system with the set of vertices $[M_0\rangle$ (i.e., the markings which are reachable from M_0) and the set of edges $\{(M, t, M') \mid M, M' \in [M_0\rangle \wedge M[t\rangle M'\}$. If an lts A is isomorphic to the reachability graph of a Petri net N, then we will also say that N *solves* A. For a place p of a Petri net $N = (P, T, F, M_0)$, let $^\bullet p = \{t \in T \mid F(t, p) > 0\}$ be its *preset*, and $p^\bullet = \{t \in T \mid F(p, t) > 0\}$ its *postset*. Analogously, for a transition t define its *preset* as $^\bullet t = \{p \in P \mid F(p, t) > 0\}$, and its *postset* as $t^\bullet = \{p \in P \mid F(t, p) > 0\}$.

3 Region Theory

This section introduces region theory and recapitulates an algorithm for Petri net synthesis from [2,4]. In this section, we fix an arbitrary (finite, deterministic, and totally reachable[2]) lts $A = (S, \rightarrow, T, s_0)$ with $T = \{t_1, \ldots t_n\}$. Also, $(S, \rightarrow', T, s_0)$ is a fixed and arbitrary spanning tree of A. Recall from its definition that this assigns a Parikh vector Ψ_s to each state $s \in S$.

A *region* of an lts $A = (S, \rightarrow, T, s_0)$ is a triple $(\mathbb{R}, \mathbb{B}, \mathbb{F}) \in (\mathbb{N}^S, \mathbb{N}^T, \mathbb{N}^T)$ such that the following holds:

$$\forall s \xrightarrow{t} s' \in \rightarrow : \mathbb{R}(s) \geq \mathbb{B}(t) \wedge \mathbb{R}(s') = \mathbb{R}(s) - \mathbb{B}(t) + \mathbb{F}(t) \tag{1}$$

Intuitively, this describes a possible place in a Petri net generating A where $\mathbb{B}(t)$, resp. $\mathbb{F}(t)$, describes the number of tokens consumed, resp. produced, by a transition $t \in T$ and $\mathbb{R}(s)$ is the number of tokens on this place in state $s \in S$. The requirement above then describes an occurrence of transition t.

For every region $(\mathbb{R}, \mathbb{B}, \mathbb{F})$, if $s \xrightarrow{\sigma} s'$ for some $s, s' \in S$ and $\sigma = t_{a_1} t_{a_2} \ldots t_{a_k} \in T^*$, then $\mathbb{R}(s') = \mathbb{R}(s) + \sum_{i=1}^{k} (\mathbb{F}(t_{a_i}) - \mathbb{B}(t_{a_i}))$ follows by induction from (1). Since we are assuming that the lts is totally reachable, $\mathbb{R}$ is thus fully determined

---

[2] The reachability graph of a Petri net is always deterministic and totally reachable. Thus, these properties can be assumed without loss of generality.

by $\mathbb{R}(s_0)$ via $\mathbb{R}(s) = \mathbb{R}(s_0) + \sum_{i=1}^{n} \Psi_s(t_i) \cdot (\mathbb{F}(t_i) - \mathbb{B}(t_i))$. We identify a region $r = (\mathbb{R}, \mathbb{B}, \mathbb{F})$ with a vector $r \in \mathbb{N}^{1+2n}$:

$$r = (r_0, \ldots, r_{2n}) = (\mathbb{R}(s_0), \mathbb{B}(t_1), \ldots, \mathbb{B}(t_n), \mathbb{F}(t_1), \ldots, \mathbb{F}(t_n))$$

The function that reconstructs the value $\mathbb{R}(s)$ for a state $s \in S$ from such a vector is given by $\mathrm{tokens}(r, s) := r_0 + \sum_{i=1}^{n} \Psi_s(t_i) \cdot (r_{n+i} - r_i)$.

With the knowledge so far we can write a predicate that ensures that a vector $x = (x_0, \ldots, x_{2n}) \in \mathbb{Z}^{1+2n}$ is the vector representation of some region of A:

$$\mathrm{is\,Region}(x) := \bigwedge_{i=0}^{2n} x_i \geq 0 \wedge \bigwedge_{s \xrightarrow{t_i} s' \in \to} \mathrm{tokens}(x, s) \geq x_i$$

$$\wedge \bigwedge_{s \xrightarrow{t_i} s' \in \to \backslash \to'} \mathrm{tokens}(x, s) + x_{n+i} - x_n = \mathrm{tokens}(x, s')$$

Recall that the definition of a region requires all elements of $\mathbb{R}$, $\mathbb{B}$ and $\mathbb{F}$ to be nonnegative. This is enforced in the first expression. The remainder represents the two conditions in (1). Note that the last condition is only required for transitions that are not in the spanning tree, because the definition of $\mathrm{tokens}(x, s)$ already guarantees this relation for the transitions in the spanning tree.

For a set R of regions, the *corresponding Petri net* $N_R = (P, T, F, M_0)$ has $P = R$ and for each $r = (\mathbb{R}_r, \mathbb{B}_r, \mathbb{F}_r) \in R$ define $F(r, t) = \mathbb{B}_r(t)$, $F(t, r) = \mathbb{F}_r(t)$ and $M_0(r) = \mathbb{R}_r(s_0)$. Note that the set of transitions is the set of labels T from the lts A. As this definition suggests, a region of a reachability graph models a possible place p in the generating Petri net. Vice versa, every place p of a Petri net gives rise to a region in the reachability graph of its Petri net. We can now give an intuitive understanding of the two conditions in (1). The first condition states that no transition in the lts may be prevented. The second condition enforces consistency between $\mathbb{R}$, $\mathbb{B}$, and $\mathbb{F}$. For example, a cycle $s \xrightarrow{\sigma} s$ in A corresponds to $M[\sigma\rangle M$ in N_R with the marking M defined by $M(r) = \mathbb{R}_r(s)$ for all $r \in R$.

For synthesizing a Petri net from A, we need to find regions such that the corresponding Petri net has a reachability graph isomorphic to the lts A. Finding regions requires separation problems to be solved. An *event/state separation problem* is a pair $(s, t) \in S \times T$ with $\neg(s \xrightarrow{t})$. This problem is *solved* by a region $(\mathbb{R}, \mathbb{B}, \mathbb{F})$ iff $\mathbb{R}(s) < \mathbb{B}(t)$, which means that t is prevented in state s. This is expressed by the predicate $\mathrm{ESSP}(r, s, t_i) := (\mathrm{tokens}(r, s) < r_i)$. A *state separation problem* is a set of two states $\{s, s'\} \subseteq S$ with $s \neq s'$ that must be distinguishable and it is *solved* by a region r with $\mathbb{R}_r(s) \neq \mathbb{R}_r(s')$. The corresponding predicate is $\mathrm{SSP}(r, s, s') := (\mathrm{tokens}(r, s) \neq \mathrm{tokens}(r, s'))$. The set *of all separation problems of* A is called SP_A. For readability, given any kind of separation problem $pr \in \mathrm{SP}_A$, we define $\mathrm{SP}(r, pr)$:

$$\mathrm{SP}(r, pr) := \begin{cases} \mathrm{ESSP}(r, s, t_i) = (\mathrm{tokens}(r, s) < r_i) & \text{if } pr = (s, t_i) \\ \mathrm{SSP}(r, s, s') = (\mathrm{tokens}(r, s) \neq \mathrm{tokens}(r, s')) & \text{if } pr = \{s, s'\} \end{cases}$$

```
Input :  lts A,  predicate additional Properties
Output :  Petri net with reachability graph isomorphic to A
begin
    R ← ∅
    for  pr ∈ SP_A:  // For each separation problem
        find  r satisfying  is Region(r) ∧ SP(r, pr) ∧ additional Properties(r)
        if  unsolvable:  return  error
        else :  R ← R ∪ {r}
    return  N_R  // Petri net corresponding to the regions R
end
```

Listing 1. A general Petri net synthesis algorithm. For now additional Properties(r) can be assumed to be always true, which results in an algorithm from [2].

Finally, a set R of regions is called *admissible* if for each separation problem a region solving it is contained in R. In this case the corresponding Petri net N_R of R has a reachability graph that is isomorphic to A, as shown in [4].

This allows to define a first formula for solving a separation problem: The separation problem pr is solvable and has a solution r, if and only if is Region(r)∧ SP(r, pr) has a solution. Based on this, a Petri net is computed by calculating solutions to all separation problems. The algorithm doing this is depicted in Listing 1. For now we will assume that additional Properties(r) is always true.

3.1 Example

As an example for the synthesis approach, consider the lts B from Fig. 1. In state s_3, the label t_2 is not enabled, so $pr = (s_3, t_2)$ is an event/state separation problem. A region r solving this problem satisfies is Region(r) ∧ SP(r, pr). Applying the definitions of SP and ESSP produces is Region(r) ∧ tokens(r, s_3) < r_2. State s_3 is reached in the spanning tree from the initial state in Fig. 1 via the word

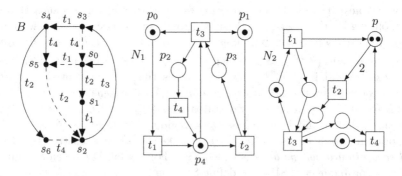

Fig. 1. A deterministic and totally reachable lts B, including one of its spanning trees. Transitions that are part of the spanning tree are drawn as straight lines. Other transitions are dashed. Two Petri nets N_1, N_2 with reachability graphs isomorphic to B are shown on the right.

$t_2 t_1 t_3$. Thus, we obtain $\mathrm{SP}(r, pr) = (\mathrm{tokens}(r, s_3) < r_2) = (r_0 + 1 \cdot (r_5 - r_1) + 1 \cdot (r_6 - r_2) + 1 \cdot (r_7 - r_3) + 0 \cdot (r_8 - r_4) < r_2)$. If we expand is $\mathrm{Region}(r)$ in a similar way, the following inequality system is produced.

All variables are non-negative $(\bigwedge r_i \geq 0)$:

$$0 \leq r_0 \quad \wedge \quad 0 \leq r_1 \quad \wedge \quad 0 \leq r_2 \quad \wedge \quad 0 \leq r_3 \quad \wedge \quad 0 \leq r_4$$
$$\wedge \quad 0 \leq r_5 \quad \wedge \quad 0 \leq r_6 \quad \wedge \quad 0 \leq r_7 \quad \wedge \quad 0 \leq r_8$$

The condition $\bigwedge \mathrm{tokens}(x, s) \geq x_i$ is satisfied. In detail this means for the initial state that labels t_1 and t_2 are allowed:

$$\wedge \quad r_1 \leq \mathrm{tokens}(r, s_0) = r_0$$
$$\wedge \quad r_2 \leq \mathrm{tokens}(r, s_0) = r_0$$

In s_1, which is reachable via t_2, label t_1 is enabled. In s_2, which is reached from s_0 via $t_2 t_1$, label t_3 is enabled:

$$\wedge \quad r_1 \leq \mathrm{tokens}(r, s_1) = r_0 + (r_6 - r_2) = \mathbb{R}(s_0) + (\mathbb{F}(t_2) - \mathbb{B}(t_2))$$
$$\wedge \quad r_3 \leq \mathrm{tokens}(r, s_2) = r_0 + (r_6 - r_2) + (r_5 - r_1)$$

In state s_3 (after $t_2 t_1 t_3$), labels t_1 and t_4 are enabled:

$$\wedge \quad r_1 \leq \mathrm{tokens}(r, s_3) = r_0 + (r_6 - r_2) + (r_5 - r_1) + (r_7 - r_3)$$
$$\wedge \quad r_4 \leq \mathrm{tokens}(r, s_3) = r_0 + (r_6 - r_2) + (r_5 - r_1) + (r_7 - r_3)$$

Next, t_2 and t_4 can fire in s_4, in s_5 label t_2 is enabled and in s_6, t_4 can fire:

$$\wedge \quad r_2 \leq \mathrm{tokens}(r, s_4) = r_0 + 2(r_5 - r_1) + (r_6 - r_2) + (r_7 - r_3)$$
$$\wedge \quad r_4 \leq \mathrm{tokens}(r, s_4) = r_0 + 2(r_5 - r_1) + (r_6 - r_2) + (r_7 - r_3)$$
$$\wedge \quad r_2 \leq \mathrm{tokens}(r, s_5) = r_0 + 2(r_5 - r_1) + (r_6 - r_2) + (r_7 - r_3) + (r_8 - r_4)$$
$$\wedge \quad r_4 \leq \mathrm{tokens}(r, s_6) = r_0 + 2(r_5 - r_1) + 2(r_6 - r_2) + (r_7 - r_3)$$

Finally, the condition $\bigwedge \mathrm{tokens}(x, s) + x_{n+i} - x_n = \mathrm{tokens}(x, s')$ needs to be satisfied for transitions that are not part of the spanning tree. This results in a couple of equalities which are all[3] equivalent to the following:

$$\wedge \quad 0 = (r_5 - r_1) + (r_6 - r_2) + (r_7 - r_3) + (r_8 - r_4)$$

The vector $r = (1, 0, 1, 1, 0, 1, 0, 0, 1)$ is a possible solution of is $\mathrm{Region}(r) \wedge \mathrm{SP}(r, (s_3, t_2))$. This corresponds to the place p_4 of N_1 in Fig. 1. Alternatively, the vector $r' = (2, 0, 2, 0, 0, 1, 0, 0, 1)$ corresponding to place p in the Petri net N_2 also is a solution. For solving other separation problems, only the single inequality for $\mathrm{SP}(r, (s_3, t_2))$ has to be replaced while is $\mathrm{Region}(r)$ stays the same. Solving all separation problems can lead, for example, to the five regions corresponding to the places in N_1.

In N_1, place p_1 prevents t_2 in states $\{s_1, s_2, s_6\}$. Place p_4 prevents t_2 and t_3 in states $\{s_1, s_3, s_6\}$ and p_3 prevents t_3 in $\{s_0, s_3, s_4, s_5\}$. The places p_0 and p_2 solve all event/state separation problems involving transition t_1, respectively t_4.

---

[3] This occurs because all smallest cycles contain each label exactly once.

4   Synthesis with Additional Properties

In this section, the general synthesis algorithm presented in Listing 1 is extended so that synthesis can be restricted to several classes of Petri nets. This is done by defining suitable predicates that can be used for the input additional Properties(r) of the algorithm. The predicates that are defined can be combined arbitrarily. Note that the predicates are constructed so that they only depend on the structure of the lts. This means that no further input is required. Some of these restrictions were already examined before, however not in the context of non-plain Petri nets.

Plain. A Petri net is called *plain* if arcs have only weights zero or one. Formally, this means that $\text{cod}(F) \subseteq \{0, 1\}$. The corresponding predicate enforces an upper limit of one for each arc weight:

$$\text{is Plain}(r) := \bigwedge_{i=1}^{2n} r_i \leq 1$$

Pure. A place p is *pure* if transitions cannot be in its preset and its postset at the same time, i.e. ${}^\bullet p \cap p^\bullet = \emptyset$. If this holds for all its places, a Petri net is called *pure*. Thus, at least one of the arc weights connecting a transition with p has to be zero:

$$\text{is Pure}(r) := \bigwedge_{i=1}^{n} (r_i = 0 \vee r_{n+i} = 0)$$

Conflict-Free. A *conflict-free* Petri net is plain and satisfies additionally $\forall p \in P : |p^\bullet| > 1 \Rightarrow p^\bullet \subseteq {}^\bullet p$. For each place, there is either just a single transition t_i consuming tokens from it ($r_i = 1 \wedge \forall k \neq i : r_k = 0$), or all transitions t_i consuming from p must also produce a token there ($r_i \leq r_{i+n}$). Specifically, the only forbidden case is $r_i = 1 \wedge r_{i+n} = 0$:

$$\text{is CF}(r) := \text{is Plain}(r) \wedge \left(\sum_{i=1}^{n} r_i = 1 \vee \bigwedge_{i=1}^{n} r_i \leq r_{i+n} \right)$$

Homogeneous. A place p is *homogeneous* if its outgoing arcs all have the same weight, i.e. $\forall t_1, t_2 \in p^\bullet : F(p, t_1) = F(p, t_2)$. In the predicate, this is expressed as pairs of weights being either zero or equal to each other:

$$\text{is Homogeneous}(r) := \bigwedge_{i=1}^{n} \bigwedge_{j=i+1}^{n} (r_i = 0 \vee r_j = 0 \vee r_i = r_j)$$

Generalized T-Net. Each place $p \in P$ has at most one transition in its preset and one in its postset, i.e. $|{}^{\bullet}p| \leq 1 \geq |p^{\bullet}|$. So, the weights of all but one transition in each $\mathbb{B}$ and $\mathbb{F}$ (of the p-region) must be zero, which can be expressed as a disjunction of all-but-one arc weight sums being zero:

$$\text{is GTNet}(r) := \bigvee_{i=1}^{n} \sum_{\substack{j=1 \\ j \neq i}}^{n} r_j = 0 \wedge \bigvee_{i=1}^{n} \sum_{\substack{j=1 \\ j \neq i}}^{n} r_{j+n} = 0$$

Generalized Marked Graph. In addition to the generalized T-net, each place $p \in P$ must be connected to two transitions, i.e. $|{}^{\bullet}p| = 1 = |p^{\bullet}|$. In our predicate, we force the potentially non-zero weights to be truly positive:

$$\text{is GMGraph}(r) := \bigvee_{i=1}^{n} \left(r_i > 0 \wedge \sum_{\substack{j=1 \\ j \neq i}}^{n} r_j = 0 \right) \wedge \bigvee_{i=1}^{n} \left(r_{i+n} > 0 \wedge \sum_{\substack{j=1 \\ j \neq i}}^{n} r_{j+n} = 0 \right)$$

Non-generalized T-Net/Marked Graph. Beyond the generalized net variant we require these nets to be plain:

$$\text{is TNet}(r) := \text{is Plain}(r) \wedge \text{is GTNet}(r)$$
$$\text{is MGraph}(r) := \text{is Plain}(r) \wedge \text{is GMGraph}(r)$$

k-Boundedness. The number of tokens on any place can never exceed $k \in \mathbb{N}$, i.e. $\forall M \in [M_0\rangle : \forall p \in P : M(p) \leq k$. Since we already have a function for counting tokens in states, we can simply define:

$$\text{is kBounded}(r, k) := \bigwedge_{s \in S} \text{tokens}(r, s) \leq k$$

Distributed according to loc. A distributed Petri net can be thought of as a structural partition of the net into several locations. Locations can send messages to each other, but these might take an arbitrary time to reach their destination. Each location has a local state and cannot query the state of other locations. Based on [6], let LOCS be some arbitrary, fixed, finite and suitable large set of so-called locations. Given a mapping: $\text{loc } T \to$ LOCS, a Petri net is *distributed according to* loc, if all $t_1, t_2 \in T$ with $\text{loc}(t_1) \neq \text{loc}(t_2)$ satisfy ${}^{\bullet}t_1 \cap {}^{\bullet}t_2 = \emptyset$ (no shared read access between locations). This means, each place/region belongs to one location. A place belonging to more than one location or to none at all does not allow any read access. This is also reflected in the following predicate. Its location related parts can be evaluated at creation time and is eliminated before giving the inequality system to a solver:

$$\text{is Distributed}(r, \text{loc}) := \bigvee_{l \in \text{LOCS}} \bigwedge_{i=1}^{n} (\text{loc}(t_i) \neq l \Rightarrow r_i = 0)$$

A similar approach is used in [3] which deals specifically with the synthesis of distributable Petri nets.

Place-output-nonbranching (ON). This is defined as $|p^\bullet| \leq 1$ for all places $p \in P$, i.e. only one transition can consume tokens from each place. This can be expressed by putting each transition into its own location via the identity location mapping with $id(t) = t$:

$$\text{is ON}(r) := \text{is Distributed}(r, id)$$

In Fig. 1, the net N_2 is ON while N_1 is not, because place p_4 has transitions t_2 and t_3 that both consume tokens from it. On the other hand, if we define a location specification loc via $\text{loc}(t_1) \neq \text{loc}(t_2) = \text{loc}(t_3) \neq \text{loc}(t_4)$ and $\text{loc}(t_1) \neq \text{loc}(t_4)$, then N_1 is distributed according to loc with the maximally possible three locations.

It can be seen that many structural properties and even the behavioural property of k-boundedness can be expressed via the predicates presented here. However, this procedure has its limit and there are properties that we cannot express easily. For example, a Petri net is a P-net if it is plain and it satisfies $|t^\bullet| \leq 1 \geq |{}^\bullet t|$ for each $t \in T$. In a P-net, each transition can consume and produce at most a single token. The P-net property cannot be checked by looking at places individually, in contrast to the properties we just defined. Thus, the P-net property can also not be expressed as a predicate on an individual region. A similar observation was made in [29] for the synthesis of P-nets with their algorithm based on integer linear programming.

Other properties that cannot easily be expressed are free-choice[4], behavioural-conflict-freeness[5], and graph-properties like weak/strong connectedness. All of these properties are, in a sense, not local to single places.

4.1 Example

In Sect. 3.1, the regions $r = (1, 0, 1, 1, 0, 1, 0, 0, 1)$ and $r' = (2, 0, 2, 0, 0, 1, 0, 0, 1)$ of the lts B from Fig. 1 were calculated. It was already noted that r corresponds to place p_4 of the net N_1 in Fig. 1 while r' represents the place p of N_2. Let's see what happens if we add the property ON (which N_1 does not fulfil) to our inequality system from Sect. 3.1. For good measure, we would also like to keep our net pure (which both N_1 and N_2 were). We do this by extending the inequality system with the predicate additional Properties$(r) = \text{is ON}(r) \wedge$ is Pure(r), compare Listing 1.

First we expand is Pure(r) to the following system:

$$(r_1 = 0 \vee r_5 = 0) \wedge (r_2 = 0 \vee r_6 = 0) \wedge (r_3 = 0 \vee r_7 = 0) \wedge (r_4 = 0 \vee r_8 = 0)$$

---

[4] Plain and two transitions with non-disjoint presets must have the same presets.
[5] For all $M \in [M_0\rangle : M[t_1\rangle \wedge M[t_2\rangle \wedge t_1 \neq t_2 \Rightarrow {}^\bullet t_1 \cap {}^\bullet t_2 = \emptyset$.

Next, we use the definitions of is $ON(r)$ and is $Distributed(r, id)$:

$$\text{is }ON(r) = \text{is }Distributed(r, id) = \bigvee_{l \in \text{LOCS}} \bigwedge_{i=1}^{n} (id(t_i) \neq l \Rightarrow r_i = 0)$$

The inner conjunction with $l = t_1$ produces $(id(t_1) \neq t_1 \Rightarrow r_1 = 0) \wedge (id(t_2) \neq t_1 \Rightarrow r_2 = 0) \wedge (id(t_3) \neq t_1 \Rightarrow r_3 = 0) \wedge (id(t_4) \neq t_1 \Rightarrow r_4 = 0)$. We can evaluate id and simplify the system to $r_2 = 0 \wedge r_3 = 0 \wedge r_4 = 0$. If this procedure is done for all locations[6], the following inequality system is generated:

$$(r_2 = 0 \wedge r_3 = 0 \wedge r_4 = 0) \vee (r_1 = 0 \wedge r_3 = 0 \wedge r_4 = 0)$$
$$\vee (r_1 = 0 \wedge r_2 = 0 \wedge r_4 = 0) \vee (r_1 = 0 \wedge r_2 = 0 \wedge r_3 = 0)$$

Due to these new conditions, the vector $r = (1, 0, 1, 1, 0, 1, 0, 0, 1)$ corresponding to place p_4 is not a solution to the system is $Region(r) \wedge SP(r, (s_3, t_2)) \wedge$ additional $Properties(r)$. On the other hand, the vector $r' = (2, 0, 2, 0, 0, 1, 0, 0, 1)$ describing the place p from the net N_2 also solves the extended system.

5   Optimization Strategies

This section presents three different algorithms. First, we introduce a heuristic that removes redundant regions, then we propose an optimization for checking state separation, and in the last part we suggest an algorithm for calculating Petri nets with a minimal number of places.

5.1   Heuristically Shrinking the Number of Places

The goal of our heuristic is to choose from its input set R of regions a small subset $R_m \subseteq R$ so that all separation problems solved by regions from R are also solved by R_m. For an admissible set of regions this means that R_m should also be an admissible set. This heuristic can be run after a Petri net was synthesized to reduce the size of the result.

For each separation problem $pr \in SP_A$ we refer to the set of regions that solve pr as $R(pr) \subseteq R$. If $R(pr)$ only contains a single region r, this region is called *required*, because it cannot be omitted from R_m while still solving pr. All required regions are elements of R_m.

From each $R(pr)$ with $|R(pr)| > 1$ we have to select at least one region for R_m. In general, this problem is NP-complete. To obtain a low complexity, we randomly select a region for a not yet solved separation problem and add it to R_m until all separation problems solved by R are also solved by R_m. If R is admissible, then R_m will also be admissible. This heuristic is shown in Listing 2.

This approach is non-deterministic, because its result depends on the order in which the separation problems are investigated and the way in which an

---

[6] In general it suffices to evaluate this disjunction for the subset of locations that can appear in the image of the location function. In our case this is $\{t_1, t_2, t_3, t_4\}$.

```
Input: lts A, set of regions R on A
Output: Set of regions solving the same separation problems
begin
    Rm ← ∅
    for pr ∈ SPA: // For each separation problem
        if |R(pr)| = 1:
            Rm ← Rm ∪ R(pr)
    for pr ∈ SPA with R(pr) ≠ ∅: // For each solved problem
        if R(pr) ∩ Rm = ∅:
            // pr is not solved by any region from Rm, so pick one
            pick any r ∈ R(pr)
            Rm ← Rm ∪ {r}
    return Rm
end
```

Listing 2. Shrinking the number of places

element r is chosen from $R(pr)$. Also, the heuristic cannot guarantee an optimal result. However, in practice the heuristic produces good results in minimizing the number of regions that are needed and can be implemented efficiently. This is evaluated in Sect. 5.4.

A similar approach is presented in algorithm 8 in [2] which calculates for each region the set of all solved separation problems and compares these sets. However, our proposed approach is more time and space efficient because we examine only a single separation problem at a time. As the results in Sect. 5.4 will show, the gained reduction is still significant.

5.2 Reducing the Computation Time for State Separation

There is a event/state separation problem for each event that is not enabled in a given state. Thus, $|S| \cdot |T|$ is an upper bound for the number of event/state separation problems. On the other hand, there is a state separation problem for any two states and thus there are $\frac{1}{2}|S|(|S| - 1)$ such problems. So, the number of state separation problems grows quadratically in the number of states while the number of event/state separation problems only grows linearly. This means state separation must be solved efficiently.

As a general rule, it is a lot faster to check if a region r solves a separation problem pr than to compute a new region r solving pr, because the check only requires the predicate $SP(r, pr)$ to be evaluated while calculating a new region means solving an inequality system in which $SP(r, pr)$ also appears. Thus, a first speed-up is gained by checking if one of the regions already found solves p before a new region is computed, which is also done in algorithm 8 from [2]. This can also be useful for checking state separation by first solving all event/state separation problems, because this already solves many state separation problems. So the remaining problem is how to quickly compute the set of unsolved state separation problems, for which we propose a new approach.

```
Input: lts A
Output: Petri net with reachability graph isomorphic to A
begin
    R ← solutions to all event/state separation problems
    for each equivalence class [r] of ≡_R:
        for every s,s' ∈ [r] with s ≠ s':
            solve {s,s'} and add result to R
    return N_R // Petri net corresponding to the regions R
end
```

Listing 3. Optimized synthesis algorithm

We define an equivalence $\equiv_r \subseteq S \times S$ from a region $r = (\mathbb{R}, \mathbb{B}, \mathbb{F})$ by $s \equiv_r s' \iff \mathbb{R}(s) = \mathbb{R}(s')$. The region r solves the state separation problem $\{s, s'\}$ iff $s \not\equiv_r s'$. The equivalence is canonically extended to a set R of regions by $\equiv_R = \bigcap_{r \in R} \equiv_r$. Since $s \not\equiv_r s'$ iff r separates these two states, it holds that $s \not\equiv_R s'$ iff some region $r \in R$ separates these states. Thus, the equivalence classes of $\equiv_R$ contain states which pairwise have unsolved state separation problems.

For calculating the equivalence classes of $\equiv_R$, $\mathbb{R}(s)$ has to be computed for all states and all regions found so far. This can be done faster than checking all state separation problems individually. The resulting algorithm is shown in Listing 3.

5.3 Finding the Minimal Number of Places

The goal of this section is to describe an algorithm that produces a Petri net with the minimal number of places possible. The algorithm is taken from [2,12] where an integer linear programming approach is used and reformulated in the presented setting, so that it can be combined with the various properties of Petri nets that were previously described. A key ingredient is a procedure that checks if a Petri net with at most ℓ places exists for which the reachability graph is isomorphic to the lts A. The value ℓ is then lowered until a minimal number of places is found.

To check if a solution with ℓ regions/places is possible, the synthesis algorithm from the previous section is modified. Instead of calculating a solution to a single separation problem p, a solution for all separation problems is computed at once. The vectors $r_1, \dots, r_\ell \in \mathbb{N}^{1+2k}$ should be ℓ regions that together form an admissible set of regions. This can be expressed as the following system:

$$\bigwedge_{i=1}^{\ell} (\text{is Region}(r_i) \wedge \text{additional Properties}(r_i)) \wedge \bigwedge_{pr \in \text{SP}_A} \bigvee_{i=1}^{\ell} \text{SP}(r_i, pr)$$

The system asserts that all r_i are regions of the lts and that for each separation problem $pr \in \text{SP}_A$ there is at least one region r_i that solves it. Thus, this system is solvable if and only if a Petri net solution with ℓ places exists. The predicate additional Properties(r_i) can again be used to require additional properties. For example, setting additional Properties(r_i) = is kBounded(r_i, 5) means that the resulting system is solvable if and only if a 5-bounded Petri net with ℓ places exists with a reachability graph isomorphic to A.

To find a minimal Petri net, we first synthesize a Petri net as before. This provides an upper bound k for the number of places that are needed. Next a solution with $k - m$ for $m = 1, 2, 3 \ldots$ places is attempted until the resulting inequality system becomes unsolvable. Then the previous solution had the minimal number of places possible.

It might be tempting to optimize this simple, linear scheme and to do a binary search for the minimal number of places. However, our experiments suggest that solving an inequality system is easier than deriving its unsolvability. The run times between these two kinds of problems varies hugely. Thus, it is in general better to do the linear search that is suggested here.

On the contrary, an optimization is possible using the fact that most separation problems are state separation problems. Our experiments show that it is often worthwhile to ignore state separation at first. In most cases, the regions computed for event/state separation already solve state separation. If this is not the case, the algorithm is repeated with these previously unsolved state separation problems. To guarantee termination, if this needs to be repeated more than once, all previously unsolved state separation problems are included in all following iterations. In the end, a feasible set of regions solving all separation problems is found, including state separation problems.

5.4 Experimental Evaluation

To evaluate the performance of the heuristics[7], some experiments were conducted. For this purpose, several classes of Petri nets were used. For each net, the reachability graph was generated and a Petri net solution was then synthesized from it in different ways. The experiments were conducted via the synthesis implementation in the tool APT [11].

We used four classes of Petri nets. The bit nets model n independent bits which can individually be set and unset. The Petri nets for words have this word and its prefixes as their only firing sequences. These words are defined inductively via $w_1 = a_1$ and for $n > 1$ it holds that $w_n = w_{n-1} a_n w_{n-1}$. This models a binary counter with n bits counting to its maximum value. The philosophers are a version of Dijkstra's dining philosophers [24] where each philosopher grabs first his left fork, then the right one, but releases forks in a single step. Finally, the rw-mutex-rn-wm is a mutual exclusion algorithm with n readers and m writers where readers are allowed simultaneous access to a shared resource. These classes of Petri nets range from highly concurrent behaviour in the bit nets to fully sequential behaviour in the binary counters. The results can be seen in Table 1.

---

[7] No comparison with other tools was done, because e.g. the proposed algorithm needs more than 10 s to solve w_9 plainly while Petrify only needs 0.01 s. Similar results are produced with GENET and rw-mutex-r8-w5. The strength of our approach is its flexibility. Thus, only the proposed heuristics are evaluated.

Table 1. Comparison of algorithms. The table shows the size of output and the run time which was limited to 1 h (except for bit-5 and phil-4). The input has $|S|$ states and is generated by a net with $|P|$ places, "base" uses no optimizations, "reuse" only computes new regions if needed, "heuristic" also applies Listing 2, and "minimal" is the algorithm from Sect. 5.3

System	$|S|$	$|P|$	Base		Reuse		Heuristic		Minimal	
bit-3	8	6	24	(1.2 s)	9	(0.7 s)	9	(0.7 s)	6	(3.1 s)
bit-4	16	8	87	(3.1 s)	25	(1.2 s)	13	(1.4 s)	8	(45.5 s)
bit-5	32	10	169	(8.2 s)	43	(2.4 s)	22	(2.5 s)	10	(4 h)
bit-6	64	12	458	(24.2 s)	77	(5.4 s)	31	(5.3 s)	-	(>1 h)
bit-7	128	14	1021	(172 s)	133	(10.9 s)	60	(9.8 s)	-	(>1 h)
bit-8	256	16	2277	(1616 s)	153	(21.6 s)	64	(20.7 s)	-	(>1 h)
word w_3	8	6	23	(0.9 s)	8	(0.5 s)	5	(0.5 s)	5	(1.1 s)
word w_4	16	8	51	(2.2 s)	14	(1.0 s)	7	(0.8 s)	7	(3.7 s)
word w_5	32	10	153	(5.7 s)	21	(1.2 s)	9	(1.4 s)	9	(19.5 s)
word w_6	64	12	408	(19.8 s)	20	(1.9 s)	11	(1.9 s)	11	(818 s)
word w_7	128	14	1046	(187 s)	34	(3.3 s)	13	(2.9 s)	-	(>1 h)
phil-2	6	8	31	(1.1 s)	14	(0.6 s)	7	(0.6 s)	5	(3.3 s)
phil-3	14	12	94	(2.3 s)	29	(1.2 s)	14	(1.2 s)	7	(40.5 s)
phil-4	34	16	286	(7.8 s)	55	(2.2 s)	22	(2.0 s)	-	(>1 day)
phil-5	82	20	838	(27.2 s)	90	(5.6 s)	39	(5.0 s)	-	(>1 h)
phil-6	198	24	2429	(343 s)	282	(13.3 s)	99	(13.3 s)	-	(>1 h)
phil-7	478	28	-	(>1 h)	320	(35.7 s)	138	(36.6 s)	-	(>1 h)
rw-mutex-r4-w1	17	11	119	(3.7 s)	23	(1.3 s)	11	(1.3 s)	5	(9.7 s)
rw-mutex-r5-w1	33	13	299	(9.3 s)	45	(2.4 s)	16	(2.5 s)	6	(103 s)
rw-mutex-r6-w1	65	15	675	(28.8 s)	39	(3.8 s)	20	(4.1 s)	-	(>1 h)
rw-mutex-r7-w1	129	17	1575	(184 s)	48	(8.5 s)	18	(8.2 s)	-	(>1 h)
rw-mutex-r8-w1	257	19	3979	(1951 s)	67	(11.1 s)	23	(12.2 s)	-	(>1 h)
rw-mutex-r4-w5	21	19	230	(5.5 s)	58	(2.2 s)	18	(1.8 s)	5	(22.1 s)
rw-mutex-r5-w5	37	21	417	(11.6 s)	75	(3.6 s)	20	(3.8 s)	6	(314 s)
rw-mutex-r6-w5	69	23	922	(32.4 s)	91	(5.3 s)	25	(5.5 s)	-	(>1 h)
rw-mutex-r7-w5	133	25	2022	(232 s)	101	(8.1 s)	28	(10.9 s)	-	(>1 h)
rw-mutex-r8-w5	261	27	4484	(2111 s)	118	(14.7 s)	32	(15.1 s)	-	(>1 h)

For each such class, instances of several sizes were measured. For the rw-mutex class, no further restrictions were imposed. For all other classes, plain Petri nets were synthesized[8]. For columns "reuse" and "heuristic", before solving

---

[8] The restriction to plain nets was chosen, because the Petri nets that generate these lts are also plain. Thus, the results can be compared with the input.

a separation problem pr, all regions $r \in R$ that were already found are first checked against $\mathrm{SP}(r, pr)$. If a solution is found, then no new region needs to be computed. The approach from Sect. 5.2 for speeding up state separation is always used.

It can be seen that calculating a minimal solution always takes longer than computing any solution at all and often runs into the time limit of one hour. This is expected since here more complicated systems have to be solved or proved unsolvable and, as was already mentioned in Sect. 5.3, deriving unsolvability takes longer than calculating a solution. It can also be seen that the other algorithms[9] almost always produce larger Petri nets.

Also, the base algorithm performs a lot worse than the other algorithms. In most cases it produces an order of magnitude more places and its execution time increases rapidly. This shows that only computing a new region when really necessary improves the execution time a lot. It can be seen that the heuristic from Sect. 5.1 to remove unnecessary places doesn't have an impact on the execution time. However, it shrinks the number of regions a lot and for the word examples achieves minimal solutions. This shows that our proposed heuristic is efficient and produces good results. While it is not shown in the table, we want to mention that the algorithm together with all heuristics can handle rw-mutex-r12-r5 in 28 min. This is an lts with 4101 states, which is a lot larger than the other lts. Without our heuristic, the time limit is already exceeded for rw-mutex-r9-w1.

Sequential systems can be handled more efficiently than concurrent systems. For example, bit-7 and word w_7 have the same size, but, except for the base algorithm, bit-7 needs more time and more places to be solved. This is presumably linked to a difference in structural complexity in Petri nets that produce these behaviour, but may warrant further investigations.

6   Conclusion

This paper extends a well-known algorithm for Petri net synthesis so that an arbitrary combination of the following properties can be required from the resulting Petri nets:

plain, pure, conflict-free, homogeneous, k-bounded for some $k \in \mathbb{N}$, generalized T-net, generalized marked graph, place-output-nonbranching, and distributed according to a location specification.

However, some properties were identified which cannot be expressed easily. Then, a heuristic was presented which can be used as a post-processing step for Petri net synthesis in general. This heuristic produces smaller Petri nets. Another heuristic speeds up the synthesis procedure. We also extended the algorithm for Petri net synthesis so that a Petri net with a minimal number of places can be calculated. This extension is compatible with the restricted classes of Petri nets that we defined before. Finally, we evaluated the performance of the presented algorithms on several examples. This showed that the heuristic has a low time overhead, but manages to remove many places from the calculated Petri nets.

---

[9] And even the Petri nets produced by hand and used for generating the lts.

Future work includes identifying further Petri net classes which can be expressed in the framework we introduced. It would also be interesting to extend this framework to properties that currently cannot be expressed. A further direction would be to improve the efficiency of the algorithm. For example, the predicate for k-boundedness has a linear size in the number of states of the lts. [4] presents polynomial algorithms for general and pure Petri nets which are also experimentally faster than the presented algorithm. This efficiency comes from exploitation of homogeneous inequalities. Extending these faster algorithms in a way similar to the presented framework is another interesting direction for further research. If this problem is overcome, then it might also be possible to extend our framework with the results for synthesis from infinite lts which also use homogeneous systems. Our heuristic for removing superfluous places is efficient and can discard many places, but the calculated Petri nets are often larger than solutions produced by hand, so there is potential for more effective approaches. Also, other notions of equivalence could be investigated. For example, we already lifted the approach that is presented here from producing Petri nets whose reachability graph is isomorphic to the input lts to producing Petri nets that are language equivalent to the input.

Acknowledgements. I would like to thank Harro Wimmel and Eike Best for their helpful comments. Special thanks go to Valentin Spreckels for the incorporation of homogeneity. Also, I am grateful for the anonymous reviewers' careful reading and valuable comments.

References

1. Badouel, E., Bernardinello, L., Darondeau, P.: Polynomial algorithms for the synthesis of bounded nets. In: Mosses, P.D., Nielsen, M., Schwartzbach, M.I. (eds.) TAPSOFT 1995. LNCS, vol. 915, pp. 364–378. Springer, Heidelberg (1995)
2. Badouel, E., Bernardinello, L., Darondeau, P.: Petri Net Synthesis. Springer, Heidelberg (2015). http://dx.doi.org/10.1007/978-3-662-47967-4
3. Badouel, E., Caillaud, B., Darondeau, P.: Distributing finite automata through Petri Net synthesis. Formal Asp. Comput. **13**(6), 447–470 (2002). http://dx.doi.org/10.1007/s001650200022
4. Badouel, E., Darondeau, P.: Theory of regions. In: Reisig, W., Rozenberg, G. (eds.) Lectures on Petri Nets I: Basic Models, Advances in Petri Nets, the Volumes are Based on the Advanced Course on Petri Nets, vol. 1491, pp. 529–586. Springer, Heidelberg (1996). http://dx.doi.org/10.1007/3-540-65306-6_22
5. Barrett, C., Stump, A., Tinelli, C.: The SMT-LIB Standard: Version 2.0. In: Gupta, A., Kroening, D. (eds.) Proceedings of the 8th International Workshop on Satisfiability Modulo Theories, Edinburgh, UK (2010)
6. Best, E., Darondeau, P.: Petri Net distributability. In: Clarke, E., Virbitskaite, I., Voronkov, A. (eds.) PSI 2011. LNCS, vol. 7162, pp. 1–18. Springer, Heidelberg (2012)
7. Best, E., Devillers, R.: Characterisation of the state spaces of live and bounded marked graph Petri Nets. In: Dediu, A.-H., Martín-Vide, C., Sierra-Rodríguez, J.-L., Truthe, B. (eds.) LATA 2014. LNCS, vol. 8370, pp. 161–172. Springer, Heidelberg (2014)

8. Best, E., Devillers, R.R.: State space axioms for t-systems. Acta Informatica **52**(2–3), 133–152 (2015). http://dx.doi.org/10.1007/s00236-015-0219-0

9. Best, E., Devillers, R.R.: Synthesis of bounded choice-free Petri Nets. In: Aceto, L., de Frutos-Escrig, D. (eds.) 26th International Conference on Concurrency Theory, CONCUR 2015, Madrid, Spain, September 1–4, 2015. LIPIcs, vol. 42, pp. 128–141. Schloss Dagstuhl - Leibniz-Zentrum fuer Informatik (2015). http://dx.doi.org/10.4230/LIPIcs.CONCUR.2015.128

10. Best, E., Schlachter, U.: Analysis of Petri Nets and transition systems. In: Knight, S., Lanese, I., Lluch-Lafuente, A., Vieira, H.T. (eds.) Proceedings 8th Interaction and Concurrency Experience, ICE 2015, Grenoble, France, 4–5 June 2015. EPTCS, vol. 189, pp. 53–67 (2015). http://dx.doi.org/10.4204/EPTCS.189.6

11. Borde, D., Dierkes, S., Ferrari, R., Gieseking, M., Göbel, V., Grunwald, R., von der Linde, B., Lückehe, D., Schlachter, U., Schierholz, C., Schwammberger, M., Spreckels, V.: APT: analysis of Petri nets and labeled transition systems. https://github.com/CvO-Theory/apt

12. Cabasino, M.P., Giua, A., Seatzu, C.: Identification of Petri Nets from knowledge of their language. Discrete Event Dyn. Syst. **17**(4), 447–474 (2007). http://dx.doi.org/10.1007/s10626-007-0025-0

13. Caillaud, B.: Synet: a synthesizer of distributable bounded Petri-nets from finite automata. https://www.irisa.fr/s4/tools/synet/

14. Carmona, J.: GENET: GEneralised NET synthesis. http://www.cs.upc.edu/~jcarmona/genet.html

15. Carmona, J.A., Cortadella, J., Kishinevsky, M.: A region-based algorithm for discovering Petri Nets from event logs. In: Dumas, M., Reichert, M., Shan, M.-C. (eds.) BPM 2008. LNCS, vol. 5240, pp. 358–373. Springer, Heidelberg (2008)

16. Carmona, J., Cortadella, J., Kishinevsky, M.: New region-based algorithms for deriving bounded petri nets. IEEE Trans. Comput. **59**(3), 371–384 (2010). http://dx.doi.org/10.1109/TC.2009.131

17. Carmona, J., Cortadella, J., Kishinevsky, M., Kondratyev, A., Lavagno, L., Yakovlev, A.: A symbolic algorithm for the synthesis of bounded petri nets. In: van Hee and Valk [27], pp. 92–111. http://dx.doi.org/10.1007/978-3-540-68746-7_10

18. Christ, J., Hoenicke, J., Nutz, A.: Proof tree preserving interpolation. In: Piterman, N., Smolka, S.A. (eds.) TACAS 2013 (ETAPS 2013). LNCS, vol. 7795, pp. 124–138. Springer, Heidelberg (2013)

19. Cortadella, J., Kishinevsky, M., Kondratyev, A., Lavagno, L., Yakovlev, A.: Petrify: a tool for manipulating concurrent specifications and synthesis of asynchronous controllers (1996)

20. Cortadella, J., Kishinevsky, M., Lavagno, L., Yakovlev, A.: Synthesizing petri nets from state-based models. In: Rudell, R.L. (ed.) Proceedings of the 1995 IEEE/ACM International Conference on Computer-Aided Design, ICCAD 1995, San Jose, California, USA, November 5–9, 1995, pp. 164–171. IEEE Computer Society/ACM (1995). http://dx.doi.org/10.1109/ICCAD.1995.480008

21. Cortadella, J., Kishinevsky, M., Lavagno, L., Yakovlev, A.: Deriving petri nets for finite transition systems. IEEE Trans. Computers **47**(8), 859–882 (1998). http://dx.doi.org/10.1109/12.707587

22. Cortadella, J., et al.: Petrify: a tool for synthesis of Petri nets and asynchronous circuits. http://www.cs.upc.edu/~jordicf/petrify/

23. Darondeau, P.: Deriving unbounded Petri Nets from formal languages. In: Sangiorgi, D., de Simone, R. (eds.) CONCUR 1998. LNCS, vol. 1466, pp. 533–548. Springer, Heidelberg (1998)

24. Dijkstra, E.W.: Hierarchical ordering of sequential processes. Acta Informatica **1**, 115–138 (1971). http://dx.doi.org/10.1007/BF00289519

25. Ehrenfeucht, A., Rozenberg, G.: Partial (set) 2-structures. Part I: basic notions and the representation problem. Acta Informatica **27**(4), 315–342 (1990). http://dx.doi.org/10.1007/BF00264611

26. Ehrenfeucht, A., Rozenberg, G.: Partial (set) 2-structures. Part II: state spaces of concurrent systems. Acta Inf **27**(4), 343–368 (1990)

27. van Hee, K.M., Valk, R. (eds.): Applications and Theory of Petri Nets, 29th International Conference, PETRI NETS 2008, Xi'an, China, 23–27, June 2008. Lecture Notes in Computer Science, vol. 5062 Springer (2008)

28. Lorenz, R., Mauser, S., Juhás, G.: How to synthesize nets from languages: a survey. In: Henderson, S.G., Biller, B., Hsieh, M., Shortle, J., Tew, J.D., Barton, R.R. (eds.) Proceedings of the Winter Simulation Conference, WSC 2007, Washington, DC, USA, December 9–12, 2007, pp. 637–647. WSC (2007). http://dx.doi.org/10.1109/WSC.2007.4419657

29. van der Werf, J.M.E.M., van Dongen, B.F., Hurkens, C.A.J., Serebrenik, A.: Process discovery using integer linear programming. In: van Hee and Valk [27], pp. 368–387. http://dx.doi.org/10.1007/978-3-540-68746-7_24

Tools

Renew 2.5 – Towards a Comprehensive Integrated Development Environment for Petri Net-Based Applications

Lawrence Cabac[✉], Michael Haustermann[✉], and David Mosteller[✉]

Department of Informatics, University of Hamburg, Hamburg, Germany
{cabac,haustermann,mosteller}@informatik.uni-hamburg.de

Abstract. RENEW (The Reference Net Workshop) is an extensible Petri net IDE that supports the development and execution of high-level Petri nets and other modeling techniques. The Reference net formalism – the major formalism for RENEW – includes concepts such as net instances, synchronous channels and seamless Java integration. It combines the advantages of Petri nets and object-oriented programming for the development of concurrent and distributed software systems. Modeling support of RENEW focuses on convenience and ease for Petri net development. An outstanding feature is the support for multi-formalism simulation. The plugin architecture of RENEW enables the developers to extend the IDE for instance with additional formalisms. Alternatively to the inline mode – within the graphical user interface – the Simulator can also be run in a headless server fashion. Several configurations of RENEW are available, which are constituted through selections of plugins providing specialized functionality for multiple platforms. In this manner the RENEW family constitutes a product line architecture. RENEW is available free of charge including the Java source code. In this contribution we provide information about RENEW's functionality and architecture as well as the development of the tool set over the last decade.

Keywords: High-level Petri nets · Nets-within-nets · Reference nets · Integrated Development Environment (IDE) · Java · Plugin architecture

1 Introduction

RENEW is a continuously developed extensible modeling and execution environment for Petri nets with various formalisms and other modeling techniques. The main formalism of RENEW is the Reference net formalism [10], which combines the concept of nets-within-nets [15] with a reference semantics and the expressive power of object-oriented programming in the form of Java. Reference nets in RENEW can handle Java objects as tokens and Java expressions in transition inscriptions to execute Java code during the simulation. With the nets-within-nets concept, it is possible to build dynamic hierarchies of arbitrary height. Multiple nets can communicate using synchronous channels, which enable the

© Springer International Publishing Switzerland 2016
F. Kordon and D. Moldt (Eds.): PETRI NETS 2016, LNCS 9698, pp. 101–112, 2016.
DOI: 10.1007/978-3-319-39086-4_7

bidirectional exchange of information. The formalism is, thus, well-suited for the implementation of concurrent software systems. RENEW is written in Java and is available for multiple platforms (including Windows, Linux and Mac). An experimental version of the simulator for Android exists. The current version 2.5 is available for download[1] free of charge including the source code [11].

This contribution presents the RENEW environment with its objectives and history (Sect. 2), a selection of features and improvements over the recent years of continuous development (Sect. 3) and a brief overview of the plugin architecture (Sect. 4). The paper is summarized in Sect. 5.

2   Objectives

Up to today the objectives of the RENEW tool and its various plugins have been widely extended. The following section gives a brief summary of the evolution of RENEW over the past recent years. This section is followed by some information about current research topics in the context of RENEW development.

2.1   History

The first official version of RENEW was released in 1999. Since then it has continuously been developed as a Petri net IDE by the TGI Group[2]. Figure 1 shows the user interface of the first release of Renew, which offers the drawing of Petri net models and the starting and stopping of the simulation. Although other formalisms than Reference nets are available, the user interface offers no means of control to switch compilers.

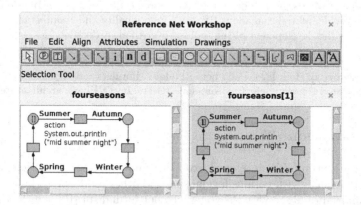

Fig. 1. RENEW 1.0 GUI, Debian 8/Java 7 together with a four seasons example (pattern and instance) featuring a simple Java inscription.

---

[1] RENEW 2.5 available at: http://www.renew.de.
[2] Theoretical Foundations Group, Department of Informatics, University of Hamburg.

The continuous development resulted in many improvements and bugfixes as well as feature enhancements. One major task has been the decoupling of editor and simulator, which started with the introduction of the separation layer in RENEW 1.6. The plugin system, introduced with the major release 2.0 in 2004 [12], enabled the extension of RENEW into various directions. RENEW was extensively applied and extended to perform agent-oriented software engineering (see following sections) and was furthermore utilized to provide a workflow management engine and clients. Besides using RENEW primarily for modeling Petri nets, plugins provide support for various modeling techniques, e.g. diagrams from UML or BPMN. Over the years RENEW evolved increasingly more into an IDE for software engineering with high-level Petri nets.

2.2 Implementing Petri Net-Based Applications

One main focus of RENEW is the execution/simulation of Reference nets. With the full support of that formalism, RENEW serves as an execution engine for net-based Java applications. Figure 2 shows a simple example net that uses Java objects, which could be part of a graphical application. In the net a frame and a button are created concurrently. After that the button is added to the frame and the frame is resized (again concurrently). When these two steps are finished the frame is displayed and in a next step disposed. This simple example gives a first impression on how to implement Petri net-based applications. With the possibility to structure multiple nets using the nets-within-nets concept, it is possible to implement even complex software systems (e.g. with the PAOSE approach, see Sect. 2.3).

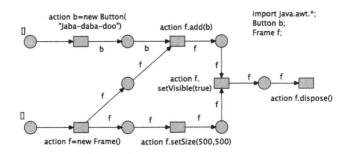

Fig. 2. Example net using Java objects.

2.3 Petri Net-Based, Agent-Oriented Software Engineering

The Petri Net-Based agent-oriented software engineering (PAOSE, [2]) is an approach to software development with an emphasis on distribution and concurrency. With the MULAN framework (multi-agent nets, [14]) Reference nets are applied as implementation artifacts for the development of multi-agent applications (MAA). To this end RENEW serves as an IDE for the development of MAA by providing the editing, debugging and simulation facilities. With its support for abstract modeling languages and the use of generative techniques to translate them into Reference nets RENEW supports the PAOSE development process in every single step from requirements engineering to system execution. RENEW is applied in the context of PAOSE as a tool for teaching and research in the field of agent-oriented software engineering.

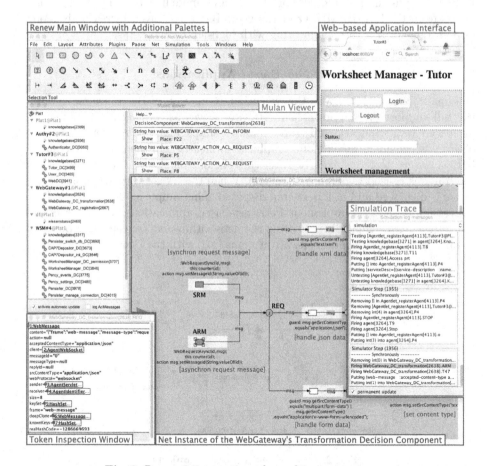

Fig. 3. Renew 2.5 execution of a multi-agent system.

Figure 3 shows the current version of the RENEW GUI together with several views on the system provided by various tools. The whole structure of the simulated PAOSE system can be inspected and navigated with the MulanViewer [3], displayed beneath the main GUI. In the structure tree the developers may inspect the agents with their sub-components. In the image the transformation decision component (DC) of the WebGateway agent is selected and details about this artifact can be inspected in the detail view (to the right of the structure tree, partly hidden). In the center/lower part a fraction of the artifact itself – the transformation DC – is displayed featuring one selected transition (ARM – asynchronous request message) and a marked place (REQ). The simulation has been halted for inspection after the transition ARM has fired through a preset local simulation breakpoint. This transition was involved in the firing step 1956 as can be inspected in the simulation log window depicted in the right. The selection of the transition in the Petri net has been done from the simulation log by using the context menu, which has been activated again for the presentation. The single token depicted as 1 on the place REQ can be inspected either by changing the representation directly in the net instance to a token bag view showing the string representation of the object or through a UML-like deep inspection of the object shown in the window located in the lower left corner of the screenshot. The token is a $WebMessge$, which contains the login data of a user that has clicked on the *login* button in the Web interface shown in the upper right corner of the screenshot. The deep inspection window is provided by the Feature Structure plugin.

Several implementations based on MULAN are available on the PAOSE Web page[3]. These include some demos, a distributed implementation of a multi-player game, and an export and diffing Web service for RENEW-compatible diagrams. The latter is presented through a stand-alone Web interface as well as integrated into the Redmine project management environment.

2.4 PAOSE Meta-Modeling

During its evolution over the years RENEW's capabilities for providing modeling support were extended beyond the initial focus on Petri nets. A great number of the additional modeling techniques are applied within the PAOSE approach. As mentioned in the previous section RENEW supports each step of the PAOSE development process from requirements engineering, over system design and specification to implementation and execution with appropriate modeling techniques [2]: we use Concept Diagrams to model agent ontologies, Use-Case Diagrams to capture the overall structure and a variant of Sequence Diagrams to model agent behavior in conversations. The latter are used to generate Reference nets, which can be executed as protocols in agent interactions. With the plugin from Haustermann [8], BPMN models can also be applied for this purpose. In our current research we are working on the RENEW Modeling and Transformation framework (RMT [13]), a framework for model-driven development of domain specific modeling languages and tools based on RENEW.

3 Highlights and Improvements

RENEW offers a wide range of features for the creation, the editing and manipulation of models as well as for execution, debugging and deployment of the

---

[3] PAOSE Web page: http://www.paose.net.

designed systems. We present a selection that – to our opinion – describes best the nature of the tool set. Although many of the presented features can not be put into one category we present the highlights as functional feature, as usability feature or as IDE related feature.

3.1 Functional Features

Multiple Formalisms. The simulator is capable of handling different formalisms. The main formalism is the Java Reference net formalism, for which different extensions exist, such as inhibitor, reset and timed arcs. The workflow net formalism, provided by an optional plugin, adds a task transition, which can be canceled during execution, so that its effect on the net can be reverted. Other formalisms provide simulation of P/T nets, feature structure nets and bool nets. Simulation is available in different modes. In the interactive simulation mode the user may control the simulation by choosing the transitions to fire and inspect each single step. The automatic simulation mode is usable for system execution and can be run with and without graphical feedback (operation as server).

Net Loading and Class Loading. RENEW features dynamic loading of nets on demand from the netpath or from the GUI. Nets may be available in the RENEW editor's format (rnw), which permits direct inspection, or as pre-compiled net system without graphical information (shadow net system), which allows a silent execution. The configurable *class reinit mode* allows to quickly develop models that combine nets and Java classes. Classes that are recompiled are reloaded at simulation start, allowing nets and Java classes to be quickly developed, tested and debugged without any restart of the environment.

Logging and Remote Monitoring. Logging in RENEW is provided through log4j. It is configurable and allows to log tool behavior and simulation events. Several plugins, which provide general or special purpose monitoring facilities may also be used for the inspection of local or remote simulations.

Graphical Editor. RENEW provides an easy to use graphical editor for Petri net models and other types of models and a simulation engine, which is seamlessly integrated into this editor. It has a plugin architecture, which makes it easily extensible. The core plugins are provided as part of the RENEW distribution. Many advanced features are supplied as optional plugins.

FreeHep Graphical Export. Since version 2.2 the graphical export relies on the FreeHep[4] libraries, which provide a wider range of formats including SVG and a high quality of output.

---

[4] The FreeHep libraries are available at https://github.com/freehep/.

3.2   Usability Features

Drag & Drop. Drag and drop support for RENEW and the navigator eases the usability by providing means to opening files or project folders directly within the editor's GUI. Additionally, images can now be added to a drawing by dropping them on the canvas.

Interaction Enhancements. The quick-draw mode has been improved to even faster draw Petri net models. Also configurable shortcuts for drawing tools and layout manipulation are available in order to combine tool selection by keyboard and positioning of net elements by the mouse.

Several drawing elements react to modifier keys during direct manipulation, so that ratios of height and width can be preserved or unified. This is for example useful when re-sizing an image.

Target Text Tool. The target text tool allows to add hyperlinks to graphical elements of a model. By this means models may be inter-linked, in order to offer simplified navigation between related models. Additionally, the usual schemes are supported through the desktop integration as well, allowing to link to Web pages (e.g. documentation/wikis) or other source code.

3.3   IDE Features

The editor has been improved over the last years and received many small usability enhancements and has evolved into an integrated development environment (IDE) for net-based software development. It contains a syntax check during editing and debugging tools, such as breakpoints or manual transitions. Furthermore the editor features desktop integration, a file navigator and image export to various formats.

Net/Diagram Diff. The net diff feature – for the first time presented in 2008 – has been added as ImageNetDiff [5,6] plugin to the optional plugins in version 2.3 and has been further enhanced for effectiveness and efficiency. It provides the functionality of diffing Petri net models and other diagrams directly within RENEW or as a Web service[5], which is used and integrated to offer this for the integrated project-management environment Redmine [1].

Quick-Fix. Syntax error notification dialogues are now enhanced to suggest possible solutions to the syntax errors, such as available methods, fields or constructors. The user can interactively choose from the provided solutions and apply the changes to the model in a quick-fix manner. Also undeclared variables are semi-automatically added to the declaration node. In Fig. 4 the variable *net*

---

[5] Available at http://paose.informatik.uni-hamburg.de/export/.

(compare with the declaration node) is not yet declared, which results in a syntax exception. The exception presents several solutions, of which the first one is currently selected. By clicking on the *apply* button (or double-clicking on the proposal) the variable will be added to the declaration node.

Refactoring. The renaming of variables in a Petri net drawing and changing of synchronous channels in net systems is now supported through the Refactoring plugin. However, these features are still under development and are still experimental.

Project Navigator. The Navigator – first introduced in version 2.3 – has been further improved. Due to a complete redesign, it provides a quicker update strategy, persistence and a filter functionality. The Navigator GUI is now extendable by plugins. On the right hand side of Fig. 4 the new Navigator GUI is displayed. The top level of buttons provides control over the content of the Navigator's tree view. The second row provides a filter for the elements in the view. Extensions may add functionality as additional buttons or as context menus. The SVN/Diff Navigator extension provides the diff of two selected Petri nets (or other models) via button and diffs against the document base via context menu. Other SVN related functionality is provided as well.

Console Plugin. The new Console plugin, which utilizes JLine[6] as library, provides many convenience enhancements for the RENEW command line in compar-

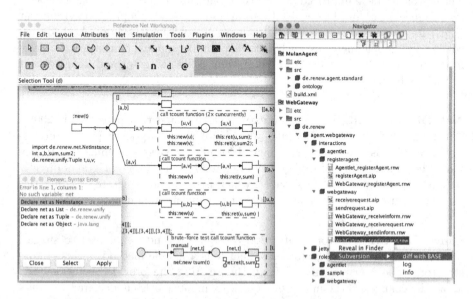

Fig. 4. RENEW Editor GUI featuring the navigator and the quick-fix functionality.

---

[6] JLine: https://github.com/jline/jline2/.

ison to the replaced Prompt plugin. The main advantages are editable command lines, tab-based command and argument completions as well as searchable and persistent command history.

Analysis. With the integration of the LoLA[7] verification tool [9] RENEW is also suited for verification tasks during modeling. So far only verification of P/T net models is provided through LoLA.

Net Components. Net components can be provided – and shared among developing teams – in order to ease recurrent modeling tasks and provide a conventionalized modeling style, which improves the readability and maintainability of net models.

Availability and OS-Integration. RENEW is available for most common platforms including Linux (and other Unices), Windows and Mac OS X. For all Platforms there exists a GUI integration into the respective Desktop environment. For Linux/X11 we provide an integration for the FreeDesktop standard and experimental debian/ubuntu packages. For Mac OS X we provide a specialized plugin for the desktop integration and an application bundle as well as a specialized installation package (DMG, disk image file).

4 Architecture

The plugin architecture – introduced in release 2.0 of RENEW – has already been presented [4,7,12]. Figure 5 shows the main parts, such as *simulator*, *graphical framework* (JHotDraw[8]), the formalism management and the Petri net IDE core. The latter extends the graphical framework as well as the simulator. On top of these core elements other plugins can be included, such as editor plugins, formalism plugins, tools that extend these formalisms and also applications, which may use Java code and Petri net code in combination.

Over the last years many plugins in various stages of maturity have been created by the maintainers or by other developers (e.g. students). Some of these extend the RENEW environment, while others extend the MULAN environment or provide multi-agent applications.

A boost for the development of plugins have been the plugins that allow the creation of plugin source folders. There exists a rather simple version of a *Plugin Development Plugin* for Renew plugins and a more elaborated version that allows the creation of multi-agent application folders – the *Use Case Components Plugin*[9]. With these plugins it is possible to create a new RENEW plugin simply by providing the name and the location of the source folder. The latter must be a valid source code repository in order to be able to compile the

---

[7] LoLA – A Low Level Petri Net Analyzer: http://www.service-technology.org.

[8] JHotDraw: http://www.jhotdraw.org.

[9] The palette of the *Use Case Components Plugin* is activated in Fig. 3.

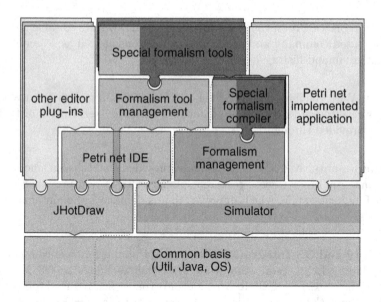

Fig. 5. RENEW's abstract architecture [7] – components as plugins.

plugin. A newly created plugin folder features already all necessary artifacts for the compilation of the plugin. These are the *Ant* build script, the plugin configuration file (*plugin.cfg*) as well as the source code folder. Additionally, a valid plugin facade class is generated. The Use Case Components Plugin also generates artifacts for the creation of MULAN applications according to a provided Coarse Design Diagram (CDD, a form of Use Case Diagram). These artifacts comprise the skeletons for agent role declarations, interaction definitions and ontology specification.

Java classes, RENEW nets and other artifacts – for instance *JavaCC* grammars or *JavaScript* files – can be added to the source code folder. The plugins may be accompanied by third party libraries and test cases.

An application that has been used heavily in the last couple of years is the above mentioned export and diff Web service. The *Mulan Export* plugin provides an agent (the *ExportAgent*) that offers the export and diff services to other agents and through the WebGateway also as a Web service to other clients. The backend of the export and diff functionality is provided by the respective RENEW plugins (FreeHep Export and ImageNetDiff). Over the last couple of years the service running as a MULAN system in an instance of RENEW has been constantly available and used, with up-times of several months. These long lasting running instances of Reference net systems and the high availability of the services show the feasibility and efficiency of the approach. Now several instances[10] of the export and diff service are running on several servers.

---

[10] A publicly available demo can reached from the PAOSE home page: http://www.paose.net.

5   Conclusion

RENEW's development has been ongoing for almost two decades. It has developed from a simulator and editor for a single high-level Petri net formalism to an integrated development environment for Java- and Petri net-based applications. The Reference net formalism and RENEW's simulator have proven themselves in various implementations to provide powerful and efficient means to develop and execute systems that include a strong focus on concurrency. Within the PAOSE context distributed, concurrency-aware systems have been implemented with the MULAN framework extension. In this environment many objectives, such as support for monitoring or specialized modeling techniques, have been provided on the grounds of the RENEW framework and were only possible through RENEW's plugin architecture.

Today RENEW exists in various configurations. Since the possibilities are growing constantly we are aiming at a product line architecture in order to ease configuration-intensive work and endorse reliable, feature-complete tool sets for multiple application domains.

Acknowledgment. We thank all developers that participated in the development of RENEW, especially Prof. Dr. Rüdiger Valk, Dr. Daniel Moldt and all of the TGI group of the Department of Informatics, University of Hamburg.

References

1. Betz, T., Cabac, L., Güttler, M.: Improving the development tool chain in the context of Petri net-based software development. In: Duvigneau, M., Moldt, D., Hiraishi, K. (eds.) Petri Nets and Software Engineering. International Workshop PNSE 2011, Newcastle upon Tyne, UK, June 2011. CEUR Workshop Proceedings, vol. 723, pp. 167–178. CEUR-WS.org, June 2011. http://CEUR-WS.org/Vol-723
2. Cabac, L.: Modeling Petri Net-Based Multi-Agent Applications, Agent Technology - Theory and Applications, vol. 5. Logos Verlag, Berlin (2010). http://www.logos-verlag.de/cgi-bin/engbuchmid?isbn=2673&lng=eng&id=
3. Cabac, L., Dörges, T., Rölke, H.: A monitoring toolset for PAOSE. In: van Hee, K.M., Valk, R. (eds.) PETRI NETS 2008. LNCS, vol. 5062, pp. 399–408. Springer, Heidelberg (2008)
4. Cabac, L., Duvigneau, M., Moldt, D., Rölke, H.: Modeling dynamic architectures using nets-within-nets. In: Ciardo, G., Darondeau, P. (eds.) ICATPN 2005. LNCS, vol. 3536, pp. 148–167. Springer, Heidelberg (2005)
5. Cabac, L., Markwardt, K., Schlüter, J.: ImageNetDiff: finding differences in models. In: Moldt, D., Ultes-Nitsche, U., Augusto, J.C. (eds.) In: Proceedings of the 7th International Workshop on Modelling, Simulation, Verification and Validation of Enterprise Information Systems - MSVVEIS 2009. Conjunction with ICEIS 2009. Milan, Italy, May 2009, pp. 156–161. INSTICC PRESS, Portugal (2009)
6. Cabac, L., Schlüter, J.: ImageNetDiff: a visual aid to support the discovery of differences in Petri nets. In: 15. Workshop Algorithmen und Werkzeuge für Petrinetze, AWPN 2008. CEUR Workshop Proceedings, vol. 380, pp. 93–98. Universität Rostock, September 2008. http://CEUR-WS.org/Vol-380/paper15.pdf

7. Duvigneau, M.: Konzeptionelle Modellierung von Plugin-Systemen mit Petrinetzen, Agent Technology - Theory and Applications, vol. 4. Logos Verlag, Berlin (2010)

8. Haustermann, M.: BPMN-Modelle für petrinetzbasierte agentenorientierte Softwaresysteme auf Basis von Mulan/Capa. Master thesis, Department of Informatics, University of Hamburg, Vogt-Kölln Str. 30, D-22527 Hamburg, September 2014

9. Hewelt, M., Wagner, T., Cabac, L.: Integrating verification into the PAOSE approach. In: Duvigneau, M., Moldt, D., Hiraishi, K. (eds.) Petri Nets and Software Engineering. International Workshop PNSE 2011, Newcastle upon Tyne, UK, June 2011. CEUR Workshop Proceedings, vol. 723, pp. 124–135. CEUR-WS.org, June 2011. http://CEUR-WS.org/Vol-723

10. Kummer, O.: Referenznetze. p. 456. Logos Verlag, Berlin (2002). http://www.logos-verlag.de/cgi-bin/engbuchmid?isbn=0035&lng=eng&id=

11. Kummer, O., Wienberg, F., Duvigneau, M., Cabac, L.: Renew - user guide (Release 2.4.2). In: Faculty of Informatics, Theoretical Foundations Group, University of Hamburg, Hamburg, January 2015. http://www.renew.de/

12. Kummer, O., Wienberg, F., Duvigneau, M., Schumacher, J., Köhler, M., Moldt, D., Rölke, H., Valk, R.: An extensible editor and simulation engine for Petri nets: RENEW. In: Cortadella, J., Reisig, W. (eds.) ICATPN 2004. LNCS, vol. 3099, pp. 484–493. Springer, Heidelberg (2004)

13. Mosteller, D., Cabac, L., Haustermann, M.: Providing petri net-based semantics in model driven-development for the renew meta-modeling framework. In: Moldt, D., Rölke, H., Störrle, H. (eds.) Petri Nets and Software Engineering. International Workshop, PNSE 2015, Brussels, Belgium, June 22–23, 2015. CEUR Workshop Proceedings, vol. 1372, pp. 99–114. CEUR-WS.org (2015). http://CEUR-WS.org/Vol-1372

14. Rölke, H.: Modellierung von Agenten und Multiagentensystemen - Grundlagen und Anwendungen, Agent Technology - Theory and Applications, vol. 2. Logos Verlag, Berlin (2004). http://logos-verlag.de/cgi-bin/engbuchmid?isbn=0768&lng=eng&id=

15. Valk, R.: Petri nets as token objects: an introduction to elementary object nets. In: Desel, J., Silva, M. (eds.) ICATPN 1998. LNCS, vol. 1420, pp. 1–25. Springer, Heidelberg (1998)

AB-QSSPN: Integration of Agent-Based Simulation of Cellular Populations with Quasi-Steady State Simulation of Genome Scale Intracellular Networks

Wojciech Ptak[1], Andrzej M. Kierzek[2], and Jacek Sroka[1(✉)]

[1] Institute of Informatics, University of Warsaw, Warsaw, Poland
{w.ptak,sroka}@mimuw.edu.pl
[2] Faculty of Health and Medical Sciences, University of Surrey, Guildford, UK
a.kierzek@surrey.ac.uk

Abstract. We present a tool for simulation of populations of living cells interacting in spatial structures. Each cell is modelled with the Quasi-Steady Petri Net that integrates dynamic regulatory network expressed with a Petri Net (PN) and Genome Scale Metabolic Networks (GSMN) where linear programming is used to explore the steady-state metabolic flux distributions in the whole-cell model.

Similar simulations have already been conducted for single cells, but we present an architecture to simulate populations of millions of interacting cells organized in spatial structures which can be used to model tumour growth or formation of tuberculosis lesions. For that we use the Spark framework and organize the computation in an agent based "think like a vertex" fashion as in Pregel like systems. In the cluster we introduce a special kind of per node caching to speed up computation of the steady-state metabolic flux.

Our tool can be used to provide a mechanistic link between genotype and behaviour of multicellular system.

1 Introduction and Objectives

Mechanistic modelling of biological systems is making increasing impact in research and industry. The ultimate goal is to predict behaviour of the system given information about its genetic blueprint and environmental conditions to which it is responding. Progress towards this goal is necessary to enable personalised and precision medicine, where diagnostics, disease prevention and therapy will be tailored to patient's genetic background and lifestyle. In the context of biotechnology and synthetic biology, computer simulation of biological systems is necessary tool for rational design of genetically engineered cells. With the advent of Next Generation Sequencing full genome sequence of any species, cell line or individual is now possible to obtain. Moreover, large number of other ~omics approaches enable measurements of the proteins, RNAs and metabolites with increasing quantitative accuracy. Availability of these data as well as legacy of

© Springer International Publishing Switzerland 2016
F. Kordon and D. Moldt (Eds.): PETRI NETS 2016, LNCS 9698, pp. 113–122, 2016.
DOI: 10.1007/978-3-319-39086-4_8

over half a century of molecular biology research further motivate mechanistic modelling of the relationship between genotype, environment and biological systems behaviour.

The Constrained Based Modelling (CBM) has achieved spectacular success in modelling metabolism at the full genome scale [2,10]. It capitalises on the fact that connectivity of a metabolic network is the best-studied sub-system within the full network of molecular interactions of the cell, and can be modelled at quasi-steady state due to time-scale separation between gene regulation (hours) and metabolism (seconds). This enables exploration of metabolic flux distributions within the GSMN consistent with stoichiometric and thermodynamic constraints as well as flux measurements and constraints formulated according to ~omics data on enzymatic gene expression [7]. The Quasi-Steady Petri Net (QSSPN) [4] algorithm has been developed to integrate Petri Net (PN) models of gene regulatory and signalling networks in the cell with steady state models of Genome Scale Metabolic Networks (GSMN). The quasi-steady state approximation is used, where for every state of dynamic, PN model the steady-state metabolic flux distribution of GSMN is explored with CBM approach. The QSSPN has been first applied to the integration a liver-specific GSMN with a qualitative model of a large-scale regulatory network responsible for homeostatic regulation of bile acid synthesis. The method was shown to be successful in simulation of individual cells.

In this paper we present AB-QSSPN a prototype tool which objective is to extends the QSSPN method to multicellular systems and provide a mechanistic link between genotype and behaviour of multicellular system. The multiscale nature of biological systems is one of the major challenges of their mechanistic modelling, especially in medical applications. The physiological state at health and disease emerges from events occurring at molecular, cellular, multicellular (tissue), organ and whole-body levels. Some of these processes, such as development, tumour growth or formation of tuberculosis lesions require spatial modelling of structures formed by millions of cells. AB-QSSPN integrates simulation of Agent Based models of multicellular systems and qualitative QSSPN models. To the best of our knowledge this is the first demonstration of the feasibility of simulation describing multicellular system and the network of gene regulatory, signalling and whole-cell scale metabolic reactions operating within each individual cell. To make this simulation possible, we capitalized on MapReduce [3] model and its open source implementation Hapdoop [1]. These recent developments in distributed computing enable reliable computation on clusters of commodity computers. As we are interested in iterative simulations we use Apache Spark [12], a new programming system which is de facto successor of MapReduce. It neatly follows a shift in the hardware used in data processing centers where the processing nodes are equipped with increasing amount of RAM memory. Spark is based on the Resilient Distributed Datasets abstraction where the data by default, if possible is kept in memory avoiding unnecessary spills to disk which are by orders of magnitude slower that in-memory operations. This allows Spark to overtake Hadoop in iterative computation similarly as HaLoop, Twister and Pregel/Giraph do. On the other hand Spark is similar to MapReduce in the way how data is grouped and shuffled between nodes. Its programming model extends the simple programming model of MapReduce with additional operations like joins and sorts and allows explicit control of data distribution with repartitions. Spark dataflows can also be composed of more steps than just map and reduce. The grouping of those steps between the group by/shuffle phases is optimized by the framework. This feature can be used in future version of our system to extend it with post-processing of the results.

In the following sections we describe QSSPN and its integration with AB model so that potential users can understand how to specify their models. The use of Petri net formalism makes it possible to make this description formal. We also present the functionality and the architecture of AB-QSSPN and a use case demonstrating application of the method to the simulation of one million liver cells undergoing metabolic reprogramming during bile acid synthesis.

AB-QSSPN is available at www.mimuw.edu.pl/~w.ptak/AB-QSSPN together with biological models on which we tested it.

2   The Model

In this section we define how we model a single cell in the Quasi-Steady Petri Net (QSSPN) algorithm and then how those cells interact within a population.

2.1   Single Cell

Essentially a cell can be thought of as a complex metabolic network of chemical reactions whose capacity is determined by gene regulation and signalling. The reactions are in the so called *steady state* so that consumption and production of metabolites is balanced. They are represented with the steady state models of GSMN. The regulatory part is represented with a PN whose state determines the bounds for the reactions, e.g., marking of places in the net represents occurrences of conditions that catalyse the reactions. For every state of the dynamic PN model the steady-state metabolic flux distribution of GSMN is explored with CBM approach, e.g., with the Flux Balance Analysis method [10] that applies linear programming. A simple overview QSSPN model adapted from [4] with the regulatory PN and the metabolism as a black box is presented in Fig. 1.

Metabolism. GSMN is represented with the stoichiometry matrix $S \in \mathbb{R}^{m \times n}$ where each column contains all the coefficients of one reaction while one row contains the coefficients for a particular metabolite in all the reactions. For example for a reaction $C_1 + 2C_4 \rightarrow C_5$, the corresponding column would contain -1 in the row for compound C_1, -2 in the row for compound C_4 and 1 in the row for compound C_5. As reactions can occur at different rates there is a vector of fluxes $v = (v_1, v_2, \ldots, v_n)$ and in the steady state it holds $Sv = 0$. The regulatory part introduces constraints for reactions of the form $a_i < v_i < b_i$. In

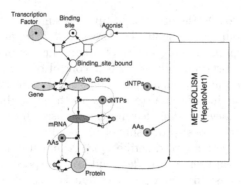

Fig. 1. A simple overview QSSPN model

practice, as there are more reactions than metabolites ($n > m$), the system of equations has infinite number of solutions even with such constraining.

To determine single points within the solution space, an objective function $Z = c^T v$ is used and we look for points that maximize this function. The coefficients of the *goal vector* c define the linear combination of fluxes through a chosen set of reactions. This can be used to look for points corresponding to maximum growth rate, or maximum ATP production, or to maximum linear combination of fluxes through a subset of reactions.

The optimization problem defined by the stoichiometry matrix S, the constraints for the reaction a and b, and the goal vector c, can be solved with linear programming libraries such as GLPK.

In the following we assume that the linear problems that we deal with always have a solution and that if there are multiple solutions we somehow choose one of them, e.g. the smallest one in the lexicographical order. We define a partial function $\mathbf{fba} : \mathbb{R}^{m \times n} \times \mathbb{R}^n \times \mathbb{R}^n \times \mathbb{R}^n \to \mathbb{R}^n$ to return this solution vector. That is, for optimisation of the linear problem for $S \in \mathbb{R}^{m \times n}$, $a \in \mathbb{R}^n$, $b \in \mathbb{R}^n$ and $c \in \mathbb{R}^n$, and its chosen solution $v \in \mathbb{R}^n$, we have $\mathbf{fba}(S, a, b, c) = v$.

Regulation. The gene regulatory and signalling networks in the cell are modelled with a PN. The existence of a token in a place means that there is "just enough" of some metabolite to trigger a reaction, thus it is possible to model interactions requiring only that some metabolites are present.

As is often in bioinformatics [11], an extra edge type, called *inhibitor edge*, is introduced to make it possible to model interactions requiring that some metabolites are not present. In the graphical notation such edges are distinguished from ordinary edges by using an empty circle in place of the arrowhead. Existence of such an edge prevents the destination transition from firing if tokens are present in the source place.

We assume the reader to be familiar with PN and its semantics and do not define it here. In the following we assume that for a PN pn its set of places is given by P_{pn}, and denote with $\mathbb{M}_{pn}$ the set of all possible markings of pn where each marking is an assignment of number of tokens for each place. We assume that a net pn defines a transition system such that $M_1 \rightarrow_{pn} M_2$ if $M_1, M_2 \in \mathbb{M}_{pn}$ and M_2 can be obtained from M_1 by firing one of its enabled transitions.

Combining Metabolism and Regulation. Now we define the interaction of metabolism with the regulatory net.

The metabolism and the regulatory net models interact both ways. One way genes regulate enzymes and enzymes regulate reactions. The other way around the production of certain metabolites influences gene expression. The core assumption is that when a change in the regulation occurs the metabolism quickly stabilises and reaches a steady state. This assumption is justified by time-scale separation between gene regulation (hours) and metabolism (seconds). Thus the metabolism has enough time to stabilise between every two firings of transitions of the regulatory Petri net. In our model the "regulatory" Petri net firing will be interleaved with metabolic phases.

After each transition firing, the marking of predefined places of the net determines the values for the constraints limiting the minimum and maximum flow for predefined reactions in the metabolism, i.e., the values of a_i and b_i for some i. Based on the modified constraints, the whole FBA optimisation is rerun several times for different goal functions to determine the optimal values of the fluxes. The values of the optimal fluxes for each goal determine the state of some predefined places in the regulatory net (regardless of their previous marking) and thus the state. This process repeats.

The user defines how a marking of the regulatory net translates to the constraints for reactions. We abstract this with functions $a, b : \mathbb{M}_{pn} \rightarrow \mathbb{R}^n$. The user also defines some g goal vectors $c_1, \dots, c_g$ and how the results of those optimizations influence the marking of the PN which we abstract with the function $reg : \mathbb{M}_{pn} \times \mathbb{R}^g \rightarrow \mathbb{M}_{pn}$. Thus, if M is the initial marking, the new marking of the regulatory net after the metabolism stabilizes is defined by $\mathbf{reg}(M, [\mathbf{fba}(\boldsymbol{S}, a(M), b(M), c_1), \dots, \mathbf{fba}(\boldsymbol{S}, a(M), b(M), c_g)])$.

The combined behaviour of a single cell is thus defined by the transition system where states are markings of the regulatory net and the system can transition from state M to state M', which we denote by $M \twoheadrightarrow M'$, if there exists $M'' \in \mathbb{M}$ such that $M \rightarrow_{pn} M'''$ and $M' = \mathbf{reg}(M'', [\mathbf{fba}(\boldsymbol{S}, a(M''), b(M''), c_1), \dots, \mathbf{fba}(\boldsymbol{S}, a(M''), b(M''), c_g)])$.

2.2 Population of Cells

In this subsection we describe how we model populations of interacting cells.

We assume the cells are placed in a three dimensional grid. A cell interacts with up to 26 cells surrounding it (6 in our experiments). The interaction mechanism is based on marking of some chosen places in the surrounding cells, if those places get marked, by the metabolic or regulatory part of the cell itself. This allows to model situations where a cell produces and introduces to the environment some protein that activates some of its and its neighbours receptors.

Let $\hat{P} \subset P$ be the set of places used for communication. The state of the whole population G is defined as a matrix of the states of the individual cells $G \in \mathbb{M}_{pn}^{k \times k \times k}$ for k being the dimension of the population grid (in practice populations of at least of million of cells are interesting with $k = 100$). A transition from the state G to state G' is possible, which we denote by $G \rightsquigarrow G'$, iff there exists $G'' \in \mathbb{M}_{pn}^{k \times k \times k}$ such that for each $1 \leq i, j, l \leq k$ it holds: (1) $G_{i,j,l} \rightarrow_{pn} G''_{i,j,l}$ for some $G''_{i,j,l}$, (2) for each $p \in (P \backslash \hat{P})$ it holds $G'_{i,j,l}(p) = G''_{i,j,l}(p)$, and (3) for each $p \in \hat{P}$ it holds $G'_{i,j,l}(p) = G''_{i,j,l}(p) + \Sigma_{i',j',l' \text{ neigh. of } i,j,k} \max(0, G''_{i',j',l'}(p) - G_{i',j',l'}(p))$.

3   Functionality

The AB-QSSPN is to the best of our knowledge the first tool enabling simulation of large multicellular systems integrated with wholegenome scale metabolic networks and dynamic models of gene regulation and signalling representing molecular processes operating within each individual cell. We have successfully tested AB-QSSPN a model of million liver cells, which is sufficient cellular population size to draw biologically meaningful conclusions. We formulated caching mechanism which allowed this calculations to be completed on a cluster of just 15 computers.

The input of AB-QSSPN is a model provided in the format of QSSPN software [4]. We provide biologically realistic example of such model on the project website. The users can examine the model in standard PN tool Snoopy [11], modify the model and rerun simulations. The user is also expected to define the set of PN places used by the cells for communication (see Sect. 2.2). Our tool reports reachability of certain states in individual cells. Users can extend the PN representing regulatory part of the cells (see Sect. 2.1) to include places representing behaviours of interest, such as homeostatic response to external perturbation. Our experiments also show how the user can pipeline AB-QSSPN and Spark for analysis of the simulation trajectories. This is another advantage of using Spark framework.

The software distribution includes scripts for running simulation on an existing spark cluster. We also provide Docker [9] images for users who would like to quickly test AB-QSSPN without configuring and running a Spark cluster. The images require minimal setup as they already provide configured AB-QSSPN, installation of HDFS and Spark with all the necessary libraries.

4   Architecture

AB-QSSPN is organized in three subprojects:

- GSMN metabolism server — implemented in C++ server that accepts GSMN problems and computes results with the GLPK linear programming solver; the server provides caching feature so that the same optimisation problems are not solved multiple times,

- QSSPN single cell simulator — implemented in C++ single cell simulator that encompasses both metabolism and regulation, it uses the metabolism server for solving GSMN problems,
- population simulator — simulator implemented in Spark that uses the agent based "think like a vertex" pattern of Pregel like systems for populations of cells, individual cells are simulated with the QSSPN single cell simulator and one per cluster node GSMN metabolism server is used to solve GSMN problems.

We use the GraphX [6] library of Spark to model populations of cells as graphs. Its operators are powerful enough to implement the Pregel computation model with its agent based "think like a vertex" pattern. The computation is organized in processing supersteps. In each superstep every cell performs one step of QSSPN simulation with regulatory PN and metabolic CB parts. Then, the cells communicate with neighbours and spread information about new tokens in places used for communication.

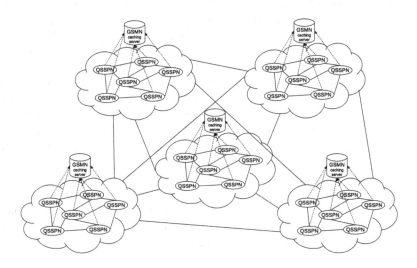

Fig. 2. Architecture of AB-QSSPN

The computation is distributed into a cluster of commodity computers by Spark. The cells in the population are partitioned by Spark between the computers see Fig. 2. The communication between cells in each node does not require network transfer. The cells from different nodes do not exchange individual messages but the framework groups the messages per node, which reduces the network overhead. We significantly speed up the processing by implementing GSMN as a separate server with a results caching feature, so that the same optimization problems are not repeated. Each computing node in the cluster has its own GSMN metabolism server instance, which minimises the network communication.

At the same time usage of GraphX allows for easier development of graph analytic pipelines which include simulation and post processing of the results like computation of statistics of how many cells reached homoeostasis in each superstep.

5 Use Case and Experimental Evaluation

5.1 Individual Cell Model

To demonstrate our AB-QSSPN approach we have constructed the model of the gene regulation, signalling, whole cell metabolism and cell-cell communication involved in homeostatic regulation of bile acid synthesis in human liver. Primary bile acids (BAs) are produced by hepatocytes as the products of cholesterol catabolism. They are vital for the intestinal absorption of lipophilic nutrients and the hepatobiliary secretion of endogenous and xenobiotic metabolites. They also act as signalling molecules and play important roles in the regulation of glucose and lipid metabolism in the enterohepatic system, and peripheral tissues. Given their global influence on the physiological state of the organism and their toxicity at high levels, it is not surprising that BA synthesis is tightly regulated and that BA homeostasis is essential for health [8]. The QSSPN model of bile acid homeostasis has been constructed and described in detail in the original QSSPN publication [4]. We modify this model in the following ways. First, we assume only two discrete states – fully active (one token) and basal (zero tokens), rather then 3 states. Second, we do not use inhibitory edges any more. All inhibitor interactions are now simulated (by using dual places). This step does not change biological meaning of the model. Third, MAP kinase pathway is now lumped into one transition. Simulations performed in our previous work [4] show that this simplification does not influence behaviour of interest. Final model has 130 places and 163 transitions in regulatory network part. The linear model of whole-cell metabolism contains 2539 reactions of 777 metabolites [5]. The model is available in AB-QSSPN distribution. The users can examine the model in standard Petri Net tool Snoopy [11], modify the model and rerun the simulations.

5.2 Multicellular Simulation of Liver Tissue

To provide Use Case for AB-QSSPN we have investigated the role of cell-to-cell communication through cytokine FGF19 on bile acid homeostasis response at tissue level. The FGF19 is produced by hepatocytes and secreted to the outside of the cell. It can then bind FGFR4 protein receptor, which triggers MAP kinase pathway. The FGF19 can act as autocrine signal, where it binds to FGFR4 receptor on the surface of the same cell that produced it, or as an paracrine signal where FGF19 produced by a particular cell binds too FGF19 receptor of others. In our previous work we did not distinguish these two signaling modes. The AB-QSSPN tool gives us for the first time opportunity to do it and to examine whether communication between cells (paracrine mode) within a volume element of liver tissue is important factor in bile acid homeostasis.

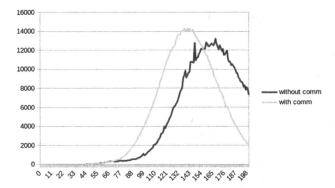

Fig. 3. Cell count by step

We have arranged 10^6 copies of the individual cell QSSPN model on the $100 \times 100 \times 100$ grid. The state of FGF19 place in a particular cell was "visible" to all 6 neighbors in the grid. The AB-QSSPN simulation has been performed using algorithm described in Sect. 2.2. Trajectory of 200 time units has been simulated on a cluster of 15 university lab computers. The state of BA_HOMEOSTASIS node, representing successful homeostatic response has been monitored. Figure 3 shows distribution of the number of steps needed to reach BA_HOMEOSTASIS for the first time. The mean number of reaction firings required to reach BA_HOMEOSTASIS decreases from 164 to 142. While the time units are arbitrary in Qualitative Petri Net simulation, the simulations demonstrate that cooperative effect of cellular communication results in faster mean response time to increasing burst of bile acid. This demonstrates that even in this relatively simple system it is important to consider cell-to-cell communication. In models of tumour growth or immune responses these effects will be more prominent. In conclusion, this Use Case demonstrates that AB-QSSPN is a unique tool for the first time enabling multiscale simulation of multicellular systems with consideration of intracellular whole-cell metabolic, gene regulatory and signaling networks. Recent advances in distributed computing applied here for the first time for QSSPN, make these simulations feasible.

6   Summary and Further Research

We have verified that AB-QSSPN architecture can be used to simulate populations of millions of cells modelled with QSSPN on only small clusters of commodity computers. As to our knowledge simulations of this scale have never been conducted so far. Such populations are biologically significant and their modelling can be useful for example while studding tumour growth where the conditions for cells in the population depend on their spacial position within the tumour. Usage of Spark framework allows for easy post processing of the simulation results, which comprise big data of states of every cell in several hundred of supersteps. Spark is ideal for aggregation and querying of data of such size.

Acknowledgements. This research was sponsored by National Science Centre based on decision DEC-2012/07/D/ST6/02492.

References

1. Apache. Hadoop. http://hadoop.apache.org/
2. Bordbar, A., Monk, J.M., King, Z.A., Palsson, B.O.: Constraint-based models predict metabolic and associated cellular functions. Nat. Rev. Genet. **15**(2), 107–120 (2014)
3. Dean, J., Ghemawat, S.: MapReduce: simplified data processing on large clusters. In: OSDI, pp. 137–150 (2004)
4. Fisher, C.P., Plant, N.J., Moore, J.B., Kierzek, A.M.: QSSPN: dynamic simulation of molecular interaction networks describing gene regulation, signalling and whole-cell metabolism in human cells. Bioinformatics **29**(24), 3181–3190 (2013). Oxford Univ Press
5. Gille, C., Bölling, C., Hoppe, A., Bulik, S., Hoffmann, S., Hübner, K., Karlstädt, A., Ganeshan, R., König, M., Rother, K., Weidlich, M., Behre, J., Holzhütter, H.-G.: HepatoNet1: a comprehensive metabolic reconstruction of the human hepatocyte for the analysis of liver physiology. Mol. Syst. Biol. **6**(1), 411 (2010)
6. Gonzalez, J.E., Xin, R.S., Dave, A., Crankshaw, D., Franklin, M.J., Stoica, I.: GraphX: graph processing in a distributed dataflow framework. In: Proceedings of the 11th USENIX Conference on Operating Systems Design and Implementation, OSDI 2014, pp. 599–613. USENIX Association, Berkeley, CA, USA (2014)
7. Lewis, N.E., Nagarajan, H., Palsson, B.O.: Constraining the metabolic genotype-phenotype relationship using a phylogeny of in silico methods. Nat. Rev. Microbiol. **10**(4), 291–305 (2012)
8. Li, T., Chiang, J.Y.L.: Bile acid signaling in liver metabolism and diseases. J. Lipids **2012** (2011)
9. Merkel, D.: Docker: lightweight linux containers for consistent development and deployment. Linux J. **2014**(239), 2 (2014)
10. Orth, J.D., Thiele, I., Palsson, B.Ø.: What is flux balance analysis? Nat. Biotechnol. **28**(3), 245–248 (2010)
11. Rohr, C., Marwan, W., Heiner, M.: Snoopy - a unifying Petri net framework to investigate biomolecular networks. Bioinformatics **26**(7), 974–975 (2010)
12. Zaharia, M., Chowdhury, M., Das, T., Dave, A., Ma, J., McCauley, M., Franklin, M.J., Shenker, S., Stoica, I.: Resilient distributed datasets: a fault-tolerant abstraction for in-memory cluster computing. In: Proceedings of the 9th USENIX Conference on Networked Systems Design and Implementation, NSDI 2012, p. 2. USENIX Association, Berkeley, CA, USA (2012)

PetriDotNet 1.5: Extensible Petri Net Editor and Analyser for Education and Research

András Vörös[1,2](✉), Dániel Darvas[1], Vince Molnár[1,2], Attila Klenik[1],
Ákos Hajdu[1,2], Attila Jámbor[1], Tamás Bartha[3], and István Majzik[1]

[1] Department of Measurement and Information Systems,
Budapest University of Technology and Economics, Budapest, Hungary
{vori,darvas,molnarv,hajdua,majzik}@mit.bme.hu
[2] MTA-BME Lendület Cyber-Physical Systems Research Group, Budapest, Hungary
[3] Institute for Computer Science and Control, Hungarian Academy of Sciences,
Budapest, Hungary
tamas.bartha@sztaki.mta.hu

Abstract. PetriDotNet is an extensible Petri net editor and analysis tool originally developed to support the education of formal methods. The ease of use and simple extensibility fostered more and more algorithmic developments. Thanks to the continuous interest of developers (especially M.Sc. and Ph.D. students who choose PetriDotNet as the framework of their thesis project), by now PetriDotNet became an analysis platform, providing various cutting-edge model checking algorithms and stochastic analysis algorithms. As a result, industrial application of the tool also emerged in recent years. In this paper we overview the main features and the architecture of PetriDotNet, and compare it with other available tools.

Keywords: Petri nets · Modelling · Simulation · Model checking · Stochastic analysis · Editor

1 Introduction and Objectives

Ordinary and coloured Petri nets are simple, yet powerful formal modelling formalisms that are covered by most undergraduate Formal Methods courses. They are widely used to demonstrate concurrency, causality and other principles of systems design. In addition, thanks to their simple syntax and semantics, Petri nets help to introduce various generic concepts, such as state space, coverability graph, invariants, reachability, temporal logic and model checking. To support active learning, a demonstrator tool is needed to give the students insight into these concepts and let them do experiments on their own.

The goal of the Formal Methods courses is to teach students the foundations. Talented students, however, are interested in diving deeper into the theoretical and algorithmic background. Petri nets have been studied for a long time, thus many analysis algorithms are described in the literature. The implementation

© Springer International Publishing Switzerland 2016
F. Kordon and D. Moldt (Eds.): PETRI NETS 2016, LNCS 9698, pp. 123–132, 2016.
DOI: 10.1007/978-3-319-39086-4_9

and improvement of these algorithms can provide interesting challenge for the students, and it also gives an opportunity for the lecturers to assess the students' skills and scientific potential. In such cases a framework should be accessible for them to experiment with advanced algorithms and methods. Unfortunately, the freely available and actively maintained Petri net editor and analysis tools have different strengths and weaknesses (see more details in Sect. 5), thus it is hard to find a single tool that is able to satisfy the above mentioned requirements of the education as well as to provide analysis algorithms that can be effectively used and extended in research.

According to these needs, PetriDotNet, our Petri net editor and analysis tool offers the following main features:

- It provides a convenient graphical editor for creating (ordinary or coloured) Petri nets. Besides simulation, the basic step to understand the dynamic behaviour of nets, it is extended with analysis of structural and dynamic properties, as well as reachability and model checking capabilities in order to support the Formal Methods courses.
- Furthermore, PetriDotNet is a simple, generic and extensible platform for new, Petri net-based algorithms that provides wide access to the Petri net data structures and the graphical user interface.

The development of PetriDotNet started as an ordinary Petri net editor in 2007 [22] as a Master's thesis project (named as Petri.NET at that time). During the last nearly ten years, the tool has been heavily modified, improved and extended, thanks to the contribution of many enthusiastic B.Sc., M.Sc. and Ph.D. students of the Fault Tolerant Systems Research Group (FTSRG) at the Budapest University of Technology and Economics.

The structure of this paper is the following. Section 2 describes the current functionality of PetriDotNet. The architecture of the tool is briefly described in Sect. 3. Next, we present some use cases in Sect. 4 and a comparison to other tools in Sect. 5. Finally, Sect. 6 discusses the installation and usage.

2   Functionality

This section overviews the main functionality of PetriDotNet and the plug-ins shipped with the tool.

Editor Features. First and foremost, PetriDotNet is an editor for Petri nets. It provides graphical editing capabilities (cf. Fig. 1) for both ordinary and well-formed coloured Petri nets (see [25] for the definition of the supported coloured Petri net variant). The tool supports Petri nets extended with inhibitor arcs, transition priorities, and places with limited token capacity. Moreover, the construction of hierarchical Petri nets is supported by allowing coarse transitions that can be refined by a subnet.

The tool provides simulation functionality (*token game*) for Petri nets, where the simulation can be manually conducted or automatically executed. The tool

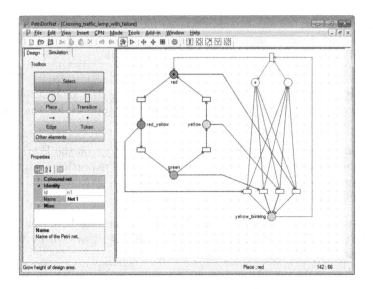

Fig. 1. The main window of PetriDotNet

is shipped with a plug-in that can perform large scale simulation, executing thousands or millions of non-deterministic firing, and then present the statistics.

To save and load the Petri nets, PetriDotNet supports two formalisms natively. The default format is PNML (Petri Net Markup Language) [15], a standard, XML-based Petri net description format. PNML is supported by various other tools, therefore this is an interface between these tools and PetriDotNet. A binary, custom file format is also supported that provides more efficient persistence for large models.

Plug-In Features. The functionality of the tool is extensible with plug-ins. Plug-ins can perform simulation tasks, provide analysis features (e.g. model checking) or export/import capabilities. Each plug-in can access the Petri net data models, use the graphical user interface, add new menu items, and call built-in PetriDotNet commands. The architecture of the tool is designed to keep the development of plug-ins simple, in order to help the users to focus on functionality instead of technology. See Sect. 3 for more details.

Export and Import Features. It is possible to export the constructed Petri nets into other Petri net formalisms, such as to the syntax of the GPenSIM[1] (General Purpose Petri Net Simulator) and the .pnt format of the INA[2] (Integrated Net Analyzer) tool. Also, the Petri net models can be translated into to the input format of SAL[3] (Symbolic Analysis Laboratory). Furthermore, import

---

[1] http://www.davidrajuh.net/gpensim/.

[2] http://www2.informatik.hu-berlin.de/lehrstuehle/automaten/ina/.

[3] http://sal.csl.sri.com/.

is also provided from the .net textual Petri net file format used by the INA/Tina[4] tools, among others. New import or export plug-ins can be developed easily as the internal model representations are simply accessible.

Formal Methods Course Plug-In. As one of the first motivations was to support the education, the framework has built in support for the following tasks:

- Calculating invariants, and displaying the results right on the Petri net,
- Generating the reachability/coverability graph, and exporting their graphical representation into image files,
- Computing various liveness properties [21].

The invariant analysis covers both P and T-invariants based on the well-known Martinez–Silva algorithm [17], and a different algorithm by Cayir and Ucer [2] that computes the bases of invariants.

Integrated Analysis Methods. In the last five years, in addition to the educational features, PetriDotNet became a Petri net analysis package providing plug-ins for a wide range of analysis methods. Among others, as detailed below, PetriDotNet supports advanced formal verification techniques based on decision diagrams and abstraction.

Saturation-Based Model Checking Algorithms. In PetriDotNet, various algorithms provide model checking based on the saturation algorithm [3–5]. The CTL model checking approaches are based on the work of Ciardo [28] and the bounded model checking approach is the extension of [27]. The LTL model checking algorithms are built on top of the ideas of [11,14]. Our research resulted in significant extensions and improvements, this way PetriDotNet currently supports novel analysis algorithms as follows:

- CTL model checking of ordinary and coloured Petri nets based on traditional and extended versions of saturation [1,25],
- Bounded CTL model checking based on a novel saturation-based algorithm, with various search strategies [10,24],
- LTL model checking based on a novel synchronous product computation algorithm [20] and incremental SCC detection [19].

CEGAR-Based Reachability Algorithms. PetriDotNet includes reachability analysis algorithms based on Counterexample-Guided Abstraction Refinement (CEGAR) [6] for ordinary Petri nets. Petri net CEGAR-based algorithms over-approximate the set of reachable states using the state equation, which is a necessary criterion for reachability. The CEGAR algorithm for Petri nets introduced in [26] was the base of our work. Our implementation includes various search strategies, adapted to the characteristics of the different models [12,13].

---

[4] http://projects.laas.fr/tina/.

Stochastic Analysis Algorithms. Recently the tool was extended to support the modelling and analysis of stochastic Petri net models. The goal was to provide a configurable stochastic analysis framework where various state space exploration, matrix representation and numerical analysis algorithms can be combined [16]. PetriDotNet provides the following stochastic analysis for ordinary stochastic Petri net models:

– Steady-state reward and sensitivity analysis,
– Transient reward analysis,
– Calculation of the mean time to reach a state partition, that is used to calculate mean-time-to-first-failure (MTFF) in dependability models.

3   Architecture

General Architectural Overview. The tool is written in C#, based on the Microsoft .NET framework. The architecture of PetriDotNet is kept as simple as reasonably possible. It is a modular tool: it provides some basic functionalities, and can be extended by various plug-ins.

The tool uses a base library defining the Petri net data structures, developed for PetriDotNet. This library contains object models for ordinary and coloured Petri nets. The PetriDotNet core contains the graphical user interface and the plug-in interface. The architecture of the tool is summarized in Fig. 2.

Plug-in Interface. To follow the previously presented educational goals, it is simple to extend PetriDotNet with a new plug-in. This allows a steep learning curve and low entry barrier, therefore the plug-in developers can focus on their algorithms, instead of the applied technologies. From the tool's point of view, a plug-in is just a .dll file in the `add-in` folder, in which at least one class implements the `IPDNPlugin` interface (see Fig. 3). Metadata about the plug-in (e.g. name, author, required PetriDotNet version) can be provided using annotations

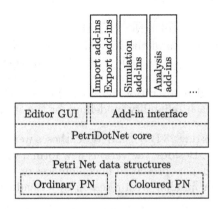

Fig. 2. High-level overview of the PetriDotNet architecture

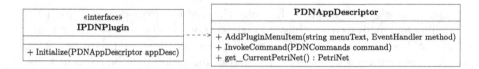

Fig. 3. PetriDotNet plug-ins

of this class (e.g. [AddinAuthor("X. Y.")]). When PetriDotNet starts, it loads all plug-ins and calls their Initialize method. In this method the plug-ins can make their menu contributions and store the application descriptor. This latter allows the plug-ins to call commands (e.g. save, load) and to access the currently active Petri net.

Being a .NET-based tool, PetriDotNet requires that the plug-ins are also implemented in one of the .NET languages. While having a graphical editor for Petri nets developed in .NET is a reasonable choice, implementing e.g. model checking algorithms seems to be uncommon, as managed languages are considered to have some overhead. However, *(i)* according to our experience the run time of the .NET-based implementations of various model checking algorithms proved to be competitive compared to their native version, and *(ii)* the development in .NET is easier and less error-prone than e.g. in C or C++ for computer engineering students, allowing them to make correct implementations in shorter time. Thus the choice of .NET can be regarded as sacrificing some run time performance in favour of development time, which is similarly important in our educational setting. If the performance needs cannot be satisfied using .NET, the plug-in can wrap or depend on a native implementation (.dll).

4   Use Cases

This section overviews the use cases where we applied PetriDotNet as an editor or an analysis tool. According to the original goals we start the overview with educational use cases, then we move on to industrial case studies.

Application in Education. PetriDotNet is used as an educational tool and a tool for the homework assignments in the Formal Methods course of the Budapest University of Technology and Economics since 2011. During this time, approximately 900 M.Sc. students attended the course. The stochastic analysis module of the tool is used for demonstration purposes in the Software and Systems Verification course to teach reliability modelling for the students.

Student Projects. To this day 23 B.Sc. and M.Sc. theses were written that applied or extended PetriDotNet. Besides, the various new formal verification algorithms resulted in 20 scientific papers presented in conferences or journals[5]. Several students who started to get familiar with research by extending and implementing

---

[5] See the complete list of related publications at http://petridotnet.inf.mit.bme.hu/publications/.

an algorithm in PetriDotNet are now Ph.D. students or planning to apply for post-graduate programmes.

Application in Industrial Cases. We are aware of various usages of our tool to model, simulate and analyse different real life systems.

– We have applied PetriDotNet to model and formally verify a safety logic of the Paks Nuclear Power Plant using saturation-based CTL model checking in [1,25]. This work validated the coloured Petri net editing capabilities and proved the efficiency of our CTL model checking algorithms, as [1] presented the first successful formal verification of the complete safety logic.
– PetriDotNet was used to model and simulate sensor nets in [18] and in the FuturICT.hu project[6].
– PetriDotNet was applied to model and study railway interlocking systems [7].
– The R3-COP project[7] applied PetriDotNet to generate test input sequences for testing the robustness of communicating autonomous robots [9].
– Initial case studies were made to apply PetriDotNet to analyse control software used at the European Organization for Nuclear Research (CERN) [8].
– Stochastic analysis and MTFF computation were used in an industrial project at our department to evaluate safety (hazard rate) of an embedded control system. The mean time to reach undetected failures or shutdown was computed in a stochastic model of a two-channel architecture with separate diagnostic facility, comparison, and time-limited degraded (single-channel) functionality.

5   Comparison with Other Tools

During the last decades several Petri net based editor and analysis tools were implemented, some of them are surveyed in [23]. In our comparison (see Table 1) we focused on the freely available, actively maintained, and/or widely used tools. The table characterizes the supported nets, the tool features, and the analysis capabilities. It illustrates that PetriDotNet is a quite versatile tool, offering the features necessary for educational purposes, and also providing sophisticated analysis capabilities [19] that allow to use it as a modelling and analysis tool in research and industrial development projects.

As a highlight, we emphasize the extensibility (plug-ins). The only other tool providing a plug-in interface is Charlie, but Charlie is strictly an analysis tool, whereas PetriDotNet contains the editing, simulation, and analysis functions in a single integrated application. Moreover, the features of the plug-ins in Charlie are more limited, while PetriDotNet plug-ins can extend all of its main functions. Other important features of PetriDotNet are the standard PNML support, the efficient state space representation, the CTL and LTL model checking, and the reward-based stochastic analysis capabilities.

---

[6] http://www.futurict.szte.hu/en/home/.
[7] http://www.r3-cop.eu/.

Table 1. Comparison of Petri net editor and analysis tools

Petri net tool	Place/Transition nets	Extended Petri nets	High-level Petri nets	Petri nets with time	Stochastic Petri nets	Continuous Petri nets	Graphical editor	Extensibility (plug-ins)	State spaces	Condensed state spaces	Token game	Fast Simulation	Net reduction	PNML support	Place/Trans. invariants	Structural analysis	Reachability graph an.	Simple performance an.	Advanced performance an.	Model checking	Free of charge
PetriDotNet	●	●	○	○	●		●	●	●		●	●		●	●	○	○	●	●	●	●
PEP	●	●	●	●			●		●	●	●		●		●	●					●
INA	●	●	●						●	●	●		●		●	●					●
Snoopy	●	●		●	●	●	●				●	●		○							●
Charlie	●	●							●	●			●		●	●	●			●	●
Marcie		●			●				●				●		●			●		●	●
PETRUCHIO	●	●	●	●	●		●		●		●	●			●			●			●
GreatSPN		●	●	●	●				●	●	●	●			●	●		●	●		●
TimeNET		●	●	●	●		●								●	○		●	●		○
CPN Tools		●	●				●		●	●	●	●			○		●	●		●	●

● – full support, ○ – partial support

In our view, having all the features summarized in Table 1 in a single, integrated, and extensible tool is a unique feature. Note that the specific features of our enhanced analysis algorithms (implemented as plug-ins) are detailed and compared to similar solutions in the respective papers (see the references in Sects. 2 and 4).

6   Installation and Usage

The installation and usage of PetriDotNet is extremely simple. After downloading the tool from our website[8], the user has to extract the tool by executing the downloaded file. After this, the tool can be started by running `PetriDotNet.exe`.

During the development, we have paid special attention to keep the main features easy to use. Using the toolbox on the left side of the window it is straightforward to create or modify Petri nets. To use the more advanced features (e.g. analysis modules), we refer the reader to the user manual, accessible on our webpage.

Installing add-ins is similarly straightforward: the files of the add-in have to be placed under the `add-in` folder of the tool. From the next startup of PetriDotNet, the add-ins will be loaded and their menu items will show up in the `Add-in` menu.

PetriDotNet is shipped with a set of analysis and import/export plug-ins. They can be accessed from the `Add-in` menu. The invariant, reachability, CTL and LTL analysis algorithms are aggregated to a common interface that can be accessed by selecting the `Net analysis` item in the `Add-in` menu.

---

[8] http://petridotnet.inf.mit.bme.hu/en/.

A set of example and benchmark models is distributed with the tool, located in the `models` folder.

Acknowledgement. The authors are grateful for all colleagues, former and present students and external users involved in the development, testing or the usage of the tool. Special thanks to Bertalan Szilvási for developing Petri.NET, the initial version of the presented tool.

This paper is partially supported by the MTA-BME Lendület 2015 Research Group on Cyber-Physical Systems and by the ARTEMIS JU and the Hungarian National Research, Development and Innovation Fund in the frame of the R5-COP and R3-COP projects.

References

1. Bartha, T., Vörös, A., Jámbor, A., Darvas, D.: Verification of an industrial safety function using coloured Petri nets and model checking. In: Proceedings of the 14th International Conference on Modern Information Technology in the Innovation Processes of the Industrial Enterprises, pp. 472–485. Hungarian Academy of Sciences (2012)

2. Cayir, S., Ucer, M.: An algorithm to compute a basis of Petri net invariants. In: 4th ELECO International Conference on Electrical and Electronics Engineering. UCTEA, Bursa, Turkey (2005)

3. Ciardo, G., Marmorstein, R., Siminiceanu, R.: The saturation algorithm for symbolic state-space exploration. Int. J. Softw. Tools Technol. Transf. **8**(1), 4–25 (2006)

4. Ciardo, G., Yu, A.J.: Saturation-based symbolic reachability analysis using conjunctive and disjunctive partitioning. In: Borrione, D., Paul, W. (eds.) CHARME 2005. LNCS, vol. 3725, pp. 146–161. Springer, Heidelberg (2005)

5. Ciardo, G., Zhao, Y., Jin, X.: Ten years of saturation: a Petri net perspective. In: Jensen, K., Donatelli, S., Kleijn, J. (eds.) Transactions on Petri Nets and Other Models of Concurrency V. LNCS, vol. 6900, pp. 51–95. Springer, Heidelberg (2012)

6. Clarke, E., Grumberg, O., Jha, S., Lu, Y., Veith, H.: Counterexample-guided abstraction refinement. In: Emerson, E.A., Sistla, A.P. (eds.) CAV 2000. LNCS, vol. 1855, pp. 154–169. Springer, Heidelberg (2000)

7. Cseh, A., Tarnai, G., Sághi, B.: Petri net modelling of signalling systems [in Hungarian, original title: Biztosítóberendezések modellezése Petri-hálókkal]. Vezetékek Világa XIX(1), 14–17 (2014)

8. Darvas, D., Fernández Adiego, B., Blanco Viñuela, E.: Transforming PLC programs into formal models for verification purposes. Internal Note CERN-ACC-NOTE-2013-0040, CERN (2013)

9. Darvas, D., Vörös, A.: Saturation-based test input generation using coloured Petri nets [in Hungarian, original title: Szaturációalapú tesztbemenet-generálás színezett Petri-hálókkal]. In: Mesterpróba 2013, pp. 48–51 (2013)

10. Darvas, D., Vörös, A., Bartha, T.: Improving saturation-based bounded model checking. Acta Cybernetica (2014, accepted, in press). http://petridotnet.inf.mit. bme.hu/publications/AC2014_DarvasEtAl.pdf

11. Duret-Lutz, A., Klai, K., Poitrenaud, D., Thierry-Mieg, Y.: Self-loop aggregation product — a new hybrid approach to on-the-fly LTL model checking. In: Bultan, T., Hsiung, P.-A. (eds.) ATVA 2011. LNCS, vol. 6996, pp. 336–350. Springer, Heidelberg (2011)

12. Hajdu, Á., Vörös, A., Bartha, T.: New search strategies for the Petri net CEGAR approach. In: Devillers, R., Valmari, A. (eds.) PETRI NETS 2015. LNCS, vol. 9115, pp. 309–328. Springer, Heidelberg (2015)

13. Hajdu, Á., Vörös, A., Bartha, T., Mártonka, Z.: Extensions to the CEGAR approach on Petri nets. Acta Cybernetica **21**(3), 401–417 (2014)

14. Heiner, M., Rohr, C., Schwarick, M.: MARCIE – model checking and reachability analysis done efficiently. In: Colom, J.-M., Desel, J. (eds.) PETRI NETS 2013. LNCS, vol. 7927, pp. 389–399. Springer, Heidelberg (2013)

15. ISO/IEC 15909-2 Systems, software engineering - High-level Petri nets - Part 2: Transfer format (2011)

16. Klenik, A., Marussy, K.: Configurable stochastic analysis framework for asynchronous systems. Scientific students' associations report, Budapest University of Technology and Economics (2015). http://petridotnet.inf.mit.bme.hu/publications/TDK2015_KlenikMarussy.pdf

17. Martínez, J., Silva, M.: A simple and fast algorithm to obtain all invariants of a generalised Petri net. In: Girault, C., Reisig, W. (eds.) Application and Theory of Petri Nets, Informatik-Fachberichte, vol. 52, pp. 301–310. Springer, Heidelberg (1982)

18. Milánkovich, A., Ill, G., Lendvai, K., Imre, S., Szabó, S.: Evaluation of energy efficiency of aggregation in WSNs using Petri nets. In: Proceedings of the 3rd International Conference on Sensor Networks, pp. 289–297. Science and Technology Publications (2014)

19. Molnár, V., Darvas, D., Vörös, A., Bartha, T.: Saturation-based incremental LTL model checking with inductive proofs. In: Baier, C., Tinelli, C. (eds.) TACAS 2015. LNCS, vol. 9035, pp. 643–657. Springer, Heidelberg (2015)

20. Molnár, V., Vörös, A., Darvas, D., Bartha, T., Majzik, I.: Component-wise incremental LTL model checking. Formal Aspects of Computing (2016, in press). doi:10.1007/s00165-015-0347-x

21. Murata, T.: Petri nets: properties, analysis and applications. Proc. IEEE **77**(4), 541–580 (1989)

22. Szilvási, B.: Development of an education tool for the Formal methods course [in Hungarian, original title: Oktatási segédeszköz fejlesztése Formális módszerek tárgyhoz]. Master's thesis, Budapest University of Technology and Economics (2008)

23. Thong, W.J., Ameedeen, M.A.: A survey of Petri net tools. ARPN J. Eng. Appl. Sci. **9**(8), 1209–1214 (2014)

24. Vörös, A., Darvas, D., Bartha, T.: Bounded saturation-based CTL model checking. Proc. Est. Acad. Sci. **62**(1), 59–70 (2013)

25. Vörös, A., Darvas, D., Jámbor, A., Bartha, T.: Advanced saturation-based model checking of well-formed coloured Petri nets. Periodica Polytechnica, Electr. Eng. Comput. Sci. **58**(1), 3–13 (2014)

26. Wimmel, H., Wolf, K.: Applying CEGAR to the Petri net state equation. In: Abdulla, P.A., Leino, K.R.M. (eds.) TACAS 2011. LNCS, vol. 6605, pp. 224–238. Springer, Heidelberg (2011)

27. Yu, A.J., Ciardo, G., Lüttgen, G.: Decision-diagram-based techniques for bounded reachability checking of asynchronous systems. Int. J. Softw. Tools Technol. Transf. **11**(2), 117–131 (2009)

28. Zhao, Y., Ciardo, G.: Symbolic CTL model checking of asynchronous systems using constrained saturation. In: Liu, Z., Ravn, A.P. (eds.) ATVA 2009. LNCS, vol. 5799, pp. 368–381. Springer, Heidelberg (2009)

Applications

Transforming CPN Models into Code for TinyOS: A Case Study of the RPL Protocol

Lars Michael Kristensen$^{(\boxtimes)}$ and Vegard Veiset

Department of Computing, Bergen University College, Bergen, Norway
lmkr@hib.no, vegard.veiset@stud.hib.no

Abstract. TinyOS is a widely used platform for the development of networked embedded systems offering a programming model targeting resource constrained devices. We present a semi-automatic software engineering approach where Coloured Petri Net (CPNs) models are used as a starting point for developing protocol software for the TinyOS platform. The approach consists of five refinement steps that allow a developer to gradually transform a platform-independent CPN model into a platform-specific model that enables automatic code generation. To evaluate our approach, we use it to obtain an implementation of the IETF RPL routing protocol for sensor networks.

1 Introduction

Model-driven software engineering [10] and verification have several attractive properties for the development of flexible and reliable software systems. In order to fully leverage modelling investments, it is desirable to use also the constructed models to obtain an implementation. Coloured Petri Nets [3] (and Petri Nets in general) constitute a general purpose modelling language supporting platform-independent modelling of concurrent systems. Hence, in most cases, such models are too abstract to be used directly to implement software. In order to bridge the gap between abstract and platform independent CPN models and the implementation of software to be deployed, the concept of *pragmatics* was introduced in [12]. Pragmatics are syntactical annotations that can be added to a CPN model and used to direct code generation for a specific platform. The contribution of this paper is an approach that exploits pragmatics in combination with a five step refinement methodology to enable code generation for the TinyOS platform.

Applications for TinyOS [7] are implemented using the nesC programming language (a dialect of C) providing an event-based split-phase programming model. An application written in nesC is organised into a wired set of modules each providing an interface consisting of commands and events. The (manual) model refinement starts from a platform independent CPN model constructed typically with the aim of specifying the protocol operation and performing model checking of the protocol design. Each step consists of a transformation that uses

© Springer International Publishing Switzerland 2016
F. Kordon and D. Moldt (Eds.): PETRI NETS 2016, LNCS 9698, pp. 135–154, 2016.
DOI: 10.1007/978-3-319-39086-4_10

the constructs of the CPN modelling language to add details to the model. Furthermore, in each step pragmatics are added that direct the code generation performed after the fifth step. The first step concentrates on the component architecture and consists of annotating CPN submodules and substitution transitions corresponding to TinyOS components, and make explicit the interfaces used and provided by components. The second step is to resolve any interface conflicts allowing components to use multiple instances of an interface. This is done by annotating CPN arcs with information providing locally unique names. The third step consists of adding type signatures to components and interfaces by creating explicit submodules for command and events, and by refining colour sets to reflect the interface signatures. The fourth step further refines the components by classifying them into four main types: timed, external, boot, and generic. The fifth step consists of refining internal component behaviour by modelling the individual commands and events such that control flow and data manipulation become explicit and organised into atomic statement blocks. After the fifth refinement step the CPN model can be used for automated code generation.

To demonstrate the practical applicability of our approach, we have conducted a case study based on the RPL routing protocol [2] developed by the Internet Engineering Task Force (IETF). The RPL protocol allows a set of sensor nodes to construct a destination-oriented directed acyclic graph which can be used for multi-hop communication. To support the automatic code generation for TinyOS, we have developed a software prototype in Java that performs a template-based model-to-text transformation on the models resulting from the fifth refinement step. The code generator performs a top-down traversal of the CPN model where code templates are invoked according to the pragmatic annotations of the CPN model elements encountered.

The rest of this paper is organised as follows. In Sect. 2 we introduce the RPL protocol and the CPN model used as a starting point for refinement. Section 3 briefly introduces the TinyOS platform and the nesC programming model that serve as the target platform for the code generation. Section 4 describes the application of the refinement steps to the RPL CPN model, and Sect. 5 discusses the code generation. Finally, in Sect. 6 we sum up conclusions and discuss related and future work. The reader is assumed to be familiar with CPN modelling concepts. An early report on our work has appeared as a poster [14]. Details omitted from this paper due to space limitations can be found in [13].

2   CPN Model of the RPL Protocol

The RPL protocol (also known as Roll) is an IPv6 routing protocol for low-power and lossy networks such as distributed sensor networks. RPL relies on so-called *Destination-Oriented Directed Acyclic Graphs* (*DODAGs*) for constructing routes connecting the nodes (devices) of the network and uses five different types of IPv6 messages for communication between the devices.

A DODAG typically only has one root node and is organised as a directed graph consisting of children and parent nodes. A child typically only has one parent, while a parent-node can have multiple children. The traffic flow in a DODAG can go in two directions: unicasted upwards in the graph from child to parent (towards the root node), or downwards by being broadcasted to all child nodes.

A DODAG is uniquely identified by the combination of a DODAGID (which is a unique number identifying the DODAG root-node), an *RPLInstanceID* (which is a unique ID identifying the network), and a *DODAGVersionNumber*. The DODAGVersionNumber is the current iteration number of the DODAG. Each node in the DODAG has an associated *rank*. An

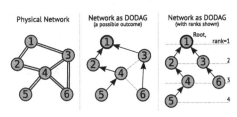

Fig. 1. Network and DODAG example.

objective function is used to determine how the nodes should choose their best parent based on attributes such as rank, DODAGVersionNumber and *DISTANCE*. Figure 1 illustrates how a network topology can be represented as a DODAG. The solid arrows in Fig. 1(middle) shows the route towards the root.

Figure 2 shows how nodes may exchange packets to join and form a DODAG using the physical network in Fig. 1(left), with one root node (root1) and five non-root nodes (nodes 2–6). The root-node (root1) is a preconfigured node and is acting as a sink in the network. Figure 2(left) shows the exchange of network packets, while Fig. 2(right) shows the current DODAG representation of the connected nodes. The nodes will send discovery requests (DIS messages) with their current rank and DODAGVersionNumber in attempt to find a DODAG to join. When a node is part of an RPL instance (has joined a DODAG) it will respond to incoming discovery requests with a discovery response (DIO message). The node will then, based on the incoming responses, pick the most suited parent according to the objective function which is used to calculate the most favourable parent. The objective function will always favour the parent with the highest DODAGVersionNumber and select the one with the lowest rank within that version of the DODAG. If a node gets multiple responses, the node will choose the parent as described by the objective function. The node will evaluate the response regardless of whether it already has a parent or not, and choose the optimal one. This is illustrated in Fig. 2 by node6.

We have constructed a baseline CPN model of RPL based on the IETF specification. The CPN model reflects how nodes in a network obtain configuration parameters (DODAGVersionNumber and rank) from neighbouring nodes and how the nodes choose their parents based on that information. Furthermore, the CPN model captures how nodes discover that their parents have disconnected. This is done by sending destination advertisements (DAO messages) explicitly asking for acknowledgements. The top-level module of the CPN model is shown in Fig. 3(left). The substitution transition Protocol in Fig. 3(left) is representing the RPL protocol logic, while the substitution transition LinkLayer represents the physical network link layer. Figure 3(right) shows the hierarchical organisation

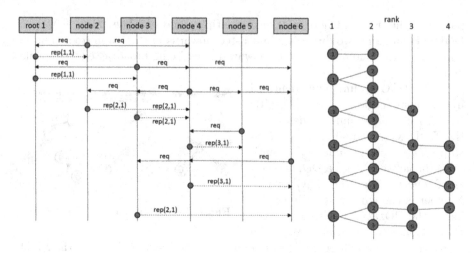

Fig. 2. Example of nodes forming a new instance of a DODAG.

of the eight modules that constitute the CPN RPL model. The top-level module RPLNetwork has two submodules: one for the link layer and one for the protocol logic as shown in Fig. 3(left). The Protocol module contains the behaviour of the routing protocol and has four submodules that specifies the protocol logic for: discovering and joining (DISDIO), sending destination advertisements (DAO), handling acknowledgements (DAOACK), and initial joining and local configuration (StartupandTimeOut). The LinkLayer module represents the link layer and is responsible for transmitting messages between the nodes and for maintaining the current physical topology of the network. Below we discuss selected representative lower-level modules in order to illustrate the abstraction level of the model that is to serve as a starting point for the refinement steps.

The protocol module shown in Fig. 4 is comprised of four substitution transitions for: discovering and joining a DODAG (DISDIO), sending packets containing payload (DAO), acknowledging packets containing payloads (DAOACK),

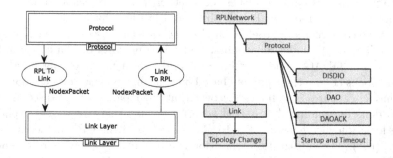

Fig. 3. The top-level module of CPN model (left) and module hierarchy (right).

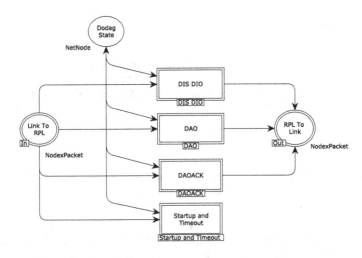

Fig. 4. The Protocol module - submodule of the top-level module in Fig. 3.

and for performing node configuration (StartupandTimeout). The port place Link-ToRPL is used for incoming packets from the link layer, and RPLToLink is used for packets being sent to the link layer, i.e., outgoing packets from the node.

The place DodagState represents the information each node currently has about the DODAG and in which state the node is in. Figure 5 shows the colour sets defined for modelling nodes and the main states of nodes. A node in our model is represented as a NetNode (see below) and has a unique identifier. The NetNode is a product of five colour sets representing: an identification number (Nodes), a rank (Rank), a version number (DodagVerNum), a parent (Nodes) and a state (STATE). The enumeration colour set STATE is used for modelling the main states that the nodes can be in. The CPN model describes three main active states that a node can be in: JOINING when trying to find and connect to an existing DODAG; JOINED when currently connected to a DODAG; and WAITING when connected to a DODAG and waiting for an acknowledgement. The CPN model encompasses two types of nodes: root nodes and non-root nodes. Both non-root nodes and root-nodes will start in a booting-state INITNODE and INITROOT, respectively. A root node will not attempt to discover or rejoin a DODAG as the root node is a preconfigured entity in the network and will be in the state ROOTJOINED until disconnected. Being a root-node allows the node to increase the version number of the DODAG. Non-root nodes will start in the JOINING state and this will enable them to probe the network to find information about the current DODAG, and thus allowing them to join.

The colour set PacketType shown in Fig. 6 is used for modelling the packets exchanged. The colour set represents each of the different types of RPL packets (messages): *DIS*, *DAO* and *DAOACK*, and *DIO*. The DIS packet contains no extra information relevant to the RPL specification and is a constant. DIO and DAOACK packets contain information about the rank and version number of

```
1  colset Nodes      = int with 0..N;
2  colset Rank       = int;                    colset DodagVerNum = int;
3
4  colset STATE = with INITROOT | INITNODE | ROOTJOINED
5                     | JOINED   | JOINING  | WAITING;
6  colset NetNode = product Nodes * Rank * DodagVerNum * Nodes * STATE;
```

Fig. 5. Colour set definitions for modelling nodes and their state.

the sender. The DAO packets (`DAOpack`) in addition to this also contain a `Data` and an option field `Options` (not shown). The option field is used to inform the receiver whether it should respond with a DAOACK or not. The `Packet` colour set contains information about the packet and the destination. The destination can either be a unicast to a single neighbour (`DEST(n)`) or a multicast to all the neighbours (`DEST(ALL)`). The `NodexPacket` is a product of the colour sets `Nodes` and `Packet` and is used to model packets going over the network with the `Nodes` component representing the source of the packet.

```
1  colset PacketType = union DIS + DAO:DAOpack +
2                            DAOACK:DAOACKpack + DIO:DIOpack;
3
4  colset DIOpack    = product Rank * DodagVerNum;
5  colset DAOpack    = product Rank * DodagVerNum * Data * Options;
6  colset DAOACKpack = product Rank * DodagVerNum;
7
8  colset Dest       = union ALL + DEST:Nodes;
9  colset Packet     = product Dest * PacketType;
10 colset NodexPacket = product Nodes * Packet;}
```

Fig. 6. Colour set definitions for modelling the RPL network packets.

The DISDIO module shown in Fig. 7 is the submodule associated with the DISDIO substitution transition in Fig. 4 and contains logic for obtaining information about a DODAG and for joining based on an objective function. The other submodules specifying protocol logic are similar in complexity and abstraction level and we therefore concentrate only on the DISDIO module. A node wanting to join the network (state JOINING) will send a DODAG Information Solicitation (DIS packet) to obtain information about nearby DODAG instances. This is done by probing the neighbouring nodes in the physical network. When a node is part of a DODAG (state JOINED) and receives a DIS packet, the node will reply with a DODAG Information Object (DIO packet). This allows new nodes to discover existing DODAGs in a network, along with obtaining information and configuration parameters of the DODAG. When a node is in the state JOINING the transition SendDISReq will be enabled, and the node will be able to send

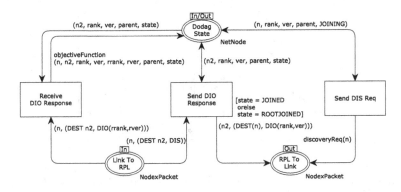

Fig. 7. The DISDIO module

out a DIS request to the network via the place RPLToLink. The packet will then be broadcast on the link layer to all the neighbouring nodes. Incoming packets will arrive on the place LinkToRPL. The SendDIOResponse transition models that when there is an incoming DIS packet, then it will trigger nodes in the state of JOINED or ROOTJOINED to reply with a DIO packet. The node receiving the DIS packet will respond with a DIO(rank,ver) packet containing the node rank and version of a DODAG. When a node receives a DIO response, it will evaluate the response against the information it already has and determine if the incoming DIO contains a better suited parent than the current one based on the objectiveFunction.

3 TinyOS and the nesC Programming Language

TinyOS is a specialised operating system that targets devices with very limited hardware capabilities such as nodes in sensor networks. TinyOS supports a wide range of *wireless sensor network* (WSN) platforms, microprocessors and peripherals. TinyOS is accompanied with a programming language dialect of C named nesC which targets the development of software systems with constraints on processing power and memory usage.

A nesC application for TinyOS consists of a *configuration* file, *components*, and *interfaces*. Interfacing in nesC is a way of structuring the software architecture of an application. The purpose of the configuration file is to *wire* (connect) components using these interfaces. Figure 8 shows the relationship between components in a simplified nesC implementation of RPL for TinyOS that we will use to introduce the basic concepts of our target platform. The squares represent components, and the triangles represent interfaces. A triangle inside of a square is an interface that the component is providing, while a triangle outside of a square represent an interface that the component uses. In this application, we have four components: MainC provides the Boot-interface used by the application as an entry point. The RPLProtocolC component constitutes the main program and the DAOC and DIOC components implement the processing of the

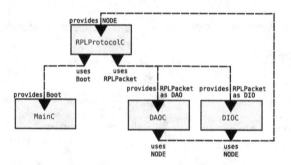

Fig. 8. Software architecture of a partial implementation of RPL for TinyOS.

network packets. Compilation of software for the TinyOS platform relies on the nesC compiler which compiles a collection of nesC files into a single C file. This C file is then compiled to binary code by a C compiler such as GCC.

The DAOC and DIOC components are handling incoming packets. To be able to decide on what to do with the incoming packets, these components need to know which state the node is in which is stored in the RPLProtocolC component. The packet processing components (DIOC/DAOC) use the NODE interface that RPLProtocolC provides to access information about the current state, rank, parent, and DODAGVersionNumber of the node. Figure 9 shows the basic nesC type definitions needed to represent the state of a node in RPL.

```
1  typedef enum {
2      INITNODE = 0, NODE = 1, JOINING = 2, JOINED = 3, WAITING = 4 ..;
3  } State;
4
5  typedef struct {
6      uint8_t id; uint8_t rank; uint8_t dodagN; uint8_t parentId;
7      State state;
8  } NetNode;
```

Fig. 9. Example of nesC datatypes for representing nodes and their state.

Components communicate with split-phase events as the application is compiled to binary code that typically is used by non-blocking hardware platforms. This means that the signal that initialises an event completes immediately. When an invoked function is done processing the request, it sends a callback (signal) to the components implementing the event-handler. This is implemented in nesC using the keywords *signal* and *event*. To invoke a function from another component nesC uses the keyword *call*. To attach an event-listener, the keyword *event* is used, and to trigger an event, the keyword *signal* is used.

A nesC interface describes events that could occur (and that should be handled) and commands that are available for use. The RPLPacket interface in

```
1  interface RPLPacket {
2     command void receive(Packet packet);
3     event void send(Packet packet); }
4
5  interface NODE {
6     command State getState();
7     command void setState(State state); }
```

Fig. 10. Example of nesC interfaces.

Fig. 10 defines a function `void receive(Packet packet)` that takes a packet as an argument and returns nothing (`void`). This function will be implemented in the component providing the interface. The `send` event defined in the interface will be signalled from the component providing the RPLPacket interface. Components using the interface will have to implement the event listener for the `void send(packet packet)` event, while the component using the interface will have access to use the function `RPLPacket.receive(..)` from the component providing the interface. The NODE interface does not use events. The function `getState()` returns a value (*State*) instead of triggering a callback using signal. This can be done safely for functionality that do not require complex or time-consuming operations.

The RPLProtocolC component in Fig. 11 uses two interfaces as shown in Fig. 8: Boot, which is a standard TinyOS interface that will give a callback when the device has booted, and RPLPacket (Line 4–5) which is an interface for sending and receiving packets. The RPLProtocolC component also provides a simple interface (NODE, Line 2) for accessing the state of the node. The keyword *command* defines a function which can have parameters and return a value.

It can be seen that the RPLProtocolC component listens to three events. The first one is the `booted()` event (Line 12) triggered by the Boot interface. This will be triggered when the TinyOS booting process is done. The next two events are callbacks from the components handling DAO and DIO packets. The `DAO.send(Packet packet)` event (Line 16) will be triggered when the DAOC component signals the `send(packet)` event. Similarly, the `DIO.send(Packet packet)` event (Line 17) will be triggered by the DIOC component.

Wiring is the concept used by nesC to connect the components by describing which components the interfaces used are connected to. The *configuration file* in Fig. 12 specifies how the components of the RPL application in Fig. 8 is wired. The RPLProtocolC is using the Boot interface from the MainC component providing callbacks when the booting process is completed (Line 5). The RPLProtocolC component is also using the two components for processing RPL packets: the DAOC and DIOC components (Line 6–7). The DAOC and DIOC components both provide the same interface but are mapped to two different name spaces in the RPLProtocolC component. The line `RPLProtocolC.DAO -> DAOC.RPLPacket` can be read as PRLProtocolC uses the RPLPacket interface

```
1   module RPLProtocolC {
2       provides interface NODE;
3       uses interface Boot;
4       uses interface RPLPacket as DAO;
5       uses interface RPLPacket as DIO; }
6   implementation {
7       NetNode node = {.id=1, .rank=0, .dodagN=0, .parentId=0, INITNODE};
8
9       command State NODE.getState() { return node.state; }
10      command void NODE.setState(State state) { node.state = state; }
11
12      event void Boot.booted() {
13          Packet packet = { .src = 2, .dest = 1, .packet = DAOpack };
14          call DAO.receive(packet);
15      }
16      event void DAO.send(Packet packet) { ... }
17      event void DIO.send(Packet packet) { ... } }
```

Fig. 11. RPLProtocolC component - example of a nesC component implementation.

```
1   configuration RPLProtocolAppC { }
2   implementation {
3       components MainC, RPLProtocolC, DAOC, DIOC;
4
5       RPLProtocolC.Boot -> MainC.Boot;
6       RPLProtocolC.DAO -> DAOC.RPLPacket;
7       RPLProtocolC.DIO -> DIOC.RPLPacket;
8       DAOC.NODE       -> RPLProtocolC.NODE; }
```

Fig. 12. Configuration file for the simplified RPL protocol implementation.

found in the DAOC component with the local identifying name DAO. DAOC uses the NODE interface provided by the RPLProtocolC component (Line 8).

4   CPN Model Refinements

The CPN model presented in Sect. 2 was created without detailed prior knowledge of the TinyOS as a target platform. The motivation for this was to keep the CPN model platform independent in order to give us a stronger indication on the generality of our refinement approach. The refinement approach that we have developed consist of five manual steps and makes it possible to use the resulting refined CPN model to automatically generate the nesC protocol application for TinyOS. The refinements rely on the use of *pragmatics* which are syntactical annotations that are eventually used to direct the code generation. The pragmatics are in our approach used to describe details related to the target platform. The pragmatic annotations can be viewed as a subtyping of CPN model elements and makes the CPN model more expressive in terms of linking elements and structure to the target platform. Aligned with [12], we use `<<type (param1, param2,...)>>` as the concrete syntax for pragmatics. The `type` describes the pragmatics type, and the `param` describes parameters.

The main elements of the refinement steps are introduced below and illustrated on the CPN model of the RPL protocol introduced in Sect. 2.

Step 1: Component Architecture. The first step is to define the architecture of the application by annotating the substitution transitions that represent TinyOS components, and by inscribing the connected CPN arcs with text specifying which TinyOS interfaces they are using or providing. The top-level module of the model was shown in Fig. 4 and is comprised of four substitution transitions with the associated submodules DISDIO, DAO, DAOACK, and StartupandTimeout modelling the protocol logic. The basic idea underlying the first refinement step is that both CPN modules and TinyOS components are encapsulating logic, and for code generation purposes TinyOS components are represented by CPN submodules. This also aligns well with the wiring of components then being represented by the socket places connecting the substitution transitions.

We introduce the `<<component>>` and `<<interface>>` pragmatics to make explicit the relationship between a TinyOS component and a CPN module. We annotate the CPN arcs with text to describe what interfaces each of the components are using and providing. This is done by inscribing arcs connected to the submodules with interface names. Figure 13 shows the result of the first refinement step which affects only the top-level of the CPN model. The substitution transitions are annotated with the `<<component>>` pragmatics, and the arcs connected to the substitution transitions are annotated with which interface they are related to. The arc going from LinkToRPL to DISDIO in Fig. 13 is inscribed with the parameter INetPacket. This is a representation of the interface that would be provided by the generated DISDIO TinyOS component.

Step 2: Resolving Interface Conflicts. The first CPN model refinement allows us to generate the overall structure of the TinyOS application with information about the components and how they are connected. However, if the same interface is used multiple times by a single component there is no way to differentiate between which interface is provided by what component. As an example, the DISDIO and DAO components in Fig. 13 both provide `INetPacket`. The second issue with interfaces after the first refinement step is that a single component cannot use multiple instances of a single interface provided by different components. As an example, the socket place LinkToRPL connecting the top level of the CPN model to the protocol submodule is acting as both an external interface for the CPN network module, and as a local interface for the submodules in the protocol module. Furthermore, the inscription on the arcs does not specify whether the interface is used or provided. The second step of the refinement is to resolve ambiguities in the way interfaces are described.

Figure 14 shows the protocol module after the second step of the refinement. To resolve the ambiguities where socket places was used as multiple interfaces,

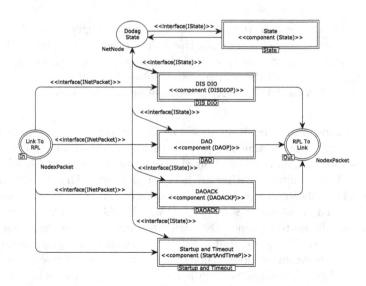

Fig. 13. Protocol annotated with pragmatics for TinyOS interfaces and components

we add an additional transition Dispatch between the incoming socket place and the places going into submodules. This effectively splits the original Link-ToRPL place into two places such that we can differentiate between the externally received packets (tokens added to the LinkToRPL place), and the packets that are processed within the application. In order to allow TinyOS components to use multiple instances of a single interface the as keyword on the arcs allows us to give interfaces local unique names. The parameters provides and uses make explicit which interfaces are being used which are being provided.

Figure 15 illustrates the nesC code that can be generated based on the second refinement step. Line 3 lists the CPN submodules annotated with the <<component>> pragmatic. The TinyOS wiring reflects the use of interface aliases, and the wiring in Line 4–6 connects the interfaces provided by DISDIO, DAO and DAOACK to the Protocol component. Lines 9–11 describes how the Protocol component uses a single interface with three distinct local names, i.e., the interface INetPacket is given a unique alias for each instance. The wiring specifies how the aliases are mapped to other components.

Step 3: Component and Interface Signatures. The second refinement has resolved the ambiguities with providing and using multiple interfaces. The third refinement step introduces types, events and commands to represent the signatures of components and interfaces. The basic idea is to exploit the relationship between CPN places and TinyOS interfaces. CPN places are used for moving tokens between CPN submodules and can be viewed as a representation of TinyOS interfaces. We use the <<interface>> pragmatic to make explicit the relationship between CPN places and TinyOS interfaces. This means that we do not need to make the assumption that all connected places are interfaces,

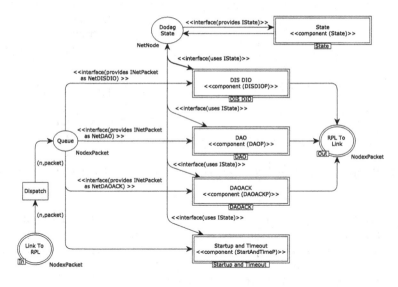

Fig. 14. Protocol module after the second refinement step.

```
 1  configuration RPLprotocolAppC { }
 2  implementation {
 3    components DISDIO, DAO, DAOACK, StartAndTimeout, State, Protocol;
 4      Protocol.DISDIO -> DISDIO.INetPacket;
 5      Protocol.DAO -> DAO.INetPacket;
 6      Protocol.DAOACK -> DAOACK.INetPacket;
 7  }
 8  module ProtocolC {
 9      provides interface INetPacket as NetDISDIO;
10      provides interface INetPacket as NetDAO;
11      provides interface INetPacket as NetDAOACK;
12  }
13  interface interface_NetPacket { ... }
14  interface interface_State { ... }
```

Fig. 15. Sketch of nesC code generated based on the second refinement step.

and the colour set of a CPN place can be used when generating the interface
signature.

The CPN model that served as a starting point made used of a highly compact modelling approach in which a small number of transitions and places is
used for modelling the behaviour. In particular, a transition executes multiple
actions at once via complex expressions on the outgoing arcs. This is illustrated
by the original DISDIO module in Fig. 7 which contains logic for handling both
DIS and DIO packets. The CPN submodule can receive packets from the Link-
ToRPL place and based on the packet type, it will either send a response by
enabling the SendDIOResponse transition or update the node status by enabling

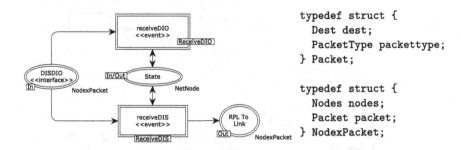

Fig. 16. Refined DISDIO module (left) and nesC data types for the interface (right).

the ReceiveDIOResponse transition. The module could also send DIS (the Send-DISReq transition) requests regardless of it receiving packets or not. In particular, there is no explicit information in the module on the command and events. In the third step we therefore also refine the model to encapsulate the logic for events and commands in individual submodules.

Figure 16(left) shows the DISDIO module after the third refinement step. Each event is represented as a substitution transition annotated with the <<event>> pragmatic. The submodules contains the logic associated with the corresponding event. The arcs describe the relationship to other interfaces, and the places connected to the submodule describe interface signatures. Figure 17 shows the generated code for the interface provided by the DISDIO component which uses the data types for the DISDIO interface shown in Fig. 16(right). The interface contains all the events and commands in a submodule annotated with the <<event>> or <<command>> pragmatics. Line 1 includes the generated header file containing the nesC types translated from the colour set of the CPN model. Line 3 corresponds to the arc between DISDIO and receiveDIO in Fig. 16, and Line 4 to the arc between DISDIO and receiveDIS.

Step 4: Component Classification. The fourth step classifies component types into components that should be executed at **boot** (startup) time, **timed** components representing tasks to be executed at a given interval, **external** components, **dispatch** components that parse network packets, and regular components triggered by event or command invocation. The classification is specified using a parameter on the component pragmatic. Figure 18 shows the refined protocol module with the component classification added. In the refined CPN

```
1  #include "global.h"
2  interface DISDIO {
3      event void receiveDIO(NodexPacket var_nodexpacket);
4      event void receiveDIS(NodexPacket var_nodexpacket); }
```

Fig. 17. Generated nesC interface signature with data types for the DISDIO module.

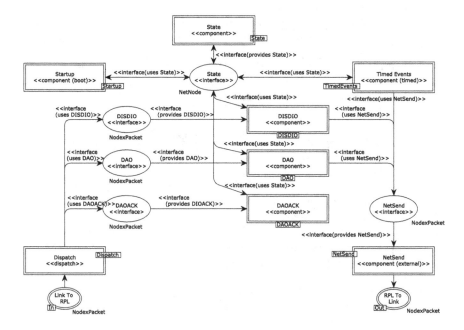

Fig. 18. The protocol module after the fourth refinement step.

model, the Startup component annotated with the boot parameter contains logic for deciding if the node should boot as a root-node or as a regular node. The timed component TimedEvents in the refined CPN model has functionality for periodically sending DIS and DAO packets, for increasing the DODAG version number, and logic for timing out while waiting for DAO acknowledgements. The components annotated with <<component (external)>> are components that will not be generated by the code generator, but which are being provided by existing TinyOS libraries on the platform. The Dispatch component is assigned to be a dispatcher for network packets. The dispatcher is an interface towards the external network, and receives the network packets and signals the correct component based on which type of packet is received.

Step 5: Internal Behaviour. The final step refines the internal behaviour of the individual commands and event handlers of components. We introduce pragmatics to describe the control flow. By having a single token move between places representing control-flow locations, we are able to obtain a clearly identifiable control flow that can be exploited for code generation purposes.

Figure 19 shows the refined receiveDIO event. The ReceiveDIO event module is a refinement of the ReceiveDIO transition in Fig. 16. Using the <<ID>> pragmatic, we obtain a clearly identifiable path of execution. The initial place of the control flow, Idle, is identifiable by having an initial marking (()). The token is moved down through the path of places annotated with the <<ID>> pragmatic. We use the <<invoke>> pragmatic to describe the signature of the event or command,

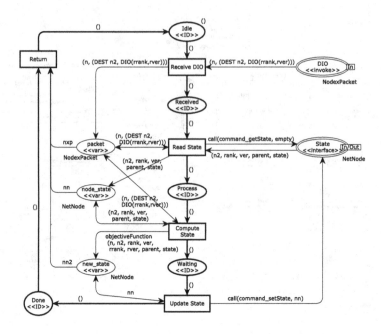

Fig. 19. Refined control-flow oriented modelling of the ReceiveDIO event module.

and the <<var>> pragmatic on places representing local variables accessed by transitions representing the control flow.

5   Code Generation and Initial Validation

We have implemented a nesC code generator that takes a CPN model refined according to the five steps in Sect. 4 as input. The code generator is implemented in Java and uses the Access/CPN framework [15] for parsing the CPN model. We outline the central elements of the code generation below.

Data Types. The colour sets used in the CPN model are mapped into equivalent nesC data types. The atomic data types UNIT, BOOL, INT and STRING colour sets are mapped directly into equivalent nesC data types. Enumeration colour sets are also translated directly. Structured colour sets (product, union, and records) are mapped into nesC structs while lists are mapped into nesC arrays.

Interfaces. The nesC interfaces are generated based on the places annotated with the <<interface>> pragmatic. As an example, the protocol module in Fig. 18 has the interface place DISDIO and an outgoing arc to the DISDIO substitution transition which specifies that it provides this interface. The code generator then uses the command and events specified inside this component (see Fig. 16) to automatically generate the interface signature (see Fig. 17).

```
1   module DISDIOC {
2      provides interface DISDIO;
3      uses interface State;
4      uses interface NetSend; }
5   implementation {
6      event void DISDIO.receiveDIO(NodexPacket var_nodexpacket) { ... }
7      event void DISDIO.receiveDIS(NodexPacket var_nodexpacket) { ... } }
```

Fig. 20. Generated code for the DISDIO component.

Components. Components are generated based on the substitution transitions annotated with the <<component>> pragmatic and the connected arcs which specifies the interfaces that the component uses and provides. As an example, Fig. 20 shows the code generated for the DISDIO component in Fig. 18 which provides the DISDIO interface and uses the State and NetSend interfaces.

Configuration and Wiring. The wiring of component and interfaces is generated based on the substitution transitions annotated with the <<component>> pragmatic and the arcs specifying the interfaces used which are mapped against the component proving the respective interfaces. Figure 21 shows the generated wiring. Line 3 lists the components in the application, and lines 5-12 show how the components are using interfaces, and which components that are providing the used interfaces.

Command and Event Behaviour. The implementation of the event and command behaviour are obtained from the corresponding module (e.g., Fig. 19) where pragmatics are used to separate the control-flow from variable updates and method invocation. The code generation is based on representing the control

```
1   configuration ConfigurationApp {}
2   implementation {
3      components DISDIOC, StartupC, DAOC, DAOACKC, StateC, TimedTasksC,
          NetSendC;
4
5      DISDIOC.State -> StateC.State;
6      DAOC.State -> StateC.State;
7      DAOACKC.State -> StateC.State;
8      TimedTasksC.State -> StateC.State;
9      StartupC.State -> StateC.State;
10     NetSendC.NetSend -> DISDIOC.NetSend;
11     NetSendC.NetSend -> DAO.NetSend;
12     NetSendC.NetSend -> TimedTasks.NetSend; }
```

Fig. 21. Generated configuration file for the wiring of components and interfaces.

flow location as a state machine and the use of code generation templates for method invocation, variable assignment, interface invocation, variable access, and method return. Figure 22 shows part of the generated nesC code for the receiveDIO event (Fig. 19).

```
1   event void DISDIO.receiveDIO(NodexPacket var_nodexpacket) {
2       NetNode new_state;
3       NetNode node_state;
4       NodexPacket packet;
5
6       packet = var_nodexpacket;
7       node_state = call State.getState();
8       new_state = objectiveFunction(...);
9       call State.setState(new_state); }
```

Fig. 22. Part of the code generated for the receiveDIO event.

To perform an initial validation of the implementation produced by the code generation we have used the TOSSIM simulation framework [1]. TOSSIM is a simulator for TinyOS with virtual sensor nodes capable of executing code without having to install the code onto a physical device. The TOSSIM framework supports the construction of simulation scenarios that captures changes in the network topology (via the creation and deletion of network links) and packet loss. TOSSIM also allows us to simulate the booting sequence of nodes running the TinyOS application. After defining the topology, the noise models and the booting sequences, we are able to simulate network nodes in the TOSSIM TinyOS environment. We simulate events in the environment by calling the runNextEvent() method of the TOSSIM environment as shown in Fig. 23.

```
1   tossim.getNode(1).bootAtTime(1800009)
2   tossim.getNode(2).bootAtTime(2000002)
3   tossim.getNode(3).bootAtTime(8008135)
4   for _ in range(60): tossim.runNextEvent()
```

Fig. 23. Simulating the behaviour of nodes in the network.

We validated the generated code by logging the events taking place in the generated code using debug channels. The resulting log files were then inspected and validated against the expected sequence of events for the simulated scenario. Figure 24 shows how we use the dbg(CHAN, msg) method to create debug channels that allow us to log events and behaviour. In Line 3, we add a debug channel called state that will be invoked when the nesC method DODAG.setState(...) is called during simulation.

```
1    event void DODAG.setState(State state) {
2        dbg("state", "%s RPL | State change: %i -> %i.\n",
3            sim_time_string(), node.state, state); }
4
5    event void Booted.booted() {
6        dbg("boot", "%s RPL | Application booted.\n",
7            sim_time_string());
8            DODAG.setState(JOINING); }
```

Fig. 24. Use of event-logging in the protocol component.

As an example, given a scenario where the nesC program boots and a node changes state from 0 (INITNODE) to 2 (JOINING) the event log file would contain the following two lines:

```
DEBUG (0): 0:0:0.0000000300 RPL | Application booted.
DEBUG (0): 0:0:0.0000000300 RPL | State change: 0 -> 2.
```

The DEBUG (0) indicates that the identifier of the node invoking the dbg() method is 0. The information following is the time of invocation (0000000300) and the debug message (RPL | Application booted).

6   Summary and Conclusions

We have suggested an approach based on pragmatics [12] that enables nesC code for the TinyOS platform to be generated from a CPN model of the application design. The approach consists of five manual refinement steps followed by automatic code generation. The main benefit offered by this approach is that it enables verification of the application model prior to code generation, and model construction efforts can be leveraged to obtain an implementation. Our case study of the RPL protocol has demonstrated the feasibility of our approach and included an initial validation of the generated code via event logging.

A detailed comparison between pragmatic-based code generation and other code generation approaches for high-level Petri nets [4–6,8,9] has already been provided in [11]. The original pragmatic-based approach to protocol software generation [12] was based on a platform-independent set of pragmatics that could be used for any target platform. This came at the price of restricting the class of CPN models that can be used for code generation. We found that the class of CPNs considered [12] was not well-suited for the TinyOS programming model and that it would be beneficial to start from more abstract application design models. We have therefore suggested a set of platform-specific pragmatics with five manual refinements steps that can serve as a basis for code generation.

There are two main directions for future work. Our refinement steps are currently only informally specified and one direction of future work is to develop formal meta-models for the intermediate models produced by the refinement steps. Another direction is automatic validation of the generated code. This will involve: (1) verification of the intermediate models in the refinement steps to check that desired behavioural properties are preserved; and (2) model-based test case derivation to overcome the limitations of manual inspection of event-logs as performed in this paper for the initial validation of the implementation.

References

1. Levis, P., et al.: TOSSIM: accurate and scalable simulation of entire TinyOS applications. In: Proceedings of SenSys 2003, pp. 126–137. ACM (2003)
2. Winter, T., et al.: RPL: IPv6 routing protocol for low-power and lossy networks. RFC 6550, 2012. Internet Engineering Task Force (2012)
3. Jensen, K., Kristensen, L.M.: Coloured Petri nets: a graphical language for modelling and validation of concurrent systems. CACM **58**(6), 61–70 (2015)
4. El Kaim, W., Kordon, F.: Code generation (Chap. 21). In: Girault, C., Valk, R. (eds.) Petri Nets for System Engineering, pp. 433–470. Springer, Berlin (2003)
5. Kristensen, L.M., Westergaard, M.: Automatic structure-based code generation from coloured Petri nets: a proof of concept. In: Kowalewski, S., Roveri, M. (eds.) FMICS 2010. LNCS, vol. 6371, pp. 215–230. Springer, Heidelberg (2010)
6. Lassen, K.B., Tjell, S.: Translating colored control flow nets into readable Java via annotated Java workflow nets. In: Proceedings of 8th CPN Workshopp (2007)
7. Levis, P.: TinyOS Programming. Cambridge University Press, Cambridge (2009)
8. Philippi, S.: Automatic code generation from high-level Petri-nets for model driven systems engineering. J. Syst. Softw. **79**(10), 1444–1455 (2006)
9. Reinke, C.: Haskell-coloured Petri nets. In: Koopman, P., Clack, C. (eds.) IFL 1999. LNCS, vol. 1868, pp. 165–180. Springer, Heidelberg (2000)
10. Silva, A.: Model-driven engineering: a survey supported by the unified conceptual model. Comput. Lang. Syst. Utilities **43**, 139–155 (2015)
11. Simonsen, K., Kristensen, L., Kindler, E.: Pragmatics annotated coloured Petri nets for protocol software generation and validation. In: Proceedings of PNSE 2015, CEUR-WS, vol. 1372, pp. 79–98 (2015)
12. Simonsen, K.I.F., Kristensen, L.M., Kindler, E.: Generating protocol software from CPN models annotated with pragmatics. In: Iyoda, J., de Moura, L. (eds.) SBMF 2013. LNCS, vol. 8195, pp. 227–242. Springer, Heidelberg (2013)
13. Veiset, V.: An Approach to Semi-Automatic Code Generation for the TinyOS Platform using CPNs. Master's thesis, Bergen University College (2014). http://home.hib.no/ansatte/lmkr/veisetthesis.pdf
14. Veiset, V., Kristensen, L.M.: Transforming platform independent CPN model into code for the TinyOS platform. In: Proceedings of PNSE 2013, CEUR-WS, vol. 989, pp. 259–260 (2013)
15. Westergaard, M.: Access/CPN 2.0: a high-level interface to coloured Petri net models. In: Kristensen, L.M., Petrucci, L. (eds.) PETRI NETS 2011. LNCS, vol. 6709, pp. 328–337. Springer, Heidelberg (2011)

Realizability of Schedules by Stochastic Time Petri Nets with Blocking Semantics

Loïc Hélouët and Karim Kecir[(⊠)]

INRIA Rennes, Rennes, France
{loic.helouet,karim.kecir}@inria.fr

Abstract. This paper considers realizability of schedules by stochastic concurrent timed systems. Schedules are high level views of desired executions represented as partial orders decorated with timing constraints, while systems are represented as elementary stochastic time Petri nets. We first consider *logical realizability*: a schedule is realizable by a net $\mathcal{N}$ if it embeds in a time process of $\mathcal{N}$ that satisfies all its constraints. However, with continuous time domains, the probability of a time process that realizes a schedule is null. We hence consider *probabilistic realizability* up to α time units, that holds if the probability that $\mathcal{N}$ logically realizes S with constraints enlarged by α is strictly positive. Upon a sensible restriction guaranteeing time progress, logical and probabilistic realizability of a schedule can be checked on the finite set of symbolic prefixes extracted from a bounded unfolding of the net. We give a construction technique for these prefixes and show that they represent all time processes of a net occurring up to a given maximal date. We then show how to verify existence of an embedding and compute the probability of its realization.

1 Introduction

Correct scheduling of basic operations in automated systems (manufacturing or transport systems,...) is a way to manage at best available resources, avoid undesired configurations, or achieve an objective within a bounded delay. Following a predetermined schedule is also a way to meet QoS objectives. For instance, changes to predetermined schedules in metro networks may cause congestion and reduce QoS. Schedules provide high-level views for correct ordering of important operations in a system, consider time issues and provide optimal dates for a production plan. They can be seen as partial orders among basic tasks, decorated with dates and timing constraints, that abstract low-level implementation details.

Designing a correct and optimal schedule for a system is a complex problem. Occurrence dates of events can be seen as variables, and correct and optimal schedules as optimal solutions (w.r.t. some criteria) for a set of constraints over these variables. Linear programming solutions have been proposed to optimize scheduling in train networks [8,9]. The size of models for real systems that run for a full day call for approximated solutions usually provided by experts. When a

© Springer International Publishing Switzerland 2016
F. Kordon and D. Moldt (Eds.): PETRI NETS 2016, LNCS 9698, pp. 155–175, 2016.
DOI: 10.1007/978-3-319-39086-4_11

high-level schedule and the low-level system that implements it are designed in a separate way, nothing guarantees that the system is able to realize the expected schedule. This calls for tools to check realizability of a schedule by a system. One can notice that optimal and realizable schedules are not necessarily robust if they impose tight realization dates to systems that are subject to random variations (delays in productions, faults...). In metro networks, trains delays are expected and are part of the normal behavior of the system. To overcome this problem, metro schedules integrate small recovery margins that avoid the network performance to collapse as soon as a train is late. Note also that for systems where time issues are defined with continuous variables, the probability to execute a given event at a precise date is zero. Furthermore, being able to realize a schedule does not mean that the probability to meet optimal objectives is high enough. Beyond logical realizability, a schedule shall hence be considered as realizable if it can be approached with a significant probability.

This paper addresses realizability of schedules by stochastic timed systems. We define schedules as labeled partial orders decorated with dates and timing constraints, and represent systems with elementary stochastic time Petri nets (STPN for short), a model inspired from [13]. We particularly emphasize on resources: non-availability of a resource (represented by a place) may block transitions. This leads to the definition of a blocking semantics for STPNs that forbids firing a transition if one of its output places is filled. We then propose a notion of realizability: a schedule S is *realizable* by an STPN $\mathcal{N}$ if S embeds in a symbolic process of $\mathcal{N}$ that meets constraints of S. We prove that upon some reasonable time progress assumption, realizability can be checked on a finite set of symbolic processes, obtained from a bounded untimed unfolding [12,16] of $\mathcal{N}$. Symbolic processes are processes of the unfolding with satisfiable constraints on occurrence dates of events. A symbolic framework to unfold time Petri nets was already proposed in [4,6] but blocking semantics brings additional constraints on firing dates of transitions. Embedding of a schedule in a process of $\mathcal{N}$ only guarantees *logical realizability*: the probabilty of a time process in which one event is forced to occur at a precise date is 0. We use transient analysis of STPNs [13] to compute the probability that a schedule is realized by a symbolic time process of $\mathcal{N}$ up to an imprecision of δ. This allows to show that $\mathcal{N}$ realizes $S \pm \delta$ with strictly positive probability, and then define a notion of *probabilistic realizability*.

The paper is organized as follows: Sect. 2 introduces schedules and our variant of stochastic time Petri nets with blocking semantics. Section 3 defines a notion of symbolic processes. Section 4 shows how to verify that a schedule is compatible with at least one process of the system and measure the probability of such realization. Due to lack of space, proofs and several technical details are provided in an extended version available at hal.inria.fr/hal-01284682.

2   Schedules and Stochastic Time Petri Nets

A schedule describes causal dependencies among tasks, and timing constraints on their respective starting dates. Schedules are defined as decorated partial orders. We allow timing constraints among tasks that are not causally related.

Definition 1 (Schedule). *A schedule over a finite alphabet $\mathcal{A}$ is a quadruple $S \triangleq \langle N, \rightarrow, \lambda, C \rangle$ where N is a set of nodes, $\rightarrow \subseteq N \times N$ is an acyclic precedence relation, $\lambda : N \rightarrow \mathcal{A}$ is a labeling of nodes, and $C : N \times N \nrightarrow \mathbb{Q}_{>0}$ is a partial function that associates a time constraint to pairs of nodes. A dating function for a schedule S is a function $d : N \rightarrow \mathbb{Q}_{\geq 0}$ that satisfies all constraints of C and $\rightarrow: \langle n, n' \rangle \in \rightarrow$ implies $d(n') \geq d(n)$, and $C(n, n') = x$ implies $d(n') - d(n) \geq x$.*

This model for schedules is inspired from [8,9]. Intuitively, if $C(n, n') = x$, then n' cannot occur earlier than x time units after n, and if $\langle n, n' \rangle \in \rightarrow$, then n (causally) precedes n'. Constraints model the minimal times needed to perform tasks and initiate the next ones in production cells, the times needed for trains to move from a station to another, etc. A schedule S is *consistent* if the graph $\langle N, \rightarrow \cup \{ \langle n, n' \rangle \mid C(n, n') \text{ is defined} \} \rangle$ does not contain cycles. Obviously, consistent schedules admit at least one dating function. A frequent approach is to associate costs to dating functions and to find optimal functions that meet a schedule. A cost example is the earliest completion date. Optimizing this cost amounts to assigning to each node the earliest possible execution date. However, these optimal schedules are not the most probable ones. For the earliest completion date objective, if an event n occurs later than prescribed by d, then all its successors will also be delayed. In real systems running in an uncertain environment (e.g., with human interactions or influenced by weather conditions), tight timings are impossible to achieve. Finding a good schedule is hence a trade-off between maximization of an objective and of the likelihood to stay close to optimal realizations at runtime.

We want to check whether a consistent schedule S with its dating function d can be realized by a system. Systems are described with a variant of Petri nets with time and probabilities, namely stochastic time Petri nets [13]. We will show how to check that (S, d) is realizable by an STPN $\mathcal{N}$, and then how to measure the probability that (S, d) is realized by $\mathcal{N}$. Roughly speaking, an STPN is a time Petri net with distributions on firing times attached to transitions. As for Petri nets, the semantics of our model moves tokens from the preset of a transition to its postset. The time that must elapse between enabling of a transition and its firing is sampled according to the distribution attached to the transition. The major difference with [13] is that we equip our STPNs with a blocking semantics. Due to blockings, stochastic time Petri nets are *safe* (1-bounded). This semantics restriction is justified by the nature of the systems we address: in production chains, places symbolize tools that can process only one item at a time. Similarly, when modeling train networks, an important security requirement is that two trains cannot occupy the same track portion, which can only be implemented with such a blocking semantics. Standard time or stochastic Petri nets do not assume a priori bounds on their markings. A way to force boundedness is to add complementary places to the original Petri net and then study it under the usual semantics [7]. However, this trick does not allow to preserve time and probability issues in STPNs with blockings.

For simplicity, we only consider closed intervals of the form $[a, b]$ with $a < b$ and open intervals of the form $[a, +\infty)$. A *probability density function* (PDF) for a continuous random variable X is a function $f_X : \mathbb{R} \to [0,1]$ that describes the relative likelihood for X to take a given value. Its integral over the domain of X is equal to 1. A *cumulative distribution function* (CDF) $F_X : \mathbb{R} \to [0,1]$ for X describes the probability for X to take a value less than or equal to a chosen value. We denote by Σ_{pdf} the set of PDFs, Σ_{cdf} the set of CDFs, and we only consider PDFs for variables representing durations, i.e., whose domains are included in $\mathbb{R}_{\geq 0}$. The CDF of X can be computed from its PDF as $F_X(x) = \int_0^x f_X(y)\, dy$. A *marking* is a function that assigns 0 or 1 token to each place $p \in P$.

Definition 2 (Stochastic Time Petri Net). *A stochastic time Petri net (STPN for short) is a tuple* $\mathcal{N} = \langle P, T, {}^{\bullet}(), ()^{\bullet}, m_0, \mathsf{eft}, \mathsf{lft}, \mathcal{F}, \mathcal{W} \rangle$ *where P is a finite set of places; T is a finite set of transitions; ${}^{\bullet}() : T \to 2^P$ and $()^{\bullet} : T \to 2^P$ are pre and post conditions depicting from which places transitions consume tokens, and to which places they output produced tokens; $m_0 : P \to \{0,1\}$ is the initial marking of the net; $\mathsf{eft} : T \to \mathbb{Q}_{\geq 0}$ and $\mathsf{lft} : T \to \mathbb{Q}_{\geq 0} \cup \{+\infty\}$ respectively specify the minimum and maximum time-to-fire that can be sampled for each transition; and $\mathcal{F} : T \to \Sigma_{pdf}$ and $\mathcal{W} : T \to \mathbb{R}_{>0}$ respectively associate a PDF and a strictly positive weight to each transition.*

For a given place or transition $x \in P \cup T$, ${}^{\bullet}x$ will be called the preset of x, and $x^{\bullet}$ the postset of x. We denote by f_t the PDF $\mathcal{F}(t)$, and by F_t the associated CDF. To be consistent, we assume that for every $t \in T$, the support of f_t is $[\mathsf{eft}(t), \mathsf{lft}(t)]$. This syntax of STPNs is similar to [13], but we equip them with a blocking semantics, defining sequences of discrete transition firings, and timed moves. We will say that a transition t is *enabled* by a marking m iff $\forall p \in {}^{\bullet}t, m(p) = 1$. We denote by $\mathsf{enab}(m)$ the set of transitions enabled by a marking m.

For a given marking m and a set of places P', we will denote by $m - P'$ the marking that assigns $m(p)$ tokens to each place $p \in P \backslash P'$, and $m(p) - 1$ tokens to each place $p \in P'$. Similarly, we will denote by $m + P'$ the marking that assigns $m(p)$ tokens to each place $p \in P \setminus P'$, and $m(p) + 1$ tokens to each place $p \in P'$. Firing a transition t is done in two steps and consists in: (1) consuming tokens from ${}^{\bullet}t$, leading to a *temporary* marking $m_{tmp} = m - {}^{\bullet}t$, then (2) producing tokens in $t^{\bullet}$, leading to a marking $m' = m_{tmp} + t^{\bullet}$.

The blocking semantics can be informally described as follows. A variable τ_t is attached to each transition t of the STPN. As soon as the preset of a transition t is marked, τ_t is set to a random value ζ_t (called the *time-to-fire* of t, or TTF for short) sampled from $[\mathsf{eft}(t), \mathsf{lft}(t)]$ according to f_t. We will assume that every CDF F_t is strictly increasing on $[\mathsf{eft}(t), \mathsf{lft}(t)]$, which allows to use *inverse transform sampling* to choose a value (see for instance [17] for details). Intuitively, this TTF represents a duration that *must* elapse before firing t once t is enabled. The value of τ_t then decreases as time elapses but cannot reach negative values. When the TTF of a transition t reaches 0, then if $t^{\bullet}$ is empty in m_{tmp}, t becomes *urgent* and has to fire unless another transition with TTF 0 and empty postset fires; otherwise (if $t^{\bullet}$ is not empty in m_{tmp}), t becomes *blocked*: its

TTF stops decreasing and keeps value 0, and its firing is delayed until the postset of t becomes empty; in the meantime, t can be disabled by the firing of another transition. The semantics of STPNs is *urgent*: time can elapse by durations that do not exceed the minimal remaining TTF of enabled transitions that are not blocked. If more than one transition is urgent, then the transition that fires is randomly chosen according to the respective weights of urgent transitions. We formalize the semantics of STPNs in terms of discrete and timed moves between *configurations* that memorize markings and TTFs for enabled transitions.

Definition 3 (Configuration of an STPN). *A configuration of an STPN is a pair $\mathcal{C}_N \triangleq \langle m, \tau \rangle$ where m is a marking, and $\tau : \mathsf{enab}(m) \to \mathbb{R}_{\geq 0}$ is a function that assigns a positive real TTF $\tau_i \triangleq \tau(t_i)$ to each transition t_i enabled by m. A transition t is* enabled *in a configuration $\langle m, \tau \rangle$ iff it is enabled by m.*

Definition 4 (Firable and Blocked Transitions). *A transition t is* firable *in $\langle m, \tau \rangle$ iff it is enabled by m, all places of its postset are empty in $m - {}^\bullet t$, and its TTF is equal to 0. We denote by $\mathsf{fira}(\langle m, \tau \rangle)$ the set of firable transitions of $\langle m, \tau \rangle$. A transition t is* blocked *in $\langle m, \tau \rangle$ iff it is enabled by m, its TTF $\tau(t)$ is equal to 0, and one of its postset places is marked in $m - {}^\bullet t$. We denote by $\mathsf{blck}(\langle m, \tau \rangle)$ the set of blocked transitions in $\langle m, \tau \rangle$.*

Timed Moves: A *timed move* $\langle m, \tau \rangle \xrightarrow{\delta} \langle m, \tau' \rangle$ lets a strictly positive duration δ elapse. To be allowed, δ must be smaller or equal to all TTFs of transitions enabled by m and not yet blocked. The new configuration $\langle m, \tau' \rangle$ decreases TTFs of every enabled and non-blocked transition t by δ time units $(\tau'(t) = \tau(t) - \delta)$. Blocked transitions keep a TTF of 0, and m remains unchanged.

Discrete Moves: A *discrete move* $\langle m, \tau \rangle \xrightarrow{t} \langle m', \tau' \rangle$ consists in firing a transition t from a configuration $\langle m, \tau \rangle$ to reach a configuration $\langle m', \tau' \rangle$. Discrete moves change the marking of a configuration, and sample new times to fire for transitions that become enabled after the move. To define the semantics of discrete moves, we first introduce newly enabled transitions.

Definition 5 (Newly Enabled Transitions). *Let m be a marking and t a transition enabled by m. A transition t' is* newly enabled *after firing of t from m iff it is enabled by marking $m' = (m - {}^\bullet t) + t^\bullet$ and either it is not enabled by $m - {}^\bullet t$ or $t' = t$. We denote by $\mathsf{newl}(m, t) \triangleq \mathsf{enab}(m') \cap (\{t\} \cup (T \setminus \mathsf{enab}(m - {}^\bullet t)))$ the set of transitions newly enabled by firing of t from m.*

The transition t fired during a discrete move is chosen among all firable transitions of $\langle m, \tau \rangle$. The new marking reached is $m' = (m - {}^\bullet t) + t^\bullet$, and τ' is obtained by sampling a new TTF for every newly enabled transition and keeping unchanged TTFs of transitions already enabled by m and still enabled by m'.

Complete operational rules for STPN moves can be found in the extended version. We will write $\langle m, \tau \rangle \to \langle m', \tau' \rangle$ iff there exists a timed or discrete move from $\langle m, \tau \rangle$ to $\langle m', \tau' \rangle$, and $\langle m, \tau \rangle \xrightarrow{*} \langle m', \tau' \rangle$ iff there exists a sequence of moves leading from $\langle m, \tau \rangle$ to $\langle m', \tau' \rangle$. An initial configuration for $\mathcal{N}$ is a configuration $\langle m_0, \tau_0 \rangle$ where τ_0 attaches a sampled TTF to each transition enabled by m_0.

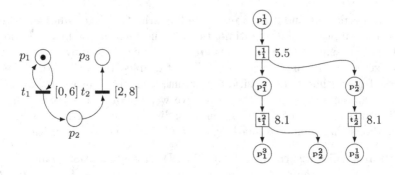

Fig. 1. (a) An example STPN $\mathcal{N}_1$ and (b) a time process of $\mathcal{N}_1$

Consider the STPN $\mathcal{N}_1$ of Fig. 1, and suppose that $\mathcal{N}_1$ is in configuration $\langle m, \tau \rangle$, with $m(p_1) = 1$, $m(p_2) = m(p_3) = 0$, $\tau(t_1) = 5.5$. From this configuration, one can let 5.5 time units elapse, and then fire t_1. After this firing, the STPN reaches marking m' with $m'(p_1) = m'(p_2) = 1$, $m'(p_3) = 0$. New TTFs d_1, d_2 are sampled for t_1, t_2, leading to a configuration $\langle m', \tau' \rangle$, where $\tau'(t_1) = d_1$ and $\tau'(t_2) = d_2$. Let us suppose that $d_1 = 1.5$ and $d_2 = 2.6$. Then one can let 1.5 time units elapse, but after this timed move, transition t_1 cannot fire, as place p_2 contains a token. $\mathcal{N}_1$ is hence in a configuration $\langle m', \tau'' \rangle$, where $\tau''(t_1) = 0$, $\tau''(t_2) = 1.1$, and t_1 is blocked. After letting 1.1 time units elapse, transition t_2 can fire, leading to marking $m''(p_1) = m''(p_3) = 1, m''(p_2) = 0$, and t_1 immediately fires at the same date.

Let us now assign probabilities to STPN moves. Randomness in STPNs semantics mainly comes from sampling of TTFs. However, when several transitions are firable from a configuration, weights are used to determine the probability for a transition to fire first. Timed moves are achieved with probability 1: once TTFs are set, there is a unique configuration allowing discrete moves. In a move $\langle m, \tau \rangle \xrightarrow{t} \langle m', \tau' \rangle$, m' is built deterministically, but τ' is obtained by sampling a random value ζ_t for each newly enabled transition t. Each ζ_t is chosen according to CDF F_t, i.e., we have $\mathbb{P}(\zeta_t \leq x) = F_t(x)$ (for any $x \in [\text{eft}(t), \text{lft}(t)]$). When more than one transition is firable from $\langle m, \tau \rangle$, the transition that fires is randomly chosen, and each transition t_k in $\text{fira}(\langle m, \tau \rangle)$ has a probability to fire $\mathbb{P}_{\text{fire}}(t_k) = \mathcal{W}(t_k) / \sum_{t_i \in \text{fira}(\langle m, \tau \rangle)} \mathcal{W}(t_i)$. Note that, as STPNs have continuous probability laws, the probability to choose a particular value ζ_t is the probability of a point in a continuous domain and is hence null. However, in the next sections, we will consider probabilities for events of the form $\tau(t_i) \leq \tau(t_j)$, which may have strictly positive probability.

STPNs define sequences of moves $\rho = (\langle m, \tau \rangle \xrightarrow{e_i} \langle m', \tau' \rangle)_{i \in 1...k}$, where e_i is a transition name in discrete moves and a real value in timed moves. Leaving probabilities for the moment, STPNs can also be seen as generators for timed words over T. A *timed word* over an alphabet $\mathcal{A}$ is a sequence $\langle a_1, d_1 \rangle \ldots \langle a_q, d_q \rangle \ldots$ in $(\mathcal{A} \times \mathbb{R}_{\geq 0})^*$, where each a_i is a letter from $\mathcal{A}$, each d_i defines the occurrence date of a_i, and $d_1, \ldots, d_q$ is an increasing sequence of positive real numbers.

Letting $i_1, \ldots, i_q$ denote the indices of discrete moves in ρ, we can build a timed word $u_\rho = \langle a_{i_1}, d_1 \rangle \ldots \langle a_{i_q}, d_q \rangle \in (T \times \mathbb{R}_{\geq 0})^q$ that associates dates to transitions firings, where $d_1 = \sum_{j < i_1} e_j$, and $d_j = d_{j-1} + \sum_{i_{j-1} < k < i_j} e_k$ for $j \in \{2, \ldots, q\}$. The *timed language* of an STPN $\mathcal{N}$ is the set $\mathcal{L}(\mathcal{N})$ of timed words associated with its sequences of moves. We denote by $\mathcal{L}_{\leq D}(\mathcal{N})$ the set of words in $\mathcal{L}(\mathcal{N})$ whose maximal date is lower than D.

As already highlighted in [2] for TPNs, timed languages give a sequential and interleaved view for executions of inherently concurrent models. A non-interleaved semantics can be defined using *time processes*, i.e., causal nets equipped with dating functions. We recall that *causal nets* are finite acyclic nets of the form $CN \triangleq \langle B, E, {}^\bullet(), ()^\bullet \rangle$, where for every $b \in B$, $|b^\bullet| \leq 1$ and $|{}^\bullet b| \leq 1$. Intuitively, a causal net contains no conflict (pairs of transition with common places in their presets) nor place receiving tokens from more than one transition.

Definition 6 (Time Process). *A time process is a tuple $TP \triangleq \langle CN, \theta \rangle$, where $CN \triangleq \langle B, E, {}^\bullet(), ()^\bullet \rangle$ is a causal net, and $\theta : E \to \mathbb{R}_{\geq 0}$ associates a positive real date to transitions of the net, and is such that $\forall e, e' \in E$ with $e^\bullet \cap {}^\bullet e' \neq \emptyset$ we have $\theta(e) \leq \theta(e')$. In time processes, places in B are called* conditions, *and transitions in E are called* events. *The* depth *of a time process is the maximal number of events along a path of the graph $\langle B \cup E, {}^\bullet() \cup ()^\bullet \rangle$. We will write $e \prec e'$ iff $e^\bullet \cap {}^\bullet e' \neq \varnothing$, and denote by $\preceq$ the transitive and reflexive closure of $\prec$.*

Intuitively, conditions in B represent occurrences of places fillings, and events in E are occurrences of transitions firings. Given an STPN $\mathcal{N}$, for every timed word $u = \langle a_1, d_1 \rangle \ldots \langle a_n, d_n \rangle$ in $\mathcal{L}(\mathcal{N})$, we can compute a time process $TP_u = \langle B, E, {}^\bullet(), ()^\bullet, \theta \rangle$. The construction described below is the same as in [2]. It does not consider probabilities and, as the construction starts from an executable word, it does not have to handle blockings either. To differentiate occurrences of transitions firings, an event will be defined as a pair $e \triangleq \langle X, t \rangle$, where t is the transition whose firing is represented e and X is the set of conditions it consumes. Similarly, a condition is defined as a pair $b \triangleq \langle p, e \rangle$, where p is the place whose filling is represented by b, and e is the event whose occurrence created b.

We denote by $\mathsf{tr}(e)$ the transition t attached to an event e, and by $\mathsf{pl}(b)$ the place p associated with a condition b. The flow relations are hence implicit: ${}^\bullet e = \{b \mid e = \langle X, t \rangle \wedge b \in X\}$, and similarly $e^\bullet = \{b \mid b = \langle p, e \rangle\}$, and for $b = \langle p, e \rangle$, ${}^\bullet b = e$ and $b^\bullet = \{e \in E \mid b \in {}^\bullet e\}$. We will then drop flow relations and simply refer to time processes as triples $TP \triangleq \langle B, E, \theta \rangle$. The time process TP_u obtained from a timed word $u = \langle t_1, d_1 \rangle \langle t_2, d_2 \rangle \ldots \langle t_k, d_k \rangle \in \mathcal{L}(\mathcal{N})$ is built inductively as follows. We assume a dummy initial event $\perp$ that initializes the initial contents of places according to m_0. We start from the initial process $TP_0 = \langle B_0, E_0, \theta_0 \rangle$ with a set of conditions $B_0 = \{(p, \perp) \mid p \in m_0\}$, a set of events $E_0 = \{\perp\}$, and a function $\theta_0 : \{\perp\} \to \{0\}$.

Let $TP_{u,i} = \langle B_i, E_i, \theta_i \rangle$ be the time process built after i steps for the prefix $\langle t_1, d_1 \rangle \ldots \langle t_i, d_i \rangle$ of u, and let $\langle t, d_{i+1} \rangle$ be the $(i + 1)^{th}$ entry of u. We denote by $\mathsf{last}(p, E_i, B_i)$ the last occurrence of place p in $TP_{u,i}$, i.e., the only condition $b = \langle p, e \rangle$ with an empty postset. Then, we have $E_{i+1} = E_i \cup \{e\}$, where $e = \langle t, X \rangle$

with $X = \{b \mid b = \mathsf{last}(p, E_i, B_i) \wedge p \in {}^\bullet t\}$ and $B_{i+1} = B_i \cup \{\langle p, e\rangle \mid p \in t^\bullet\}$. We also set $\theta(e) = d_{i+1}$. The construction ends with $TP_u = TP_{u,|u|}$.

Figure 1(b) is an example of a time process for STPN $\mathcal{N}_1$. In this example, event t_i^j (resp. condition p_i^j) denotes the jth occurrence of transition t_i (resp. place p_i). This time process corresponds to the time word $u = \langle t_1, 5.5\rangle\langle t_2, 8.1\rangle\langle t_1, 8.1\rangle \in \mathcal{L}(\mathcal{N}_1)$. It contains causal dependencies among transitions (e.g., from t_1^1 to t_2^1). Event t_1^2 cannot occur before t_2^1 as t_1 cannot fire as long as place p_2 is filled. However, this information is not explicit in the process. The timed language $\mathcal{L}(\mathcal{N})$ of a TPN can be reconstructed as the set of linearizations of its time processes. In these linearizations, ordering of events considers both causality and dates of events: e must precede $e' \neq e$ in a linearization of a process if $\theta(e) < \theta(e')$ or if $e \preceq e'$. With blocking semantics, some causality and time-preserving interleavings may not be valid timed words of $\mathcal{L}(\mathcal{N})$: in the process of Fig. 1(b), t_1^2 cannot occur before t_2^1, even if both transitions have the same date. A correct ordering among events with identical dates in a process TP_u can however be found by checking that a chosen ordering does not prevent occurrence of other transitions.

3   Unfolding of STPNs

A time process emphasizes concurrency but only gives a partial order view of a *single* timed word. Many time processes of $\mathcal{N}_1$ have the same structure as the process of Fig. 1(b), but different dating functions. Indeed, there can be uncountably many time processes with identical structure, but different real dates. It is hence interesting to consider symbolic (time) processes, that define constraints on events dates instead of exact dates. Similarly, to avoid recomputing the structural part of each symbolic process, we will work with *unfoldings*, i.e., structures that contain all symbolic processes of an STPN, but factorize common prefixes. Symbolic unfoldings were introduced for TPNs in [18] and used in [5]. In this section, we show how to unfold STPNs with blockings and extract symbolic processes out of this unfolding. Our aim is to find the minimal structure that represents prefixes of all symbolic processes that embed a schedule of known duration. We show that if a system cannot execute arbitrary large sets of events without progressing time, unfolding up to some bounded depth is sufficient.

Definition 7 (Time Progress). *An STPN $\mathcal{N}$ guarantees time progress iff there exists $\delta \in \mathbb{Q}_{>0}$ such that $\forall t \in T, i \in \mathbb{N}$, and for every time word $u = \langle t_1, d_1\rangle \ldots \langle t^i, \theta_1\rangle \ldots \langle t^{i+1}, \theta_2\rangle \ldots \langle t_k, d_k\rangle \in \mathcal{L}(\mathcal{N})$ where t^i denotes the ith occurrence of t, we have $\theta_2 - \theta_1 \geq \delta$.*

Time progress is close to non-Zenoness property, and is easily met (e.g., if no transition has an earliest firing time of 0). Any execution of duration Δ of an STPN that guarantees time progress is a sequence of at most $|T| \cdot \lceil \frac{\Delta}{\delta} \rceil$ transitions.

As in processes, unfoldings will contain occurrences of transitions firings (a set of events E), and occurrences of places fillings (a set of conditions B). We associate to each event $e \in E$ positive real valued variables $\mathsf{doe}(e)$, $\mathsf{dof}(e)$ and

$\theta(e)$ that respectively define the enabling, firability and effective firing date of the occurrence of transition $\mathsf{tr}(e)$ represented by event e. Similarly, we associate to each condition b positive real valued variables $\mathsf{dob}(b)$ and $\mathsf{dod}(b)$ that respectively represent the date of birth of the token in place $\mathsf{pl}(b)$, and the date at which the token in place $\mathsf{pl}(b)$ is consumed. We denote by $\mathsf{var}(E, B)$ the set of variables $\bigcup_{e \in E} \mathsf{doe}(e) \cup \mathsf{dof}(e) \cup \theta(e) \cup \bigcup_{b \in B} \mathsf{dob}(b) \cup \mathsf{dod}(b)$ (with values in $\mathbb{R}_{\geq 0}$). A *constraint* over $\mathsf{var}(E, B)$ is a boolean combination of atoms of the form $x \bowtie y$, where $x \in \mathsf{var}(E, B)$, $\bowtie \in \{<, >, \leq, \geq\}$ and y is either a variable from $\mathsf{var}(E, B)$ or a constant value. A set of constraints C over a set of variables V is *satisfiable* iff there exists at least one valuation $v : V \to \mathbb{R}$ such that replacing each occurrence of each variable x by its valuation $v(x)$ yields a tautology. We denote by $\mathrm{SOL}(C)$ the set of valuations that satisfy C.

Definition 8 (Unfolding). *A (structural) unfolding of an STPN $\mathcal{N}$ is a pair $\mathcal{U} \triangleq \langle E, B \rangle$ where E is a set of events and B a set of conditions.*

Unfoldings can be seen as processes with branching. As for processes, each event $e \in E$ is a pair $e = \langle {}^\bullet e, \mathsf{tr}(e) \rangle$ where ${}^\bullet e \subseteq B$ is the set of predecessor conditions of e (the conditions needed for e to occur). A condition $b \in B$ is a pair $b \triangleq \langle {}^\bullet b, \mathsf{pl}(b) \rangle$ where ${}^\bullet b \subseteq E$ is the predecessor of b, i.e., the event that created condition b. We assume a dummy event $\bot$ that represents the origin of the initial conditions in an unfolding. Function ${}^\bullet()$, $()^\bullet$, $\mathsf{pl}()$ and $\mathsf{tr}()$ keep the same meaning as for time processes. The main change between processes and unfoldings is that conditions may have several successor events. Using relations $\prec$ and $\preceq$ as defined for processes, we define the *causal past* of $e \in E$ as $\uparrow e \triangleq \{e' \in E \mid e' \preceq e\}$. A set of events $E' \subseteq E$ is *causally closed* iff $\forall e \in E', \uparrow e \subseteq E'$. We extend this notion to conditions. Two events e, e' are in *conflict*, and write $e \sharp e'$, iff ${}^\bullet e \cap {}^\bullet e' \neq \varnothing$. A set of events $E' \subseteq E$ is *conflict free* if it does not contain conflicting pairs of events. Two events e, e' are *competing* iff $\mathsf{tr}(e)^\bullet \cap \mathsf{tr}(e')^\bullet \neq \varnothing$ (they fill a common place).

Definition 9 (Pre-processes of an Unfolding). *A pre-process of a finite unfolding $\mathcal{U} = \langle E, B \rangle$ is a pair $\langle E', B' \rangle$ such that $E' \subseteq E$ is a maximal (i.e., there is no larger pre-process containing E', B'), causally closed and conflict free set of events, and $B' = {}^\bullet E' \cup E'^\bullet$. $\mathcal{PE}(\mathcal{U})$ denotes the set of pre-processes of $\mathcal{U}$.*

We say that a condition $b \in B$ is *maximal* in $\mathcal{U} = \langle E, B \rangle$ or in a pre-process of $\mathcal{U}$ when it has no successor event ($b^\bullet = \varnothing$), and denote the set of maximal conditions of B by $\mathsf{max}(B)$. As for time processes construction, given a finite pre-process $\langle E', B' \rangle \in \mathcal{PE}(\mathcal{U})$, and a place p of the considered STPN, we denote by $\mathsf{last}(p, E', B')$ the maximal occurrences of place p w.r.t. $\prec$ in $\langle E', B' \rangle$. A *cut* of a pre-process is an unordered set of conditions. We denote by $Cuts(E, B)$ the set of cuts of pre-process $\langle E, B \rangle$.

Unfolding an STPN up to depth K is performed inductively, without considering time. We will then use this structure to find processes. Timing issues will be considered through addition of constraints on occurrence dates of events.

Structural Unfolding: Following [12], we inductively build unfoldings $\mathcal{U}_0, \ldots, \mathcal{U}_K$. Each step k adds new events at depth k and their postset to the preceding unfolding $\mathcal{U}_{k-1}$. We start with the initial unfolding $\mathcal{U}_0 \triangleq \langle \varnothing, B_0 \rangle$ where $B_0 = \{ \langle \bot, p \rangle \mid p \in m_0 \}$. Each induction step that builds $\mathcal{U}_{k+1}$ from $\mathcal{U}_k$ adds new events and conditions to $\mathcal{U}_k$ as follows. Letting $\mathcal{U}_k = \langle E_k, B_k \rangle$ be the unfolding obtained at step k, we have $\mathcal{U}_{k+1} = \langle E_k \cup \hat{E}, B_k \cup \hat{B} \rangle$ where $\hat{E} \triangleq \{ \langle B, t \rangle \in (2^{B_k} \times T) \setminus E_k \mid \exists \langle X, Y \rangle \in \mathcal{PE}(\mathcal{U}_k), B \subseteq Cuts(X, Y), {}^\bullet t = \mathsf{pl}(B) \}$, and $\hat{B} \triangleq \{ \langle e, p \rangle \in \hat{E} \times T \mid e = \langle B, t \rangle \in \hat{E} \wedge p \in t^\bullet \}$. Intuitively, $\hat{E}$ adds an occurrence of a transition if its preset is contained in the set of conditions representing the last occurrences of places contained in some pre-process of $\mathcal{U}_k$, and $\hat{B}$ adds the conditions produced by $\hat{E}$.

The structural unfolding of an STPN does not consider timing issues nor blockings. Hence, an (untimed) pre-process of $\mathcal{PE}(\mathcal{U}_K)$ need not be the untimed version of a time process obtained from a word in $\mathcal{L}(\mathcal{N})$. Indeed, urgent transitions can forbid firing of other conflicting transitions. Similarly, blockings prevent an event from occurring as long as a condition in its postset is filled. They may even prevent events in a pre-process from being executed if a needed place is never freed. We will show later that, once constrained, time processes of $\mathcal{N}$ are only prefixes of pre-processes in $\mathcal{PE}(\mathcal{U}_K)$ with associated timing function. To introduce timing aspects, we now attach constraints on events and conditions of pre-processes as follows:

Constraints: Let $\mathcal{U}_K = \langle E_K, B_K \rangle$ be the unfolding of an STPN $\mathcal{N}$ up to depth K, and let $E \subseteq E_K$ be a conflict free and causally closed set of events, and $B = {}^\bullet E \cup E^\bullet$ (B is contained in B_K). We define $\Phi_{E,B}$ as the set of constraints attached to events and conditions in E, B, assuming that executions of $\mathcal{N}$ start at a fixed date d_0. Constraints must be set to guarantee that occurrence dates of events are compatible with the earliest and latest firing times of transitions in $\mathcal{N}$, and that urgency or blocking is never violated. Let us first define the constraints associated with each condition $b = \langle e, p \rangle$. Recalling that variable $\mathsf{dob}(b)$ represents the date at which condition b is created, $\Phi_{E,B}$ must impose that for every $b \in B_0$, $\mathsf{dob}(b) = d_0$.

For all other conditions $b = \langle e, p \rangle$, as the date of birth is exactly the occurrence date of e, we set $\mathsf{dob}(b) = \theta(e)$ for every $b = \langle e, p \rangle$. Despite this equality, we will use both variables $\theta(e)$ and $\mathsf{dob}(b)$ for readability reasons. Recall that $\mathsf{dod}(b)$ is a variable that designates the date at which a place is emptied by some transition firing, $\mathsf{dod}(b)$ is hence the occurrence date of an event that has b as predecessor. Within a conflict free set of events, this event is unique. In the considered subset of conditions B, several conditions may represent fillings of the same place, and B can hence be partitioned into $B_1 \uplus B_2 \uplus \cdots \uplus B_{|P|}$, where conditions in B_i represent fillings of place p_i. Due to blocking semantics, all conditions in a particular subset $B_i = \{ b_{i,1}, b_{i,2}, \ldots, b_{i,k} \}$ must have disjoint existence dates, that is for every $j, j' \in \{ 1, 2, \ldots, k \}$ with $j \neq j'$, the intersection between $[\mathsf{dob}(b_{i,j}), \mathsf{dod}(b_{i,j})]$ and $[\mathsf{dob}(b_{i,j'}), \mathsf{dod}(b_{i,j'})]$ is either empty, or limited to a single value. This constraint can be encoded by the disjunction:

no-overlap$(b_{i,j}, b_{i,j'}) \triangleq$
$$\begin{cases} \mathsf{dod}(b_{i,j}) \le \mathsf{dob}(b_{i,j'}) \lor \mathsf{dod}(b_{i,j'}) \le \mathsf{dob}(b_{i,j}) & \text{if } b_{i,j}{}^{\bullet} \ne \varnothing \land b_{i,j'}{}^{\bullet} \ne \varnothing, \\ \mathsf{dod}(b_{i,j}) \le \mathsf{dob}(b_{i,j'}) & \text{if } b_{i,j}{}^{\bullet} \ne \varnothing \land b_{i,j'}{}^{\bullet} = \varnothing, \\ \mathsf{dod}(b_{i,j'}) \le \mathsf{dob}(b_{i,j}) & \text{otherwise.} \end{cases}$$

Note that if $b_j \preceq b_{j'}$, then the constraint among events and transitions immediately ensures $\mathsf{dob}(b_{j,i}) \le \mathsf{dod}(b_{j,i}) \le \mathsf{dob}(b_{j',i}) \le \mathsf{dod}(b_{j',i})$. However, we need to add a consistency constraint for every pair of concurrent conditions $b_{i,j}, b_{i,j'}$ that belong to the same B_i. Hence, calling $I(b_{i,j}, E, B)$ the set of conditions that represent the same place as $b_{i,j}$ and are concurrent with $b_{i,j}$ in $\langle E, B \rangle$, we have to ensure the constraint non-blocking$(b_{i,j}) \triangleq \bigwedge_{b_{i,j'} \in I(b_{i,j}, E, B)}$ no-overlap$(b_{i,j}, b_{i,j'})$. In words, condition $b_{i,j}$ does not hold during the validity dates of any concurrent condition representing the same place. In particular, a time process of $\mathcal{N}$ cannot contain two maximal conditions with the same place.

Let us now consider the constraints attached to events. An event $e = \langle B, t \rangle$ is an occurrence of a firing of transition t that needs conditions in B to be fulfilled to become enabled. Calling $\mathsf{doe}(e)$ the date of enabling of e, we necessarily have $\mathsf{doe}(e) = \max\{\mathsf{dob}(b) \mid b \in B\}$. Event e is firable at least $\mathsf{eft}(t)$ time units, and at most $\mathsf{lft}(t)$ time units after being enabled. We hence have $\mathsf{doe}(e) + \mathsf{eft}(t) \le \mathsf{dof}(e) \le \mathsf{doe}(e) + \mathsf{lft}(t)$. However, execution of e does not always occur immediately when e is firable. Execution of e occurs after e is firable, as soon as the places filled by e are empty, i.e., e occurs at a date $\theta(e)$ that guarantees that no place in $t^{\bullet}$ is occupied. This is guaranteed by attaching to every event e the constraints $\theta(e) = \mathsf{dob}(b_1), \theta(e) = \mathsf{dob}(b_2), \ldots, \theta(e) = \mathsf{dob}(b_k)$, where $\{b_1, b_2, \ldots b_k\} = e^{\bullet}$, and constraints non-blocking(b_1), non-blocking$(b_2), \ldots,$ non-blocking(b_k). Last, as semantics of STPNs is urgent, once firable, e has to fire at the earliest possible date. This is encoded by the constraint $\theta(e) = \min\{x \in \mathbb{R}_{\ge 0} \mid x \notin \,]\mathsf{dob}(b), \mathsf{dod}(b)[$ for some $b \in \bigcup I(b_i) \land x \ge \mathsf{dof}(e)\}$. Figure 2 shows the effect of blocking and possible free firing dates for some event with a condition b in its postset. Horizontal lines represent real lines, and intervals values in interval $[\mathsf{dob}(b_i), \mathsf{dod}(b_i)]$ for $i \in 0, 1, 2$. Suppose that $I(b) = \{b_0, b_1, b_2\}$. Then $[\mathsf{dob}(b), \mathsf{dod}(b)]$ have to be fully inscribed in one of these thick segments. An event with b in its postset can occur only at dates contained in these thick segments.

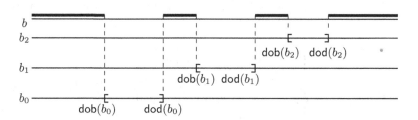

Fig. 2. Constraints on dates of birth of tokens in a shared place.

Written differently,

$$\theta(e) = \begin{cases} \mathsf{dof}(e) \text{ if } \bigwedge_{b \in I(b_1) \cup \ldots I(b_k)} \mathsf{dof}(e) \leq \mathsf{dob}(b), \text{ and} \\ \min\{\mathsf{dod}(b) \mid \forall b' \in \bigcup_{b_i \in e} {}^\bullet I(b_i), \mathsf{dod}(b) \notin \,]\mathsf{dob}(b'), \mathsf{dod}(b')[\} \text{ otherwise.} \end{cases}$$

This formula can be translated in boolean combinations of inequalities over variables of $\mathsf{var}(E, B)$. Similarly, event $e = \langle B, t \rangle$ must occur before all its conflicting events. If an event e' in conflict with e is executed, at least one condition in B is consumed, and e cannot occur in a time process containing e'. We hence need the additional constraint $\bigwedge_{e' \sharp e} \mathsf{notMoreUrg}(e, e')$ to guarantee that there exists no other event that is forced to occur before e due to urgency. We define $\mathsf{notMoreUrg}(e, e')$ as the following constraint:

$\mathsf{notMoreUrg}(e, e') \triangleq \theta(e) \geq \mathsf{doe}(e') + \mathsf{lft}(\mathsf{tr}(e')) \Rightarrow \mathsf{tiled}(e, e') \vee \bigvee_{e'' \| e} \mathsf{preempts}(e', e'')$

where $\mathsf{tiled}(e, e') \triangleq \mathsf{free}(e') \cap [\mathsf{doe}(e') + \mathsf{lft}(\mathsf{tr}(e')), \theta(e)] = \varnothing$, $e'' \| e$ refers to events that are concurrent with e in the considered set of events E, $\mathsf{free}(e') = \mathbb{R}_{\geq 0} \setminus \{[\mathsf{dob}(b), \mathsf{dod}(b)] \mid \exists b' \in e'^\bullet, b \in I(b')\}$ is the set of intervals in which places attached to conditions in $e'^\bullet$ are empty, and $\mathsf{preempts}(e', e'') \triangleq \theta(e'') \leq \min(]\mathsf{doe}(e') + \mathsf{lft}(\mathsf{tr}(e')), \theta(e)[\cap \mathsf{free}(e'))$ means e'' disabled e' by consuming a condition in ${}^\bullet e''$.

Constraint $\mathsf{notMoreUrg}(e, e')$ means that if e' is in conflict with e, then at least one condition in ${}^\bullet e'$ is consumed before e' can fire, or if e' becomes firable before e fires, the urgent firing of e' is delayed by blockings so that e can occur. As for constraint attached to blockings, $\mathsf{notMoreUrg}(e, e')$ can be expressed as a boolean combination of inequalities. One can also notice that $\mathsf{notMoreUrg}(e, e')$ can be expressed without referring to variables attached to event e' nor $e'^\bullet$, as $\mathsf{doe}(e') = \max_{b_i \in {}^\bullet e'} \mathsf{dob}(b_i)$ and the intersection of $I(b)$ and $e'^\bullet$ is void.

For causally closed sets of events and conditions $E \cup B$ contained in some pre-process of $\mathcal{U}_K$, the constraint $\Phi_{E,B}$ applying on events and conditions of $E \cup B$ is now defined as $\Phi_{E,B} = \bigwedge_{x \in E \cup B} \Phi_{E,B}(x)$ where:

$$\forall b \in B, \Phi_{E,B}(b) = \mathsf{non\text{-}blocking}(b) \wedge \begin{cases} \mathsf{dob}(b) = d_0 \text{ if } b \in B_0, \text{ and } b \text{ is maximal,} \\ \mathsf{dob}(b) = d_0 \wedge \mathsf{dob}(b) \leq \mathsf{dod}(b) \text{ if } b \in B_0, \\ \mathsf{dob}(b) = \theta({}^\bullet b) \text{ if } b \notin B_0 \text{ and } b \text{ is maximal,} \\ \mathsf{dob}(b) = \theta({}^\bullet b) \wedge \mathsf{dob}(b) \leq \mathsf{dod}(b) \text{ otherwise.} \end{cases}$$

$$\forall e \in E, \Phi_{E,B}(e) = \begin{cases} \quad \mathsf{doe}(e) = \max_{b \in {}^\bullet e} \mathsf{dob}(b) \\ \wedge \quad \mathsf{doe}(e) + \mathsf{eft}(\mathsf{tr}(e)) \leq \mathsf{dof}(e) \leq \mathsf{doe}(e) + \mathsf{lft}(\mathsf{tr}(e)) \\ \wedge \quad \mathsf{dof}(e) \leq \theta(e) \wedge \bigwedge_{b \in {}^\bullet e} \mathsf{dod}(b) = \theta(e) \\ \wedge \quad \bigwedge_{b \in {}^\bullet e} \theta(e) = \mathsf{dob}(b) \\ \wedge \quad \bigwedge_{e' \sharp e} \mathsf{notMoreUrg}(e, e') \end{cases}$$

We can now define symbolic processes, and show how instantiation of their variables define time processes of $\mathcal{N}$. Roughly speaking, a symbolic process is a prefix of a pre-process of $\mathcal{U}_K$ (it is hence a causal net) decorated with a *satisfiable* set of constraints on occurrence dates of events. Before formalizing symbolic processes, let us highlight three important remarks. **Remark 1:** an unfolding up to depth K misses some constraints on occurrence dates of events due to blockings by conditions that do not belong to $\mathcal{U}_K$ but would appear in some larger unfolding $\mathcal{U}_{K'}$, with $K' > K$. We will however show (Propositions 1 and 2 that with time progress assumption, unfolding $\mathcal{N}$ up to a sufficient depth guarantees that all constraints regarding events with $\theta(e) \leq D$ are considered. This allows to define symbolic processes representing the time processes of $\mathcal{N}$ that are executable in less than D time units. **Remark 2:** unfoldings consider depth of events, and not their dates. Hence, if a process contains an event e occurring at some date greater than d, and another event e' that belongs to the same pre-process and becomes urgent before date d, then e' must belong to the process, even if it lays at a greater depth than e. **Remark 3:** Every pre-process $\langle E, B \rangle$ of $\mathcal{U}_K$ equipped with constraint $\Phi_{E,B}$ is not necessarily a symbolic process. Indeed, some events in a pre-process might be competing for the same resource. Consider for instance the STPN of Fig. 3(a)). Its unfolding is represented in (b), and two of its (symbolic) processes in (c) and (d). For readability, we have omitted constraints. One can however notice that there exists no symbolic process containing two occurrences of transition t_3, because conditions p_4^1 and p_4^2 are maximal and represent the same place p_4.

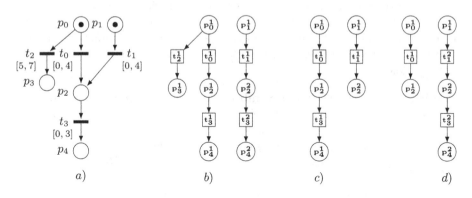

Fig. 3. An STPN with conflicts and blockings (a), its symbolic unfolding (b), and two of its symbolic processes (c) and (d).

Definition 10 (Prefixes of an Unfolding). *Let $SPP = \langle E, B \rangle$ be a preprocess of $\mathcal{U}_K$. A symbolic prefix of SPP is a triple $\langle E', B', \Phi_{E',B'} \rangle$ where $E' \subseteq E$ is a causally closed set of elements contained in E, and $B' = {}^\bullet E' \cup E'^\bullet$.*

Symbolic prefixes are causally closed parts of pre-processes, but their constraints inherited from the unfolding $\mathcal{U}_K$ may not be satisfiable.

Definition 11 (Symbolic Processes). *A symbolic process of* $\mathcal{U}_K$ *is a triple* $\mathcal{E}^s = \langle E', B', \Phi_{E',B'} \rangle$ *where* $\langle E', B', \Phi_{E',B'} \rangle$ *is a symbolic prefix of some pre-process* $PP = \langle E, B \rangle$ *of* $\mathcal{U}_K$, $\Phi_{E',B'}$ *is satisfiable, and* E' *is maximal w.r.t. urgent events firing in* PP, *that is for every* $f \in B'^{\bullet} \cap E$, *and letting* $C_f = \mathsf{pl}^{-1}(f^{\bullet}) \cap B'$ *denote the set of conditions whose place appears in the postset of* e, *the following constraint is not satisfiable.*

$$\Phi_{\max}(f) \triangleq \begin{cases} \Phi_{E',B'} \\ \wedge \ \theta(f) \leq \max_{e' \in E'} \theta(e') \ \text{(f fires before the last event in E')} \\ \wedge \ \mathsf{eft}(f) + \max_{b \in {}^{\bullet}f} \mathsf{dob}(b) \leq \theta(f) \ \text{(f is urgent)} \\ \wedge \ \bigvee_{X \in 2^{C_f}} \max_{x \in X} \mathsf{dod}(x) \leq \theta(f) \leq \min_{x \in C_f \setminus X} \mathsf{dob}(x) \\ \quad \text{(f is not blocked for the whole duration of the process)} \end{cases}$$

Intuitively, $\Phi_{\max}(f)$ means that f, that is not in the symbolic process, becomes urgent, is not blocked by conditions in B', and has to fire before the execution of the last event in E'. If $\Phi_{\max}(f)$ is satisfiable, then f should appear in the process. A crux in the construction of symbolic processes of $\mathcal{U}_K$ is to find appropriate maximal and causally closed sets of events with satisfiable constraints. This can be costly: as illustrated by the example of Fig. 3, satisfiability of constraints is not monotonous: the constraints for processes in Fig. 3(c,d) are satisfiable. However, adding one occurrence of transition t_3 yields unsatisfiable constraints. Satisfiability of a prefix of size n hence does not imply satisfiability of a larger prefix of size $n + 1$. The converse implication is also false: if a constraint of a prefix of size n is not satisfiable, appending a new event may introduce, blockings, delay urgent transitions, yielding satisfiability of a constraint on a prefix of size $n + 1$. So, satisfiability of constraints is not a criterion to stop unfolding.

Definition 12 (Executions of Symbolic Processes). *Let* $\mathcal{E}^s = \langle E, B, \Phi \rangle$ *be a symbolic process of an unfolding* $\mathcal{U}_K$. *An execution of* $\mathcal{E}^s$ *is a time process* $TP = \langle E, B, \theta \rangle$ *where* θ *is a solution for* Φ. *For a chosen* θ, *we denote by* $\mathcal{E}^s_\theta = \langle E, B, \theta \rangle$ *the time process obtained from* $\mathcal{E}^s$. $TP = \langle E, B, \theta \rangle$ *is a time process of* $\mathcal{U}_K$ *if there exists a symbolic process* $\mathcal{E}^s = \langle E, B, \Phi \rangle$ *of* $\mathcal{U}_K$ *s.t. TP is an execution of* $\mathcal{E}^s$.

Informally, symbolic pre-processes select maximal conflict-free sets of events in an unfolding. Symbolic processes extract executable prefixes from symbolic pre-processes, and executions attach dates to events of symbolic processes to obtain time processes. In the rest of the paper, we respectively denote by $\mathcal{E}^s(\mathcal{U}_K)$ and by $\mathcal{E}(\mathcal{U}_K)$ the set of symbolic processes and time processes of $\mathcal{U}_K$.

We can now show that upon time progress hypothesis, unfoldings and their symbolic processes capture the semantics of STPNs with blockings. Given an STPN that guarantees time progress with a minimal elapsing of δ time units between successive occurrences of every transition, and given a maximal date D, we want to build an unfolding $\mathcal{U}^D$ of $\mathcal{N}$ that contains all events that might be executed before D, but also all places and events which may impact firing dates of these events. We can show that $\mathcal{U}^D$ is finite and its processes are of depth $H = \lceil \frac{D-d_0}{\delta} \rceil \cdot |T|$ at most.

Let $b = \langle e, p \rangle$ be a condition of an unfolding $\mathcal{U}_n$ obtained at step n. Let block(b) be the set of conditions that may occur in the same process as b, represent the same place, and are not predecessors or successors of b in any unfolding $\mathcal{U}_{n+k}$ obtained from $\mathcal{U}_n$. Clearly, dates of birth and death of conditions in block(b) may influence the date of birth and death of b, or even prevent b from appearing in the same process as some conditions in block(b). However, in general, block(b) need not be finite, and at step n, block(b) is not fully contained in a pre-process of $\mathcal{U}_n$. Fortunately, upon time progress assumption, we can show that elements of block(b) that can influence dob(b) appear in some bounded unfolding $\mathcal{U}_K$.

Proposition 1. *Let $\mathcal{N}$ be a STPN guaranteeing time progress of δ time units (between consecutive occurrences of each transition). For every date $D \in \mathbb{R}_{\geq 0}$ and condition b in an unfolding $\mathcal{U}_n$, there exists $K \geq n$ s.t. $\{b' \in$ block$(b) \mid$ dob$(b') \leq D\}$ is contained in $\mathcal{U}_K$.*

This proposition means that if some event cannot occur at dof(e) due to a blocking, then one can discover all conditions that prevent this firing from occuring in a bounded extension of the current unfolding.

Proposition 2. *Let $\mathcal{N}$ be a STPN guaranteeing time progress of δ time units. The set of time processes executable by $\mathcal{N}$ in D time units are prefixes of time processes of $\mathcal{U}_K$, with $K = \lceil \frac{D}{\delta} \rceil \cdot |T|^2$ containing only events with date $\leq D$.*

4   Realizability of Schedules

We can now address realizability of a schedule S, i.e., a high-level description of operations of a system and of their timing constraints can be realized by a system represented as a STPN $\mathcal{N}$ depicting low-level operations and distributions over possible delays between enabledness and firing of transitions. The connection between operations in S and $\mathcal{N}$ is defined via a realization function.

Definition 13 (Realization Function). *A realization function for a schedule S and an STPN $\mathcal{N}$ is a map $r : \mathcal{A} \to 2^T$ that associates a subset of transitions from T to each letter of $\mathcal{A}$, and such that $\forall a \neq a' \in \mathcal{A}, r(a) \cap r(a') = \varnothing$.*

A realization function describes which low-level actions implement a high-level operation of a schedule. Each letter a from $\mathcal{A}$ can be interpreted as an operation performed through the firing of any transition from the subset of transitions $r(a)$. Allowing $r(a)$ to be a subset of T provides some flexibility in the definition of schedules: in a production cell, for example, a manufacturing step a for an item can be implemented by different processes on different machines. Similarly, in a train network, a departure of a train from a particular station in the schedule can correspond to several departures using different tracks, which is encoded with several transitions in an STPN. Realization functions hence relate actions in schedules to several transitions in an STPN. The condition on realization functions prevents ambiguity by enforcing each transition to appear at most once in the image of r. Note that $r(\mathcal{A}) \subseteq T$, that is the realization of a schedule may need many intermediate steps that are depicted in the low-level description of a system, but are not considered in the high-level view provided by a schedule. We will call transitions that belong to $r(\mathcal{A})$ *realizations* of $\mathcal{A}$.

Definition 14 (Embedding, Realizability). *Let* $S = \langle N, \rightarrow, \lambda, C \rangle$ *be a schedule,* $\mathcal{E}^s = \langle E, B, \Phi \rangle$ *be a symbolic process of* $\mathcal{N}$ *and* $r : N \rightarrow T$ *be a realization function. We say that* S *embeds into* $\mathcal{E}^s$ *(w.r.t.* r *and* d*) and write* $S \hookrightarrow \mathcal{E}^s$ *iff there exists an injective function* $\psi : N \rightarrow E$ *such that:*

$$\begin{cases} \forall n \in N, \mathsf{tr}(\psi(n)) \in r(\lambda(n)) \\ \forall \langle n, n' \rangle \in \rightarrow, \psi(n) \preceq \psi(n') \\ \nexists f \leq \psi(\min(n)), \mathsf{tr}(f) \in r(\mathcal{A}) \\ \forall e \leq f \leq g, e = \psi(n) \wedge g = \psi(n'') \wedge \mathsf{tr}(f) \in r(\mathcal{A}) \\ \qquad\qquad \Rightarrow \exists n', f = \psi(n') \wedge n \rightarrow^* n' \rightarrow^* n'' \end{cases}$$

S embeds in $\mathcal{E}^s$ iff there is a way to label every node n of S by a letter from $r(\lambda(n))$ and obtain a structure that is contained in some restriction of a prefix of $\mathcal{E}^s$ to events that are realizations of actions from $\mathcal{A}$ and to a subset of its causal ordering. Note that there can be several ways to embed S into a process of $\mathcal{N}$.

Definition 15 ((Boolean) Realizability). *Let* d *be a dating function for a schedule* S*,* r *be a realization function.* S *is* realizable by $\mathcal{E}^s$ *(w.r.t.* r *and* d*) iff there exists an embedding* ψ *from* S *to* $\mathcal{E}^s$*, and furthermore,* $\Phi_{\psi,S,d} \triangleq \Phi \wedge \bigwedge_{n \in N} \theta(\psi(n)) = d(n)$ *is satisfiable.* S *is* realizable by $\mathcal{N}$ *(w.r.t.* r *and* d*) iff there exists a symbolic process* $\mathcal{E}^s$ *such that* S *is realizable by* $\mathcal{E}^s$*.*

We write $\mathcal{E}^s \models S$ when S is realizable by $\mathcal{E}^s$, and $\mathcal{N} \models S$ when S is realizable by $\mathcal{N}$. An algorithm to compute a set $\Psi_{S,\mathcal{E}^s}$ of embeddings of a schedule S in a process $\mathcal{E}^s$ is provided in the extended version. Once $\Psi_{S,\mathcal{E}^s}$ is obtained, it remains to show that for at least one embedding $\psi \in \Psi_{S,\mathcal{E}^s}$, $\Phi_{\psi,S,d}$ is satisfiable to prove that S is realizable by $\mathcal{E}^s$. We can then compute the set of symbolic processes $\mathcal{E}^S \triangleq \{\mathcal{E}^s_0, \mathcal{E}^s_1, \ldots, \mathcal{E}^s_{N-1}\}$ of $\mathcal{U}_K$ that embed S and similarly for each $\mathcal{E}^s_i \in \mathcal{E}^S$ the set of possible embedding functions $\Psi_i \triangleq \{\psi_{i,0}, \psi_{i,1}, \ldots, \psi_{i,N_i-1}\}$ for which the constraints $\Phi_{\psi_{i,j},S,d}$ are satisfiable.

To illustrate the construction of unfoldings and of processes, let us consider the example of Fig. 4. This toy example depicts two train carousels that serve stations. Line 1 serves stations A, B and C, and line 2 serves stations D, B' and C'. Both lines share a common track portion between stations B, C and B', C', and line 1 uses two trains. A possible required schedule (top left of the figure) is that one train leaves every 10 time units from station A on line 1, starting from date 10, and one train leaves station C' every 10 time units, but starting from date 15. Departures from A are nodes labeled by d_A and departures from C' are nodes labeled by $d_{C'}$. The bottom left picture shows the aspect of both lines and stations. The center picture is an STPN model for this example, and we set $r(d_A) = \{t_5\}$ and $r(d_{C'}) = \{t_9\}$. We do not precise distributions, and focus on the structural unfolding, on the right of the figure. Note that the topmost occurrence of place OK, that plays the role of a boolean flag in a critical section can be both consumed by occurrences t_1^1 and t_1^2 of transition t_1, which is a standard conflict. However, as events t_4^1 and t_4^2 both output a token in place A, their firing times may influence one another even though they are not in conflict.

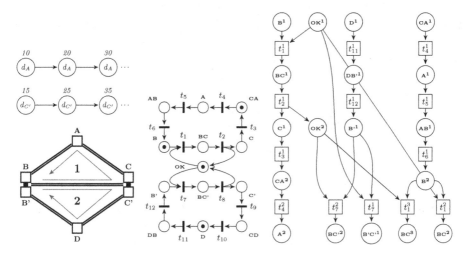

Fig. 4. A toy example: realizability of a partial schedule for two train carrousels with shared track portions.

Let us now show that boolean realizability is not always a precise enough notion to characterize feasability of a schedule. Consider the STPN of Fig. 5, and the two symbolic processes: one in which transition t_1 fires, and another one in which t_2 fires. The probability of the first process is the probability that a value v_1 sampled to assign a TTF for t_1 is smaller or equal to another value v_2 sampled independently to assign a TTF for t_2. Clearly, the probability that $v_1 \leq v_2$ is equal to the probabilty that $v_1 \in [0, 1]$. The probability of the second process is equal to the probability that $v_1 \geq v_2$, but the set of values allowing this inequality is restricted to a single point $v_1 = 1, v_2 = 1$. Conforming to continous probability distribution semantics, the probability of this point is equal to zero. A schedule composed of a single node n with date 1 such that $r(\lambda(n)) = \{t_2\}$ is realizable according to Definition 14, but with *null probability*. A more accurate notion of realizability is to require that schedules embed into symbolic processes of $\mathcal{U}_K$ with strictly positive probability.

This raises a second issue: requiring a schedule to be realized with an exact timing also leads to realizations with null probabilities. Consider the former example: a schedule composed of a single node n, a realization function r s.t. $r(\lambda(n)) = \{t_2\}$, and a dating function d s.t. $d(n) = 2$. Assign interval $[0, 3]$ to transition t_1 in the STPN of Fig. 5(a) and interval $[1, 4]$ to transition t_2.

The probability that t_2 fires from the initial marking is equal to the probability that $v_1 \geq v_2$, which is not null (we will explain later how to compute the probability of such domain and the joint probability of v_1, v_2), and is equal to the probability of the domain for values of v_1, v_2 depicted by the colored zone in Fig. 5(b). However, within this continuous domain of possible values, the probability to fire t_2 exactly at precise date 2 as required by dating function d is still null. We hence consider realizability of a schedule up to some admissible imprecision α. Once an injection ψ from a schedule S to a symbolic process $\mathcal{E}^s$ is found, the constraint to meet becomes: $\Phi_{\psi,S,d\pm\alpha} = \Phi \wedge \bigwedge_{n \in N} \max(d(n) - \alpha, 0) \leq \theta(\psi(n)) \leq d(n) + \alpha$.

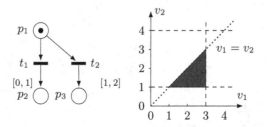

Fig. 5. (a) An example STPN (b) A domain for $\tau(t_1), \tau(t_2)$ allowing firing of t_2.

Definition 16 (Probabilistic Realizability). *A schedule with maximal date D is realizable with non-null probability iff there exists an embedding ψ of S into a symbolic process $\mathcal{E}^s$ of $\mathcal{U}_K$ s.t. $\mathbb{P}(\mathcal{E}^s \wedge \text{SOL}(\Phi_{\psi,S,d\pm\alpha})) > 0$.*

Intuitively, this definition requires that a symbolic process embeds S, and that the probability that this process is executed and satisfies all timing constraints imposed by the STPN and by the dating function is non-null. This probability can be evaluated using a transient execution tree, as proposed in [13]. Roughly speaking, nodes of this tree are abstract representations of time domains for sampled values attached to enabled transitions (this is the usual notion of state class, already used in [3,15] to analyze time Petri nets). In addition to state classes, transient tree nodes contain abstract representations of probability distributions. If the definition of distribution is appropriately chosen, for instance, using truncated sums of exponentials of the form

$$f(x) = \begin{cases} \sum c_k x^{a_k} e^{-\lambda_k x} & \text{if } x \in [a, b] \\ 0 & \text{otherwise} \end{cases}$$

then the distributions obtained by projection, multiplication, or variable elimination can still be encoded as sums of exponentials, and memorized using a finite set of parameters. The probability to fire a particular transition from a state and move to a successor node is computed as an integration over the time domains allowing this transition to fire first. The children of a node give a probabilistic distribution on possible classes of successor states. As time progress is guaranteeed in our model, a finite tree representing executions of an STPN or of one of its processes up to some bounded duration can be built. As explained in [13], the sum of probabilities attached to all paths of the tree can be used to compute the probability of some properties. In our case, the sum of probabilities of all paths that end with the execution of a chosen symbolic process gives the probability to realize this process. Details on construction of a transient tree are provided in the extended version.

5   Conclusion

Related Work: we have addressed realizability of partially ordered timed schedules by timed and stochastic concurrent systems with blocking semantics. Realizability in a timed setting has been addressed as a timed game problem [11], with a boolean answer. The objective in this work is to check whether a player in a timed game has a strategy to ensure satisfaction of a formula written in a timed logic called Metric Interval Temporal Logic. Brought back to the setting of realizability of schedules, the work of [11] can be used to answer a boolean realization question, by translating a schedule to a formula. However, the work of [11] lies in an interleaved setting: a sequential formula cannot differentiate interleaved and concurrent actions. It does not address randomness in systems and hence cannot quantify realizability. Scheduling of train networks was already addressed as a contraint satisfaction problems [8]. The input of the problem is given as an alternative graph (that can be seen as some kind of unfolding of a systems's behavior, decorated with time constraints. The algorithms in [8] use a branch and bound algorithm to return an optimal schedule for the next 2 h of operation of a train network, but do not consider randomness.

Realizability is also close to diagnosis. Given a log (a partial observation of a run of a system), and a model for this system, diagnosis aims at finding all possible runs of the model of the system whose partial observation complies with the log. Considering a log as a schedule, the ability to compute a diagnosis implies realizability of this high-level log by the model. Diagnosis was addressed for stochastic Petri nets in [1]. In this work, the likelihood of a process that complies with an observation is evaluated, and time is seen as a sequence of discrete instants. Diagnosis was addressed for timed Petri nets in [4], where unfolding of a timed Petri net is built to explain an observed log. [10] proposes temporal patterns called chronicles that represent possible evolutions of an observed system. A chronicle is a set of events, linked together by time constraints. The diagnosis framework explains stream of time-stamped events as combinations of chronicles. Assembling chronicles is some kind of timed unfolding. However, event streams are not a concurrent model, and chronicles extraction does not consider randomness.

Schedulability can also be seen as conformance of an expected behavior (the schedule) to an implementation (the Petri net model). Conformance was defined as a timed input output conformance relation (tIOCO) relation between timed input/output automata in [14]. More precisely, $\mathcal{A}_1$ tIOCO $\mathcal{A}_2$ iff after some timed word, the set of outputs produced by $\mathcal{A}_1$ is included in the outputs produced by $\mathcal{A}_2$. This relation cannot be verified in general (as inclusion of timed automata languages is not decidable), but can be tested. Boolean realizability can be seen as some kind of conformance test. Note however that tIOCO is defined for an interleaved timed model without probabilization of transitions.

Assessment: The techniques described in this work first build an unfolding $\mathcal{U}_K$ up to a depth K that depends on the maximal date appearing in the schedule, find symbolic processes of $\mathcal{U}_K$ that embed the schedule, and then check that at least one of them has non-null probability. So far, we did not consider complexity issues. The size of an unfolding can grow exponentially w.r.t. its depth. Checking satisfiability of a set of constraints with disjunctions can also be costly. Satisfiability of constraints is not monotonous and hence cannot be used to stop unfolding. However, embedding verification and unfolding can be done jointly: one can stop a branch of unfolding as soon as a schedule does not embed in the pre-process on this branch. Most of the constraints presented in this paper can be simplified, and refer mainly to event variables. One can also notice that atoms in constraints are rather simple inequalities, which could simplify their verification. Computation of realization probability for processes can also be improved. We use the transient tree construction of [13], that builds a symbolic but *interleaved* representation of some processes. This is obviously very costly. We are currently investigating ways to evaluate probabilities of symbolic processes in a non-interleaved setting.

As future work, we would like to implement and improve this realizability verification framework, and use it as a basis to prove more properties. For instance, it might be interesting to prove that a schedule can be realized while ensuring that the overall sum of delays w.r.t the expected schedule does not exceed some threshold. Another improvement would be to provide means to compute an exact value for the realization probability. We are also interested in the design of controllers that maximize the probability of realization.

References

1. Aghasaryan, A., Fabre, E., Benveniste, A., Boubour, R., Jard, C.: Fault detection and diagnosis in distributed systems: an approach by partially stochastic Petri nets. Discrete Event Dyn. Syst. **8**(2), 203–231 (1998)
2. Aura, T., Lilius, J.: Time processes for time Petri nets. In: Azéma, P., Balbo, G. (eds.) ICATPN 1997. LNCS, vol. 1248, pp. 136–155. Springer, Heidelberg (1997)
3. Berthomieu, B., Diaz, M.: Modeling and verification of time dependent systems using time Petri nets. IEEE Trans. Softw. Eng. **17**(3), 259–273 (1991)
4. Chatain, T., Jard, C.: Symbolic diagnosis of partially observable concurrent systems. In: de Frutos-Escrig, D., Núñez, M. (eds.) FORTE 2004. LNCS, vol. 3235, pp. 326–342. Springer, Heidelberg (2004)

5. Chatain, T., Jard, C.: Time supervision of concurrent systems using symbolic unfoldings of time Petri nets. In: Pettersson, P., Yi, W. (eds.) FORMATS 2005. LNCS, vol. 3829, pp. 196–210. Springer, Heidelberg (2005)

6. Chatain, T., Jard, C.: Complete finite prefixes of symbolic unfoldings of safe time Petri nets. In: Donatelli, S., Thiagarajan, P.S. (eds.) ICATPN 2006. LNCS, vol. 4024, pp. 125–145. Springer, Heidelberg (2006)

7. Cortadella, J., Kishinevsky, M., Lavagno, L., Yakovlev, A.: Synthesizing Petri nets from state-based models. In: ICCAD 1995, pp. 164–171 (1995)

8. D'Ariano, A., Pacciarelli, D., Pranzo, M.: A branch and bound algorithm for scheduling trains in a railway network. Eur. J. Oper. Res. $183(2)$, 643–657 (2007)

9. D'Ariano, A., Pranzo, M., Hansen, I.A.: Conflict resolution and train speed coordination for solving real-time timetable perturbations. IEEE Trans. Intell. Transp. Syst. $8(2)$, 208–222 (2007)

10. Dousson, C.: Extending and unifying chronicle representation with event counters. In: ECAI 2002, pp. 257–261 (2002)

11. Doyen, L., Geeraerts, G., Raskin, J.-F., Reichert, J.: Realizability of real-time logics. In: Ouaknine, J., Vaandrager, F.W. (eds.) FORMATS 2009. LNCS, vol. 5813, pp. 133–148. Springer, Heidelberg (2009)

12. Esparza, J., Römer, S., Vogler, W.: An improvement of McMillan's unfolding algorithm. Form. Meth. Syst. Des. $20(3)$, 285–310 (2002)

13. Horváth, A., Paolieri, M., Ridi, L., Vicario, E.: Transient analysis of non-Markovian models using stochastic state classes. Perform. Eval. $69(7)$, 315–335 (2012)

14. Krichen, M., Tripakis, S.: Conformance testing for real-time systems. Form. Meth. Syst. Des. $34(3)$, 238–304 (2009)

15. Lime, D., Roux, O.H.: Model checking of time Petri nets using the state class timed automaton. J. Discrete Event Dyn. Syst. $16(2)$, 179–205 (2006)

16. McMillan, K.L.: A technique of state space search based on unfolding. Form. Meth. Syst. Des. $6(1)$, 45–65 (1995)

17. Rubinstein, R.Y., Kroese, D.P.: Simulation and the Monte Carlo Method, 2nd edn. Wiley, London (2008)

18. Semenov, A.L. Yakovlev, A.: Verification of asynchronous circuits using time Petri net unfolding. In: DAC, pp. 59–62 (1996)

ABCD: A User-Friendly Language
for Formal Modelling and Analysis

Franck Pommereau[✉]

IBISC, University of Évry, 23 Boulevard de France, 91037 Évry Cedex, France
franck.pommereau@ibisc.univ-evry.fr

Abstract. This paper presents an algebra of coloured Petri nets called
the *Asynchronous Box Calculus with Data*, or ABCD for short. ABCD
allows to model complex systems using a user-friendly and high-level
syntax. In particular, parts of the model can be directly programmed
in Python [21], which allows to embed complex computation and data
values within a model. A compiler for ABCD is shipped with the toolkit
SNAKES [16,18] and ABCD has been used for years, which is quickly surveyed. This paper is the first complete and formal presentation of the
language and its semantics. It also presents uses cases of ABCD for the
modelling and analysis of various systems.

Keywords: Formal modelling · High-level models · Petri nets semantics

1   Introduction

The *Asynchronous Box Calculus with Data*, or ABCD for short, is an algebra of
Petri net, *i.e.*, a process algebra with a Petri net semantics [17]. With respect to
the other algebras of the family like the *Petri Box Calculus* [2,3], ABCD is a high-
level modelling language: its semantics is based on high-level Python-coloured
Petri nets, that can be composed and transformed using various operations like
the terms of a process algebra. With respect to other members of the family,
ABCD is asynchronous, *i.e.*, does not have the transition synchronisation operation *à la* CCS; however, it could be added easily if needed. An important aspect
of ABCD is that it uses Python as a concrete programming language to provide
data, expressions and computation. The syntax of ABCD is inspired from that
of Python but separated even if it actually embeds the fragment for expressions
(Python expressions may be used in ABCD). A compiler is distributed within the
SNAKES toolkit [16,18] and allows to build a Petri net from ABCD source code.

This paper provides the first complete and formal definition of ABCD, *i.e.*, its
syntax and semantics. Only informal introductions though examples had been
published so far, the most complete of which being [17, pages 30–33]. Other
contributions of this paper are: a definition of Python-coloured Petri nets with
read/fill/flush-arcs, a presentation of the ABCD compiler and simulator, and a
short survey of ABCD use cases for research and teaching to showcase its usability.

© Springer International Publishing Switzerland 2016
F. Kordon and D. Moldt (Eds.): PETRI NETS 2016, LNCS 9698, pp. 176–195, 2016.
DOI: 10.1007/978-3-319-39086-4_12

The next section presents the syntax of ABCD together with its intuitive semantics. The formal semantics is defined in Sect. 3 as a translation of ABCD terms into Petri nets. Section 5 describes the compiler and the interactive simulator. Section 4 presents existing applications of ABCD. Finally, the paper ends on a conclusion with perspectives. This paper assumes no particular knowledge about Python, however, a good Python tutorial is available online [20].

2   Modelling with ABCD

Figure 1 shows an ABCD model of the dining philosophers problem with four philosophers. We use it to introduce the main concepts of ABCD. Line 1, a *buffer* called forks is *declared*, it is a typed container that will initially hold the four integers 0 to 3 (whose type is int in Python), each of which models a fork identifier. Line 3–4, a *sub-process* called philo is declared. It is parametrised by the two values of the left and right fork that a particular philosopher has to use. Line 4 is the *process expression* for a philosopher that consists of three *atomic actions* enclosed between square brackets and connected with *control-flow operators*. The first atomic action is "[forks−(left), forks−(right)]" and specifies that value left is consumed (thus the "−") from buffer forks and, at the same time, value right is also consumed in the same buffer. This atomic action is composed sequentially (operator ";") with another atomic action that produces (thus the "+") the two same values into the same buffer. Then, the sequence itself is composed in a loop (operator "∗") with atomic action "[False]", which means that the sequence can be arbitrarily repeated until "[False]" is executed to finish the loop (and here the whole process). However, "[False]" is an atomic actions that can never be executed so we actually have an infinite loop. Finally, Line 6 defines the *main process* of the model that composes in parallel (operator "|") four *instances* of sub-process philo with parameters chosen to arrange the philosophers on a circle.

```
1  buffer forks : int = 0, 1, 2, 3
2
3  net philo ( left , right ):
4      ([ forks−( left ), forks−(right )]  ;  [ forks+( left ), forks+(right )]) ∗ [False]
5
6  philo (0, 1) | philo (1, 2) | philo (2, 3) | philo (3, 0)
```

Fig. 1. A model of four dining philosophers where a generic philosopher is specified as a parametrised sub-process.

More generally, an ABCD model consists of a *process* description comprising optional *declarations* (in particular sub-processes and resources) and a main *process expression*. Sub-process can themselves include declarations that are local to them, *i.e.*, cannot be used from outside the sub-process. The full grammar of ABCD is given in Fig. 2 and is commented in the rest of the section.

⟨*spec*⟩	::= ⟨*global*⟩ ↵ ⟨*spec*⟩	global declaration
	| ⟨*local*⟩ ↵ ⟨*spec*⟩	local declaration
	| ⟨*proc*⟩	process
⟨*global*⟩	::= import_stmt	Python import statement
	| **symbol** name { "," name}	symbols declaration
	| **typedef** name ":" ⟨*type*⟩	type declaration
	| **const** name "=" expr	constant declaration
⟨*local*⟩	::= **buffer** name ":" ⟨*type*⟩ "=" expr	buffer declaration
	| **net** name "(" ⟨*params*⟩? ")":" ↪ ⟨*sub*⟩ ↩	sub-process declaration
⟨*sub*⟩	::= ⟨*local*⟩ ↵ ⟨*sub*⟩	local declarations
	| ⟨*proc*⟩	behaviour specification
⟨*type*⟩	::= name	native Python type
	| ⟨*type*⟩ "&" ⟨*type*⟩	intersection
	| ⟨*type*⟩ "|" ⟨*type*⟩	union
	| ⟨*type*⟩ "*" ⟨*type*⟩	cross-product
	| **enum** "(" expr {"," expr} ")"	enumerated type
	| ⟨*cont*⟩ "(" ⟨*type*⟩ {"," ⟨*type*⟩} ")"	container type
⟨*cont*⟩	::= name "(" ⟨*type*⟩ ")"	collection type
	| "dict(" ⟨*type*⟩ "," ⟨*type*⟩ ")"	dictionary type
⟨*params*⟩	::= name {"," ⟨*params*⟩}	value parameter
	| name ":" **buffer** {"," ⟨*params*⟩}	buffer parameter
⟨*proc*⟩	::= ⟨*proc*⟩ "|" ⟨*proc*⟩	parallel composition
	| ⟨*proc*⟩ ";" ⟨*proc*⟩	sequential composition
	| ⟨*proc*⟩ "+" ⟨*proc*⟩	choice composition
	| ⟨*proc*⟩ "*" ⟨*proc*⟩	iteration
	| "(" ⟨*proc*⟩ ")"	nested process
	| name "(" ⟨*args*⟩? ")"	anonymous net instance
	| name "::" name "(" ⟨*args*⟩? ")"	named net instance
	| "[True]"	always possible action
	| "[False]"	always blocking action
	| "[" ⟨*access*⟩ {"," ⟨*access*⟩} "]"	unconditional action
	| "[" ⟨*access*⟩ {"," ⟨*access*⟩} **if** expr "]"	conditional action
⟨*access*⟩	::= name "+(" expr ")"	production
	| name "-(" expr ")"	consumption
	| name "?(" expr ")"	test
	| name "<>(" expr "=" expr ")"	swap
	| name ">>(" name ")"	flush
	| name "<<(" expr ")"	fill
⟨*args*⟩	::= expr {"," ⟨*args*⟩}	arguments

Fig. 2. The syntax of ABCD, where: ⟨···⟩ denotes non-terminals, ↵ denotes a newline; import_stmt is a Python import statement; **bold** face denotes keywords; name is an arbitrary Python name (*i.e.*, an identifier); expr is an arbitrary Python expression; "..." denotes literals; {···} denotes parts that can be repeated zero or more times; ...? denotes parts that can be omitted; ↪ denotes a newline followed by an indented block; ↩ denotes a newline at the end of an indented block.

2.1   Global Declarations

These are declarations that are only allowed at the top level of the specification, *i.e.*, not within a sub-process.

A Python *import statement* [20, Sect. 6] allows to make visible names defined in an external Python module. For instance, using "**import** math" allows to use function "math.factorial" in expressions; statement "**from** math **import** *" gives a direct access to function "factorial" and others, without the prefix "math.".

Defining *symbols* is a way to create unique named values in a model. For instance, "**symbol** OPEN, CLOSE" defines names "OPEN" and "CLOSE" that have opaque values, distinct from every other existing values.

It is also possible to define *new types*, *i.e.*, give a name to a type, using the "**typedef**" declaration. Types in ABCD are sets of values and can be specified using a rich type algebra, see ⟨*type*⟩ in the grammar. Basically, a type is a Python class, for instance "int" or "str", and corresponds to the set of all the objects of this class. Two classes are worth mentioning: "object" is Python's universal class, *i.e.*, any value an "object" instance; "BlackToken" is a class with a single value "dot" that implements the Petri nets black token. Building more complex types is possible using union, intersection and cross-product of types; two more constructions deserve explanation. Enumerated types are defined as sets of values, for instance "**enum**(1, 2,"hello")" defines a type with only the three enumerated values. Container types are Python collections whose content is constrained, for instance "tuple(int)" denotes the set of tuples of integers; "list" and "set" are the two other supported simple containers. Finally, Python dictionaries (*i.e.*, mappings) are also supported containers, for instance "dict(int, str)" denotes the set of dictionaries whose keys are integers and values are strings.

Other global declarations are *constants*. For instance, "**const** foo = 42" defines the name "foo" whose value is 42. Contrasting with symbols, constants have known values that can be exploited in the model, for instance, "foo+2" is a correct expression when "foo" has been declared as above.

2.2   Buffers

Resources in ABCD are stored in *buffers*, *i.e.*, unbounded and unordered data containers that can be accessed from the process that declares the buffer as well as from any of its sub-processes. In the semantics, they correspond to (coloured) places. A buffer is declared using keyword **buffer** and is given:

- a *name* that is an identifier that will be used in process expressions to access the buffer;
- a *type* that restricts the values allowed in the buffer;
- an *initial content* given as an expression that is interpreted as a series of values initially stored in by the buffer.

The following ABCD code shows the declarations of two buffers:

```
1   buffer foo : int = ()
2   buffer bar : str ="hello", "world"
```

The first line declares a buffer named "foo", whose type is "int" the set of integers and whose initial content is empty since "()" denotes the empty tuple in Python. The second line declares a buffer named "bar" whose type is "str" the set of strings and that initially contains the two strings "hello" and "world".

2.3 Sub-processes

An important feature of ABCD is to provide *parametrised sub-process* that can be instantiated later on. A sub-process is declared using keyword "**net**" followed by a name and a list of parameters. For instance "**net** sub (a, b): ↦ " introduces a sub-process called sub that is parametrised by two values "a" and "b". If a parameter needs to be a buffer, this must be explicit, like in "**net** sub (a, b: **buffer**): ↦ " where "b" is now a buffer parameter. The specification of a sub-process is given in an indented block after the first line, it comprises local declarations and a process expression that specifies the behaviour. We will see later on how sub-processes are instantiated within a process expression.

2.4 Process Expressions

These specify the *behaviour of a (sub-)process*. The most basic behaviours are *atomic actions* and are enclosed in square brackets "[···]". In the semantics, atomic actions correspond to Petri nets transitions. The simplest ones are "[True]" that can always be executed and has no effect on buffers, and "[False]" that can never be executed and is always blocking. We have seen and example using "[False]" above and will see one with "[True]" later on.

More complex actions are formed as lists of *buffer accesses* and an *optional execution condition*. Each buffer access is given as a buffer name, a symbol to specify the access type and an expression to specify the data accessed. For instance, "buf+(2∗n)" specifies that the atomic action, when executed, creates in buffer "buf" a value that is the result of evaluation expression "2∗n". "buf-(x)" allows to consume from the buffer a value that is bound to variable "x". An actual value may be used instead of variable "x" to consume a known value. It is also possible to use patterns, like in "buf-(x,y,0)" that consumes a triple whose first and second elements are bound to x and y respectively and whose third element must be 0. Currently, patterns may only be nested tuples, allowing to decompose the consumed values. Note that it is not possible to specify an arbitrary expression to be consumed because this would require to solve an arbitrary equation, which is not possible in general. Two other access types are: test "?" that behaves like consumption except that is does not actually consume the value; and swap that is a shorthand for consumption plus production, for instance, "buf<>(x=x+1)" can be replaced by "buf-(x), buf+(x+1)".

Then come two accesses handling multiple tokens. First, the flush "buf>>(v)" empties buffer "buf" and binds the multiset of its content to variable "v". Note that this is possible even if the buffer is empty in which case "v" is bound to the empty multiset, this gives a possible implementation of a test for zero using "[..., buf>>(v) **if** not v]" where "v" used as a Boolean expression is true if and only if it is not empty. Next, the fill operation produces values into a buffer: using "buf<<(expr)", expression "expr" is evaluated and iterated over as a collection so that each of its value is added to "buf". (Note that this does not overwrite existing values in the buffer, it just adds new content.) For instance, one may increment all the values within a buffer using a single atomic action: "[buf>>(v), buf<<(x+1 **for** x **in** v)]" where expression "x+1 **for** x **in** v" is a Python *comprehension* [20, Sect. 5.1.4].

A *guard* may be specified at the end of an atomic action, using keyword "if" followed by an expression. This allows the execution only if the expression evaluates to true. The scope of the variables used within an action is limited to this action. Variables are bound thanks to buffer accesses that consume or test values in buffers (*i.e.*, "−", "?", ">>" and the left-hand side of "<>"), free variables in other accesses and in the guard are forbidden.

Actions can be composed using four *control-flow operators* and parentheses: ";" is the sequential composition allowing to execute first its left-hand side process and then its right-hand side process; "|" is the parallel composition allowing to execute two processes concurrently; "+" is the choice composition allowing to execute only one of the two processes it composes; "∗" is the iteration allowing to execute repeatedly its left-hand side process (including zero times) followed by exactly one execution of its right-hand side process. Action "[False]" is often used at the right-hand side of an iteration to create an infinite loop, like in "[buf−(x), buf−(y), buf+(x) **if** y % x == 0] ∗ [False]" which implements a sieve of Eratosthenes.

Finally, a process may also include *instances* of previously declared sub-processes (*i.e.*, nets). A term composed of the net name followed by a list of effective arguments is replaced by the whole sub-process in which all the parameters have been substituted by the arguments. Such an instance may be named to simplify the access to its places in the Petri net semantics. Imagine for example a buffer "mybuf" declared inside a sub-process "mynet" parametrised by three values, when building instance "mynet(1,2,3)", the resulting copy of "mybuf" is normally called "mynet(1,2,3).mybuff". By using a named instance, one can simplify this, for example, instance "foo::mynet(1,2,3)" gives rise to buffer "foo.mybuff" and a place with the same name in the Petri net semantics.

Note that within a process expression, spaces and newlines are not significant, only indentation must be respected. And within a process nested in parentheses, even indentation is not significant anymore. This allows to choose clearer presentation for process expressions, as for instance in the example of Sect. 4.1.

3   Petri Net Semantics of ABCD

We define now the Petri nets semantics of ABCD, and first the variant of Petri nets we use: an algebra of Python-coloured Petri nets extended with read/fill/flush-arcs, and supporting control-flow compositions. This class of Petri nets corresponds to *Petri nets with control-flow* as defined in [17, Sects. 2.1 to 2.3] in which the originally abstract colour domain has been concretized as the Python language, and with an extension to support read/fill/flush-arcs.

3.1   Python-Coloured Petri Nets

A Python-coloured Petri net (PCPN) involves values, variables and expressions. These objects are defined by the Python programming language and, because we do not want to defined them here, abstracted away as follows:

- $\mathbb{D}$ is the set of *data* values, *i.e.*, all the possible Python objects, including "dot" that implements "•";
- $\mathbb{D}_\perp \stackrel{\mathrm{df}}{=} \mathbb{D} \uplus \{\perp\}$ is the set of data enriched with a special "undefined" value;
- $\mathbb{V}$ is the set of *variables*, *i.e.*, all the possible Python identifiers;
- $\mathbb{E}$ is the set of *expressions*, involving values, variables and appropriate operators according the syntax of Python. Let $e \in \mathbb{E}$, we denote by *vars*(e) the set of variables from $\mathbb{V}$ involved in e. Moreover, variables or values are valid (simple) expressions, *i.e.*, we have $\mathbb{D} \cup \mathbb{V} \subset \mathbb{E}$.

We make no assumption about the typing or syntactical correctness of values or expressions. Instead, we assume that any expression can be evaluated, possibly to $\perp$ (undefined). More precisely, a *binding* is a partial function $\beta : \mathbb{V} \to \mathbb{D}$. Let $e \in \mathbb{E}$ and β be a binding, we denote by $\beta(e)$ the evaluation of e under β. For instance, if $\beta_1 \stackrel{\mathrm{df}}{=} \{x \mapsto 1, y \mapsto 2\}$, we have $\beta_1(x + y) = 3$. With $\beta_2 \stackrel{\mathrm{df}}{=} \{x \mapsto 1, y \mapsto \text{"2"}\}$, Python raises an exception upon evaluation, which corresponds in our setting to $\beta_2(x + y) = \perp$; similarly, if the domain of β does not include *vars*(e) then $\beta(e) \stackrel{\mathrm{df}}{=} \perp$. The application of a binding to evaluate an expression is naturally extended to sets and multisets of expressions.

In the following, given a set X, we denote by $X^\star$ the set of multisets over X. We use the standard notations for multisets, $+$ for sum, $-$ for difference, $\leq$ for inclusion, etc., as well as an extended set notation $\{\cdots\}$.

Definition 1 (Python-Coloured Petri Nets). *A* Python-coloured Petri net *(*PCPN *) is a tuple* (S, T, ℓ, α) *where:*

- S *is the finite set of* places;
- T, *disjoint from* S, *is the finite set of* transitions;
- ℓ *is a* labelling *function such that:*
  - *for all* $s \in S$, $\ell(s) \subseteq \mathbb{D}$ *is the* type *of* s, *i.e.*, *the set of values that* s *is allowed to carry,*
  - *for all* $t \in T$, $\ell(t) \in \mathbb{E}$ *is the* guard *of* t, *i.e.*, *a condition for its execution,*
  - *for all* $(x, y) \in (S \times T) \cup (T \times S)$, $\ell(x, y) \in \mathbb{E}^\star$ *is the* arc *from* x *to* y. *Arcs from* $S \times T$ *(resp.* $T \times S$*) are called* input arcs *(resp.* output arcs*);*
- α *is the* arc type *function that associates to each arc in* $(S \times T) \cup (T \times S)$ *a function* $\mathbb{D}^\star \times \mathbb{D}^\star \to \mathbb{D}_\perp^\star$ *that takes the marking of a place plus the evaluation of an arc annotation and returns the actual multiset of consumed or produced tokens. In particular we shall use four functions:*
  - $\alpha_= \stackrel{\mathrm{df}}{=} (m, a \mapsto a)$ *for a* regular *arc;*
  - $\alpha_? \stackrel{\mathrm{df}}{=} (m, a \mapsto \emptyset$ *if* $a \leq m$ *else* $\{\perp\})$ *for a* read *arc;*
  - $\alpha_{\gg} \stackrel{\mathrm{df}}{=} (m, a \mapsto a$ *if* $a = m$ *else* $\{\perp\})$ *for a* flush *arc;*
  - $\alpha_{\ll} \stackrel{\mathrm{df}}{=} (m, a \mapsto \sum_{x \in a} iter(x))$ *for a* fill *arc, where* iter *is a function that builds a multiset from the elements in collection* x *(set, list, ...).* □

As usual, Petri nets are depicted as graphs in which places are round nodes, transitions are square nodes, and arcs are directed edges with arrow tips depending on the arc types: $\rightarrow$ for regular, — for read, $\twoheadrightarrow$ for flush (input arcs) or fill (output arc). Empty arcs, *i.e.*, arcs such that $\ell(x, y) = \emptyset$, are not depicted.

Definition 2 (Markings and Firing). *Let $N \overset{\text{df}}{=} (S, T, \ell, \alpha)$ be a* PCPN. *A marking M of N is a function on S that maps each place s to a finite multiset over $\ell(s)$ representing the tokens in s. A transition $t \in T$ is enabled at a marking M and a binding β, which is denoted by $M[t, \beta\rangle$, iff the following conditions hold:*

- *M has enough tokens, i.e., for all $s \in S$, $\alpha(s, t)(M(s), \beta(\ell(s, t))) \leq M(s)$;*
- *the guard is satisfied, i.e., $\beta(\ell(t)) = \mathsf{True}$;*
- *place types are respected, i.e., for all $s \in S$, $\alpha(t, s)(M(s), \beta(\ell(t, s)))$ is a multiset over $\ell(s)$.*

If $t \in T$ is enabled at marking M and binding β, then t may fire and yield a marking M' defined for all $s \in S$ as $M'(s) \overset{\text{df}}{=} M(s) - \alpha(s, t)(M(s), \beta(\ell(s, t))) + \alpha(t, s)(M(s), \beta(\ell(t, s)))$. This is denoted by $M[t, \beta\rangle M'$. □

We may observe how the various arc types are implemented:

- $\alpha_=$ always returns the evaluation of the arc $\beta(\ell(s, t))$ or $\beta(\ell(t, s))$ so we fall back to the definition given in [17, Definition 1];
- on an input arc, $\alpha_?$ requires that the tokens from $\beta(\ell(s, t))$ are actually in the marking of s but then it returns $\emptyset$ so no token is consumed. But if some tokens are not in the place, returning $\{\bot\}$ forbids the firing because $\bot \notin \ell(s)$ by definition. Returning $\emptyset$ unconditionally would not work because it would be like removing the arc;
- on an input arc also, $\alpha_{>>}$ forces to find β such that $\beta(\ell(s, t)) = M(s)$ so that all the marking is consumed;
- finally, on an output arcs, $\alpha_{<<}$ transforms a collection of multisets (or other collection types) into the sum of these multisets which is how fill arcs are expected to behave.

3.2 Petri Nets Compositions

To implement control-flow operations, PCPN are equipped with control-flow operations adapted from the Petri Box Calculus [2] and Petri Net Algebra [3]. We refer to [17, Sect. 2.3] for a complete definition and give here a summary.

First, places of a PCPN are separated into *control-flow* and *data* places. To do so, PCPN are equipped with an additional labelling function σ that returns for each place its *status* which may be for control-flow places: e for an entry place that is marked when the PCPN starts its execution; x for an exit place that is marked when the PCPN has finished its execution; i for an internal place when the PCPN is in an intermediary state. For data places, status may be ε for an anonymous data place or an arbitrary label *name* $\notin \{\mathsf{e}, \mathsf{i}, \mathsf{x}, \varepsilon\}$ for a named data place. Control-flow places must have type $\{\bullet\}$ and data places may have arbitrary types.

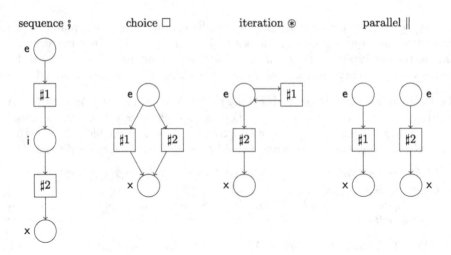

Fig. 3. The four operator nets [17, Fig. 3 in Sect. 2.3].

Then, control-flow operations are defined from the *operator nets* shown in Fig. 3. Intuitively, each transition $\sharp i$ in an operator net is to be replaced with the i-th operand net of the specified operation. To do so, we consider in turn each place in the operator net and use its arcs to collect in the operand net the places to be combined. For instance, take the internal place of the sequence operator net to compute $N_1 \, \sfrac{9}{} \, N_2$: it is an output of $\sharp 1$ so we collect the exit places of N_1; it is also an input place of $\sharp 2$ so we collect the entry places of N_2. The sets of collected places are then composed using a cross-product and become internal places in the resulting net because we considered an internal place in the operator net. The same principle is applied for every place of the operator net which results in a composition of N_1 and N_2 whose control-flow places have been combined to implement the required control-flow. To finish the control-flow operation, we have to glue together (adding the markings) all the named data places that have the same name (usually one such place comes from each operand name), so that each named place is present only once. Anonymous data places are left untouched because they are considered local to each operand net.

One more operation is needed for our purpose, this is *name hiding* $N/\underline{name}$ that replaces the status of every place named $\underline{name}$ with ε, making it anonymous and no more mergeable upon control-flow compositions.

3.3   From ABCD to Petri Nets

The translation of ABCD to PCPN is defined through a recursive function *net* that takes two arguments: an environment that is used to collect information about ABCD declarations encountered so far, and a fragment of ABCD source code that remains to be compiled. The environment is a mapping from declared names to various information about the corresponding declarations. Look for instance at the first rule in Fig. 4: when a symbol declaration is found, this is

symbol definition
$net(env, \text{“symbol } name_1, \dots, name_k \hookleftarrow tail\text{”})$
$\quad \stackrel{\text{df}}{=} net(env + \{name_1 \mapsto [\text{symbol}], \dots, name_k \mapsto [\text{symbol}]\}, \text{“}tail\text{”})$

type definition
$net(env, \text{“typedef } name \;:\; type \hookleftarrow tail\text{”})$
$\quad \stackrel{\text{df}}{=} net(env + \{name \mapsto [\text{type}, type(env, type)]\}, \text{“}tail\text{”})$

buffer definition
$net(env, \text{“buffer } name : type = expr \hookleftarrow tail\text{”})$
$\quad \stackrel{\text{df}}{=} N_{buffer} \parallel net(env + \{name \mapsto [\text{buffer}, type(type), expr]\}, \text{“}tail\text{”})$

net definition
$net(env, \text{“net } name(par_1, \dots, par_k) : \looparrowright sub \looparrowleft tail\text{”})$
$\quad \stackrel{\text{df}}{=} net(env + \{name \mapsto [\text{net}, sub, par_1, \dots, par_k]\}, \text{“}tail\text{”})$

constant definition
$net(env, \text{“const } name = expr \hookleftarrow tail\text{”})$
$\quad \stackrel{\text{df}}{=} net(env + \{name \mapsto [\text{const}, expr]\}, \text{“}tail\text{”})$

parallel composition
$net(env, \text{“}proc_1 \mid proc_2\text{”}) \stackrel{\text{df}}{=} net(env, \text{“}proc_1\text{”}) \parallel net(env, \text{“}proc_2\text{”})$

sequential composition
$net(env, \text{“}proc_1 \,;\, proc_2\text{”}) \stackrel{\text{df}}{=} net(env, \text{“}proc_1\text{”}) \,\fatsemi\, net(env, \text{“}proc_2\text{”})$

choice composition
$net(env, \text{“}proc_1 + proc_2\text{”}) \stackrel{\text{df}}{=} net(env, \text{“}proc_1\text{”}) \,\square\, net(env, \text{“}proc_2\text{”})$

iteration
$net(env, \text{“}proc_1 * proc_2\text{”}) \stackrel{\text{df}}{=} net(env, \text{“}proc_1\text{”}) \,\circledast\, net(env, \text{“}proc_2\text{”})$

nested process
$net(env, \text{“}(proc)\text{”}) \stackrel{\text{df}}{=} net(env, proc)$

always possible action
$net(env, \text{“}[\text{True}]\text{”}) \stackrel{\text{df}}{=} N_{\text{True}}$

always blocking action
$net(env, \text{“}[\text{False}]\text{”}) \stackrel{\text{df}}{=} N_{\text{False}}$

unconditional action
$net(env, \text{“}[access_1, \dots access_k]\text{”}) \stackrel{\text{df}}{=} net(env, \text{“}[access_1, \dots access_k \text{ if True}]\text{”})$

conditional action
$net(env, \text{“}[access_1, \dots access_k \text{ if } expr]\text{”}) \stackrel{\text{df}}{=} N_{action}$

anonymous net instance
$net(env, \text{“}name(arg_1, \dots, arg_k)\text{”})$
$\quad \stackrel{\text{df}}{=} net(env, \text{“}[\![sub \mid par_1 \leftarrow arg_1, \dots, par_k \leftarrow arg_k]\!]\text{”})/\underline{buf1}/ \cdots /\underline{bufn}$
$\quad$ where $env(name) = [\text{net}, sub, par_1, \dots, par_k]$
$\quad$ and $\underline{buf1}, \dots, \underline{bufn}$ are the names of the buffers declared inside net $name$

named net instance
$net(env, \text{“}alias :: name(arg_1, \dots, arg_k)\text{”})$
$\quad \stackrel{\text{df}}{=} \langle\!\langle net(env, \text{“}name(arg_1, \dots, arg_k)\text{”}) \mid name(arg_1, \dots, arg_k) \leftarrow alias \rangle\!\rangle$

Fig. 4. Translation rules of the PCPN semantics of ABCD.

simply recorded in the environment and the translation proceeds with the rest of the code. Type definition is treated similarly but the value of the type is recorded also, it is computed using an auxiliary function *type*. We will not detail it because it is both straightforward and an implementation detail (interested readers may look at module snakes.typing that is used for this purpose [16]). Buffer definition starts to build parts of the resulting Petri net: the net returned by translating the rest of the code is composed in parallel with a net N_{buffer} that consists of a single data place, whose type, status and marking is exactly the type, name and initial content of the buffer respectively. When applying the composition, this will result in merging this place with another empty copy (see the translations of actions below) in order to initialise the marking. The next six rules are straightforward.

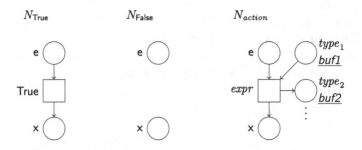

Fig. 5. Base nets for atomic actions.

Then come two rules to build simple actions: "[True]" (resp. "[False]") is translated to a net N_{True} (resp N_{False}) depicted in Fig. 5. Then, an unconditional action is just a conditional action with a true guard. Conditional action itself is implemented by a simple Petri net N_{action} as sketched in Fig. 5:

- it has one entry place and one exit place, connected by a single transition whose guard is exactly the guard of the action;
- for each buffer access, there is a data place named and typed as the buffer (which is known from the environment) to implement the buffer, and an arc with the appropriate type:
  - $\alpha_=$ on an input arc for a consumption ("−"),
  - $\alpha_=$ on an output arc for production ("+"),
  - $\alpha_?$ on an input arc for a test ("?"),
  - $\alpha_{>>}$ on an input arc for a flush (">>"),
  - $\alpha_{<<}$ on an output arc for a fill ("<<"),
  - a swap ("<>") is decomposed into the corresponding pair of consumption and production;
- multiple regular arcs to (resp. from) the same buffer are merged, *i.e.*, there annotations is summed. Multiple read arcs and multiple fill arcs are merged as well. Multiple arcs with the same direction but of one of the other types or of mixed types are forbidden. For instance we cannot flush twice a place nor we can flush it and at the same time consume one token from it.

Finally, net instances are built as follows:

- function *net* is called recursively on the content *sub* of the net declaration in which we substitute each parameter par_i with the effective argument arg_i, which is denoted by $[\![sub \mid par_1 \leftarrow arg_1, \ldots, par_k \leftarrow arg_k]\!]$;
- the data places for all the buffer declared inside the net are hidden so that they become private to the resulting Petri net and no more mergeable;
- if the net instance is named, its nodes are renamed by replacing the prefix $name(arg_1, \ldots, arg_k)$ with the name *alias* of the instance, which is denoted by $\langle\!\langle \cdots \mid name(arg_1, \ldots, arg_k) \leftarrow alias \rangle\!\rangle$.

Definition 3 (Semantics of ABCD). *Given function net as defined above, the complete semantics of an* ABCD *specification "spec" is the* PCPN *returned by* $net(\{\}, \text{"spec"})$ *in which all the entry places are marked with a single "•".*   □

Note that we did not include import statement in the semantics because it does not change the net itself. It is rather an implementation detail and just consists in making the imported names available in the execution environment of the Petri net. This is made also for constants and symbols.

4   Applications and Use Cases

This section presents uses of ABCD for scientific applications and for teaching. The first one is detailed to provide a complete example of an actual ABCD model. The next examples will be partly presented due to space limitation, so chosen fragments will be showed to illustrate particular points we would like to discuss.

4.1   Critical Systems

A model of a railroad crossing system with multiple tracks has been developed in ABCD in order to generate Petri nets for the model-checking contest (MCC) 2012 [11,12]. The purpose of the MCC is to compare model-checkers on a variety of models with a scaling parameter, *i.e.*, a parameter allowing to tune the size of the model and of its state space. For the railroad model, the idea was to develop a model that is generic with respect to the number of tracks, each track being a net instance. However, as one may have remarked with the dining philosophers model of Fig. 1, ABCD has no mechanism to instantiate a number of processes that depends on a parameter: in the case of the philosophers, we have to explicitly instantiate a statistically chosen number of nets. In the case of the railroad model, this was solved using a template engine that allowed to generate ABCD source code for any number of tracks, each such ABCD file was then converted to a Petri net. Below, we show the model for two tracks, it is easy to figure out how this can be parametrised (actually, only the first and last lines need to be changed).

The model is based on three nets to model respectively: a pair of gates; generic tracks with a green/red light to control the progression of trains; and a controller to count the trains and operate the gates. The model starts with various declarations: number of tracks, values and type for the state of the gates, then all the global buffers. Note line 5 how a comment is inserted just like in Python: "#this comment extends until the end of the line ⏎". Note also that in source code below, the omitted lines are all blank. Buffer "green" stores the number of each track that has a green light, so that a red light is modelled by the absence of the corresponding token. Other buffers are dedicated to the communication between the components: "enter" receives the track numbers on which a trains approaches the gates; "leave" receives the track numbers on which a train leaves the gates; "down" allows to ask the gates to go down; "up" allows to ask the gates to go up; "done" is used by the gates to notify the controller that they have finished a command.

```
 1   const NUM = 2
 2   symbol OPEN, MOVING, CLOSED
 3   typedef gatestate : enum(OPEN, MOVING, CLOSED)
 4
 5   # green lights on tracks
 6   buffer green : int = range(NUM)
 7   # tracks -> controller
 8   buffer enter : int = ()
 9   buffer leave : int = ()
10   # controller -> gates
11   buffer down : BlackToken = ()
12   buffer up : BlackToken = ()
13   # gates -> controller
14   buffer done : gatestate = ()
```

The gates are modelled with a net that has a private buffer "state" reflecting the current position of the gates. The associated process is a repeated sequence of four actions: wait for the request to go down and start proceed it; arrive down and notify the controller; wait for the request to go up and start proceed it; arrive up and notify the controller.

```
16   net gates () :
17       buffer state : gatestate = OPEN
18       ([down-(dot), state<>(OPEN=MOVING)]
19       ; [state<>(MOVING=CLOSED), done+(CLOSED)]
20       ; [up-(dot), state<>(CLOSED=MOVING)]
21       ; [state<>(MOVING=OPEN), done+(OPEN)])
22       * [False]
```

The model for the tracks has the same structure. A local buffer "crossing" is marked when a train is crossing the road and a series of actions executed repeatedly corresponds to the successive steps of the progression of a train: approach the gates and switch the green light to red; start crossing the road only on a green light and switch it back to red; leave the crossing zone.

```
24   net track ( this ) :
25       buffer crossing : BlackToken = ()
26       ([enter+(this), green-(this)]
27       ; [green-(this), crossing+(dot)]
28       ; [crossing-(dot), leave+(this)])
29       * [False]
```

Then, the model for the controller is composed of one buffer "count" to count the trains present in the supervised zone, one buffer "waiting" to record on which track a train is waiting for the green light, and one process that can repeatedly execute one of four behaviours: detect the first train approaching ("c == 0" line 34) and ask the gates to go down, then wait until they arrive down and give the green light to the train that triggered this behaviour; count another train approaching (line 36) and give it the green light; count a train leaving the zone while there are still other trains in the zone ("c > 1" line 37); detect that the last train leaves the zone ("c == 1" line 37), ask the gates to go up and wait until this order is executed. When a train leaves, the corresponding light is turned green again so another train is allowed to approach on this track. Without this mechanism, we could have an accumulation of tokens in buffer "leave".

```
31   net controller () :
32       buffer count : int  = 0
33       buffer waiting : int = ()
34       (([enter-(num), count<>(c=c+1), down+(dot), waiting+(num) if c == 0]
35       ; [done-(CLOSED), waiting-(num), green+(num)])
36       + [enter-(num), count<>(c=c+1), green+(num) if c > 0]
37       + [leave-(num), green+(num), count<>(c=c-1) if c > 1]
38       + ([leave-(num), green+(num), count<>(c=c-1), up+(dot) if c == 1]
39       ; [done-(OPEN)]))
40       * [False]
```

The complete system is just a parallel composition of instances of these nets: one pair of gates, one controller and several tracks.

```
42   # all components in parallel
43   gates() | controller () | track(0) | track(1)
```

On the Petri net obtained from this model, safety (1) and liveness (2) LTL properties may be verified using Neco-SPOT model-checker [9]:

$$\forall 0 \leq i \leq 1: \ G\big(\text{track}(i).\text{crossing} \neq \emptyset \Rightarrow \text{gates}().\text{state} = \{\text{CLOSED}\}\big) \qquad (1)$$

$$G\big(\text{gates}().\text{state} = \{\text{CLOSED}\} \Rightarrow F(\text{gates}().\text{state} = \{\text{OPEN}\})\big) \qquad (2)$$

where G and F are respectively the *globally* and *eventually* modalities. Note that Neco actually requires slight changes to the model presented above because it does not support dot or parentheses in place names (so buffers "crossing" and "state" need to be replaced with global buffers), symbols (to be replaced with constants) nor enumerated types (to be replaced with "int"), see [15].

4.2 Security Protocols

A massively parallel CTL* model-checker for models of security protocols has been developed in [10]; a side product of this work has been the actual modelling of a bunch of security protocols, which has been made using ABCD. We show here two excerpts of a model of the Needham-Schroeder public key protocol [13], it is not needed to present it to understand our purpose, it is enough to know that some agents are exchanging encrypted messages in the presence of an attacker.

```
1  # implementation of a Dolev-Yao attacker
2  from dolev_yao import *
```

First, a Python module called "dolev_yao" is imported, it contains the definition of various symbols ("CRYPT", "PUB", "PRIV" and "NONCE") used to make a symbolic treatment of cryptography (*i.e.*, replace actual computation of cryptographic operations with terms that express it, which is a classical treatment of cryptography when modelling protocols) as well as a class "Spy" that implements a Dolev-Yao attacker [8]. Such an attacker has an infinite memory and computational power, however, it cannot break the cryptography that is assumed perfect. So it can capture messages exchanged by the other agents, gain knowledge (*i.e.*, learn) by decomposing messages, decrypt messages when it has the key to do so, recompose or encrypt messages, and inject new messages on the network. Recomposition leads in practice to infinite computation because just one object may be assembled into sequences of arbitrary sizes. The classical solution to bound the computation is to restrict compositions of objects to patterns that actually appear in the protocol: indeed, other sequences are useless to produce because no other agent in the system would ever use them as a valid message.

Modelling such an attacker is actually not difficult, but it requires to implement the learning actions discussed above, which immediately leads to state space explosion because we expose in the model all the intermediate steps of a fixed point computation (*i.e.*, the attacker applies each learning action until it cannot learn anything new). Instead of this, using ABCD, we *implement* (*i.e.*, program) the Dolev-Yao attacker directly in Python and have an efficient execution of this learning phase on a single transition. So, in the case of the Needham-Schroeder protocol, we have a simple model of the attacker as follows:

```
25  net Mallory (this, agents) :
26    buffer knowledge : object = ([this, (NONCE, this), (PRIV, this)]
27                          + [(PUB, a) for a in agents]
28                          + agents)
29    # Dolev-Yao engine, bound by the protocol signature
30    buffer spy : object = Spy((CRYPT, (PUB, int), int, (NONCE, int)),
31                              (CRYPT, (PUB, int), (NONCE, int), (NONCE, int)),
32                              (CRYPT, (PUB, int), (NONCE, int)))
33    # capture on message and learn from it
34    ([spy?(s), nw-(m), knowledge>>(k), knowledge<<(s.learn(m, k))]
35    # loose message or inject another one (may be the same)
36    ; ([True] + [spy?(s), knowledge?(x), nw+(x) if s.message(x)]))
37    * [False]
```

Buffer "knowledge" stores all the information learnt by the attacker; initially, this is information about itself, plus the public keys and identities of the other agents. Buffer "spy" stores an instance of class "Spy" that implements the Dolev-Yao learning mechanism. This class is instantiated with the signature of the protocol, that is, the types of all the possible messages, here also presented in a symbolic way (*i.e.*, as terms). Then, the process executed by the attacker is always the same for any protocol, it repeatedly execute a sequence of two behaviours:

– line 34, capture a message on the network "nw-(m)", learn from it and the previous knowledge by calling method "Spy.learn", and enrich the knowledge with decomposed and recomposed messages;
– line 36, immediately loop with "[True]" which causes a message loss, or inject a new message on the network using method "Spy.message" to check that a syntactically correct message is actually injected (anything else would yield additional states for nothing).

This example illustrates well how in ABCD programming and modelling can nicely complement each other. Not only this is simpler for the modeller, but also it leads to more efficient verification because it reduces state spaces a lot. Of course, the programmed part has to be correct but in this case, it is only 100 lines of simple Python that can be carefully written and scrutinised as well as thoroughly tested. In particular, we have verified that known attacks are detected, which shows that our Dolev-Yao attacker is at least as good as that implemented by specialised tools like Avispa [1]. On the other hand, when functions of the system are programmed and model-checking is applied, we can consider that this code has a good level of certification because it has been intensely exercised without triggering a bug nor producing an invalid run from the model-checking point of view. In other word, this code is part of the model and is verified just like the ABCD part.

ABCD has been initially developed for the purpose of modelling an industrial peer-to-peer storage system whose security needed to be assessed [5,19]. The kind of models we obtain for such a use case is similar to models of security protocols, the main difference is that we model identical peers instead of distinct partners with distinct roles. However, additionally to model-checking in the Dolev-Yao perspective, we have used statistical analysis of large sets of random traces to assess quantitative properties; in particular, we obtained the number of file loss with respect to the number of malicious peers connected to the system (a typical case where the yes/no answer of a model-checker is not enough).

4.3   Teaching Formal Modelling and Verification

The most recurring use of ABCD is for teaching: it is used for years at the university of Évry to teach formal modelling to master students in computer science. They are presented models like those discussed above and they must produce such models themselves.

This experience has shown that ABCD is not easier nor harder to understand by such students than coloured Petri nets. However, when it comes to actually produce models, students are much more successful and efficient using ABCD. In particular, sub-processes are naturally adopted and the models produced tend to be clearly structured, contrasting with Petri net models that quickly become random-looking and completely wrong. Clearly, the similarity of the syntax of ABCD with that of programming languages helps a lot to this respect. The interactive simulator is also very much appreciated because it allows an immediate feedback during the process of modelling.

5   Implementation, Compilation and Simulation

ABCD is implemented in SNAKES [16,18] as a compiler that takes ABCD source code as its input and has various possible outcomes: pictures, SNAKES' variant of PNML,[1] or an interactive simulator that allows to execute a model in a user-friendly graphical user-interface. A naive reachability model-checker is also implemented but we will not describe it, and actually we did not describe the related parts in the syntax, because it is intended to be replaced with something more general, robust and efficient. The compiler can be invoked from a command line interface or from a Python program in which case the constructed Petri net object is returned as an instance of SNAKES' PetriNet class.

The compiler is a rather straightforward implementation of the rules presented in Fig. 4, extended with syntactic and semantic constraints checks.

The interactive simulator is an important feature of the ABCD compiler, it is often the main tool invoked by users during the design of a model, just like a programmer invokes the compiler and make dry runs to exercise programs. The simulator has been completely reworked recently and is now displayed as a responsive Web user interface: when simulation is asked from the compiler, a Web page opens in which all the interaction takes place. Figure 6 show the main parts of this simulator (hiding a menu with a few auxiliary features):

- at the top is a player that allows to automatically run a chosen number of actions randomly selected, with a controlled speed;
- in the left column, under the ABCD label, the ABCD source code is displayed and enabled actions are highlighted. This is static information that will not evolve with the execution (apart from the highlighting);
- in the right column, a dynamic tree view of the model allows the user to observe and control the execution. Because a sub-process may have many instances, it is necessary to display separately each instance so that it can be controlled separately and its state (*i.e.*, the content of its buffers) can be displayed separately. In the example of Fig. 6 that shows a simulation of the specification from Fig. 1 (restricted to two philosophers for readability), we can see the instances of "**net** philo", each with its actions in various enabling states. For instance, among the two actions of the first instance, only the

---

[1] Which is not valid PNML in the case of the coloured models obtained from ABCD [18].

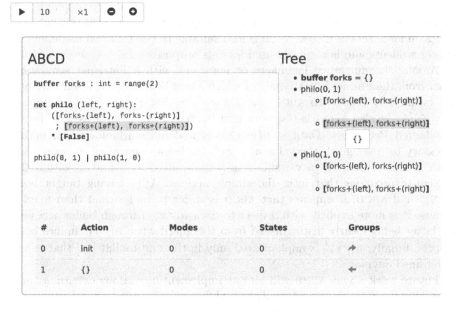

Fig. 6. A screenshot of (part of) the Web user interface.

second one is enabled for only one possible mode that is {} here because there is no variables;

– finally, at the bottom is the trace executed so far. Using the arrow in the right-most column, it is possible to navigate into the trace in order to update the tree view to the state it had just before the corresponding action has been executed; it is also possible to restart a new trace from this point.

The architecture of the simulator is modular and flexible and it is possible to adapt it to simulate Petri nets based formalisms others than ABCD. For instance, we have developed a similar simulator for models of biological regulatory networks [6,7] where the state is a plot of concentration levels of the regulated products (on the y axe) with respect to time (on the x axe). To do so, it is necessary to provide some HTML code that provides the presentation of the model and its state, and some JavaScript code to translate the interactions with them into appropriate calls to the simulation engine, as well as to implement the updates requested by the engine.

6   Conclusion

We have presented ABCD, a modelling language that is mixing the Python programming language and a process algebras. We have defined the Petri nets semantics of ABCD, targeting a Python-coloured variant of Petri nets extended with read-, flush- and fill-arcs. All this is implemented and freely available with the toolkit SNAKES. Use cases of ABCD have showed its suitability to qualitative analysis through model-checking as well as to quantitative analysis through statistics on large sets of traces. ABCD is also suitable to teach formal modelling to master students and is regularly used for this purpose.

Among the numerous languages or notations with a Petri net semantics, apart from the PBC and PNA family of which ABCD is a member, essentially one can be directly related to ABCD: the *Basic Petri Net Programming Notation*, $B(PN)^2$ [4], is also a process algebra and its semantics is expressed in terms of coloured Petri nets. Data in $B(PN)^2$ is stored into variables which makes necessary to distinguish the value of a variable before and after the execution of an atomic action. So, a variable x is actually used as $'x$ and x' within the Boolean expressions that form the atomic actions. After having taught both $B(PN)^2$ and ABCD, it appears that ABCD is easier to understand than $B(PN)^2$ because it is more explicit with respect to data storage through buffer accesses, the latter being clearly distinguished from the guard when $B(PN)^2$ unifies both aspects. Finally, $B(PN)^2$ is implemented only in the PEP toolkit [14] that is not maintained anymore.

Future work about ABCD will aim at implementing various extensions and improving its connection with analysis tools.

Considered extensions include: *buffer capacities* to block actions that would add (resp. remove) too much tokens to (resp. from) a buffer; *arrays of buffers* to declare k identical buffers at the same time, where k is a constant; *parametric composition* to compose identical processes depending on a parameter, for instance to compose the k tracks of the railroad example of Sect. 4.1 where k is a constant; *dynamic threads of executions* like suggested in [17, Sect. 4.3] allowing to create dynamic instances of sub-processes with abort/suspend/resume capabilities and to emulate function calls (including recursive calls); *syntax for raw Petri nets* allowing to include arbitrary Petri nets within an ABCD model, which is sometimes useful when control-flow is over-constraining; *inhibitor access* to leverage the inhibitor arcs already implemented in SNAKES. These extensions will be included in a demand driven fashion: they are identified to be potentially useful but the actual need for them has not been too crucial so far to trigger the effort of implementing them.

Two ways are envisaged to improve the usability of ABCD for analysis. First, we would like to ease the invocation of Neco-SPOT [9] to support direct model-checking of LTL formulas on ABCD models, this will require some work on Neco itself that currently has a few blocking limitations as explained above. Then, we are already working on a fast multi-core simulation engine coupled with automatic execution-related data collection for statistical analysis. Currently, this is a manual process with an inefficient execution of the traces, and so, building even simple statistics is quite a tedious process.

Finally, we will continue to model systems using ABCD in the context of research projects as well as for teaching because it has proved to be a good tool for these purposes.

References

1. Armando, A., et al.: The AVISPA tool for the automated validation of internet security protocols and applications. In: Etessami, K., Rajamani, S.K. (eds.) CAV 2005. LNCS, vol. 3576, pp. 281–285. Springer, Heidelberg (2005)
2. Best, E., Devillers, R., Hall, J.G.: The box calculus: a new causal algebra with multi-label communication. In: Rozenberg, G. (ed.) Advances in Petri Nets 1992. LNCS, vol. 609, pp. 21–69. Springer, Heidelberg (1992)
3. Best, E., Devillers, R., Koutny, M.: Petri Net Algebra. Springer, Heidelberg (2001)
4. Best, E., Hopkins, R.P.: $B(PN)^2$ - a basic Petri net programming notation. In: Bode, A., Reeve, M., Wolf, G. (eds.) PARLE 1993 Parallel Architectures and Languages Europe. LNCS, vol. 694, pp. 379–390. Springer, Heidelberg (1993)
5. Chaou, S., Utard, G., Pommereau, F.: Evaluating a peer-to-peer storage system in presence of malicious peers. In: Proceedings of HPCS 2011. IEEE Computer Society (2011)
6. Delaplace, F., Di Giusto, C., Giavitto, J.L., Klaudel, H., Spicher, A.: Activity networks with delays application to toxicity analysis. Technical report hal-01152719, I3S, Univ. Nice Sophia Antipolis (2015)
7. Di Guisto, C., Klaudel, H., Delaplace, F.: Systemic approach for toxicity analysis. In: Proceedings of BioPPN 2014. CEUR Workshop Proceedings, vol. 1159 (2014)
8. Dolev, D., Yao, A.C.: On the security of public key protocols. IEEE Trans. Inf. Theory **29**(2), 198–208 (1983)
9. Fronc, Ł., Duret-Lutz, A.: LTL model checking with Neco. In: Van Hung, D., Ogawa, M. (eds.) ATVA 2013. LNCS, vol. 8172, pp. 451–454. Springer, Heidelberg (2013)
10. Gava, F., Pommereau, F., Guedj, M.: A BSP algorithm for on-the-fly checking CTL* formulas on security protocols. J. Supercomput. **69**, 629–672 (2014)
11. Kordon, F., Buchs, D., Garavel, H., Hillah, L.: MCC 2016 - models. http://mcc.lip6.fr/models.php
12. Kordon, F., Linard, A., Buchs, D., Colange, M., Evangelista, S., Fronc, Ł., Hillah, L.M., Lohmann, N., Paviot-Adet, E., Pommereau, F., Rohr, C., Thierry-Mieg, Y., Wimmel, H., Wolf, K. (eds.): Raw report on the model-checking contest at Petri nets 2012. CoRR arXiv:1209.2382, September 2012
13. Needham, R.M., Schroeder, M.D.: Using encryption for authentication in large networks of computers. Commun. ACM **21**(12), 993–999 (1978)
14. Parallel Systems Group, University of Oldenburg: The PEP tool. http://peptool.sourceforge.net
15. Pommereau, F.: Model-checking with ABCD and Neco. https://goo.gl/FLVItx
16. Pommereau, F.: The SNAKES toolkit. http://www.ibisc.univ-evry.fr/fpommereau/SNAKES/ with sources at http://github.com/fpom/snakes
17. Pommereau, F.: Algebras of Coloured Petri Nets. Lambert Academic Publishing, Germany (2010)
18. Pommereau, F.: SNAKES: a flexible high-level Petri nets library. In: Devillers, R., Valmari, A. (eds.) PETRI NETS 20115. LNCS, vol. 9115, pp. 254–265. Springer, Switzerland (2015)
19. Sanjabi, S., Pommereau, F.: Modelling, verification, and formal analysis of security properties in a P2P system. In: Proceedings of COLSEC 2010. IEEE Digital Library, IEEE Computer Society (2010)
20. The Python Software Foundation: The Python tutorial. http://docs.python.org/tutorial
21. The Python Software Foundation: Python website. http://www.python.org

Health Monitoring of a Planetary Rover Using Hybrid Particle Petri Nets

Quentin Gaudel[1], Pauline Ribot[1], Elodie Chanthery[1(✉)],
and Matthew J. Daigle[2]

[1] LAAS-CNRS, Université de Toulouse, CNRS, INSA, UPS, Toulouse, France
{quentin.gaudel,pauline.ribot,elodie.chanthery}@laas.fr
[2] NASA Ames Research Center, Moffett Field, CA 94035, USA
matthew.j.daigle@nasa.gov

Abstract. This paper focuses on the application of a Petri Net-based diagnosis method on a planetary rover prototype. The diagnosis is performed by using a model-based method in the context of health management of hybrid systems. In system health management, the diagnosis task aims at determining the current health state of a system and the fault occurrences that lead to this state. The Hybrid Particle Petri Nets (HPPN) formalism is used to model hybrid systems behavior and degradation, and to define the generation of diagnosers to monitor the health states of such systems under uncertainty. At any time, the HPPN-based diagnoser provides the current diagnosis represented by a distribution of beliefs over the health states. The health monitoring methodology is demonstrated on the K11 rover. A hybrid model of the K11 is proposed and experimental results show that the approach is robust to real system data and constraints.

Keywords: Diagnosis · Hybrid systems · Model-based monitoring · Health management · Uncertainty · Petri Nets · Particle filter

1 Introduction

Real systems have become so complex that it is often impossible for humans to capture and explain their behaviors as a whole, especially when they are exposed to failures. *System health management* or *prognostics and health management* (PHM) aims at developing tools that can support operator tasks, reducing the global costs due to unavailability and repair actions, but also optimizing the mission reward by replanning or reconfiguring the system [23].

An efficient health monitoring technique has to be adopted to determine the health state of the system at any time by using diagnostics and prognostics techniques. A diagnosis method is used to determine the current health state and identify the possible causes of failures that lead to this state by reasoning on observations. Prognosis is used to predict the future health states and the dates of the occurrences of the faults that lead to these states.

© Springer International Publishing Switzerland 2016
F. Kordon and D. Moldt (Eds.): PETRI NETS 2016, LNCS 9698, pp. 196–215, 2016.
DOI: 10.1007/978-3-319-39086-4_13

A system is considered as a *hybrid system* if it exhibits both *discrete and continuous dynamics* [13]. Sensor data and commands are designated as continuous or discrete observations on the system. Hybrid systems are usually described as a multi-mode system composed of an underlying discrete-event system (DES) representing the mode changes and various underlying continuous dynamics associated with each mode [3]. A discrete state of the DES coupled to a continuous evolution (continuous dynamics) represents a mode (or operational condition) of the system. The changes of modes are then associated with occurrences of *events*. The system *discrete state* is the current discrete state of the DES. The evolution of the system *continuous state* depends on continuous dynamics associated with the current system mode.

In most industrial systems, if the degradation is not observable, it is estimated as fault occurrence probabilities. The degradation thus depends on the stress level of the current health mode of the system and, in some cases, also relies on the current continuous state and also on the analysis of the events that occurred on the system [11]. Because of these dependencies, we consider the degradation as a hybrid characteristic. We thus defined the evolution of this hybrid characteristic as *hybrid dynamics* and its current value as the *hybrid state*. We extend the multi-mode system by associating underlying hybrid dynamics (e.g. degradation laws) with each mode. The definition of a *mode* is thus enriched and is a combination of a discrete state of the DES with continuous dynamics and hybrid dynamics [9]. The *state* of the hybrid system is the combination of its discrete, continuous and hybrid states.

Our previous works introduced a framework called *Hybrid Particle Petri Nets* (HPPN). [10] proposed to use HPPN to both model the system, which is hybrid but also uncertain, and track its current health state with a diagnoser representation. The methodology uses information about the system degradation that is a significant advantage to compute a more accurate diagnosis and to perform prognosis. In [11], we tested the proposed approach on a simulated three-tank system.

The main contribution of this paper is to expose results of the implemented HPPN-based health monitoring method on the K11 planetary rover prototype. The K11 is a testbed developed by NASA Ames Research Center and is used for diagnostics and prognostics purposes [1,7,8,23]. A hybrid model of the rover is proposed, based on the discretization of its health evolution. Experimental results are given, illustrating how the methodology is robust to real system data and constraints. The method exposed in [11] have been improved. It is hence recalled and new notions are precised, such as the definition of events, the mode scores or the scale parameters for example.

This paper is organized as follows. Section 2 presents related works on diagnosis of hybrid systems. Section 3 recalls and deepens the health monitoring methodology based on the modeling of the system and the generation of a diagnoser by using HPPN. Section 4 focuses on the application of the proposed methodology on the K11 planetary rover prototype. It provides the K11 hybrid model and exposes the experimental results and performance metrics. Conclusions and future works are discussed in the final section.

2   Related Works

In [5], we extended the diagnosis approach proposed in [3] in order to integrate diagnosis and prognosis for hybrid systems. The approach uses hybrid automata and stochastic models for the system degradation. Diagnosis is performed using a Discrete Event System (DES) approach. The DES-oriented diagnosis framework, however, explodes in the number of states and it does not seem to be the most suited for the incorporation of the prognosis task. Prognosis is indeed a probabilistic prediction process and is highly subject to uncertainty. The health monitoring task usually has to take into account the different sources of uncertainty, such as model approximation, partial observability of the system and measurement noise. Diagnosis should help the decision making process. In case of ambiguity in diagnosis results, the traditional diagnoser fails at providing relevant information. By taking all uncertainty sources into account, the method we propose succeeds in quantifying each diagnosis result.

The diagnoser approach was introduced in [21]. The diagnoser is basically a monitor that is able to process any possible observable event that occurs in the system. It consists in recording these observations and providing the set of possible faults whose occurrence is consistent with the observations. However, this approach is restricted to DES and does not manage uncertainty. Some approaches extend the diagnoser to DES modelled by Petri Nets. A distributed version of the diagnoser is proposed in [12]. In [4], the authors study the diagnosability of a system, inspired by the diagnosability approach for finite state automata proposed by [21]. However, none of these approaches take into account continuous aspects, nor consider uncertainty in the system. In [22], an approach for the localization of intermittent faults by dealing with partial observability in the discrete event framework is proposed. The method is based on Petri Nets that model the normal functioning of the system observable behavior. A localization mechanism, based on the diagnoser approach, points out the set of events potentially responsible for the faults.

Some works try to take into account uncertainty. In [15], a particle filtering technique is used to estimate the state of a hybrid system modeled as a hybrid automaton. Uncertainty related to discrete events is not taken into account and the system degradation is not considered. The authors of [20] use partially observed Petri Nets. Partially observed Petri Nets are transformed into an equivalent labelled Petri net and an online monitor is built to diagnose faults and provide beliefs (degrees of confidence) regarding the occurrences of faults. However, this approach is limited because it only takes into account uncertainty in the diagnosis results, not about the model or the event observations. In [2], the authors propose to reduce the explosion of the state space by introducing generalized markings (negative tokens) to take into account uncertainty about the firing of transitions. The stochastic Petri Nets are used in [14] to build a formal model of each component of an integrated modular avionics architecture. However, for all these approaches, no continuous aspect in the model is taken into account.

In [24], the Modified Particle Petri Nets (MPPN) formalism is used to get a more compact representation and to capture all uncertainties related to the system, the observations and the diagnosis results. MPPN are an extension of particle Petri Nets [17] that combine a discrete event model (Petri Net) with a continuous model (differential equations). The main advantage of MPPN is that uncertainties about both discrete and continuous dynamics are taken into account. A particle filter is used to integrate probabilities in the continuous state estimation process. Tokens are duplicated during the online process to model uncertainty on the event occurrences. The duplication, however, disturbs the distribution over the continuous state. In addition, there is no mention of the health state notion for the system. In [9], we apply the MPPN formalism to health monitoring and highlight the inability to capture hybrid characteristics. In [10], we extend MPPN into HPPN in order to monitor hybrid characteristics and solve the continuous distribution issue. HPPN are used to monitor a three-tank system, for which system degradation evolves according to the valves configurations.

This paper focuses on the application of the health monitoring methodology on the K11 rover, that is subject to the inherent uncertainty of real systems. In previous works, health monitoring and diagnosis was applied to the K11 rover. In [18], two diagnosis algorithms were applied, Qualitative Event-based Diagnosis (QED) [6], and the Hybrid Diagnosis Engine (HyDE) [19]. QED performs diagnosis based on reasoning over symbols representing qualitative deviations of the sensor signals with respect to model-predicted values. Sensor and process noise are handled by using an observer to estimate the current system state, however no uncertainty in the symbols computed for diagnosis is considered, and all diagnostic hypotheses are viewed as equally likely. HyDE is a consistency-based diagnosis engine that uses hybrid and stochastic models and reasoning. Reasoning is performed by hypothesizing alternative system trajectories inferred from the transition and behavior models of the system, and considers a priori fault probabilities and mode transition probabilities. Both diagnosis algorithms were used to diagnose parasitic load, motor friction, and voltage sensor faults in simulation. In [23], QED diagnosed parasitic load faults and voltage sensor faults in real-world scenarios.

3   Hybrid System Health Monitoring

This section recalls the methodology proposed in [11] to perform model-based health monitoring of hybrid systems.

We are interested in modeling changes in system dynamics when one or several anticipated faults occur. The *health modes* are the hybrid system modes and represent different health conditions. As long as the system does not encounter any fault, it is in a *nominal mode*. Tracked faults are assumed to be permanent, i.e. once a fault happens, the system moves from a nominal mode to a *degraded mode* or faulty mode. Without repair, the system ends in a *failure mode* in which it is not operational anymore.

The proposed diagnosis solution is a two-step method. The first offline step is to model the considered system using the HPPN framework (see Sect. 3.1) and to generate the HPPN-based diagnoser (see Sect. 3.2). Then the online process initializes the diagnoser marking and uses consecutive observations to update it and compute the diagnosis at any time (see Sect. 3.2).

Example 1. Throughout Sect. 3, an example of a mobile robot, described in Fig. 1, is used to illustrate the definitions and concepts.

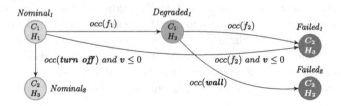

Fig. 1. Mobile robot description.

The system is described with an oriented graph, in which the nodes represent the health modes and the arcs represent the mode changes. Variables that can be observed or estimated with observations are in bold.

The robot mission is to move without encountering an obstacle or failure, until it reaches a specific area and is turned off. The initial mode is $Nominal_1$: the robot is not degraded and is moving in a non-hostile zone. Its velocity v can be estimated with continuous dynamics C_1 and continuous observations, and is positive. Two faults are expected and the robot degradation is estimated as fault occurrence probabilities with hybrid dynamics H_1, in which the probabilities increase with time.

When the (discrete and observable) on-off command *turn off* occurs, the robot stops and its velocity decreasing to 0. The robot enters in mode $Nominal_2$, where its motor is turned off and its velocity thus stays 0 (continuous dynamics C_2). Because the robot is turned off, the fault occurrence probabilities stagnate, following hybrid dynamics H_3.

Fault f_2 represents the disconnection of the robot motor. Its occurrence leads the system to the failure mode $Failed_1$. The occurrence of f_2 implies the robot stops, so its velocity decreases to 0. Once the motor is disconnected, the robot has the same continuous and hybrid dynamics (C_2 and H_3) as if it was turned off.

Fault f_1 represents the entrance in a hostile zone and in mode $Degraded_1$. The robot is still moving at the same velocity (C_1). The physical conditions, however, imply that the probability of occurrence of f_2 increases more significantly than in mode $Nominal_1$. This is defined with hybrid dynamics H_2.

From mode $Degraded_1$, the robot can still enter in mode $Failed_1$ with fault f_2 occurrence but it does not match with any condition on the velocity in that case (see arc between $Degraded_1$ and $Failed_1$). The velocity estimation is considered less accurate in the hostile zone than in the non-hostile zone, indeed.

Finally, the hostile zone contains obstacles. The robot can encounter a wall, that stops the robot but not its motor. In that case, the mission fails and the robot enters in failure mode $Failed_2$. This event $wall$ is not predictable (not estimated with probabilities) but is observable with an environmental on-off sensor. Even if the mission is compromised and the robot is not moving anymore (C_2), its motor is still on so the degradation laws remain the same (H_2).

3.1 Hybrid System Modeling

We propose to model the system by using the *Hybrid Particle Petri Nets* (HPPN) formalism, introduced in [10].

Hybrid Particle Petri Nets. The HPPN formalism is an extension of Petri Nets.

A HPPN is defined as a tuple $\langle P, T, A, \mathcal{A}, E, X, H, C, \mathcal{F}, \Omega, M_0 \rangle$ where:

- P is the set of places, partitioned into numerical places P^N, symbolic places P^S and hybrid places P^H,
- T is the set of transitions,
- $A \subset P \times T \cup T \times P$ is the set of arcs,
- $\mathcal{A}$ is the set of arc annotations,
- E is the set of event labels,
- $X \subset \mathbb{R}^n$ is the state space of the continuous state vector, with $n \in \mathbb{N}$ the number of continuous state variables,
- $H \subset \mathbb{R}^m$ is the state space of the hybrid state vector, with $m \in \mathbb{N}$ the number of hybrid state variables,
- C is the set of dynamic equation sets associated with numerical places, representing continuous dynamics,
- $\mathcal{F}$ is the set of dynamic equation sets associated with hybrid places, representing hybrid dynamics,
- Ω is the set of conditions associated with transitions,
- M_0 is the initial marking of the Petri net.

The marking M_k of the HPPN at time k is composed of tokens, that can be symbolic, numerical or hybrid tokens:

$$M_k = \{M_k^S, M_k^N, M_k^H\}. \tag{1}$$

Symbolic places model the discrete states of the system and are marked by configurations. Σ is the sets of events of the system. An event $e \in \Sigma$ is a couple (v, k) where $v \in E$ is an event label and k the time of occurrence of e. A *configuration* δ_k^i with $i \in \{1, ..., |M_k^S|\}$ is a symbolic token at time k and represents a possible set of events b_k^i that occurred on the system until time k. $b_k^i = \{e_j\}$ with $j \in \{1, ..., |b_k^i|\}$ and for any event $e_j = (v, \kappa)$, $\kappa \leq k$.

A numerical place $p^N \in P^N$ is associated with a set of dynamic equations $C(p^N)$ modeling system continuous dynamics and its corresponding model noise and measurement noise. They are marked with particles. A *particle* π_k^i, with $i \in \{1, ..., |M_k^N|\}$ is a numerical token at time k and represents a possible continuous state $x_k^i \in X$ of the system at time k.

A hybrid place $p^H \in P^H$ is associated with a set of dynamic equations $H(p^H)$ modeling system hybrid dynamics. They are marked with hybrid tokens. A *hybrid token* h_k^i, with $i \in \{1, ..., |M_k^H|\}$ is linked with a configuration δ_k^j and a particle π_k^i, and represents a possible hybrid state $d_k^i \in H$ of the system at time k.

The initial marking M_0 of a HPPN carries the system initial states b_0, x_0 and d_0.

A condition $\Omega(t)$ associated with a transition $t \in T$ is a Boolean function that combines tests on the values of the tokens in the input places of t. Let $^\circ t$ (t°) designate the set of input (output) places of t. A condition must involves at least one token in each place in $^\circ t$. A condition involving more than one type of tokens can be satisfied only if the tokens are linked with hybrid tokens. If $\Omega(t)$ involves a configuration δ_k, it can deal with the occurrence of an event labeled with $v \in E$ (faults, mission events, interaction with the environment, ...). In that case, it takes the form $occ(b_k, v)$, to test if the set of events b_k of δ_k contains the event (v, k). A condition $\Omega(t)$ that involves a particle π_k can concern the continuous state. For example, $c(x_k) < B$ tests if the constraint equation c on the numerical state vector x_k of π_k is greater than a threshold B. In the same way, a condition involving a hybrid token h_k can deal with the hybrid state by constraining the hybrid state vector d_k of h_k, e.g. $\varsigma(d_k) \geq \beta$. Finally, a condition that involves more than one token can be a Boolean expression combining two or the three kinds of conditions above, e.g. $\Omega(t)(\delta_k, \pi_k, h_k) = occ(b_k, v) \wedge (c(x_k) < B) \vee (\varsigma(d_k) \geq \beta)$.

An annotation $\varrho \in \mathcal{A}$ is associated with any arc $a \in A$ that connects a transition t to a symbolic place p^S. It is an assignment function defined as follows: if $\Omega(t)$ deals with the occurrence of an event labeled with $v \in E$, $\varrho(\delta^i)$ adds the event (v, k) to the event set b^i of δ^i, when δ^i is moved to p^S after the firing of t at time k.

Health Modeling. With the definition of the HPPN above, it is possible to build a health-oriented model of a hybrid system. We consider the system modes as health modes (nominal, degraded and failure modes). Symbolic places represent the different discrete health states of the system. Numerical (resp. Hybrid) places represent various system continuous (resp. hybrid) dynamics. Health modes are thus combinations of discrete states, continuous dynamics and hybrid dynamics. Transitions model changes of health modes, so any transition $t \in T$ must have three places (one of each type) in its sets of input places and three places in its set of output places. Two transitions cannot have both the same set of input places and the same set of output places.

An anticipated fault is represented by an unobservable event $f \in \Sigma_{uo} \subset \Sigma$, where Σ_{uo} is the set of unobservable events. Fault events are abstractions of changes of health mode that might be unobservable or difficult to describe as conditions on the continuous state.

Finally, we use conditions to model the change of health modes and then let the degradation state affect the system evolution. For example, if the degradation is modeled by a fault occurrence probability, a condition on the hybrid state can be a Boolean function satisfied if the probability is higher than a given threshold.

Example 2. The HPPN-based model of the mobile robot is presented in Fig. 2. Symbolic places are represented by places with regular thicknesses, while numerical and hybrid places are represented by places with medium and large thicknesses, respectively. Arcs that connect transitions and symbolic (numerical and hybrid) places are represented by solid (dashed and dotted) arrows.

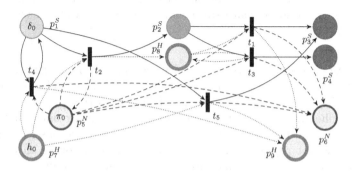

Fig. 2. Health-oriented model of the mobile robot using HPPN.

We decompose the five health modes of the robot into four symbolic places, two numerical places and three hybrid places. Four discrete health states are identified from the robot description (Fig. 1). One nominal state, one degraded state, and two different failure states are represented by the four symbolic places p_1^S, p_2^S, p_3^S and p_4^S, respectively. The two numerical places p_5^N and p_6^N represent the continuous dynamics C_1 and C_2. The three hybrid places p_7^H, p_8^H and p_9^H represent the hybrid dynamics H_1, H_2 and H_3, respectively. Five transitions represent the health mode changes. For example, transition t_4 represents the change from mode $Nominal_1$ to mode $Nominal_2$ so ${}^\circ t_4 = \{p_1^S, p_5^N, p_7^H\}$ and $t_4^\circ = \{p_1^S, p_6^N, p_9^H\}$.

The initial mode is $Nominal_1$ so δ_0, π_0 and h_0 are in p_1^S, p_5^N and p_7^H, respectively. At time $k = 0$, no event has occurred, so $b_0 = \{\}$. The only estimated state is the velocity, so $x_0 = [v_0]^T$ with $v_0 > 0$ because the velocity is initially positive. The initial fault occurrence probabilities $\rho_0^{f_1}$ and $\rho_0^{f_2}$ are very low. Thus, $d_0 = [\rho_0^{f_1}, \rho_0^{f_2}]^T$ with $\rho_0^{f_1} = 0.01$ and $\rho_0^{f_2} = 0.05$.

The condition $\Omega(t_4)(\delta_k, \pi_k, h_k) = occ(b_k, turn\ off) \wedge (x_k^0 \leq 0)$ tests if an event labeled with $turn\ off$ occurred at time k and if v_k is 0. We assume that a fault occurs if its probability of occurrence is greater than 0.9. Consequently, the condition associated with transition t_2 is $\Omega(t_2)(\delta_k, \pi_k, h_k) = occ(b_k, f_1) \vee (d_k^0 > 0.9)$. With the same reasoning, we obtain $\Omega(t_1)(\delta_k, \pi_k, h_k) = occ(b_k, f_2) \vee (d_k^1 > 0.9)$, $\Omega(t_3)(\delta_k, \pi_k, h_k) = occ(b_k, f_2) \wedge (x_k^0 \leq 0) \vee (d_k^1 > 0.9)$ and $\Omega(t_5)(\delta_k, \pi_k, h_k) = occ(b_k, wall)$.

3.2 Hybrid System Diagnosis

In a health monitoring context, diagnosis aims at tracking the system current *health state*. The system health state is the combination of its discrete, continuous and hybrid states. In earlier work, we proposed to build a *diagnoser* from a HPPN model [9]. The HPPN-based diagnoser is generated based on the HPPN specifying the system model. It is a HPPN that monitors both the system behavior and degradation under uncertainty. Its online process takes as inputs the set of observations on the system. The output of the diagnoser at any time k is an estimation of the system health state that takes the form of a marking of the diagnoser $\Delta_k = \hat{M}_k$.

Uncertainty. Several types of uncertainty are taken into account. Knowledge-based uncertainty must be taken into account because the model does not reflect perfectly reality, as for the symbolic part of the model than the numerical one. Due to the inherent imprecision of sensors, we also consider uncertainty about observations. Regarding the symbolic aspects, the possible observation of an event that has not really occurred and the non observation of an observable event that occurred are taken into account. Symbolic uncertainty is dealt with using *pseudo-firing* (i.e. duplication) of tokens [17,24]. Numerical uncertainty embodies the fact that the numerical values are imprecise. It is often dealt with through an estimator, that aims at estimating the continuous state according to model noise and measurement noise. We use particle filters to estimate the continuous state through the set of particles of the HPPN. The links between the configurations and the particles, provided by the hybrid tokens, are used to prevent the particle distribution to be disturbed by pseudo-firing.

Diagnoser Generation. Let us suppose that the health-oriented system model is a HPPN given by a tuple $\langle P, T, A, \mathcal{A}, E, X, H, C, \mathcal{F}, \Omega, M_0 \rangle$ as defined in Sect. 3.1.

The set of places of the diagnoser remains the same as the one of the model. Concerning the conditions associated with transitions, two aspects have to be taken into account. First, any Boolean function dealing with an event occurrence that is part of a condition $\Omega(t)$ is removed from it, in order to manage symbolic uncertainty (see Sect. 3.2). Arc annotations, however, are conserved to monitor event occurrences. Secondly, conditions on the hybrid state must also be substituted because a diagnoser works with observations (the degradation is estimated but not corrected with observations).

To improve computational performance, transitions of the HPPN are transformed following several rules defined in [11]. Basically, some transitions are merged and other are created in a way that the HPPN is separated in two levels. The *behavioral level* contains only the symbolic and numerical places, while the *hybrid level* contains the hybrid places. New transitions (called *hybrid transitions* in previous works) connect hybrid places. A hybrid token $h_k \in \hat{M}_k^H$ is moved from one hybrid place to another if it satisfies a condition associated with hybrid transition. Theses conditions are called *hybrid conditions* in previous work. The satisfaction of a hybrid condition depends on the places in which δ_k and π_k belong at time k, where δ_k and π_k are the configuration and the particle associated with h_k.

Example 3. Figure 3 shows the two levels of the HPPN-based diagnoser of the mobile robot example. The hybrid places are isolated and the hybrid transitions $\{t_i^H\}$ with $i \in \{6, ..., 11\}$ are added to the net. The condition associated to t_2 becomes $\Omega(t)(\delta_k, \pi_k) = \top$, a function returning *true* for any δ_k and π_k, because it does not depend on the continuous state. With the same reasoning, $\Omega(t_1)$ and $\Omega(t_3)$ become also $\top$, while $\Omega(t_4)$ and $\Omega(t_5)$ become $x_k^0 \leq 0$. Then transitions t_1 and t_3 (t_4 and t_5) have been merged because they were associated with the same condition, they have the same input places $\{p_2^S, p_5^N\}$ ($\{p_1^S, p_5^N\}$) and the numerical place p_6^N in their set of output places. The merging of t_4 and t_5 into t_{45} is useful to monitor at time k the possibilities to be in mode $Failed_1$ (δ_k^1, $\{\pi_k^i\}$ and $\{h_k^j\}$) and the one to be in mode $Failed_2$ (δ_k^2, $\{\pi_k^i\}$ and $\{h_k^l\}$) with the same set of particles $\{\pi_k^i\}$. This is particularly convenient because the particle filtering computation time increases with the number of particles.

Diagnoser Marking. In particle filtering, the number of particles defines the precision of the filter. A *possible mode* of the system is represented by a set of tokens composed of a configuration, n_k particles, and the n_k hybrid tokens that link the configuration to the particles, where n_k is representative of the

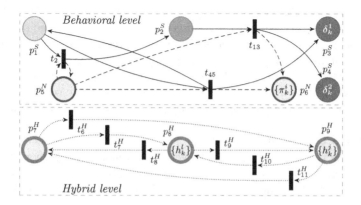

Fig. 3. HPPN-based diagnoser of the mobile robot.

precision associated to the monitoring of the mode at time k. The initial marking $M_0 = \{M_0^S, M_0^N, M_0^H\}$ represents the system's initial mode. It is composed of one configuration with value b_0, n_0^N particles with value x_0 and n_0^N hybrid tokens with value d_0, where n_0^N is the initial number of particles. The estimated marking at time k, $\hat{M}_k = \{\hat{M}_k^S, \hat{M}_k^N, \hat{M}_k^H\}$ where $\hat{M}_k = \hat{M}_{k|k}$, represents all the possible modes at time k. As long as only one mode is considered in the initial marking, two possible modes cannot share the same configuration, at any time k. However, two possible modes can share the same set of particles if they have the same continuous dynamics but different discrete states (see Example 3). As a consequence, the performance of the diagnoser regarding the uncertainty management is improved, in a way that the number of calculations is reduced where it can be. This is particularly true during the online process.

Diagnoser Process. The online process of the diagnoser is based on the evolution of the marking and on particle filters. A prediction step and a correction step are performed on the tokens to compute the marking of the diagnoser $\hat{M}_k$ at time k according to the observations $O_k = O_k^S \cup O_k^N$, where O^S and O^N respectively represent the observations corresponding to the symbolic part and the numerical part.

The prediction step aims at determining all possible next states of the diagnoser $\hat{M}_{k+1|k}$. It is based on the firing of the enabled transitions and on the update of the token values. All the enabled transitions are fired according to the rules described in [10]. This implies the assumption that a single event can occur at time k. The event set b_k of a configuration δ_k moved through an arc $a \in A$ during the transition firing, is updated according to the annotation $\mathcal{A}(a)$. The value x of a particle π is updated according to the continuous dynamics associated to the numerical place $p^N \in P^N$ in which π belongs after the transition firing. Noise is added during the particle value update to take into account uncertainty about model continuous dynamics. The value d of a hybrid token h is updated according to the hybrid dynamics associated to the hybrid place $p^H \in P^H$ in which h belongs after the transition firing.

The correction step updates the predicted marking $\hat{M}_{k+1|k}$ to the estimated marking $\hat{M}_{k+1|k+1}$ according to new observations O_{k+1}. It is based on the computation of the scores of all the possible modes represented by the marking and on the resampling of the tokens depending on the scores of the possible modes they represent. The scores of all possibles modes are computed with Pr^S and Pr^N, the probability distributions over the symbolic and the continuous states, respectively. Pr^S is the configuration weights. A configuration weight is computed as the inverse of exponential of the distance between the configuration event set and $O_{k+1}^- = \{O_\kappa | \kappa \leq k+1\}$, the set of symbolic observations until $k+1$. Pr^N is the normalized particle weights, calculated according to the distance between the particle values and numerical observations O_{k+1}^N. Then, the score of one possible mode is computed using a weighted function of the sum of its particle weights and its configuration weight:

$$Score(\delta_k^i, \{\pi_k^j\}, \{h_k^l\}) = \alpha \times Pr^S(\delta_k^i) + (1-\alpha) \times \sum_{j=1}^{n_k^N} Pr^N(\pi_k^j). \qquad (2)$$

where $\alpha \in [0,1]$ is the coefficient indicating the global confidence of the symbolic part relatively to the numerical part and $n_k^N = |\{\pi_k^j\}|$ is the number of particles considered for the given possible mode. The score of a possible mode is always between 0 and 1. A decision making process associates a new number of particles n_{k+1}^N to each set of particles, according to the best score of all the possible modes it belongs (see Sect. 3.2) and three scale parameters, denoted n_{min}^N, n_{suff}^N and n_{max}^N, of the HPPN. Each set of particles is then resampled with its associated n_{k+1}^N particles, like in classical particle filter. Parameters n_{min}^N and n_{suff}^N are respectively the minimum and the sufficient numbers of particles (but also hybrid tokens) to monitor a possible mode. It means that any n_{k+1}^N is chosen to satisfy the predicate $n_{min}^N \leq n_{k+1}^N \leq n_{suff}^N$. Parameter n_{max}^N is the maximum number of particles (hybrid tokens) available to monitor all possible modes. It means the total number of particles after the resampling is always less than or equal to n_{max}^N. During the resampling, hybrid tokens linked to duplicated particles are duplicated while those linked to deleted particles are deleted. Finally, configurations that are no longer linked with any hybrid tokens are deleted. The correction mechanism highlights that the hybrid tokens, in addition to estimate the hybrid state, prevent the particle distribution of one possible mode to be disturbed by the particle distributions of the other possible modes. In particle filtering, the number of particles defines the precision of the filter but is also a computational performed factor. The HPPN scale parameters thus compromise the number of possible modes to monitor and the precision granted to each one of them, relative to the available computational power (n_{max}^N can be set up to fulfill performance constraints).

The diagnosis Δ_k is deduced from the marking of the diagnoser at time k:

$$\Delta_k = \hat{M}_k = \{\hat{M}_k^S, \hat{M}_k^N, \hat{M}_k^H\}. \qquad (3)$$

It represents the distribution of beliefs over the current health mode and how this mode has been reached. In other words, the marking $\hat{M}_k$ indicates the belief over the continuous state, the fault occurrences and the system degradation. The HPPN-based diagnoser results include the results of a classical diagnoser in terms of fault occurrences. In a classical diagnoser, however, every possible diagnosis has the same belief degree. A HPPN-based diagnoser handles more uncertainty and evaluates the ambiguity according to the tokens places and values.

4   Case Study

This section focuses on the application of the proposed methodology on the K11 planetary rover prototype. The K11 is a four-wheeled rover designed as a platform for testing power-efficient rover architectures in Antarctic conditions [16].

The K11 has then been redesigned by NASA Ames Research Center for diagnostics and Prognostics-enabled Decision Making research [1, 7, 23]. It has been transformed into a testbed to simulate some fault occurrences and failures. In this work, it is studied as a functional rover exposed to failures and executing missions.

4.1 Rover Description

The K11 rover is powered by twenty-four 2.2 Ah lithium-ion single cell batteries. A typical mission of the rover consists in visiting and performing desired science functions at a set of waypoints, before joining its charging station. A decision making module (DM) is responsible for determining the order in which to visit the waypoints according to the terrain map, the waypoint positions and rewards, and the rover conditions. The rover has four wheels, denominated by their location: the front-left (FL) wheel, the front-right (FR) wheel, the back-left (BL) wheel and the back-right (BR) wheel. Each wheel is driven by an independent 250 W graphite-brush motor, with control performed by a single-axis digital motion controller. An onboard laptop computer runs the control and data acquisition software. The rover is a skid-steered vehicle, meaning that the wheels cannot be steered and the rover is rotated by commanding the wheel speeds on the left and right sides to different values. The battery management system provides battery charging and load balancing capabilities. It also sends voltage and temperature measurements for each of the individual cells to the onboard computer. The data acquisition module collects current and motor temperature measurements and sends them to the onboard computer. The motor controllers send back motion data such as commanded speeds and actual speeds. More details on the rover can be found in [1].

All the continuous observations on the rover and the list of faults we consider in this study are presented in Table 1. Four signals command the wheels with a proportional-integral-derivative controller and the set of sensors returns 61 measurement signals. Several fault types have been implemented on the testbed and are related to the power system (battery), the electro-mechanical system (motors, controller), and the sensors (drift, bias, scaling or failure).

The K11 rover has no discrete actuator or discrete sensor and thus has mostly been studied as a continuous system, where faults were defined as constraints on the continuous state. We propose to abstract anticipated faults into unobservable events. The multi-mode system that describes the rover health evolution is presented in Fig. 4. To simplify the description, only a part of the multi-mode system is shown. The modes corresponding to consecutive fault occurrences are not included and only the front-left motor is considered.

The rover is in mode $Nominal_1$ with continuous dynamics C_1 as long as no fault has occurred. Fault f_1 occurrence represents the *end of discharge* (EOD) of the battery, i.e. the date when the battery is too discharged to power the system. This is assumed to occur when the battery voltage is lower than 3.25 V and it leads to the mission failure (mode $Failed_1$ with continuous dynamics C_5).

Table 1. Continuous commands, continuous measurements, and fault types on the K11

Command type	Comments	Units
Wheel speed	Commanded speeds for wheels on the same side are the same	rad/s
Measurement type	Comments	Units
Wheel speed	One for each wheel	rad/s
Total current	A current sensor on the power bus	A
Motor current	One for each motor	A
Motor temperature	One for each motor	°C
Battery temperature	One for each battery cell	°C
Battery voltage	One for each battery cell	V
Fault event labels	Fault descriptions	Effects
f_1	Battery charge depletion	Lead to failure
f_2	Parasitic electric load	Increase battery drain
f_3, f_4, f_5, f_6	Increased motor frictions	Increase battery drain and motor temperatures
f_7, f_8, f_9, f_{10}	Motor overheating	Lead to failure
$f_{11}, f_{12}, f_{13}, f_{14}$	Failed motor temperature sensors	Unable to estimate motor temperatures

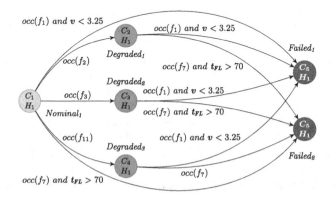

Fig. 4. Streamlined description of the rover health evolution.

Fault f_2 represents the emergence of a parasitic battery load arising from an electrical submodule continuously engaged, for example. The parasitic load increases the total current and thus the battery drain (mode $Degraded_1$ with continuous dynamics C_2), which causes the system to reach the EOD prematurely. Fault f_3 (f_4, f_5 and f_6) represents an increased friction of the FL (FR, BL and BR) motor. The increased friction induces the need for a larger amount of current to satisfy the same speed (mode $Degraded_2$ with continuous dynamics C_3). Furthermore, the load demands will be higher, raising the motor temperature. The most feared scenario for a motor is an overheating. In such case, the heat will eventually destroy the insulation of the windings, causing electrical shorts and leading to motor failure. The overheating of the FL (FR, BL and BR) motor is represented by fault f_7 (f_8, f_9 and f_{10}). The occurrence of any one of these faults leads to the rover failure (mode $Failed_2$ with continuous dynamics C_5) and thus represents the rover *end of life* (EOL). A motor is assumed to overheat when its temperature exceeds $70\,°C$. The motor temperatures are measured by four sensors. These sensors, however, are known to fail unexpectedly, sending inconsistent values. These failures are represented by faults f_{11} f_{12}, f_{13} and f_{14}. We consider that the temperature model is not accurate enough without a correction step with observations. As a consequence, once f_{11} (f_{12}, f_{13} and f_{14}) has occurred, the occurrence of fault f_7 (f_8, f_9 and f_{10}) does not match with any condition on the FL (FR, BL and BR) motor temperature (see the arc between $Degraded_3$ and $Failed_2$). In Fig. 4, mode $Degraded_3$ with continuous dynamics C_4 represents the mode where the temperature sensor of the FL motor has failed. The rover has no hybrid state to monitor, so all modes have the same hybrid dynamics H_1, which corresponds to the identity dynamics.

4.2   Rover Modeling

Considering all the motors and the consecutive fault combinations, we identified 192 modes and 240 mode changes. The HPPN-based model of the rover has 241 places (192 symbolic, 48 numerical places, 1 hybrid place) and 240 transitions. The HPPN-based diagnoser has the same number of places and transitions. The merging step of the diagnoser generation does not reduce the number of transitions (specific to the case study) but still the hybrid place is removed from the transition inputs and outputs, reducing the complexity of the net. Because there is only one hybrid place, there is no hybrid transition. The underlying DES of the multi-mode system and HPPN-based model and diagnoser of the K11 rover are available at https://homepages.laas.fr/echanthe/PetriNets2016.

The nominal continuous model is represented as a set of differential equations that unifies the battery model with the rover motion model and the temperature models. It can be converted to a discrete-time representation and solved with a sample time of $1/20$ s, while continuous observation sampling is about 1 s. We consider 30 state variables for the rover, including the rover 3-dimensional position, its relative angle position, the wheel control errors, the motor temperatures and motor winding temperatures. The 24 batteries are lumped into a single one to only consider 5 battery state variables (3 charges, the temperature and the voltage) instead of 120. The battery model has been validated with experimental data in previous works [7,23]. Unifying the battery model with motion and temperatures, however, increases uncertainty about the rover model.

Fault f_2 occurrence and effect are modeled as a time varying parameter. The parasitic battery load is captured as an additional current reaching a value between 1.5 A and 4.5 A from value 0 A in a few seconds after the fault occurrence. First, two parameters are added to the continuous state vector to monitor both the duration since the fault occurrence and the additional current value. Then, the uncertain rise of the additional current is modeled by adding a Gaussian noise, with a mean and standard deviation values starting respectively at 3 and 0.3, and decreasing to 0 while the duration since the fault occurrence increases.

Finally, the temperature model is quite uncertain so temperature measurements are assumed to be reliable when sensors are not failed. We model fault $f_{11}, f_{12}, f_{13}, f_{14}$ by increasing significantly the motor temperature sensor noise because failed sensors only send inconsistent large values with no pattern. Fault f_3, f_4, f_5 and f_6 and increased motor frictions can be modeled with time varying parameters (as additional motor resistances) like f_2 but are not monitored in this study.

4.3 Results

The HPPN framework is implemented in Python 3.4. The tests were performed on a 4 Intel(R) Core(TM) i5-4590 CPU at 3.30 GHz with 16 GB of RAM and running GNU/Linux (Linux 3.13.0 − 74, x86_64). In order to reduce computation time, the token value update step is multithreaded on the 4 physical cores. The rest of this implementation only uses one core.

Two scenarios studied in [23] are considered in this work. The rover mission is to visit a maximum of 12 waypoints and to go back to its starting position. All waypoints have different associated rewards. In nominal conditions, the rover DM system returns a 5-waypoints path, starting and finishing at the same position. For all scenarios, the K11 rover starts at 0 s with batteries fully charged and with all components at the ambient temperature. The K11 rover currently has, however, 2 motor temperature sensors (FL and BL) failed. These faults do affect the monitoring but not the physical system, so the DM returns the same path as in nominal conditions.

The sensors faults are diagnosed in one sampling period by the diagnoser if we consider the initial mode to be unknown. We assume to know the rover initial degraded mode.

For the sake of clarity, in the rest of the paper, modes are designated with representative keywords of the rover state. For example, the initial mode is designated as *Sensor BL FL fault*. The initial number of particles and hybrid tokens is $n_0^N = 100$. Finally, due to the high uncertainty related to the unified model of the rover, we set the scale parameters to $(n_{min}^N, n_{suff}^N, n_{max}^N) = (40, 80, 6000)$.

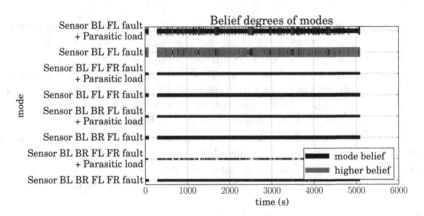

Fig. 5. Scenario 1: mode belief at any time (Color figure online).

Scenario 1. In Scenario 1, no fault occurs. The rover successfully executes its mission. Figure 5 presents the distribution of beliefs over the current health mode at any time.

The belief degree of a possible mode is its score computed with Eq. 2 and α set to 0.5. Any belief degree is between 0 and 1, but the sum of the belief degrees of all possible modes is not 1. In Fig. 5, the maximum belief degree of a mode at any time is represented by the thickness of the line and the highest belief degree of all the modes is plotted in blue. The gap between 81 s and 281 s corresponds to a break during the experiment. The figure shows that the diagnoser keeps the real mode *Sensor BL FL fault* in its set of candidates and assigns it the highest belief degree almost all along the scenario. Other modes are also highly considered by the diagnoser at any time because of the model-based uncertainty.

Scenario 2. In Scenario 2, a battery parasitic load occurs between 660 s and 695 s, and the DM system cancels the visit of the farthest waypoint. Fault f_2 occurrence is immediately detected by the diagnoser (Fig. 6). After 678 s, the possibility of being in mode *Sensor BL FL fault + Parasitic load* is the highest until the end of the mission. The fault load is estimated (most likely) at 1.39 A at 678 s, 1.73 A at 679 s, 2.16 A at 683 s and 2.16 A at 3906 s. A zoom between 570 s and 760 s on the trajectories of the modes that are still possible at 3906 s (Fig. 7) shows that fault f_2 is believed to occur between 631 s and 694 s, and most likely between 677 s and 689 s. These results are consistent with our analysis of the measured total current.

Faults are always detected in one sampling period because the HPPN considers all possibilities during the online process prediction step and keeps the matching marking during the correction step. The results show that the diagnoser grants most of the time but not always, the highest belief to the real mode. The diagnosis, however, carries all the explanation of the observations as a distribution of beliefs, and then the real mode is always considered in the set

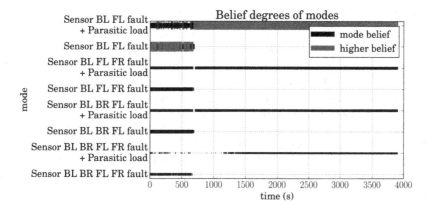

Fig. 6. Scenario 2: mode belief at any time.

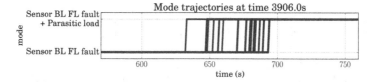

Fig. 7. Scenario 2: trajectories of possible modes at time 3906 s.

of candidates. This illustrates the robustness of the HPPN-based diagnoser to the rover model and data. The average diagnosis computation time and token number are 13.3 s and 8801.4, respectively. These metrics point out the diagnosis computation time remains acceptable compared to the system model computational complexity. The maximum RAM used by Scenarios 1 and 2 are 140.7 MB and 141.8 MB.

The case study results show that HPPN-based diagnosis is robust to real system data and constraints and adaptable to systems without discrete observations nor degradation knowledge.

5 Conclusion

This work applies the approach of health monitoring based on Hybrid Particle Petri Nets to a real case study, the K11 planetary rover prototype. The HPPN approach is particularly useful to take into account knowledge-based and observation-based uncertainty. The HPPN-based diagnoser deals with event occurrence possibility and knowledge imprecision. It monitors both discrete and continuous dynamics, as well as hybrid characteristics, such as degradation, in order to introduce concepts that will be useful to perform prognosis and health management of hybrid systems under uncertainty. In addition, diagnosis results can be used as probability distributions for decision making.

Then, the methodology was applied on the K11 rover. A hybrid model of the rover has been proposed by discretizing its health evolution and defining fault events. The model and diagnoser have been generated and two scenarios have been tested to illustrate the proposed method advantages. The diagnoser results are consistent with the expected ones and show that HPPN-based diagnosis is robust to real system data and constraints and adaptable to systems without discrete observations nor degradation knowledge.

In future work, futher scenarios will be tested. We also aim at formalizing and developing a prognosis process that will interleave diagnosis and prognosis methods to obtain more accurate results. The HPPN-based prognostics methodology will be defined and tested on a three-tank system as well as on the K11 rover.

References

1. Balaban, E., Narasimhan, S., Daigle, M.J., Roychoudhury, I., Sweet, A., Bond, C., Celaya, J.R., Gorospe, G.: Development of a mobile robot test platform and methods for validation of prognostics-enabled decision making algorithms. Int. J. Prognostics Health Manag. 4(006), 1–19 (2013)
2. Basile, F., Chiacchio, P., Tommasi, G.D.: Fault diagnosis and prognosis in Petri Nets by using a single generalized marking estimation. In: 7th IFAC Symposium on Fault Detection, Supervision and Safety of Technical Processes, Spain (2009)
3. Bayoudh, M., Travé-Massuyes, L., Olive, X.: Hybrid systems diagnosis by coupling continuous and discrete event techniques. In: IFAC World Congress, Korea, pp. 7265–7270 (2008)
4. Cabasino, M.P., Giua, A., Seatzu, C.: Diagnosability of discrete-event systems using labeled Petri Nets. IEEE Trans. Autom. Sci. Eng. 11(1), 144–153 (2014)
5. Chanthery, E., Ribot, P.: An integrated framework for diagnosis and prognosis of hybrid systems. In: 3rd Workshop on Hybrid Autonomous System, Italy (2013)
6. Daigle, M., Roychoudhury, I., Bregon, A.: Qualitative event-based diagnosis applied to a spacecraft electrical power distribution system. Control Eng. Pract. 38, 75–91 (2015)
7. Daigle, M., Roychoudhury, I., Bregon, A.: Integrated diagnostics and prognostics for the electrical power system of a planetary rover. In: Annual Conference of the PHM Society, USA (2014)
8. Daigle, M., Sankararaman, S., Kulkarni, C.S.: Stochastic prediction of remaining driving time and distance for a planetary rover. In: IEEE Aerospace Conference (2015)
9. Gaudel, Q., Chanthery, E., Ribot, P., Le Corronc, E.: Hybrid systems diagnosis using modified particle Petri Nets. In: 25th International Workshop on Principles of Diagnosis, Austria (2014)
10. Gaudel, Q., Chanthery, E., Ribot, P.: Health monitoring of hybrid systems using hybrid particle Petri Nets. In: Annual Conference of the PHM Society, USA (2014)
11. Gaudel, Q., Chanthery, E., Ribot, P.: Hybrid particle Petri Nets for systems health monitoring under uncertainty. Int. J. Prognostics Health Manag. 6(022), 1–20 (2015)
12. Genc, S., Lafortune, S.: Distributed diagnosis of place-bordered Petri Nets. IEEE Trans. Autom. Sci. Eng. 4(2), 206–219 (2007)

13. Henzinger, T.: The theory of hybrid automata. In: 11th Annual IEEE Symposium on Logic in Computer Science, pp. 278–292 (1996)
14. Jianxiong, W., Xudong, X., Xiaoying, B., Chuang, L., Xiangzhen, K., Jianxiang, L.: Performability analysis of avionics system with multilayer HM/FM using stochastic Petri Nets. Chin. J. Aeronaut. **26**(2), 363–377 (2013)
15. Koutsoukos, X., Kurien, J., Zhao, F.: Monitoring and diagnosis of hybrid systems using particle filtering methods. In: 15th International Symposium on Mathematical Theory of Networks and Systems, USA (2002)
16. Lachat, D., Krebs, A., Thueer, T., Siegwart, R.: Antarctica rover design and optimization for limited power consumption. In: 4th IFAC Symposium on Mechatronic Systems (2006)
17. Lesire, C., Tessier, C.: Particle Petri Nets for aircraft procedure monitoring under uncertainty. In: Ciardo, G., Darondeau, P. (eds.) ICATPN 2005. LNCS, vol. 3536, pp. 329–348. Springer, Heidelberg (2005)
18. Narasimhan, S., Balaban, E., Daigle, M., Roychoudhury, I., Sweet, A., Celaya, J., Goebel, K.: Autonomous decision making for planetary rovers using diagnostic and prognostic information. In: 8th IFAC Symposium on Fault Dectection, Supervision and Safety of Technical Processes, Mexico, pp. 289–294 (2012)
19. Narasimhan, S., Browston, L.: HyDE - a general framework for stochastic and hybrid modelbased diagnosis. In: 18th International Workshop on Principles of Diagnosis, pp. 162–169 (2007)
20. Ru, Y., Hadjicostis, C.N.: Fault diagnosis in discrete event systems modeled by partially observed Petri Nets. Discrete Event Dyn. Syst. **19**(4), 551–575 (2009)
21. Sampath, M., Sengupta, R., Lafortune, S., Sinnamohideen, K., Teneketzis, D.: Diagnosability of discrete-event systems. IEEE Trans. Autom. Control **40**(9), 1555–1575 (1995)
22. Soldani, S., Combacau, M., Subias, A., Thomas, J.: On-board diagnosis system for intermittent fault: application in automotive industry. In: 7th IFAC International Conference on Fieldbuses and Networks in Industrial and Embedded Systems, vol. 7-1, pp. 151–158 (2007)
23. Sweet, A., Gorospe, G., Daigle, M., Celaya, J.R., Balaban, E., Roychoudhury, I., Narasimhan, S.: Demonstration of prognostics-enabled decision making algorithms on a hardware mobile robot test platform. In: Annual Conference of the PHM Society, USA (2014)
24. Zouaghi, L., Alexopoulos, A., Wagner, A., Badreddin, E.: Modified particle Petri Nets for hybrid dynamical systems monitoring under environmental uncertainties. In: IEEE/SICE International Symposium on System Integration, pp. 497–502 (2011)

Conformance Checking

Merging Alignments for Decomposed Replay

H.M.W. Verbeek[(✉)] and W.M.P. van der Aalst

Department of Mathematics and Computer Science,
Eindhoven University of Technology, Eindhoven, The Netherlands
{h.m.w.verbeek,w.m.p.v.d.aalst}@tue.nl

Abstract. In the area of process mining, conformance checking aims
to find an optimal alignment between an event log (which captures the
activities that actually have happened) and a Petri net (which describes
expected or normative behavior). Optimal alignments highlight discrep-
ancies between observed and modeled behavior. To find an optimal alignment, a potentially challenging optimization problem needs to be solved
based on a predefined cost function for misalignments. Unfortunately,
this may be very time consuming for larger logs and models and often
intractable. A solution is to decompose the problem of finding an optimal
alignment in many smaller problems that are easier to solve. Decomposition can be used to detect conformance problems in less time and provides a lower bound for the costs of an optimal alignment. Although the
existing approach is able to decide whether a trace fits or not, it does not
provide an overall alignment. In this paper, we provide an algorithm that
is able to provide such an optimal alignment from the decomposed alignments if this is possible. Otherwise, the algorithm produces a so-called
pseudo-alignment that can still be used to pinpoint non-conforming parts
of log and model. The approach has been implemented in ProM and
tested on various real-life event logs.

1 Introduction

The ultimate goal of *process mining* [2] is to gain process-related insights based
on an *event log* created by some system. Such an event log contains a sequence of
events for every case that was handled by the system. As an example, an event
could be as follows:

On October 1st, 2011, the resource 112 has completed the activity a_1.

A sequence of events contained in an event log is commonly referred to as a *trace*.
From the data associated with the trace, we can derive for which particular case
the activity a_1 was completed.

Within process mining, the field of *process conformance* [2, 4, 5, 7–11, 13, 15,
17] deals with checking to what extent a process model (like a Petri net) and an
event log conform to each other, that is, how well they match. For this sake, the
event log is first replayed on the Petri net *as best as possible*, which results in
an *optimal alignment* between both. Such an optimal alignment relates events

© Springer International Publishing Switzerland 2016
F. Kordon and D. Moldt (Eds.): PETRI NETS 2016, LNCS 9698, pp. 219–239, 2016.
DOI: 10.1007/978-3-319-39086-4_14

in the event log to activities (transition labels) in the Petri net in the best-possible way. Based on this optimal alignment, conclusions can then be drawn on important metrics like *fitness* (how well does the event log conform to the Petri net?), *precision* (how well does the Petri net conform to the event log?), and *generalization* (how well does the Petri net conform to the system?).

A cutting-edge algorithm to compute an alignment is the *cost-based replayer* [3], which finds a *cost-minimal* alignment between the event log and the Petri net. Although this algorithm is very efficient and effective for smaller logs and smaller nets, it has problems when dealing with larger logs and larger nets. To speed up problematic replays, a *decomposition technique* has been proposed in [1]. This decomposition technique decomposes an overall log and an overall Petri net into a collection of decomposed logs and a collection of matching decomposed Petri nets, and guarantees that the decomposed costs (the costs of the replaying the decomposed logs on the decomposed nets) equal 0 if and only if the non-decomposed costs (the costs of replaying the overall log on the overall net) equal 0. *Hence, the approach is able to accurately identify deviating and non-deviating traces, often in a fraction of the time.* Furthermore, this technique guarantees that the decomposed costs are a lower bound for the non-decomposed costs.

An open issue for the decomposition approach is that it does not prescribe how to *merge the decomposed alignments* into an overall alignment, if possible. Whereas the replay of the overall log on the overall net results in an overall alignment, replaying the decomposed logs on the decomposed nets results in a collection of decomposed alignments. By merging these decomposed alignments into an overall alignment, which may be much faster than computing the non-decomposed alignment, one can also obtain diagnostic information on where the event log and the Petri net do not match. This paper introduces an algorithm to merge decomposed alignments into an overall alignment, again if possible. If not possible, then the algorithm will result in a so-called *pseudo-alignment*, which is a relaxation of the regular alignment. Such pseudo-alignments provide valuable diagnostic information and help to diagnose the misalignments.

The core of this algorithm consists of 3 alignment rules and 2 pseudo-alignment rules. Only applying the alignment rules will result in an alignment, but might not be feasible as in certain situations no alignment rule can be applied anymore. In such situations, we can apply a pseudo-alignment rule, but then the result will be a pseudo-alignment.

The approach has been implemented in ProM and has been applied to a large collection of logs and models showing that the constructed (pseudo-)alignments indeed help to diagnose conformance problems.

The remainder of this paper is organized follows. First, Sect. 2 provides the preliminaries, that is, logs, nets, alignments, and the decomposition. Second, Sect. 3 introduces our alignment merge, that is, the 3 alignment rules and the 2 pseudo-alignment rules. Third, Sect. 4 introduces the implementation of the merge. Fourth, Sect. 5 discusses the benefits of using the algorithm. Fifth, Sect. 6 concludes the paper.

2 Preliminaries

2.1 Logs

In this paper, we consider *activity logs*, which are an abstraction of the *event logs* as found in practice. An *activity log* is a collection of traces, where every trace is a sequence of *activities* [2]. Table 1 shows the example activity log L_1, which contains information about 20 cases, for example, 4 cases followed the trace $\langle a_1, a_2, a_4, a_5, a_8 \rangle$. In total, the log contains $13 + 17 + 9 + 2 \times 9 + 9 + 4 \times 5 + 9 + 9 + 5 + 5 + 17 + 3 \times 5 + 5 + 5 = 156$ activities.

Definition 1 (Universe of Activities). *The set $\mathcal{A}$ denotes the universe of activities.*

To capture an activity log, we use multi-sets. If S is a set of objects, then $\mathcal{B}(S)$ is a multi-set of objects, that is, if $B \in \mathcal{B}(S)$ and $o \in S$, then object o occurs $B(o)$ times in multi-set B.

Definition 2 (Activity Log). *Let $A \subseteq \mathcal{A}$ be a set of activities. An activity log L over A is a multi-set of activity traces over A, that is, $L \in \mathcal{B}(A^*)$.*

2.2 Nets

A Petri net is a modelling formalism that contains three different types of elements: *places*, *transitions*, and *arcs* [16]. Figure 1 shows an example Petri net containing 10 places (p_1 through p_{10}), 11 transitions (t_1 through t_{11}), and 24 arcs.

Table 1. An example activity log L_1 in tabular form.

Trace	Frequency
$\langle a_1, a_2, a_4, a_5, a_6, a_2, a_4, a_5, a_6, a_4, a_2, a_5, a_7 \rangle$	1
$\langle a_1, a_2, a_4, a_5, a_6, a_3, a_4, a_5, a_6, a_4, a_3, a_5, a_6, a_2, a_4, a_5, a_7 \rangle$	1
$\langle a_1, a_2, a_4, a_5, a_6, a_3, a_4, a_5, a_7 \rangle$	1
$\langle a_1, a_2, a_4, a_5, a_6, a_3, a_4, a_5, a_8 \rangle$	2
$\langle a_1, a_2, a_4, a_5, a_6, a_4, a_3, a_5, a_7 \rangle$	1
$\langle a_1, a_2, a_4, a_5, a_8 \rangle$	4
$\langle a_1, a_3, a_4, a_5, a_6, a_4, a_3, a_5, a_7 \rangle$	1
$\langle a_1, a_3, a_4, a_5, a_6, a_4, a_3, a_5, a_8 \rangle$	1
$\langle a_1, a_3, a_4, a_5, a_8 \rangle$	1
$\langle a_1, a_4, a_2, a_5, a_6, a_4, a_2, a_5, a_6, a_3, a_4, a_5, a_6, a_2, a_4, a_5, a_8 \rangle$	1
$\langle a_1, a_4, a_2, a_5, a_7 \rangle$	3
$\langle a_1, a_4, a_2, a_5, a_8 \rangle$	1
$\langle a_1, a_4, a_3, a_5, a_7 \rangle$	1
$\langle a_1, a_4, a_3, a_5, a_8 \rangle$	1

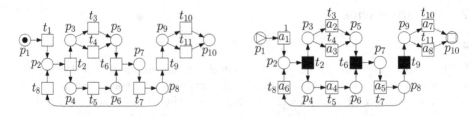

Fig. 1. A Petri net.   **Fig. 2.** An accepting Petri net N_1.

Definition 3 (Petri Net). *A Petri net is a 3-tuple (P, T, F) where P is a set of places, T is a set of transitions such that $P \cap T = \emptyset$, and $F \subseteq (P \times T) \cup (T \times P)$ is a set of arcs.*

For our purposes, we extend Petri nets with labels, an initial marking, and a set of final markings, yielding an *accepting* Petri net. Figure 2 shows an accepting Petri net based on the example Petri net, with labels (like a_1 and a_8), an initial marking ($[p_1]$), and one final marking ($[p_{10}]$).

The labels are used to link transitions in the Petri net to activities in an activity log. As an example, transition t_1 is linked to activity a_1. Transitions that are linked to log activities are called *visible* transitions. Transitions that are not linked to a log activity, like transition t_2, are called *invisible* transitions. These invisible transitions are linked to a dummy activity named τ. Note that $\tau \notin \mathcal{A}$.

Definition 4 (Accepting Petri Net). *Let $A \subseteq \mathcal{A}$ be a set of activities. An accepting Petri net over the set of activities A is a 6-tuple (P, T, F, l, I, O) where (P, T, F) is a Petri net, $l \in T \to (A \cup \{\tau\})$ is a labeling function that links every transition onto an activity (possibly the dummy activity τ), $I \in \mathcal{B}(P)$ is an initial marking, and $O \subseteq \mathcal{B}(P)$ is a set of final markings.*

As a result of the labeling, we can obtain an *activity sequence* from a transition sequence by removing all invisible transitions while replacing every visible transition with its label. For example, the example transition sequence $\langle t_1, t_2, t_3 \rangle$ yields $\langle a_1, a_2 \rangle$ as activity sequence.

The initial marking and final markings are included because process mining considers complete traces and not a prefix-closed language. When replaying an activity log on a Petri net, the Petri net needs to have an initial marking to start with, and final markings to conclude whether the replay has reached a proper final marking. In the example, a replay of some trace starts from marking $[p_1]$, and the replay will be successful if and only if the marking $[p_{10}]$ is reached.

2.3 Alignments

A *trace alignment* [2,3] links activities in a trace onto transitions in a Petri net. As an example, Fig. 3 shows a possible trace alignment for the trace

a_1	τ	a_2	a_3	a_4	τ	a_5	a_6	τ	a_7	a_8
t_1	t_2	t_3	$\gg$	t_5	t_6	t_7	$\gg$	t_9	t_{10}	$\gg$
0	0	0	10	0	0	0	10	0	0	10

Fig. 3. A trace alignment extended with costs for the trace $\langle a_1, \ldots, a_8 \rangle$ and net N_1. Every column corresponds to a move, where the top row contains the activity, the middle row the transitions, and the bottom row the costs of this activity-transition pair.

$\langle a_1, a_2, a_3, a_4, a_5, a_6, a_7, a_8 \rangle$ and the accepting Petri net N_1. We use $\gg$ to denote the *lack* of a visible transition in an alignment. For example, the occurrence of activity a_3 was not matched by a firing of transition t_4 in the net. In such a case, we use $\gg$ to indicate that no corresponding transition was fired. Likewise, although not present in this example, it is possible that transition t_4 was fired but that this was not matched by an occurrence of activity a_3 in the log. In such a case, we also use $\gg$ but now to indicate that no corresponding activity occurred.

The occurrence of a_1 matches the firing of transition t_1 (this is a so-called *synchronous move*, as both the log and the net can advance), then we need to fire the transition t_2 in the net which has no counterpart in the log (a so-called *invisible model move*), followed by another synchronous move for a_2 and t_3, after which we need to skip the activity a_3 (a so-called *log move*) as there is no transition enabled in the net that matches this activity, etc. Note that we require the transition sequence in the middle row of the alignment to lead from the initial marking of the net to some final marking.

Definition 5 (Legal Moves). *Let $A \subseteq \mathcal{A}$ be a set of activities, let $\sigma \in A^*$ be an activity trace over A, and let $N = (P, T, F, l, I, O)$ be an accepting Petri net over A. The set of legal moves of A and N is the union of the sets $\{(a, t) | a \in A \land t \in T \land l(t) = a\}$ (synchronous moves), $\{(a, \gg) | a \in A\}$ (log moves), $\{(\gg, t) | t \in T \land l(t) \in A\}$ (visible model moves), and $\{(\tau, t) | t \in T \land l(t) = \tau\}$ (invisible model moves).*

Definition 6 (Trace Alignment). *Let $A \subseteq \mathcal{A}$ be a set of activities, let $\sigma \in A^*$ be an activity trace over A, and let $N = (P, T, F, l, I, O)$ be an accepting Petri net over A. A trace alignment h for trace σ on net N is a sequence of legal moves $(a, t) \in ((A \cup \{\tau, \gg\}) \times (T \cup \{\gg\}))$ such that:*

- $\sigma = h \upharpoonright_A^1$ *and*
- *For some $o \in O$ it holds that $I [h \upharpoonright_T^2 \rangle o$,*

where

$$h \upharpoonright_A^1 = \begin{cases} \langle \rangle & \text{if } h = \langle \rangle; \\ \langle a \rangle \cdot \overline{h} \upharpoonright_A^1 & \text{if } h = \langle (a, t) \rangle \cdot \overline{h} \text{ and } a \in A; \\ \overline{h} \upharpoonright_A^1 & \text{if } h = \langle (a, t) \rangle \cdot \overline{h} \text{ and } a \notin A; \end{cases}$$

and

$$h\lceil_T^2 = \begin{cases} \langle\rangle & \text{if } h = \langle\rangle; \\ \langle t\rangle \cdot \overline{h}\lceil_T^2 & \text{if } h = \langle(a,t)\rangle \cdot \overline{h} \text{ and } t \in T; \\ \overline{h}\lceil_T^2 & \text{if } h = \langle(a,t)\rangle \cdot \overline{h} \text{ and } t \notin T; \end{cases}$$

The bottom row in Fig. 3 shows the possible *costs* of every move. In this example, a synchronous move costs 0, a visible model move costs 4, an invisible model move costs 0, and a log move costs 10. The total costs for the example alignment is 30.

Definition 7 (Costs Structure). *Let $A \subseteq \mathcal{A}$ be a set of activities, and let $N = (P, T, F, l, I, O)$ be an accepting Petri net over A. A cost structure $\$$ for A and N is a function that maps every legal move of A and N onto a (non-negative) natural number.*

Typically, the costs of all synchronous moves and all invisible model moves are set to 0, as then a perfect match has costs 0. The user then only needs to set the costs for the log moves and the visible model moves. If these costs would be set to 10 and 4 for all transitions and activities, then we would have that $\$(\gg, t_3) = 4$, $\$(a_2, \gg) = 10$, and $\$(a_2, t_3) = 0$.

Definition 8 (Costs of Trace Alignment). *Let $A \subseteq \mathcal{A}$ be a set of activities, let $\sigma \in A^*$ be an activity trace over A, let $N = (P, T, F, l, I, O)$ be an accepting Petri net over A, let $h = \langle(a_1, t_1), \ldots, (a_n, t_n)\rangle$ be a trace alignment (of length n) for σ and N, and let $\$$ be a cost structure for A and N. The costs of trace alignment h, denoted $\$h$, is defined as the sum of the costs of all legal moves in the alignment, that is, $\$h = \sum_{i \in \{1,\ldots,n\}} \$(a_i, t_i)$.*

If no other alignment results in lower costs, the alignment is called *optimal*. There may exist multiple optimal alignments for a single trace. For example, the alignment as shown in Fig. 3 is optimal, but the alignment as shown in Fig. 4 is also optimal.

Definition 9 (Optimal Trace Alignment). *Let $A \subseteq \mathcal{A}$ be a set of activities, let $\sigma \in A^*$ be an activity trace over A, let $N = (P, T, F, l, I, O)$ be an accepting Petri net over A, let h be a trace alignment for σ and N, and let $\$$ be a cost structure for A and N. The trace alignment h is called optimal if there exists no other trace alignment h' such that $\$h' < \$h$.*

a_1	τ	a_2	a_3	a_4	τ	a_5	a_6	τ	a_7	a_8
t_1	t_2	$\gg$	t_4	t_5	t_6	t_7	$\gg$	t_9	$\gg$	t_{11}
0	0	10	0	0	0	0	10	0	10	0

Fig. 4. Another optimal trace alignment for the trace $\langle a_1, a_2, a_3, a_4, a_5, a_6, a_7, a_8 \rangle$ and Petri net N_1 (now t_4 and t_{11} fire rather than t_3 and t_{10}).

A *log alignment* is a trace alignment for every trace in the activity log, an *optimal log alignment* is an optimal trace alignment for every trace in the activity log. As a result of a log alignment, any trace in the log can be mapped to the transition sequence that best matches this trace. As an example, an optimal trace alignment for the trace $\langle a_1, a_2, a_4, a_5, a_6, a_2, a_4, a_5, a_6, a_4,$ $a_2, a_5, a_7 \rangle$ from log L_1 could include the transition sequence $\langle t_1, t_2, t_3, t_5, t_6, t_7,$ $t_8, t_2, t_3, t_5, t_6, t_7, t_8, t_5, t_2, t_3, t_6, t_7, t_9, t_{10} \rangle$ in net N_1, and the costs of this alignment would be 0.

Definition 10 ((Optimal) Log Alignment). *Let $A \subseteq \mathcal{A}$ be a set of activities, let $L \in \mathcal{B}(A^*)$ be an activity log over A, and let $N = (P, T, F, l, I, O)$ be an accepting Petri net over A. A log alignment H for log L and net N is a function that maps every possible trace $\sigma \in L$ to a trace alignment. A log alignment is called optimal if and only if all its trace alignments are optimal.*

Clearly, log L_1 can be perfectly aligned to net N_1, as there exists an alignment where all trace alignments have costs 0. Using such a log alignment, it is possible to project the date and information that is present in a log onto the net, and obtain average durations between activities, an animation with the token replay, etc.

2.4   Decomposition

The overall net and the overall log can be decomposed in a number of decomposed nets and decomposed logs, in such a way that (1) the costs of the optimal overall alignment is 0 if and only if the costs of every optimal decomposed alignment is 0, and (2) the accumulated costs of the decomposed alignments are a lower bound for the costs of the overall alignment [1]. This allows us to decompose an overall alignment problem into a number of decomposed alignment problems, which can possibly be solved much faster, while still providing certain guarantees.

Figure 5 shows the five decomposed nets that result from decomposing the net N_1. For an in-depth description of such decompositions, we refer to [1]. For this paper, it is sufficient to know that (1) every visible transition occurs in one or more decomposed nets, (2) for every label all different transitions sharing

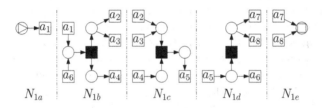

Fig. 5. Decomposed nets obtained by decomposing the net N_1. Nets N_{1b}, N_{1c}, N_{1d}, and N_{1e} have the empty marking as initial marking, while the nets N_{1a}, N_{1b}, N_{1c}, and N_{1d} have the empty marking as the only final marking.

that label occur in a single decomposed net, and (3) that every place, invisible transition, and arc occurs in only a single decomposed net. As such, a token can only flow from one decomposed net to another decomposed net through firing some visible transition, which is hence observable in the log.

Based on the activity sets as present in these decomposed nets, five decomposed logs will be created. Every decomposed log contains as many traces as the overall log, but every trace in a decomposed log contains only those activities that are present in the corresponding net. As an example, Table 2 shows the decomposed log resulting from filtering log L_1 using the decomposed net N_{1b}, that is, the net that corresponds to the set of activities $\{a_1, a_2, a_3, a_4, a_6\}$.

Table 2. Decomposed log for activities $\{a_1, a_2, a_3, a_4, a_6\}$ in tabular form. This is the log that would be replayed on the decomposed net N_{1b} as shown in Fig. 5.

Trace	Frequency
$\langle a_1, a_2, a_4, a_6, a_2, a_4, a_6, a_4, a_2 \rangle$	1
$\langle a_1, a_2, a_4, a_6, a_3, a_4, a_6, a_4, a_3, a_6, a_2, a_4 \rangle$	1
$\langle a_1, a_2, a_4, a_6, a_3, a_4 \rangle$	3
$\langle a_1, a_2, a_4, a_6, a_4, a_3 \rangle$	1
$\langle a_1, a_2, a_4 \rangle$	4
$\langle a_1, a_3, a_4, a_6, a_4, a_3 \rangle$	2
$\langle a_1, a_3, a_4 \rangle$	1
$\langle a_1, a_4, a_2, a_6, a_4, a_2, a_6, a_3, a_4, a_6, a_2, a_4 \rangle$	1
$\langle a_1, a_4, a_2 \rangle$	4
$\langle a_1, a_4, a_3 \rangle$	2

By replaying every decomposed log on the corresponding decomposed net, we obtain optimal decomposed alignments, say h_1 to h_n. From [1] we know that the costs of these optimal decomposed alignments are guaranteed to be 0 if and only if the costs of an optimal overall alignment (of the overall log on the overall net) is 0. Furthermore, we know from [1] that we can use these decomposed alignments to obtain a lower bound for the costs of the overall alignment.

Figure 6 shows the usefulness of the decomposition approach. It shows the required computation times[1] and numbers of activities for the *DMKD 2006*, *BPM 2013*, and *IS 2014* data sets [12,14,15]. These data sets contain in total 59 cases of varying size, ranging from 12 to 429 activities, from 500 to 2000 traces, with varying numbers of mismatching traces (from 0 % to 50 %). Obviously, the decomposed replay is more robust when it comes to computation times, while it provides the same guarantee as mentioned earlier. For larger events logs and models, computing optimal alignments can take days and is often

---

[1] All tests are performed on a desktop computer with an Intel Core-i7-4770 CPU at 3.40 GHz, 16 GB of RAM, running Windows 7 Enterprise (64-bit), and using a 64-bit version of Java 7 where 4 GB of RAM was allocated to the Java VM.

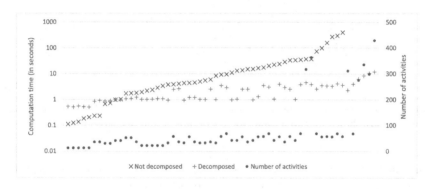

Fig. 6. Computation times and numbers of activities for the replay on some data sets. The non-decomposed replay did not finish in 10 min for some cases, typically the cases with many different activities.

intractable. For example, for some of the cases that did not finish in 10 min it is known that they also do not finish within 12 h [15], or that they do not finish because they run out of memory. If the net has a suitable decomposition, replay time may thus be reduced from more than 12 h or infeasible to 10 s.

As a result of this replay, we will have a collection of decomposed alignments and a lower bound for the costs. To be able to diagnose the mismatches between the log and the net, we want to be able to merge the decomposed alignments into an overall alignment, and project that overall alignment onto the log or the net. Note that as a result of the guarantees of the decomposition, a trace has no costs in the overall alignment if and only if it has costs in the decomposed alignments.

3   Merging Alignments

This section introduces an algorithm to merge a coherent set of decomposed alignments, that is, a set of alignments that result from replaying decomposed logs on corresponding decomposed nets. Please note that the costs of the merged alignment are simply the accumulation of the costs of the decomposed alignments [1]. As a result, when merging the alignments we do not need to take the costs into account. Instead, we can focus on the diagnostic value of the merged alignment.

To explain issues at hand for this step, we assume that we need to replay the trace $\langle a_1, a_2, a_3, a_4, a_5, a_6, a_7, a_8 \rangle$ on the net N_1 (see Fig. 2). Figure 3 shows an optimal overall alignment for this trace, which shows that the optimal costs for replaying this trace are 30. Figure 7 shows a set of possible optimal decomposed alignments, obtained by replaying the decomposed logs on the decomposed nets (see Fig. 5). Accumulating the costs from these decomposed alignments yields costs 27, which is caused by the fact that net h_{1d} can do the model move $(\gg, t_7)$ instead of the more expensive log move $(a_6, \gg)$.

The algorithm needs to merge these five decomposed alignments into one overall alignment, if possible. To do so, the algorithm takes the trace, an empty

a_1		a_1	τ	a_2	a_3	a_4	a_6		a_2	a_3	a_4	τ	a_5		a_5	a_6	$\gg$	τ	a_7	a_8		a_7	a_8
t_1		t_1	t_2	t_3	$\gg$	t_5	$\gg$		$\gg$	t_4	t_5	t_6	t_7		t_7	t_8	t_7	t_9	t_{10}	$\gg$		t_{10}	$\gg$
0		0	0	0	5	0	5		5	0	0	0	0		0	0	2	0	0	5		0	5
h_{1a}				h_{1b}							h_{1c}						h_{1d}					h_{1e}

Fig. 7. Possible optimal decomposed alignments. h_{1b} is an optimal alignment for the decomposed log shown in Table 2 and the decomposed net N_{1b}, etc.

alignment, and the five decomposed alignments, and works its way through the trace and the decomposed alignment while building up the overall alignment:

- The algorithm first encounters the activity a_1 in the trace, which is covered by two decomposed alignments (h_{1a} and h_{1b}). Fortunately, both decomposed alignments agree on a synchronous move on a_1 and transition t_1, so the algorithm adds the legal move (a_1, t_1) to the overall alignment and advances both the trace and the decomposed alignments.

- The algorithm then encounters the activity a_2, which is also covered by two decomposed fragments (h_{1b} and h_{1c}). However, h_{1b} is not yet ready to accept a_2 as it first needs to do an invisible model move on the transition t_2. Therefore, the algorithm first adds the invisible model move $(\gg, t_2)$ to the overall alignment and advances the state of h_{1b}. Then, unfortunately, the algorithm notices that h_{1b} and h_{1c} disagree on the move on a_2, as h_{1b} suggests a synchronous move (on transition t_3) while h_{1c} suggests a log move. In case of such a conflict, we can either take an *optimistic* approach (by selecting the least expensive move) or a *pessimistic* approach (by selecting the most expensive move). In the remainder of this paper, we will use the pessimistic approach, as the optimistic approach tends to mask mismatches by selecting, in case of a conflict, moves without costs. Clearly, when diagnosis is the goal, one should not mask possible problems, but one should stress them. So, the algorithm adds the log move $(a_2, \gg)$ to the overall alignment and advances the state of the trace and both h_{1b} and h_{1c}.

- Activity a_3 is handled by the algorithm in a similar way as a_2, as h_{1b} and h_{1c} again disagree. Note that as a result, the algorithm now has added two log moves for a_2 and a_3 to the overall alignment, which leads to a transition sequence that is not executable in the overall net, and to an overall alignment which is (by definition) not a proper alignment. For this reason, we introduce so-called pseudo-alignments, which are alignments except for the fact that the trace does not need to be executable in the net. The result of merging the decomposed alignments at hand would then be a pseudo-alignment instead of an alignment.

- Etc.

This result of this merging is visualized in Fig. 8. In this figure, the middle row shows the *alignment of alignments* that results from merging the decomposed alignments. In this row, the legal moves that have been ignored (because they were in conflict and were less expensive, like (a_2, t_3), or because they were

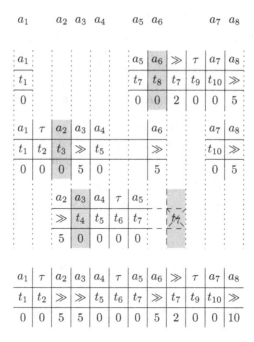

Fig. 8. Alignment of the decomposed alignments for obtaining the overall pseudo-alignment. The top row shows the trace that we need to align in the net. The middle row shows the optimal decomposed alignments of Fig. 7 laid out in such a way that the activities match in the vertical direction. Note that the ordering in the vertical direction of these decomposed alignments is of no importance. The bottom row shows the pseudo-alignment that results from merging these decomposed alignments.

missing, like a move on t_7) are indicated with a grey background. The overall pseudo-alignment (see the bottom row in Fig. 8) follows directly from this alignment of decomposed alignments by taking in every column a legal move that has no grey background, and by accumulating the costs in every column.

To avoid the introduction of the same concepts in the formal definitions over and over again, we first define a base setting for these formal definitions. This definition is to be used as a preamble for all other definitions in this section.

Definition 11 (Base Setting). *The base setting for this section is as follows:*

- *$A \subseteq \mathcal{A}$ denotes a set of activities,*
- *L denotes an activity log over A,*
- *σ denotes an activity trace from L,*
- *$N = (P, T, F, l, I, O)$ denotes an accepting Petri net over A,*
- *$\$$ denotes a cost structure for A and N,*
- *h denotes an optimal trace alignment of σ for A and N, given $\$$,*
- *n equals the number of decomposed nets obtained by decomposing N,*
- *for every $i \in \{1, \ldots, n\}$:*
  - *A^i denotes the set of activities of the i-th decomposed net,*
  - *L^i denotes the log obtained from L by filtering out all activities not in A^i,*

- σ^i denotes the activity trace from L^i obtained from L by filtering out all activities not in A^i,
- $N^i = (P^i, T^i, F^i, l^i, I^i, O^i)$ denotes the i-th decomposed net obtained by decomposing N as explained in [1], where $P^i \subseteq P$, $T^i \subseteq T$, $F^i \subseteq F$, $\forall_{t \in T^i} l^i(t) = l(t)$, $I^i = I \cap P^i$, and $O^i = \{o \cap P^i | o \in O\}$,
- h^i denotes an optimal trace alignment of σ^i for L^i and N^i.

First, we introduce the space of alignments that we are interested in, that is, the collection of overall alignments that fit the decomposed alignments. Later on, we introduce the algorithm that returns an alignment from this space.

Definition 12 (Merged Trace Alignment). The trace alignment h' is a merged trace alignment of $h^1, \ldots, h^n$ if and only if $\forall_{i \in \{1, \ldots, n\}} h' \downarrow_{A^i} = h^i$, where $h' \downarrow_{A^i}$ is defined as follows:

$$h' \downarrow_{A^i} = \begin{cases} \langle \rangle & \text{if } h' = \langle \rangle; \\ \langle (a, t) \rangle \cdot \overline{h'} \downarrow_{A^i} & \text{if } h' = \langle (a, t) \rangle \cdot \overline{h'} \text{ and } a \in A^i \vee t \in T^i; \\ \overline{h'} \downarrow_{A^i} & \text{if } h' = \langle (a, t) \rangle \cdot \overline{h'} \text{ and } a \notin A^i \wedge t \notin T^i; \end{cases}$$

For decomposed alignments that conflict on some legal move no such merged trace alignment exists.

Observation 1. (A merged trace alignment may not exist) For arbitrary decomposed alignments $h^1, \ldots, h^n$, a merged trace alignment h' may not exist.

See Fig. 8: Either we have the legal move (a_2, t_3) or the legal move $(a_2, \gg)$. In the former case, the decomposed alignment that contains the legal move $(a_2, \gg)$ cannot be matched. In the latter case, the decomposed alignment that contains the legal move (a_2, t_3) cannot be matched.

In such cases, to get any result of merging the decomposed alignments, we need to let go of the requirement that for some $o \in O$ it holds that $I[\sigma\rangle o$, that is, the result is not an alignment, but a *pseudo-alignment*.

Definition 13 (Trace Pseudo-Alignment). A trace pseudo-alignment h for trace σ on net N is a sequence of legal moves $(a, t) \in (A \cup \{\tau, \gg\}) \times (T \cup \{\gg\}))$ such that $\sigma = h \upharpoonright_A^1$, where $h \upharpoonright_A^1$ is defined as in Definition 6.

In a pseudo alignment we drop the second requirement in Definition 6. Using these pseudo-alignments, the algorithm can handle conflicts between the decomposed alignments. A merged pseudo alignment has only legal moves for:

- Each activity in the log trace. In case of conflicts, the cheapest legal move is selected for the overall pseudo-alignment.
- A model move that all agree on. Note that, by definition, for an invisible model move all agree, as there is only one decomposed net that contains this transition.

Definition 14 (Merged Trace Pseudo-Alignment). The trace pseudo-alignment h' is a merged trace pseudo-alignment of $h^1, \ldots, h^n$ if and only if

$\forall_{i\in\{1,\ldots,n\}}h'\!\downarrow_{A^i} = h^i$, where $h'\!\downarrow_{A^i}$ is defined as follows:

$$
h'\!\downarrow_{A^i} = \begin{cases}
\langle\rangle & \text{if } h' = \langle\rangle; \\
\langle(a,t')\rangle \cdot \overline{h'}\!\downarrow_{A^i} & \text{if } h' = \langle(a,t)\rangle \cdot \overline{h'} \text{ and } a \in A^i, \\
& \text{for some } t' \text{ such that } \$(a,t') \geq \$(a,t); \\
\langle(x,t)\rangle \cdot \overline{h'}\!\downarrow_{A^i} & \text{if } h' = \langle(x,t)\rangle \cdot \overline{h'}, \ x \in \{\tau,\gg\}, \text{ and } t \in T^i; \\
\overline{h'}\!\downarrow_{A^i} & \text{if } h' = \langle(\gg,t)\rangle \cdot \overline{h'} \text{ and } t \in T^i; \\
\overline{h'}\!\downarrow_{A^i} & \text{if } h' = \langle(a,t)\rangle \cdot \overline{h'} \text{ and } a \notin A^i \text{ and } t \notin T^i;
\end{cases}
$$

As a result, in case of conflicting legal moves, the most expensive legal move is selected to be included in the overall pseudo-alignment (see the second item). Of course, this *selected* legal move will not match some *unselected* legal moves, which most likely *breaks* the execution of the transition sequence in the net. Furthermore, note that it is possible to *ignore* visible model moves (see the fourth item). This is required for completeness as otherwise we cannot deal with a conflict for such transitions. For example, observe that the decomposed alignment h_{1d} includes the legal move $(\gg, t_7)$, which is not matched in the decomposed alignment h_{1c}. Having $(\gg, t_7)$ in the corresponding position in h' would work for h_{1d}, but not for h_{1c}. Likewise, not having it would work for h_{1c}, but not for h_{1d}. To solve this problem, we decide *to have* $(\gg, t)$ in h' (for sake of diagnosis) and to compensate for this using this fourth item.

Theorem 1 (A merged trace pseudo-alignment always exists). *For arbitrary decomposed alignments $h^1, \ldots, h^n$, a merged trace pseudo-alignment h' always exists.*

Proof. Assume that such an h' does not exist, and assume that we could find a prefix of h' such that the projection of this prefix onto every A^i does result in a prefix of h^i. Obviously, the empty prefix satisfies this requirement. Now, assume that we cannot extend this prefix anymore, that is, we cannot add a new legal move, while a final marking has not been reached yet. This can obviously not involve an invisible transition, as there can be no conflict on such transition. Likewise, this can also not involve a visible transition contained in only one decomposed alignment. However, this can also not involve a shared visible transition that is *enabled* by all sharing decomposed alignments, as then we could simply take a most expensive of the legal moves proposed by these alignments. As a result, this can only happen in case at least one of the sharing alignments expects another shared visible transition first. Such a shared visible transition cannot correspond to a model move, as otherwise we could use the fourth item to continue, as explain above. As a result, there should be a conflict with synchronous moves. But this clearly contradicts the fact that every decomposed alignment adheres to the order of these transitions in the original trace. Therefore, it cannot be that we cannot extend the prefix, unless we have reached a final marking.

Theorem 2 (A merged trace pseudo-alignment may not be an alignment). *Let the trace pseudo-alignment h' be a merged trace pseudo-alignment of $h^1, \ldots, h^n$. Then h' may not be a trace alignment for L and N.*

Proof. See Fig. 8: We added the legal move $(a_2, \gg)$ as this is more expensive than adding (a_2, t_3). In a similar fashion, we also added $(a_3, \gg)$. As a result, neither t_3 nor t_4 is present in the transition sequence of the alignment. But, clearly, net N_1 requires either t_3 to t_4 to fire to reach the final marking. Hence the resulting transition sequence σ does not satisfy the requirement that $I[\sigma\rangle o$, for some $o \in O$.

Based on these definitions, we first introduce three alignment stitching rules, followed by two pseudo-alignment stitching rules. The alignment stitching rules construct a merged trace alignment, if possible. If this succeeds, we know that the result is again an alignment, and that the reported costs are exact, and not just a lower bound. Otherwise, we need a pseudo-alignment stitching rule to be able to continue, but this will result in a pseudo-alignment, and the reported costs will only be a lower bound.

Definition 15 (Stitching Function Y). *Let $\mathcal{H}$ be the set of all possible trace pseudo-alignments of L and N, and let $\mathcal{H}^i$ be the set of all possible trace alignments of L^i and N^i. The function $Y \in (\mathcal{H} \times A^* \times \mathcal{H}^1 \times \ldots \times \mathcal{H}^n) \to \mathcal{H}$ returns the first argument concatenated by the merged trace pseudo-alignment of the third and following arguments $(h^1, \ldots, h^n)$, where the second argument (σ) is used to guide the stitching. As a result, $Y(\langle\rangle, \sigma, h^1, \ldots, h^n)$ returns the merged trace pseudo-alignment of $h^1, \ldots, h^n$.*

The first alignment stitching rule is a simple rule that detects when the algorithm is done: If the trace and all decomposed alignments have been dealt with completely.

Alignment Stitching Rule 1 (All Done)

$$Y(h', \langle\rangle, \langle\rangle, \ldots, \langle\rangle) = h'$$

The second alignment stitching rule is a rule that allows the algorithm to continue if all relevant decomposed alignments agree on the first activity in the trace. If so, this activity is now dealt with and so are the corresponding legal moves in the relevant decomposed alignments. For the irrelevant decomposed alignments, nothing changes.

Alignment Stitching Rule 2 (Activity w/o Conflict)

$$\begin{aligned}
&\textit{If } \sigma = \langle a \rangle \cdot \overline{\sigma} \textit{ and } t \in (T \cup \{\gg\}) \\
&\textit{and } \forall_{i \in \{1, \ldots, n\}} (a \in A^i) \Rightarrow (h^i = \langle(a, t)\rangle \cdot \overline{h^i}) \\
&\textit{and } \forall_{i \in \{1, \ldots, n\}} (a \notin A^i) \Rightarrow (h^i = \overline{h^i}) \\
&\textit{then } Y(h', \sigma, h^1, \ldots, h^n) = Y(h' \cdot \langle(a, t)\rangle, \overline{\sigma}, \overline{h^1}, \ldots, \overline{h^n})
\end{aligned}$$

The third alignment stitching rule is a rule that allows the algorithm to continue if all relevant decomposed alignments agree on a next model move. If so, these legal moves are now dealt with. Note that the set of relevant decomposed alignments differs per model move, as this set comprises all decomposed alignments where the corresponding decomposed net contains the transition involved in the selected legal move. As a result, multiple legal model moves could be a candidate for applying this rule. Note that this indicates that the candidate transitions are now all enabled, that is they are concurrent.

Alignment Stitching Rule 3 (Transition w/o Conflict)

$$\begin{aligned}
&\textit{If } t \in T \textit{ and } x \in \{\tau, \gg\} \\
&\textit{and } \forall_{i \in \{1,\ldots,n\}} (t \in T^i) \Rightarrow (h^i = \langle (x,t) \rangle \cdot \overline{h^i}) \\
&\textit{and } \forall_{i \in \{1,\ldots,n\}} (t \notin T^i) \Rightarrow (h^i = \overline{h^i}) \\
&\textit{then } Y(h', \sigma, h^1, \ldots, h^n) = Y(h' \cdot \langle (\tau,t) \rangle, \sigma, \overline{h^1}, \ldots, \overline{h^n})
\end{aligned}$$

As mentioned before, applying these rules will result in an alignment if the algorithm ends and Rule 1 can be applied. However, it may be that no rule is applicable before reaching the end of one or more decomposed alignments.

Theorem 3 (Alignment Stitching Rules Result in an Alignment). *Provided that the application of the alignment stitching rules ends, that is, if at the end Rule 1 is applied, then the result of applying these rules is an alignment merged trace alignment, that is, a trace alignment.*

Proof. By construction, the alignment stitching rules append h' with a legal move (a, t) if and only if all relevant decomposed alignments h^i agree on this legal move. See also [1].

If conflicts between activities and/or transitions do occur, the algorithm can use one of the following rules to continue. However, by applying these rules, we know that the end result will not be an alignment. As we favor alignments, over pseudo-alignments, we only apply the following stitching rules if the previous stitching rules can not be applied.

The first pseudo-alignment stitching rule is a rule that allows the algorithm to continue if the relevant decomposed alignments disagree on the next legal move containing the first activity in the trace, that is, a synchronous or log move. If so, the most expensive of the conflicting legal moves is added to the resulting pseudo alignment, the activity in the trace is now dealt with, and so are all the conflicting moves in the relevant decomposed alignment.

Pseudo-Alignment Stitching Rule 1 (Activity w/ Conflict)

$$\begin{aligned}
&\textit{If } \sigma = \langle a \rangle \cdot \overline{\sigma} \textit{ and } R = \{i \in \{1,\ldots,n\} | a \in A^i\} \textit{ and } m \in R \\
&\textit{and } \forall_{i \in R} (t^i \in (T^i \cup \{\gg\})) \wedge h^i = \langle (a, t^i) \rangle \cdot \overline{h^i} \wedge \$(a, t^m) \geq \$(a, t^i)) \\
&\textit{and } \forall_{i \in \{1,\ldots,n\} \setminus R} h^i = \overline{h^i} \\
&\textit{then } Y(h', \sigma, h^1, \ldots, h^n) = Y(h' \cdot \langle (a, t^m) \rangle, \overline{\sigma}, \overline{h^1}, \ldots, \overline{h^n})
\end{aligned}$$

In this definition, R can be interpreted as the set of (indices of) *relevant* decomposed alignments, and m can be interpreted as the (index of the) relevant decomposed alignment with *maximal* costs.

The second pseudo-alignment stitching rule is a rule that allows the algorithm to continue if the relevant decomposed alignments disagree on a next model move. If so, one of these model moves is selected, and added to the pseudo-alignment, and all corresponding model moves are now dealt with.

Pseudo-Alignment Stitching Rule 2 (Transition w/ Conflict)

$$\begin{aligned}
&\textit{If } t \in T \textit{ and } l(t) \in A \\
&\textit{and } R = \{i \in \{1, \ldots, n\} | h^i = \langle(\gg, t)\rangle \cdot \ldots\} \textit{ and } R \neq \emptyset \\
&\textit{and } \forall_{i \in R} h^i = \langle(\gg, t)\rangle \cdot \overline{h^i} \\
&\textit{and } \forall_{i \in \{1, \ldots, n\} \setminus R} h^i = \overline{h^i} \\
&\textit{then } Y(h', \sigma, h^1, \ldots, h^n) = Y(h' \cdot \langle(\gg, t)\rangle, \sigma, \overline{h^1}, \ldots, \overline{h^n})
\end{aligned}$$

In this definition, again R can be interpreted as the set of (indices of) *relevant* decomposed alignments.

Note that both rules are not deterministic, as there may be more activities or multiple visible transitions that satisfy the preamble. In such a case, one can select any of these activities or transitions, apply the rule using that activity or transition, and continue.

Theorem 4 (Stitching Rules Are Complete). *Applying all five rules ends, and the result of applying them is a merged trace pseudo-alignment.*

Proof. By construction, Pseudo-alignment Stitching Rule 1 appends h' with a legal move (a, t) if and only if it is the most expensive option, which corresponds 1-to-1 with the second item of the merged trace pseudo-alignment. As a result, this rule deals effectively with conflicting synchronous moves and conflicting log moves (as t^i is allowed to be $\gg$). Also by construction, Pseudo-alignment Stitching Rule 2 allows to *add* a conflicting model move, as it may add such a model move to h' while not adding it to some h^i. This correspond 1-to-1 with the fourth item of the conflicting merged trace alignment. As a result, the rule deals effectively with conflicting model moves. What remains is the proof that Alignment Stitching Rule 1 can be applied at some point in time (algorithm ends). Assume that the stitching blocks at some point in time, while σ starts with a. If all corresponding h^i's start with the same legal move, then Alignment Stitching Rule 2 can be applied. If these h^i's start with conflicting legal moves, then Pseudo-alignment Stitching Rule 1 can be applied. As a result, to have no stitching rule applicable at this moment, some of these h^i's need to start with a model move, that is, with some (τ, t^i) or $(\gg, t^i)$. In case of (τ, t^i), Alignment Stitching Rule 3 can be applied, as t^i only occurs in T^i. Otherwise, in case of $(\gg, t^i)$, Pseudo-alignment Stitching Rule 2 can be applied. Hence, the stitching cannot block.

We now have everything in place for the merge algorithm, which simply keeps on checking whether the rules as provided earlier (in the order given) can be applied. As soon as it detects a rule that it can apply, it applies that rule and starts over again by checking whether the rules can be applied. In the end, the first rule is applied, which provides us with the result: either a pseudo-alignment or a proper alignment.

Fig. 9. Screenshot of the result of the decomposed replay (left-hand side) and of the result of the non-decomposed replay (right-hand side). Both alignments are projected onto the overall log.

4   Implementation

The alignment merge as described in the previous section has been implemented in the "LogAlignment" package of ProM 6 [19]. This "LogAlignment" package[2] is part of the "DivideAndConquer" framework [18] in ProM 6 that supports decomposed discovery and decomposed replay.

In the framework, a single replay (that is, on overall alignment of every trace in a log on a net) has a timeout of 10 min. In Fig. 6 we already noted that some non-decomposed replays did not finish within this time. This timeout of 10 min is set to prevent a single replay to take almost forever. Experiences indicated that only rarely a replay finishes successfully after more than these 10 min [14,15]. In case of a decomposed replay, this timeout is enforced in a progressive way. If one of the decomposed replays has failed, then the resulting pseudo-alignment will be empty. For this reason, after one of the decomposed replays has exceeded the timeout, the timeout will be set to 0 min. This effectively prevents time being spent in decomposed replays that are not needed anyway as the resulting pseudo-alignment is already known to be empty.

Figure 9 shows two screenshots: one of the result of the decomposed replay and the alignment merge, and one of the result of the non-decomposed replay. The resulting (pseudo-)alignments have both been projected onto the overall log. This figure shows that the decomposed replay followed by the alignment merge successfully matches all synchronous moves (the lighter and green chevrons), and also most of the visible model moves (the darker and purple chevrons).

---

[2] See https://svn.win.tue.nl/repos/prom/Packages/LogAlignment/Trunk.

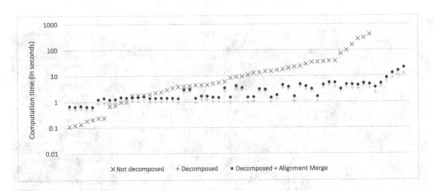

Fig. 10. Computation times for the replay and the alignment merge on the data sets.

5   Discussion

Figure 10 shows the computation time needed for the decomposed replay extended with the alignment merge for the three data sets introduced earlier. For sake of reference, this figure also includes the computation time needed for both the non-decomposed replay and the decomposed replay. Clearly, in many cases, doing a decomposed replay followed by an alignment merge is faster than doing a non-decomposed replay. As a result, a pseudo-alignment can be returned in a fraction of the time it would take to return an alignment. Note that, for every data set used, the computation of a pseudo-alignment would take up to 20 s, whereas the computation of an alignment might take more than 10 min, that is, days [14,15].

If the decomposed alignments do no incur any costs, then there exists an alignment that is the result of the merge [1]. For this alignment, it is guaranteed that there are no conflicts when merging. As a result, in such cases, the algorithm as introduced in this paper is guaranteed to return an alignment instead of only a pseudo-alignment.

If the decomposed alignments do incur costs, then it is still possible that an optimal alignment is returned by the stitching algorithm: If at every step during the stitching all relevant decomposed alignments agree on a next legal move, then the result will be an alignment. Note that this alignment may still incur costs, as every relevant decomposed alignment may agree on the move to be a log move, or in case all misalignments are local. As a result, in certain cases if costs are incurred, the algorithm will return an alignment, and this alignment will have the same costs as the non-decomposed alignment [1].

Figure 11 shows that in general it is not possible to obtain an alignment in every case. The dashed line in this net indicates the only way this net can be decomposed into nets: The first decomposed net (N_a) contains all transitions labeled a and the second net (N_d) contains all transitions labeled d. Now assume that the trace at hand is the empty trace and that every model move costs 4. The optimal alignment for N_a contains only the legal move $(\gg, t_c)$ (with costs 2), whereas the optimal alignment for N_d contains only $(\gg, t_b)$ (also with costs 2). Clearly, there is no alignment in the overall net that has lower costs than the costs (4) of these two

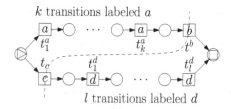

Fig. 11. An example net for which there is no proper alignment.

model moves: The upper branch would cost $4 \times k + 2$, the lower branch $2 + 4 \times l$. This example also shows that we cannot give an upper bound for an overall alignment using the decomposed alignment, as k and l could be arbitrary high.

At the moment, the cost-based replay algorithm results in on overall optimal alignment. As a result, it is conceivable that for two decomposed replays two optimal decomposed alignments are returned which have conflicts, while there would also be two optimal decomposed alignments that do not conflict. In case of the conflicting decomposed alignments, the algorithm returns a pseudo-alignment, whereas it would return an alignment if the alignments do not conflict. As such, it would be beneficial for the merge algorithm if the replay algorithm would return *all* optimal alignments instead of only *one*. If so, then the merge algorithm could return an alignment in more cases, although of course this would take more time as the algorithm would have to check possibly many combinations of decomposed alignments.

6   Conclusions

This paper has introduced an algorithm to merge decomposed alignments. In general, the result of the algorithm will be a pseudo-alignment, that is, an alignment except for the fact that it may not be executable in the net. However, if the decomposed alignments agree with each other, then the algorithm returns a proper optimal alignment. In case of a perfect match between the log and the net, then these decomposed alignments will always agree with each other [1], and hence the result of the algorithm will be an alignment. In case of mismatches between the log and the net, the result many still be an alignment, but then all decomposed alignments need to agree.

This paper has also shown that, especially for logs and nets that contain many activities, the computation of a (non-decomposed) alignment takes longer than the computations of the decomposed alignments and the time it takes to merge them. As the pseudo-alignment that results from the decomposed approach can still be used effectively to diagnose mismatches, it will often be more convenient to use this approach.

In case the algorithm returns a proper alignment, then the costs of this alignment are exact, that is, it equals the costs obtained through a non-decomposed replay. In case the algorithm does not return an alignment but a pseudo-alignment, then the costs of this alignment are a lower bound for the costs obtained through a non-decomposed replay.

In the future, we want to see whether heuristics exist that help the merge into obtaining *better* (pseudo-)alignments. As is, the current algorithm contains non-determinism, in which case it has several alternatives to proceed. For example, there could be multiple visible model moves to merge next. Possibly, using some local heuristic, we can select a next merge action which *most likely* results in a (pseudo-)alignment that better matches the overall alignment one would get by doing a non-decomposed replay. Note that the better this match, the better the gain of using the non-decomposed replay.

Also, we want to extend the stitching rules with rules that allow for different ways of decomposing the net. The decomposition introduced in [1] takes care that every invisible transition ends up in a single decomposed net. As a result, there can be no conflict that involves invisible transitions. However, different decomposition approaches may not guarantee this. As an example take a decomposition approach where a decomposed net is obtained by simply hiding (that is, making invisible) those visible transitions that are not relevant for this decomposed net. For such a decomposition approach, every transition occurs in every decomposed net, only some visible transitions will be made invisible. Of course, if some visible transition has been made invisible in some decomposed net, then there will definitely be a conflict when merging the alignment. This gets even more complicated if the decomposition approach first reduces the decomposed nets, for example, by using existing Petri net reduction rules [6,16]. Then some invisible transitions will be present in only some decomposed nets, and some of them might also have visible counterparts in other decomposed nets.

Finally, an interesting idea is to recompose decomposed nets and decomposed logs in case their decomposed alignments have many conflicts. By recomposing the nets and the logs, we remove these conflicts but obtain a slightly larger recomposed net and recomposed log. As this recomposed net and recomposed log might still be much smaller than the overall net and overall log, the decomposed replay might still be much faster than the overall replay.

References

1. van der Aalst, W.M.P.: Decomposing Petri Nets for process mining: a generic approach. Distrib. Parallel Databases **31**(4), 471–507 (2013). http://dx.doi.org/10.1007/s10619-013-7127-5
2. van der Aalst, W.M.P.: Process Mining: Discovery, Conformance and Enhancement of Business Processes, 1st edn. Springer, Heidelberg (2011)
3. van der Aalst, W.M.P., Adriansyah, A., van Dongen, B.F.: Replaying history on process models for conformance checking and performance analysis. Wiley Interdisc. Rev.: Data Min. Knowl. Discov. **2**(2), 182–192 (2012). http://dx.doi.org/10.1002/widm.1045
4. Adriansyah, A., van Dongen, B.F, van der Aalst, W.M.P.: Conformance checking using cost-based fitness analysis. In: Proceedings of the 2011 IEEE 15th International Enterprise Distributed Object Computing Conference, EDOC 2011, pp. 55–64. IEEE Computer Society, Washington, DC (2011). http://dx.doi.org/10.1109/EDOC.2011.12

5. Adriansyah, A., Sidorova, N., van Dongen, B.F.: Cost-based fitness in conformance checking. In: 2011 11th International Conference on Application of Concurrency to System Design (ACSD), pp. 57–66, June 2011
6. Berthelot, G.: Transformations and decompositions of nets. In: Brauer, W., Reisig, W., Rozenberg, G. (eds.) Advances in Petri Nets 1986, Part I. LNCS, vol. 254, pp. 360–376. Springer, Heidelberg (1987)
7. vanden Broucke, S.K.L.M., De Weerdt, J., Vanthienen, J., Baesens, B.: Determining process model precision and generalization with weighted artificial negative events. IEEE Trans. Knowl. Data Eng. **26**(8), 1877–1889 (2014)
8. Calders, T., Günther, C.W., Pechenizkiy, M., Rozinat, A.: Using minimum description length for process mining. In: Proceedings of the 2009 ACM Symposium on Applied Computing, SAC 2009, pp. 1451–1455. ACM, New York (2009). http://doi.acm.org/10.1145/1529282.1529606
9. Cook, J.E., Wolf, A.L.: Software process validation: quantitatively measuring the correspondence of a process to a model. ACM Trans. Softw. Eng. Methodol. **8**(2), 147–176 (1999). http://doi.acm.org/10.1145/304399.304401
10. De Weerdt, J., De Backer, M., Vanthienen, J., Baesens, B.: A robust f-measure for evaluating discovered process models. In: 2011 IEEE Symposium on Computational Intelligence and Data Mining (CIDM), pp. 148–155, April 2011
11. Goedertier, S., Martens, D., Vanthienen, J., Baesens, B.: Robust process discovery with artificial negative events. J. Mach. Learn. Res. **10**, 1305–1340 (2009). http://dl.acm.org/citation.cfm?id=1577069.1577113
12. Maruster, L., Weijters, A.J.M.M., van der Aalst, W.M.P., Van Den Bosch, A.: A rule-based approach for process discovery: dealing with noise and imbalance in process logs. Data Min. Knowl. Disc. **13**(1), 67–87 (2006). http://dx.doi.org/10.1007/s10618-005-0029-z
13. Muñoz-Gama, J., Carmona, J.: A fresh look at precision in process conformance. In: Hull, R., Mendling, J., Tai, S. (eds.) BPM 2010. LNCS, vol. 6336, pp. 211–226. Springer, Heidelberg (2010). http://dx.doi.org/10.1007/978-3-642-15618-2_16
14. Muñoz-Gama, J., Carmona, J., van der Aalst, W.M.P.: Conformance checking in the large: partitioning and Topology. In: Daniel, F., Wang, J., Weber, B. (eds.) BPM 2013. LNCS, vol. 8094, pp. 130–145. Springer, Heidelberg (2013)
15. Muñoz-Gama, J., Carmona, J., van der Aalst, W.M.P.: Single-entry single-exit decomposed conformance checking. Inf. Syst. **46**, 102–122 (2014). http://dx.doi.org/10.1016/j.is.2014.04.003
16. Murata, T.: Petri nets: properties, analysis and applications. Proc. IEEE **77**(4), 541–580 (1989)
17. Rozinat, A., van der Aalst, W.M.P.: Conformance checking of processes based on monitoring real behavior. Inf. Syst. **33**(1), 64–95 (2008). http://www.sciencedirect.com/science/article/pii/S030643790700049X
18. Verbeek, H.M.W.: Decomposed process mining with divide-and-conquer. In: BPM 2014 Demos, vol. 1295, pp. 86–90. CEUR-WS.org (2014). http://ceur-ws.org/Vol-1295/paper11.pdf
19. Verbeek, H.M.W., Buijs, J.C.A.M., van Dongen, B.F., van der Aalst, W.M.P: ProM 6: the process mining toolkit. In: Proceedings of BPM Demonstration Track 2010, vol. 615, pp. 34–39. CEUR-WS.org (2010). http://ceur-ws.org/Vol-615/paper13.pdf

Anti-alignments in Conformance Checking – The Dark Side of Process Models

Thomas Chatain[1(✉)] and Josep Carmona[2]

[1] LSV, ENS Cachan, CNRS, INRIA, Université Paris-Saclay, Cachan, France
`chatain@lsv.ens-cachan.fr`
[2] Universitat Politècnica de Catalunya, Barcelona, Spain
`jcarmona@cs.upc.edu`

Abstract. Conformance checking techniques asses the suitability of a process model in representing an underlying process, observed through a collection of real executions. These techniques suffer from the well-known state space explosion problem, hence handling process models exhibiting large or even infinite state spaces remains a challenge. One important metric in conformance checking is to asses the precision of the model with respect to the observed executions, i.e., characterize the ability of the model to produce behavior unrelated to the one observed. By avoiding the computation of the full state space of a model, current techniques only provide estimations of the precision metric, which in some situations tend to be very optimistic, thus hiding real problems a process model may have. In this paper we present the notion of *anti-alignment* as a concept to help unveiling traces in the model that may deviate significantly from the observed behavior. Using anti-alignments, current estimations can be improved, e.g., in precision checking. We show how to express the problem of finding anti-alignments as the satisfiability of a Boolean formula, and provide a tool which can deal with large models efficiently.

1 Introduction

The use of process models has increased in the last decade due to the advent of the process mining field. Process mining techniques aim at discovering, analyzing and enhancing formal representations of the real processes executed in any digital environment [1]. These processes can only be observed by the footprints of their executions, stored in form of *event logs*. An event log is a collection of traces and is the input of process mining techniques. The derivation of an accurate formalization of an underlying process opens the door to the continuous improvement and analysis of the processes within an information system.

Among the important challenges in process mining, *conformance checking* is a crucial one: to assess the quality of a model (automatically discovered or manually designed) in describing the observed behavior, i.e., the event log. Conformance checking techniques aim at characterizing four quality dimensions: fitness, precision, generalization and simplicity [2]. For the first three dimensions,

© Springer International Publishing Switzerland 2016
F. Kordon and D. Moldt (Eds.): PETRI NETS 2016, LNCS 9698, pp. 240–258, 2016.
DOI: 10.1007/978-3-319-39086-4_15

the *alignment* between the process model and the event log is of paramount importance, since it allows relating modeled and observed behavior [3].

Given a process model and a trace in the event log, an alignment provides the run in the model which mostly resembles the observed trace. When alignments are computed, the quality dimensions can be defined on top [3,4]. In a way, alignments are optimistic: although observed behavior may deviate significantly from modeled behavior, it is always assumed that the least deviations are the best explanation (from the model's perspective) for the observed behavior.

In this paper we present a somewhat symmetric notion to alignments, denoted as *anti-alignments*. Given a process model and a log, an anti-alignment is a run of the model that mostly deviates from any of the traces observed in the log. The motivation for anti-alignments is precisely to compensate the optimistic view provided by alignments, so that the model is queried to return highly deviating behavior that has not been seen in the log. In contexts where the process model should adhere to a certain behavior and not leave much exotic possibilities (e.g., banking, healthcare), the absence of highly deviating anti-alignments may be a desired property to have in the process model.

We cast the problem of computing anti-alignments as the satisfiability of a Boolean formula, and provide high-level techniques which can for instance compute the most deviating anti-alignment for a certain run length, or the shortest anti-alignment for a given number of deviations.

Using anti-alignments one cannot only catch deviating behavior, but also use it to improve some of the current quality metrics considered in conformance checking. For instance, a highly-deviating anti-alignment may be a sign of a loss in precision, which can be missed by current metrics as they bound considerably the exploration of model state space for the sake of efficiency [5].

Anti-alignments are related to the *completeness of the log*; a log is complete if it contains all the behavior of the underlying process [1]. For incomplete logs, the alternatives for computing anti-alignments grows, making it difficult to tell the difference between behavior not observed but meant to be part of the process, and behavior not observed which is not meant to be part of the process. Since there exists already some metrics to evaluate the completeness of an event log (e.g., [6]), we assume event logs have a high level of completeness before they are used for computing anti-alignments.

To summarize, the contributions of the paper are now enumerated.

- We propose the notion of anti-alignment as an effective way to explore process deviations with respect to observed behavior.
- We present an encoding of the problem of computing anti-alignments into SAT, and have implemented it in the tool DARKSIDER.
- We show how anti-alignments can be used to provide an estimation of precision that uses a different perspective from the current ones.

The remainder of the paper is organized as follows: in the next section, a simple example is used to emphasize the importance of computing anti-alignments.

Then in Sect. 3 the basic theory needed for the understanding of the paper is introduced. Section 4 provides the formal definition of anti-alignments, whilst Sect. 5 formalizes the encoding into SAT of the problem of computing anti-alignments and Sect. 6 presents some adaptions of the notion of anti-alignments. In Sect. 7, we define a new metric, based on anti-alignments, for estimating precision of process models. Experiments are reported in Sect. 8, and related work in Sect. 9. Section 10 concludes the paper and gives some hints for future research directions.

2   A Motivating Example

Let us use the example shown in Fig. 1 for illustrating the notion of anti-alignment. The example was originally presented in [7]. The modeled process describes a realistic transaction process within a banking context. The process contains all sort of monetary checks, authority notifications, and logging mechanisms. The process is structured as follows (Fig. 1 (top) shows a high-level overview of the complete process): it is initiated when a new transaction is requested, opening a new instance in the system and registering all the components involved. The second step is to run a check on the person (or entity) origin of the monetary transaction. Then, the actual payment is processed differently, depending of the payment modality chosen by the sender (cash, cheque and payment). Later, the receiver is checked and the money is transferred. Finally, the process ends registering the information, notifying it to the required actors and authorities, and emitting the corresponding receipt. The detailed model, formalized as a Petri net, is described in the bottom part of the figure.

Assume that a log which contains different transactions covering all the possibilities with respect of the model in Fig. 1 is given. For this pair of model and log, no highly deviating anti-alignment will be obtained since the model is a precise representation of the observed behavior. Now assume that we modify a bit the model, adding a loop around the alternative stages for the payment. Intuitively, this (malicious) modification in the process model may allow to pay several times although only one transfer will be done. The modified high-level overview is shown in Fig. 2. Current metrics for precision (e.g., [5]) will not consider this modification as a severe one: the precision of the model with respect to the log will be very similar before or after the modification.

Clearly, this modification in the process models comes with a new highly deviating anti-alignment denoting a run of the model that contains more than one iteration of the payment. This may be considered as a certification of the existence of a problematic behavior allowed by the model.

3   Preliminaries

Definition 1 ((Labeled) Petri Net). *A (labeled) Petri Net [8] is a tuple* $N = \langle P, T, \mathcal{F}, m_0, \Sigma, \lambda \rangle$, *where P is the set of places, T is the set of transitions*

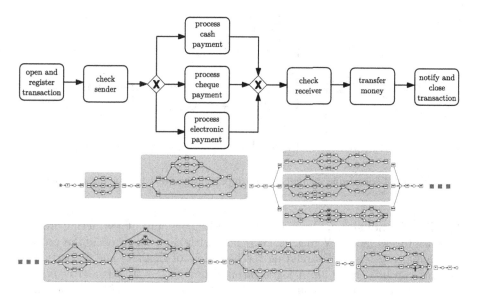

Fig. 1. Running example (adapted from [7]). Overall structure (top), process model (bottom).

(with $P \cap T = \emptyset$), $\mathcal{F} : (P \times T) \cup (T \times P) \rightarrow \{0,1\}$ is the flow relation, m_0 is the initial marking, Σ is an alphabet of actions and $\lambda : T \rightarrow \Sigma$ labels every transition by an action.

A marking is an assignment of a non-negative integer to each place. If k is assigned to place p by marking m (denoted $m(p) = k$), we say that p is marked with k tokens. Given a node $x \in P \cup T$, we define its pre-set $^\bullet x := \{y \in P \cup T \mid (x,y) \in F\}$ and its post-set $x^\bullet := \{y \in P \cup T \mid (y,x) \in F\}$.

A transition t is *enabled* in a marking m when all places in $^\bullet t$ are marked. When a transition t is enabled, it can *fire* by removing a token from each place in $^\bullet t$ and putting a token to each place in $t^\bullet$. A marking m' is *reachable* from m if there is a sequence of firings $t_1 t_2 \ldots t_n$ that transforms m into m', denoted by $m[t_1 t_2 \ldots t_n\rangle m'$. A sequence of actions $a_1 a_2 \ldots a_n$ is a *feasible sequence* (or *run*, or *model trace*) if there exists a sequence of transitions $t_1 t_2 \ldots t_n$ firable from m_0 and such that for $i = 1 \ldots n$, $a_i = \lambda(t_i)$. Let $\mathcal{L}(N)$ be the set of feasible sequences of Petri net N. A *deadlock* is a reachable marking for which no transition is enabled. The set of reachable markings from m_0 is denoted by $[m_0\rangle$, and form a graph called *reachability graph*. A Petri net is *k-bounded* if no marking in $[m_0\rangle$ assigns more than k tokens to any place. A Petri net is *safe* if it is 1-bounded. In this paper we assume safe Petri nets.

An event log is a collection of traces, where a trace may appear more than once. Formally:

Definition 2 (Event Log). *An event log L (over an alphabet of actions Σ) is a multiset of traces $\sigma \in \Sigma^*$.*

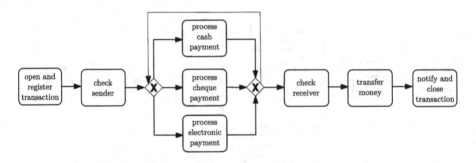

Fig. 2. Model containing a highly deviating anti-alignment for the log considered.

Quality Dimensions. Process mining techniques aim at extracting from a log L a process model N (e.g., a Petri net) with the goal to elicit the process underlying a system S. By relating the behaviors of L, $\mathcal{L}(N)$ and S, particular concepts can be defined [9]. A log is *incomplete* if $S \backslash L \neq \emptyset$. A model N *fits* log L if $L \subseteq \mathcal{L}(N)$. A model is *precise* in describing a log L if $\mathcal{L}(N) \backslash L$ is small. A model N represents a *generalization* of log L with respect to system S if some behavior in $S \backslash L$ exists in $\mathcal{L}(N)$. Finally, a model N is *simple* when it has the minimal complexity in representing $\mathcal{L}(N)$, i.e., the well-known *Occam's razor principle*.

4 Anti-alignments

The idea of anti-alignments is to seek in the language of a model N what are the runs which differ a lot with all the observed traces. For this we first need a definition of distance between two traces (typically a model trace, i.e. a run of the model, and an observed log trace). Relevant definitions about alignments can be found in [3]. Let us start here with a simple definition. We will discuss other definitions in Sect. 6.

Definition 3 (Hamming Distance *dist*). *For two traces* $\gamma = \gamma_1 \ldots \gamma_n$ *and* $\sigma = \sigma_1 \ldots \sigma_n$, *of same length* n, *define* $dist(\gamma, \sigma) := \left| \{ i \in \{1 \ldots n\} \mid \gamma_i \neq \sigma_i \} \right|$.

Definition 4. *In order to deal with traces of different length, we define for every trace* $\sigma = \sigma_1 \ldots \sigma_p$ *and* $n \in \mathbb{N}$, *the trace* $\sigma_{|1 \ldots n}$ *as:*

- $\sigma_{|1 \ldots n} := \sigma_1 \ldots \sigma_n$, *i.e. the trace* σ *truncated to length* n, *if* $|\sigma| \geq n$,
- $\sigma_{|1 \ldots n} := \sigma_1 \ldots \sigma_p \cdot w^{n-p}$, *i.e. the trace* σ *padded to length* n *with the special symbol* $w \notin \Sigma$ (w *for 'wait'*), *if* $|\sigma| \leq n$.

Notice that the two definitions coincide when $p = n$ *and give* $\sigma_{|1 \ldots n} := \sigma$.

In the sequel, we write $dist(\gamma, \sigma)$ for $dist(\gamma, \sigma_{|1 \ldots |\gamma|})$.

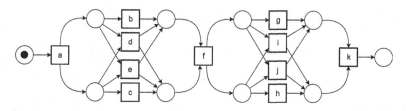

Fig. 3. The process model (taken from [10]) has the anti-alignment $\langle a, b, c, f, i, k \rangle$ for the log $L = \{\langle a,b,c,f,g,h,k \rangle, \langle a,c,b,f,g,h,k \rangle, \langle a,c,b,f,h,g,k \rangle, \langle a,b,c,f,h,g,k \rangle, \langle a,e,f,i,k \rangle, \langle a,d,f,g,h,k \rangle, \langle a,e,f,h,g,k \rangle\}$.

Definition 5 (Anti-alignment). *An (n,m)-anti-alignment of a model N w.r.t. a log L is a run $\gamma \in \mathcal{L}(N)$ such that*

- $|\gamma| = n$ *and*
- *for every $\sigma \in L$, $dist(\gamma, \sigma) \geq m$.*

Notice that, in this definition, only σ is truncated or padded. In particular this means that γ is compared to the prefixes of the observed traces. The idea is that a run γ which is close to a prefix of an observed trace is good, while a run γ which is much longer than an observed trace σ cannot be considered close to σ even if its prefix $\gamma_{|1\ldots|\sigma|}$ is close to σ.

Example 1. For instance, for the Petri net shown in Fig. 3, and the log $L = \{\langle a,b,c,f,g,h,k \rangle, \langle a,c,b,f,g,h,k \rangle, \langle a,c,b,f,h,g,k \rangle, \langle a,b,c,f,h,g,k \rangle, \langle a,e, f,i,k \rangle, \langle a,d,f,g,h,k \rangle, \langle a,e,f,h,g,k \rangle\}$, the run $\langle a,b,c,f,i,k \rangle$ denotes an $(6,2)$-anti-alignment. Notice that for $m \geq 3$ there are no anti-alignments for this example.

Lemma 1. *If the model has no deadlock, then for every $n \in \mathbb{N}$, for every $m \in \mathbb{N}$, if there exists a (n,m)-anti-alignment γ, then there exists a $(n+1,m)$-anti-alignment. Moreover, for $n \geq \max_{\sigma \in L} |\sigma|$, there exists a $(n+1, m+1)$-anti-alignment.*

Proof. It suffices to fire one transition t enabled in the marking reached after γ; $\gamma \cdot t$ is a $(n+1, m)$-anti-alignment since for every $\sigma \in L$, $dist(\gamma \cdot t, \sigma) \geq dist(\gamma, \sigma)$. When $n \geq \max_{\sigma \in L} |\sigma|$, we have more: $dist(\gamma \cdot t, \sigma) \geq 1 + dist(\gamma, \sigma)$ (because the t is compared to the padding symbol w), which makes $\gamma \cdot t$ a $(n+1, m+1)$-anti-alignment.   □

Corollary 1. *If the model has no deadlock, (and assuming that the log L is a finite multiset of finite traces), then for every $m \in \mathbb{N}$, there is a least n for which a (n,m)-anti-alignment exists. This n is less than or equal to $m + \max_{\sigma \in L} |\sigma|$.*

Lemma 2. *The problem of finding a (n,m)-anti-alignment is NP-complete. (Since n and m are typically smaller than the length of the traces in the log, we assume that they are represented in unary.)*

Proof. The problem is clearly in NP: checking that a run γ is a (n,m)-anti-alignment for a net N and a log L takes polynomial time.

For NP-hardness, we propose a reduction from the problem of reachability of a marking M in a 1-safe acyclic[1] Petri net N, known to be NP-complete [11,12]. The reduction is as follows: equip the 1-safe acyclic Petri net N with complementary places[2]: a place $\overline{p}$ for each $p \in P$, with $\overline{p}$ initially marked iff p is not, $\overline{p} \in {}^\bullet t$ iff $p \in t^\bullet \setminus {}^\bullet t$, and $\overline{p} \in t^\bullet$ iff $p \in {}^\bullet t \setminus t^\bullet$. Now M is reachable in the original net iff $M \cup \{\overline{p} \mid p \in P \setminus M\}$ is reachable in the complemented net (and with the same firing sequence).

Notice that, since N is acyclic, each transition can fire only once; hence, the length of the firing sequences of N is bounded by the number of transitions $|T|$.

Add now a new transition t_f with ${}^\bullet t_f = t_f{}^\bullet = M \cup \{\overline{p} \mid p \in P \setminus M\}$. Transition t_f is firable if and only if M is reachable in the original net, and in this case, t_f may fire forever. As a consequence the new net (call it N_f) has a firing sequence of length $|T| + 1$ iff M is reachable in N.

It remains to observe that a firing sequence of length $|T| + 1$ is nothing but a $(|T| + 1, 0)$-anti-alignment for N_f and the empty log. Then M is reachable in N iff such anti-alignment exists. $\square$

5   Computation of Anti-alignments

In order to compute a (n,m)-anti-alignment of a net N w.r.t. a log L, our tool DARKSIDER constructs a SAT formula $\Phi_m^n(N, L)$ and calls a SAT solver (currently MINISAT [13]) to solve it. Every solution to the formula is interpreted as a run of N of length n which has at least m misalignments with every log in L.

The formula $\Phi_m^n(N, L)$ characterizes a (n,m)-anti-alignment γ:

- $\gamma = \lambda(t_1) \ldots \lambda(t_n) \in \mathcal{L}(N)$, and
- for every $\sigma \in L$, $dist(\gamma, \sigma) \geq m$.

5.1   Coding $\Phi_m^n(N, L)$ Using Boolean Variables

The formula $\Phi_m^n(N, L)$ is coded using the following Boolean variables:

- $\tau_{i,t}$ for $i = 1 \ldots n$, $t \in T$ (remind that w is the special symbol used to pad the logs, see Definition 4) means that transition $t_i = t$.
- $m_{i,p}$ for $i = 0 \ldots n$, $p \in P$ means that place p is marked in marking M_i (remind that we consider only safe nets, therefore the $m_{i,p}$ are Boolean variables).
- $\delta_{i,\sigma,k}$ for $i = 1 \ldots n$, $\sigma \in L$, $k = 1, \ldots, m$ means that the kth mismatch with the observed trace σ is at position i.

---

[1] A Petri net is acyclic if the transitive closure $\mathcal{F}^+$ of its flow relation is irreflexive.
[2] In general the net does not remain acyclic with the complementary places.

The total number of variables is $n \times (|T| + |P| + |L| \times m)$.

Let us decompose the formula $\Phi_m^n(N, L)$.

- The fact that $\gamma = \lambda(t_1) \ldots \lambda(t_n) \in \mathcal{L}(N)$ is coded by the conjunction of the following formulas:
  - Initial marking:

$$\left(\bigwedge_{p \in M_0} m_{0,p} \right) \wedge \left(\bigwedge_{p \in P \setminus M_0} \neg m_{0,p} \right)$$

  - One and only one t_i for each i:

$$\bigwedge_{i=1}^{n} \bigvee_{t \in T} \left(\tau_{i,t} \wedge \bigwedge_{t' \in T} \neg \tau_{i,t'} \right)$$

  - The transitions are enabled when they fire:

$$\bigwedge_{i=1}^{n} \bigwedge_{t \in T} \left(\tau_{i,t} \implies \bigwedge_{p \in {}^\bullet t} m_{i-1,p} \right)$$

  - Token game (for safe Petri nets):

$$\bigwedge_{i=1}^{n} \bigwedge_{t \in T} \bigwedge_{p \in t^\bullet} \left(\tau_{i,t} \implies m_{i,p} \right)$$

$$\bigwedge_{i=1}^{n} \bigwedge_{t \in T} \bigwedge_{p \in {}^\bullet t \setminus t^\bullet} \left(\tau_{i,t} \implies \neg m_{i,p} \right)$$

$$\bigwedge_{i=1}^{n} \bigwedge_{t \in T} \bigwedge_{p \in P, p \notin {}^\bullet t, p \notin t^\bullet} \left(\tau_{i,t} \implies (m_{i,p} \iff m_{i-1,p}) \right)$$

- Now, the constraint that γ deviates from the observed traces (for every $\sigma \in L$, $dist(\gamma, \sigma) \geq m$) is coded as:

$$\bigwedge_{\sigma \in L} \bigwedge_{k=1}^{m} \bigvee_{i=1}^{n} \delta_{i,\sigma,k}$$

with the $\delta_{i,\sigma,k}$ correctly affected w.r.t. $\lambda(t_i)$ and σ_i:

$$\bigwedge_{\sigma \in L} \bigwedge_{k=1}^{m} \bigwedge_{i=1}^{n} \left(\delta_{i,\sigma,k} \iff \bigvee_{t \in T, \; \lambda(t) = \sigma_i} \tau_{i,t} \right)$$

and that for $k \neq k'$, the kth and k'^{th} mismatch correspond to different i's (i.e. a given mismatch cannot serve twice):

$$\bigwedge_{\sigma \in L} \bigwedge_{i=1}^{n} \bigwedge_{k=1}^{m-1} \bigwedge_{k'=k+1}^{m} \neg(\delta_{i,\sigma,k} \wedge \delta_{i,\sigma,k'})$$

5.2   Size of the Formula

In the end, the first part of the formula $(\gamma = \lambda(t_1)\ldots\lambda(t_n) \in \mathcal{L}(N))$ is coded by a Boolean formula of size $O(n \times |T| \times |N|)$, with $|N| := |T| + |P|$.

The second part of the formula (for every $\sigma \in L$, $dist(\gamma, \sigma) \geq m$) is coded by a Boolean formula of size $O(n \times m^2 \times |L| \times |T|)$.

The total size for the coding of the formula $\Phi_m^n(N, L)$ is

$$O\left(n \times |T| \times \left(|N| + m^2 \times |L|\right)\right).$$

5.3   Solving the Formula in Practice

In practice, our tool DARKSIDER builds the coding of the formula $\Phi_m^n(N, L)$ using the Boolean variables $\tau_{i,t}$, $m_{i,p}$ and $\delta_{i,\sigma,k}$.

Then we need to transform the formula in conjunctive normal form (CNF) in order to pass it to the SAT solver MINISAT. We use Tseytin's transformation [14] to get a formula in conjunctive normal form (CNF) whose size is linear in the size of the original formula. The idea of this transformation is to replace recursively the disjunctions $\phi_1 \vee \cdots \vee \phi_n$ (where the ϕ_i are not atoms) by the following equivalent formula:

$$\exists x_1, \ldots, x_n \quad \begin{cases} x_1 \vee \cdots \vee x_n \\ \wedge\, x_1 \implies \phi_1 \\ \wedge\, \ldots \\ \wedge\, x_n \implies \phi_n \end{cases}$$

where $x_1, \ldots, x_n$ are fresh variables.

In the end, the result of the call to MINISAT tells us if there exists a run $\gamma = \lambda(t_1)\ldots\lambda(t_n) \in \mathcal{L}(N)$ which has at least m misalignments with every observed trace $\sigma \in L$. If a solution is found, we extract the run γ using the values assigned by MINISAT to the Boolean variables $\tau_{i,t}$.

5.4   Finding the Largest m for n

It follows directly from Definition 5 that, for a model N and a log L, every $(n, m + 1)$-anti-alignment is also a (n, m)-anti-alignment.

Notice also that, by Definition 5, there cannot exist any $(n, n + 1)$-anti-alignment and that, assuming that the model N has a run γ of length n, this run is a $(n, 0)$-anti-alignment (otherwise there is no (n, m)-anti-alignment for any m).

(Under the latter assumption), we are interested in finding, for a fixed n, the largest m for which there exists a (n, m)-anti-alignment, i.e. the run of length n of the model which deviates most from all the observed traces. Our tool DARK-SIDER computes it by dichotomy of the search interval for m: $[0, n]$.

5.5   Finding the Least n for m

If the model N has no deadlock, then by Corollary 1, for every $m \in \mathbb{N}$, there is a least n for which a (n, m)-anti-alignment exists.

Then it is relevant to find, for a fixed m, the least n for which there exists a (n, m)-anti-alignment, i.e. (the length of) the shortest run of N which has at least m mismatches with any observed trace.

Corollary 1 tells us that the least n belongs to the interval $[m, m + \max_{\sigma \in L} |\sigma|]$. Then it can be found simply by dichotomy over this interval. However, in practice, when $\max_{\sigma \in L} |\sigma|$ is much larger than m, the dichotomy would require to check the satisfiability of $\Phi_m^n(N, L)$ for large values of n, which is costly.

Therefore our tool DARKSIDER proceeds as follows: it checks the satisfiability of the formulas $\Phi_m^m(N, L)$, then $\Phi_m^{2m}(N, L)$, then $\Phi_m^{4m}(N, L)$... until it finds a p such that $\Phi_m^{2^p m}(N, L)$ is satisfiable. Then it starts the dichotomy over the interval $[m, 2^p m]$.

6   Relaxations of Anti-alignments

6.1   Limiting the Use of Loops

A delicate issue with anti-alignments is to deal with loops in the model N: inserting loops in a model is a relevant way of coding the fact that similar traces were observed with a various number of iterations of a pattern. Typically, if the log contains traces ac, abc, $abbc$, ..., $abbbbbbbc$, it is fair to propose a model whose language is ab^*c.

However a model with loops necessarily generate (n, m)-anti-alignments even for large m: it suffices to take the loops sufficiently many more times than what was observed in the log. Intuitively, these anti-alignments are cheated and one does not want to blame the model for generating them, i.e., the model correctly generalizes the behavior observed in the event log. Instead, it is interesting to focus the priority on the anti-alignments which do not use the loops too often.

Our technique can easily be adapted so that it limits the use of loops when finding anti-alignments. The simplest idea is to add a new input place (call it $bound_t$) to every transition t; the number of tokens present in $bound_t$ in the initial marking determines how many times t is allowed to fire. The drawback of this trick is that the model does not remain 1-safe, and our tool currently deals only with 1-safe nets.

An alternative is to duplicate the transition t with t', t''... (all labeled $\lambda(t)$) and to allow only one firing per copy (using input places $bound_t$, $bound_{t'}$... like before, but now we need only one token per place).

Finally, another way to limit the use of loops is to introduce appropriate constraints directly in the formula $\Phi_m^n(N, L)$.

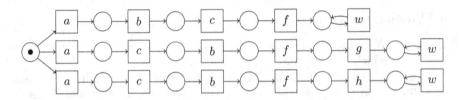

Fig. 4. The net N_L for $L = \{\langle a, b, c, f \rangle, \langle a, c, b, f, g \rangle, \langle a, c, b, f, h \rangle\}$.

6.2   Improving the Notion of Distance

A limitation of our technique as presented above, concerning the application to process mining, is that it relies on a notion of distance between γ and σ which is too rigid: indeed, every symbol of γ_i is compared only to the exact corresponding symbol σ_i. This puts for instance the word $abababab$ at distance 10 from $babababa$. In process mining techniques often other distances are usually preferred (see for instance [3]), typically Levenshtein's distance (or edit distance), which counts how many deletions and insertions of symbols are needed to obtain σ starting from γ.

We propose here an intermediate definition where every γ_i is compared to all the σ_j for j sufficiently close to i.

Definition 6 ($dist_d$). *Let $d \in \mathbb{N}$. For two traces $\gamma = \gamma_1 \ldots \gamma_n$ and $\sigma = \sigma_1 \ldots \sigma_n$, of same length n, we define*

$$dist_d(\gamma, \sigma) := \left| \{ i \in \{1 \ldots n\} \mid \forall\, i - d \le j \le i + d \quad \gamma_i \ne \sigma_j \} \right|$$

Notice that $dist_0$ corresponds to the Hamming distance.

This definition is sufficiently permissive for many applications, and we can easily adapt our technique to it, simply by adapting the constraints relating the $\delta_{i,\sigma,k}$ with the $\lambda(t_i)$ in the definition of $\Phi_m^n(N, L)$.

6.3   Anti-alignments Between Two Nets

Our notion of anti-alignments can be generalized as follows:

Definition 7. *Given $n, m \in \mathbb{N}$ and two labeled Petri nets N and N' sharing the same alphabet of labels Σ, we call (n, m)-anti-alignment of N w.r.t. N', a run N of length n which is at least at distance m from every run of N'.*

Our problem of anti-alignment for a model N and a log L corresponds precisely to the problem of anti-alignment of N w.r.t. the net N_L representing all the traces in L as disjoint sequences, all starting at a common initial place end ending by a loop labeled w, like in Fig. 4.

We show below that the problem of finding anti-alignments between two nets can be reduced to solving a 2QBF formula, i.e. a Boolean formula with an alternation of quantifiers, of the form $\exists \ldots \forall \ldots \phi$.

Solving 2QBF formulas is intrinsically more complex than SAT formulas (Σ_2^P-complete [15] instead of NP-complete) and 2QBF solvers are usually far from being as efficient as SAT solvers.

Anyway, the notion of anti-alignments between two nets allow us to modify the net N_L in order to code a better notion of distance, for instance inserting optional wait loops at desired places in the logs. Possibly also, one can replace N_L by another net which represents a large set of runs very concisely.

2QBF solvers are usually far from being as efficient as SAT solvers. As a matter of fact, we first did a few experiments with the 2QBF encoding, but for efficiency reasons we moved to the SAT encoding. Anyway we plan to retry the 2QBF encoding in a near future, with a more efficient 2QBF solver and some optimizations, in order to benefit from the flexibility offered by the generalization of the anti-alignment problem.

2QBF Coding. Finding a (n, m)-anti-alignment of a net N w.r.t. a net N' corresponds to finding a run $\gamma \in \mathcal{L}(N)$ such that $|\gamma| = n$ and for every $\sigma \in \mathcal{L}(N')$, $dist(\gamma, \sigma) \geq m$. This is encoded by the following 2QBF formula:

$$\exists (\tau_{i,t})_{\substack{i=1...n \\ t \in T}}, (m_{i,p})_{\substack{i=0...n \\ p \in P}}$$

$$\forall (\tau'_{i,t'})_{\substack{i=1...n \\ t' \in T'}}, (m'_{i,p'})_{\substack{i=0...n \\ p' \in P'}}, (\delta_{i,k})_{\substack{i=1...n \\ k=1...m}}$$

$$\left\{ \begin{array}{l} \lambda(t_1) \ldots \lambda(t_n) \in \mathcal{L}(N) \\ \wedge\ \lambda'(t'_1) \ldots \lambda'(t'_n) \in \mathcal{L}(N') \\ \wedge\ \Delta \end{array} \right\} \implies \bigwedge_{k=1}^{m} \bigvee_{i=1}^{n} \delta_{i,k}$$

where:

- the variables $\tau_{i,t}$ and $m_{i,p}$ encode the execution of N like for the coding into SAT (see Sect. 5.1); $\tau'_{i,t'}$ and $m'_{i,p'}$ represent the execution of N';
- $\delta_{i,k}$ means that the kth mismatch between the two executions is at position i;
- the constraints that $\lambda(t_1) \ldots \lambda(t_n) \in \mathcal{L}(N)$ and $\lambda'(t'_1) \ldots \lambda'(t'_n) \in \mathcal{L}(N')$ are coded like in Sect. 5;
- Δ is a formula which says that the variables $\delta_{i,k}$ are correctly affected w.r.t. the values of the $\tau_{i,t}$ and $\tau'_{i,t'}$. Δ is the conjunction of:
  - there is a mismatch at the ith position iff $\lambda(t_i) \neq \lambda'(t'_i)$:

$$\bigwedge_{i=1}^{n} \left((\bigvee_{k=1}^{m} \delta_{i,k}) \iff \bigvee_{\substack{t \in T, t' \in T' \\ \lambda(t) \neq \lambda'(t')}} (\tau_{i,t} \wedge \tau'_{i,t'}) \right)$$

  - a mismatch cannot serve twice:

$$\bigwedge_{k=1}^{m-1} \bigwedge_{k'=k+1}^{m} \neg(\delta_{i,k} \wedge \delta_{i,k'})$$

7   Using Anti-alignments to Estimate Precision

In this section we will provide two ways of using anti-alignments to estimate precision of process models. First, a simple metric will be presented that is based only on the information provided by anti-alignments. Second, a well-known metric for precision is introduced and it is shown how the two metrics can be combined to provide a better estimation for precision.

7.1   A New Metric for Estimating Precision

There are different ways of incorporating the information provided by anti-alignments that can help into providing a metric for precision. One possibility is to focus on the number of misalignments for a given maximal length n, i.e., find the anti-alignment with bounded length that maximizes the number of mismatches, using the search techniques introduced in the previous section. Formally, let n be the maximal length for a trace in the log, and let $max^n(N, L)$ be the maximal number of mismatches for any anti-alignment of length n for model N and log L. In practice, the length n will be set to the maximal length for a trace in the log, i.e., only searching anti-alignments that are similar in length with respect to the traces observed in the log. We can now define a simple estimation metric for precision:

$$a^n(N, L) = 1 - \frac{max^n(N, L)}{n}$$

Clearly, $max^n(N, L) \in [0 \ldots n]$ which implies $a^n \in [0 \ldots 1]$.

For instance, let the model be the one in Fig. 5 (top-left), and the log $L = [\sigma_1, \sigma_2, \sigma_3, \sigma_4, \sigma_5]$ also shown in the figure. Since maximal length n for L is 6, $max^6(N, L) = 3$, corresponding to the run $\langle a, c, b, i, b, i \rangle$. Hence, $a^n = 1 - \frac{3}{6} = 0.5$.

Lemma 3 (Monotonicity of the Metric a^n). *Observing a new trace which happens to be already a run of the model, can only increase the precision measure. Formally: for every N, L and for every $\sigma \in \mathcal{L}(N)$, $a^n(N, L \cup \{\sigma\}) \geq a^n(N, L)$.*

Proof. Clearly, every (n, m)-anti-alignment for $(N, L \cup \{\sigma\})$ is also a (n, m)-anti-alignment for (N, L). Consequently $max^n(N, L \cup \{\sigma\}) \leq max^n(N, L)$ and $a^n(N, L \cup \{\sigma\}) \geq a^n(N, L)$. $\square$

7.2   The Metric a_p

In [4,5] the metric *align precision* (a_p) was presented to estimate the precision a process model N (a Petri net) has in characterizing observed behavior, described by an event log L. Informally the computation of a_p is as follows: for each trace σ from the event log, a run γ of the model which has minimal number of deviations

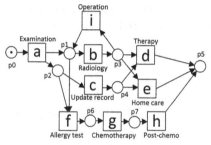

trace	one-optimal	all-optimal
$\sigma_1 = \langle a \rangle$	$\langle a, f, g, h \rangle$	$\langle a, f, g, h \rangle$
		$\langle a, c, b, e \rangle$
		$\langle a, c, b, d \rangle$
		$\langle a, b, c, d \rangle$
		$\langle a, b, c, e \rangle$
$\sigma_2 = \langle a, b, c, d \rangle$	$\langle a, b, c, d \rangle$	$\langle a, b, c, d \rangle$
$\sigma_3 = \langle a, c, b, e \rangle$	$\langle a, c, b, e \rangle$	$\langle a, c, b, e \rangle$
$\sigma_4 = \langle a, f, g, h \rangle$	$\langle a, f, g, h \rangle$	$\langle a, f, g, h \rangle$
$\sigma_5 = \langle a, b, i, b, c, d \rangle$	$\langle a, b, i, b, c, d \rangle$	$\langle a, b, i, b, c, d \rangle$

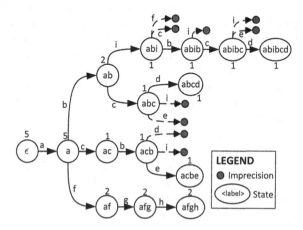

Fig. 5. Example taken from [5]. Initial process model N (top-left), optimal alignments for the event log $L = [\sigma_1, \sigma_2, \sigma_3, \sigma_4, \sigma_5]$ (top-right), automaton $\mathcal{A}_{\Gamma(N,L)}$ (bottom).

with respect to σ is computed (denoted by $\gamma \in \Gamma(N, \sigma)$), by using the techniques from [3][3]. Let

$$\Gamma(N, L) := \bigcup_{\sigma \in L} \Gamma(N, \sigma)$$

be the set of model traces optimally aligned with traces in the log. An automaton $\mathcal{A}_{\Gamma(N,L)}$ can be constructed from this set, denoting the model's representation of the behavior observed in L. Figure 5 describes an example of this procedure. Notice that each state in the automaton has a number denoting the weight, directly related to the frequency of the corresponding prefix, e.g., in the automaton of Fig. 5, $w(ab) = 2$ and $w(acb) = 1$.

For each state s in $\mathcal{A}_{\Gamma(N,L)}$, let $a_v(s)$ be the set of available actions, i.e., possible direct successor activities according to the model, and $e_x(s)$ be the set of executed actions, i.e., activities really executed in the log. Note that, by construction $e_x(s) \subseteq a_v(s)$, i.e., the set of executed actions of a given state is

---

[3] Note that more than one run of the model may correspond to an optimal alignment with log trace σ, i.e., $|\Gamma(N, \sigma)| \geq 1$. For instance, in Fig. 5 five optimal alignments exist for trace $\langle a \rangle$. For the ease of explanation, we assume that $|\Gamma(N, \sigma)| = 1$.

always a subset of all available actions according to the model. By comparing these two sets in each state the metric a_p can be computed:

$$a_p(\mathcal{A}_{\Gamma(N,L)}) = \frac{\sum\limits_{s \in Q} w(s) \cdot |e_x(s)|}{\sum\limits_{s \in Q} w(s) \cdot |a_v(s)|}$$

where Q is the set of states in $\mathcal{A}_{\Gamma(N,L)}$. This metric evaluates to 0.780 for the automaton of Fig. 5.

Drawbacks of the Metric a_p. A main drawback of metric a_p relies in the fact that it is "short-sighted", i.e., only one step ahead of log behavior is considered in order to estimate the precision of a model. Graphically, this is illustrated in the automaton of Fig. 5 by the red states being successors of white states.

A second drawback is the lack of monotonicity, a feature that metric a^n has: observing a new trace which happens to be described by the model may unveil a model trace which has a large number of escaping arcs, thus lowering the precision value computed by a_p.

For instance, imagine that in the example of Fig. 5, the model has another long branch starting as a successor of place p_0 and allowing a large piece of behaviour. Imagine that this happens to represent a possible behaviour of the real system; simply, it has not been observed yet. This branch starting at p_0 generates a new escaping arc from the initial state of $\mathcal{A}_{\Gamma(N,L)}$, but the metric a_p does not blame a lot for this: only one more escaping point.

Now, when a trace σ corresponding to the new behaviour is observed (proving somehow that the model was right!): after this observation, the construction $\mathcal{A}_{\Gamma(N,L\cup\{\sigma\})}$ changes dramatically because it integrates the new observed trace. In consequence, if the corresponding branch in the model enables other transitions, then the model is going to be blamed for many new escaping points while, before observing σ, only one escaping point was counted.

7.3   Combining the Two Metrics

In spite of the aforementioned problems, metric a_p has proven to be a reasonable metric for precision in practice. Therefore the combination of the two metrics can lead to a better estimation of precision: whilst a_p focuses globally to count the number of escaping points from the log behavior, a^n focuses on searching globally the maximal deviation one of those escaping points can lead to.

$$a_p^n(N,L) = \alpha \cdot a_p(\mathcal{A}_{\Gamma(N,L)}) - \beta \cdot a^n(N,L)$$

with $\alpha, \beta \in \mathbb{R}_{\geq 0}$, $\alpha + \beta = 1$. Let us revisit the example introduced at the beginning of this section, which is a transformation of the model in Fig. 5 but that contains an arbitrary number of operations before the Post-chemo. If $\beta = 0.2$, then a_p^n will evaluate to 0.508, a mid value that may explicit the precision problem represented by the anti-alignment computed.

8   Experiments

We have implemented a prototype tool called DARKSIDER which implements the techniques described in this paper[4] Given a Petri net N and a log L, the tool is guided towards the computation of anti-alignments in different settings:

- Finding an anti-alignment of length n with at least m mismatches ($\Phi_m^n(N, L)$).
- Finding the shortest anti-alignment necessary for having at least m mismatches ($\Phi_m(N, L)$).
- Finding the anti-alignment of length n with maximal mismatches ($\Phi^n(N, L)$).

Results are provided in Table 1. We have selected two considerably large models, initially proposed in [7,16]. The table shows the size of the models (number of places and transitions), the number of traces in the log and the size of the alphabet of the log. Then the column labeled as n establishes the length imposed for the derived anti-alignment. In this columns values always start with the maximal length of a trace in the corresponding log e.g., for the first log of the prAm6 benchmark the length of any trace is less or equal to 41. Then the column m determines the minimal number of mismatches the computed anti-alignment should have. Finally, the results on computing the three formulas described above on these parameters are provided. For $\Phi_m^n(N, L)$, it is reported whereas the formula holds. For $\Phi_m(N, L)$, it is provided the length of the shortest anti-alignment found for the given number of mismatches (m). Finally, for $\Phi^n(N, L)$ we provide the number of mismatches computed for the given length (n).

For each benchmark, two different logs were used: one containing most of the behavior in the model, and the same log but where cases describing some important branch in the process model are removed. The results clearly show that using anti-alignments highly deviating behavior can be captured, e.g., for the benchmark prAm6 a very deviating anti-alignment (39 mismatches out of 41) is computed when the log does not contains that behavior in the model, whereas less deviating anti-alignments can be found for the full log (19 mismatches out of 41)[5].

9   Related Work

The seminal work in [2] was the first one in relating observed behavior (in form of a set of traces), and a process model. In order to asses how far can the model deviate from the log, the *follows* and *precedes* relations for both model and log are computed, storing for each relation whereas it *always* holds or only *sometimes*. In case of the former, it means that there is more variability. Then, log and model follows/precedes matrices are compared, and in those matrix cells where

---

[4] The tool is available at http://www.lsv.ens-cachan.fr/~chatain/darksider.

[5] Since in the current implementation we do not incorporate techniques for dealing with the improved distance as explained in Sect. 5, we still get a considerably deviating anti-alignment for the original log.

Table 1. Experiments for different models and logs.

benchmark	$|P|$	$|T|$	$|L|$	A_L	n	m	$\Phi_m^n(N,L)$	$\Phi_m(N,L)$	$\Phi^n(N,L)$
prAm6	347	363	761	272	41	1	✓	3	39
					41	5	✓	7	
					21	1	✓	3	19
					21	5	✓	7	
			1200	363	41	1	✓	4	19
					41	5	✓	8	
					21	1	✓	4	15
					21	5	✓	8	
BankTransfer	121	114	989	101	51	1	✓	8	32
					51	10	✓	17	
					21	1	✓	8	14
					21	10	✓	17	
			2000	113	51	1	✓	15	16
					51	10	✓	37	
					21	1	✓	15	5
					21	10	✗	37	

the model has a *sometimes* relation whilst the log has an *always* relation indicate that the model allows for more behavior, i.e., a lack of precision. This technique has important drawbacks: first, it is not general since in the presence of loops in the model the characterization of the relations is not accurate [2]. Second, the method requires a full state-space exploration of the model in order to compute the relations, a stringent limitation for models with large or even infinite state spaces.

In order to overcome the limitations of the aforementioned technique, a different approach was proposed in [4]. The idea is to find *escaping arcs*, denoting those situations where the model starts to deviate from the log behavior, i.e., events allowed by the model not observed in the corresponding trace in the log. The exploration of escaping arcs is restricted by the log behavior, and hence the complexity of the method is always bounded. By counting how many escaping arcs a pair (model, log) has, one can estimate the precision of a model. Although being a sound estimation for the precision metric, it may hide the problems we are considering in this paper, i.e., models containing escaping arcs that lead to a large behavior.

Less related is the work in [17], where the introduction of *weighted artificial negative events* from a log is proposed. Given a log L, an artificial negative event is a trace $\sigma' = \sigma \cdot a$ where $\sigma \in L$, but $\sigma' \notin L$. Algorithms are proposed to weight the confidence of an artificial negative event, and they can be used to estimate the precision and generalization of a process model [17]. Like in [4], by only considering one step ahead of log/model's behavior, this technique may not catch serious precision/generalization problems.

10 Conclusions and Future Work

In this paper the new concept of anti-alignments is introduced as a way to catch deviations a process model may have with respect to observed behavior. We show how the problem of computing anti-alignments can be casted as the satisfiability of a Boolean formula, and have implemented a tool which automates this encoding. Experimental results performed on large models show the usefulness of the approach, being able to compute deviations when they exist.

This work starts a research direction based on anti-alignments. We consider that further steps are needed to address properly some important extensions. First, it would be interesting to put anti-alignments more in the context of process mining; for that it may be required that models have also defined a clear final state, and anti-alignments should be defined accordingly in this context. Also, the distance metric may be adapted to incorporate the log frequencies, and allow it to be less strict with respect to trace deviations concerning individual positions, loops, etc. Alternatives for the computation of anti-alignments will also be investigated. Finally, the use of anti-alignments for estimating the generalization of process models will be explored.

Acknowledgments. We thank Boudewijn van Dongen for interesting discussions related to this work. This work has been partially supported by funds from the Spanish Ministry for Economy and Competitiveness (MINECO), the European Union (FEDER funds) under grant COMMAS (ref. TIN2013-46181-C2-1-R).

References

1. van der Aalst, W.M.P.: Process Mining - Discovery Conformance and Enhancement of Business Processes. Springer, Heidelberg (2011)
2. Rozinat, A., van der Aalst, W.M.P.: Conformance checking of processes based on monitoring real behavior. Inf. Syst. **33**(1), 64–95 (2008)
3. Adriansyah, A.: Aligning observed and modeled behavior. Ph.D. thesis, Technische Universiteit Eindhoven (2014)
4. Munoz-Gama, J.: Conformance checking and diagnosis in process mining. Ph.D. thesis, Universitat Politecnica de Catalunya (2014)
5. Adriansyah, A., Munoz-Gama, J., Carmona, J., van Dongen, B.F., van der Aalst, W.M.P.: Measuring precision of modeled behavior. Inf. Syst. E-Bus. Manag. **13**(1), 37–67 (2015)
6. Yang, H., van Dongen, B.F., her Hofstede, A.H.M., Wynn, M.T., Wang, J.: Estimating completeness of event logs. Technical report BPM-12-04, BPM Center (2012)
7. van den Broucke, S.K.L.M., Munoz-Gama, J., Carmona, J., Baesens, B., Vanthienen, J.: Event-based real-time decomposed conformance analysis. In: Meersman, R., Panetto, H., Dillon, T., Missikoff, M., Liu, L., Pastor, O., Cuzzocrea, A., Sellis, T. (eds.) OTM 2014. LNCS, vol. 8841, pp. 345–363. Springer, Heidelberg (2014)
8. Murata, T.: Petri nets: properties, analysis and applications. Proc. IEEE **77**(4), 541–574 (1989)

9. Buijs, J.C.A.M., van Dongen, B.F., van der Aalst, W.M.P.: Quality dimensions in process discovery: the importance of fitness, precision, generalization and simplicity. Int. J. Coop. Inf. Syst. **23**(1), 1440001 (2014)

10. van der Aalst, W.M.P., Kalenkova, A., Rubin, V., Verbeek, E.: Process discovery using localized events. In: Devillers, R., Valmari, A. (eds.) PETRI NETS 2015. LNCS, vol. 9115, pp. 287–308. Springer, Heidelberg (2015)

11. Stewart, I.A.: Reachability in some classes of acyclic Petri nets. Fundam. Inform. **23**(1), 91–100 (1995)

12. Cheng, A., Esparza, J., Palsberg, J.: Complexity results for 1-safe nets. Theor. Comput. Sci. **147**(1&2), 117–136 (1995)

13. Eén, N., Sörensson, N.: An extensible SAT-solver. In: Giunchiglia, E., Tacchella, A. (eds.) SAT 2003. LNCS, vol. 2919, pp. 502–518. Springer, Heidelberg (2004)

14. Tseytin, G.S.: On the complexity of derivation in propositional calculus. In: Slisenko, A. (ed.) Studies in Constructive Mathematics and Mathematical Logic, Part II. Seminars in Mathematics. Steklov Mathematical Institute, pp. 115–125 (1970) Translated from Russian: Zapiski Nauchnykh Seminarov LOMI, vol. 8, pp. 234–259 (1968)

15. Kleine Büning, H., Bubeck, U.: Theory of quantified Boolean formulas. In: Biere, A., Heule, M., van Maaren, H., Walsh, T. (eds.) Handbook of Satisfiability: vol. 185. Frontiers in Artificial Intelligence and Applications, pp. 735–760. IOS Press, Amsterdam (2009)

16. Munoz-Gama, J., Carmona, J., van der Aalst, W.M.P.: Single-entry single-exit decomposed conformance checking. Inf. Syst. **46**, 102–122 (2014)

17. van den Broucke, S.K.L.M., Weerdt, J.D., Vanthienen, J., Baesens, B.: Determining process model precision and generalization with weighted artificial negative events. IEEE Trans. Knowl. Data Eng. **26**(8), 1877–1889 (2014)

Time and Stochastic Models

Probabilistic Time Petri Nets

Yrvann Emzivat[1,3](✉), Benoît Delahaye[2], Didier Lime[1], and Olivier H. Roux[1]

[1] UMR CNRS 6597, École Centrale de Nantes, IRCCyN, Nantes, France
{Yrvann.Emzivat,Didier.Lime,Olivier-H.Roux}@irccyn.ec-nantes.fr
[2] UMR CNRS 6241, Université de Nantes, LINA, Nantes, France
Benoit.Delahaye@univ-nantes.fr
[3] Renault S.A.S., Technocentre Renault, Guyancourt, France

Abstract. We introduce a new model for the design of concurrent stochastic real-time systems. Probabilistic time Petri nets (PTPN) are an
extension of time Petri nets in which the output of tokens is randomised.
Such a design allows us to elegantly solve the hard problem of combining
probabilities and concurrency. This model further benefits from the con-
cision and expressive power of Petri nets. Furthermore, the usual tools for
the analysis of time Petri nets can easily be adapted to our probabilistic
setting. More precisely, we show how a Markov decision process (MDP)
can be derived from the classic atomic state class graph construction.
We then establish that the schedulers of the PTPN and the adversaries
of the MDP induce the same Markov chains. As a result, this construction notably preserves the lower and upper bounds on the probability of
reaching a given target marking. We also prove that the simpler original
state class graph construction cannot be adapted in a similar manner for
this purpose.

Keywords: Time Petri nets · Probabilistic systems · State classes ·
Markov decision processes

1 Introduction

Many highly critical applications, like autonomous vehicles, require the use of
modelling tools that integrate concurrency, real-time constraints and probabilities. Designing such models is challenging for they require the development
of new algorithms that combine both real-time and probabilistic verification
techniques. Continuous-time Markov chains [1], continuous-time Markov decision processes [2], probabilistic timed automata [3], Markov automata [4] and
stochastic timed automata [5] are but a few examples of models that were introduced with the intention of formally verifying probabilistic real-time systems.
In particular, the product of probabilistic timed automata [6,7] provides the
medium for concurrency in a real-time constrained environment. Yet, none of
the aforementioned formalisms are adapted to the modelling of systems that
exhibit variables whose bounds cannot be inferred. In contrast, the blending of
concurrency and of such dynamical bounds is inherent to Petri net models.

© Springer International Publishing Switzerland 2016
F. Kordon and D. Moldt (Eds.): PETRI NETS 2016, LNCS 9698, pp. 261–280, 2016.
DOI: 10.1007/978-3-319-39086-4_16

Petri nets were enhanced through the use of stochastic temporal parameters and exponential distributions of firing times in [8,9] for the modelling of *concurrent* probabilistic real-time systems. The time Petri net model was extended by adding a probability density-function to the static firing interval of each non-deterministic transition [10]. These *stochastic time Petri nets* generalise time Petri nets [11] and involve the extension of the state class graph of [12] in order to account for stochastic information in each state class.

While stochastic time Petri nets are a powerful formalism in terms of expressivity and conciseness, we argue that the randomisation of transition rates is not necessarily required, while a randomisation of tokens in subsequent places might be needed. For example, a component failure in a gracefully degrading system can be linked to the firing of a transition whose rate is not necessarily subject to some random phenomenon, but whose outcome needs to be specified in terms of token generation. The *extended stochastic Petri nets* introduced in [13] allow firing times to belong to an arbitrary distribution and output places to be randomised, but they still require stringent restrictions, including the randomisation of transition rates.

In this paper, we introduce *probabilistic time Petri nets* (PTPN) as a new modelling formalism. By enhancing the forward incidence mapping of a classic time Petri net in such a way that transitions are mapped to a set of distributions of markings, we are able to extend the class of time Petri nets to a wider class of nets. The output arcs of a transition are effectively replaced with stacks of probabilistic hyperarcs. Each hyperarc contributes to the generation of tokens in output places of the transition. When a transition is fired in a PTPN, one hyperarc is chosen in each stack according to some probability distribution. A resulting marking emerges from this combination of choices. In fact, a time Petri net is a probabilistic time Petri net if the firing of any given transition almost surely leads to a certain marking.

The tools that are used for the analysis of time Petri nets can easily be adapted to our probabilistic setting. Here, we conform the classic atomic state class graph construction [14] to our class of nets in order to isolate the properties of a PTPN into a finite Markov decision process (MDP). We prove that this MDP induces the same Markov chains as the semantics of the PTPN, up to isomorphism. As a result, this construction preserves the lower and upper bounds on the probability of reaching a given marking. This allows us to make use of the extensive set of tools that are used for the study of MDPs in order to thoroughly study the probabilistic real-time reachability problem in the context of PTPNs. The construction we put forward is quite complex, for it is based on the atomic state class graph. Unfortunately, we prove that the simpler original state class graph construction cannot be adapted to our setting as it does not preserve these lower and upper probability bounds.

Outline. We introduce the syntax and the semantics of probabilistic time Petri nets in Sect. 2 and consider the verification of PTPNs against reachability properties in Sect. 3. We conclude the present work in Sect. 4 and suggest directions for future research.

2   Probabilistic Time Petri Nets

2.1   Preliminaries

We denote the set of natural numbers by $\mathbb{N}$, the set of rational numbers by $\mathbb{Q}$ and the set of real numbers by $\mathbb{R}$. We consider 0 to be an element of $\mathbb{N}$ and let $\mathbb{N}^* = \mathbb{N} \setminus \{0\}$. For $n \in \mathbb{N}$, we let $[\![0, n]\!]$ denote the set $\{i \in \mathbb{N} \mid i \leq n\}$. The set of real intervals that have rational or infinite endpoints is denoted $\mathscr{I}(\mathbb{Q}_+)$. A *clock valuation* over a set T is a mapping $v : T \to \mathbb{R}_+$, where $\mathbb{R}_+$ denotes the set of non-negative real numbers. We let 0_T denote the clock valuation that assigns 0 to every clock in T. For $d \in \mathbb{R}_+$, we let $v + d$ be the clock valuation that satisfies $(v + d)(t) = v(t) + d$ for every clock t in the domain of v.

For a given set X, let $\mathscr{P}(X)$ denote the power set of X. The *characteristic (or indicator) function* of $A \in \mathscr{P}(X)$, denoted $\chi_A : X \to \{0, 1\}$, is defined as

$$\chi_A(x) = \begin{cases} 1 & \text{if } x \in A, \\ 0 & \text{if } x \notin A. \end{cases}$$

Given two arbitrary sets E and F, let F^E denote the set of functions from E to F. When F is an ordered set, we define a partial order $\preceq$ on F^E by $f \preceq g$ if $f(x) \leq g(x)$ for all $x \in E$.

A *discrete probability distribution* over a countable set X is a function $\mu : X \to [0, 1]$ such that $\sum_{x \in X} \mu(x) = 1$. The *support* of a discrete probability distribution μ, denoted $Supp(\mu)$, is the preimage of the interval $]0, 1]$ under μ. For an arbitrary set X, we define $\mathscr{D}ist_X$ to be the set of functions $\mu : X \to [0, 1]$ such that $Supp(\mu)$ is a countable set and μ restricted to $Supp(\mu)$ is a discrete probability distribution. For $x_0 \in X$, let the discrete probability distribution denoted δ_{x_0} be the *Dirac measure* which assigns probability 1 to x_0:

$$\delta_{x_0}(x) = \chi_{\{x_0\}}(x) = \begin{cases} 1 & \text{if } x = x_0, \\ 0 & \text{if } x \neq x_0. \end{cases}$$

2.2   Probabilistic Time Petri Nets

This section introduces the syntax and the semantics of *probabilistic time Petri nets*. Intuitively, a probabilistic time Petri net is a time Petri net in which every non-deterministic choice involves the resolution of a probabilistic experiment. Such experiments are described explicitly by means of discrete probability distributions. In a typical time Petri net, these probability distributions are Dirac measures. In other words, any given state of a time Petri net has a successor that is uniquely determined by a chosen course of action. This is generally not the case for probabilistic time Petri nets, which extend the class of time Petri nets as a result.

Syntax of a Probabilistic Time Petri Net.

Definition 1 (Probabilistic Time Petri Net (PTPN)). *A probabilistic time Petri net is a quintuple* $\mathcal{N} = (P, T, Pre, Post, I)$ *where*

- *P is a finite, non-empty set of* places,
- *T is a finite set of* transitions *such that $T \cap P = \phi$,*
- *$Pre : T \rightarrow \mathbb{N}^P$ is the backward incidence mapping,*
- *$Post : T \rightarrow \mathscr{P}(\mathscr{D}ist_{\mathbb{N}^P})$ is the forward incidence mapping, and*
- *$I : T \rightarrow \mathscr{I}(\mathbb{Q}_+)$ is a function assigning a firing interval to each transition.*

An element of $\mathbb{N}^P$ is called a *marking* of the net. A marking denotes a distribution of *tokens* in the places of the net. The forward incidence mapping *Post* specifies a *finite* set of probability distributions of markings for every transition of the net. For a given transition t, we assume that the probability distributions in $Post(t)$ are associated with *independent* random variables. These random variables each contribute to the production of tokens in subsequent places when that transition is fired. Moreover, we assume that the support of each discrete probability distribution in $Post(t)$ is finite.

A distribution in $Post(t)$ is represented graphically by a stack of *hyperarcs*. A hyperarc is labelled with a probability before it is split into a set of arcs that lead to a set of *output places*. These arcs contain information about the number of tokens that are generated in each one of these places when that hyperarc is selected.

Definition 2 (Marked Probabilistic Time Petri Net). *A marked probabilistic time Petri net is a sextuple $\mathcal{N} = (P, T, Pre, Post, I, \rho_{\mathcal{N}})$ where*

- *$(P, T, Pre, Post, I)$ is a probabilistic time Petri net, and*
- *$\rho_{\mathcal{N}} \in \mathscr{D}ist_{\mathbb{N}^P}$ is the distribution of initial markings of the net.*

The experiment that yields the initial marking of the net is only conducted once. Any marking belonging to the support of $\rho_{\mathcal{N}}$ is *an* initial marking of the net. The value $\rho_{\mathcal{N}}(M)$ specifies the probability that *the* initial marking of the net is indeed M.

Example 1. In order to grasp the intuition behind the proposed model, let us consider the probabilistic time Petri net depicted in Fig. 1. Transition T_2 of the net displays two probability distributions. The first distribution either generates one token in P_1, three tokens in P_3 and one token in P_4 with probability a, or two tokens in P_4, one token in P_5 and one token in P_6 with probability b. No token is generated with probability $c = 1 - a - b$. The second distribution generates one or two tokens in P_6 with probability p and $1 - p$ respectively. Since these distributions are associated with independent random variables, it follows that the firing of T_2 leads to the consumption of one token in P_1 and two tokens in P_2, and the generation of two tokens in P_4, one token in P_5 and three tokens in P_6 with probability $b(1 - p)$.

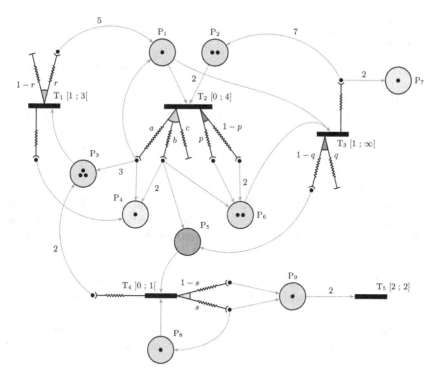

Fig. 1. A marked probabilistic time Petri net in its initial state, given by $\rho_{\mathcal{N}} = \delta_{(1,2,3,1,0,2,1,1,1)}$

The following paragraph introduces the terminology of probabilistic time Petri nets as well as important notations that are used throughout this paper. Let $\mathcal{N} = (P, T, Pre, Post, I)$ be a probabilistic time Petri net. A *state* of the net $\mathcal{N}$ is described by an ordered pair (M, v) in $\mathbb{N}^P \times \mathbb{R}_+^T$, where M is a marking of $\mathcal{N}$ and v is a clock valuation over the set of transitions T. In practice, clock valuations are only defined for transitions that are enabled.

- A transition $t \in T$ is said to be *enabled* by a given marking $M \in \mathbb{N}^P$ if M supplies t with at least as many tokens as required by the backward incidence mapping Pre. We define the set $\mathscr{E}(M)$ of transitions that are enabled by the marking M as
$$\mathscr{E}(M) = \{t \in T \mid M \succeq Pre(t)\}.$$

- A transition $t \in T$ is said to be *firable* from a given state (M, v) if the transition t is enabled by M and if its clock is assigned a value that lies within its firing interval. We define the set $\mathscr{F}(M, v)$ of transitions that are firable from the state (M, v) as
$$\mathscr{F}(M, v) = \{t \in \mathscr{E}(M) \mid v(t) \in I(t)\}.$$

- A time delay $d \in \mathbb{R}_+$ is said to be *compliant* with a given state (M, v) if every transition that is firable from $(M, v + d')$ for some time delay $d' \in [0, d]$ stays firable until $(M, v + d)$. We define the set $\mathscr{C}(M, v)$ of time delays that are compliant with the state (M, v) as

$$\mathscr{C}(M, v) = \{d \in \mathbb{R}_+ \mid \forall t \in T, t \notin \mathscr{F}(M, v+d) \Rightarrow \forall d' \in [0, d], t \notin \mathscr{F}(M, v+d')\}.$$

– An action $(d, t) \in \mathbb{R}_+ \times T$ is said to be *feasible* from a given state (M, v) if the time delay d leads the net to a state from which t is firable. We define the set $\Phi(M, v)$ of actions that are feasible from the state (M, v) as

$$\Phi(M, v) = \{(d, t) \in \mathbb{R}_+ \times T \mid d \in \mathscr{C}(M, v) \text{ and } t \in \mathscr{F}(M, v + d)\}.$$

When adopting a purely semantical standpoint, an element of the set T is best referred to as a *trial*, through the medium of an underlying probability distribution μ_t. Informally, a trial t induces the production of tokens in the net each time it is conducted, by providing alternatives that lead to one marking or another.

– Let $t \in T$ be a transition of $\mathcal{N}$. The discrete probability distributions in $Post(t)$ are associated with random variables that can take one of many values. By definition, these values are endowed with a non-zero probability. An *alternative* is a function f that chooses a value for each one of these random variables. Formally, we define the set $\mathscr{A}(t)$ of *alternatives* provided by the transition t as follows:

$$\mathscr{A}(t) = \{f : Post(t) \to \mathbb{N}^P \mid \forall \mu \in Post(t), f(\mu) \in Supp(\mu)\}.$$

– An *outcome* of a given trial t is a marking ω of $\mathcal{N}$ which results from the choices of some alternative in $\mathscr{A}(t)$. This marking ω accounts for the tokens that are to be generated in each output place of t. We define the set $\Omega(t)$ of outcomes of the trial t as

$$\Omega(t) = \left\{\omega \in \mathbb{N}^P \mid \exists f \in \mathscr{A}(t), \omega = \sum_{\mu \in Post(t)} f(\mu)\right\}.$$

– For a given outcome $\omega \in \Omega(t)$, we define the non-empty set $\mathscr{A}(\omega)(t) \subseteq \mathscr{A}(t)$ of alternatives that lead to it as

$$\mathscr{A}(\omega)(t) = \left\{f \in \mathscr{A}(t) \mid \omega = \sum_{\mu \in Post(t)} f(\mu)\right\}.$$

Let us now provide the formal definition of the probability distribution μ_t that governs a trial $t \in T$. Intuitively, the probability of reaching a given outcome $\omega \in \Omega(t)$ is the sum of the probabilities of all the alternatives leading to ω. Since the probability distributions in $Post(t)$ are assumed to be independent, the probability that an alternative is chosen is the product of the probabilities of all the independent choices it makes. Formally, μ_t is defined as follows:

Definition 3. *Let* $(P, T, Pre, Post, I)$ *be a probabilistic time Petri net. The discrete probability distribution that governs a trial* $t \in T$ *is a function* $\mu_t : \Omega(t) \to [0, 1]$ *that assigns probabilities to the outcomes of* t *as follows:*

$$\mu_t : \omega \to \sum_{f \in \mathscr{A}(\omega)(t)} \left(\prod_{\mu \in Post(t)} \mu\big(f(\mu)\big) \right).$$

Lemma 1. *Let* $(P, T, Pre, Post, I)$ *be a probabilistic time Petri net. For a given trial* $t \in T$*, the function* μ_t *is a discrete probability distribution over* $\Omega(t)$*.*

The probabilistic time Petri nets depicted in Fig. 2 have different structures. Yet they are equivalent from a semantical standpoint, since the discrete probability distribution μ_{T_1} is the same in both nets. In fact, every probabilistic time Petri net can be canonicalised into a probabilistic time Petri net such that $Post(t)$ is a singleton for every transition t.

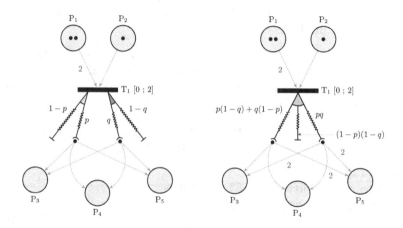

Fig. 2. Two syntactically different probabilistic time Petri nets that are equivalent from a semantical standpoint

It is worth noting that a probabilistic time Petri net is equivalent to a time Petri net if $Supp(\mu_t)$ is a singleton for all trials t. A time Petri net can therefore be interpreted as a probabilistic time Petri net whose transitions yield a single combination of hyperarcs, or similarly, whose trials each lead to a single outcome.

Semantics of a Probabilistic Time Petri Net. A probabilistic time Petri net $\mathcal{N}$ has the following operational behaviour. The distribution $\rho_{\mathcal{N}}$ yields the initial marking M_0 of the net $\mathcal{N}$ and subsequently, the initial state $(M_0, 0_T)$ of $\mathcal{N}$. When in a given state, the net can either fire an enabled transition or let time flow. Doing so changes the state of the net. An enabled transition is firable if and only if its clock value lies within its firing interval. Furthermore, a time delay must always be compliant with the current state of the net. In other words, time can flow as long as otherwise enabled transitions are not disabled in the process. This behaviour is typical in the context of *strong time semantics* and conveys the notion of urgency. As such, the behaviour of a probabilistic time Petri net is similar to that of a classic time Petri net. Once a choice has been made, however, the next state is selected in a probabilistic manner. The difference therefore lies in the way the subsequent state of the net is computed once the non-determinism has been resolved.

- If the net chooses to let a certain amount of time d to elapse, then the marking remains the same while the clock values of the enabled transitions are increased by that particular amount.
- If the net chooses to fire a certain transition t, tokens are removed from the current marking according to the mapping $Pre(t)$ while the outcome of the trial t generates additional ones. Moreover, the clocks associated with the transition t and with any transition that has been disabled by the removal of the $\sum_{p \in P} Pre(t)(p)$ tokens are reset and disabled. Finally, the clocks associated with newly enabled transitions are activated. This includes those that were previously disabled.

The semantics of a probabilistic time Petri net is defined as a probabilistic timed transition system. Probabilistic timed transition systems can be considered an extension of Markov decision processes that account for the flow of time, leading to a potentially uncountable set of states. Formally:

Definition 4 (Probabilistic Timed Transition System (PTTS)). *A probabilistic timed transition system is a quadruple (Q, ρ, T, W) where*

- *Q is a set of* states,
- *$\rho \in \mathscr{D}ist_Q$ is the distribution of* initial states,
- *T is a set of* trials, *and*
- *$W : Q \times (T \cup \mathbb{R}_+) \to \mathscr{D}ist_Q$ is a (partial) probabilistic transition function.*

We now formally introduce the semantics of marked probabilistic time Petri nets in terms of probabilistic timed transition systems.

Definition 5 (Semantics of a Marked Probabilistic Time Petri Net). *The semantics of a marked probabilistic time Petri net $\mathcal{N} = (P, T, Pre, Post, I, \rho_{\mathcal{N}})$ is a probabilistic timed transition system $S_{\mathcal{N}} = (Q, \rho_{S_{\mathcal{N}}}, T, W)$ where*

- *$Q \subseteq \mathbb{N}^P \times \mathbb{R}_+^T$ is the set of* states *of the net $\mathcal{N}$,*
- *$\rho_{S_{\mathcal{N}}} : Q \to [0, 1]$ is the distribution of* initial states, *defined for $(M, v) \in Q$ by*

$$\rho_{S_{\mathcal{N}}}(M, v) = \rho_{\mathcal{N}}(M) \times \chi_{\{0_T\}}(v) \ , \ and$$

- *$W : Q \times (T \cup \mathbb{R}_+) \to \mathscr{D}ist_Q$ is the (partial)* piecewise *probabilistic transition function that defines continuous time transition relations over $Q \times \mathbb{R}_+$ and discrete transition relations over $Q \times T$.*

1. *W is defined for $((M,v),d) \in Q \times \mathbb{R}_+$ if and only if the delay d is compliant with the state (M,v). In that case, let $W((M,v),d)$ be the Dirac measure $\delta_{(M,v')}$, where the clock valuation v' is defined for all transitions t' enabled by the marking M by*

$$v'(t') = v(t') + d.$$

2. *W is defined for $((M,v),t) \in Q \times T$ if and only if the transition t is firable from the state (M,v). In that case, let $W((M,v),t) = \tilde{\mu}_t$, where $\tilde{\mu}_t \in \mathscr{D}ist_Q$ is defined as follows:*
   - *Let $(M',v') \in Q$. The state (M',v') lies in $Supp(\tilde{\mu}_t)$ if and only if the two following conditions are met:*
     * *there exists an outcome $\omega_{M'} \in \Omega(t)$ such that*

$$M' = (M - Pre(t)) + \omega_{M'} \qquad (1)$$

     * *the clock valuation v' is defined for all transitions t' enabled by the marking M' by*

$$v'(t') = v(t') \times (1 - \chi_t(t')) \times \chi_{\mathscr{E}(M-Pre(t))}(t') \qquad (2)$$

   - *Suppose that $(M',v') \in Supp(\tilde{\mu}_t)$. We define the image of (M',v') by the formula*

$$\tilde{\mu}_t(M',v') = \mu_t(\omega_{M'}).$$

Figure 3 depicts a probabilistic time Petri net and a fragment of its semantics. Clock valuations are not represented.

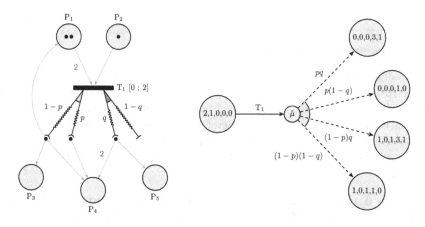

Fig. 3. Correspondence between the transitions of a probabilistic time Petri net and the trials of its semantics

3   The Probabilistic Real-Time Reachability Problem

A state is said to be *reachable* if there exists a sequence of transition relations that leads a probabilistic time Petri net from one of its initial states to that particular one. When considering a given system, one might want to express the fact that certain unwanted events are unlikely to happen when it operates. If that system is modelled as a probabilistic time Petri net, those unwanted events are formally represented by a certain set of states. Proving whether a given set of states can be reached with a certain probability or not is at the core of the *probabilistic real-time reachability problem for probabilistic time Petri nets.* Quantitative reachability properties enable us to assert that the probability of reaching certain unwanted states is sufficiently small and that the probability of achieving a certain desired system behaviour is above a given threshold.

We artificially introduce $(d_{\mathcal{N}}, t_{\mathcal{N}})$ as an action that the probabilistic time Petri net $\mathcal{N}$ performs when it decides that it will never fire a transition again. We let $d_{\mathcal{N}}$ be a real number that is strictly greater than the greatest real endpoint of any firing interval in $\{I(t) \mid t \in T\}$ and let $t_{\mathcal{N}}$ be a fictitious trial that does not belong to the set T. Intuitively, we want $(d_{\mathcal{N}}, t_{\mathcal{N}})$ to be a feasible action whenever the firing intervals of the transitions enabled in the current state of the net have no upper bound.

Subsequently, we define the extended set $\tilde{\Phi}(M, v)$ of actions that are feasible from a given state (M, v) by setting $\tilde{\Phi}(M, v) = \Phi(M, v) \cup \{(d_{\mathcal{N}}, t_{\mathcal{N}})\}$ if $\mathscr{C}(M, v) = \mathbb{R}_+$, and $\tilde{\Phi}(M, v) = \Phi(M, v)$ otherwise. We let $\tilde{T} = T \cup \{t_{\mathcal{N}}\}$ denote the *extended set of trials* and extend the domain of the partial piecewise probabilistic transition function W to take $(d_{\mathcal{N}}, t_{\mathcal{N}})$ into account as follows:

$$W((M, v + d_{\mathcal{N}}), t_{\mathcal{N}}) = \delta_{(M, v + d_{\mathcal{N}})}.$$

3.1   Paths and Schedulers

The possible evolution of a probabilistic time Petri net is described formally by a *path*. Reasoning about probabilities of sets of paths relies on the resolution of non-determinism, which is performed by a *scheduler*. The paths describe the potential computations that are obtained by resolving both the non-deterministic and probabilistic choices in the underlying probabilistic timed transition system. In other words, a path is a sequence of trials that are performed at certain dates. These trials carry the net over a set of states.

Definition 6 (Path in a Probabilistic Timed Transition System). *Let $S_{\mathcal{N}} = (Q, \rho_{S_{\mathcal{N}}}, T, W)$ be the semantics of a marked probabilistic time Petri net $\mathcal{N} = (P, T, Pre, Post, I, \rho_{\mathcal{N}})$.*

- *A finite path in the probabilistic timed transition system $S_{\mathcal{N}}$ is a finite sequence*

$$q_0 \xrightarrow{d_1, t_1} q_1 \xrightarrow{d_2, t_2} \cdots \xrightarrow{d_n, t_n} q_n$$

where $q_0 \in Supp(\rho_{S_{\mathcal{N}}})$, $n \in \mathbb{N}$ and for all $i \in [\![0, n-1]\!]$,

$$\begin{cases} q_i = (M_i, v_i) \in Q, \\ (d_{i+1}, t_{i+1}) \in \tilde{\Phi}(M_i, v_i), \\ q_{i+1} \in Supp(W((M_i, v_i + d_{i+1}), t_{i+1})). \end{cases}$$

The integer n is called the length *of the path. A finite path in $S_{\mathcal{N}}$ is an element of $Supp(\rho_{S_{\mathcal{N}}}) \times ((\mathbb{R}_+ \times T) \times Q)^*$. We denote by $Path^*_{(S_{\mathcal{N}})}$ the set of finite paths in the probabilistic timed transition system $S_{\mathcal{N}}$.*

– *An* infinite path *in the probabilistic timed transition system $S_{\mathcal{N}}$ is an infinite sequence*

$$q_0 \xrightarrow{d_1, t_1} q_1 \xrightarrow{d_2, t_2} q_2 \xrightarrow{d_3, t_3} \dots$$

such that $q_0 \xrightarrow{d_1, t_1} q_1 \xrightarrow{d_2, t_2} \dots \xrightarrow{d_n, t_n} q_n \in Path^*_{(S_{\mathcal{N}})}$ for all $n \in \mathbb{N}$.
An infinite path in $S_{\mathcal{N}}$ is an element of $(Q \times (\mathbb{R}_+ \times T))^\infty$. We denote by $Path^\infty_{(S_{\mathcal{N}})}$ the set of infinite paths in the probabilistic timed transition system $S_{\mathcal{N}}$.

The resolution of all non-deterministic choices in a probabilistic time Petri net is described formally by a scheduler. A scheduler chooses a feasible action $\tilde{\Phi}(M, v)$ in any state (M, v) of the net, but does not have any influence on the probability that one marking or another will be reached once that action has been chosen.

Definition 7 (Scheduler for a Probabilistic Timed Transition System).
Let $S_{\mathcal{N}} = (Q, \rho_{S_{\mathcal{N}}}, T, W)$ be the semantics of a marked probabilistic timed transition system $\mathcal{N} = (P, T, Pre, Post, I, \rho_{\mathcal{N}})$.
For a given finite path $\pi = q_0 \xrightarrow{d_1, t_1} q_1 \xrightarrow{d_2, t_2} \dots \xrightarrow{d_n, t_n} q_n$ in $S_{\mathcal{N}}$, let $last(\pi)$ denote the state q_n.

– *A* scheduler *for the probabilistic timed transition system $S_{\mathcal{N}}$ is a (total) function $\mathfrak{S} : Path^*_{(S_{\mathcal{N}})} \to (\mathbb{R}_+ \times T) \cup \{(d_{\mathcal{N}}, t_{\mathcal{N}})\}$ such that for all finite paths π in $S_{\mathcal{N}}$*

$$\begin{cases} \mathscr{C}(last(\pi)) \neq \mathbb{R}_+ \Rightarrow \mathfrak{S}(\pi) \in \Phi(last(\pi)), \\ \mathscr{C}(last(\pi)) = \mathbb{R}_+ \Rightarrow \mathfrak{S}(\pi) \in \tilde{\Phi}(last(\pi)). \end{cases}$$

A finite or infinite path $\pi = q_0 \xrightarrow{d_1, t_1} q_1 \xrightarrow{d_2, t_2} \dots$ of $S_{\mathcal{N}}$ is called a $\mathfrak{S}$-path if $\mathfrak{S}(\pi_{|i}) = (d_{i+1}, t_{i+1})$ for all prefixes $\pi_{|i}$ (the path $\pi_{|i}$ denotes the finite prefix of π of length i). We let $Path^*_{\mathfrak{S}}$ denote the (countable) set of finite $\mathfrak{S}$-paths.

The behaviour of a probabilistic time Petri net that is subject to a scheduler $\mathfrak{S}$ can be formalised by a *Markov chain* [15]. Intuitively, this Markov chain unfolds the net into as many trees as there are elements in $Supp(\rho_{\mathcal{N}})$.

Definition 8 (Markov Chain of a PTPN Induced by a Scheduler). *Let $S_{\mathcal{N}} = (Q, \rho_{S_{\mathcal{N}}}, T, W)$ be the semantics of a marked probabilistic time Petri net $\mathcal{N} = (P, T, Pre, Post, I, \rho_{\mathcal{N}})$.*

A scheduler $\mathfrak{S}$ of $S_{\mathcal{N}}$ induces a Markov chain $\mathcal{M}_{\mathfrak{S}} = (Path^*_{\mathfrak{S}}, \rho_{\mathfrak{S}}, \mathbf{P}_{\mathfrak{S}})$ where

- *$\rho_{\mathfrak{S}} \in \mathcal{D}ist_{Path^*_{\mathfrak{S}}}$ is the distribution of initial paths of the chain. Its support is equal to the finite paths in $S_{\mathcal{N}}$ of length 0 that are also initial states of the probabilistic timed transition system $S_{\mathcal{N}}$. For all $(M_0, 0_T) \in Supp(\rho_{\mathfrak{S}})$,*

$$\rho_{\mathfrak{S}}((M_0, 0_T)) = \rho_{S_{\mathcal{N}}}(M_0, 0_T) = \rho_{\mathcal{N}}(M_0).$$

- *$\mathbf{P}_{\mathfrak{S}} : Path^*_{\mathfrak{S}} \to \mathcal{D}ist_{Path^*_{\mathfrak{S}}}$ is the (total) probabilistic transition function of $\mathcal{M}_{\mathfrak{S}}$. For $\lambda \in Path^*_{\mathfrak{S}}$, the support of $\mathbf{P}_{\mathfrak{S}}(\lambda)$ is the set of $\mathfrak{S}$-paths of the form $\pi \xrightarrow{\mathfrak{S}(d,t)} q$. For $(\pi, q) \in Path^*_{\mathfrak{S}} \times Q$,*

$$\mathbf{P}_{\mathfrak{S}}(\pi)(\pi \xrightarrow{\mathfrak{S}(d,t)} q) = \tilde{\mu}_t(q).$$

Example 2. Let us consider the marked probabilistic time Petri net depicted in Fig. 4, whose initial marking is given by $\rho_{\mathcal{N}} = \delta_{(1,0,0,1,0,0,0)}$. Since the enabled transition T_4 is not firable before date 2, all paths in $\mathcal{N}_1$ start with the resolution of the trial T_1, which either generates a token in P_2 or in P_3. Every scheduler must first choose when to fire that transition. Depending on the outcome of the trial T_1, a scheduler is not presented with the same opportunities. Let us consider a scheduler $\mathfrak{S}_1$ that chooses to fire T_1 immediately. If a token ends up in P_2, then $\mathfrak{S}_1$ is constrained by the deterministic trial T_3 which ends up being performed at date 1. If a token ends up in P_3, then $\mathfrak{S}_1$ must let time flow before performing either T_2 or T_4.

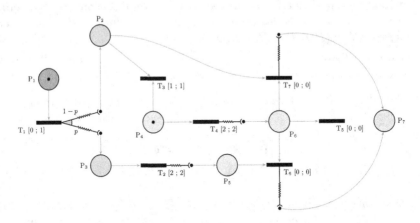

Fig. 4. The probabilistic time Petri net $\mathcal{N}_1$

Suppose that we are interested in reaching the place P_7. Our target set consists of every marking M for which $M(P_7) > 0$. Figure 5 depicts the choices scheduler $\mathfrak{S}_1$ makes as it resolves all non-determinism before reaching P_7 with probability p. While scheduler $\mathfrak{S}_1$ does exhibit a path leading to a target marking, we would like to thoroughly study the likelihood of reaching those particular markings.

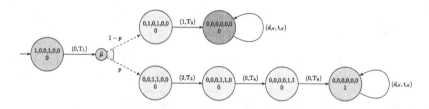

Fig. 5. Abridged representation of the scheduler $\mathfrak{S}_1$

Intuitively, the deterministic trials T_3 and T_5 must be avoided at all costs if P_7 is to be reached. This stems from the fact that these trials eliminate the tokens that are needed to fire T_6 or T_7. To avoid T_3, the trial T_1 must necessarily be resolved at date 1 and no sooner than that. To avoid T_5, the trial T_1 must necessarily be resolved at date 0, without delay. Schedulers that do not fire T_1 at date 0 or at date 1 never reach P_7. Therefore, the minimum probability of reaching P_7 is 0. Since a scheduler has no influence over the outcome of T_1, it has no way of knowing if firing T_1 at date 0 or at date 1 is best. As a result, the probability of reaching P_7 can be no greater than $max(p, 1 - p)$.

The probabilistic real-time reachability problem consists in the establishment of these lower and upper probability bounds. The whole set of schedulers of a probabilistic time Petri net is considered in order to compute these bounds, as they cover every possible resolution of non-determinism. This corresponds to a worst-case analysis.

3.2   Markov Decision Processes

Since a probabilistic time Petri net evolves in a dense-time environment, there are usually infinitely many schedulers as soon as a single firing interval is a proper interval. To compute the lower and upper probability bounds by ranging over all schedulers, we proceed to a natural grouping of states that leads to the formation of *state classes*. This enables us to capture the information we need in a finite graph, called a state class graph, which can then be used to apply formal verification techniques. The state space of the net thus takes the form of a Markov decision process. Formally:

Definition 9 (Markov Decision Process (MDP)). *A Markov decision process is a quadruple $(C, \rho, A, \mathbf{P})$ where*

- *C is the (countable) set of states of the process,*
- *$\rho \in \mathscr{D}ist_C$ is the distribution of initial states of the process,*
- *A is the set of actions of the process, and*
- *$\mathbf{P} : C \times A \to \mathscr{D}ist_C$ is the (partial) probabilistic transition function.*

For a given state c of a Markov decision process, we define the set $\Sigma(c)$ of actions that are enabled in the state c as

$$\Sigma(c) = \{\alpha \in A \mid \mathbf{P}(c, \alpha)\text{is defined}\}.$$

The assumption that $\Sigma(c) \neq \phi$ for all $c \in C$ is a conventional requirement in the literature that is not specific to our setting [15].

As for probabilistic time Petri nets, the paths in a Markov decision process resolve both probabilistic and non-deterministic choices.

Definition 10 (Path in a Markov Decision Process). *Let $\mathcal{M} = (C, \rho, A, \mathbf{P})$ be a Markov decision process.*

– *A* finite *path in the Markov decision process $\mathcal{M}$ is a finite sequence*

$$c_0 \xrightarrow{\alpha_1} c_1 \xrightarrow{\alpha_2} \ldots \xrightarrow{\alpha_n} c_n$$

where for all $i \in [\![0, n-1]\!]$,

$$\begin{cases} c_i \in C, \\ \alpha_{i+1} \in \Sigma(c_i), \\ c_{i+1} \in Supp(\mathbf{P}(c_i, \alpha_{i+1})). \end{cases}$$

The integer n is called the length *of the path. A finite path in $\mathcal{M}$ is an element of $Supp(\rho) \times (A \times C)^*$. We denote by $Path^*_{(\mathcal{M})}$ the set of finite paths in the Markov decision process $\mathcal{M}$.*

– *An* infinite *path in the Markov decision process $\mathcal{M}$ is an infinite sequence*

$$c_0 \xrightarrow{\alpha_1} c_1 \xrightarrow{\alpha_2} c_2 \xrightarrow{\alpha_3} \ldots$$

where $c_0 \xrightarrow{\alpha_1} c_1 \xrightarrow{\alpha_2} \ldots \xrightarrow{\alpha_n} c_n \in Path^*_{(\mathcal{M})}$ for all $n \in \mathbb{N}$.
An infinite path in $\mathcal{M}$ is an element of $(C \times A)^\infty$. We denote by $Path^\infty_{(\mathcal{M})}$ the set of infinite paths in the Markov decision process $\mathcal{M}$.

An adversary of a Markov decision process fulfils the same function a scheduler does for a probabilistic time Petri net.

Definition 11 (Adversary of a Markov Decision Process). *Let $\mathcal{M} = (C, \rho, A, \mathbf{P})$ be a Markov decision process.*
For a given finite path $\sigma = c_0 \xrightarrow{\alpha_1} c_1 \xrightarrow{\alpha_2} \ldots \xrightarrow{\alpha_n} c_n$ in $\mathcal{M}$, let $last(\sigma)$ denote the state c_n.

– *An* adversary *of the Markov decision process $\mathcal{M}$ is a (total) function $\Lambda : Path^*_{(\mathcal{M})} \to A$ such that for all finite paths $\sigma = c_0 \xrightarrow{\alpha_1} c_1 \xrightarrow{\alpha_2} \ldots \xrightarrow{\alpha_n} c_n$ in $Path^*_{(\mathcal{M})}$*

$$\Lambda(\sigma) \in \Sigma(last(\sigma)).$$

A finite or infinite path $\sigma = c_0 \xrightarrow{\alpha_1} c_1 \xrightarrow{\alpha_2} \ldots \xrightarrow{\alpha_n} c_n$ of $\mathcal{M}$ is called a Λ-path if $\Lambda(\sigma_{|i}) = \alpha_{i+1}$ for all prefixes $\sigma_{|i}$ of σ (the path $\sigma_{|i}$ denotes the finite prefix of σ of length i). We let $Path^*_\Lambda$ denote the (countable) set of finite Λ-paths.

– An adversary Λ of the Markov decision process $\mathcal{M}$ induces a Markov chain $\mathcal{M}_\Lambda = (Path_\Lambda^*, \rho_\Lambda, \mathbf{P}_\Lambda)$ where

• ρ_Λ is the distribution of initial paths of the chain. Its support is equal to the finite paths in $\mathcal{M}$ of length 0 that are also initial states of the process. For all $c \in Supp(\rho_\Lambda)$,

$$\rho_\Lambda(c) = \rho(c).$$

• $\mathbf{P}_\Lambda : Path_\Lambda^* \to \mathscr{D}ist_{Path_\Lambda^*}$ is the (total) probabilistic transition function of $\mathcal{M}_\Lambda$. For $\sigma \in Path_\Lambda^*$, the support of $\mathbf{P}_\Lambda(\sigma)$ is the set of Λ-paths of the form $\sigma \xrightarrow{\Lambda(\sigma)} c$. For $(\sigma, c) \in Path_\Lambda^* \times C$,

$$\mathbf{P}_\Lambda(\sigma)(\sigma \xrightarrow{\Lambda(\sigma)} c) = \mathbf{P}(last(\sigma), \Lambda(\sigma))(c).$$

3.3   The Probabilistic Strong State Class Graph

Time Petri nets typically generate an infinite state space. The *linear state class graph* was introduced in [11] and [12] in order to capture linear time temporal properties of time Petri nets in a finite graph. Intuitively, each class is an element of $\mathbb{N}^P \times \mathscr{P}(\mathbb{R}^T)$ which captures all the states that are reachable from an initial state class by firing schedules of a given support. Since there are generally infinitely many supports, state classes are then considered modulo some equivalence relation. The graph thus becomes *finite* if the net is *bounded*.

The probabilistic strong state class graph extends the construction methods that are proposed in the literature to account for the probabilistic nature of PTPNs. The following definition introduces *strong state classes* for probabilistic time Petri nets and details how the successor of a class is obtained when firing a given transition.

Definition 12 (Strong State Classes). *Let $S_\mathcal{N} = (Q, \rho_{S_\mathcal{N}}, T, W)$ be the semantics of a marked probabilistic time Petri net $\mathcal{N} = (P, T, Pre, Post, I, \rho_\mathcal{N})$. The set of* strong state classes *is defined as follows:*

1. *For a given transition t of the net $\mathcal{N}$, we define the set $\Delta(t)$ of decoupled trials of t as $\Delta(t) = \{t_\omega \in \mathscr{D}ist_{\mathbb{N}^P} \mid \exists \omega \in Supp(\mu_t), t_\omega = \delta_\omega\}$ and denote by $T_\Delta = \bigcup_{t \in T} \Delta(t)$ the set of decoupled trials in $S_\mathcal{N}$.*

2. *For a given initial state $q_0 \in Supp(\rho_{S_\mathcal{N}})$, we define a cover $C_{q_0} = \bigcup_{\tau \in T_\Delta^*} c_\tau$ of Q inductively by $c_\varepsilon = \{q_0\}$ and*

$$c_{\tau t_\omega} = \left\{ \begin{array}{l} (M', v') \in \mathbb{N}^P \times \mathbb{R}_+^T \mid \exists (M, v) \in c_\tau, \exists (d, t) \in \Phi(M, v), \\ t_\omega \in \Delta(t) \text{ and } v' = v + d \text{ and } M' = (M - Pre(t)) + \omega \end{array} \right\}$$

The classes $c_{\tau t_\omega}$ are the successors of the state class c_τ.

3. *The cover C_{q_0} denotes the set of nodes of the tree that is generated by q_0. We must account for all the trees that are generated by an initial state of the net and thus let*

$$C = \bigcup_{q_0 \in Supp(\rho_{S_\mathcal{N}})} C_{q_0}.$$

Let $c \in C$ be a state class in which the shared marking is M. We say that a transition $t \in \mathscr{E}(M)$ is *firable* from the state class c if there exists a state $q \in c$ such that t is firable from q. The *probabilistic strong state class graph* (which remains *finite* if the net is *bounded*) is defined as follows:

Definition 13 (Probabilistic Strong State Class Graph). *Let* $S_N = (Q, \rho_{S_N}, T, W)$ *be the semantics of a marked probabilistic time Petri net* $N = (P, T, Pre, Post, I, \rho_N)$.

The probabilistic strong state class graph *of the net* N *is a Markov decision process* $\mathscr{M} = (C, \rho, \tilde{T}, \mathbf{P})$ *where*

- C *is the set of* strong state classes,
- $\rho : C \to [0, 1]$ *is the distribution of initial classes of the graph.*
  The support of ρ *is equal to the set of singletons* $\{q_0\}$, *where* $q_0 \in Supp(\rho_{S_N})$.
  For all $(M_0, 0_T) \in Supp(\rho_{S_N})$,

$$\rho(\{(M_0, 0_T)\}) = \rho_{S_N}(M_0, 0_T) = \rho_N(M_0).$$

- $\mathbf{P} : C \times \tilde{T} \to \mathscr{D}ist_C$ *is the (partial) transition probability function.*
  1. $\mathbf{P}$ *is defined for* $(c, t) \in C \times T$ *if and only if the transition* t *is firable from the state class* c. *In that case, let* $\mathbf{P}(c, t) = \widehat{\mu}_t$, *where* $\widehat{\mu}_t \in \mathscr{D}ist_C$ *is defined as follows:*
     - *Let* $c' \in C$. *The class* c' *lies in* $Supp(\widehat{\mu}_t)$ *if and only if* c' *is the successor of* c *for some decoupled transition* $t_\omega \in \Delta(t)$.
     - *Suppose that* $c' \in Supp(\widehat{\mu}_t)$. *We define the image of* c' *by the formula*

$$\widehat{\mu}_t(c') = \mu_t(\omega).$$

  2. $\mathbf{P}$ *is defined for* $(c, t) \in C \times \{t_N\}$ *if and only if* $\mathscr{C}(q) = \mathbb{R}_+$ *for some* $q \in c$. *In that case,* $\mathscr{C}(q) = \mathbb{R}_+$ *for all* $q \in c$ *since all the states in* c *have the same marking. We define the image of* (c, t_N) *by the formula*

$$\mathbf{P}(c, t_N) = \delta_c.$$

The probabilistic strong state class graph of the probabilistic time Petri net N_1 is represented in Fig. 6. Each class is represented by a node, which is labelled with the marking that all states share in that particular class. Here, strong state classes are considered modulo an equivalence relation $\equiv$ that asserts that two classes are equivalent if they denote the same set of states. For the sake of clarity, time domains are not represented.

Let us now consider the adversary Λ_1 of the probabilistic state class graph of N_1, depicted in Fig. 7. Depending on the outcome of the trial T_1, it either performs the untimed sequence of actions $T_1 \to T_4 \to T_7$ or the untimed sequence $T_1 \to T_2 \to T_4 \to T_6$ before reaching a target state. However, there is no scheduler for N_1 that can perform both of these paths since the path $T_1 \to T_4 \to T_7$ can only be performed when T_1 is fired at date 1 while the path $T_1 \to T_2 \to T_4 \to T_6$ can only be performed when T_1 is fired at date 0. As a result, the probabilistic strong state class graph potentially generates duplicitous adversaries, which display a probability of reaching target states greater than that of any scheduler.

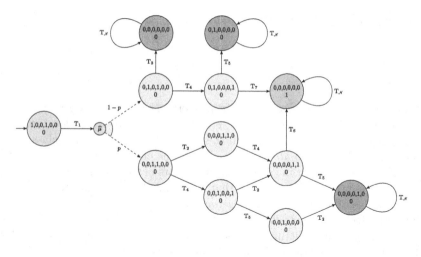

Fig. 6. The probabilistic strong state class graph of the probabilistic time Petri net $\mathcal{N}_1$

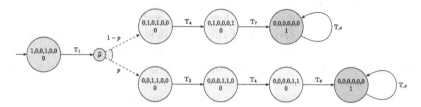

Fig. 7. Abridged representation of the duplicitous adversary Λ_1

3.4 The Probabilistic Atomic State Class Graph

The reason why the probabilistic strong state class graph fails to produce proper adversaries lies in the way time and probabilities are intertwined in probabilistic time Petri nets. A graph that better captures the effect the firing date of probabilistic trials has on future actions is needed in order to solve the probabilistic real-time reachability problem.

Berthomieu and Vernadat introduced the atomic state class graph for time Petri nets in order to preserve their branching time temporal properties in a finite graph [14]. The construction of this graph can be adapted for probabilistic time Petri nets to preserve the adversaries we need. Let us consider the following properties of interest for state class graphs:

- (EE) For all classes $c, c' \in \mathbb{N}^P \times \mathscr{P}(\mathbb{R}^T)$ and for all $t \in \Sigma(c)$,

$$c \xrightarrow{t} c' \in Path^*_{(\mathcal{M})} \iff \exists q \in c, \exists q' \in c', \exists d \in \mathbb{R}_+, \begin{cases} (d,t) \in \Phi(q) \\ q \xrightarrow{(d,t)} q' \in Path^*_{(S_{\mathcal{N}})} \end{cases}$$

– (AE) For all classes $c, c' \in \mathbb{N}^P \times \mathscr{P}(\mathbb{R}^T)$ and for all $t \in \Sigma(c)$,

$$c \xrightarrow{t} c' \in Path^*_{(\mathscr{M})} \implies \forall q \in c, \exists q' \in c', \exists d \in \mathbb{R}_+, \begin{cases} (d,t) \in \Phi(q) \\ q \xrightarrow{(d,t)} q' \in Path^*_{(S_{\mathcal{N}})} \end{cases}$$

State class graphs typically satisfy property (EE) and so does the probabilistic strong state class graph. The *probabilistic atomic state class graph* we introduce in this section is built from the probabilistic strong state class graph, by refining its classes into *atomic* ones. An atomic class is a state class in which each state has a successor in each of the successors of that class. Intuitively, each atomic class captures all the states that are reachable from an initial state by firing schedules of a given support *during certain time windows*.

The algorithm that details how to split strong state classes into atomic ones can be found in [14]. Splitting a class c replaces it with a pair of classes which both inherit the predecessors of c and the successors of c that they can still reach. This technically causes multiple hyperarcs leaving the predecessors of c to have the same label. However, each one of these hyperarcs is implicitly augmented with a time interval. This time window corresponds to the set of delays that enforce property (EE) in each one of the states it leads to. Since no time delay is shared among those hyperarcs, any ambiguity is lifted.

This stable refinement enforces property (AE) in the probabilistic atomic state class graph, which once again takes the form of a Markov decision process $\mathscr{M}_A = (C_A, \rho_A, \tilde{T}, \mathbf{P}_A)$. However, this graph is usually significantly bigger than the probabilistic state class graph from which is it built. The probabilistic atomic state class graph of the probabilistic time Petri net $\mathcal{N}_1$ is represented in Fig. 8.

The proof of the following theorem is omitted due to lack of space.

Theorem 1. *Let $\mathcal{N} = (P, T, Pre, Post, I, \rho_N)$ be a bounded marked probabilistic time Petri net, let $S_N = (Q, \rho_{S_N}, T, W)$ be its semantics and let $\mathscr{M}_A = (C_A, \rho_A, \tilde{T}, \mathbf{P}_A)$ be the probabilistic atomic state class graph of $\mathcal{N}$.*

1. *Let Λ be an adversary of the Markov decision process $\mathscr{M}_A$. There exists a scheduler for the probabilistic timed transition system S_N that induces the same Markov chain as Λ up to isomorphism.*
2. *Conversely, let $\mathfrak{S}$ be a scheduler for the probabilistic timed transition system S_N. There exists an adversary of the Markov decision process $\mathscr{M}_A$ that induces the same Markov chain as $\mathfrak{S}$ up to isomorphism.*

As a result of theorem 1, the probabilistic real-time reachability problem can be solved by computing the probability of reaching a target state for every adversary of the probabilistic atomic state class graph (with the tools commonly used for Markov decision processes). For example, it can easily be shown that the sought probability bounds for reaching P7 in the net $\mathcal{N}_1$ (Fig. 4) are indeed 0 and $max(p, 1-p)$, by considering all the adversaries of its probabilistic atomic state class graph (Fig. 8). In fact, an array of algorithms can now be used to prove that the net verifies the following properties:

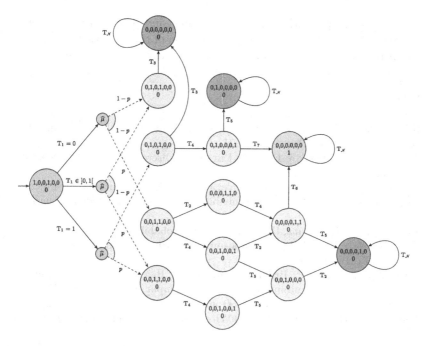

Fig. 8. The probabilistic atomic state class graph of the PTPN $\mathcal{N}_1$

- **reachability**: the net $\mathcal{N}_1$ can reach P_7 with probability (at least) 0.5,
- **inevitability**: the net $\mathcal{N}_1$ inevitably leaves P_1 with probability 1,
- **time bounded reachability**: the net $\mathcal{N}_1$ can reach P_7 within two time units with probability 0.5,
- **bounded response**: the net $\mathcal{N}_1$ inevitably reaches P_5 or P_7 within two time units with probability 1 after reaching the marking $(0, 0, 1, 1, 0, 0, 0)$.

4   Conclusion

We have introduced a new formalism for the modelling of concurrent probabilistic real-time systems. This new model extends time Petri nets by enhancing the forward incidence mapping with sets of probability distributions. Probabilistic time Petri nets natively integrate time, concurrency and probabilities. In the spirit of probabilistic timed automata [16], we have restricted all random phenomena to the discrete behaviour of a time Petri net. Time and concurrency are still resolved in a non-deterministic manner. We have shown how the atomic state class graph construction of TPNs can be adapted to our model and how this enables us to recover a Markov decision process that induces the same Markov chains as the semantics of the PTPN. Therefore, the use of a wide range of tools for the analysis of PTPN is made available to us. We have also proved that the simpler non-atomic state class graph construction cannot be adapted in a similar manner.

Future work includes the addition of timing and probability parameters in probabilistic time Petri nets, the implementation of the proposed method in our tool Roméo and the application of this model to the automotive industry.

References

1. Stewart, W.J.: Introduction to the Numerical Solutions of Markov Chains. Princeton University Press, Princeton (1994)
2. Puterman, M.L.: Markov Decision Processes: Discrete Stochastic Dynamic Programming. Wiley, London (1994)
3. Kwiatkowska, M., Norman, G., Segala, R., Sproston, J.: Automatic verification of real-time systems with discrete probability distributions. Theoret. Comput. Sci. **282**(1), 101–150 (2002)
4. Eisentraut, C., Hermanns, H., Zhang, L.: On probabilistic automata in continuous time. In: 25th Annual IEEE Symposium on Logic in Computer Science (LICS), pp. 342–351. IEEE (2010)
5. Bertrand, N., Bouyer, P., Brihaye, T., Menet, Q., Baier, C., Größer, M., Jurdziński, M.: Stochastic timed automata. Log. Meth. Comput. Sci. **10**(4), 6 (2014)
6. Kwiatkowska, M., Norman, G., Sproston, J.: Probabilistic model checking of deadline properties in the IEEE 1394 FireWire root contention protocol. Formal Aspects of Comput. **14**(3), 295–318 (2003)
7. Kwiatkowska, M., Norman, G., Parker, D.: PRISM 4.0: verification of probabilistic real-time systems. In: Gopalakrishnan, G., Qadeer, S. (eds.) CAV 2011. LNCS, vol. 6806, pp. 585–591. Springer, Heidelberg (2011)
8. Marsan, M.A., Conte, G., Balbo, G.: A class of generalized stochastic Petri nets for the performance evaluation of multiprocessor systems. ACM Trans. Comput. Syst. **2**(2), 93–122 (1984)
9. Molloy, M.K.: Discrete time stochastic Petri nets. IEEE Trans. Softw. Eng. **11**(4), 417–423 (1985)
10. Vicario, E., Sassoli, L., Carnevali, L.: Using stochastic state classes in quantitative evaluation of dense-time reactive systems. IEEE Trans. Softw. Eng. **35**(5), 703–719 (2009)
11. Berthomieu, B., Diaz, M.: Modeling and verification of time dependent systems using time Petri nets. IEEE Trans. Soft. Eng. **3**, 259–273 (1991)
12. Berthomieu, B., Menasche, M.: An enumerative approach for analyzing time Petri nets: In: Mason, R.E.A. (ed.) Information Processing: Proceedings of the IFIP Congress, vol. 9 of IFIP Congress Series, pp. 41–46 (1983)
13. Dugan, J.B., Trivedi, K.S., Geist, R.M., Nicola, V.F.: Extended stochastic Petri nets: applications and analysis. Technical report, DTIC Document (1984)
14. Berthomieu, B., Vernadat, F.: State class constructions for branching analysis of time Petri nets. In: Garavel, H., Hatcliff, J. (eds.) TACAS 2003. LNCS, vol. 2619, pp. 442–457. Springer, Heidelberg (2003)
15. Baier, C., Katoen, J.: Principles of Model Checking. MIT Press, Cambridge (2008)
16. Norman, G., Parker, D., Sproston, J.: Model checking for probabilistic timed automata. Formal Meth. Syst. Des. **43**(2), 164–190 (2013)

Efficient Decomposition Algorithm for Stationary Analysis of Complex Stochastic Petri Net Models

Kristóf Marussy[1], Attila Klenik[1], Vince Molnár[2], András Vörös[2(✉)], István Majzik[1], and Miklós Telek[3]

[1] Department of Measurement and Information Systems, Budapest University of Technology and Economics, Budapest, Hungary
[2] MTA-BME Lendület Cyber-Physical Systems Research Group, Budapest, Hungary
vori@mit.bme.hu
[3] MTA-BME Information Systems Research Group, Budapest, Hungary

Abstract. Stochastic Petri nets are widely used for the modeling and analysis of non-functional properties of critical systems. The state space explosion problem often inhibits the numerical analysis of such models. Symbolic techniques exist to explore the discrete behavior of even complex models, while block Kronecker decomposition provides memory-efficient representation of the stochastic behavior. However, the combination of these techniques into a stochastic analysis approach is not straightforward. In this paper we integrate saturation-based symbolic techniques and decomposition-based stochastic analysis methods. Saturation-based exploration is used to build the state space representation and a new algorithm is introduced to efficiently build block Kronecker matrix representation to be used by the stochastic analysis algorithms. Measurements confirm that the presented combination of the two representations can expand the limits of previous approaches.

Keywords: Stochastic Petri nets · Stationary analysis · Block kronecker decomposition · Numerical algorithms · Symbolic methods

1 Introduction

Stochastic analysis provides information about the quantitative aspects of models and is used for the analysis of non-functional properties of critical systems. Stochastic Petri nets are widely used in reliability, availability and performability modelling to capture the stochastic behaviours and the analysis questions are answered with the help of Markovian analysis. However, successful stochastic analysis is often prevented by the *state space explosion problem*: in addition to the complexity of traditional qualitative analysis, stochastic computations require more involved data structures and numerical algorithms. To successfully tackle these problems, efficient algorithms are needed.

© Springer International Publishing Switzerland 2016
F. Kordon and D. Moldt (Eds.): PETRI NETS 2016, LNCS 9698, pp. 281–300, 2016.
DOI: 10.1007/978-3-319-39086-4_17

Many efficient techniques exist in the literature for the exploration and storage of the state space of Petri net models. One of the most efficient is the so-called saturation algorithm which uses a special iteration strategy for the state space traversal and stores the state space representation symbolically in decision diagrams [13]. On the other hand, numerical algorithms for Markovian analysis neccesitates the representation of the stochastic behaviours.

The infinitesimal generator matrix describes the behaviours of stochastic Petri nets and the underlying Markov chains. The size of the matrix is quadratic in the number of reachable states of the system. This implies a quadratic storage complexity in case the matrix is directly represented in a dense form. Sparse matrix formats, such as Compressed Column Storage (CCS) [3, Sect. 4.3.1], reduce memory requirements to be proportional to the transitions in the system. However, even sparse storage techniques tend to fail quickly due to state space explosion.

Potential Kronecker methods [8] divide the large matrix representation into smaller matrices using only local information. Computations are then performed with the local matrices and vectors. Unfortunately, using local information leads to storing probabilities for unreachable states. This may cause problems in some numerical solver algorithms as well as increases storage requirements.

In contrast, *actual Kronecker methods* [5,8,18] apply additional conversions and computations to handle unreachable states in the encoding. This yields higher implementation complexities and computational overhead.

The basis of our work is *block Kronecker decomposition* which imposes a hierarchical structure on the reachable state space to solve the issue of unreachable potential states [4,7,9].

Several algorithms have been developed that use variations of decision diagrams to represent the infinitesimal generator. Matrix diagrams [12,21] generalize the Kronecker representation to arbitrary matrices and not necessarily Kronecker consistent model partitions. Multi-Terminal Decision Diagrams (MTDDs) can store both the generator matrix [20] and the vector of state probabilities [19] by extending decision diagrams with terminal nodes corresponding to real numbers. Multiplicative Edge-valued Multilabel Decision Diagrams (EV*MDDs) [25] can provide up to exponential space savings compared to MTDDs by storing matrix and vector entries as edge labels instead of terminal nodes.

While vector-matrix products can be handled with symbolic approaches easily, more elaborate matrix access becomes difficult. For example, efficient access of a single column of the symbolic descriptor requires the introduction of caching strategies [26].

As it turns out from the literature, the combination of efficient state space traversal and matrix representation techniques into a stochastic analysis approach is not straightforward. In this paper we elaborate an idea of Buchholz [10] to construct the matrix representation of the stochastic behaviour from symbolic state space representation. In addition to the initial idea of Buchholz [10], we further extended the method by employing partition refinement instead of hashing and we also proved correctness of the algorithm formally. The stochastic analysis framework uses saturation-based exploration to build the state space representation and the new algorithm builds the block Kronecker matrix representation to be used by the stochastic analysis algorithms. Measurements confirm that the presented combination of the two representations can expand the limits of previous approaches.

2 Background

In this section, we overview the basic formalisms and scope of our work. At first, a stochastic Petri net based formalism is introduced. Kronecker algebra and multivalued decision diagrams are also discussed.

2.1 Stochastic Petri Nets

Stochastic Petri Nets extend Petri nets by assigning exponentially distributed random delays to transitions [1]. After the delay associated with an enabled transition is elapsed the transition fires and transition delays are reset.

Definition 1. *A Stochastic Petri Net is a pair SPN = $\langle PN, \Lambda \rangle$, where PN is a Petri net and $\Lambda : T \to \mathbb{R}^+$ maps the set of transitions to transition rates. PN may contain inhibitor arcs but no priority specifications.*

The stochastic behaviours of a stochastic Petri net are defined by an underlying continuous-time Markov chain (CTMC). The Markov chain associated with an SPN is a stochastic process $X(\tau) \in \mathrm{RS}$, $\tau \geq 0$, where RS is the set of reachable markings of the underlying Petri net.

We will only consider the case when the Petri net is bounded, hence $n = |\mathrm{RS}| < \infty$. In order to establish the transformation between the Petri net and its underlying Markov chain, we have to define a mapping from states to indices. A bijection $\iota : \mathrm{RS} \to \{0, 1, \ldots, n-1\}$ exists between the reachable markings and a set of indices. This allows representing the distribution of $X(\tau)$ as a vector

$$\boldsymbol{\pi}(\tau) \in \mathbb{R}^n, \quad \boldsymbol{\pi}(\tau)[x] = \Pr(X(\tau) = \iota^{-1}(x)),$$

i.e. $\boldsymbol{\pi}(\tau)[\iota(M)]$ is the probability that the SPN is in the marking M at time τ.

The time evolution of the $X(\tau)$ is described by the differential equation

$$\frac{\partial \boldsymbol{\pi}(\tau)}{\partial \tau} = \boldsymbol{\pi}(\tau)\, Q, \tag{1}$$

where $Q \in \mathbb{R}^{n \times n}$ is the *infinitesimal generator matrix* of the CTMC associated with the stochastic Petri net.

Off-diagonal elements $q[x, y]$ of Q ($0 \leq x, y < n$ and $x \neq y$) contain the rate of exponentially distributed transitions from the marking $\iota^{-1}(x)$ to $\iota^{-1}(y)$. Diagonal elements $q[x, x]$ are calculated such that $Q\mathbf{1}^\mathrm{T} = \mathbf{0}^\mathrm{T}$, where $\mathbf{1}$ and $\mathbf{0} \in \mathbb{R}^n$ are vectors with every element equal to 1 and 0, respectively. That is,

$$q[x, y] = \begin{cases} -\sum_{z=0, z \neq x}^{n-1} q[x, z] & \text{if } x = y, \\ \sum_{\iota^{-1}(x)[t\rangle\iota^{-1}(y)}^{t \in T} \Lambda(t) & \text{if } x \neq y. \end{cases} \tag{2}$$

The notation $\iota^{-1}(x)$ $[t\rangle$ $\iota^{-1}(y)$ indicates that the transition t can be fired in the marking $\iota^{-1}(x)$ to assume the marking $\iota^{-1}(y)$.

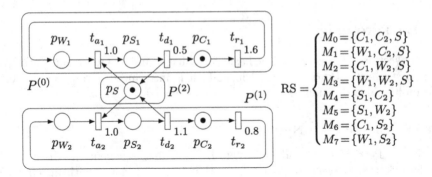

Fig. 1. Example stochastic Petri net with superposed partitions.

Example 1. In Fig. 1 we introduce the *SharedResource* model which will serve as a running example throughout this paper.

The model consists of a single shared resource S and two consumers. Each consumer can be in one of the following states: C_i (calculating locally), W_i (waiting for resource) and S_i (using shared resource). The transitions r_i (request resource), a_i (acquire resource) and d_i (done) correspond to behaviors of the consumers. The net has 8 reachable states, which are also shown in Fig. 1. As the net is 1-bounded, only the marked places are listed for each state.

The net is annotated with exponentially distributed transition rates. The clients have different request (1.6 and 0.8) and completion (0.5 and 1.1, respectively) rates, while both clients have an acquire rate of 1.0.

2.2 Superposed Stochastic Petri Nets

As the decomposition method in our approach fits the concept of superposed Petri nets, we use it in the rest of the paper.

Definition 2. *A Superposed Stochastic Petri Net (SSPN) is a pair SSPN = $\langle SPN, \mathcal{P} \rangle$, where $\mathcal{P} = \{P^{(0)}, P^{(1)}, \ldots, P^{(J-1)}\}$ is the partitioning of the set of places P in the underlying Petri net of SPN such that $P = P^{(0)} \sqcup \cdots \sqcup P^{(J-1)}$ [15].*

The partition $P^{(j)}$ is called the jth *local net* or *component* of SSPN. A *local marking* $M^{(j)} \colon P^{(j)} \to \mathbb{N}$ is obtained from a *global marking* $M \colon P \to \mathbb{N}$ by restricting the domain to $P^{(j)}$, i.e. $M^{(j)} = M|_{P^{(j)}}$.

The *local reachable state space* of the jth local net contains the restrictions of the globally reachable markings $\mathrm{RS}^{(j)} = \{M^{(j)} : M \in \mathrm{RS}\}$.

We will assume a bijection $\iota^{(j)} \colon RS^{(j)} \to \{0, 1, \ldots, n_j\}$ from local markings to an index set, where $n_j = |\mathrm{RS}^{(j)}|$. Let the notation $x^{(j)}$ refer to the local marking $\left(\iota^{(j)}\right)^{-1}(x)$.

If $\mathbf{x} = \langle x[0], x[1], \ldots, x[J-1] \rangle$ is a vector of indices, then let the notation

$$M = \langle\!\langle \mathbf{x} \rangle\!\rangle = \langle\!\langle (x[0])^{(0)}, (x[1])^{(1)}, \ldots, (x[J-1])^{(J-1)} \rangle\!\rangle$$

refer to the marking M with the property $M^{(j)} = (x[j])^{(j)}$ for all j, i.e. M is the marking obtained by joining the local markings indexed by $\mathbf{x}$. We extend this notation to take sets of local states and yield a set of markings.

The *potential state space*

$$\mathrm{PS} = \langle\!\langle \mathrm{RS}^{(0)}, \mathrm{RS}^{(1)}, \ldots, \mathrm{RS}^{(J-1)} \rangle\!\rangle$$

is isomorphic to the Cartesian product of local state spaces. More concretely, each $M \in \mathrm{PS}$ can be identified with a vector of indices $\mathbf{x}$ such that $M = \langle\!\langle \mathbf{x} \rangle\!\rangle$, i.e. M can be obtained by joining some local states for each component. This vector is the state coding of M expressed by the function $\iota(M) : \mathrm{PS} \to \mathbb{N}^J$, $\iota(\langle\!\langle \mathbf{x} \rangle\!\rangle) = \mathbf{x}$.

Let us write $x^{(j)} [t\rangle y^{(j)}$ if there is a reachable marking $M_x \in \mathrm{RS}$ such that

$$M_x|_{P^{(j)}} = x^{(j)}, \quad M_x [t\rangle M_y, \quad M_y|_{P^{(j)}} = y^{(j)},$$

i.e. there is a global state transition that takes the jth local net from the state $x^{(j)}$ to $y^{(j)}$. It is important to note that superposed stochastic Petri nets are *Kronecker consistent*: if $x^{(j)} [t\rangle y^{(j)}$ and $x^{(j)} [t\rangle z^{(j)}$, then $y^{(j)} = z^{(j)}$.

Example 2. The *SharedResource* SPN in Fig. 1 contains three partitions. The local nets $P^{(0)}$ and $P^{(1)}$ correspond to the two clients, while $P^{(2)}$ contains the shared resource. The local state spaces of the components are

$$RS^{(0)} = \begin{cases} 0^{(0)} = \{C_1\} \\ 1^{(0)} = \{W_1\} \\ 2^{(0)} = \{S_1\} \end{cases}, \quad RS^{(1)} = \begin{cases} 0^{(1)} = \{C_2\} \\ 1^{(1)} = \{W_2\} \\ 2^{(1)} = \{S_2\} \end{cases}, \quad RS^{(2)} = \begin{cases} 0^{(2)} = \{S\} \\ 1^{(2)} = \emptyset \end{cases}.$$

The reachable states can be factored over the local state spaces, e.g. the marking $M_4 = \{S_1, C_2\} = \langle\!\langle 2^{(0)}, 0^{(1)}, 1^{(2)} \rangle\!\rangle$. However, the potential state space PS contains $|\mathrm{RS}^{(0)}| \cdot |\mathrm{RS}^{(1)}| \cdot |\mathrm{RS}^{(2)}| = 3 \cdot 3 \cdot 2 = 18$ states, 10 more than the reachable state space RS. For example, the marking $\langle\!\langle 2^{(0)}, 2^{(1)}, 0^{(2)} \rangle\!\rangle = \{S_1, S_2, S\}$, which violates mutual exclusion, is not reachable, although it is in PS.

2.3   Decision Diagrams

Multivalued decision diagrams (MDDs) [13] provide a compact, graph-based representation for boolean functions defined over Cartesian products of domains.

Definition 3. *A quasi-reduced ordered multivalued decision diagram (MDD) encoding the function $f(x[0], x[1], \ldots, x[J-1]) \in \{0,1\}$, where the domain of each variable $x[j]$ is $D^{(j)} = \{0, 1, \ldots, n_j - 1\}$, is a tuple $MDD = \langle V, \underline{r}, \underline{0}, \underline{1}, level, child \rangle$, where*

- $V = \bigcup_{i=0}^{J} V_i$ is a finite set of nodes, where $V_0 = \{\underline{0}, \underline{1}\}$ are the terminal nodes, the rest of the nodes $V_N = V \setminus V_0$ are nonterminal nodes;
- level: $V \to \{0, 1, \ldots, J\}$ assigns nonnegative level numbers to each node, i.e. $V_i = \{\underline{v} \in V : level(\underline{v}) = i\}$;
- $\underline{r} \in V_J$ is the root node;
- $\underline{0}, \underline{1} \in V_0$ are the zero and one terminal nodes;
- child: $\left(\bigcup_{i=1}^{J} V_i \times D^{(i-1)}\right) \to V$ is a function defining edges between nodes labeled by the items of the domains, such that either $child(\underline{v}, x) = \underline{0}$ or $level(child(\underline{v}, x)) = level(\underline{v}) - 1$ for all $\underline{v} \in V$, $x \in D^{(level(\underline{v})-1)}$;
- if $\underline{n}, \underline{m} \in V_j, j > 0$ then the subgraphs formed by the nodes reachable from $\underline{n}$ and $\underline{m}$ are either non-isomorphic, or $\underline{n} = \underline{m}$.

According to the semantics of MDDs, $f(\mathbf{x}) = 1$ if the node $\underline{1}$ is reachable from $\underline{r}$ through the edges labeled with $x[0], x[1], \ldots, x[J-1]$,

$$f(x[0], x[1], \ldots, x[J-1]) = 1 \iff$$
$$child(child(\ldots child(\underline{r}, x[J-1]) \ldots, x[1]), x[0]) = \underline{1}.$$

Definition 4. A quasi-reduced ordered edge-valued multivalued decision diagram (EDD) [22] encoding the function $g(x^{(0)}, x^{(1)}, \ldots, x^{(J-1)}) \in \mathbb{N}$ is a tuple $EDD = \langle V, \underline{r}, \underline{0}, \underline{1}, level, child, label \rangle$, where

- $MDD = (V, \underline{r}, \underline{0}, \underline{1}, level, child)$ is a quasi-reduced ordered MDD;
- label: $\left(\bigcup_{i=1}^{J} V_i \times D^{(i-1)}\right) \to \mathbb{N}$ is an edge label function.

According to the semantics of EDDs, the function g is evaluated by summing edge labels along the path from $\underline{r}$ to $\underline{1}$. Formally,

$$g(\mathbf{x}) = \begin{cases} undefined & \text{if } f(\mathbf{x}) = 0, \\ \sum_{j=0}^{J-1} label(\underline{n}^{(j)}, x[j]) & \text{if } f(\mathbf{x}) = 1, \end{cases}$$

where f is the function associated with the underlying MDD and $\underline{n}^{(j)}$ are the nodes along the path to $\underline{1}$, i.e. $\underline{n}^{(J-1)} = \underline{r}$, $\underline{n}^{(j)} = child(\underline{n}^{(j+1)}, x[j+1])$.

Symbolic State Spaces. Symbolic techniques involving MDDs can efficiently store large reachable state spaces of superposed Petri nets. Reachable states $M \in$ RS are associated with state codings $\iota(M) = \mathbf{x}$. The function $f : PS \to \{0, 1\}$ can be stored as an MDD where $f(\mathbf{x}) = 1$ if and only if $\langle\langle \mathbf{x} \rangle\rangle \in$ RS. The domains of the MDD are the local state spaces $D^{(j)} = RS^{(j)}$.

Similarly, EDDs can efficiently store the mapping between symbolic state encodings $\mathbf{x}$ and reachable state indices $x = \iota(\langle\langle \mathbf{x} \rangle\rangle)$ as the function $g(\mathbf{x}) = x$. This mapping is used to refer to elements of state probability vectors and the sparse generator matrix Q when these objects are created and accessed [12].

Some iteration strategies for MDD state space exploration are *breath-first search* and *saturation* [13].

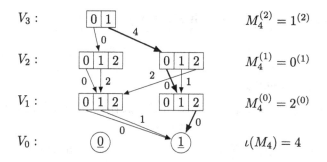

Fig. 2. EDD state space mapping of the *SharedResource* model.

Example 3. The EDD displayed in Fig. 2 describes the reachable state space of the *SharedResource* model from Example 2. Edges to $\underline{0}$ were omitted for clarity.

The edge labels allow computation of the indexing function ι for a given state. For example, to find the index of the marking $M_4 = \langle\!\langle 2^{(0)}, 0^{(1)}, 1^{(2)}\rangle\!\rangle$, we can follow the edges corresponding to the local states to $\underline{1}$ and sum their labels to find $\iota(M_4) = 4 + 0 + 0 = 4$. In contrast, if we follow the edges corresponding to the unreachable state $\langle\!\langle 2^{(0)}, 2^{(1)}, 0^{(2)}\rangle\!\rangle$, $\underline{0}$ is reached instead of $\underline{1}$.

2.4   Kronecker Algebra

In linear algebra, the Kronecker product operation may be used to build large matrices from smaller ones. It therefore plays an important role in the stochastic analysis of Markovian systems, where Kronecker products of matrices may help reducing the memory requirements of the infinitesimal generator matrix Q.

Definition 5. *The* Kronecker product $A \otimes B$ *of matrices* $A \in \mathbb{R}^{n_1 \times m_1}$ *and* $B \in \mathbb{R}^{n_2 \times m_2}$ *is the matrix* $C \in \mathbb{R}^{n_1 n_2 \times m_1 m_2}$, *where*

$$c[i_1 n_1 + i_2, j_1 m_1 + j_2] = a[i_1, j_1]b[i_2, j_2].$$

The SHUFFLE family of algorithms [5] allows efficient evaluation of vector-matrix products of the form

$$\mathbf{v} \cdot (A^{(0)} \otimes A^{(1)} \otimes \ldots \otimes A^{(J-1)}).$$

The factors $A^{(j)} \in \mathbb{R}^{n_j \times m_j}$ together represent an $n_0 n_1 \cdots n_{J-1} \times m_0 m_1 \cdots m_{J-1}$ matrix in the J-way Kronecker product.

Recent developments include the SLICE [16] and SPLIT [14] algorithms for vector-descriptor products, which allow parallel implementation while retaining the beneficial properties of the SHUFFLE algorithm.

3 Stochastic Petri Net Stationary Analysis

In this section the used stochastic analysis approach is introduced.

3.1 Analysis Workflow

The tasks performed by stochastic analysis tools that operate on stochastic Petri nets, can be often structured as follows (Fig. 3).

1. *State space exploration.* The reachable state space of the Petri net is explored to enumerate the possible behaviors of the model. For superposed stochastic Petri nets, this step includes the exploration of the local state spaces of the component as well as the possible global combinations of states.
2. *Descriptor generation.* The *infinitesimal generator matrix* Q is built in order to describe the Markov chain $X(t)$ over the reachable states of the stochastic Petri net.
3. *Numerical solution.* Numerical algorithms obtain probability vectors $\boldsymbol{\pi}$ from the matrix Q.
4. *Engineering measure calculation.* The studied performance measures are calculated from the output of the previous step. The expected values of most measures of interest can be obtained as weighted sums of state probabilities.

In stochastic model checking, where the desired system behaviors are expressed in stochastic temporal logics [2,6], these analytic steps are called as subrouties to evaluate propositions.

In the steady-state analysis of continuous-time Markovian stochastic systems, the steady state solution

$$\boldsymbol{\pi}(0) = \boldsymbol{\pi}_0, \quad \frac{\partial \boldsymbol{\pi}(\tau)}{\partial \tau} = \boldsymbol{\pi}(\tau)\, Q, \quad \boldsymbol{\pi} = \lim_{\tau \to \infty} \boldsymbol{\pi}(\tau) \tag{3}$$

of Eq. 1 is sought, where $\boldsymbol{\pi}_0$ describes the initial probability distribution and $\boldsymbol{\pi}$ is the stationary solution. If the CMTC is irreducible, i.e. there is a nonzero probability of transitioning from any state to any other, $\boldsymbol{\pi}$ is independent from $\boldsymbol{\pi}_0$ and is the initial solution of the system of linear equations

$$\boldsymbol{\pi}\, Q = \mathbf{0}, \quad \boldsymbol{\pi} \mathbf{1}^{\mathrm{T}} = 1. \tag{4}$$

Example 4. The utilization of the shared resource in the *SharedResource* SPN, presented in Fig. 1, can be calculated as the sum

$$U = \pi[\iota(M_4)] + \pi[\iota(M_5)] + \pi[\iota(M_6)] + \pi[\iota(M_7)]$$

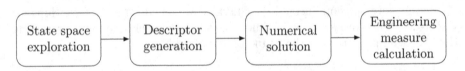

Fig. 3. Stochastic analysis workflow.

after obtaining π from Eq. (4). Notice that the resource is in use in the reachable markings M_4, M_5, M_6 and M_7.

To solve Eq. (4), the matrix Q and the vector π must be stored. Additionally, the numerical algorithm may reserve additional vectors for intermediate storage.

3.2 Infinitesimal Generator Matrix Storage

In this section the basic complexity issues behind our developments are summarized. Traditional methods use sparse or dense matrix storage methods.

Dense and Sparse Matrices. The infinitesimal generator matrix Q of a stochastic Petri net is an $n \times n$ matrix of real numbers, where n is the number of reachable states. The storage of Q thus requires memory proportional to the square of the state space size if a dense matrix form is used.

Sparse matrix representation [3, Sect. 4.3.1], reduces memory requirements to $O(\text{NZ})$, where NZ is the number of nonzero elements in Q.

Kronecker Decomposition. To alleviate the high memory requirements of Q, the Kronecker decomposition for a superposed SPN expresses the infinitesimal generator matrix as a sum of Kronecker products. Let

$$Q = Q_O + Q_D, \quad Q_D = \text{diag}\{-Q\mathbf{1}^T\}, \tag{5}$$

where Q_O and Q_D are the off-diagonal and diagonal parts of Q, respectively. The off-diagonal part may be written as

$$Q_O = \sum_{t \in T} \Lambda(t) \bigotimes_{j=0}^{J-1} Q_t^{(j)}. \tag{6}$$

The matrix $Q_t^{(j)} \in \mathbb{R}^{n_j \times n_j}$ describes the effects of the transition t on the jth local net. If $t \in p^\bullet \cup {}^\bullet p \cup p^\circ$ for some $p \in P^{(j)}$, i.e. t is connected to a place in the jth local net with an input, output or inhibitor arc,

$$q_t^{(j)}[x, y] = \begin{cases} 1 & \text{if } x^{(j)} \, [t\rangle \, y^{(j)}, \\ 0 & \text{otherwise.} \end{cases} \tag{7}$$

If t is not adjacent to the jth local net, $Q_t^{(j)}$ is set to an $n_j \times n_j$ identity matrix.

3.3 Block Kronecker Decomposition

In this section, we review the concept of block Kronecker decomposition and hierarchical structuring of the state space from [7], which divides big monolithic matrices into smaller pieces by the use of *macro states*.

Let $\widetilde{\mathrm{RS}}^{(j)}$ denote the *local macro states* of the jth local net of an SSPN. Elements of $\widetilde{\mathrm{RS}}^{(j)}$ form a partition of the local state space $\mathrm{RS}^{(j)}$ of the jth component, i.e. $\mathrm{RS}^{(j)} = \bigsqcup \widetilde{\mathrm{RS}}^{(j)}$.

The macro state indexing function $\tilde{\imath}^{(j)}: \widetilde{\mathrm{RS}}^{(j)} \to \{0, 1, \dots, \tilde{n}_j - 1\}$ assigns a unique index to every macro state, where $\tilde{n}_j = |\widetilde{\mathrm{RS}}^{(j)}|$. We use the notation $\widetilde{m}^{(j)}$ to refer to $(\tilde{\imath}^{(j)})^{-1}(m) \subseteq \mathrm{RS}^{(j)}$.

A vector $\mathbf{m} = \langle m[0], m[1], \dots, m[J-1] \rangle$ is a *global macro state index* if

$$\langle\!\langle \widetilde{m[0]}^{(0)}, \widetilde{m[1]}^{(1)}, \dots, \widetilde{m[J-1]}^{(J-1)} \rangle\!\rangle \subseteq \mathrm{RS},$$

i.e. a subset of reachable markings is isomorphic to a Cartesian product of local macro states. Such subset is called a *global macro state*.

Hierarchical structuring of the reachable state space expresses RS as a disjoint union of global macro states $\widetilde{\mathrm{RS}} = \{\tilde{0}, \tilde{1}, \dots, \tilde{n} - 1\}$.

The bijection $\tilde{\imath}: \widetilde{\mathrm{RS}} \to \{0, 1, \dots, \tilde{n} - 1\}$ assigns indices to global macro states such that $\tilde{\imath}^{-1}(m) = \tilde{m}$, while the function $\boldsymbol{\imath}: \widetilde{\mathrm{RS}} \to \mathbb{N}^J$ assings their respective global macro state index vectors.

Since each global macro state has the structure of a Cartesian product of local macro states, the Kronecker product may be used to construct a matrix of state transitions between two global macro states.

Let $\mathbf{m}$ and $\mathbf{k}$ be two reachable global macro state indices. The matrix $Q_t^{(j)}[m[j], k[j]]$ is obtained from $Q_t^{(j)}$ in Eq. (7) by only keeping the rows that correspond to $m[j]^{(j)}$ and the columns that correspond to $k[j]^{(j)}$. The matrix

$$Q_O[m, k] = \sum_{t \in T} \Lambda(t) \bigotimes_{j=0}^{J-1} Q_t^{(j)}[m[j], k[j]] \tag{8}$$

describes the states transitions from the macro state $\tilde{\imath}^{-1}(m)$ to $\tilde{\imath}^{-1}(k)$, where m and k are the indices of global macro states with index vectors $\mathbf{m}$ and $\mathbf{k}$, respectively.

We can finally express the infinitesimal generator matrix Q as a block matrix with $\tilde{n} \times \tilde{n}$ blocks. Let the $\langle m, k \rangle$th block of the off-diagonal part Q_O be $Q_O[m, k]$ as defined in Eq. (8) above. Then it can be seen that the matrix

$$Q = Q_O + Q_D, \quad Q_D = \mathrm{diag}\{-Q\mathbf{1}^T\} \tag{9}$$

is equivalent to the matrix Q in Eq. (2).

Example 5. The state space of the *SharedResource* model in Fig. 1 may be hierarchically structured as follows.

Recall from Example 2 that the model has three local nets, two corresponding to the clients with three local states each and a local net with two local states corresponding to the shared resource. We may partition the local state spaces into local macro states as

$$\widetilde{\mathrm{RS}}^{(0)} = \begin{cases} \tilde{0}^{(0)} = \{0^{(0)}, 1^{(0)}\} \\ \tilde{1}^{(0)} = \{2^{(0)}\} \end{cases}, \quad \widetilde{\mathrm{RS}}^{(1)} = \begin{cases} \tilde{0}^{(1)} = \{0^{(1)}, 1^{(1)}\} \\ \tilde{1}^{(1)} = \{2^{(1)}\} \end{cases}, \quad \widetilde{\mathrm{RS}}^{(2)} = \begin{cases} \tilde{0}^{(2)} = \{0^{(2)}\} \\ \tilde{1}^{(2)} = \{1^{(2)}\} \end{cases}.$$

Observe that, for each component j, the macro state $\tilde{0}^{(j)}$ contains local states that are reachable when the shared resource is not in use, while $\tilde{1}^{(j)}$ corresponds to the allocation of the resource.

The global reachable state space is then partitioned into global macro states as

$$\widetilde{RS} = \{\langle\langle\tilde{0}^{(0)}, \tilde{0}^{(1)}, \tilde{0}^{(2)}\rangle\rangle, \langle\langle\tilde{0}^{(0)}, \tilde{1}^{(1)}, \tilde{1}^{(2)}\rangle\rangle, \langle\langle\tilde{1}^{(0)}, \tilde{0}^{(1)}, \tilde{1}^{(2)}\rangle\rangle\},$$

i.e. any state that does not require use of the shared resource is reachable when the shared resource is available, while if one of the clients allocates the resource, the other cannot simultaneously acquire it.

Macro State Construction. Let us introduce the notation

$$\hat{\mathbf{x}}^{(j)} = \langle x[0], x[1], \ldots, x[j-1], x[j+1], \ldots, x[J-1]\rangle.$$

Suppose that the reachable marking M is coded by the vector of local state indices $\mathbf{x} = \iota(M)$, i.e. $M = \langle\langle\mathbf{x}\rangle\rangle$. Then the vector $\hat{\mathbf{x}}^{(j)}$ contains the local state indices of all components except the jth.

The *environment* of a local state $x^{(j)}$ is the set of vectors

$$\text{env}\, x^{(j)} = \{\hat{\mathbf{z}}^{(j)} : M \in RS, \mathbf{z} = \iota(M), z[j] = x\}, \tag{10}$$

i.e. the local state combinations of other local nets that result in reachable markings together with $x^{(j)}$. We define the equivalence relation $\sim^{(j)} \subseteq RS^{(j)} \times RS^{(j)}$,

$$x^{(j)} \sim^{(j)} y^{(j)} \quad \Longleftrightarrow \quad \text{env}\, x^{(j)} = \text{env}\, y^{(j)}. \tag{11}$$

The equivalence classes $RS^{(j)}/\sim^{(j)}$ define the local macro states $\widetilde{RS}^{(j)}$. Now we can construct the equivalence relation $\sim \subseteq RS \times RS$,

$$M \sim K \quad \Longleftrightarrow \quad M^{(j)} \sim^{(j)} K^{(j)} \text{ for all } j = 0, 1, \ldots, J-1,$$

i.e. two markings are equivalent if all their local nets belong to the same local macro states. The set of global macro states is the partition $\widetilde{RS} = RS/\sim$.

Explicit Macro State Algorithm. The original hierarchical structuring algorithm proposed by Buchholz is based on a bit array representation of the potential state space PS [7].

Algorithm 1 shows local and global macro state generation. The environment env $x^{(j)}$ is represented explicitly as a row of the reshaped bit array $\mathbf{B}$. Nonzero elements correspond to reachable states.

Lexicographic ordering is used to make local states with equal environments adjacent. After extracting local macro states from the bit array, only a single representant of every local macro state is kept. This both accelerates further iterations of the algorithm and results in reduced bit array at the end that has a nonzero element for every combination of local states that is reachable. Note that the permutations used to reorder local states must be stored in order to recover the global macro state indices.

Note that storage of the bit array requires $O(|PS|)$ memory, therefore the bit array based macro state generation is unsuitable for extremely large potential state spaces due to memory requirements.

Algorithm 1: Bit array based macro state construction.

Input: Reachable state space RS, reachable local states $RS^{(j)}$
Output: Local macro states $\widetilde{RS}^{(j)}$, global macro states $\widetilde{RS}$

1 Allocate an array of bits $\mathbf{B} \in \{0,1\}^{n_0 \times n_1 \times \cdots \times n_{J-1}}$
2 **foreach** $M \in RS$ **do** $\mathbf{x} \leftarrow \iota(M)$; $B[x[0], x[1], \ldots, x[J-1]] \leftarrow 1$
3 **for** $j \leftarrow 0$ **to** $J - 1$ **do**
4   Reshape $\mathbf{B}$ into a matrix with n_j, where the xth row corresponds to the local state $x^{(j)} \in RS^{(j)}$ and its environment env $x^{(j)}$
5   Sort the rows of the matrix lexicographically
6   Partition the rows such that equal rows form local macro states $\widetilde{RS}^{(j)}$
7   Discard all but one representant row for each local macro state $\widetilde{m}^{(j)}$
8 Nonzero elements of the resulting bit array $\mathbf{B}$ are correspond to the reachable global macro states $\widetilde{RS}$

---

4 Symbolic Decomposition Algorithm

In this section, we present our symbolic decomposition algorithm that allows the construction of macro state spaces without explicit enumeration and storage of the potential state space PS.

4.1 Description

The memory requirements and run time of bit array based macro state decomposition may be significantly improved by the use of symbolic state space storage

---

Algorithm 2: Local macro state construction by partition refinement.

Input: Symbolic state space MDD
Output: Local macro states $\widetilde{RS}^{(j)}$

1 **for** $j \leftarrow 0$ **to** $J - 1$ **do**
2   Initialize the empty queue Q and $Done \leftarrow \{RS^{(j)}\}$
3   **foreach** $\underline{n} \in V_{j+1}$ **do**
4   **foreach** $S \in Done$ **do** ENQUEUE(Q, S)
5      $Done \leftarrow \emptyset$
6   **while** $\neg$EMPTY(Q) **do**
7        $S \leftarrow$ DEQUEUE(Q); $S_1 \leftarrow \emptyset$; $S_2 \leftarrow \emptyset$
8   Let x_0 be any element of S and $\underline{m} \leftarrow child(\underline{n}, x_0)$
9   **foreach** $x \in S \setminus \{x_0\}$ **do**
10   **if** $\underline{m} = child(\underline{n}, x)$ **then** $S_1 \leftarrow S_1 \cup \{x\}$
11          $S_2 \leftarrow S_2 \cup \{x\}$
12   **if** $S_2 \neq \emptyset$ **then** ENQUEUE(Q, S_2)
13        $Done \leftarrow Done \cup \{S_1\}$
14    $\tilde{n}_j \leftarrow |Done|$; $\widetilde{RS}^{(j)} \leftarrow Done$

instead of a bit vector. Algorithm 2 constructs the local macro states from the MDD representation of the state space.

The algorithm partitions the local states $RS^{(j)}$ of every component of the stochastic Petri net into local macro states. In order to perform this operation, the nodes in the levels $V_1, V_2, \ldots, V_J$ of the MDD corresponding to the state space RS must be provided. While symbolic techniques often share nodes between multiple MDDs, in Algorithm 2 the sets V_j should contain only nodes reachable from the root $\underline{r}$ corresponding to RS. These sets can be extracted from a shared MDD container by e.g. depth first search starting at $\underline{r}$.

The lines 2–13 implement partition refinement for $RS^{(j)}$ based on the local states associated with the edges between nodes in V_{j+1} and V_j, i.e. the jth level of the MDD.

The candidate macro state partition $Done$ is initialized to contain only $RS^{(j)}$. Then, the lines 5–12 refine the candidate macro states for each node $\underline{n} \in V_{j+1}$ according to the associated local states of the arcs starting at $\underline{n}$. After moving the sets from $Done$ to the queue Q, every candidate macro state $S \in Q$ is split into S_1 and S_2. Arcs from $\underline{n}$ with local states $x \in S_1$ all go to some node $\underline{m} \in V_j$. The candidate macro state S_1 is added to the new $Done$ partition. Arcs from $\underline{n}$ with local states $y \in S_2$ may not be all parallel, therefore S_2 is placed back to Q if it is nonempty.

After Q becomes empty and no new S_2 is enqueued, edges starting at $\underline{n}$ which correspond to $x \in S$ all go to the same $\underline{m}_S \in V_j$ for all candidate macro states $S \in Done$. No two candidate macro states $S \neq S'$ have $\underline{m}_S = \underline{m}_{S'}$ due to the construction of the partition refinement. Moreover, this property also holds for nodes $\underline{n}' \in V_{j+1}$ processed in lines 5–12 before $\underline{n}$. Hence macro states in the final partition $Done$ constructed in lines 2–13 are all parallel in the sense that $child(\underline{n}, x) = child(\underline{n}, y)$ for all $\underline{n} \in V_{j+1}$ and $x, y \in S \in Done$.

In Subsect. 4.2 we will prove that the final partition $Done$ is indeed the set of local macro states $\widetilde{RS}^{(j)}$.

Algorithm 2, unlike Algorithm 1, does not output the global macro state space $\widetilde{RS}$. An MDD representation of $\widetilde{RS}$ may be obtained by replacing every arc x with the index m of the local macro state such that $x^{(j)} \in \widetilde{m}^{(j)}$. The original state space MDD can be recovered by the opposite operation, which replaces m with parallel arcs $x_0, x_1, \ldots$ having $\widetilde{m}^{(j)} = \{x_0^{(j)}, x_1^{(j)}, \ldots\}$.

Example 6. Figure 4 shows the MDD state space of the *SharedResource* model, its local macro state decomposition and the MDD representation of the global macro states.

The edges corresponding to local states that belong to the same local macro state are parallel for *all* parent nodes on a level. This is represented in the figure with ellipses connecting the edges. In the global macro state MDD, these parallel edge sets collapse to a single edge, as every edge from the original MDD is replace with its macro state.

Block Kronecked decomposition of the infinitesimal generator Q can be performed based on the sets of macro states $\widetilde{RS}^{(j)}$ obtained by the partition refinement. By enumerating paths in the macro state MDD, global macro states $\widetilde{RS}$

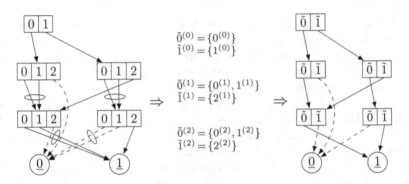

$$\tilde{0}^{(0)} = \{0^{(0)}\}$$
$$\tilde{1}^{(0)} = \{1^{(0)}\}$$

$$\tilde{0}^{(1)} = \{0^{(1)}, 1^{(1)}\}$$
$$\tilde{1}^{(1)} = \{2^{(1)}\}$$

$$\tilde{0}^{(2)} = \{0^{(2)}, 1^{(2)}\}$$
$$\tilde{1}^{(2)} = \{2^{(2)}\}$$

Fig. 4. Symbolic macro state construction for the *SharedResource* model.

can be listed. Moreover, the macro state MDD can be turned into an EDD for mapping indices between block Kronecker and sparse representations, which is described in Subsect. 4.3.

4.2 Proof of Correctness

To show the correctness of the partition of the local states $\mathrm{RS}^{(j)}$ into macro states $\widetilde{\mathrm{RS}}^{(j)}$, we will use the notations of above and below substates from [13]:

Definition 6. *The set of* above *substates coded by the node $\underline{n}$ is*

$$\mathcal{A}(\underline{n}) \subseteq \{\langle x[j+1], x[j+2], \dots, x[J-1]\rangle \in D^{(j+1)} \times D^{(j+2)} \times \cdots \times D^{(J-1)}\},$$
$$\mathbf{x} \in \mathcal{A}(\underline{n}) \iff child(child(\dots child(\underline{r}, x[J-1])\dots, x[j+2]), x[j+1]) = \underline{n},$$

where $j = level(\underline{n}) - 1$, i.e. $\mathcal{A}(\underline{n})$ is the set of all paths in the MDD from $\underline{r}$ to $\underline{n}$.

Definition 7. *The set of* below *substates coded by the node $\underline{n}$ is*

$$\mathcal{B}(\underline{n}) \subseteq \{\langle x[0], x[1], \dots, x[j]\rangle \in D^{(0)} \times D^{(1)} \times \cdots \times D^{(j)}\},$$
$$\mathbf{x} \in \mathcal{B}(\underline{n}) \iff child(child(\dots child(\underline{n}, x[j])\dots, x[1]), x[0]) = \underline{1},$$

where $j = level(\underline{n}) - 1$, i.e. $\mathcal{B}(\underline{n})$ is the set of all paths in the MDD from $\underline{n}$ to $\underline{1}$.

Proposition 1. *If $\underline{n}$ and $\underline{m}$ are distinct nonterminal nodes of a quasi-reduced ordered MDD, $\mathcal{A}(\underline{n}) \cap \mathcal{A}(\underline{m}) = \emptyset$ and $\mathcal{B}(\underline{n}) \neq \mathcal{B}(\underline{m})$.*

Proof. We prove the statements by contradiction. Let $\mathbf{a} \in \mathcal{A}(\underline{n}) \cap \mathcal{A}(\underline{m})$. If we follow the path $\mathbf{a}$ from $\underline{r}$ we arrive at $\underline{n}$ because $\mathbf{a} \in \mathcal{A}(\underline{n})$. However, we also arrive at $\underline{m}$, because $\mathbf{a} \in \mathcal{A}(\underline{m})$. Since $\underline{n} \neq \underline{m}$, such $\mathbf{a}$ cannot exist. $\mathcal{A}(\underline{n})$ and $\mathcal{A}(\underline{m})$ must be disjoint.

Now suppose that there are $\underline{n}, \underline{m} \in V_N$ such that $\mathcal{B}(\underline{n}) = \mathcal{B}(\underline{m})$. Because the set of paths $\mathcal{B}(\underline{n})$ fully describes the subgraph reachable from $\underline{n}$, this means the subgraphs reachable from $\underline{n}$ and $\underline{m}$ are isomorphic. This is impossible since the MDD is quasi-reduced. $\mathcal{B}(\underline{n})$ and $\mathcal{B}(\underline{m})$ must be distinct. $\qquad\square$

Proposition 2. *The environment of the local state $x^{(j)}$, defined in Eq. (10), may be written as*

$$\operatorname{env} x^{(j)} = \{ \langle\!\langle \mathbf{b}, \mathbf{a} \rangle\!\rangle : \underline{n} \in V_{j+1},\, \mathbf{a} \in \mathcal{A}(\underline{n}),\, \mathbf{b} \in \mathcal{B}(child(\underline{n}, x^{(j)})) \}.$$

Proof. Any reachable state $\langle\!\langle \mathbf{z} \rangle\!\rangle \in \mathrm{RS}$ that has $z[j] = x$ is represented by a path from $\underline{r}$ to $\underline{1}$ in the MDD that passes through a pair of nodes $\underline{n} \in V_{j+1}$ and $\underline{k} = child(\underline{n}, x^{(j)})$. Therefore, some path $\mathbf{a} \in \mathcal{A}(\underline{n})$ must be followed from $\underline{r}$ to reach $\underline{n}$, then after traversing the edge between $\underline{n}$ and $\underline{k}$, some path $\mathbf{b} \in \mathcal{B}(\underline{k})$ must be followed from $\underline{k}$ to $\underline{1}$.

This means all paths from $\underline{r}$ to $\underline{1}$ containing $x^{(j)}$ are of the form $\mathbf{z} = (\mathbf{b}, x, \mathbf{a})$ and the converse also holds. Thus, $\hat{\mathbf{z}}^{(j)} = \langle \mathbf{a}, \mathbf{b} \rangle$ holds for some $\mathbf{a}$ and $\mathbf{b}$ defined as above for all reachable states $\mathbf{z}$. □

The relation $\sim^{(j)}$ over $\mathrm{RS}^{(j)}$ can be expressed with $\mathcal{A}(\underline{n})$ and $\mathcal{B}(\underline{n})$ in a way that can be handled with symbolic techniques.

Proposition 3. *The relation $x^{(j)} \sim^{(j)} y^{(j)}$ can be formulated as*

$$x^{(j)} \sim^{(j)} y^{(j)} \iff edges(x, j) = edges(y, j),$$
$$\text{where } edges(z, j) = \{ \langle \underline{n}, child(\underline{n}, z) \rangle : \underline{n} \in V_{j+1} \}.$$

Proof. Recall that $x^{(j)} \sim^{(j)} y^{(j)}$ is defined as $\operatorname{env} x^{(j)} = \operatorname{env} y^{(j)}$ in Eq. (11). Let X and Y be the environments of $x^{(j)}$ and $y^{(j)}$, respectively, so that $x^{(j)} \sim^{(j)} y^{(j)}$ holds if and only if $X = Y$. Define

$$X(\underline{n}) = \{ \mathbf{b} : \langle \mathbf{b}, \mathbf{a} \rangle \in X,\, \mathbf{a} \in \mathcal{A}(\underline{n}) \}, \qquad Y(\underline{n}) = \{ \mathbf{b} : \langle \mathbf{b}, \mathbf{a} \rangle \in Y,\, \mathbf{a} \in \mathcal{A}(\underline{n}) \}.$$

Observe that $X = Y$ if and only if $X(\underline{n}) = Y(\underline{n})$ for all $\underline{n} \in V_{j+1}$, because the sets $\{ X(\underline{n}) \times \mathcal{A}(\underline{n}) \}_{\underline{n} \in V_{j+1}}$ and $\{ Y(\underline{n}) \times \mathcal{A}(\underline{n}) \}_{\underline{n} \in V_{j+1}}$ are partitions of X and Y.
According to Proposition 2,

$$X(\underline{n}) = \mathcal{B}(child(\underline{n}, x)), \qquad\qquad Y(\underline{n}) = \mathcal{B}(child(\underline{n}, y)).$$

Thus, $X(\underline{n}) = Y(\underline{n})$ if and only if $child(\underline{n}, x) = child(\underline{n}, y)$, because the $\mathcal{B}$-sets are distinct for each node. Hence $X(\underline{n}) = Y(\underline{n})$ for all $\underline{n} \in V_{j+1}$ is equivalent to the statement $edges(x, j) = edges(y, j)$. □

Proposition 3 can be interpreted as the statement that $x^{(j)} \sim^{(j)} y^{(j)}$ if and only if the MDD edges corresponding to $x^{(j)}$ are always parallel, i.e. from the node $\underline{n}$ they all go to the same node $\underline{m}(\underline{n})$, which only depends on $\underline{n}$, for all $\underline{n} \in V_{j+1}$.

4.3   Symbolic State Indexing

The last step of the stochastic analysis workflow is the calculation of engineering measures by weighted sums of state probabilities, which were obtained by

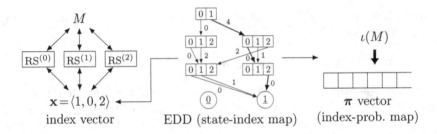

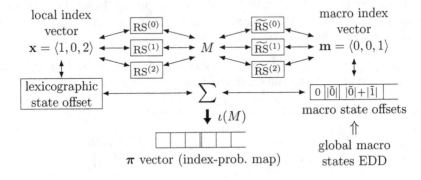

Fig. 5. Index manipulations for EDD-based state spaces.

Fig. 6. Index manipulations for EDD-based macro state spaces.

the numerical solution algorithm. This requires iteration over all states and the corresponding indices of the probability vector.

In this section, we review techniques for state-index mapping in superposed stochastic Petri nets. An implementation of the mapping is presented for macro state decompositions in symbolic form.

The EDD-based state-index mapping is depicted in Fig. 5. A vector of local macro state indices is formed by observing the local states of the components. Both forward and reverse mapping between linear indices $\iota(M)$ of the probability vector and index vectors $\mathbf{x}$ is possible [12].

In block Kronecker decompositions, the generator matrix, as well as the vector $\boldsymbol{\pi}$ is partitioned according to the global macro states $\widetilde{\mathrm{RS}}$. Within a partition, markings are ordered lexicographically by their local state indices. Although it is possible to construct an EDD representing this ordering, it can easily grow large, due to the intertwined ordering.

To efficiently store the index mapping (Fig. 6), a macro state offset vector $\mathbf{o}$ of length $\tilde{n}$ is populated with the starting offsets of the global states by enumeration of the global macro state space. The ith marking in the lexicographic ordering within the global macro state $\tilde{m}$ has the linear index $x = o[m] + i$. Conversion between linear macro state indices m and macro state index vectors $\mathbf{m}$ is performed by an EDD, analogously to the mapping in Fig. 5.

5   Evaluation

The decomposition algorithms were implemented in the PetriDotNet modelling framework, which supports structural analysis of Petri nets, saturation-based CTL and LTL model checking and reachability checking as well as Markovian stochastic analysis. The algorithms may be used in Markovian transient, sensitivity and time-to-first-failure analysis in addition to steady state analysis.

Our symbolic block Kroncker decomposition approach is compared with sparse generator matrices and the explicit block Kronecker decomposition algorithm by Buchholz [7]. The explicit decomposition algorithm was executed on an explicit representation of the state space as a hash table, while symbolic algorithms used saturation and MDDs. Steady-state analysis was performed using the BiCGSTAB [24] numerical linear equation solver with a tolerance of 10^{-10}.

Running time was limited to 1 h on virtual machines with 8 execution threads and 30 GiB memory.

Three scalable families of models were used in the evaluation:

- The *SR* family of models are upscaled variants of the *SharedResource* model that served as a running example throughout this paper. The model was extended with additional clients, moreover, the number of tokens was increased. In *SR-Sym*, each transition rate is set to 1.0, while in *SR-Asym*, different rates were chosen for the transitions.
- The *KanBan* SPN models from [11] describe the kanban manufacturing system with various resource pool sizes.
- Members of the *Cloud* family are SPN performability models of a cloud architecture [17]. Scaling of the state space is achieved by changing the number of physical and virtual machines. Some aspects of the models from [17] were modified, as our tool currently does not support the GPSN formalism.

The models in several SPN formats and the PetriDotNet 1.5 tool are available at our website[1]

Table 1 shows the measured execution times and memory usages. The execution time of the decomposition algorithm t_{macro}, the construction of the generator matrix t_{gen} and the BiCGSTAB solver t_{solve} is displayed, as well as the peak memory usage M_{peak}. Minimum values of every measure are emphasised in bold for each model.

The symbolic decomposition algorithm was executed under 100 ms for all the studied models, even in cases when the BiCGSTAB algorithm timed out. Block Kronecker based analysis with symbolic state space also consumed the least amount of memory, except in a single variation of the *KanBan* model.

Matrix construction was also fastest with symbolic decomposition. While the same matrices are constructed after explicit decomposition, the matrices were built slower based on the explicit state space than on MDDs due to fast access to the decision diagram data structures.

---

[1] https://inf.mit.bme.hu/en/petridotnet/stochasticanalysis.

Table 1. Measurement results.

Model	States	Sparse			Explicit BK				Symbolic BK			
		t_{gen}	t_{solve}	M_{peak}	t_{macro}	t_{gen}	t_{solve}	M_{peak}	t_{macro}	t_{gen}	t_{solve}	M_{peak}
SR-Sym	26 464	147 ms	**296 ms**	40 M	464 ms	562 ms	303 ms	55 M	**23 ms**	**142 ms**	370 ms	**38 M**
	842 051	2 s	**10 s**	296 M	22 s	11 s	**10 s**	1035 M	**23 ms**	**582 ms**	12 s	**98 M**
	$1.1 \cdot 10^7$	24 s	182 s	3404 M	530 s	183 s	231 s	12 G	**24 ms**	**5 s**	155 s	**791 M**
	$8.2 \cdot 10^7$	215 s	1985 s	25 G	Timed out				**26 ms**	**31 s**	1612 s	**5563 M**
SR-Asym	26 464	132 ms	**482 ms**	42 M	455 ms	402 ms	580 ms	57 M	**26 ms**	**125 ms**	638 ms	**39 M**
	842 051	2 s	**17 s**	296 M	22 s	10 s	20 s	1035 M	**23 ms**	**519 ms**	21 s	**99 M**
	$1.1 \cdot 10^7$	22 s	327 s	3404 M	540 s	246 s	463 s	12 G	**27 ms**	**6 s**	285 s	**793 M**
	$8.2 \cdot 10^7$	217 s	Timed out		Timed out				**31 ms**	**32 s**	Breakdown	
KanBan	58 400	181 ms	**1 s**	51 M	250 ms	847 ms	3 s	77 M	**24 ms**	**130 ms**	2 s	**45 M**
	454 475	1 s	**11 s**	181 M	1 s	4 s	31 s	448 M	**26 ms**	**285 ms**	19 s	**171 M**
	$2.5 \cdot 10^6$	5 s	**81 s**	**388 M**	6 s	28 s	240 s	2276 M	**22 ms**	**1 s**	124 s	**780 M**
	$1.1 \cdot 10^7$	33 s	**436 s**	3727 M	31 s	138 s	1274 s	10 G	**25 ms**	**5 s**	737 s	**3591 M**
Cloud	$2.7 \cdot 10^6$	38 s	446 s	5846 M	119 s	48 s	913 s	3361 M	**64 ms**	**4 s**	278 s	**291 M**
	$2.0 \cdot 10^7$	Out of memory			2021 s	464 s	Timed out		**29 ms**	**9 s**	Timed out	
	$1.3 \cdot 10^8$	Out of memory			Timed out				**32 ms**	**75 s**	Timed out	
	$8.2 \cdot 10^8$	Out of memory			Timed out				**42 ms**	**574 s**	Out of memory	

The state space data structure must be kept in memory throughout the numerical solution, because it is needed in the phase of engineering measure evaluation. Thus, BiCGSTAB ran slower after explicit decomposition due to the pressure on the garbage collector (GC) caused by the larger size of the state space data structures. For smaller models, numerical solution with sparse matrices was faster than with block Kronecker matrices. However, for larger models the decomposed matrix utilized the memory bandwidth and caches more efficiently.

The sole difference between the *Sym* and *Asym* versions of the *SR* models are the transition rates, which only affected the numerical solution time. The structure of the state space remained identical.

Failures of BiCGSTAB included exhaustion of the time limit and the available memory. In the largest *SR-Asym* model, a numerical breakdown condition occurred. This condition may be handled by switching to a more stable solver, such as Jacobi or Gauss–Seidel iteration [23, Sect. 2.2]. These solvers are also implemented in the PetriDotNet framework.

6   Conclusion and Future Work

In this paper we introduced an efficient stochastic analysis approach using symbolic algorithms to explore the possible behaviours of the system and decomposition-based stochastic analysis algorithms to efficiently compute stationary measures of stochastic Petri nets. In our work we established an efficient mapping technique which can bridge the gap between the encoded state space representation and the decomposition-based numerical algorithms. This algorithm supports the analysis of Petri net models with huge state spaces and complex behaviours. Measurements on models with various sizes and characteristics showed the effectiveness of the introduced approach and the benefits of the new mapping algorithm.

In the future, we plan to further extend our stochastic analysis framework with other numerical solution algorithms such as the SPLIT algorithm for Kronecker products. In addition, we will also investigate GPU and distributed implementation of the available algorithms.

Acknowledgement. This work was partially supported by the ARTEMIS JU and the Hungarian National Research, Development and Innovation Fund in the frame of the R5-COP project. This research was partially performed within the framework of the grant of the Hungarian Scientific Resarch Fund (grant no. OTKA K101150).

References

1. Ajmone Marsan, M.: Stochastic Petri nets: an elementary introduction. In: Rozenberg, G. (ed.) Advances in Petri Nets 1989, Covers the 9th European Workshop on Applications and Theory in Petri Nets, held in Venice, Italy in June 1988, Selected Paper. LNCS, vol. 424, pp. 1–29. Springer, Heidelberg (1988)
2. Baier, C., Katoen, J.P., Hermanns, H.: Approximative symbolic model checking of continuous-time Markov chains. In: Baeten, J.C.M., Mauw, S. (eds.) CONCUR, 1999 Concurrency Theory. LNCS, vol. 1664, pp. 146–161. Springer, Heidelberg (1999)
3. Barrett, R., Berry, M.W., Chan, T.F., Demmel, J., Donato, J., Dongarra, J., Eijkhout, V., Pozo, R., Romine, C., Van der Vorst, H.: Templates for the Solution of Linear Systems: Building Blocks for Iterative Methods, vol. 43. SIAM, Philadelphia (1994)
4. Bause, F., Buchholz, P., Kemper, P.: A toolbox for functional and quantitative analysis of DEDS. In: Puigjaner, R., Savino, N.N., Serra, B. (eds.) TOOLS 1998. LNCS, vol. 1469, p. 356. Springer, Heidelberg (1998)
5. Benoit, A., Plateau, B., Stewart, W.J.: Memory-efficient Kronecker algorithms with applications to the modelling of parallel systems. Future Gener. Comp. Syst. **22**(7), 838–847 (2006)
6. Bianco, A., de Alfaro, L.: Model checking of probabilistic and nondeterministic systems. In: Thiagarajan, P.S. (ed.) FSTTCS 1995. LNCS, vol. 1026, pp. 499–513. Springer, Heidelberg (1995)
7. Buchholz, P.: Hierarchical structuring of superposed GSPNs. IEEE Trans. Softw. Eng. **25**(2), 166–181 (1999)
8. Buchholz, P., Ciardo, G., Donatelli, S., Kemper, P.: Complexity of memory-efficient Kronecker operations with applications to the solution of Markov models. INFORMS J. Comput. **12**(3), 203–222 (2000)
9. Buchholz, P., Kemper, P.: On generating a hierarchy for GSPN analysis. SIGMETRICS Perform. Eval. Rev. **26**(2), 5–14 (1998)
10. Buchholz, P., Kemper, P.: Kronecker based matrix representations for large Markov models. In: Baier, C., Haverkort, B.R., Hermanns, H., Katoen, J.-P., Siegle, M. (eds.) Validation of Stochastic Systems: A Guide to Current Research. LNCS, vol. 2925, pp. 256–295. Springer, Heidelberg (2004)
11. Ciardo, G., Jones, R.L., Miner, A.S., Siminiceanu, R.: Logical and stochastic modeling with SMART. In: Kemper, P., Sanders, W.H. (eds.) TOOLS 2003. LNCS, vol. 2794, pp. 78–97. Springer, Heidelberg (2003)

12. Ciardo, G., Miner, A.S.: A data structure for the efficient Kronecker solution of GSPNs. In: The 8th International Workshop on Petri Nets and Performance Models, 1999, pp. 22–31. IEEE (1999)

13. Ciardo, G., Zhao, Y., Jin, X.: Ten years of saturation: a Petri net perspective. In: Jensen, K., Donatelli, S., Kleijn, J. (eds.) Transactions on Petri Nets and Other Models of Concurrency V. LNCS, vol. 6900, pp. 51–95. Springer, Heidelberg (2012)

14. Czekster, R.M., Rose, C., Fernandes, P.H.L., de Lima, A.M., Webber, T.: Kronecker descriptor partitioning for parallel algorithms. In: McGraw, R.M., Imsand, E.S., Chinni, M.J. (eds.) Proceedings of the 2010 Spring Simulation Multiconference, SpringSim 2010, Orlando, Florida, USA, 11–15, April 2010, p. 242. SCS/ACM (2010)

15. Donatelli, S.: Superposed generalized stochastic Petri nets: Definition and efficient solution. In: Valette, R. (ed.) Application and Theory of Petri Nets 1994. LNCS, vol. 815, pp. 258–277. Springer, Heidelberg (1994)

16. Fernandes, P., Presotto, R., Sales, A., Webber, T.: An alternative algorithm to multiply a vector by a Kronecker represented descriptor. In: 21st UK Performance Engineering Workshop, pp. 57–67 (2005)

17. Ghosh, R.: Scalable stochastic models for cloud services. Ph.D. thesis, Duke University (2012)

18. Kemper, P.: Numerical analysis of superposed GSPNs. IEEE Trans. Softw. Eng. **22**(9), 615–628 (1996)

19. Kwiatkowska, M., Mehmood, R., Norman, G., Parker, D.: A symbolic out-of-core solution method for Markov models. Electron. Notes Theoret. Comput. Sci. **68**(4), 589–604 (2002)

20. Kwiatkowska, M., Norman, G., Parker, D.: Probabilistic symbolic model checking with PRISM: a hybrid approach. Int. J. Softw. Tools Technol. Transfer **6**(2), 128–142 (2004)

21. Miner, A.S.: Efficient solution of GSPNs using canonical matrix diagrams. In: 9th International Workshop on Petri Nets and Performance Models, 2001, pp. 101–110. IEEE (2001)

22. Roux, P., Siminiceanu, R.: Model checking with edge-valued decision diagrams. In: Muñoz, C.A. (ed.) Second NASA Formal Methods Symposium - NFM 2010, Washington D.C., USA, 13–15 April 2010. Proceedings. NASA Conference Proceedings, vol. NASA/CP-2010-216215, pp. 222–226 (2010)

23. Stewart, W.J.: Probability, Markov Chains, Queues, and Simulation: The Mathematical Basis of Performance Modeling. Princeton University Press, Princeton (2009)

24. Van der Vorst, H.A.: Bi-CGSTAB: a fast and smoothly converging variant of Bi-CG for the solution of nonsymmetric linear systems. SIAM J. Scientific Stat. Comput. **13**(2), 631–644 (1992)

25. Wan, M., Ciardo, G., Miner, A.S.: Approximate steady-state analysis of large Markov models based on the structure of their decision diagram encoding. Performance Eval. **68**(5), 463–486 (2011)

26. Zhao, Y., Ciardo, G.: A two-phase Gauss-Seidel algorithm for the stationary solution of EVMDD-encoded CTMCs. In: Ninth International Conference on Quantitative Evaluation of Systems, QEST 2012, London, United Kingdom, 17–20 September 2012, pp. 74–83. IEEE Computer Society (2012)

Decidable Classes of Unbounded Petri Nets with Time and Urgency

S. Akshay[1(✉)], B. Genest[2], and L. Hélouët[3]

[1] Department of Computer Science and Engineering,
IIT Bombay, Mumbai, India
akshayss@cse.iitb.ac.in
[2] CNRS, IRISA, Rennes, France
blaise.genest@irisa.fr
[3] INRIA, Campus de Beaulieu, Rennes, France
loic.helouet@inria.fr

Abstract. Adding real time information to Petri net models often leads to undecidability of classical verification problems such as reachability and boundedness. For instance, models such as Timed-Transition Petri nets (TPNs) [22] are intractable except in a bounded setting. On the other hand, the model of Timed-Arc Petri nets [26] enjoys decidability results for boundedness and control-state reachability problems at the cost of disallowing urgency (the ability to enforce actions within a time delay). Our goal is to investigate decidable classes of Petri nets with time that capture some urgency and still allow unbounded behaviors, which go beyond finite state systems.

We present, up to our knowledge, the first decidability results on reachability and boundedness for Petri net variants that combine unbounded places, time, and urgency. For this, we introduce the class of Timed-Arc Petri nets with restricted Urgency, where urgency can be used only on transitions consuming tokens from bounded places. We show that control-state reachability and boundedness are decidable for this new class, by extending results from Timed-Arc Petri nets (without urgency) [2]. Our main result concerns (marking) reachability, which is undecidable for both TPNs (because of unrestricted urgency) [20] and Timed-Arc Petri Nets (because of infinite number of "clocks") [25]. We obtain decidability of reachability for unbounded TPNs with restricted urgency under a new, yet natural, timed-arc semantics presenting them as Timed-Arc Petri Nets with restricted urgency. Decidability of reachability under the intermediate marking semantics is also obtained for a restricted subclass.

1 Introduction

Petri nets are a simple yet powerful formalism modeling distributed systems. Several extensions have been proposed to enrich them with timing constraints, and allow specification of real-time behaviors. We first discuss the decidability and expressivity of two main variants: *Timed-Transition Petri Nets (TPNs)* [22] and *Timed-Arc Petri Nets* [26].

© Springer International Publishing Switzerland 2016
F. Kordon and D. Moldt (Eds.): PETRI NETS 2016, LNCS 9698, pp. 301–322, 2016.
DOI: 10.1007/978-3-319-39086-4_18

TPNs can constrain each transition with a timing interval. To be fireable, a transition needs to have been enabled for an amount of time in the given interval [22]. Further, when a transition has been enabled for the maximal amount of time according to its associated interval, it must fire. This is called *urgency*. Formally, a (continuous, positive valued) *clock* is associated to each transition. Hence the number of such clocks is bounded by the number of transitions. Although the number of clocks is bounded, most problems (reachability, control-state reachability, boundedness) are undecidable for TPNs [20], as two counter machines can easily be encoded. To obtain decidability, usually one has to either restrict to bounded TPNs [7], where the number of tokens in any place is bounded, or give up urgency [24]. In the latter case, the untimed language of a TPN without urgency, also known as its weak-time semantics, is the language of the associated Petri net without timing constraints, weakening the interest of TPNs.

Timed-Arc Petri Nets, also called Timed Petri Nets, associate a (continuous, positive valued) age to each token [2,26]. The number of continuous values is thus a priori unbounded. Each arc from a place to a transition can be constrained by a timing interval, meaning that only tokens with age in the interval can be consumed by this transition. Timed-Arc Petri Nets as explained in [2,18] cannot encode urgency. Although the number of token ages is unbounded, the theory of well structured transition systems [17] can be applied because of monotonicity (a token is allowed to stay forever at a place). Thus, control-state reachability (whether a place can be filled with at least one token) and boundedness (whether the number of tokens in places are always bounded) are decidable for Timed-Arc Petri Nets [2]. However, the (marking) reachability problem (whether a particular marking is ever reachable) is undecidable [25].

The two models have incomparable expressive power. TPNs can produce a token exactly every unit of time using urgency, while Timed-Arc Petri Nets cannot. On the other hand, Timed-Arc Petri Nets can express *latency* requirements, while TPNs cannot: indeed, TPNs (under the intermediate marking semantics) cannot track [6,9] the ages of an unbounded number of tokens (having slightly different ages) and consume each of them with a delay or latency of at least two time units after their creation.

Our goal in this paper is to examine the trade-off between expressivity and decidability in this setting of unbounded Petri nets with time. We start by considering a framework which is expressive enough to specify both these characteristics of *latency* and *urgency*. We aim to identify subclasses which are decidable while retaining at least a restricted form of this expressivity. To do this, we introduce *Timed-Arc Petri Nets with Urgency*, extending Timed-Arc Petri Nets with explicit urgency requirements, à la Merlin [22], forcing transitions to fire if they remains enabled for long enough.

Unsurprisingly, most problems are undecidable as soon as urgency is used on unbounded places (Proposition 1, and [19]). In earlier works, decidability results have been obtained by either imposing a bound on the number of tokens (e.g., [7,15]) or removing urgency completely (e.g., [21,24]). Here, we consider classes of Timed-Arc Petri Nets and of TPNs *with restricted Urgency* to obtain decidability. More specifically, transitions consuming tokens exclusively from bounded places can use urgency; other transitions consuming tokens from at least one unbounded place do not have urgency constraints. Using restricted urgency does *not* make the untimed language of a TPN with restricted Urgency the same as the language of the associated untimed Petri Net. Thus, these classes with restricted Urgency differ from TPNs with weak-time semantics [24], where all urgency constraints are ignored.

We present to our knowledge the first decidability results for a Petri net variant combining time, urgency and unbounded places. First, for the general class of Timed-Arc Petri Nets with restricted Urgency, we obtain decidability of *control-state reachability* (Theorem 1), i.e., whether a given place can ever be filled, and of boundedness. This extends decidability results [2] on Timed-Arc Petri Nets (without urgency). Our main result concerns the *decidability of (marking) reachability*. Reachability is undecidable for Timed-Arc Petri Nets (without any urgency), due to the presence of unboundedly many "clocks" (timed tokens) [25], and also for TPNs (because of unrestricted urgency) [20]. This leads us to consider TPNs *with restricted urgency*, which inherently use a bounded number of "clocks". We define a new *timed-arc semantics* for TPNs, presenting them as a subclass of Timed-Arc Petri Nets with Urgency, in the spirit of the time on token semantics of [11]. We then obtain our *main* result: reachability is decidable for TPNs with restricted Urgency under our new timed-arc semantics (Theorem 2). This allows us to decide reachability for channel systems with specified latency assuming that there is a bound on the *throughput* of the channel (i.e., on the number of messages transfered per unit of time). While our proof for deciding reachability does not adapt to the intermediate marking semantics, we obtain decidability of reachability under the intermediate marking semantics for the subclass of TPNs with restricted constraints (Theorem 3). This class forbids specifying upper and lower bounds on transitions leaving unbounded places. We summarize the decidability and expressivity results in the table below.

Table 1. Classes of systems and their associated decidability and expressivity. The italicized rows are new results in this paper. R stands for restricted form of expressivity.

Class of (unbounded) systems	Decidability		Expressivity	
	Reachability	Control-state Reach	Urgency	Latency
Timed-Arc Petri Nets with Urgency	×	×	✓	✓
Timed-Arc Petri Nets with restricted Urgency	×	✓	R	✓
Timed-Arc Petri Nets	×	✓	×	✓
TPNs	×	×	✓	×
TPNs with restricted constraints	✓	✓	R	×
TPNs with restricted Urgency under new timed-arc semantics	✓	✓	R	R

Related Work. In [19], Timed-Arc Petri Nets were extended with urgent transitions and place invariants. In contrast to our model where a timed or discrete move is always allowed in any configuration, deadlocked configurations can be reached in [19], where no discrete move is possible, and elapsing time is forbidden. Further, urgent transitions of [19] must fire as soon as they are enabled, which corresponds to the special case of having urgency 0 in our model. Urgency has also been modeled using Black transitions in generalized stochastic nets [4] and priorities in [8], but these nets cannot model latency constraints. For TPNs, the alternative multiple server semantics [9] has been proposed to model latency, but this makes the number of clocks unbounded.

Our focus in this paper is to address decidability issues. We obtain decidability for systems with (restricted) urgency *and* unbounded places. As far as we know, in all earlier results and in particular in [4,8,19,21,24], decidability is ensured only when urgency is completely disallowed, or places are all bounded. Further, our framework is powerful enough to capture systems of timed finite state machines communicating through *bag channels* [12,13], with urgency, throughput and latency characteristics of channels, and still yields decidability results.

Structure of the Paper. Section 2 introduces Timed-Arc Petri Nets with Urgency (Timed-Arc PNU), their semantics, and gives examples of communication channels that can be represented with this new model. Section 3 examines decidability issues for Timed-Arc PNU and introduces restrictions for decidability of control-state reachability and boundedness. Section 4 addresses the reachability problem for Timed-Arc Petri Nets and TPNs with restricted urgency and gives the main decidability results. Section 5 provides a proof of the main theorem followed by discussion and the conclusion.

2   Timed-Arc Petri Nets with Urgency

We will denote by $\mathbb{Q}_{\geq 0}$ the set of positive rational numbers, and by $\mathcal{I}(\mathbb{Q}_{\geq 0})$ the set of intervals over $\mathbb{Q}_{\geq 0} \cup \{\infty\}$. These intervals can be of the form (a, b), $(a, b]$, $[a, b)$, or $[a, b]$. We will denote by $\mathbb{M}_\mathbb{R}$ the set of *multisets* of positive real numbers. For two multisets A and B, we denote by $A \sqcup B$ the disjoint union of A and B, i.e., the multiset that gathers elements of multisets A and B without deleting identical elements. Similarly, we define $A \setminus B$ as the operation that removes from A exactly one occurrence of each element of B (if it exists).

We introduce our main model, Timed-Arc Petri Nets with urgency constraints. The model is based on a semantics using *timed markings* $m : P \to \mathbb{M}_\mathbb{R}$ which associate to each place a multiset describing the ages of all the tokens in this place.

Definition 1. *A Timed-Arc Petri Net with Urgency, denoted* Timed-Arc PNU, *is a tuple* $\mathcal{N} = (P, T, {}^\bullet(), ()^\bullet, m_0, \gamma, U)$ *where*

- *P is a set of places, T is a set of transitions, m_0 is the initial timed marking,*
- *${}^\bullet() : T \to P$ and $()^\bullet : T \to P$ are respectively, the backward and forward flow relations indicating tokens consumed/produced by each transition.*

- $\gamma : P \times T \to \mathcal{I}(\mathbb{Q}_{\geq 0})$ *is a set of* token-age constraints on arcs *and*
- $U : T \to \mathbb{Q}_{\geq 0} \cup \{\infty\}$ *is a set of* urgency constraints on transitions.

For a given arc constraint $\gamma(p,t) = [\alpha(p,t), \beta(p,t)]$ we will call $\alpha(p,t)$ the lower bound and $\beta(p,t)$ the upper bound of $\gamma(p,t)$. Such constraints mean that the transition t is enabled when for each place p of its preset ${}^{\bullet}t$, there is a token in p of age in $\gamma(p,t)$, i.e., between $\alpha(p,t)$ and $\beta(p,t)$. The urgency constraint $U(t)$ means that a transition must fire if t has been enabled (by its preset of tokens) for $U(t)$ units of time. A Timed-Arc Petri Net [2] can be seen as a Timed-Arc PNU with $U(t) = \infty$ for all $t \in T$. Note that we do not label transitions, hence each transition can be seen as labeled by its unique name.

As an example, consider the Timed-Arc PNU $\mathcal{N}_1$ of Fig. 1. Places are represented by circles, transitions by narrow rectangles, and flow relations by arcs between places and transitions. Urgency of a transtion is represented below the transition (in the example, transition t_3 has urgency 3). Arc constraints γ are represented as intervals below arcs. When unspecified, an arc constraint is set to $[0, \infty)$ and an urgency constraint to ∞ (e.g. $U(t_2) = \infty$). Intuitively, Fig. 1 depicts a process $p1$ that sends an unbounded number of messages to a process $p2$ through a channel. A message is sent at least every five time units (t.u.) because of the urgency constraint on t_1. Latency (or delay) for each message is at least 2 t.u. before being received, and the maximal throughput (or rate) of the channel is between 1 message every t.u. and 1 message every 4 t.u. Changing constraint $[2, \infty)$ into $[2, 100]$ models message loss, i.e., messages not received after 100 t.u. are considered lost. *Formal Semantics of Timed-Arc PNU:* We now define the semantics of a Timed-Arc PNU $\mathcal{N} = (P, T, {}^{\bullet}(), ()^{\bullet}, m_0, \gamma, U)$ in terms of timed markings and discrete and timed moves. For a given place p and timed marking m, we will let age_p denote real values from $m(p)$ depicting the age of one token in place p. Note that as $m(p)$ is a multiset, two tokens in a place p may have identical ages.

We say that a transition t is *enabled* from a timed marking m if, for each $p \in {}^{\bullet}t$, there exists $age_p \in m(p)$ such that $age_p \in \gamma(p,t)$. A transition t is said to be *urgent* from a timed marking m if $\forall p \in {}^{\bullet}t, \exists age_p \in m(p)$ such that $\alpha(p,t) + U(t) \leq age_p \leq \beta(p,t)$, i.e., if the preset of t has tokens at least $U(t)$

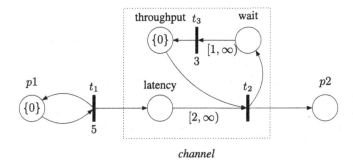

Fig. 1. Timed-Arc Petri net with urgency $\mathcal{N}_1$.

time units older than required by $\gamma(p,t)$. Let t be an urgent transition from m. This implies that t is enabled. Further, as formally defined below, presence of urgent transitions disallows time from elapsing. Thus, there will exist a place $p \in {}^\bullet t$ such that the oldest token $age_p \in m(p)$ with $age_p \leq \beta(p,t)$ will satisfy $age_p = \alpha(p,t) + U(t)$. An urgent transition t will force occurrence of a discrete move, but not necessarily of this transition t as several transitions can be enabled (or even urgent) at the same time. Formally, the semantics of Timed-Arc PNU is decomposed into timed moves and discrete moves.

Timed moves symbolize elapsing of δ time units from a timed marking in the following way: for a given timed marking m, we denote by $m + \delta$ the timed marking obtained by adding δ to the age of every token: if $m(p) = \{age_1, \ldots, age_k\}$, then $(m + \delta)(p) = \{age_1 + \delta, \ldots, age_k + \delta\}$. A *timed move* of $\delta > 0$ time units is allowed from m if for every $0 \leq \delta' < \delta$, the timed marking $m + \delta'$ has no urgent transition, and we denote $m \xrightarrow{\delta} m + \delta$ such timed moves.

Discrete moves represent firings of transitions from a marking m. One can fire transition t from marking m and reach marking m', denoted $m \xrightarrow{t} m'$ iff t is enabled and for each place p, we have $m'(p) = (m(p) \setminus S_p) \sqcup S'_p$, where

- $S_p = \{age_p\}$ where $age_p \in m(p) \cap \gamma(p,t)$ if $p \in {}^\bullet t$, and $S_p = \emptyset$ otherwise.
- $S'_p = \{0\}$ if $p \in t^\bullet$, and $S'_p = \emptyset$ otherwise.

A Timed-Arc PNU $\mathcal{N}$ defines a timed transition system $\llbracket \mathcal{N} \rrbracket$ whose states are timed markings and transitions are discrete and timed moves. A *run* of $\mathcal{N}$ is a sequence $m_1 a_1 m_2 \cdots m_n$ where, for all $i \in \{1, \ldots, n\}$, m_i is a timed marking of $\mathcal{N}$ and $a_i \in (\mathbb{R}_{>0} \cup T)$, such that $m_i \xrightarrow{a_i} m_{i+1}$ is a timed ($a_i \in \mathbb{R}_{>0}$) or discrete ($a_i \in T$) move. We will denote by $\mathsf{Reach}(\mathcal{N})$ the set of reachable timed markings of $\mathcal{N}$ (starting from m_0). An *(untimed) marking* is a function from P to $\mathbb{N}$. For a timed marking m, we will denote by $m^\sharp : P \to \mathbb{N}$ the untimed marking that associates to every place $p \in P$ the number of tokens in $m(p)$. A place $p \in P$ of a Timed-Arc PNU is called *bounded* if there exists an integer K such that for every timed marking $m \in \mathsf{Reach}(\mathcal{N})$, $m^\sharp(p) \leq K$ and $\mathcal{N}$ is *bounded* if all its places are bounded.

3   Undecidable and Decidable Problems for Timed-Arc PNU

In this paper we will tackle the decidability of the following problems:

- Reachability: given a Timed-Arc PNU $\mathcal{N}$, given an (untimed) marking m, does there exists a timed marking $m' \in \mathsf{Reach}(\mathcal{N})$ with $m'^\sharp = m$?
- Control State reachability (also called place-reachability): given a Timed-Arc PNU $\mathcal{N}$ and a place p, does there exist $m \in \mathsf{Reach}(\mathcal{N})$ with $m^\sharp(p) \geq 1$?
- Boundedness: given a Timed-Arc PNU $\mathcal{N}$, does there exist K such that for all $m \in \mathsf{Reach}(\mathcal{N})$, we have $m^\sharp(p) \leq K$ for all places p?

Proposition 1. *Control State reachability, Reachability and Boundedness are undecidable for Timed-Arc PNU.*

Proof (sketch). Reachability is undecidable for Timed-Arc PNU since it is already undecidable for Timed-Arc Petri nets [25]. Because of urgency, control state reachability and boundedness are also undecidable for Timed-Arc PNU. As the proofs closely follow the proofs of undecidability for TPNs [20], we do not detail them here (see also [19] for the proof for Timed-Arc Petri Nets with age invariants). □

To obtain decidability, two main approaches have been explored. The first involves dropping all urgency requirements. For Timed-Arc PNU, doing so we get back Timed-Arc Petri Nets and their decidability results. For TPNs, this corresponds to the weak semantics [24], under which the reachable (untimed) markings are the markings reachable by the associated (untimed) Petri net. The second approach considers only bounded nets [15] (see also bounded TPNs [7]). Our goal in this paper is to define restrictions for Timed-Arc PNU that ensure decidability for models combining urgency and unbounded nets. This allows us to verify networks of timed systems communicating via unbounded channels with specified latency and throughput such as the one shown in Fig. 1.

3.1 Restricted Urgency

We now define our subclass of Timed-Arc PNU. Let $\mathcal{N} = (P, T, {}^\bullet(), ()^\bullet, m_0, \gamma, U)$ be a Timed-Arc PNU. We start by defining the untimed Petri net associated with $\mathcal{N}$ as $\overline{\mathcal{N}} = (P, T, {}^\bullet(), ()^\bullet, m_0)$, by just dropping the timing constraints. We also define the restriction of $\mathcal{N}$ to a subset of places $P_b \subseteq P$ as the Timed-Arc PNU $\mathcal{N}_{P_b} = (P_b, T, {}^\star()_{P_b}, ()^\star{}_{P_b}, m'_{0P_b}, \gamma_{P_b}, U)$, where ${}^\star()_{P_b}, ()^\star{}_{P_b}, m'_{0P_b}, \gamma_{P_b}$ are respectively restriction of ${}^\bullet(), ()^\bullet, m_0, \gamma$ to $P_b \times T, T \times P_b$ and P_b. For a timed marking m of $\mathcal{N}$, we define the timed marking m_{P_b} of $\mathcal{N}_{Pb}$ with $m_{P_b}(p) = m(p)$ for all $p \in P_b$. We observe that if the places that are projected away do not use urgency then every run of $\mathcal{N}$ is also a run in the projected net $\mathcal{N}_{P_b}$. Formally,

Lemma 1. *Assume that for each transition $t \in T$ with $U(t) < \infty$, we have ${}^\bullet t \subseteq P_b$. Then for every run $m_0 a_1 \cdots a_n m_n$ of $\mathcal{N}$, $m_{0,P_b} a_1 \cdots a_n m_{n,P_b}$ is a run of $\mathcal{N}_{P_b}$.*

Proof. Let $\rho = m_0 a_1 \dots a_n m_n$ be a run of $\mathcal{N}$. Consider, for the sake of contradiction, the smallest i for which we do not have $m_{i-1,P_b} \xrightarrow{a_i} m_{i,P_b}$. The only possibility is to contradict urgency because discrete moves satisfy $m_{i-1,P_b} \xrightarrow{a_i} m_{i,P_b}$. Hence we must have $a_i = \delta$ and for some $\delta' < \delta$, there exists a transition t with urgency $U(t) = k < \infty$ and for all input places $p \in P_b$ of t, there is at least one token of age at least k in $(m_{P_b,i} + \delta')(p)$. Now, by assumption, ${}^\bullet t \subseteq P_b$. That is, there are no other places (from P_u) that can be in the preset of t. Hence, by definition of urgency, $m_i \xrightarrow{\delta} m_{i+1}$ is not a valid timed move in $\mathcal{N}$ either, which is a contradiction. □

Note that the converse is not true in general: a run of $\mathcal{N}_{P_b}$ needs not be a run of $\mathcal{N}$. We can now define our decidable subclass of Timed-Arc PNU. It is mainly based on the notion of *restricted urgency*, which intuitively means that urgency can be enforced only on the bounded part of the system.

Definition 2. *A* Timed-Arc Petri Net with restricted Urgency *(denoted* Timed-Arc PNrU*) is a triple* $(\mathcal{N}, P_u, P_b)$*, where* $\mathcal{N} = (P, T, {}^\bullet(), (){}^\bullet, m_0, \gamma, U)$ *is a Timed-Arc PNU, and* $P_u \sqcup P_b = P$ *is a partition of places of* $\mathcal{N}$ *such that:*

- *for each transition* $t \in T$ *with* $U(t) < \infty$*, we have* ${}^\bullet t \subseteq P_b$ *and,*
- *the (untimed) Petri Net* $\overline{\mathcal{N}_{P_b}}$ *associated with* $\mathcal{N}_{P_b}$ *is bounded.*

Intuitively, in a Timed-Arc PNrU $(\mathcal{N}, P_u, P_b)$, urgency can only be used by transitions consuming tokens from structurally bounded places. As an example, consider the net $\mathcal{N}_1$ from Fig. 1. Let $P_b = \{p1, \text{wait}, \text{throughput}\}$ and $P_u = \{\text{latency}, p2\}$ be a partition of places in P. The (unbounded) places in P_u do not use urgency and the (untimed) Petri Net $\overline{\mathcal{N}_{P_b}}$ is a 1-bounded Petri Net. Hence $\mathcal{N}_1$ is a Timed-Arc PNrU.

Checking membership in Timed-Arc PNrU, i.e., checking whether a Timed-Arc PNU is with restricted Urgency, is decidable. This immediately follows from the fact that it is decidable whether a place of a Petri Net is bounded. Given $\mathcal{N}$, it suffices to define $P_b = \bigcup_{U(t)<\infty} {}^\bullet t$, and to check that $\overline{\mathcal{N}_{P_b}}$ is a bounded (untimed) Petri Net. Though we will often refer to places in P_u as "unbounded places", this only means the contents of these places can be unbounded, not that they must be. On the other hand, places of P_b are bounded in $\mathcal{N}$:

Lemma 2. *Let* $(\mathcal{N}, P_u, P_b)$ *be a Timed-Arc PNrU. Then every* $p \in P_b$ *is bounded in* $\mathcal{N}$*.*

Proof. Let K be the bound on the number of tokens in $\overline{\mathcal{N}_{P_b}}$. For the sake of contradiction, if $p \in P_b$ was not bounded in $\mathcal{N}$, there would exist a reachable marking m with more than K tokens in p. Let $m_0 a_1 \cdots a_n m_n$ be a run reaching $m_n = m$. Then by Lemma 1, $m_{0,P_b} a_1 \cdots a_n m_{n,P_b}$ is a run of $\mathcal{N}_{P_b}$, and thus of $\overline{\mathcal{N}_{P_b}}$, and m_{n,P_b} has more than K tokens in p, a contradiction with $\overline{\mathcal{N}_{P_b}}$ being K bounded.   □

We next turn to the (un)decidable properties for this subclass of Timed-Arc PNrU.

Theorem 1. *Control-State reachability and Boundedness are decidable for Timed-Arc PNrU. However, reachability is undecidable for Timed-Arc PNrU.*

Proof (sketch). The decidability of control-state reachability and boundedness for Timed-Arc PNU is adapted from [1,2], by defining a well-quasi order over the markings and using the theory of well structured transition systems [17]. The well quasi order $\preceq$ is defined in the following way. First, we define a region abstraction for markings of Timed-Arc PNrU. This abstraction is a combination of regions of a finite timed automaton representing the behavior of the net on its bounded part, and regions representing symbolically the markings of the unbounded places of the net. This set of regions is equipped with a comparison relation $\preceq$ that requires equality on the region bounded part, and comparable contents on the unbounded part. This relation is compatible with markings comparison and is a well-quasi order. We can then define a successor relation among regions that is an abstract representation of moves of a Timed-Arc PNrU. Regions equipped with their ordering and this successor relation form a well-structured transition system and hence control-state reachability and boundedness are decidable. Details are omitted as the construction is rather similar to [1,2]. The undecidability of reachability for Timed-arc PNrUs follows directly from the undecidability of reachability for Timed-Arc Petri nets [1,25].   □

We remark that the results of the above Theorem 1 can easily be extended to a strictly larger class of Timed-Arc PNUs, where $\mathcal{N}_{P_b}$ is bounded instead of $\overline{\mathcal{N}_{P_b}}$. However, checking membership in this extended class is not decidable as boundedness is not decidable for Timed-Arc PNU.

4   Decidability of the Reachability Problem

In this section we tackle the decidability of the reachability problem. On one hand, reachability is undecidable for Timed-Arc Petri Nets [25], and thus for Timed-Arc PN(r)Us, because an unbounded number of clocks can be encoded, one for each token. On the other hand, Timed-transition Petri Nets (TPNs) [22] only use a bounded number of clocks (one per transition), even if the places have unboundedly many tokens. Nevertheless, (unrestricted) urgency makes reachability undecidable for TPNs [20]. To obtain decidability of reachability, we thus consider classes of TPNs with restricted urgency.

4.1   Timed-Transition Petri Nets (TPNs)

Timed-transition Petri Nets (TPNs for short), also called Time Petri Nets, introduced in [22], associate time intervals to transitions of a Petri net. Formally, a TPN $\mathcal{N}$ is a tuple $(P, T, {}^{\bullet}(), ()^{\bullet}, m_0, I)$ where P is a finite set of *places*, T is a finite set of *transitions*, ${}^{\bullet}(), ()^{\bullet} : P \to T$ are the *backward* and *forward* flow relations respectively, $m_0 \in \mathbb{N}^P$ is the *initial* (untimed) marking, and $I : T \mapsto \mathcal{I}(\mathbb{Q}_{\geq 0})$ maps each transition to a *firing interval*. We denote by $A(t)$ (resp. $B(t)$) the lower bound (resp. the upper bound) of interval $I(t)$. A *configuration* of a TPN is a pair (m, ν), where m is an untimed *marking* (recall that in untimed markings, $m(p)$ is the number of tokens in p), and $\nu : T \to \mathbb{R}_{\geq 0}$ associates a real value to each transition. A transition t is *enabled* in a marking m if $m \geq {}^{\bullet}t$. We denote by $En(m)$ the set of enabled transitions in m. The valuation ν associates to each enabled transition $t \in En(m)$ the amount of time that has elapsed since this transition was last newly enabled. An enabled transition t is *urgent* if $\nu(t) \geq B(t)$, with $B(t)$ the upper bound of $I(t)$. An example of a TPN is depicted in Fig. 2 below.

We first recall the intermediate marking semantics [5,7] for TPNs defined using timed and discrete moves between configurations. A *timed move* consists of letting time elapse in a configuration. For (m, ν), $\nu + \delta$ is defined by $\nu + \delta(t) = \nu(t) + \delta$, for all $t \in En(m)$. A timed move from (m, ν) to $(m, \nu + \delta)$, denoted $(m, \nu) \xrightarrow{\delta} (m, \nu+\delta)$, is allowed if for every $0 \leq \delta' < \delta$, the configuration $(m, \nu+\delta')$

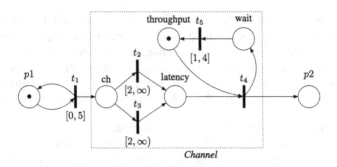

Fig. 2. A TPN $\mathcal{N}_2$.

has no urgent transition. A *discrete move* consists of firing an enabled transition t that has been enabled for a duration that fulfills the time constraint attached to t. We have $(m, \nu) \xrightarrow{t} (m', \nu')$ if $t \in En(m)$, $\nu(t) \in I(t)$ and $m' = m - {}^\bullet t + t^\bullet$, for ν' defined below. We call intermediate marking the marking $m - {}^\bullet t$ which is obtained after t consumes tokens from its preset but did not create new ones yet. We will say that a transition $t' \in En(m')$ is *newly enabled* by firing of t if either $t' = t$, or $t' \notin En(m - {}^\bullet t)$, i.e. is not enabled in the intermediate marking $m - {}^\bullet t$. Now, we define $\nu'(tt) = 0$ if tt is newly enabled, and $\nu'(tt) = \nu(tt)$ for all $tt \in En(m)$ but not newly enabled. That is, for a transition t both consuming and producing a token in p having a single token, a transition t' with $p \in {}^\bullet t'$ is disabled then newly enabled when t is fired.

This classical semantics of TPN is somewhat similar to that of Timed-Arc PNU, but is based on configurations instead of timed markings. The only continuous values kept in the configuration of a TPN are in ν. Hence, only $|T|$ "clock" values are kept, and configurations cannot keep track of the exact time elapsed since their creation for arbitrary number of tokens. In particular, a TPN under the intermediate marking semantics cannot encode latency for an unbounded number of tokens [9] (for instance, the property that tokens are consumed at least 2 units of time after each of them is created). More generally, it is not simple to model a channel with specified latency and throughput with the intermediate marking semantics of TPNs. For instance, TPN $\mathcal{N}_2$ in Fig. 2 seems to model a channel with a latency of 2 time units and throughput (rate) of at most 1 message per time unit. However, if a token reaches place ch at date 0 and another at date 1.9, then both can be consumed at time 2, though only one of them has spent two time units at ch, hence it does not faithfully encode a latency of 2.

4.2   A New Timed-Arc Semantics for TPNs

We now introduce a new *timed-arc semantics* in order to model channels with latency and throughput, presenting TPNs as Timed-arc PNUs. The core idea is that the timed-arc semantics takes into account the age of tokens in input places. Formally, we define Timed($\mathcal{N}$), the Timed-Arc PNU associated with

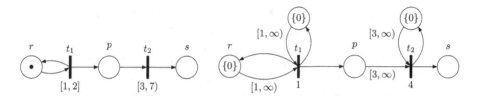

Fig. 3. A TPN $\mathcal{N}_3$ (left) which is timed bisimilar to $Timed(\mathcal{N}_3)$ (right).

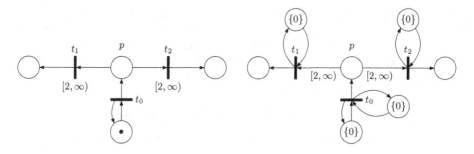

Fig. 4. A TPN $\mathcal{N}_4$ (left) which is not bisimilar to $Timed(\mathcal{N}_4)$ (right).

the TPN $\mathcal{N} = (P, T, {}^{\bullet}(), ()^{\bullet}, m_0, I)$. Intuitively, $\mathrm{Timed}(\mathcal{N})$ preserves all places and transitions of $\mathcal{N}$, adds one place p_t per transition t, adds p_t to the pre and post flow of t, and adapts the timing constraints. Figures 3 and 4 display TPNs $\mathcal{N}_3, \mathcal{N}_4$ on the left and $Timed(\mathcal{N}_3)$, $Timed(\mathcal{N}_4)$ on the right. We define $\mathrm{Timed}(\mathcal{N}) = (P', T, {}^{\star}(), ()^{\star}, m_0', \gamma, U)$ where:

- $P' = P \cup P_T$ with $P_T = \{p_t \mid t \in T\}$.
- ${}^{\star}(), ()^{\star}$ extend respectively ${}^{\bullet}(), ()^{\bullet}$ in the following way: $p \in {}^{\star}t$ iff $p = p_t$ or $p \in {}^{\bullet}t$ and $p \in t^{\star}$ iff $p = p_t$ or $p \in t^{\bullet}$.
- For all t, for $I(t) = [A(t), B(t)]$, we let $U(t) = B(t) - A(t)$ and for all $p \in {}^{\star}t$, we set $\gamma(p, t) = [A(t), +\infty)$ (for $I(t) = (A(t), B(t)]$ we let $\gamma(p, t) = (A(t), +\infty)$),
- We let $m_0'(p) = 0^{m_0(p)}$ for all $p \in P$ and $m_0'(p_t) = \{0\}$ for all transitions t.

TPN $\mathcal{N}_2$ under the timed-arc semantics, i.e., $\mathrm{Timed}(\mathcal{N}_2)$, represents the channel with latency 2 and maximal throughput of 1 message per time unit, which is also modeled by the Timed-arc PNU of Fig. 1. Indeed, a token can be sent from place ch to place $latency$ by either transition only when it is at least 2 time units old, preserving the latency requirement.

The new timed-arc semantics is close in spirit to the time-on-token semantics of [11], which was defined for 1-safe TPNs. In case of 1-safe TPNs as well as in examples such as net $\mathcal{N}_3$, this semantics is bisimilar to the classical intermediate marking semantics [11]. However, in general, the behaviors of $\mathcal{N}$ and $\mathrm{Timed}(\mathcal{N})$

differ. Consider for instance the TPN $\mathcal{N}_4$ in Fig. 4. Consider the execution of $\mathcal{N}_4$ where t_0 fires twice: first at date 0 and then at date 1. At date 2, both t_1 and t_2 have been enabled for 2 time units ($\nu(t_1) = \nu(t_2) = 2$), hence any one of them can fire. Let t_1 fire. Now, t_1 cannot fire again immediately as it is newly enabled (hence $\nu'(t_1) = 0$), but t_2 can fire immediately after t_1, because $\nu'(t_2) = 2$ (in particular, it is not newly enabled by firing t_1 as there are two tokens in the input place p, i.e., $m(p) - {}^\bullet t(p) = 2 - 1 = 1$).

In contrast, in Timed($\mathcal{N}_4$), if t_0 is fired at date 0 and again at date 1, then at date 2, $m(p) = \{1, 2\}$, and any one of t_1 or t_2 can fire. Just as in the execution of $\mathcal{N}_4$, let t_1 fire. After this firing of t_1, the other transition t_2 cannot fire because $m'(p) = \{1\}$ and $1 < 2$. It is only at date 3 that t_2 can fire. At date 3, transition t_1 cannot fire because $m''(p_{t_1}) = \{1\}$, and $1 < 2$. This illustrates that the behaviors of $\mathcal{N}_4$ and Timed($\mathcal{N}_4$) can indeed differ in general. In the following, we will use the timed-marking semantics in the general case, where it does not coincide with the intermediate marking semantics.

4.3   Reachability for TPNs Under the Timed-Arc Semantics

Reachability is undecidable for general TPNs because of unrestricted urgency [20], under the timed-arc or the intermediate marking semantics. We now introduce two natural restrictions to urgency to allow decidability.

Definition 3. *Let $\mathcal{N} = (P, T, {}^\bullet(), ()^\bullet, m_0, I)$ be a TPN and $P = P_u \sqcup P_b$ be a partition of its places such that the (untimed) Petri Net $\overline{\mathcal{N}_{P_b}}$ associated with $\mathcal{N}_{P_b}$ is bounded.*

- *$\mathcal{N}$ is called a TPN with restricted urgency if for each transition $t \in T$ with an upper bound $B(t) < \infty$ on its firing interval, we have ${}^\bullet t \subseteq P_b$.*
- *$\mathcal{N}$ is called a TPN with restricted constraints if for each transition $t \in T$ with a non trivial firing interval $I(t) \neq [0, \infty)$ we have ${}^\bullet t \subseteq P_b$.*

The class of TPNs with restricted constraints is strictly contained in the class of TPNs with restricted urgency. As an example, the TPN $\mathcal{N}_2$ on Fig. 2 is a TPN with restricted urgency but not a TPN with restricted constraints, since there is an arc from the unbounded place ch to transition t_2 with constraints $[2, \infty)$, i.e., a constraint with non-trivial lower bound and no upper (urgency) bound. As for Timed-Arc PNU, checking whether a TPN is with restricted urgency or with restricted constraints is decidable, since checking boundedness of (untimed) Petri Nets is decidable.

Now, if $\mathcal{N}$ is a TPN with restricted Urgency, then Timed($\mathcal{N}$) is a Timed-Arc PNrU, ensuring that boundedness and control-state reachability are decidable. We can now state our main result, namely Theorem 2: reachability is decidable for TPNs with restricted urgency *under timed-arc semantics* (e.g. Timed($\mathcal{N}_2$) from Fig. 2 is in this class). TPNs with restricted urgency *under timed-arc seman-tics* can model networks of (finite-state) *timed* systems with unrestricted urgency, communicating through bag channels [12,13], specifying maximal throughput and minimal latency, assuming that the throughput is not infinite. Indeed, it suffices to modify the TPN in Fig. 2 with $\lceil \frac{x}{\delta} \rceil$ transitions from ch to *latency* in order to model a channel with latency at least x and throughput at most δ messages per unit of time.

Theorem 2. *Let $\mathcal{N}$ be a TPN with restricted urgency. Then the reachability, boundedness and control-state reachability problems are decidable for Timed($\mathcal{N}$).*

The next section is devoted to the proof of Theorem 2. In essence, we show that although the *timed-arc semantics* of TPNs "formally" uses an unbounded number of clocks, a complex reduction allows to consider only a bounded number of clocks. This step is crucial in the proof of Theorem 2, and we believe that this technique can be generalized and re-used for other problems in related contexts.

5   Proof of Theorem 2

Let $(\mathcal{N}, P, Q)$, with $\mathcal{N} = (P \cup Q, T, {}^\bullet(), ()^\bullet, m_0, I)$ be a TPN with restricted Urgency, P (resp. Q) the set of bounded (resp. unbounded) places. In this section, we show how to check if a given (untimed) marking is reachable in Timed($\mathcal{N}$). The intuitive idea is that, under restricted urgency, a transition t which has an unbounded place from Q in its preset, has no urgency/upper constraint. Hence to fire t, it suffices to check the lower bound constraint, i.e., to check that some tokens (among an unbounded number) in its pre-places are old enough. Now, the crucial point is that to check this lower-bound, we need the ages of only a bounded number of tokens, as there are a finite number of transitions, and for each transition t, its associated "clock" p_t is reset after it is fired.

Formally, the proof (of Theorem 2) is in two steps: we first convert the TPN with restricted urgency $\mathcal{N}$ to a TPN with restricted constraints $\mathcal{N}'$ such that Timed($\mathcal{N}$) and Timed($\mathcal{N}'$) have the same set of reachable markings. In the second step, we obtain a Petri Net that is bisimilar to Timed($\mathcal{N}'$), which implies the decidability of reachability.

Step 1: Construction of the TPN with Restricted Constraints $\mathcal{N}'$. In order to obtain a TPN with restricted constraints $\mathcal{N}'$ from $\mathcal{N}$, we will keep (an overapproximation of) ages for a bounded number of tokens from each unbounded place $p \in Q$. For that, we will use $|T| \times |Q|$ gadgets $(C_p^t)_{t \in T, p \in Q}$.

Gadget C_p^t, associated with place $p \in Q$ and transition $t \in T$ (with $p \in {}^\bullet t$), is a TPN with restricted constraints. Each gadget is similar: it has 2 places, 0_p^t and 1_p^t, and in the initial marking the token is at 0_p^t. There is an associated transition $start_p^t$: we have ${}^\star start_p^t = \{p, 0_p^t\}$ and $start_p^{t\,\star} = \{1_p^t\}$, with the timing constraint $I'(start_p^t) = [0, \infty)$. That is, $\mathcal{N}'$ will non-deterministically guess the transition that will fire. The gadget for a fixed transition t and place p is shown in Fig. 5. Every transition t reading from an (unbounded) place $p \in Q$ is transformed to

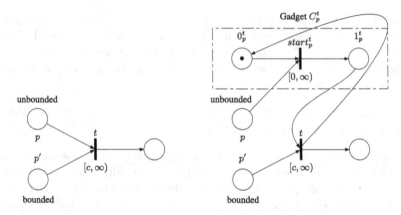

Fig. 5. Step 1 of proof: converting (part of) TPN with restricted urgency $\mathcal{N}$ to restricted constraints $\mathcal{N}'$

read from (bounded) place 1_p^t of gadget C_p^t instead. That is, if a transition t reads from unbounded places $\{p_1, \cdots, p_k\} = {}^\bullet t \cap Q$, then we have ${}^\star t = {}^\bullet t \setminus \{p_1, \cdots, p_k\} \cup \{1_{p_j}^t \mid j \le k\}$ and $t^\star = t^\bullet \cup \{0_{p_j}^t \mid j \le k\}$. The timing constraint is left unchanged: $I'(t) = I(t)$. We obtain $\mathcal{N}' = (P', T', {}^\star(), ()^\star, m_0', I')$:

- $P' = P \cup Q \cup \{0_p^t, 1_p^t \mid p \in P, t \in T\}$,
- $T' = T \cup \{start_p^t \mid t \in T, p \in Q\}$,
- ${}^\star(), ()^\star, I'$ as defined above, and
- $m_0'(p) = m_0(p)$ for $p \in P$, and $m_0'(0_p^t) = 1$, $m_0'(1_p^t) = 0$ for all t, p.

It is clear that $\mathcal{N}'$ is a TPN with restricted constraints, with the same set $Q' = Q$ of unbounded places as for all t' with ${}^\star t' \cap Q' \ne \emptyset$, we have $t' = start_p^t$ for some $t \in T$, and thus $I(t') = [0, \infty)$.

The idea of the gadget is the following. Let $m \in \mathsf{Reach}(\mathsf{Timed}(\mathcal{N}))$, t be a transition with $I(t) = [a, \infty)$ and $p \in Q \cap {}^\bullet t$ be an unbounded place. $m(p_t)$ is the time elapsed since the last firing of t. For firing t, we need to have both $m(p_t) \ge a$ and $age_p \ge a$, i.e., we need $min(m(p_t), age_p) \ge a$. In other words, keeping $min(m(p_t), age_p)$ instead of age_p is sufficient to know whether t is enabled. This is implemented in $\mathsf{Timed}(\mathcal{N}')$, as there can be only one token in $1_p^{t'}$, and its age $m'(1_p^{t'})$ is never older than $m'(p_t)$, as $start_p^t$ can happen only after t fired (0_p^t filled when t fired).

We now show that $\mathsf{Timed}(\mathcal{N}')$ preserves the set of reachable untimed markings of $\mathsf{Timed}(\mathcal{N})$. We start by defining a map f from untimed markings of $\mathsf{Timed}(\mathcal{N}')$ to untimed markings of $\mathsf{Timed}(\mathcal{N})$. Recall that for a timed marking m, $m^\sharp$ refers to the untimed marking obtained by counting the number of tokens in each place. Let $m' \in \mathsf{Reach}(\mathsf{Timed}(\mathcal{N}'))$. For each place $p \in P \cup Q$ of $\mathsf{Timed}(\mathcal{N})$, we define:

$$f(m'^\sharp)(p) = \begin{cases} m'^\sharp(p) + \sum_{t \in T} m'^\sharp(1_p^t) & \text{if } p \in Q \\ m'^\sharp(p) & \text{otherwise} \end{cases}$$

First, we show that Timed($\mathcal{N}'$) can reach only untimed markings corresponding to untimed markings of Timed($\mathcal{N}$):

Lemma 3. *Let m' be a timed marking in* Reach(*Timed*($\mathcal{N}'$)). *Then there exists a timed marking $m \in$ Reach(Timed($\mathcal{N}$)) with $f(m'^{\sharp}) = m^{\sharp}$.*

Proof. We will prove by induction on the length of a path that if one can reach m' in Timed($\mathcal{N}'$), then one can reach m in Timed($\mathcal{N}$) such that:

1. for all $p \in P \cup \{p_t \mid t \in T\}$, $m(p) = m'(p)$,
2. for all $q \in Q$, letting T_q be the set of $t \in T$ such that $m'(1_q^t) \neq \emptyset$, we have $m(q) = m'(q) \sqcup \{age_1, \cdots age_k\}$ and there exists a bijection $g : T_q \mapsto [1, k]$ with $m'(1_q^t) \leq age_{g(t)}$ for all $t \in T_q$.

When these two conditions are met, we say that m *satisfies the hypothesis wrt m'*. It is easy to see that $f(m'^{\sharp}) = m^{\sharp}$ whenever m satisfies the hypothesis wrt m'.

For $m' = m'_0$, we have trivially that m_0 satisfies the hypothesis wrt m'_0. We can now proceed by induction on the length of run needed to reach m'. Let m' be a reachable marking of Timed($\mathcal{N}'$). A path reaching m' ends with a move $m'' \xrightarrow{e} m'$, where e can be a timed move, a firing of a transition $start_p^t$, or a firing of a transition t of the original net. Hence, m'' is reached in less steps than m'. We can hence apply the induction hypothesis, i.e., one can reach m in Timed($\mathcal{N}$) with:

1. for all $p \in P \cup \{p_t \mid t \in T\}$, $m(p) = m''(p)$,
2. for all $q \in Q$, letting T_q be the set of $t \in T$ such that $m''(1_q^t) \neq \emptyset$, we have $m(q) = m''(q) \sqcup \{age_1, \cdots age_k\}$ and there exists a bijection $g : T_q \mapsto [1, k]$ with $m''(1_q^t) \leq age_{g(t)}$ for all $t \in T_q$.

For a given bijection g, we denote by $g''(1_q^t) = age_{g(t)}$ the function that relates tokens in places of the form 1_q^t with token $age_{g(t)}$ in m.

Case $e = start_q^t$: We know that m satisfies the hypothesis wrt m'' by hypothesis and want to show that m satisfies the hypothesis wrt m' as well. The conditions are true for all $p \notin \{q, 0_q^t, 1_q^t\}$, as for these places, $m'(p) = m''(p)$. Last, $m(q) = m''(q) \sqcup \{age_1, \ldots, age_k\}$ and we have a bijection $g : T_q \mapsto [1, k]$. Now, we have $m'(q) = m''(q) \sqcup \{age_0\}$ for the token age_0 which is consumed by $start_q^t$ from q. Hence $m(q) = m'(q) \sqcup \{age_0, age_1, \ldots, age_k\}$, and one can extend $g : T_q \mapsto [1, k]$ to $g' : T_q \cup \{t_q\} \mapsto [0, k]$ by setting $g'(t) = 0$. As $m'(1_q^t) = 0$, we indeed have $age_0 \geq m'(1_q^t)$. Hence m satisfies the hypothesis wrt m'.

Case $e = \delta$ (time elapses by δ units): We note that urgency is not violated in m'' by elapsing δ units of time. Now, since for all $p \in P$ we have $m(p) = m''(p)$, and transitions leaving (unbounded) places of Q have no urgency, urgency is not violated in m either by elapsing δ units of time. Thus $m + \delta$ is reachable in *Timed*($\mathcal{N}$). Finally, it is easy to see that $m + \delta$ satisfies the hypothesis wrt $m' = m'' + \delta$.

Case $e = t$ for some $t \in T$: If ${}^{\bullet}t$ has only bounded places, since $m(p) = m''(p)$ for all bounded places p, one can fire t from m to obtain a marking m^+ which satisfies the hypothesis wrt m' and we are done. Else, $\bullet t \cap Q \neq \emptyset$ and $I(t) = [a, +\infty)$ for some $a \in \mathbb{R}_{\geq 0}$. For all $q \in \bullet t \cap Q$, we have $m''(1_q^t) \geq a$ as t can be fired from m''. Taking the token $g''(1_q^t)$ of $m(q)$, we have $g''(1_q^t) \geq m''(1_q^t) \geq a$ for each $q \in \bullet t \cap Q$. Further, since $m(p) = m''(p)$ for all $p \in P \cup \{p_t \mid t \in T\}$, we have that t is enabled from m. We now carefully define a particular marking m^+ of Timed($\mathcal{N}$) which can be obtained from m by firing t. First, for every $q \in \bullet t \cap Q$, we delete the token $g''(1_q^t)$ of $m(q)$. Then for all $p \in \bullet t \cap (P \cup \{p_t \mid t \in T\})$, we define age_p the age of token removed from $m''(p)$ to $m'(p)$, and remove it from $m(p)$ as well. Finally, for every place p of $t^\bullet$, we create a token of age 0 in $m(p)$. It is now easy to check that m^+ satisfies the hypothesis wrt m'. □

Next, we show that every untimed marking of Timed($\mathcal{N}$) can be simulated in Timed($\mathcal{N}'$):

Lemma 4. *Let m be a timed marking in* Reach($Timed(\mathcal{N})$). *Then one can reach in* Timed($\mathcal{N}'$) *any timed marking m' with:*

(1) for all $p \in P \cup \{p_t \mid t \in T\}$, we have $m'(p) = m(p)$ and

(2) for all $t \in T, p \in Q$, we have either $m'(0_p^t) = \emptyset$ or $m'(0_p^t) = m'(p_t)$, and

(3) for all $q \in Q$, letting $T_q' = \{t \in T \mid m'(1_q^t) \neq \emptyset\}$, we have $m(q) = m'(q) \sqcup \{age_t \mid t \in T_q'\}$ with $m'(1_q^t) = min(m(p_t), age_t)$ for all $t \in T_q'$.

Proof (sketch). We proceed by induction on the length of run reaching m in $\mathcal{N}$. For a run of length 0, this is trivial. Assume that m is reached after a move $m^- \xrightarrow{e} m$. Let m' be any marking satisfying the conditions (1–3) above wrt m. We will show that we can reach m' in Timed($\mathcal{N}'$).

Assume that e is a timed move that lets $\delta > 0$ units of time elapse. Hence, for every place $p \in P \cup Q$, and every token $age_p \in m(p)$, $age_p \geq \delta$. We have $m^- = m - \delta$. We first show that for all $p' \in P'$ and all $age_p' \in m'(p')$, $age_p' \geq \delta$. This is easy to see for $p' \in P \cup \{p_t \mid t \in T\}$ as $m(p') = m'(p')$, and hence also for $p' \in \{0_p^t \mid t \in T, p \in Q\}$. For $p \in Q$, we have $m'(q) \sqsubseteq m(q)$. Further, for all $t \in T, p \in Q$ with $m'(1_p^t) \neq \emptyset$, we have $m'(1_p^t) = \{min(m(p_t), age_p)\}$ with $age_p \in m(p)$. As $m(p_t) \geq \delta$ and $age_p \geq \delta$, we have $m'(1_p^t) \geq \delta$. Thus, $age' \geq \delta$ for all $p' \in P'$ and all $age' \in m'(p')$. We can now define the timed marking $m'' = m' - \delta$. It is then easy to check that m'' satisfies the conditions (1–3) above wrt to m^-, and so, we can apply the induction hypothesis and conclude that m'' is reachable in Timed($\mathcal{N}'$).

Now, we show that waiting δ units of time from m'' is allowed in Timed($\mathcal{N}'$). That is, we show that it does not violate any urgency: Suppose not, i.e., suppose the urgency of some transition t was violated. Then, this would imply that $I(t) = [a, b]$ and thus $\bullet t \subseteq P$ contains only bounded places. As m^- and m'' coincide on bounded places, this would also violate urgency on m^-, a contradiction with a δ timed move being allowed from m^-. Hence δ units of time can elapse from m'', reaching marking m'. Thus m' is reachable in Timed($\mathcal{N}'$).

Finally, the case of a discrete move e firing a transition t can be handled by a similar analysis, which completes the proof of this lemma. □

Now observe that for all places p, we have $\sum_{t \in T} m'^{\sharp}(1_p^t) \leq |T|$. Thus fixing an untimed marking c, there exist only a finite number of untimed markings $m'^{\sharp}$ such that $f(m'^{\sharp}) = c$. Combining Lemmas 3 and 4, we obtain:

Proposition 2. *Let c be an untimed marking of Timed($\mathcal{N}$). Let c' be any untimed marking of Timed($\mathcal{N}'$) with $f(c') = c$. Then c is reachable in Timed($\mathcal{N}$) iff c' is reachable in Timed($\mathcal{N}'$).*

This completes the first step of the proof of Theorem 2.

Step 2: From the TPN with Restricted Constraints $\mathcal{N}'$ to a Petri Net $\mathcal{N}''$. Now we show that for a TPN with restricted constraints $\mathcal{N}'$, it is decidable whether a marking c' is reachable in Timed($\mathcal{N}'$), by reducing $\mathcal{N}'$ to an equivalent (untimed) Petri net. As marking reachability is decidable for Petri nets, this completes the proof of Theorem 2.

Proposition 3. *For any TPN with restricted constraints $\mathcal{N}'$, one can construct a Petri Net $\mathcal{N}''$ such that $\mathcal{N}''$ and Timed($\mathcal{N}'$) are (untimed) bisimilar.*

Proof. Given a TPN with restricted constraints $\mathcal{N}'$, we first construct a 1-bounded (untimed) Petri Net $\mathcal{N}_1$ which is bisimilar to Timed($\mathcal{N}_B'$), where $\mathcal{N}_B$ is the bounded part of $\mathcal{N}$. Formally, we have the following lemma.

Lemma 5. *If $\mathcal{N}_B$ is a K-bounded TPN, for some positive integer K, we can construct a 1-bounded Petri Net $\mathcal{N}_1$ such that $\mathcal{N}_1$ and Timed($\mathcal{N}_B$) are (untimed) bisimilar.*

Proof (sketch). The proof of this lemma is easily obtained by building a timed automaton bisimilar to Timed($\mathcal{N}_B$) and interpreting its regions as places of a 1-safe Petri Net [19], adapting a result for the intermediate semantics of TPNs [14].

After building the Petri net $\mathcal{N}_1 = (P_1, T_1, {}^{\bullet}(), ()^{\bullet}, m_1^0)$ we add the unbounded places of $\mathcal{N}'$. Formally, we build the Petri net $\mathcal{N}_2 = (P_2, T_1, {}^{\star}(), ()^{\star}, m_2^0)$ with:

- The set P_2 of places of $\mathcal{N}_2$ is $P_2 = P_1 \cup P_u$, for P_u the unbounded places of Timed($\mathcal{N}'$).
- Initial marking m_2^0 is the union of m_1^0 and of the restriction of the initial marking of Timed($\mathcal{N}'$) to its set P_u of unbounded places.
- The set of transitions of $\mathcal{N}_2$ is the set T_1 of transitions of $\mathcal{N}_1$. Concerning the flow relations, for $t_1 \in T_1$ and its corresponding transition $t \in T$ in the original net Timed($\mathcal{N}'$), we have $p \in {}^{\star}t_1$ if:
  - $p \in P_1$ and $p \in {}^{\bullet}t_1$ (arc from p to t_1 in $\mathcal{N}_1$), or
  - $p \in P_u$ and there is an arc from p to t in Timed($\mathcal{N}'$).
  We have $p \in t_1{}^{\star}$ if $p \in P_1$ and $p \in t_1{}^{\bullet}$, or if $p \in P_u$ and there is an arc from t to p in Timed($\mathcal{N}'$).

With this, we have the following lemma:

Lemma 6. *Timed($\mathcal{N}'$) and $\mathcal{N}_2$ are (untimed) bisimilar.*

Proof. A timed marking m of $\text{Timed}(\mathcal{N}')$ can be decomposed as $m = m_b \cup m_u$, where m_b is the restriction of m to bounded places, and m_u the restriction to unbounded places. Similarly, a marking of $\mathcal{N}_2$ can be decomposed as $m_2 = m_1 \cup m'_u$ by restriction to bounded and unbounded places respectively. From Lemma 5 and from the construction of $\mathcal{N}'$, we know that $\text{Timed}(\mathcal{N}_B)$ is bisimilar to $\mathcal{N}'$. Let $R_{B,1}$ be the unique largest bisimulation between timed markings of $\text{Timed}(\mathcal{N}_B)$ and markings of $\mathcal{N}'$.

We denote by R a relation from timed markings of $\text{Timed}(\mathcal{N})$ to markings of $\mathcal{N}_2$ defined as follows. Let $m = m_b \cup m_u$ be a marking of $\text{Timed}(\mathcal{N})$ and $m_2 = m_1 \cup m'_u$ be a marking of $\mathcal{N}_2$. Then, $(m, m_2) \in R$ iff $(m_b, m_1) \in R_{B,1}$, and $m'_u = m_u^{\sharp}$. Obviously, we have $(m_0, m_2^0) \in R$. We can now prove that R is a bisimulation.

Let $(m, m_2) \in R$. Assume that $m \xrightarrow{\delta} m+\delta \xrightarrow{t} m'$ in $\mathcal{N}$. Thus $m_b \xrightarrow{\delta} m_b+\delta \xrightarrow{t} m'_b$ in $\mathcal{N}_b$ with m'_b the bounded part of m'. Furthermore, $m_u^{\sharp} \geq {}^{\bullet}t \cap P_u$. Thus we have $m_1 \xrightarrow{t} m'_1$ in $\mathcal{N}_1$, and furthermore, $(m'_1, m'_b) \in R_{B,1}$. By definition of $\mathcal{N}_2$, firing t results in a flow of tokens among places of P_u that is identical (regardless of ages) in $\mathcal{N}$ and in $\mathcal{N}_2$, so we indeed have $m_1 \cup m_u^{\sharp} \xrightarrow{t} m'_1 \cup m'^{\sharp}_u$. Furthermore $m'^{\sharp}_u = m'_u$, so $(m', m'_1 \cup m'^{\sharp}_u) \in R$.

Conversely, assume that $m_2 \xrightarrow{t} m'_2$. We denote $m_2 = m_1 \cup m_3$ and $m'_2 = m'_1 \cup m'_3$ where m_3, m'_3 denote respectively the projections of m_2 and m'_2 on P_u. In particular, as t can fire, we have $m_1 \xrightarrow{t} m'_1$. So, there exists a reachable marking m'_b of $\text{Timed}(\mathcal{N}_B)$ such that $(m'_b, m'_1) \in R_{B,1}$ and there exists δ such that $m_b \xrightarrow{\delta} m_b+\delta \xrightarrow{t} m'_b$. In particular, δ does not violate any urgency constraints in the bounded part of the net.

Now, $\mathcal{N}'$ is a TPN with restricted constraints. This means that all urgency constraints are in the bounded part of $\mathcal{N}$. Hence, $m \xrightarrow{\delta} m + \delta$ does not violate any urgency constraints. Now, to show that R is a bisimulation, we want to show that $m + \delta \xrightarrow{t} m'$ is possible in $\mathcal{N}'$, for some m'_u with $m' = m'_b \cup m'_u$ and $(m'_u)^{\sharp} = m'_3$. To see this, we start by noting that, since $(m, m_2) \in R$, with $m_2 = m_1 \cup m_3$, we have $m^{\sharp}(p) = m_3(p) \geq 1$ for all $p \in P_u \cap {}^{\bullet}t$. Also, we have trivially that $m^{\sharp}(p) = m_b^{\sharp}(p) \geq 1$ for all $p \in P_B \cap {}^{\bullet}t$ as t is enabled from m_1, and $(m_b, m_1) \in R_{B,1}$. Thus t is enabled. Now, $m + \delta$ respects all the timings constraints of t: as $\mathcal{N}'$ is a TPN with restricted constraints, all constraints apply to the bounded part. Transition t is enabled from m_1, thus t can fire from $m + \delta$. For the unbounded part, firing of t can consume any token in places of $P_u \cap {}^{\bullet}t$ and we easily get $(m'_u)^{\sharp} = m'_3$. For the bounded part, we choose to consume the tokens consumed during the transition $m_b + \delta \xrightarrow{t} m'_b$. We thus obtain $m' = m'_b + m'_u$, and $(m', m'_2) \in R$. Hence R is a bisimulation relation. □

We can then conclude that the net $\mathcal{N}_2$, as constructed above, is bisimilar to $\text{Timed}(\mathcal{N}')$ and hence satisfies the properties required by the proposition. Thus, setting $\mathcal{N}_2$ to be the net $\mathcal{N}''$, we obtain the proof of Proposition 3. □

From Proposition 2, we have that for every TPN $\mathcal{N}$ with restricted urgency, one can build (Step 1) a TPN $\mathcal{N}'$ with restricted constraints that has the same set of reachable markings. Then Proposition 3 shows that one can design (Step 2) a Petri net that is bisimilar to $\mathcal{N}'$. As reachability is decidable for Petri nets, this allows to conclude the proof of Theorem 2.

5.1   Discussion

Let us now observe some salient points regarding the proof of Theorem 2 and in particular, how it relies on several features of the considered nets. First, the proof works only for nets with restricted urgency. If urgency is not restricted, one can easily model unbounded counters with places, and zeros tests with urgency, which yields undecidability of reachability, control-state reachability and boundedness. Second, Step 1 of the proof of Theorem 2 works only with a timed-arc semantics. The main idea in this step was to simulate clocks with gadgets as in Fig. 5, that need to be assembled to obtain nets with restricted constraints, which are equivalent (i.e., have the same set of behaviors). However, for TPNs under the intermediate semantics, assembling the gadgets leads to nets that are not equivalent.

Step 2 of the proof works for both the intermediate and the timed-arc semantics. Thus, starting from a TPN with restricted constraints, we get decidability of reachability for TPNs with intermediate semantics as stated in the following Theorem 3. However, as seen earlier, this class does not allow to model channels with latency constraints.

Theorem 3. *Let $\mathcal{N}$ be a TPN with restricted constraints. Then the reachability, boundedness and control-state reachability problems are decidable for $\mathcal{N}$.*

Proof (sketch). The proof of Theorem 3 is obtained by a simple adaptation of Proposition 3 from Sect. 5, which shows that for any TPN with restricted constraints $\mathcal{N}$, one can construct a Petri Net $\mathcal{N}'$ that is (untimed) bisimilar. □

Finally, our proof works only when the considered systems can be implemented with a bounded number of clocks (in order to get a bounded number of gadgets in the proof). This approach would not work for systems modeling channels with latency *and* unbounded throughput, which require nets with an unbounded number of clocks to be specified. Decidability of reachability for such classes is left open.

6   Conclusion

In this paper, we considered extensions of Timed-Arc Petri Nets and subclasses of TPNs to express urgency and latency constraints, while obtaining decidability results for unbounded systems. Decidability is obtained when urgency is used only in the bounded part of the system. This led us to consider a timed-arc semantics for general TPNs, defined via a Timed-Arc Petri Nets with Urgency. This new timed-arc semantics allows TPNs to model restricted forms of latency, namely, unbounded latency in a channel can be modeled when the throughput of

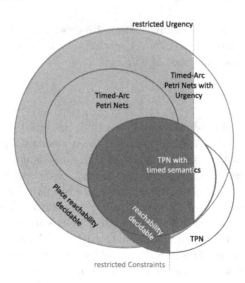

Fig. 6. Inclusion of classes of time/Timed-Arc Petri Nets with urgency w.r.t. timed bisimilarity.

this channel is bounded, as well as urgency requirements. Further, the new timed-arc semantics is also interesting as decidability of reachability can be proved for a class of TPNs larger with the timed-arc semantics than with the intermediate marking semantics. Table 1 in the Introduction summarizes the decidability results as well as expressiveness in terms of which (subclasses of) models allow latency and urgency. The *relative expressiveness* of classes (wrt timed bisimilarity) is summarized in Fig. 6, where we also emphasize their decidability status. While Timed-Arc Petri nets are contained in Timed-Arc Petri nets with restricted Urgency, Timed Arc Petri nets (with restricted Urgency) and TPNs are disjoint classes of models. For the entire subclass of Timed-Arc Petri nets with restricted Urgency, reachability is decidable. However, outside this class, i.e. without restriction on the use of urgency, control-state reachability and boundedness are undecidable. Further, with a timed-arc semantics, TPNs fall back into the class of Timed-Arcs PNs with Urgency. And by restricting urgency and under this timed-arc semantics, we obtain decidability of reachability. Further, as a subclass of Timed-Arcs PNs with restricted Urgency, control-state reachability and boundedness are decidable. Finally, the class of TPNs under their intermediate marking semantics does not enjoy decidability results. However, by restricting to the class of TPNs with restricted constraints, one gets decidability of reachability and control-state reachability. The decidability of reachability for TPNs with restricted urgency under intermediate marking semantics remains open.

As future work, we plan to study robustness properties, i.e., whether the system can withstand infinitesimal timing errors, as has been extensively studied for timed automata [10, 16, 23], etc. We would like to extend the study started for TPNs (e.g. [3]) to Timed-Arc Petri Nets with restricted Urgency.

Acknowledgments. We thank the anonymous reviewers for their helpful suggestions which led to significant improvements in the presentation of this article. This work was partially supported by Indo-French CEFIPRA project AVERTS, by DST-INSPIRE faculty award [IFA12-MA-17], and by the DISTOL associated team of INRIA.

References

1. Abdulla, P.A., Mahata, P., Mayr, R.: Dense-timed Petri nets: checking zenoness, token liveness and boundedness. J. Logical Methods Comput. Sci. **3**(1) (2007)
2. Abdulla, P.A., Nylén, A.: Timed Petri nets and BQOs. In: Colom, J.-M., Koutny, M. (eds.) ICATPN 2001. LNCS, vol. 2075, p. 53. Springer, Heidelberg (2001)
3. Akshay, S., Hélouët, L., Jard, C., Reynier, P.-A.: Robustness of time Petri nets under guard enlargement. In: Finkel, A., Leroux, J., Potapov, I. (eds.) RP 2012. LNCS, vol. 7550, pp. 92–106. Springer, Heidelberg (2012)
4. Bause, F., Kritzinger, P.S.: Stochastic Petri Nets - An Introduction to the Theory, 2nd edn. Vieweg (2002)
5. Bérard, B., Cassez, F., Haddad, S., Lime, D., Roux, O.H.: Comparison of different semantics for time Petri nets. In: Peled, D.A., Tsay, Y.-K. (eds.) ATVA 2005. LNCS, vol. 3707, pp. 293–307. Springer, Heidelberg (2005)
6. Bérard, B., Cassez, F., Haddad, S., Lime, D., Roux, O.H.: The expressive power of time Petri nets. TCS **474**, 1–20 (2013)
7. Berthomieu, B., Diaz, M.: Modeling and verification of time dependent systems using time Petri nets. IEEE Trans. Softw. Eng. **17**(3), 259–273 (1991)
8. Berthomieu, B., Peres, F., Vernadat, F.: Bridging the gap between timed automata and bounded time Petri nets. In: Asarin, E., Bouyer, P. (eds.) FORMATS 2006. LNCS, vol. 4202, pp. 82–97. Springer, Heidelberg (2006)
9. Boucheneb, H., Lime, D., Roux, O.H.: On multi-enabledness in time Petri nets. In: Colom, J.-M., Desel, J. (eds.) PETRI NETS 2013. LNCS, vol. 7927, pp. 130–149. Springer, Heidelberg (2013)
10. Bouyer, P., Markey, N., Sankur, O.: Robustness in timed automata. In: Abdulla, P.A., Potapov, I. (eds.) RP 2013. LNCS, vol. 8169, pp. 1–18. Springer, Heidelberg (2013)
11. Chatain, T., Jard, C.: Back in time Petri nets. In: Braberman, V., Fribourg, L. (eds.) FORMATS 2013. LNCS, vol. 8053, pp. 91–105. Springer, Heidelberg (2013)
12. Clemente, L., Herbreteau, F., Stainer, A., Sutre, G.: Reachability of communicating timed processes. In: Pfenning, F. (ed.) FOSSACS 2013 (ETAPS 2013). LNCS, vol. 7794, pp. 81–96. Springer, Heidelberg (2013)
13. Clemente, L., Herbreteau, F., Sutre, G.: Decidable topologies for communicating automata with FIFO and bag channels. In: Baldan, P., Gorla, D. (eds.) CONCUR 2014. LNCS, vol. 8704, pp. 281–296. Springer, Heidelberg (2014)
14. D'Aprile, D., Donatelli, S., Sangnier, A., Sproston, J.: From time Petri nets to timed automata: an untimed approach. In: Grumberg, O., Huth, M. (eds.) TACAS 2007. LNCS, vol. 4424, pp. 216–230. Springer, Heidelberg (2007)
15. David, A., Jacobsen, L., Jacobsen, M., Srba, J.: A forward reachability algorithm for bounded timed-arc Petri nets. In: SSV 2012, EPTCS, vol. 102, pp. 125–140 (2012)

16. De Wulf, M., Doyen, L., Markey, N., Raskin, J.-F.: Robust safety of timed automata. Formal Methods Syst. Des. **33**(1–3), 45–84 (2008)
17. Finkel, A., Schnoebelen, P.: Well-structured transition systems everywhere!. TCS **256**(1–2), 63–92 (2001)
18. Haddad, S.: Time and timed Petri nets. In: Disc Ph.D. School 2011 (2011). http://www.lsv.ens-cachan.fr/~haddad/disc11-part1.pdf
19. Jacobsen, L., Jacobsen, M., Møller, M.H., Srba, J.: Verification of timed-arc Petri nets. In: Černá, I., Gyimóthy, T., Hromkovič, J., Jefferey, K., Královič, R., Vukolić, M., Wolf, S. (eds.) SOFSEM 2011. LNCS, vol. 6543, pp. 46–72. Springer, Heidelberg (2011)
20. Jones, N.D., Landweber, L.H., Lien, Y.E.: Complexity of some problems in Petri nets. Theor. Comput. Sci. **4**(3), 277–299 (1977)
21. Mateo, J.A., Srba, J., Sørensen, M.G.: Soundness of timed-arc workflow nets. In: Ciardo, G., Kindler, E. (eds.) PETRI NETS 2014. LNCS, vol. 8489, pp. 51–70. Springer, Heidelberg (2014)
22. Merlin, P.M.: A study of the recoverability of computing systems. Ph.D. thesis, University of California, Irvine, CA, USA (1974)
23. Puri, A.: Dynamical properties of timed automata. DEDS **10**(1–2), 87–113 (2000)
24. Reynier, P.-A., Sangnier, A.: Weak time Petri nets strike back!. In: Bravetti, M., Zavattaro, G. (eds.) CONCUR 2009. LNCS, vol. 5710, pp. 557–571. Springer, Heidelberg (2009)
25. Ruiz, V.V., Gomez, F.C., de Frutos-Escrig, D.: On non-decidability of reachability for timed-arc Petri nets. In: PNPM, pp. 188–196. IEEE Computer Society (1999)
26. Walter, B.: Timed Petri-nets for modelling and analysing protocols with real-time characteristics. In: Proceedings of PSTV, pp. 149–159 (1983)

Structural Methods

Structural Place Invariants for Analyzing the Behavioral Properties of Nested Petri Nets

Leonid W. Dworzanski and Irina A. Lomazova$^{(\boxtimes)}$

National Research University Higher School of Economics,
Myasnitskaya ul. 20, 101000 Moscow, Russia
leo@mathtech.ru, ilomazova@hse.ru

Abstract. Nested Petri nets (NP-nets) is an extension of the Petri nets formalism within the "nets-within-nets" approach. Due to tokens with individual behavior and the mechanism of synchronization NP-nets are convenient for modeling multi-agent and adaptive systems, flexible workflow nets, and other systems with mobile interacting components and dynamic structure.

In contrast to classical Petri nets, there is still a lack of analysis methods for NP-nets. In this paper we show, that the classical Petri nets analysis technique based on place invariants can be extended to NP-nets. This paper defines place invariants of NP-nets, which link several NP-net components and allow to prove crucial behavioral properties directly from the NP-net structure. An algorithm for computing NP-net invariants is presented and illustrated with an example of EJB system verification.

Keywords: Nested Petri nets · Place invariants · Behavioral properties · Structural analysis methods

1 Introduction

Nested Petri nets (NP-nets) [18] is an extension of high-level Petri nets according to the "nets-within-nets" approach. Nets within nets are extensively studied in the Petri net literature, as a formalism for modeling active objects, mobility and dynamics in distributed systems [1, 11, 15, 26].

NP-nets is a convenient formalism for modeling systems of dynamic interacting agents: an agent is represented by a net token, while agents are distributed in a system net. Levels in NP-nets are coordinated via synchronized transitions (simultaneous firing of transitions in adjacent levels of the model). Because of a loosely-coupled multilevel structure, NP-nets can be used for effective modeling of adaptive distributed systems [9, 10, 17, 19, 25], systems of mobile robots [22], sensor networks of mobile agents [3], innovative space systems architecture [4], productive and reconfigurable manufacturing systems [14, 23, 28]. To make this

This work is supported by the Basic Research Program of the National Research University Higher School of Economics and Russian Foundation for Basic Research, project No. 16-37-00482 mol_a.

© Springer International Publishing Switzerland 2016
F. Kordon and D. Moldt (Eds.): PETRI NETS 2016, LNCS 9698, pp. 325–344, 2016.
DOI: 10.1007/978-3-319-39086-4_19

formalism not only convenient for modeling and simulation, but applicable for securing correctness of complex systems, analysis methods should be developed.

In contrast with classical Petri nets, there is still lack of analysis methods for NP-nets, though some efforts were done in this direction. In the work [6] the approach to checking properties of NP-nets by translating them into colored Petri nets was developed. The practical value of the translation is determined by the comprehensive tool support for analysis of colored Petri nets. In [27] a verification method based on translating recursive nested Petri nets into PROMELA language and applying SPIN model checker is described. The compositional approach to inferring liveness and boundedness of NP-nets from liveness and boundedness of NP-nets separate components was introduced in [7].

One of the essential tools to analyze Petri nets behavior is based on place invariants (P-invariants), i.e. the properties of a Petri net that are invariant under transitions firings. Such invariant properties are crucial for reasoning about different behavioral properties of Petri nets such as boundedness, deadlock-freeness, reachability, and domain specific properties. First definitions of invariants were introduced for the standard interpretations of Petri nets — place/transition-nets (P/T-nets) [16], predicate/transition-nets (Pr/T-nets) [8], colored Petri nets [12]. In the last of these works the organization scheme of a duplicate database system was modeled with Pr/T-nets and colored Petri nets and several crucial for correctness properties were proven using invariant analysis.

As for NP-nets, a bounded NP-net can be translated into a classical Petri net (P/T-net) with the same behavior. So we can apply place invariant technique for classical Petri nets to find invariants of NP-nets. But the size of the obtained P/T-net can be exponentially larger than the size of the NP-net. If the original NP-net is unbounded, then such reduction is just impossible, since it has been proven [21] that NP-nets are strictly more expressive than P/T-nets. This determines the need for new analysis means that exploit the structure of NP-nets instead of reducing them to P/T-nets.

Classical place invariants for separate NP-net components (a system net, net tokens) can be used for deducing properties describing their autonomous behavior, but for properties concerning coordinated behavior of the whole system we need a new definition of place invariants, as well as a new method for computing these invariants, and heuristics for deducing meaningful properties from them.

In classical Petri nets invariants assign weights to places. For NP-nets we need a more complex framework of weights. In the definition we propose each place in a system net gets two weights: a weight for token counting and a weight for net token markings. For net tokens a weight is ascribed to a pair of places: a place in a net token and a place in the system net, in which it is located. Due to this the invariants capture the relationship between the components.

In this paper we introduce a definition of NP-nets place invariants, an algorithm to compute them, and give an example of using invariants for inferring a crucial property of system behavior.

2 Motivating Example

Enterprise JavaBeans (EJB) is a widely used powerful framework that address the concerns of persistence, transaction integrity, object-relation mapping, inter-process communication in distributed systems. EJB technology allows to build complex multi-agent systems, where agents are represented as enterprise beans In this section we model an EJB system with nested Petri nets formalism.

The modeled system is a multi-agent financial forecasting system (Fig. 4), i.e. it is a set of agents making financial forecasts at client's requests. The agents collect and analyze data relevant to the client request, update values of corresponding financial indices, and provide a final forecast to the client. Agents obtain domain specific data from a huge database of analytical information. Indices are updated by requests to the external index service. There are three kinds of agents — forecasters, data agents, and index update agents. Their behavior is modeled by the element nets E_1, E_2, E_3 respectively (Figs. 1, 2 and 3). For brevity, by $N{:}pl$ ($N{:}\mathbf{tr}$) we will denote the place pl (the transition $\mathbf{tr}$) of the net N.

Forecasting agents (tokens of type E_1) are the main agents of the forecasting system. In the initial state they residue in the forecasting agents pool ($SN{:}forecasters$). The agents are waiting ($E_1{:}waiting$) for client requests ($SN{:}requests$). When client requests evolve ($SN{:}\mathbf{client\ req}$), they are placed into the requests pool ($SN{:}requests$). If there are available agents in the agents pool then the system allocates ($SN{:}\mathbf{allocate}$) an agent to serve a request.

Data mining that precedes forecasting usually demands processing huge amounts of data. The database with the comprehensive collection of analytical data is stored on a dedicated server ($SN{:}DB\ server, SN{:}DB\ agents, SN{:}DB\ querying, SN{:}DB\ data\ retrieved$). The allocated agent ($SN{:}allocated\ agents$) moves ($SN{:}\mathbf{move\ to\ DB}$) to the database server ($SN{:}DB\ server$). The internal state of the forecasting agent (E_1) changes correspondingly (from $E_1{:}allocated$ to $E_1{:}DB\ server$ by $E_1{:}\mathbf{move\ to\ DB}$). Since large data queries are served locally on the dedicated DB server, the net traffic and time for data mining are reduced. When a forecasting agent reaches the $DB\ server$, it requests ($E_1{:}\mathbf{query\ DB}$ $\mathbf{agent}$) data by making a local call ($SN{:}\mathbf{local\ call}$) to a database agent (DB agent). DB agents take care of database routine procedures. They are modeled roughly, since we focus on the forecasting agents behavior. In the initial state DB agents are located in the pool for DB agents ($SN{:}DB\ agents$). When a forecasting agent requests data, the DB agent responding to the request ($E_2{:}\mathbf{request}$) starts querying the underlying database ($SN{:}DB\ querying, E_2{:}querying$). When the database has returned the information ($E_2{:}\mathbf{DB\ return}, SN{:}retrieve$) a DB agent sends the result ($E_2{:}result$) to the forecasting agent ($SN{:}\mathbf{local\ ret}$, $E_2{:}\mathbf{transfer}$) that retrieves and analyzes data ($E_1{:}\mathbf{retrieve\ data}$). After that, the database agent moves to the initial pool and waits for other requests.

Then, the forecasting agent starts to update financial indices ($E_1{:}updating$ $indices$), that are needed for precise forecasting. The indices are updated by sending asynchronous requests to index agents ($SN{:}index\ agents$). The agent has three different financial indices. Each index can be in the up-to-date state ($E_1{:}up\text{-}to\text{-}date_1, E_1{:}up\text{-}to\text{-}date_2, E_1{:}up\text{-}to\text{-}date_3$) or outdated ($E_1{:}outdated_1,$

E_1:*outdated$_2$*, E_1:*outdated$_3$*). The agent's value of index can become out of date (E_1:**outdate$_1$**, E_1:**outdate$_2$**, E_1:**outdate$_3$**), when the agent is waiting in the pool (*SN*:forecasters, *SN*:**outdate**). While the second and the third indices are free and public, the first requires a paid subscription to the financial index web services. The index service provider provides license tokens for the fixed number of simultaneous requests. The system keeps license tokens in a license tokens pool (*SN*:*license tokens*). To start indices update the agent gets a license token (*SN*:**get license**, E_1:**get license**) or skips the step (*SN*:**license not needed**, E_1:**license not needed**), if the first index value is up-to-date.

When the agent has obtained a license token (E_1:*license obtained*), it puts an asynchronous request (*SN*:**req$_{1-3}$**, E_1:**req$_{1-3}$**) for each outdated index to the input queues (*SN*:*queue$_{1-3}$*) of index agents (*SN*:*index agents*). In the initial state index agents are waiting (E_3:*waiting*) for index requests. An index agent receives requests (*SN*:**recv$_{1-3}$**, E_3:**recv$_{1-3}$**) from the system queues (*SN*:*queue$_{1-3}$*) and passes them to its internal buffers (E_3:*buffer$_{1-3}$*). When there is a request in an internal buffer, the index agent starts to proceed (E_3:**proceed$_{1-3}$**) the request. The agent queries (E_3:*WS querying$_{1-3}$*) external web-services that provide financial indices. The returned (E_3:**return$_{1-3}$**) index value is stored in the output buffers (E_3:*index$_{1-3}$*). From the output buffers the index value is sent (E_3:**send$_{1-3}$**, *SN*:**send$_{1-3}$**) to the corresponding system queue (*SN*:*result$_{1-3}$*). The forecasting agent updates its internal index values (*SN*:**upd$_{1-3}$**, E_1:**upd$_{1-3}$**) from the result queues. For the first index the procedure is a bit different. The license tokens are paid resources. Since only three simultaneous requests can be issued, they form the bottleneck of the system. The forecasting agent should release the license token (*SN*:**put license**, E_1:**release license**) immediately after receiving an answer (E_1:**received$_1$**) from an index agent. When all indices are in the up-to-date states, the agent moves directly (*SN*:**updated**, E_1:**updated**) to the forecasting phase (*SN*:*forecasting agents*, E_1:*forecasting*). After the forecast is completed, (E_1:*transferring*) the transferring of results starts. When the results are transferred (*SN*:**send result**, E_1:**transferred**) to the client, the agent returns back to the initial pool and waits for another client request.

The agents represent major types of EJB components — stateless (DB agents), stateful (forecasting agents), and message-driven beans (index agents). The described model is an example of modeling enterprise software architecture concepts by means of NP-nets. The system behavior should possess some good properties, such as deadlock freeness, boundedness, reversibility, etc. Otherwise we need to fix the system and rebuild the model. For our example one of such behavioral properties is the restriction on the number of simultaneous requests sent to the subscribed index service. It is a crucial property, since violation of the agreement with the service provider may lead to extra charges or to the abrogation of the contract. The important aspect here is that this property concerns different levels of the system. Initially a license token resides in the system net in *SN*:*license tokens* pool. A forecaster agent removes the license token from the pool and puts it into the internal place *license obtained*. Then the license token is passed back and forth to an index agent through the system net *queue*, and returned back to the pool.

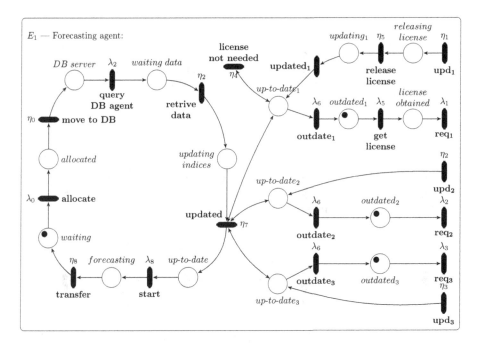

Fig. 1. The element net of a forecasting agent.

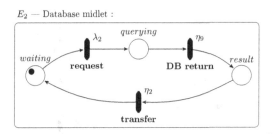

Fig. 2. The element net of a DB agent.

So, the invariant for proving the preservation of license tokens should involve the system net, forecaster and index agent elementary nets. Another important aspect is that these license tokens should be used efficiently. So we have to prove that forecasters do not leave dangling requests and return license tokens to the license pool as soon as possible. Another quite different important characteristic of the system is the ratio of the number of forecasters to the number of database agents querying the database. This characteristic helps to predict the number of needed database agents and the load of the database. These and some other properties can be proven by NP-nets invariants. In the Sect. 6 we show how NP-net invariants can be used for proving such properties.

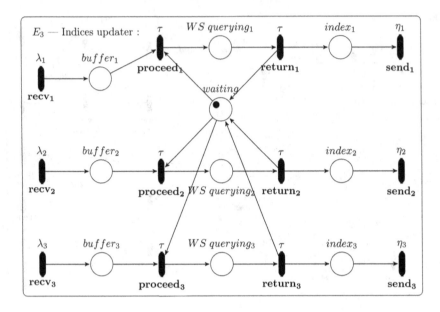

Fig. 3. The element net of an index updating agent.

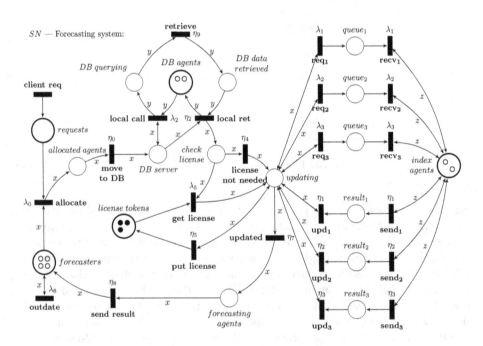

Fig. 4. The forecasting system: the system net SN.

3   Preliminaries

By $\mathbb{N}$ we denote the set of natural numbers including zero. For a set S, a *bag (multiset)* m over S is a mapping $m : S \to \mathbb{N}$. The set of all bags over S is also denoted by $\mathbb{N}^S$. We use $+$ and $-$ for the sum and the difference of two bags, $\|m\|$ for the number of all elements in m taking into account the multiplicity, and $=, <, >, \leq, \geq$ for comparisons of bags, which are defined in the standard way. We overload the set notation writing $\emptyset$ for the empty bag and $\in$ for the element inclusion.

Petri nets is a well-known formalism for concurrent systems modeling. In this section we give the definition of colored Petri nets (CP-nets) parameterized with a value universe U. We slightly adapted the classical definition of colored Petri nets [13] by addition of transition labels. As well a colored function for places is defined using the notion of types, and a colored function for transitions is defined using expressions over the simple additive language *Expr*. So, each place is mapped to a type, which is a subset of U. We assume a language *Expr* for arcs expressions over a set *Var* of variables and a set *Con* of constants with some fixed interpretation $\mathcal{I}$, such that for any type-consistent evaluation $\nu : Var \to U$ the value $\mathcal{I}(e, \nu) \in \mathbb{N}^U$ of an expression $e \in Expr$ is defined. We also assume a set *Lab* of labels for transitions such that $\tau \notin Lab$. The label τ is the special "silent" label, while labels from *Lab* mark externally observable firings.

Definition 1 (Colored Petri net). *A* colored net *over the universe U is a 6-tuple $(P, T, F, \upsilon, \gamma, \Lambda)$, where*

- P *and T are disjoint finite sets of* places, *respectively* transitions;
- $F \subseteq (P \times T) \cup (T \times P)$ *is a set of* arcs;
- $\upsilon : P \to 2^U$ *is a place typing* function, *mapping P to the subsets of U;*
- $\gamma : F \to Expr$ *is an arc labelling* function;
- $\Lambda : T \to Lab \cup \{\tau\}$ *is a transition labelling* function.

For an element $x \in P \cup T$ an arc (y, x) is called an *input* arc, and an arc (x, y) an *output* arc; a *preset* $^\bullet x$ and a *postset* $x^\bullet$ are subsets of $P \cup T$ such that $^\bullet x = \{y | (y, x) \in F\}$ and $x^\bullet = \{y | (x, y) \in F\}$. Given a CP-net $N = (P, T, F, \upsilon, \gamma, \Lambda)$ over the universe U, a *marking* in N is a function $m : P \to \mathbb{N}^U$, s.t. $m(p) \in \mathbb{N}^{\upsilon(p)}$ for $p \in P$. A pair $\langle N, m \rangle$ of a CP-net and a marking is called a *marked net*.

Let $N = (P, T, F, \upsilon, \gamma, \Lambda)$ be a CP-net. A transition $t \in T$ is *enabled* in a marking m iff $\exists \nu \forall p \in P : (p, t) \in F \Rightarrow m(p) \geq \mathcal{I}(\gamma(p, t), \nu)$. Here $\nu : Var \to U$ is a variable evaluation, called also a *binding*. An enabled transition t may *fire* yielding a new marking $m'(p) = m(p) - \mathcal{I}(\gamma(p, t), \nu) + \mathcal{I}(\gamma(t, p), \nu)$ for each $p \in P$ (denoted $m \xrightarrow{t} m'$). The set of all markings reachable from a marking m (via a sequence of firings) is denoted by $\mathcal{R}(m)$.

As usual, a marked colored net defines a transition system which represents the observable behavior of the net.

4   Nested Petri Nets

In this section we give the definition of *nested Petri nets (NP-nets)*.

Nested Petri nets (NP-nets) are colored Petri nets over a special universe [18,19]. This universe consists of elements of some finite set S (called atomic tokens) and marked Petri nets (called net tokens). For simplicity we consider here only two-level NP-nets, where net tokens are classical place-transition nets.

Let S be a finite set of atomic objects. For a colored PN N by $\mathcal{M}(N, S)$ we denote the set of all marked nets, obtained from N by adding markings over the universe S. Let then $N_1, \ldots, N_k$ be colored PNs over the universe S. Define a universe $\mathcal{U}(N_1, \ldots, N_k) = S \cup \mathcal{M}(N_1, S) \cup \cdots \cup \mathcal{M}(N_k, S)$ with types $S, \mathcal{M}(N_1, S), \ldots, \mathcal{M}(N_k, S)$. We denote $\Omega(N_1, \ldots, N_k) = \{S, \mathcal{M}(N_1, S), \ldots, \mathcal{M}(N_k, S)\}$. By abuse of notation we say, that a place p with a type $\mathcal{M}(N, S)$ is typed by N.

Definition 2 (Nested Petri net). *Let Lab be a set of transition labels and let* $N_1, \ldots, N_k$ *be colored PNs over the universe S, where all transitions are labeled with labels from $Lab \cup \{\tau\}$.*

An NP-net is a tuple $NP = \langle N_1, \ldots, N_k, SN \rangle$, *where* $N_1, \ldots, N_k$ *are called element nets, and SN is called a system net. A system net* $SN = \langle P_{SN}, T_{SN}, F_{SN}, \upsilon, \gamma, \Lambda \rangle$ *is a colored PN over the universe* $\mathcal{U} = \mathcal{U}(N_1, \ldots, N_k)$, *where places are typed by elements of* $\Omega = \Omega(N_1, \ldots, N_k)$, *transition labels are from $Lab \cup \{\tau\}$, and an arc expression language Expr is defined as follows.*

Let Con be a set of constants interpreted over $\mathcal{U}$ and Var – a set of variables, typed with Ω-types. Then an expression in Expr is a multiset of elements over $Con \cup Var$ of the same type with two additional restrictions for each transition $t \in T_{SN}$:

1. *constants or multiple instances of the same variable are not allowed in input arc expressions of t;*
2. *each variable in an output arc expression for t occurs in one of the input arc expressions of t.*

Note that removing the first restriction on system net arc expressions makes NP-nets Turing-powerful [18], since without this restriction there would be a possibility to check, whether inner markings of two tokens in a current marking are equal, and hence to make a zero-test. The second restriction excludes infinite branching in a transition system, representing a behavior of an NP-net.

The interpretation of constants from *Con* is extended to the interpretation $\mathcal{I}$ of expressions under a given binding of variables in the standard way.

We call a marked element net a net token, and an element from S an atomic token. A marking in an NP-net is defined as a marking in its system net. So, a marking $m : P_{SN} \rightarrow \mathbb{N}^{\mathcal{U}}$ in an NP-net maps each place in its system net to a multiset of atomic tokens or net tokens of appropriate type.

A behavior of an NP-net is composed of three kinds of steps (firings). An *element-autonomous step* is the firing of a transition t, labeled with τ, in one of the net tokens of the current marking according to the usual firing rule for colored

Petri nets. Formally, let m be a marking in an NP-net NP, $\alpha = (N, \mu) \in m(p)$ — a net token residing in the place $p \in P_{SN}$ in m. Let also t be enabled in α and $\mu \xrightarrow{t} \mu'$ in α. Then the element-autonomous step $s = \{t[\alpha]\}$ is enabled in m and the result of s-firing is the new marking m', s.t. for all $p' \in P_{SN} \setminus p$: $m'(p') = m(p')$, and $m'(p) = m(p) - \alpha + (N, \mu')$. Note, that such a step changes only the inner marking in one of the net tokens.

A *system-autonomous step* is the firing of a transition $t \in T_{SN}$, labeled with τ, in the system net according to the firing rule for colored Petri nets, as if net tokens were just colored tokens without an inner marking. Formally, the system-autonomous step $s = \{t\}$ is enabled in a marking m iff there exists a binding $\nu : Var \rightarrow \mathcal{U}$, such that $\forall p \in P_{SN} : (p, t) \in F_{SN} \Rightarrow m(p) \geq \mathcal{I}(\gamma(p, t), \nu)$.

The result of s-firing is the new marking $m'(p) = m(p) - \mathcal{I}(\gamma(p, t), \nu) + \mathcal{I}(\gamma(t, p), \nu)$ for each $p \in P_{SN}$ (denoted $m \xrightarrow{s} m'$).

An autonomous step in a system net can move, copy, generate, or remove tokens involved in the step, but doesn't change their inner markings.

A *(vertical) synchronization step* is the simultaneous firing of a transition $t \in T_{SN}$, labeled with some $\lambda \in Lab$, in the system net together with firings of transitions $t_1, \ldots, t_q$ ($q \geq 1$) also labeled with λ, in all net tokens involved in (i.e. consumed by) this system net transition firing.

Formally, let m be a marking in an NP-net NP, a transition $t \in T_{SN}$ be labeled with λ and enabled in m via binding ν as a system-autonomous step. We say that a net token α is involved in t-firing via binding ν iff $\alpha \in \mathcal{I}(\gamma(p, t), \nu)$ for some $p \in {}^{\bullet}t$. Let then $\alpha_1 = (N_{i1}, \mu_1), \ldots, \alpha_q = (N_{iq}, \mu_q)$ be all net tokens involved in the firing of t via binding ν, and for each $1 \leq j \leq q$ there is a transition t_j, labeled with λ in N_{ij}, such that t_j is enabled in μ_j, and $\mu_j \xrightarrow{t_j} \mu'_j$ in N_{ij}. Then the synchronization step $s = \{t, t_1[\alpha_1], \ldots, t_q[\alpha_q]\}$ is enabled in m for NP, and the result of s-firing is the new marking m' defined as follows. For each $p \in P_{SN}$: $m'(p) = m(p) - \mathcal{I}(\gamma(p, t), \nu) + \mathcal{I}(\gamma(t, p), \nu')$, where for a variable x: $\nu(x) = (N, \mu)$ implies $\nu'(x) = (N, \mu')$.

Figure 5 gives an example of a synchronization step. The left part of this picture shows a marked fragment of a system net. Here a transition t has two input places p_1 and p_2, and two output places p_3 and p_4. In the current marking the place p_1 contains three net tokens, two of them, α_1 and α_3, are explicitly depicted. The place p_2 contains two net tokens, the structure and the marking of one of them are shown in the picture. Only the synchronization step is allowed here, since all transitions are labeled with the synchronization label λ. A possible binding of variables x, y, z in the input arc expressions is $x = \alpha_1, y = \alpha_2$ and $z = \alpha_3$. Then the transitions t in the system net, t_1 in α_1, t_1 in α_3, and t_2 in α_2 fire simultaneously. The resulting marking m' is shown on the right side of the picture. According to the output arc expressions after t-firing two copies of α_1 appear in p_3, the net token α_3 disappears, α_2 with a new marking is transported into the place p_4, and a new net token α_c appears in p_4 being a value of the net constant c.

A transition labeled with $\lambda \in Lab$ in a system net consumes net tokens with enabled transitions labeled with λ. To exclude obviously dead transitions we add

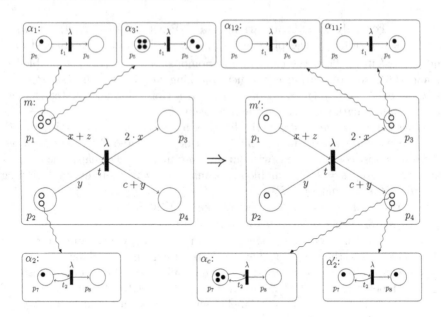

Fig. 5. An example of a synchronization step.

to our definition of NP-nets the following syntactical restriction: for each system net transition t labeled with $\lambda \neq \tau$, and for each $p \in {}^\bullet t$, p is typed by an element net with at least one transition labeled with λ.

Thus a step is a set of transitions (a one-element set in the case of an autonomous step). We write $m \xrightarrow{s} m'$ for a step s converting the marking m into the marking m'. By $Steps(NP)$ we denote the set of all (potential) steps in NP.

A run in an NP-net NP is a sequence $\rho = m_0 \xrightarrow{s_1} m_1 \xrightarrow{s_2} \ldots$, where $m_0, m_1, \ldots$ are markings, m_0 is an initial marking, and $s_1, s_2, \ldots$ are steps in NP. For a sequence of steps $\sigma = s_1, \ldots s_n$ we write $m \xrightarrow{\sigma} m'$, and say that m' is reachable from m, if $m = m_0 \xrightarrow{s_1} m_1 \ldots \xrightarrow{s_n} m_n = m'$. By $\mathcal{R}(NP, m)$ we denote the set of all markings reachable from m in NP, and by abuse of notations we write $\mathcal{R}(NP)$ for the set of all markings reachable in NP from its initial marking.

Note that net tokens of the same type (i.e., with the same net structure) are not distinguished in a system net autonomous firing. This follows from the first input arc expressions restriction for NP-nets, which eliminates comparing inner markings of net tokens. Moreover, since all tokens in a system net place are of the same type, enabledness of an autonomous transition in a system net depends only on the numbers of tokens in its input places, and a system net considered as a separate component is actually similar to a p/t-net.

For further details on NP-nets see [18,20]. Note, however, that here we consider a typed variant of NP-nets, where a type is instantiated to each place.

5   Place Invariants of Nested Petri Nets

Invariant analysis is considered as one of the very basic analysis tools for different kinds of Petri nets. Invariants were introduced for place/transition-nets (P/T-nets) as linear weight functions on P/T-nets markings [16]. The values of such functions are invariant under marking transformations induced by transitions firings. Later on invariants were generalized to predicate/transition-nets (Pr/T-nets) [8]. This required substituting integer weights with integer polynomials over tokens values to capture invariants of Pr/T-nets with individual tokens. In [12] it was suggested to use linear functions over set of colors as invariant functions for colored Petri nets.

To define the invariant weight function for an NP-net we take into account its structure. Element nets are classical Petri nets with transitions labeled by synchronization labels. An element-autonomous step produces a new net token marking according to the classical Petri net firing rules, but the effect of this firing for the behavior of the whole system may depend on the system net place, in which the net token resides. So, for an element net $\langle P_N, T_N, F_N \rangle$ residing in the place p in the system net we define a weight function $\mathcal{W}(p)$ just as for a classical Petri nets [16]:

$$\mathcal{W}(p) : P_N \to \mathbb{Z}$$

A system net in an NP-net should be treated in a different way, since we are to take into account net tokens markings. Hence, for each place we introduce two weights: w_t and w_m, where w_t is the weight of black tokens or net tokens without taking into account their internal markings, and w_m is the coefficient for a net token internal marking weight. Thus the presence and the internal marking of a net token are weighed with different coefficients. The overall weight function for an NP-net is defined as follows:

Definition 3 (NP-net weight function). *Let $NP = \langle N_1, \ldots, N_k, SN \rangle$ be an NP-net. Let $w_t : P_{SN} \to \mathbb{Z}$ and $w_m : P_{SN} \to \mathbb{Z}$ be weight functions that take each system net place $p \in P_{SN}$ to an integer number.*

To each place $p \in P_{SN}$ typed with the element net $N = \langle P_N, T_N, F_N \rangle$, the function $\mathcal{W}$ assigns a weight function that maps P_N into $\mathbb{Z}$. Let $\widehat{\mathcal{W}}(p) : \mathcal{M}(N) \to \mathbb{Z}$ be the linear extension of $\mathcal{W}(p)$ to the markings of N defined in the standard way

$$\forall \mu \in \mathcal{M}(N) : \widehat{\mathcal{W}}(p)(\mu) = \sum_{q \in P_N} \mu(q) \cdot \mathcal{W}(p)(q)$$

The weight function of NP is

$$W(m) = \sum_{p \in P_{SN}} \left(\|m(p)\| \cdot w_t(p) + \sum_{\alpha \in m(p)} w_m(p) \cdot \widehat{\mathcal{W}}(p)(\mu_\alpha) \right) \qquad (1)$$

where μ_α is the internal marking of the net token α.

An NP-net weight function W is parameterized by the functions w_t, w_m, and $\mathcal{W}$. A weight function W is an invariant for an NP-net iff the value of W is not changed by any transition firing (any step). So, to define invariants for NP-nets we consider all three kinds of NP-net steps and infer constraints that guarantee the invariance of W under NP-net steps.

Let $NP = \langle N_1, \ldots, N_k, SN, m_0 \rangle$ be an NP-net. An element autonomous step $\{t\}$ consists of a single transition t in a net-token $\alpha = (N, \mu)$ from a system net place p_{SN}. While firing $m_0 \xrightarrow{t} m$, the transition t consumes $\gamma(p, t)$ tokens from each $p \in {}^\bullet t$ and produces $\gamma(t, p)$ tokens into each $p \in t^\bullet$. The difference between the weighted sums $W(m_0)$ and $W(m)$ consists of the changed elements that correspond to these tokens. As the net token α wasn't moved to another system place, $W(m_0)$ and $W(m)$ differ only in the part $w_m(p_{SN})\widehat{\mathcal{W}}(p_{SN})(\mu_\alpha)$ of (1). By canceling $w_m(p_{SN})$ we obtain the next equation:

$$\sum_{p \in {}^\bullet t} \widehat{\mathcal{W}}(p_{SN})(p) \cdot \gamma(p, t) = \sum_{p \in t^\bullet} \widehat{\mathcal{W}}(p_{SN})(p) \cdot \gamma(t, p) \tag{2}$$

The left part of this equation corresponds to the consumed tokens, the right part to the produced tokens. The equation represents the equality of the weight subtracted from and added to the overall weight $W(m_0)$. The residue part of $W(m_0)$ is not affected; hence, the equation ensures the invariance of W relative to the element autonomous step firing.

A system autonomous step consists of a single system net transition t_{SN}. The transition t_{SN} consumes $\gamma(p, t_{SN})$ black or net tokens from each $p \in {}^\bullet t_{SN}$ and produces $\gamma(t_{SN}, p)$ black tokens, net tokens, or net constants to each $p \in t_{SN}^\bullet$. Let us consider the internal weights of consumed and produced net tokens. System autonomous step produces net tokens in output places by cloning net tokens with their internal markings consumed from the input places with respect to the arc inscriptions variables. The internal weight of a net token consumed by the variable x on an input arc of t_{SN} can be compensated only by the weight of net tokens produced by entries of x on output arcs of t_{SN}. This becomes clear if we consider the step $\{t\}$ in the Fig. 5 and assume that t is labeled by τ and the variables z, y are assigned to zero marked net tokens. Then the internal weight of the consumed net token bound to x can be compensated only by the sum of internal weights of two net tokens produced by two x entries in the arc $\langle t, p_3 \rangle$ expression. Moreover, the sum elements corresponding to different internal places of the net tokens are linearly independent. If we suppose that the marking of a consumed net token α with all empty places except a fixed place p, and the markings of net tokens produced by x entries are the same as the marking of α (i.e. all places except p are empty), then the weight of tokens in the place p of α can be compensated only by the weight of the tokens in the place p of the produced net tokens. So, for each variable x on the input arc $\langle p_{SN}, t_{SN} \rangle$ and for each place p of the x's element net it should be:

$$w_m(p_{SN}) \cdot \mathcal{W}(p_{SN})(p) = \sum_{q \in t_{SN}^\bullet} w_m(q) \cdot \|\gamma(\langle t_{SN}, q \rangle)\|_x \cdot \mathcal{W}(q)(p), \tag{3}$$

where $\|\gamma(\langle t_{SN}, q\rangle)\|_x$ is the number of x entries in the expression $\gamma(\langle t_{SN}, q\rangle)$. The sum elements with w_t coefficients of the weight function W do not depend on the internal markings of the consumed tokens. The weight of a net constant on an outgoing arc of t_{SN} does depend on its own internal marking, but has the same value for each firing and doesn't depend on the internal marking of any consumed net token. To ensure the invariance of the weight of the elements that do not depend on the internal markings of the consumed tokens, we obtain the next equation:

$$\sum_{p \in \bullet t_{SN}} w_t(p) \cdot \|\gamma(\langle p, t_{SN}\rangle)\|$$

$$= \sum_{p \in t_{SN}\bullet} \left(w_t(p) \cdot \|\gamma(\langle t_{SN}, p\rangle)\| + w_m(p) \cdot \sum_{c \in Con(\langle t_{SN}, p\rangle)} \widehat{W}(p)(c) \right), \tag{4}$$

where $\|\gamma(\langle p, t_{SN}\rangle)\|$ is the overall number of all variables and constants entries in the expression $\gamma(\langle p, t_{SN}\rangle)$.

Vertical synchronization step $s = \{t_{SN}, t_1[\alpha_1], \ldots, t_q[\alpha_q]\}$ consists of a system net transition t_{SN} and the transitions $t_1, \ldots, t_q$ of consumed net tokens $\alpha_1, \ldots, \alpha_q$. We start from the internal weights of the consumed net tokens places. Due to the same argument as for a system autonomous step, we have the same equation for the weights of consumed and produced net tokens places; for each variable x on the input arc $\langle p_{SN}, t_{SN}\rangle$ and for each place p of the x's element net:

$$w_m(p_{SN}) \cdot W(p_{SN})(p) = \sum_{q \in t_{SN}\bullet} w_m(q) \cdot \|\gamma(\langle t_{SN}, q\rangle)\|_x \cdot W(q)(p) \tag{5}$$

The case of other weights is more interesting. The number of tokens consumed from an internal place p by an internal transition t_i does not depend on m_0, but depends only on the multiplicity of the input arc $\langle p, t\rangle$. Therefore, the weights of consumed and produced internal tokens are included into the equation for internal marking-independent weights. Together with weights w_t, they form the following equation:

$$\sum_{p \in \bullet t_{SN}} w_t(p) \cdot \|\gamma(\langle p, t_{SN}\rangle)\| + \sum_{t_i \in \{t_1, \ldots, t_q\}} \sum_{p \in \bullet t_i} w_m(p_{\alpha_i}) \cdot W(p_{\alpha_i})(p) \cdot \gamma(p, t_i)$$

$$= \sum_{p \in t_{SN}\bullet} \left(w_t(p) \cdot \|\gamma(\langle t_{SN}, p\rangle)\| + w_m(p) \cdot \sum_{c \in Con(\langle t_{SN}, p\rangle)} \widehat{W}(p)(c) \right)$$

$$+ \sum_{t_i \in \{t_1, \ldots, t_q\}} \sum_{p \in t_i\bullet} w_m(p_{\alpha_i}) \cdot W(p_{\alpha_i})(p) \cdot \gamma(t_i, p) \tag{6}$$

Since all possible steps in NP-net are considered, by exhaustion, (2)–(6) equations guarantee the invariance of the weight function (1).

Definition 4 (NP-net place invariant). *The tuple $I = \langle w_t, w_m, \mathcal{W} \rangle$ is a place invariant of an NP-net NP, if it satisfies the equations (2)–(6).*

Theorem 1 (Fundamental property of place invariants). *Let $I = \langle w_t, w_m, \mathcal{W} \rangle$ be a place invariant of an NP-net NP. Then the weight function W_I is an invariant on the reachability sets of NP, i.e. $\forall m \in \mathcal{R}_{NP}(m_0) : W_I(m) = W_I(m_0)$.*

Proof. Let $m \in \mathcal{R}_{NP}(m_0)$, then $m_0 \xrightarrow{\sigma} m$, where σ is a sequence of steps $s_1, m_1, s_2, m_2, ..., s_n, m$. If s_i is an elementary autonomous step, then the equation (2) ensures $W(m_{i-1}) = W(m_i)$; the equations (4),(3) ensure invariance of the weight function under system autonomous steps; (5),(6) ensure invariance under vertical synchronization steps. Then, by induction on the number of steps, we prove the invariance of the weight function for all intermediate markings m_i.

The fundamental property provides the opportunity to infer non-reachability of markings, i.e. if two markings do not agree on the invariant weight function, then either of them is not reachable from another one [5]. We use this in the next section for proving some behavioral properties of the financial predicting system.

We would like to note, that the weights of consumed tokens that do not depend on the internal marking can be balanced only with weights of produced token that do not depend on the internal marking. The consumed weights that depend on the marking of an internal place can be balanced only with corresponding weights that depend on the marking of the place. For example, if a transition t_{SN} removes net tokens, i.e. there is a variable x on an input arc (p, t_{SN}) of the transition, but no entries of x on output arcs, then by the equation (4) the weights of internal places $\mathcal{W}$ of the element net E_p are all equal to 0. This is not so obvious, because it might seem that it is possible to compensate the weight of the consumed net token with the weights of the net tokens produced by other variables, net constants, or even black tokens.

6   Invariant Analysis of NP-nets

In this section we demonstrate application of introduced invariants for analysis of behavioral properties important for our NP-net model example (Sect. 2).

We consider in details the property, which concerns a restriction on the number of simultaneous requests sent to the subscribed index service. This is a crucial restriction, as a violation of the agreement with the service provider may lead to extra charges or to an abrogation of the contract. Requests are sent by index agents. The property can be formulated as follows:

The index agents can simultaneously send not more than 3 requests to the external index service.

The place *WS querying$_1$* of the E_3 elementary net models the index agent state in which the agent is waiting for the response to a sent request. The sum of tokens in the internal places *WS querying$_1$* of all index agents net-tokens represents the number of requests currently sent to the subscribed index service. According to the contract this number should be not greater than 3.

License tokens are stored in the place *license tokens* of the *SN* system net of the model. License tokens are carried from the license tokens pool to an index agent by a forecasting agent (E_1). A forecasting agent receives a license token via a firing of *SN*:**get license** transition. Then the forecasting agent can send a request to an index agent by firing E_1 : **req₁**, but only if it has a license token.

If we find the intrinsic dependence between the number of tokens in *WS querying₁* places of all index agents on the initial number of tokens in *license tokens*, then we can use this dependence to prove the property. Formally, we need to prove $\forall m \in \mathcal{R}(m_0) : (\sum_{\alpha \in m(p_0)} m_\alpha(p_1)) \leq m_0(p_2)$, where p_0, p_1, and p_2 denote *index agents*, *WS querying₁*, and *license tokens* places, correspondingly. Since the initial marking contains 3 tokens in *SN:license tokens* there will be at most 3 tokens in *WS querying₁* places. It should be noted that this sum consists of weighted tokens in all index agent tokens, not the sum of tokens of one index agent. Intuitively, since the tokens flow between SN, E_1, and E_3 nets, the needed invariant should be distributed among all these nets.

The property can be proven with the invariant I_1 specified by the following weights $\langle w^t, w^m, W = \{w^{E_1}, w^{E_3}\}\rangle$:

- w_t maps places {*license tokens, queue₁, result₁* to 1, and other places to 0;
- w_m maps places {*check license,updating,index agents, forecasting agents, forecasters, allocated agents, DB server*} to 1, and others to 0;
- the weight function w^{E_1} for the system net places {*check license, updating, forecasting agents, forecasters, allocated agents, DB server*} maps places {*releasing license,license obtained*} of the element net E_1 to 1, others to 0;
- the weight functions w^{E_3} for the system net place *index agents* maps places {*buffer₁, WS querying₁, index₁*} of the element net E_3 to 1, and others to 0.

The initial marking m_0 of the example NP-net is depicted in the Fig. 4. For all net tokens in m_0 their initial markings are shown in the Figs. 1, 2 and 3. The number of simultaneous requests to the index service is the sum of all tokens in the place *WS querying¹* in all index agents net tokens. But this sum is the part of the positive sum W_{I_1} determined by I_1. Hence, since all elements are positive, the subsum is always not greater than the sum $W_{I_1}(m)$ for each reachable marking m. Since $W_{I_1}(m_0)$ equals 3 and is invariant, the number of simultaneously sent requests is always not greater than 3, what we wanted to prove.

The property says that the number of sent requests is not greater than some given number. We also need to check if the number of DB agents querying the database is precisely equal to the number of forecasting agents requesting analytical datum. The subtle difference from the previous property is that the former concerns the upper bound on the number of simultaneous requests, while this property requires precise equality between the numbers of querying and waiting agents. We want to ensure that there are no redundant processing DB agents and no waiting agents that won't receive response. The invariant, that proves this is $\langle w_m, w_t, W = \{w^{E_1}, w^{E_2}\}\rangle$, where $w_t = 0$; w_m maps places {*DB server,*

DB querying, DB data retrieved} to 1; maps the place *waiting data* to 1; w^{E_2} maps the places *querying* and *result* to -1.

The following properties have been also proven for our NP-net model example with the help of invariants:

1. A forecasting agent does not leave dangling tokens, when it moves from the updating to the forecasting phase.
2. The number of DB agents querying the database is equal to the number of forecasters waiting for the response.
3. An updating process can be only in one of the following states: E_1:*up-to-date*$_1$, E_1:*outdated*$_1$, E_1:*license obtained*, SN:*queue*$_1$, E_3:*buffer*$_1$, E_3:*WS querying*$_1$, E_3:*index*$_1$, SN:*result*$_1$, E_1:*releasing license*, E_1:*updating*$_1$ (such properties are called "metamorphosis" of tokens in [8].
4. The number of asynchronous requests to external web services is not greater than 3 times the number of forecasters in the initial marking.
5. The system is bounded except the client requests queue.
6. If the paid financial index is outdated, then forecasting agent may enter updating state only with a license token.

The common general approach to proving a behavioral property of a system with invariants is as follows: first obtain a collection of invariants sufficient to prove the property, check that the property is valid in the initial marking of the system, and then by invariance infer that it is valid in all reachable markings. The common heuristic to find such collection of invariants is that the collection should cover the places involved in the property statement.

The main advantage of the invariant method is that we prove a property for arbitrary amount of agents with the only assumption that in the initial marking they reside in the initial pools and the markings of agents tokens are the same as in the given example. We cannot prove the property for all such initial markings with classical model checking technique as it proves the property only for a given finite combination of agents. To scale the results obtained with model checking to arbitrary amount of agents we need to apply semi-automatic techniques — parameterized model checking or k-induction based techniques [2].

7 Algorithm for Computing NP-nets Place Invariants

Place-invariants of different kinds of Petri nets are usually computed as solutions of matrix equations defined as $C \cdot x = 0$, where C is the incidence matrix of the Petri net, 0 is zero vector, and x is the decision solution of the equation. An incidence matrix can be in different forms for different kinds of Petri nets, i.e. it is just a matrix over integers for classical place-transition nets, or a matrix over functions or algebraical terms for colored or algebraic Petri nets [12,24].

The method suggested in this paper is a variation of the method of indeterminate coefficients, where the solution of the equations induced by transitions is assumed in a form of weight function containing a number of unknown weights.

Algorithm 1. Algorithm for computing NP-nets place invariants equations

---

Input : $NP = \langle N_1, \ldots, N_k, SN \rangle$, $SN = \langle P_{SN}, T_{SN}, F_{SN}, \upsilon, \gamma, \Lambda \rangle$

Output: $\mathcal{E} = \{e_1, e_2 \ldots e_n\}$ — set of equations

/* we shortcut $\mathcal{W}(p)(q)$ by w_q^p, $w_t(p)$ by w_p^t, $w_m(p)$ by w_p^m */

1   **begin**

2     $\mathcal{E} \leftarrow \emptyset$;

3   /* Autonomous elementary steps equations (2)   */

4   **foreach** $p \in \{p \mid p \in P_{SN}\ \&\ \upsilon(p) = \langle P, T, F \rangle\}$ **do**

5   **foreach** $t \in \{t \mid t \in T\ \&\ \Lambda(t) = \tau\}$ **do**

6        $left \leftarrow \emptyset$; $right \leftarrow \emptyset$;

7   **foreach** $\langle q, t \rangle \in F$ **do** insert $\|\gamma(\langle q, t \rangle)\| \cdot w_q^p$ into $left$;

8   **foreach** $\langle t, q \rangle \in F$ **do** insert $\|\gamma(\langle t, q \rangle)\| \cdot w_q^p$ into $right$;

9   insert $\sum\limits_{l \in left} l = \sum\limits_{r \in right} r$ into $\mathcal{E}$

10   /* Elementary nets places weights equations (5),(3)   */

11   **foreach** $t \in T_{SN}$ **do**

12      $left \leftarrow \emptyset$; $right \leftarrow \emptyset$;

13   **foreach** $\langle p, t \rangle \in F_{SN}$ **do**

14   **foreach** $x \in \gamma(\langle p, t \rangle)$ **do**

15   **foreach** $q \in \{q \mid \upsilon(p) = \langle P, T, F \rangle\ \&\ q \in P\}$ **do**

16           $left \leftarrow w_p^m \cdot w_q^p$; $right \leftarrow \emptyset$;

17   **foreach** $\langle t, p' \rangle \in \{\langle t, p' \rangle \in F_{SN} \mid |\gamma(\langle t, p' \rangle)|_x > 0\}$ **do**

18   insert $w_{p'}^m \cdot w_q^{p'} \cdot |\gamma(\langle t, p' \rangle)|_x$ into $right$;

19   insert $\sum\limits_{l \in left} l = \sum\limits_{r \in right} r$ into $\mathcal{E}$

20   /* Synchronization (6) and sys. autonomous (4) steps equations */

21   **foreach** $t \in T_{SN}$ **do**

22      $left_{SN} \leftarrow \emptyset$; $right_{SN} \leftarrow \emptyset$;

23   **foreach** $\langle p, t \rangle \in F_{SN}$ **do** insert $w_p^t \cdot |\gamma(\langle p, t \rangle)|$ into $left_{SN}$;

24   **foreach** $\langle t, p \rangle \in F_{SN}$ **do**

25   insert $w_p^t \cdot |\gamma(\langle t, p \rangle)|$ into $right_{SN}$;

26   **foreach** $c \in \{c \mid c \in Con(\langle t, p \rangle)\ \&\ c = \langle \langle P, T, F \rangle, m_0 \rangle\}$ **do**

27   **foreach** $q \in P$ **do** insert $w_p^m \cdot w_q^p \cdot m_0(p)$ into $right_{SN}$;

28   **if** $\Lambda(t) = \tau$ **then** insert $\sum\limits_{l \in left_{SN}} l = \sum\limits_{r \in right_{SN}} r$ into $\mathcal{E}$;

29   **else foreach** $\{\langle t_1^1 \ldots t_{n_1}^1 t_1^k \ldots t_{n_k}^k \rangle \in (T_1)^{n_1} \times \cdots \times (T_k)^{n_k} \mid$
       $\{p_1, \ldots, p_k\} = {}^\bullet t\ \&\ \forall j \in \overline{1, k} : n_j = |\gamma(\langle p_j, t \rangle)|$
       $\&\ \upsilon(p_j) = \langle P_j, T_j, F_j \rangle\ \&\ \forall l \in \overline{1, n_j} : \Lambda(t_l^j) = \Lambda(t)\}$ **do**

30        $left \leftarrow left_{SN}$; $right \leftarrow right_{SN}$;

31   **foreach** $t_l^j \in \langle t_1^1 \ldots t_{n_1}^1 t_1^k \ldots t_{n_k}^k \rangle$ **do**

32   **foreach** $q \in {}^\bullet t_l^j$ **do** insert $w_{p_j}^m \cdot w_q^{p_j} \cdot |\gamma(\langle q, t_l^j \rangle)|$ into $left$;

33   **foreach** $q \in t_l^{j\,\bullet}$ **do** insert $w_{p_j}^m \cdot w_q^{p_j} \cdot |\gamma(\langle t_l^j, q \rangle)|$ into $right$;

34   insert $\sum\limits_{l \in left} l = \sum\limits_{r \in right} r$ into $\mathcal{E}$

35   ;

The algorithm consists of 4 steps. The result of the first 3 steps is a set of equations that correspond to all possible steps in a given NP-net. By substituting a new variable for each product term containing w_m we obtain a system of linear equations. Now the solutions can be obtained by the well-known methods of linear algebra.

Algorithm (*Computing place invariants*). The algorithm computes weights of the place invariant function for a given NP-net $NP = \langle N_1, \ldots, N_k, SN \rangle$. For each transition of the NP-net, it extracts the corresponding (2)–(6) equations from the NP-net structure. The solutions of the extracted system of equations $\mathcal{E}$ are weight tuples, which determine all possible invariants. The more detailed pseudo-code of the algorithm is given in Algorithm 1.

Step 1. For each elementary autonomous transition of every element net, build a firing equation (2) and add it to $\mathcal{E}$ (lines 4–9).

Step 2. For each variable of every system autonomous transition, extract a firing Eq. 4 or 5 and add it to $\mathcal{E}$ (lines 11–19).

Step 3. For each variable of every system autonomous transition, extract a firing Eq. 3 and add it to $\mathcal{E}$. For each possible vertical synchronization step of every vertical synchronization transition extract a firing Eq. 6 and add it to $\mathcal{E}$ (lines 21–35).

Step 4. Find the solutions of the system of equations $\mathcal{E}$. Each solution of $\mathcal{E}$ corresponds to an invariant of NP.

Thus, similar to the classical case place invariants for NP-nets can be effectively represented and computed with the help of standard linear algebraic methods. Inferring properties from place invariants requires informal model analysis and even some insight. However, heuristic approaches can be developed for some classes of properties. This is a subject for further research.

8   Conclusion

In this paper we have defined place invariants of NP-nets, provided an algorithm for computing invariants, and demonstrated how they can be used for analysis of NP-nets by the example of a financial forecasting system.

The main contribution is that despite of the dynamic structure of NP-nets, i.e. the components of an NP-net move within the system, it is still possible to find structural invariants capturing informational/material flows between different levels of NP-nets.

The authors would like to thank the anonymous referees for valuable and very helpful comments.

References

1. Bednarczyk, M.A., Bernardinello, L., Pawłowski, W., Pomello, L.: Modelling mobility with Petri hypernets. In: Fiadeiro, J.L., Mosses, P.D., Orejas, F. (eds.) WADT 2004. LNCS, vol. 3423, pp. 28–44. Springer, Heidelberg (2005). doi:10. 1007/978-3-540-31959-7_2

2. Bloem, R., et al.: Decidability of parameterized verification. Synth. Lect. Distrib. Comput. Theory **6**(1), 1–170 (2015). doi:10.2200/S00658ED1V01Y201508DCT013
3. Chang, L. et al.: Applying a nested Petri net modeling paradigm to coordination of sensor networks with mobile agents. In: Proceedings of Workshop on Petri Nets and Distributed Systems, Xian, China, pp. 132–145 (2008)
4. Cristini, F., Tessier, C.: Nets-within-nets to model innovative space system architectures. In: Haddad, S., Pomello, L. (eds.) PETRI NETS 2012. LNCS, vol. 7347, pp. 348–367. Springer, Heidelberg (2012). doi:10.1007/978-3-642-31131-4_19
5. Desel, J., Neuendorf, K.-P., Radola, M.-D.: Proving nonreachability by modulo-invariants. Theoret. Comput. Sci. **153**(1–2), 49–64 (1996). doi:10.1016/0304-3975(95)00117-4
6. Dworzański, L.W., Lomazova, I.: CPN tools-assisted simulation and verification of nested Petri nets. Autom. Control Comput. Sci. **47**(7), 393–402 (2013). doi:10.3103/S0146411613070201
7. Dworzański, L.W., Lomazova, I.A.: On compositionality of boundedness and liveness for nested Petri nets. Fundamenta Informaticae **120**(3–4), 275–293 (2012). doi:10.3233/FI-2012-762
8. Genrich, H.J., Lautenbach, K.: The analysis of distributed systems by means of predicate/transition-nets. In: Kahn, G. (ed.) Semantics of Concurrent Computation. LNCS, vol. 70, pp. 123–146. Springer, Heidelberg (1979)
9. van Hee, K.M., Lomazova, I.A., Oanea, O., Serebrenik, A., Sidorova, N., Voorhoeve, M.: Nested nets for adaptive systems. In: Donatelli, S., Thiagarajan, P.S. (eds.) ICATPN 2006. LNCS, vol. 4024, pp. 241–260. Springer, Heidelberg (2006). doi:10.1007/11767589_14
10. van Hee, K.M., et al.: Checking properties of adaptive workflow nets. Fundamenta Informaticae **79**(3–4), 347–362 (2007)
11. Hoffmann, K., Ehrig, H., Mossakowski, T.: High-level nets with nets and rules as tokens. In: Ciardo, G., Darondeau, P. (eds.) ICATPN 2005. LNCS, vol. 3536, pp. 268–288. Springer, Heidelberg (2005)
12. Jensen, K.: Coloured Petri nets and the invariant-method. Theoret. Comput. Sci. **14**, 317–336 (1981)
13. Jensen, K., Kristensen, L.M.: Coloured Petri Nets - Modelling and Validation of Concurrent Systems. Springer, Heidelberg (2009). doi:10.1007/b95112
14. Kahloul, L., Djouani, K., Chaoui, A.: Formal study of reconfigurable manufacturing systems: a high level Petri nets based approach. In: Mařík, V., Lastra, J.L.M., Skobelev, P. (eds.) HoloMAS 2013. LNCS, vol. 8062, pp. 106–117. Springer, Heidelberg (2013). doi:10.1007/978-3-642-40090-2_10
15. Köhler, M., Farwer, B.: Object nets for mobility. In: Kleijn, J., Yakovlev, A. (eds.) ICATPN 2007. LNCS, vol. 4546, pp. 244–262. Springer, Heidelberg (2007). doi:10.1007/978-3-540-73094-1_16
16. Lautenbach, K.: Linear algebraic techniques for place/transition nets. In: Brauer, W., Reisig, W., Rozenberg, G. (eds.) Petri Nets: Central Models and Their Properties. LNCS, vol. 254, pp. 142–167. Springer, Heidelberg (1986). doi:10.1007/978-3-540-47919-2_7
17. Lomazova, I.A.: Modeling dynamic objects in distributed systems with nested Petri nets. Fundamenta Informaticae **51**(1–2), 121–133 (2002)
18. Lomazova, I.A.: Nested Petri nets - a formalism for specification and verification of multi-agent distributed systems. Fundamenta Informaticae **43**(1), 195–214 (2000)
19. Lomazova, I.A.: Nested Petri nets for adaptive process modeling. In: Avron, A., Dershowitz, N., Rabinovich, A. (eds.) Pillars of Computer Science. LNCS, vol. 4800, pp. 460–474. Springer, Heidelberg (2008). doi:10.1007/978-3-540-78127-1_25

20. Lomazova, I.A.: Nested Petri nets: multi-level and recursive systems. Fundamenta Informaticae **47**(3–4), 283–293 (2001)
21. Lomazova, I.A., Schnoebelen, P.: Some decidability results for nested Petri nets. In: Bjorner, D., Broy, M., Zamulin, A.V. (eds.) PSI 1999. LNCS, vol. 1755, p. 208. Springer, Heidelberg (2000). doi:10.1007/3-540-46562-6_18
22. Lopez-Mellado, E., Almeyda-Canepa, H.: A three-level net formalism for the modelling of multiple mobile robot systems. In: IEEE International Conference on Systems, Man and Cybernetics, vol. 3, pp. 2733–2738 (2003). doi:10.1109/ICSMC.2003.1244298
23. Lopez-Mellado, E., Villanueva-Paredes, N., Almeyda-Canepa, H.: Modelling of batch production systems using Petri nets with dynamic tokens. Math. Comput. Simul. **67**(6), 541–558 (2005). doi:10.1016/j.matcom.2004.07.005
24. Schmidt, K.: On the computation of place invariants for algebraic Petri nets. In: Desel, J. (ed.) Structures in Concurrency Theory, pp. 310–325. Springer, Heidelberg (1995). doi:10.1007/978-1-4471-3078-9_21
25. Tărăbuţă, O.: Use of Petri nets system concept in modeling dynamics with increased complexity. In: 2011 15th International Conference on System Theory, Control, and Computing (ICSTCC), pp. 1–6, October 2011
26. Valk, R.: Object Petri nets using the nets-within-nets paradigm. In: Desel, J., Reisig, W., Rozenberg, G. (eds.) Lectures on Concurrency and Petri Nets. LNCS, vol. 3098, pp. 819–848. Springer, Heidelberg (2004). doi:10.1007/978-3-540-27755-2_23
27. Venero, M.L.F., da Silva, F.S.C.: Model checking multi-level and recursive nets. Softw. Syst. Model., 1–28 (2016)
28. Zhang, L., Rodrigues, B.: Nested coloured timed Petri nets for production configuration of product families. Int. J. Prod. Res. **48**(6), 1805–1833 (2010). doi:10.1080/00207540802585329

Author Index

Printed in the United States
by Baker & Taylor Publisher Services